OXFORD WORLD'S CLASSICS

# THE OXFORD SHAKESPEARE

*General Editor* · Stanley Wells

The Oxford Shakespeare offers new and authoritative editions of Shakespeare's plays in which the early printings have been scrupulously re-examined and interpreted. An introductory essay provides all relevant background information together with an appraisal of critical views and of the play's effects in performance. The detailed commentaries pay particular attention to language and staging. Reprints of sources, music for songs, genealogical tables, maps, etc. are included where necessary; many of the volumes are illustrated, and all contain an index.

JOHN JOWETT, the editor of *Richard III* in the Oxford Shakespeare, is Reader in Shakespeare Studies at the Shakespeare Institute, Birmingham.

D0205779

## THE OXFORD SHAKESPEARE

*Currently available in paperback*

| | |
|---|---|
| *All's Well that Ends Well* | *Measure for Measure* |
| *Anthony and Cleopatra* | *The Merchant of Venice* |
| *As You Like It* | *The Merry Wives of Windsor* |
| *Coriolanus* | *A Midsummer Night's Dream* |
| *Cymbeline* | *Much Ado About Nothing* |
| *Hamlet* | *Richard III* |
| *Henry V* | *Romeo and Juliet* |
| *Henry IV, Part 1* | *The Taming of the Shrew* |
| *Henry IV, Part 2* | *The Tempest* |
| *Julius Caesar* | *Titus Andronicus* |
| *King Henry VIII* | *Troilus and Cressida* |
| *King John* | *Twelfth Night* |
| *Love's Labour's Lost* | *The Two Noble Kinsmen* |
| *Macbeth* | *The Winter's Tale* |

*The rest of the plays and poems are forthcoming*

OXFORD WORLD'S CLASSICS

WILLIAM SHAKESPEARE

# *The Tragedy of King Richard III*

*Edited by*
JOHN JOWETT

OXFORD
UNIVERSITY PRESS

# OXFORD
UNIVERSITY PRESS

Great Clarendon Street, Oxford OX2 6DP

Oxford University Press is a department of the University of Oxford.
It furthers the University's objective of excellence in research, scholarship,
and education by publishing worldwide in

Oxford New York

Athens Auckland Bangkok Bogotá Buenos Aires Calcutta
Cape Town Chennai Dar es Salaam Delhi Florence Hong Kong Istanbul
Karachi Kuala Lumpur Madrid Melbourne Mexico City Mumbai
Nairobi Paris São Paulo Shanghai Singapore Taipei Tokyo Toronto Warsaw

with associated companies in Berlin Ibadan

Oxford is a registered trade mark of Oxford University Press
in the UK and in certain other countries

Published in the United States
by Oxford University Press Inc., New York

© John Jowett 2000

The moral rights of the author have been asserted

Database right Oxford University Press (maker)

First published as an Oxford World's Classics paperback 2000

British Library Cataloguing in Publication Data

Data available

Library of Congress Cataloging in Publication Data

Data available

ISBN 0–19–818245–7 (hbk.)
ISBN 0–19–283993–4 (pbk.)

1 3 5 7 9 10 8 6 4 2

Typeset by Jayvee,
Trivandrum, India
Printed in Spain by Book Print S.L.

# ACKNOWLEDGEMENTS

Throughout the preparation of this edition Stanley Wells as general editor has combined selfless rigour with humanity and care. Christine Buckley was a superb copy-editor and more; her accuracy, knowledge, and scholarship have improved the edition in many ways.

My work was facilitated by a period of study leave from the University of Birmingham. My most immediate resource has been the Shakespeare Institute Library, where Jim Shaw, Kate Welch, and various assistants gave unstinting help. I have been aided too by Marian Pringle, Sylvia Morris, and others at the Shakespeare Centre Library, and by staff at the Folger Shakespeare Library, the Bodleian Library, and the British Library.

I am in debt to all at the Shakespeare Institute and elsewhere who have provided information, exchanged ideas, given encouragement, and provided outlets for work in progress. These include Iska Alter, Roberta Barker, Susan Brock, Clara Calvo, Ralph Cohen, Gillian Day, Paul Edmondson, Speed Hill, Grace Ioppolo, Christa Jansohn, Ann Kaegi, Adrian Kiernander, Wendy Lamoreaux, Amelia Mariette, Robert Ormsby, Eric Rasmussen, Gary Taylor, Steven Urkowitz, Elaine Walker, and Eric Wilson. My colleagues Russell Jackson and Martin Wiggins have been repeatedly generous with their knowledge. Peter Holland, M. J. Kidnie, and Kristin Lucas made detailed and constructive comments on the Introduction.

This edition is for my parents, Dorothy Jowett and Jack Jowett.

JOHN JOWETT

# CONTENTS

# Contents

# LIST OF ILLUSTRATIONS

# INTRODUCTION

*Richard III* is conspicuously a performance piece, and in many ways it is about the nature of performance. The play was critical in developing a new and spectacular symbiosis between William Shakespeare, as actor-turned-dramatist, and Richard Burbage, the aspiring actor for whom Shakespeare probably wrote the dominating role of Richard III. It is on account of this role, at once flamboyant, beguiling, and terrifying, that the play has always been celebrated as a centrepiece of the dramatic traditions influenced by Shakespeare.

In this introduction, the history of the play's fortunes in performance, presented on pp. 72–110, is essential to my account of Richard as a dramatic figure. Earlier sections consider the origins, making, and shaping of the play. Here Shakespeare's most important accomplice is literary rather than theatrical; he is Sir Thomas More, whose *History of Richard III* is the main source for Shakespeare's play. Shakespeare reshapes this prose account of Richard as tyrant into the language and conventions of the theatre. The resulting play gives us to understand that there was a man in history who lived and became king, and it amazes us at the precocity of theatre in giving a figure who is so much that man and yet so estranged from him.

These are masculine scenarios, whereby the predominantly male agents in late medieval politics are represented by male writers. The resulting play was originally acted in a theatre whose actors were, as was usual, all men and boys. Yet *Richard III* presents a feminized community, presided over by three queens and a queen mother. It stretches beyond the living present, to remember, include, and empower the dead. At first this is a community of victims, but as the play moves forward it becomes an active force in disabling and defeating Richard. At the military–political level, the play shows Henry Earl of Richmond's overthrow of Richard in battle at Bosworth Field. Because Richmond founded the Tudor line of monarchs and was Queen Elizabeth's grandfather, his victory seems to define *Richard III* as a restatement of Tudor political orthodoxy. Yet Richmond is insubstantial as a dramatic role. Richard is defeated in non-military ways: because, for example, kingship is an empty goal, because memory and knowledge of his crimes are actively instrumental in his downfall, and because his sardonic hostility to others cannot for ever stave off his participation in a social and moral world. It is the women who identify or implement these causes of defeat.

The play's theatricality does not detract from its seriousness as an engagement with history and as a study in malevolent tyranny. Though it addresses the topic of seduction as a political art, it indicates, optimistically, that resistance to Richard can succeed. Before that happens, Richard thrives by exploiting a background of fear and generating a foreground of false security. Richard's victims are usually those lulled into thinking that he is an ally, perhaps even a friend. If the play suggests to contemporary audiences a relevance to modern totalitarian regimes, it does so as a study in the politics of false hope and complicity. It shows how the courage to oppose can be silenced, though only temporarily.

Sir Thomas More as the chronicler of the historical narrative and Richard Burbage as the persuasive actor can be taken to typify Shakespeare's involvement with others, from his past and present, in the making of *Richard III*. The works of writers such as Seneca, Thomas Sackville, Thomas Kyd, Christopher Marlowe, Edmund Spenser, Philip Sidney, and John Lyly are echoed more locally, enriching the play with an allusive literary quality and defining its claim as a work of art over and above the immediate needs of the stage. Actors and theatre personnel less conspicuous than Burbage, together with the more general material conditions of the Elizabethan theatre such as the structure of the playhouse, the background of aristocratic patronage, and the conditions of theatre regulation and censorship, all these both enable the play and at the same time set limits on it. Beyond the theatre, there are those who participated in remaking *Richard III* as a printed text for readers. The substantially variant versions published in the First Quarto of 1597 (Q1) and the First Folio of 1623 (F) had passed through manuscript transcription and the intricate and time-consuming process of hand-printing. To some extent the differences between these texts no doubt reflect alterations made by Shakespeare, but his activities as a reviser cannot be separated from larger processes of alteration for the stage that would have centrally involved other members of the theatre company as well. The present edition endorses the play as a product of shared performance as well as a product of dramatic authorship, following the text that seems closest to the play as it would have been staged, the First Quarto.

The shapers, makers, and performers lead the play towards its reception. Written literature depends on readers,[1] and there is no theatre without audiences. *Richard III* takes us into a theatre of showmanship and seduction; but that is Richard's project. The play as a whole instructs in the necessity of resistance. *Richard III* enables us, as its potentially active and critical receptors, to experience in full the conflict between the morality and amorality of theatre. And it leaves to readers and performers the possibilities of constructing diverse *Richard III*s that reflect their tastes, their skills, their places in culture and history.

## Taking Shape

*Date, Theatre Companies, and Patrons.* *Richard III* was clearly written in the early 1590s. A number of considerations help to place it more exactly within this period, though there is no evidence or argument that is entirely compelling. The play exercises a control over dramatic materials that is seen only incipiently in the earlier Henry VI trilogy, and yet shows stylistic and rhetorical traits of Shakespeare's early writing before the plays such as *A Midsummer Night's Dream* of the 'lyrical' period, 1594–6. *Richard III* builds on events shown in *Richard Duke of York* (otherwise known as *3 Henry VI*), and must have been written and performed after it. The earlier play was written in or by 1592, for a line from it is travestied in the pamphlet *Greene's Groatsworth of Wit*, entered in the Stationers' Register on 20 September of that year.[2] So *Richard Duke of York* must presumably have reached the stage before plague caused the London theatres to be closed down on 23 June. Unfortunately the *Groatsworth* allusion provides no terminus for the dating of *Richard III*, though the recent views that the writing of *Richard Duke of York* belongs to 1591 or early 1592 might suggest a date of several months later for *Richard III*.[3]

[1] For a transcript of one early Scottish reader's annotations, see Yamada.

[2] 'Tiger's heart wrapped in a player's hide', mocking *Richard Duke of York* 1.4.138, 'tiger's heart wrapped in a woman's hide'.

[3] Taylor, in *Textual Companion*, p. 112; Michael Hattaway, ed., *The Third Part of King Henry VI* (Cambridge, 1993), pp. 52–60. Harold Brooks suggests a line of influence running from *Richard III* to Marlowe's *Edward II*: 'Marlowe and Early Shakespeare', in *Christopher Marlowe*, ed. Brian Morris (1968), pp. 65–94. This

3

Marco Mincoff has put forward a plausible but impressionistic argument that Shakespeare absorbed the influence of Seneca and worked out an understanding of tragic structure while writing *Titus Andronicus*, and that he had this experience behind him by the time he came to work on *Richard III*.[1] *Titus* has in recent years been placed at either 1592 or 1593–4.[2] In response to Mincoff's discussion it is possible to argue that *Richard III* shows itself to be a transitional work taking Shakespeare from chronicle-style history plays towards Senecan tragedy. Significant here is the Senecan element at work in earlier texts dealing with the period of history depicted in the play.[3] It would therefore remain a hazardous business to deduce the date of *Richard III* from *Titus*, even if the date of *Titus* could be stabilized.

The question of theatre patronage is relevant because it encourages a date of composition of about 1592, and it has significance for the play in its own right. Before the formation of the Lord Chamberlain's Men in 1594, Shakespeare may have acted and written plays for the theatre company known as Lord Strange's Men. *Richard III*, along with other Shakespeare plays of the period, looks as though it was written with this company and its patron in mind. Ferdinando Lord Strange, patron of the theatre company named after him, was a descendant of the play's Lord Stanley. Shakespeare alters More's account of events to present Stanley in a favourable light.[4] For instance, a tactful silence surrounds his role in crushing Buckingham's uprising and his enrichment with lands from Buckingham's estate as Richard's reward. History is altered by making it the lord rather than his brother Sir William who leads

play must, of course, have been written before Marlowe was killed on 30 May 1593, and is usually also put at *c*. 1592. Taylor (*Textual Companion*, p. 116) argues that the parallels are too commonplace and/or that they could run from play to play in either direction. See also Commentary to 1.2.207.

[1] Marco Mincoff, *Shakespeare: The First Steps* (Sofia, 1976), pp. 110–37.

[2] For 1592: Taylor, *Textual Companion*, pp. 113–15; for 1593–4: Bate, ed., *Titus*, pp. 69–79, and Alan Nelson, 'George Buc, William Shakespeare, and the Folger *George a Greene*', *SQ* 49 (1998), 74–83.

[3] See below, pp. 23–4. Another possible influence is Thomas Legge's Latin academic play *Ricardus Tertius*, acted at St John's College, Cambridge, in the 1580s. *Ricardus Tertius* anticipates Shakespeare's play by including a scene showing Richard's seduction of Anne. G. B. Churchill makes an overstated case for its influence on Shakespeare, in *Richard the Third up to Shakespeare* (Berlin, 1900), p. 497.

[4] For details, and for hypothesized contact between Shakespeare and Lord Strange before Shakespeare became a player in London, see Honigmann, *Lost Years*, p. 64.

the main Stanley force at the Battle of Bosworth, and a favourable gloss is applied to Stanley's wait-and-see policy.

The Stanley family thrived from the Wars of the Roses until Shakespeare's time through acts of political opportunism.[1] Stanley's presentation as a figure of reluctant and constrained allegiance to Richard that resolves itself into intuitive and active moral allegiance to Richmond might have held a particular resonance to Lord Strange. Shakespeare's play reflects on the miseries of enforced loyalty to the wrong cause, and, although Stanley is amongst the culpable peers who silently abandon Hastings to his fate in 3.4, in other respects he is discreetly vindicated. Moreover, the end of the play, in which the houses of Lancaster and York are to be united through marriage, would have acquired distinctive overtones in the context of patronage by Lord Strange. He was himself the issue of a major dynastic marriage between Margaret Clifford, great-granddaughter of Richmond, and Henry, fourth Earl of Derby. He was therefore a descendant of both Richmond and the play's Stanley.[2] By concentrating entirely on Richmond and Stanley, the ending would have been able to foreshadow the union of Tudor and Stanley alongside the union of Lancaster and York.

Yet the ancestors of another theatre patron, the Earl of Pembroke, are also subject to eulogistic distortion. Late in the play, his ancestors Sir Walter Herbert and the Earl of Pembroke seem to be introduced solely so that they can be associated with Richmond and praised.[3] The passages in question are not firmly integrated with the rest of the play, and, relatively speaking at least, they look like afterthoughts. Amongst the men of name who resort to Richmond 'At Pembroke or at Ha'rfordwest, in Wales' are 'Sir Walter Herbert, a renownèd soldier' and 'redoubted Pembroke'. The names are amongst those scattered across the accounts of events leading to the Battle of Bosworth in Shakespeare's sources,

---

[1] The Elizabethan Stanley family was widely known for its Catholic sympathies, whilst Lord Strange had kept himself on the right side of official polity by helping to hunt down Catholic suspects. From either the Catholic or Protestant point of view his loyalty was in question. See also Peter Thomson, *Shakespeare's Professional Career* (Cambridge, 1992), pp. 23–4.

[2] See the family tree in Thomson, pp. 32–3.

[3] The play's praise of the Pembroke family is also a reason *against* dating it as a Lord Chamberlain's play of 1594, as does, for example, Bate, in his edition of *Titus*, pp. 78–9. The Lord Chamberlain Henry Carey's son 'was engaged in hostile wrangles with Pembroke from the autumn of 1593 until 1595': Andrew Gurr, *The Shakespearian Playing Companies* (Oxford, 1996), p. 272.

but the catalogue in *Richard III* is selected and distilled in such a way as to make praise of the Pembroke family unmistakable. Apart from the short catalogue of the dead in the final scene, it is the only such listing of characters not involved in the action, and it comes in a passage (4.5.8–15) that could be cut out without loss.

What's more, the source material is augmented in 5.4 where, for no apparent reason, Richmond sends a message to Pembroke asking him to attend him on the night before the battle at two o'clock in the morning. This is something of a loose end, as the telescoped but continuous night sequence offers no opportunity for such an interview to take place. The purpose seems to be to strengthen the impression that Pembroke is a key figure militarily in the establishment of the Tudor monarchy, and the future king's closest confidant. In the Folio, the second Pembroke passage is again preceded by a mention of Herbert. This time Herbert, on stage with Richmond's followers, is picked out as one of Richmond's three night-time companions: 'My Lord of Oxford, you Sir *William Brandon*, | And your [*sic*] Sir *Walter Herbert* stay with me' (after 5.4.4). Perhaps this attention to Herbert and Pembroke was because Henry Herbert, second Earl of Pembroke, was patron of the company now envisaged as about to perform it.

In view of the generous praise of Stanley and the briefer, more gratuitous praise of Pembroke, one might reasonably conclude that Shakespeare was hedging his bets. This assumes that the manuscript on which the Folio text is based represents the play before its first performances, and therefore that the text does not simultaneously represent different points in its stage history. There are other possibilities. The manuscript could have been updated with the two discrete 'Pembroke' passages if, for example, it was about to be gifted to the Earl himself, or indeed if the manuscript underwent minor revision with a view to a delayed first performance or a revival by Pembroke's Men.

Apart from the cut-off date imposed by the publication of the First Quarto in 1597, no other factor has more weight in determining where *Richard III* is placed in the chronology of Shakespeare's writing and the annals of stage history than these internal allusions. Andrew Gurr makes a case for Shakespeare working as an actor with Pembroke's Men in 1592–3.[1] The association between

---

[1] Gurr, p. 271.

Shakespeare and Pembroke's Men is strong and yet threaded with peculiarities.[1] The relationship between Pembroke's and Strange's is also uncertain. As against Gurr's theory that the new company was founded on rivalry, George, amongst others, has argued that it was an offshoot company. This would be consistent with Gurr's own inference that *The Contention* (otherwise known as *2 Henry VI*) and *Richard Duke of York* began as Strange's plays and then went to Pembroke's,[2] and also with the mixed complexion of praise in *Richard III*.

Whatever the historical particularities, the Quarto text itself indicates that a play initially written as if for Strange's Men is given finishing touches towards its close that make it suitable for the new Pembroke company; then later, like Shakespeare's other pre-1594 plays (or at least those that are extant), it appears in the hands of the Chamberlain's Men. These details highlight 1592, the year in which Pembroke's Men was formed, as the most probable date of composition.

*Richard Duke of York*, *1 Henry VI*, *Richard III*, and *Titus Andronicus* all vie for a place in the period immediately before the closing of the theatres on account of the plague. But Shakespeare may have contributed only a minor part to the collaborative *1 Henry VI*, and

---

[1] The company's financial manager Philip Henslowe records performances of 'harey the vj', on 3 March 1592, and on fourteen subsequent days until 19 June. This is usually understood to be *1 Henry VI*, but the identification is not entirely secure, and in any case this 'Shakespeare' play is probably a collaboration with other dramatists (Gary Taylor, 'Shakespeare and Others', *Medieval and Renaissance Drama in England 7*, ed. Leeds Barroll (1995), 145–205). *The Taming of A Shrew*, as printed in the Quarto of 1594, names Pembroke's Men as the acting company on the title-page. This text, however, can be regarded as an independent and anonymous play in its own right, having only limited connection with the Folio's *The Taming of the Shrew*. As compared with the *Shrew* plays, the 1595 text of *Richard Duke of York* is much closer to the Folio equivalent *3 Henry VI*; nevertheless, it is considerably independent, and it has traditionally been described as 'bad' or memorially reconstructed. As for *Titus Andronicus*, though the textual situation is relatively straightforward, the circumstances of production are confused. The 1594 Quarto names three companies, 'the Earle of *Darbie*, Earle of *Pembrooke*, and Earle of *Sussex* their Seruants'. Editors have been receptive to David George's view that the three companies mounted a joint performance (David George, 'Shakespeare and Pembroke's Men', *SQ* 32 (1981), 305–23; Eugene M. Waith, in his 1984 Oxford edition of *Titus Andronicus*, p. 8; Bate, ed., *Titus*, pp. 74–5), but a summary stage history recording three productions cannot be discounted. The case for the Pembroke company's owning the *Titus* playbook is slight but suggestive: it was this company who were discarding manuscripts for publication in 1594.

[2] Gurr, p. 262.

probably had some help from George Peele in writing *Titus*.[1] *Richard Duke of York* can be assigned to 1591, and the later dating of *Titus* takes it too out of 1592. Nothing contradicts the assumption that *Richard III* was mostly written in or before mid 1592, but was completed in the preliminary state represented in the Folio text only after the formation of Pembroke's Men. Strange's Men were performing at the Rose playhouse from February until the plague closure in June. As Philip Henslowe's *Diary* provides a full record of the plays they put on, we can be fairly sure that Strange's Men did not perform *Richard III* in this period.[2] If Pembroke's were the first company to stage the play, it might have begun its life on stage during the company's 1592 tour of the provinces. Its first appearance in a London playhouse might perhaps have been postponed by the plague at least until Christmas. This offers a possible explanation as to why the theatrically allusive pamphlets of 1592 such as Thomas Nashe's *Pierce Penniless* and *Greene's Groatsworth of Wit* make no reference to it. But there are many 'if's in such an account; uncertainty remains.

*The First Tetralogy*. *Richard III* concludes a sequence that Shakespeare had begun in the historical plays mentioned above. Those treating the reign of Henry VI were first published under the titles *The First Part of Henry the Sixth* (the First Folio title, there being no earlier printed text), *The First Part of the Contention Between the Houses of York and Lancaster* (in the First Folio *The Second Part of Henry VI*, in this edition *The Contention*), and *The True Tragedy of Richard Duke of York and the Good King Henry the Sixth* (in the First Folio *The Third Part of Henry VI*, in this edition *Richard Duke of York*). The second and third of these plays depict the Wars of the Roses between the dynastic houses of Lancaster and York, showing a period of political chaos that lent short-lived power to those who temporarily triumphed on the battlefield. Henry VI's disinclination to rule allows a succession of warlords to rise and fall. His

---

[1] Taylor, 'Shakespeare and Others'; Brian Boyd, 'Common Words in *Titus Andronicus*', *Notes and Queries*, 240 (1995), 300–7; MacD. P. Jackson, 'Stage Directions and Speech Headings in Act I of *Titus Andronicus* Q (1594)', *Studies in Bibliography*, 49 (1996), 134–48.

[2] Henslowe records four performances by Sussex's Men of a play called *Buckingham* between 30 December 1593 and 27 January 1594, but this seems unlikely to be Shakespeare's *Richard III*.

purchase on the crown is rarely secure, and at times he loses it. Margaret, the dispossessed voice of the past in *Richard III*, appears as a marital trophy of Henry's conquests in France in *1 Henry VI*, then as Henry's queen, powerbroker, and the mistress of Suffolk in *The Contention*, and then as Amazonian warrior replacing the king as leader of the Lancastrian forces in *Richard Duke of York*. Her part in tormenting and murdering the captive Duke of York is well remembered in *Richard III*. Because King Henry is present in *Richard III* only as a corpse and a ghost, Margaret is the sole figure who remains alive in all four plays.

As for Richard, he first appears towards the end of *The Contention*, and in *Richard Duke of York* quickly establishes himself as the most violent and determined warrior of the Duke's three surviving sons. At first he is a loyal supporter of his father and his brother Edward, who by the end has become king. Richard the hardy warrior evolves into something more complex, beguiling, and repulsive in the soliloquy that ends 3.2.[1] This speech initiates Shakespeare's portrayal of Richard from a psychological standpoint, a man rejected by women on account of the 'chaos' of his body. Finding himself 'like one lost in a thorny wood' he determines to 'hew my way out with a bloody axe' so that he can 'catch the English crown', a task that will require the skills of the self-transformer Proteus as well as sheer violence. The play ends with Richard helping to stab Henry's son Edward on the battlefield at Tewkesbury and single-handedly murdering Henry himself in the Tower of London. In the closing moments, comparing himself to Judas, he kisses his brother's son, the infant Prince Edward. It is a clear sign that Richard's future axe-strokes will be aimed at his own family.

So the ground is laid for *Richard III*, which will bring the entire tetralogy to an end. In this play the Lancastrian faction is represented only by two stranded women, Anne and Margaret. Richard will settle all scores, with the effect that his death purges the strife of the past. The conflict is no longer between two houses almost equally weighted in military might. Richard might be considered an effect or product of the conflictual world that came before him,

---

[1] See the section quoted below, p. 35. I cannot exclude the possibility that Richard's speeches here and at the end of 5.6 were added or expanded after Shakespeare wrote *Richard III*.

a sump into which factious malice has dropped to be distilled. The monstrousness of one man can eventually, through his death at Richmond's hands, engender peace and a sense of national community. This stable resolution is something that the earlier chronicle form resists. The Tudor monarchy established by Richmond will belong to a new era. The savage engine of medieval history can be arrested. Memory will no longer entail unsettled grievance and the desire for retribution. Conditions have come into being whereby a line can be drawn under the past. The audience of Shakespeare's here and now can remember events for their mythic quality across a gap of time.

*Touching Those Times.* Twentieth-century criticism was often much occupied with stating or challenging the place of the First Tetralogy within Tudor political thought. *Richard III* itself is the most crucial of these plays because it shows the first Tudor monarch coming to power, and because it gives the sequence shape and closure. To E. M. W. Tillyard and Lily B. Campbell, Shakespeare's history plays, including the 'Second Tetralogy' of *Richard II*, *1* and *2 Henry IV*, and *Henry V*, restate a providential view of history whereby the Wars of the Roses are a delayed punishment on the nation for Henry IV's deposition of Richard II; a peaceful and ordered polity is restored with the killing of Richard III, who encapsulates all that is opposed to God's will. Shakespeare is an apologist who echoes this view of history as it had been articulated most clearly in the chronicles from which Shakespeare drew his material.[1] This view has been challenged from a number of directions. A keynote was sounded by A. P. Rossiter, who realized that Richard's appeal as a stage character decisively complicated the play's political and moral significance. He contrasted Richard as 'a huge triumphal stage personality' with him as a figure within 'a rigid Tudor *schema* of retributive justice'.[2] Nicholas Brooke similarly found ambivalence in the 'gigantic scheme' of history. He stressed its ritualistic patterns, which he found 'explicitly Christian' and at the same time 'repulsive'. Richard, in accordance with the Christian scheme, derives from the 'Vice' of the old morality plays, but

[1] E. M. W. Tillyard, *Shakespeare's History Plays* (1944); Lily B. Campbell, *Shakespeare's 'Histories'* (San Marino, 1947).

[2] A. P. Rossiter, *Angel With Horns* (1961), pp. 1–22 (p. 2).

grows beyond this role to become a heroic exemplar of humankind as beings able to exert will; the world is 'poorer for his loss'.[1]

Other critics, such as David Bevington, saw the plays of the First Tetralogy as dealing analogically with political topics that concerned thinkers of Shakespeare's time rather than as explanatory linear narratives.[2] This approach enables a more secular reading of the plays' politics. It applies more immediately to the Henry VI plays than to the more obviously teleological *Richard III*, though here too it can act as a useful corrective. Recent historical approaches to Shakespeare's plays have usefully drawn attention to the interplay between theatre and state politics in Elizabethan England. Work flowing from Marjorie Garber's influential study has placed psychoanalytic interpretation and considerations of gender in the foreground, showing how these cannot be separated from the arena of politics as traditionally defined.[3] *Richard III* emerges from these various interpretations as a more complex and contradictory work than Tillyard would have recognized. It remains a play very much about history, but the term 'history' itself has been complicated by critics' attention to concepts such as performance, representation, and gender.

If, at first sight, Shakespeare seems to restate the tenets of Tudor orthodoxy, this may be because it was virtually impossible to do otherwise. The times were, in Ben Jonson's words, 'somewhat queasy to be touched'.[4] In 1589 the Privy Council sought to scrutinize all stage plays because the actors had taken upon themselves 'certain matters of divinity and state unfit to be suffered'.[5] Shakespeare, writing a few years later, would have been aware that he was negotiating troublesome ground that was critical to the Tudor claim to the right to govern. His freedom to vary on the received accounts was limited. He would be conscious that matters fit for perusal in books would not automatically be fit for display on the

---

[1] Nicholas Brooke, *Shakespeare's Early Tragedies* (1968), pp. 78–9.

[2] David Bevington, *Tudor Drama and Politics* (Cambridge, Mass., 1968).

[3] Marjorie Garber, 'Descanting on Deformity', in *Shakespeare's Ghost Writers* (New York and London, 1987), 28–51. See also Barber and Wheeler, pp. 86–124; Charnes; and Jean E. Howard and Phyllis Rackin, *Engendering a Nation* (London and New York, 1997).

[4] Ben Jonson, *Sejanus his Fall*, ed. Philip J. Ayres (Manchester, 1990), 1.82.

[5] The document is reproduced in E. K. Chambers, *The Elizabethan Stage*, 4 vols. (Oxford, 1923), iv. 306–7.

popular stage, and that the approach he adopted would count as much as the subject matter itself.

Historically, the death of Edward IV ushered in the reign of a boy-king Edward V, aged only twelve. Factional disputes made it possible for Richard quickly to consolidate his power-base and become Protector.[1] Appealing to the need for stability and impugning Edward with bastardy, he dislodged the uncrowned and unanointed Edward, and was himself crowned king. Meanwhile Edward and his brother were held in the Tower and effectively imprisoned. According to the Tudor accounts, they were murdered at the instigation of Richard, though this has been frequently disputed. Rosemary Horrox suggests that the rebellion of August 1483 aimed at rescuing the princes from the Tower provides a plausible context for Richard deciding to kill the princes. She comments, 'The princes appear to conform to the pattern established by earlier deposed kings, who remained alive until a rebellion in their favour demonstrated that they were still a threat.'[2] Shakespeare's sources do not mention the rebellion. They inform us that Richard's coronation led to a renewed outbreak of dynastic warfare, first in Buckingham's revolt in October 1483 (a major event that Shakespeare represents only perfunctorily), then in the armed uprising in support of Henry Tudor, Earl of Richmond, in 1485. Richard was killed at the Battle of Bosworth Field, and Richmond became Henry VII, the first Tudor king.

These events were related in the series of interconnected narrative accounts known collectively as the Tudor chronicles. They established a new historiography that helped to provide an ideological basis for Tudor power. From smaller-scale beginnings in manuscript, the chronicles expanded into an immense record of national history reproduced in print, and indeed these huge books owe their very existence to the young and burgeoning technology of the printing press. The last and longest of them, the 1587 edition of Raphael Holinshed's *Chronicles*, was to become the source for more plays of the period than any other book.[3]

---

[1] Shakespeare follows More in playing down the aristocratic support for Richard. His rise to power seems to depend on a shaky alliance with the London citizens, making it an offence to the feudal model of kingship.

[2] Rosemary Horrox, *Richard III: A Study of Service* (Cambridge, 1989), p. 151 and n. 52.

[3] Private communication from Martin Wiggins.

The textual genealogy of the chronicles dealing in part with the events represented in *Richard III* is a complex subject in its own right.[1] A version of More's *History* was published in Richard Grafton's 'Continuation' to *The Chronicle of John Hardyng* (1543). Grafton's main source for the period was the *Anglica Historia*, written early in the century by More's Italian friend Polydore Vergil and published in Basel in 1534. He departed from Vergil in order to incorporate More's own account, and so he embedded More within a larger historical narrative.

Shakespeare's most immediate sources were two even lengthier synthetic compilations: Edward Hall's chronicle of 1548 and 1550, with its programmatic title *The Union of the Two Noble and Illustre Families of Lancaster and York*, and its expanded successor Holinshed's *Chronicles* in the second edition of 1587. Though Hall owes much to Grafton, some of Hall's translation of Vergil was independent, and Hall was prepared to introduce new matter. He followed Grafton's example of switching from Vergil to More then back to Vergil, and referred to the same manuscript of More.

Holinshed's account of Richard III is largely copied from Hall's. However, the edition of More's works prepared by his nephew William Rastell had appeared in the interim (1557), and Holinshed introduced new details from it. There are numerous local departures from Hall, and the second edition imported more fragments of new material. For most of Shakespeare's *Richard III* his most regular source of information is not obvious, as Hall and Holinshed supply the same information. There are aspects of plot and vocabulary that have specific links with both chronicles, and there is no immediately clear pattern to their distribution.[2]

The chronicles played a major role in the Tudor mapping out of nationhood. They impress on their readers the sheer significance of English history as a topic crucial to the discursive formulation of an independent English national identity, and they lock the fortunes of the nation firmly to the person and personality of the reigning king. Though often tendentious, their account would have been the one widely acknowledged version of events. Henry VII

---

[1] For a fuller account, see Alison Hanham, *Richard III and his Early Historians, 1483–1535* (Oxford, 1975), pp. 198–219.

[2] Churchill, *Richard the Third up to Shakespeare*; Edleen Begg, 'Shakespeare's Debt to Hall and to Holinshed in *Richard III*', *Studies in Philology*, 32 (1935), 189–96.

probably commissioned Vergil's *Anglica Historia*. Grafton published Hardyng's *Chronicle* and Hall's *Union* within a few years of Henry VIII's dissolution of the monasteries. The *Union* in particular contributed to a new ideological infrastructure based on the monarch, consciously set in place after Henry's break with the Church of Rome.

The chronicles can therefore be regarded as chapters of a newly articulated national history hung up, like the armour in the opening soliloquy of *Richard III*, for monuments. However, their place was not necessarily secure. In 1555, two years after the Catholic Queen Mary came to the throne, Hall's chronicle was suppressed.[1] Protestants began to be persecuted in the same year. Nothing could show more clearly how the chronicles were contingent upon the politics of the moment.

It is worth remembering, then, that, from the standpoint of an Elizabethan reader, the writer of More's *History* could be seen as not only a major humanist scholar but also a martyr who died at the hands of Henry VIII for his loyalty to the Church of Rome. The *History* was first published in its own right two years after the Marian suppression of Hall, in Rastell's laudatory edition of More's works. The edition as a whole was issued not so much for the merit of the works themselves as for the Catholic doctrines they could be taken to embody.[2] Much depends on context. In the Rastell edition, More's *History* might have been read analogically in relation to Henry VIII as a tyrant who responded to legitimate resistance by executing his opponents. Shakespeare would have been aware of More as a Catholic humanist. He would have been especially alert to the ambivalence of his narrative if, as has been argued, he had pro-Catholic sympathies.[3]

Hall and Holinshed both clearly identify where More's *History* is incorporated into their larger narratives, even at the expense of disrupting their own organization of material.[4] In Holinshed, the chapter on Edward V is headed, 'The History of King Edward V and

---

[1] Annabel M. Patterson, *Reading Holinshed's 'Chronicles'* (Chicago, 1994), p. 251.

[2] Alistair Fox, *Sir Thomas More: History and Providence* (Oxford, 1982), p. 254.

[3] Honigmann, *Lost Years*, pp. 114–25.

[4] For More's own sources, see Richard S. Sylvester, ed., *The History of Richard III* (Sir Thomas More, *Complete Works*, vol. 2; New Haven and London, 1963), pp. lxv–lxxx.

King Richard III unfinished, written by Master Thomas More then one of the under-sheriffs of London, about the year of our Lord 1513, according to a copy of his own hand, printed among his other works'. Here the debt to More is advertised so insistently that the heading promises that his *History* will break through the arrangement of chapters according to the reigns of monarchs. As it happens, the beginning of Richard III's reign prompts a new chapter as usual. After some eight pages a note in the margin records that 'Here endeth Sir Thomas More, and this that follows is taken out of Master Hall'.

More's account breaks off, apparently unfinished, soon after Richard becomes king. Consequently, the strong sense of closure effected by Shakespeare through the killing of Richard and the accession of Richmond is entirely absent. Despite his demonization of Richard, More might have resisted developing a specifically pro-Tudor polemic, which would be hard to avoid if the life-history were seen through to its conclusion.[1] By the time More wrote the *History* he might already have had doubts about Henry VIII, the monarch he served. Richard as the antitype of the Tudor king might begin to look like his analogue.

Some such awareness even finds oblique expression in Holinshed. The 1587 edition adds after the account of Hastings's execution the following comment: 'Thus began he to establish his kingdom in blood, growing thereby in hatred of the nobles, and also abridging both the line of his life and the time of his regiment; for God will not have bloodthirsty tyrants' days prolonged, but will cut them off in their ruff, according to David's words: "Impio, fallaci, avidoque caedis | Fila mors rumpet viridi in iuventa" (*Buchanan, in Psalm* 55)' ('For the man who is wicked, false, and eager for slaughter, death breaks the thread of life in vigorous youth'). In this passage Richard becomes a wider model of the monarch who oversteps sanctioned authority. The biblical paraphrase might justify the killing of a tyrant, any tyrant. Holinshed cites Psalm 55, which denounces tyranny in words that have particular relevance to Richard's judicial murder of Hastings: 'He laid his hands upon such as be at peace with him, and he brake his covenant. | The words of his mouth were softer than butter, having war in his heart; his words were smoother than oil, and yet be they very swords . . . And as for them,

---

[1] Sylvester, pp. xcviii–civ.

thou, O God, shalt bring them unto the pit of destruction. | The bloodthirsty and deceitful men shall not live out half their days. | Nevertheless, my trust shall be in thee, O Lord.' This song of suffering is given an implicit active, political gloss by citing it in the Latin metrical paraphrase of the opponent of tyranny and defender of tyrannicide, George Buchanan (Paris, 1566; London, 1580). Buchanan may have been invoked for his reputation as a radical in these matters. Further, a precise reference back to More himself is possible. In his Latin academic drama *Baptistes* (first published in England in 1577, translated as *Tyrannical Government* in 1642) Buchanan allegorizes Henry VIII as the archetypal tyrant Herod, and his executed victim Sir Thomas More as John the Baptist.[1] If the allusion to *Baptistes* holds, the implications are considerable. More, as author of the narrative of Hastings's execution, would seem to anticipate his own death at the instigation of Henry VIII. So the revision in the second edition of Holinshed offers momentarily to subvert the pro-Tudor polemic of the chronicle as a whole.

The description of Richard in More and the chronicles remains that of a tyrant whose physique reflects his criminality, and that became the received picture. Shakespeare may have been familiar from his schooldays with a brief propagandist distillation of the chronicle account headed 'King Richard III, the Cruel Tyrant' in Richard Reynoldes's grammar-school primer, *The Foundation of Rhetoric* (1563).[2] Amongst early audiences too, this book would have been more widely read than the large and expensive tomes of Hall and Holinshed. The account of Richard III, given as a stylistic example of historical narrative, was a compact if overstated account of his 'cruel tyranny'.

By and large, until Sir George Buc's defence of Richard was published in 1646, this view of Richard was almost uncontested. However, a tract anticipating Buc's position did circulate in manuscript in the sixteenth century.[3] The later Elizabethan copies

[1] 'I represented the accusation and death of Thomas More, as far as the similarity of the subject-matter allowed, and I provided a portrait of tyranny at that time': Buchanan, quoted in I. D. McFarlane, *Buchanan* (1981), p. 384.

[2] T. W. Baldwin, *William Shakespeare's small Latine & Lesse Greeke* (Urbana, 1943), pp. 43–4, 311–12. See Commentary to 3.1.69–78.

[3] Preserved in British Library, Add. MS 29307, Duke of Devonshire's library, MS 44 P. 23892, Huntington Library, MS 199, and Folger Library, MS 49.10. See W. Gordon Zeeveld, 'A Tudor Defense of Richard III', *PMLA* 55 (1940), 946–57. Quotations from Zeeveld's transcripts.

of this favourable account of Richard show awareness of him as a figure who had been presented on stage, claiming that 'Malicious credulity rather embraceth the partial writings of indiscreet chroniclers and witty playmakers than his laws and actions, the most innocent and impartial witnesses.' Yet the Elizabethan revisions also open up the possibility that the tract's defence is an ironic hoax, by introducing the hedging conclusion that 'for all this, know I hold this but as a paradox'. The text stayed out of print in Queen Elizabeth's reign, but Sir William Cornwallis appropriated it as one of his *Essays and Paradoxes* (1616); here the ironic reading is formalized, not least in Cornwallis's title. If Shakespeare knew of this submerged and sometimes anxiously qualified defence tradition, he responded to it cryptically or not at all.

The events of Richard's rise to power and reign touched on some of the most sensitive issues in early modern political thinking, the basis and nature of the power invested in a monarch. There is, moreover, a potentially dangerous fracture-line between two approaches to the subject matter that entail two ways of thinking about the past. One, the 'teleological', sees events leading forward towards the present as an ordained outcome. The other, the 'analogical', sees events as a metaphorical vehicle for exploring the concerns of the Elizabethan present. They potentially conflict in the lessons they teach, as well as in their assumptions about historical process. The extended chronicle account was obviously teleological, but the unfinished account from More conspicuously embedded within it was more open to analogical reading.

Could Richard's overthrow by Henry Tudor, Earl of Richmond and first of the Tudor kings, be justified? The view expressed in the 'Homily against Disobedience' read from the pulpits of English churches throughout the land was that rebellion against the monarch was forbidden: 'The wicked judge Pilate said to Christ, "Knowest thou not that I have power to crucify thee, and have power also to loose thee?" Jesus answered, "Thou couldest have no power at all against me except it were given thee from above." Whereby Christ taught us plainly that even the wicked rulers have their power and authority from God, and therefore it is not lawful for their subjects to withstand them, although they abuse their power.'[1]

---

[1] Quotations from early texts are modernized, as here, unless cited for their material documentary significance.

That doctrine reinforced royal authority in the here-and-now, but applied awkwardly to Richmond's overthrow of Richard. So an analogical reading of the events potentially contradicts the teleological reading. Moreover, Richmond's hereditary claim to the throne was weaker than Richard's. There is scope for arguing that Richard is legitimate and therefore Richmond the usurper. And according to some Tudor political thinkers, whereas a usurper could be overthrown, a despotic king had to be endured.

In More's account Richard is a usurper as well as a despot. That Richard arranged for the young princes to be murdered in the Tower is probable, though unproven. Perhaps more to the point is the way this crime is used to demonize Richard. Comparable crimes by other rulers were not treated as signs that the ruler was a delinquent tyrant. More turns the weakly evidenced supposition into fact, and draws the necessary conclusion from it: 'certain it is that he contrived their [the princes'] destruction, with the usurpation of the regal dignity upon himself'.[1]

Potentially, there are technical difficulties here, for Richard did not kill the princes in order to become king, and Prince Edward had not been crowned.[2] But More's argument does not focus on technicalities. In practice, the asserted certainty that Richard is a usurper merges with the portrait of him as a monstrous tyrant. Richard can be seen as a murderer of innocent children. As such, his affinities lie with archetypal figures such as the biblical tyrant and child-slayer Herod.[3] His crimes are multiplied. Richard cannot credibly be blamed for Clarence's death as More at least suggests. More also emphasizes Richard's physical deformity as a supposed measure of his evil inner being. Richard is unlikely to have been as misshapen as More describes him. As one moves away from More to the wider canvas of Tudor historiography, Richmond's killing of Richard can then become a symbolic act of purging the realm,

---

[1] Holinshed, p. 363. This is More's only use in the *History* of 'usurp' and its cognates. Holinshed ends his account of the reign with an afterword making the same connection: 'Thus far Richard the usurper, unnatural uncle to Edward the Fifth and Richard Duke of York, brethren' (p. 479). Shakespeare's play uses the word nine times, though not always with reference to Richard.

[2] Sixteenth-century books portraying English monarchs showed Edward V with the crown emblematically hovering above his head instead of sitting on it. See John Rastell, *Pastime for People* (c.1529–30), F5ᵛ.

[3] More reserves the phrase 'traitorous tyranny' for Richard's murder of the princes (Holinshed, p. 402). For Herod as an implied analogue in *Richard III*, see Commentary to 4.3.2–3 and 4.3.9.

1. The Family of Henry VII, with St George and the Dragon. Lady Elizabeth opposite Henry VII (Richmond). Artist unknown; probably painted by order of Henry VII *c*.1503.

like St George slaying the dragon (see fig. 1). Along with his marriage to Lady Elizabeth, his status as national saviour compensates for his shaky claim to the throne. So the sensitivity of the subject did not make it incapable of representation. On the contrary, it becomes essential to depict it openly and vigorously, indeed in lurid colours.

For his part, Shakespeare played up to the image of a villainous and deformed Richard. The 'facts' of the play are uglier than those of his sources, but Shakespeare complicates things by making Richard charismatic and attractive in spite of them.

'*As it were stage plays*'. For Shakespeare, the chronicles would have suggested a mode for conceptualizing English history that is detailed, grand in scale, and structured. Yet it can scarcely be doubted that Shakespeare's encounter with More in the source material fuelled the difference in the dramatization of history between the Henry VI plays and *Richard III*. Shakespeare engages more fully with More than the surrounding account, responding to More as a source of structured narrative episodes. This applies especially to the pages in Holinshed from which extracts are printed in Appendix E.

More's *History* scarcely claims to be history as we would now (albeit sceptically) understand the term. As a record of historical events it is informed by way of structure, style, mood, and even content by classical historiography, in particular the accounts of Tiberius written by Suetonius and Tacitus.[1] It is also crammed with tendentiousness. In manipulating historical actuality More acted neither naively nor ineptly. Indeed he helped to lay the foundations of modern historiography by moving away from a tabular chronicle of dates, events, and documents, towards a conception of history as an admonitory narrative of people acting out their lives under the eye of God. Stopping well short of the end of Richard's life, More closes:

I have heard by credible report of such as were secret with his chamberlain that after this abominable deed done [the murder of the princes] he never had a quiet mind[2] . . . He never thought himself sure. Where he went abroad, his eyes whirled about, his body privily fenced, his hand ever upon his dagger . . . so was his restless heart continually tossed and tumbled with the tedious impression and stormy remembrance of his abominable deed.

More gives guarded substantiation to the details he narrates, but the substantiation also admits the scope for doubt. That difficult object of historical representation, Richard's bad conscience, is all to the point. His alleged disturbance of mind lends credibility to his responsibility for the 'abominable deed' and builds a bridge between the event and its moral meaning. More is engaged in an imaginative reconstruction of a human subjectivity. To this extent, the foundations of his portrait lie in a percept rather than in knowable facts.

[1] Sylvester, pp. lxxxvi–xcviii.
[2] Holinshed (1587) adds some general moralization on 'a guilty conscience'.

More's *History* had various qualities that anticipate Shakespeare's play: interest in the psychology of human motivation, political insight, ethical perspective, depth of texture, subtle irony, and dramatic immediacy. He explicitly uses the metaphor of drama: 'in a stage play, all the people know right well that one playing the sultan is percase a souter [for instance a cobbler]. . . . And so they said these matters be king's games, as it were stage plays, and for the more[1] part played upon scaffolds.' That is the note on which More closes one of his most dramatically executed passages, his description of Richard's pretended reluctance to be king before the citizens at Baynard's Castle (see Appendix E, Passage 3). More's point is that the onlookers knew better than to intervene in affairs of state: Richard's speech is impressive enough as a performance for it to be accepted as a king's game, but no one is deluded into thinking it sincere. For the dissimulation to work, the audience too must dissemble, and they recognize their unavoidable complicity. Nevertheless, the whole point of Richard's speech, and Buckingham's before it, is that the citizens' assent was not easily won, and even needed falsification. In More's account, acting skills achieve an outcome against the odds. Translate this into a real stage-play, and the drama is immediately both urgent and complex. The play's own activity of playing becomes, within the story it tells, the route to kingship itself. Meanwhile a theatre audience is able to enjoy and admire the charade as a piece of daring theatrical skill in a way More's citizens and the play's citizens could not, assured that they do not face the same kind of consequences. The shift from one medium to another helps to release a Richard at which More can only hint: actor, manipulator, entertainer, and conniver. Because this Richard presents himself as friend of the audience, he threatens to eclipse Richard the hateful tyrant.

*History and Tragedy.* To describe *Richard III* as a history play is to suggest that it appeals to those who are interested in the political events of late medieval England. As has been suggested, the play is perhaps now more relevant as a study of history as representation, of the politics of historical narrative. But it is also, as it is

---

[1] Thus Rastell and Holinshed. For 'more', Hall reads 'most'. If not authorial, 'more' might conceivably involve wordplay on More's name by way of allusion to his execution.

proclaimed on the Q1 title-page, a tragedy. This broadens its appeal. In Shakespeare's time tragedy was sometimes seen as provoking a tearful response that reached out specifically to female auditors as well as men.[1] In more recent times, the play has often appealed as political tragedy to audiences with no particular interest in the events of English history.

Shakespeare's dramatization of the chronicles introduces major episodes early in the play that are almost entirely fictional, a massive prologue sequence written in an imaginative, poetic, and classically informed style. Richard's seduction of Anne in 1.2 sets him firmly in place as the play's driving force, and the murder of Clarence in 1.4 explores areas of human subjectivity whose oblique relevance to Richard becomes clear by the end. Despite his debt to the chronicles for historical information, Shakespeare's account of events after the murder of the young princes is organized around fictional encounters: first Richard's confrontation with the two queens and his mother in 4.4, and then the ghosts' appearance to Richard and Richmond on the eve of the Battle of Bosworth. Hall and Holinshed supply little more than intermittent historical anchor-points for a drama that shows a process of nemesis as it bears upon the subjectivity of Richard himself. This is the process set in place early in Shakespeare's play, before it comes into direct engagement with More's account, and continued after those central episodes. So the play assumes its own form as a variant on the revenge tragedy by manipulating and altering the structures of its historical sources.

It is in these respects that the promise on the title-page of Q1 that it will present a tragedy is fulfilled. In Hall's chronicle the chapter heading for the reign is already given the generic marker: 'The Tragical Doings of King Richard the Third'. Before Shakespeare and Marlowe, 'history' was not a formal subdivision of dramatic writing in any recognized sense. The 1623 Folio gathered a third of Shakespeare's plays under the heading of (English) histories, creating the impression that he single-handedly defined a new subgenre. But the head-title still calls *Richard III* a 'Tragedy'.

Categories intermix in another source text for *Richard III*, the *Mirror for Magistrates*, a homiletic work that sets material from the chronicles and elsewhere in rhyming stanzas.[2] The *Mirror* is

[1] Howard and Rackin, pp. 101–4.
[2] First published in 1559; progressively expanded editions in 1563, 1578, and 1587.

22

divided into numbered sections described as 'tragedies',[1] each dealing with the fall of a particular historical figure. 'In this narrow courtiers' world', Emrys Jones writes, 'the ambitious scheme and climb, enjoy a few hours of power and suddenly plunge into an abyss.'[2] That is the nature of tragedy as the *Mirror* defines it. In loose, rule-of-thumb terms, following the Renaissance distinction between political and private virtue, 'history' becomes 'tragedy' in the *Mirror* because it is particularized around the misdeeds or fall of a single figure. This practical reduction of the difference to a matter of emphasis in non-dramatic contexts opened the way for popular drama to embrace the term 'history' as it sought ways to describe its own heterogeneous practices.

There are direct borrowings from Seneca in the imagery of passages such as Clarence's dream.[3] Other major non-historical passages draw on Seneca, an influence reflected in the technical device of stichomythia in the exchange of short speeches between Richard and Anne in 1.2. It is found again in the dramatic configuration of this scene and others. The wooing of Anne probably owes something to the wooing of Megara by the murderer-king Lycus in Seneca's *Hercules Furens*; Shakespeare seems to draw on his *Hippolytus* for Richard's gambit of offering Anne his sword. Situations in 4.4 echo *Troades*: Seneca's group of women lamenting the destruction of Troy anticipates Shakespeare's gathering of women who have lost children at Richard's hands, with the Duchess of York equivalent to Hecuba, the mother of the ill-omened Paris, grief-stricken by the destruction his life has caused.[4] The effect is to ground the play in the fundamental and violent dramatic tropes of the Senecan world. *Richard III* is in this way aligned with tragedy of implacable fate on a classical model.[5] Events echo within the play itself, and its recourse to prophecy and ghosts makes the action seem inexorable. Here Christian exegesis is

---

[1] The term, though not usual in the titles of the poems, is found repeatedly in the introductory prose addresses between the poems.

[2] Jones, p. 193.     [3] See Brooks, 'Antecedents'.

[4] For these and other suggestions of Senecan influence, see Harold F. Brooks, '*Richard III*: Unhistorical Amplifications', *Modern Language Review*, 75 (1980), 721–37. See also Commentary to 1.2.159–68, 1.4.44, 48, 1.4.225, and 4.2.63–4.

[5] In the background to Seneca are the tragedies of Euripides, but, although Shakespeare arguably catches something of the spirit of Euripides, it seems doubtful that he knew the plays.

challenged by glimpses of a view of humanity as tortured and lost, strangers to the idea of redemption.

However, Shakespeare avoids the stage convention that gives formal privilege to a Senecan perspective in other Elizabethan plays. Thomas Kyd's *The Spanish Tragedy* was first published in 1592, at about the time Shakespeare was writing *Richard III*, though it had evidently reached the London stage some years before. It represents a startling attempt to impose an insistent if ironized Senecan framework on an action that takes place in a Renaissance court. The call for revenge is initiated in the Induction, where, recalling the dialogue between the Ghost of Tantalus and the Fury in Seneca's *Thyestes*, the ghost of the recently killed Don Andrea petitions the figure of Revenge himself. A Senecan otherworld is given a comparable formal representation in the opening of the Queen's Men's play *The True Tragedy of Richard III* (published in 1594), which is influenced by *The Spanish Tragedy* and is in turn an influence on Shakespeare's *Richard III*. At the opening of *True Tragedy* an induction consisting of a dialogue between Truth and Poetry begins after the Ghost of Clarence enters calling for revenge. The figure of Truth, who appears also in John Pickering's early Senecan revenge play *Horestes* (1567), represents in *True Tragedy* the domestication of classical tragedy, offering 'A tragedy in England done but late' (l. 14).[1] Another text that cross-fertilizes the classics and the English events of the play is Sackville's verse 'Induction' added in the 1563 edition of *Mirror for Magistrates*. The late medieval vision of tragic history is given a Virgilian coloration when the poet is conducted on a journey through Hades. Shakespeare might have noted the passage when writing Clarence's classically informed dream vision of being drowned and transported to the underworld in 1.4, especially if

[1] Truth is also a choric figure in *Two Lamentable Tragedies*, a domestic drama written in its extant form no earlier than 1594 and attributed on the 1601 title-page to Robert Yarington. The plot in which two ruffians are hired to murder a boy in the woods has some resemblance to the murders of Clarence and the young princes in *Richard III* (though partly because both draw on *Leir*; see Martin Wiggins, *Journeymen in Murder* (Oxford, 1991), pp. 116–21). The Children in the Wood plot is closely related to the ballad 'The Norfolk Gentleman his Last Will and Testament' (also known as 'The Children in the Wood'), entered in the Stationers' Register on 15 October 1595, first extant edition *c*.1635, and quoted as an analogue to *Richard III* in New Variorum *Richard III*, ed. Horace Howard Furness, Jr. (Philadelphia and London, 1908), pp. 612–15.

he had already remarked on the Senecan ghost of Clarence in *True Tragedy*.

Both source texts offer a formal device of an Induction, but this is something that Shakespeare rejected. He had probably already experimented with the framing device in a comic context in *The Taming of the Shrew*, in which the 'Induction' involving Sly leads to Sly witnessing the main action involving Katherine and Petruccio. In *Richard III*, Richard's opening speech describes his gathering and ultimately tragic plots as 'inductious', but he is a Machiavellian and mortal human being, not an underworld spirit. He might be thought of as 'playing' the induction much as he later describes himself as playing 'like' the Vice (3.1.82). A slightly more formal Induction opens the play's final movement in 4.4, where Margaret describes herself as witness to a 'dire induction'. In the exchange between the grieving women that follows, the Duchess of York's phrase 'poor mortal living ghost' (4.4.21) pinpoints the relationship between the Senecan otherworld and the world these women inhabit.

*The Spanish Tragedy* was the foremost example of the revenge play as it had been developed by the English professional theatre. *Richard III* shares the sense that normal life has been disrupted by something horrible and otherly. It is not simply Richard, but the process he enacts. As in *The Spanish Tragedy*, the figure who is initially singled out as a wrongdoer initially prospers. 'Brought'st thou me hither to increase my pain?' the ghost of Andrea demands of Revenge halfway through *The Spanish Tragedy* (2.6.1). In *Richard III*, initial wrongdoings similarly take place before the play starts. From Margaret's point of view most of the other characters are ripe for punishment too, and Richard prospers by becoming her avenging demon. In the interim, the house of York and the Greys will suffer in ways that they, like the Spanish courtiers, fail to understand, and the primary target of revenge will temporarily triumph. The difference is that the horrible otherworld is merely intimated in the language in which Richard's origins are described. Whereas the devious and clutching otherworld is a fact of the narrative in *The Spanish Tragedy*, in *Richard III* it is an impression: perhaps merely how characters imagine themselves, perhaps—even less—simply the figures of speech by which they express their anguish.

Shakespeare borrows the elaborately patterned language

developed in plays such as *The Spanish Tragedy* and Kyd's *Soliman and Perseda*.[1] For example, repetition, antithesis, and other rhetorical devices in 1.2 heighten the erotic tension and at the same time intimate the dangers of entrapment; the seduction scene (2.2) in *The Spanish Tragedy* has similar characteristics. The web of rhetoric in *Richard III* effectively suggests a world in which events, as much as language, are locked into patterns of grim inevitability. Of course, that represents only one extreme of the play's stylistic range. At the other extreme are the wit, irony, irreverence and aggression of Richard's speech. There is, therefore, contestation of style and of ideational poetics. We might feel unsure as to whether the Senecan frame of reference is an elaborate and sustained figure of speech or a reality.

Shakespeare avoided the extremes of horror and violence that would accompany a drama by Seneca if it were acted on the stage. Richard's victims die off stage. The scene of Clarence's death is only a partial exception. Though the weapons are lunged, Clarence evidently meets his final end in the butt of malmsey and, fulfilling his prophetic dream, dies off stage of drowning. If so, the only death we actually see will be Richard's. It is Richard too who voluntarily endures the sword-point at his throat in 1.2. He survives that moment to massacre others, but the play habitually draws back from the moment of execution or butchery. After 1.2, in marked contrast with *The Spanish Tragedy* or Shakespeare's *Titus Andronicus*, the scenes of lamentation are not enacted before corpses or mutilated bodies. Violence curtails life fearfully, but it does not make life grotesque or reduce the human person to a dismemberable piece of flesh. The very influence of plays such as *The Spanish Tragedy*, and the very use of Senecan apparatus such as dreams of the underworld and stage ghosts, help to measure out the extent to which *Richard III* has rejected some of the more reductively 'Senecan' aspects of the Elizabethan revenge play. The nominal revenger Richmond sees nothing and suffers nothing, proceeding to his silently motivated task in tranquillity.

---

[1] See A. R. Braunmuller, 'Early Shakespearean Tragedy and Its Contemporary Context', in *Shakespearean Tragedy*, ed. Malcolm Bradbury and David Palmer, Stratford-upon-Avon Studies, 20 (1984), pp. 97–128. For *Soliman and Perseda*, see Kyd, *Works*, ed. Frederick S. Boas (Oxford, 1901).

*Barabas and the Vice.* As for Richard, his energy, buoyancy, and gaiety place him at a distance from a Hieronimo or a Titus. Richard makes murder a game, a joke. His antecedents do not lie primarily in Seneca or Kyd, nor can they be confined to More's portrayal. His capacity to isolate himself from the action, to manipulate events, and to form a special relationship with the audience all reflect his consanguinity with Marlowe's Barabas in *The Jew of Malta* (*c.*1590) and, behind him, the Vice of medieval drama.

At the beginning of *Richard III* the audience first sees an actor alone on stage. He is not a formal prologue who supplies narrative context, but presents a character who is temporarily abstracted from a social world that does not yet exist. Of Shakespeare's major protagonists, Richard is the only one to begin the play addressing the audience. It helps, of course, that the audience would largely have known of Richard either from his appearance in *Richard Duke of York* or from prior awareness of history. But there was also a recent precedent for a play beginning with a soliloquy in *The Jew of Malta*. Marlowe confronted the challenge of opening the play with an abstracted figure by having Machiavel introduce Barabas in a formal prologue. Unlike Barabas, the historical Machiavelli was already notorious as a subversive and atheistic political theorist; Machiavel's self-introduction is sufficient. He is then able figuratively, perhaps literally, to point to his adherent Barabas, who is revealed in his study at the end of the Prologue. The audience is presented with an exemplum of Machiavellian doctrine. Moreover, Barabas's isolation on stage during his first soliloquy, and the piles of gold and silver with which he surrounds himself, betoken his alienated social and economic relationship with others. As Jew and as Machiavellian he is an outsider, and his relations with others will be characterized by mutual and aggressive hostility.

What Marlowe set in place so carefully Shakespeare could use to advantage. The isolation, its meaning, the implication that the on-stage figure will propel himself into a socio-political world that he will confront with hostility—all these are already implied. And this helps to initiate the audience's superior understanding of Richard as compared with his relatively naive opponents and victims. Then there are questions of tone. Barabas counterbalanced a rhapsodic account of his own wealth with a scathing depreciation of 'vulgar trade', as though the idea of material goods gave access to a visionary fantasy of the idea of opulence itself. He is sardonic in himself, and he is presented with a measure of sarcasm too. In the opening soliloquy of *Richard III* there is a comparable, if more restrained, sarcasm on the part of the speaker in relation to the social world he first describes. The exact nuance of Richard's voice is unnervingly uncertain, for he rails against things and people that are yet to come into view. The sonorous vocality of his words with their rich and perhaps studied eloquence is tinged with unspecifiable irony. He plays with our knowledge and with our ignorance. Should we laugh?—We are not sure, and yet audiences are quickly readied to respond to an innuendo, an intonation, or a glance.

Richard's immediate sociality in relation to the audience reflects his isolation within the play. What marks him out as separate from his world identifies him as special to us. Here too the opening refers back to Marlowe. Where Barabas would have worn the caricatural Jew's nose, Richard probably wore a comparably distorting hump on his back. His words almost immediately confirm that he too is set apart from his social world, he too is the engine of the play's plot devices, he too is the Machiavellian villain who makes the paradoxical but emphatic demand on the audience's interest and attention.

Richard also owes something of his sociality to Barabas. In a moment of unique and apparently unfeigned involvement with another person, he says to Buckingham:

> My other self, my counsel's consistory,
> My oracle, my prophet, my dear cousin!
> I like a child will go by thy direction.
> 
> (2.2.120–2)

There are echoes here of the co-operation between the Machiavellian villain Barabas and his accomplice Ithamore in Marlowe's *Jew of Malta*, though the terms 'cousin' and 'servant' mark out a significant difference in social relationship:

> Come near, my love, come near, thy master's life,
> My trusty servant, nay, my second self!
> For I have now no hope but even in thee,
> And on that hope my happiness is built.
> 
> (*Jew of Malta* 3.4.14–17)

Barabas and Richard use such hyperbole to weld together their alliances in crime. Both partnerships degenerate into rivalry that causes the accomplice to lose his life. The phrase 'my other self' was proverbial for friendship, and indeed it had potential homo-erotic implications to which Marlowe and perhaps Shakespeare respond. That Richard should engage in such mutuality might be puzzling, were it not that it complements his earlier narcissistic fantasy. Buckingham is indeed another self, taking on Richard's characteristics as a Protean actor. He states more emphatically than Richard himself his skills in the trade:

> I can counterfeit the deep tragedian:
> Speak, and look back, and pry on every side,
> Tremble and start at wagging of a straw
>
> (3.5.6–8)

and later, 'I'll play the orator' (3.5.93). Both speeches echo Richard's own great self-defining soliloquy invoking Proteus and Machiavelli in *Richard Duke of York* at 3.2.124–95: 'I can . . . Change shapes with Proteus for advantages, | And set the murderous Machiavel to school' (ll. 191–3), 'I'll play the orator' (l. 188). When Richard's victims are isolated individuals such as Anne and Clarence, he can play to them alone. When the audience is an assembly of citizens representative of society at large he needs to perform in relation to another performer. It is a reminder of the full dynamic of the actual theatre, in which a whole company of actors performs to a large audience.

The humorous or even sardonic edge to the episodes between Richard and Buckingham also glances back to Barabas and Ithamore. The two players of deep tragedy are sometimes a comic double act. Their silencing of opposition also attempts to marginalize the voices of human suffering and political reality. Hastings's last line, 'They smile at me that shortly shall be dead' (3.4.108), is placed strategically just before Richard and Buckingham enter in their absurd rotten armour (3.5.0.1–2) and then go on to intimidate the Mayor of London with the executed Hastings's head. However, in this respect Richard and Buckingham never entirely monopolize the action. The final word on Hastings is left to the Scrivener in 3.6, and to Hastings himself when he returns as a ghost.

Buckingham is something more than a professional colleague and something other than a mirror image. He can seem to draw some of Richard's energy from him, showing a political intelligence and an ability to take the initiative that suggest a limit to Richard's dynamism. In some productions Buckingham has appeared brisk and even dominating, a theatrical manager threatening to make Richard his puppet, an interpretation supported by Richard's offer to go by his direction (2.2.122). Yet Buckingham eventually goes to his death, which suggests that he has miscalculated his ability to control Richard. Richard might have quietly kept the upper hand all along. Fritz Kortner, for instance, played a Svengali-like Richard to Rudolf Forster's passive Buckingham, an equivalent to the mesmerized girl singer Trilby in George Du Maurier's story.[1] Ambiguity in the lines of dependence and manipulation is intrinsic to the villain–accomplice relationship as Marlowe had defined it. By any reading, Richard's dependence is a form of vulnerability, for even a Svengali needs a Trilby to perform at his behest. Moreover, the friendship cannot be sustained. Whether Buckingham is primarily interested in his promised reward or more perturbed by Richard's plan to kill the princes is unclear, but the rift that opens between them straight after the coronation ensures that kingship will bring Richard only a new kind of isolation.

Shakespeare therefore extends the psychological possibilities intimated in Marlowe's Barabas. Barabas himself had been based on a far less psychologized figure, the 'Vice' of the medieval and Tudor morality play. The Vice was an allegorical representation of a sin sent by the devil to tempt humanity. Richard makes the lineage clear towards the beginning of his intrigue against the princes, when in an aside he describes himself as 'like the formal Vice Iniquity' (3.1.82).[2] The name is both apt to Richard and allusive, for the Vice is called Iniquity in *Nice Wanton* (licensed for print 1560) and *Darius* (printed 1565), and later in Jonson's *The Devil is an Ass* (1616). But the morality plays developed the Vice as a grim jester, a conniver with the audience, an equivocator, a disguiser, a weeping feigner of empathy and grief, and a misleader of youth. His language is familiar, jocular, and sprinkled with oaths ('By the mass, ye will climb the ladder! | Ah, sirrah, I love a wench that can be wily': *Nice Wanton*, ll. 232–3); he plots and intrigues ('If thou tell no tales, but hold thy tongue, | I will set thee at liberty, ere it be

---

[1] Published in 1894; adapted for the theatre by Paul Potter and the actor-manager Herbert Beerbohm Tree in 1895.

[2] See in particular Bernard Spivack, *Shakespeare and the Allegory of Evil* (New York and London, 1958).

long, | Though thou be judged to die anon': *Nice Wanton*, ll. 367–9).[1] Richard shares all of these qualities, and they enable him to offset the play's formal and potentially static rhetoric by explosively breaking into the action and so violently propelling the plot forward. His downright and demotic language in lines such as 'And yet to win her, all the world to nothing? Ha?' (1.2.223) reflects his affinity with the conniving Vice.[2] His common touch, his deflating irreverence, his resort to soliloquies and asides, his schemes, his quips, wit, double meanings, and wordplay, all these bond him with the audience and show his allegiance with the Vice.[3] Marlowe's Barabas is another such figure. So too, later, would be Iago in Shakespeare's *Othello*.

Richard acknowledges his kinship. His dagger is not merely a weapon; it harks back to the crude wooden stage property wielded by his antecedent.[4] But Richard's dagger is dangerous, and he describes himself as merely *like* the formal Vice. This recognition of similitude also admits difference. Richard enacts a sarcastic, mobile, and detached variant on Margaret's serious vision of him as hell's agent on earth. He can both behave theatrically and take part in a morality play that shows the overarching conflict between God and the devil.

In so far as he acts out a Vice role that itself involves acting to the audience, he can scarcely be taken seriously as a member of the play's royal family. He aligns himself with the plebeian actor performing the role, behaving like a charlatan, as though he were immune from consequences. Actors have sometimes brought out affinities with the clown or court jester (fig. 10), and in the 1972 production at the Deutsches Theater, Berlin, Manfred Wekwerth combined Brechtian alienation-effect with Robert Weimann's explication of the role of the Vice, creating a formalized distinction between the character Richard Gloucester and the Vice who steps out of the play to address the audience directly.[5] As performer, Richard

[1] *Nice Wanton*, in *English Moral Interludes*, ed. Glynne Wickham (London and Totowa, NJ, 1976), pp. 143–62.

[2] Robert Weimann, 'Performance-Game and Representation in *Richard III*', in *Textual and Theatrical Shakespeare*, ed. Edward Pechter (Iowa, 1996), pp. 66–85.

[3] Ralph Berry, 'Richard III: Bonding the Audience', in *Mirror up to Shakespeare*, ed. J. C. Gray (Toronto and London, 1984), pp. 114–27.

[4] See Commentary to 3.1.111.

[5] Lawrence Gunter, 'Shakespeare on the East German Stage', in *Foreign Shakespeare*, ed. Dennis Kennedy (Cambridge, 1993), pp. 109–39.

has the appeal of letting us the audience in on the lofty workings of state, and showing us from a robustly mocking perspective that the great are paltry and weak. Whatever Richard does carries the implication that anyone sufficiently skilled could do the same. There are no mysteries. No person and no situation intrinsically commands respect. Humorous though it may be, his wit is a form of aggression, enfeebling his opponents and bolstering Richard himself in relation to them. Where he claims to be a 'plain man' of 'simple truth', he is furthest from plain truth. He concedes as much to the audience, who, like Clarence and Hastings, feel they have a special rapport with him. As with the Vice, the audience itself should be on its guard, for, as John W. Blanpied puts it, '*we* are the prize, to control us the object of the larger performance'.[1]

*Re-formation, Deformation.* As the most infamous monarch in English history, the home-grown example of a tyrant, Richard bears with him a pre-formed historical being, what Linda Charnes suggestively calls a notorious identity.[2] Sir Thomas More and the other Tudor historians made Richard mythic, and he appears on stage ready to fulfil or challenge expectations. Richard is above all playing himself, or, rather, outplaying the Richard of Tudor historical memory.

In accordance with his project of vilifying Richard, Sir Thomas More described him as 'evil-featured of limbs, crook-backed, the left shoulder much higher than the right'.[3] More's vocabulary is telling in itself: the limbs are, as it were, wicked of feature rather than simply ugly; *crook* or *crooked* can mean 'deviating from rectitude', and the left side of the body, here dominating, was associated with evil.[4] The Richard on stage himself indicates similar physical traits: he has a limp (1.1.23), his arm is withered (3.4.73–4), and his back has the appearance of a pedlar's pack or a saddle for a trained ape (3.1.130–1).

Actors have always had to confront the physical demands and interpretative implications of how they play Richard's deformity.

---

[1] John W. Blanpied, *Time and the Artist in Shakespeare's English Histories* (Newark, Del., and London, 1983), p. 97.

[2] Linda Charnes, *Notorious Identity* (Cambridge, Mass., and London, 1993).

[3] Hall, *King Edward V*, 1ᵛ. For 'evil', Holinshed has 'ill'.

[4] More exaggerated ('much') and reversed John Rous's statement that Richard had 'uneven shoulders, the right being higher than the left'.

It can obstruct an actor from realizing a dynamically energetic interpretation of the role, and Edwin Forrest's physical and ebullient Richard retained little trace of it. Ian McKellen showed Richard struggling to suppress his difficulties; his military uniform and overcoat gave an outward semblance of stiff-backed symmetry, leaving his disability to reveal itself in unguarded side-profiles and in his pained awkwardness managing buttons with his withered hand. A restrained lump on Simon Russell Beale's shoulder could jut his head forward with thick-necked aggression. But, like some other Richards, he stumbled on his bad leg as he stepped up to the throne in 4.2; courtiers rushed to help him out of his moment of dangerous embarrassment. Antony Sher approached the role seeking prosthetic realism, but ended up with a caricatural hump.[1] It was heaved above black crutches that offset his restrictions by giving him a grotesque mobility (fig. 9). As king he abandoned the crutches and was barely able to walk. Sher's visually extreme presence nevertheless communicated physical and emotional pain, and reminders that Richard suffers physically can offer moments of vividly corrective insight into his cruel monstrosity. In contrast, Alan Howard's excessive focus on facial and bodily deformity, reflecting a twisted and unempathetic mind, was accused of exaggerated showmanship. Howard's bad leg, encased in a steel surgical boot, was dragged along by a chain.

The able-bodied actor is, unavoidably, presenting a figure who is described as disabled. Though Colley Cibber described the late seventeenth-century actor Samuel Sandford as 'having a low and crooked person' and so 'naturally made for' the role, Richard's physical characteristics generally belong to the role as acted rather than the body of the actor.[2] As a result, the very appearance of Richard with limp or hunchback or twisted body has become a hallmark of acting as a process of transformation.[3] Over two centuries ago Samuel Johnson made the point in caricature, rumbustiously describing 'a great player' as 'a fellow who claps a

---

[1] Antony Sher, *Year of the King* (1985), pp. 108–17, 222.

[2] *An Apology for the Life of Colley Cibber* (1739), ed. Edmund Bellchambers (1822), pp. 139, 144.

[3] All the more so if the actor is a woman, as in the 1998 Shenandoah Shakespeare Express production. According to Ralph Cohen (private correspondence), Kate Norris readily melted into the role. She was perhaps able to do so because the role itself is intrinsically theatrical.

hump on his back, and a lump on his leg, and cries "I am Richard the Third"'.[1] Richard's histrionic self-definitions as the jolly lover or the fair-proportioned prince might remind an audience that the underlying figure is himself an enactment. There were similar complications when a female dramatic character played in the Elizabethan theatre by a boy, such as Rosalind or Viola, assumed the disguise of a young man. But all Elizabethan plays contained cross-gender acting, and many included female characters disguised as male. Richard's appearance is singular, a metatheatrical function in its own right.

Richard's traits as an actor, as a refigured portrait, and as an agent of evil are all cognate, and they all open up spaces for him beyond the more flat and stable world that the other characters inhabit. The complex texture of the dramatic role depends on the interplay between Richard as a reportraiture and Richard as a figure of immediacy, energy, and presence. Deformity gives a physical immediacy to the historical person and to the Vice that precede him alike. At the same time deformity is the defining bodily characteristic of his character in the play-world's here-and-now.

If the fiction is accepted at face value, Richard's physical attributes are part of a human predicament. Renaissance accounts of 'monsters' are dealing with something more sensational and altogether less readily accommodated to the sphere of humanity.[2] Nevertheless, there are momentary hints that Richard appears on earth as a horrible parodic inversion of Jesus Christ:

> From forth the kennel of thy womb hath crept
> A hell-hound that doth hunt us all to death.
> That dog that had his teeth before his eyes,
> To worry lambs and lap their gentle bloods,
> That foul defacer of God's handiwork
> Thy womb let loose, to chase us to our graves.
>
> (4.4.44–9) ·

[1] James Boswell, *Life of Johnson* (1791), ed. R. W. Chapman (Oxford, 1904; repr. 1980), p. 863.

[2] A compendious early modern account of 'monstrous' births is to be found in Ambroise Paré's *Profitable Treatise* (Paris, 1577), but it was not translated into English until 1634. A number of comparable examples are to be found in Konrad Lycosthenes' *Prodigiorum* (Basel, 1557), translated into English by Stephen Bateman as *The Doom Warning All Men to the Judgement* (1581).

This Richard comes from hell to unleash a plague of suffering. His body is the merest hint of an appalling origin.

The hints of hellish monstrosity are kept under control, for Richard must also be psychologically plausible, intelligent, and amusing. Nevertheless, Richard himself draws attention to his physical shape at the very outset, offering it as a cause rather than a symptom. The text invites the player to use his body as a prop around which to perform. In his opening speech, almost masochistically, as if the words were injuries, he marks himself verbally as deformed. If this reinforces his visual appearance, it also, and more importantly, has consequences for his character, as we are invited to consider a narrative of self: he is 'a villain' who boasts that 'Plots have I laid' (1.1.30, 32). Even before he was born he was 'curtailed' of fair proportion (1.1.18). He was cheated by Nature, who is imagined as a dissembling woman. There is a clear reminiscence of the soliloquy in which Richard comes to life as a deformed monster in *Richard Duke of York*:

> Why, love forswore me in my mother's womb,
> And, for I should not deal in her soft laws,
> She did corrupt frail nature with some bribe
> To shrink mine arm up like a withered shrub,
> To make an envious mountain on my back—
> Where sits deformity to mock my body—
> To shape my legs of an unequal size,
> To disproportion me in every part,
> Like to a chaos, or an unlicked bear whelp
> That carries no impression like the dam.
> And am I then a man to be beloved?
> (*Richard Duke of York* 3.2.153–63)

'Love' in this earlier soliloquy has some suggestion of the Christian God: Richard is deprived of grace. But his mind is on sexual love. The feminized 'love' of which he speaks veers away from God. She is the malicious prime mover in a conspiracy of the female that denies him access to women as sexual partners.

The soliloquy that opens *Richard III* is not quite a paraphrase of the earlier one. The myth of origin through the desertion of 'love' has all but disappeared. Richard's misshapenness is simply put down to 'dissembling nature', who seems to have little more to do than deliver Richard from the uterus prematurely. The self-portrait is more naturalistic and modern. If he results from a capriciousness of nature, his birth is thereby reclaimed for the natural order of things, and his evil is an effect of it. The animal spirits or libidinal energies are frustrated, and resentment turns them towards malicious acts. That is a conscious and perhaps chosen outcome. Evil is a consequence, not a cause. For Richard, as a Machiavellian spirit who senses that he is wronged in his birth, what matters is not virtue but *virtù*—skill and genius. In his own myth of selfhood, his disadvantages make him a villain, and the role of villain seems to generate the skills demanded of it.

There is a consistency between Richard's verve in playing the outrageously effective suitor and his exclusion from love. The roles he acts mark out definitively what he cannot be—which is something he discovers about kingship too. His relations with women are consistently hostile, based either on cynical manipulation or on determination to blame them.[1] His withered body is a symptom of imperfect maturation in the womb and a cause of exclusion from love. It becomes the physical link between two aspects of his misogyny, hostility to the maternal and aversion to female sexuality. One might adduce, for example, Richard's blatantly invented fiction about his withered arm at 3.4.72–7. In this new myth the malignant forces that Richard blames are no longer feminized abstractions that curtail him before his birth. They are actual women, the Queen and Mistress Shore, characterized as 'monstrous witch' and whore. This disturbingly implausible story supposes a most unlikely alliance between the King's wife and his mistress. He claims that disruptive femininity has withered his arm, and so, typically, he shifts monstrousness from himself to the women.[2]

Richard has no objective pathological origin. There is the underdeveloped Richard 'unfinished, sent before my time | Into this breathing world scarce half made up' (1.1.20–1), the victim of nature who grows into resentment and wickedness as a result. Then

[1] A line of psychological speculation would be to enquire as to the effect on Richard of Margaret's part in tormenting and killing his father. By such light, his interpretations of his deformity might be seen as effects of identifying Margaret as a wildly aberrant alternative mother figure.

[2] On Richard's employment of women as scapegoats, see Madonne M. Miner, '"Neither Mother, Wife, nor England's Queen": The Roles of Women in *Richard III*', in *The Woman's Part*, ed. Carolyn Ruth Swift Lenz, Gayle Greene, and Carol Thomas Neely (Urbana and London, 1980), pp. 35–55.

there is the overdeveloped Richard ominously born with his teeth, preternaturally ready to bite. Faced with these half-articulated and competing theories—and they have some resemblance to the 'teleological' and 'analogical' readings of history discussed above—we can scarcely opt for one and reject the other. The figure of Richard is always a point of conflict between different versions of deformation and re-formation.

Mark Thornton Burnett has pointed out that there are 'precise connections between parthenogenesis, the monstrous birth and the artist', and that 'The single author's work is invariably figured as a monstrous delivery'.[1] The artist's conception of his or her work is not in the downright way of creation, and Sidney's description of art is entirely congruent with the birth of Richard: the poet makes 'things either better than nature bringeth forth [i.e. gives birth to], or, quite anew, forms such as never were in nature, as the Heroes, Demigods, Cyclops, Chimeras, Furies, and such like'.[2] The more Richard defies nature and seeks to determine himself as an autonomous being, the more he asserts himself as a creature fashioned by the poet. This, after all, is what qualifies the spontaneity of all actors' roles. But, as we have seen, the authorship of Richard is neither exclusive to himself nor exclusive to Shakespeare. Historians and historiography itself are part of the making.

## Episodes on the Edge of History

*Structuring Absences.*[3] Richard, witty and monstrous, plays against and eventually within the post-Senecan world described and determined by Margaret. Here, death creates absence, and memory sustains it. Richard deals in death, but cannot cope with memory. His spirit is revolutionary, in that his emphasis on the destroying moment of here and now crumples up and eradicates the past. In declaring his intention to make amends for killing Anne's

---

[1] Mark Thornton Burnett, '"Strange and woonderfull syghts": *The Tempest* and the Discourses of Monstrosity', *Shakespeare Survey 50* (1997), 187–99; p. 196.

[2] Philip Sidney, *A Defence of Poetry*, ed. J. A. Van Dorsten (1966), p. 23. The *Defence* was written *c.*1579 and circulated in manuscript before publication in 1595.

[3] I borrow this phrase most immediately from Hodgdon, who applies it to the figure of Lady Elizabeth (p. 111).

husband and her father by becoming Anne's husband and her father (1.1.153–5), he attempts to expunge memory as an active force in the present. In this he will ultimately fail, as the ghosts will make manifest to him.

When the play opens it looks back to two earlier murders staged in the final scenes of *Richard Duke of York*: the stabbing of Prince Edward after the Battle of Tewkesbury, and Richard's murder of Henry VI in the Tower. Richard temporarily exculpates himself from blame for both incidents. In 1.2 he effectively blames Anne by saying that he acted out of love for her. But the memories linger, particularly those of Prince Edward. The Tewkesbury incident as remembered in *Richard III* is altered from both the version given in the chronicles and the version staged in *Richard Duke of York*. The change allows the event to precipitate the pattern of deaths in the new play. In contrast with the event as previously staged, Richard becomes the prime culprit, and Rivers and Dorset (or Grey) are retrospectively added to the standers-by. In effect, Richard will become king by purging the others who were present. Seen from this point of view, his marriage to Anne, the victim's widow, places him, despite his own responsibility for the deed, in the prime position of revenger.[1] Richard will be an effective scourge of those more passively implicated in the stabbing at Tewkesbury. The moment he trespasses beyond this role as avenger of Tewkesbury is when he kills two more innocent sons of another king. At the same moment he rejects and dooms Anne, turning his ambitions to taking Lady Elizabeth as wife in her place. The remaining action follows through fate's retribution against the scourge himself, who was, after all (by the play's revisionary account), the active killer of Prince Edward.

Perhaps a seemly reticence influenced Shakespeare's decision not to stage the turning-point, the killing of the Prince Edward and the young Duke of York. Or perhaps he wished to avoid staging an episode that had been prominent in *The True Tragedy of Richard III*. But the absence of the scene can be understood in terms of the play's own action and structure. Shakespeare treats the execution of the princes as ineffable, beyond stage representation

---

[1] Compare *The Spanish Tragedy*, where Bel-Imperia effectively appoints Horatio to become revenger for the death of her lover Don Andrea by choosing Horatio as her new lover.

entirely. The murders become, like those of Henry VI and his son, unstaged actions that assume a mythic quality in the way they bear upon events and consciousness in the play's two major halves. The princes will be hailed after their deaths as saintly and innocent, and they are treated with reticence in their deaths. Whereas in 3.1 the audience sees on the stage a pair of pert adolescent youths, in 4.3 Tyrrell tearfully memorializes twinned alabaster babes. It is a set-piece speech of high artifice, setting Tyrrell's own account as well as the murders' narrative and re-enactment between the stage audience and the carefully distanced event.

The murders of two kings' sons, two Edwards, two heirs to the throne, are the prime acts of violence that drive the two halves of the play. At Tewkesbury, the Yorkists went beyond the bounds of acceptable military conduct. In the aftermath of Tewkesbury, Richard both unwittingly avenges those more or less passively responsible for Edward's death and garners all the guilt for himself. Having secured the crown by these same acts, he then doubles the curses against himself by committing a second killing of young innocents, this time two of them at once. The final structuring absence is Lady Elizabeth, sister of the young princes and the only possible guarantor that the cycle of retribution and civil war will end. The 'true succeeder', the absent Elizabeth, allows the play to glance beyond its own matter to the monarch reigning when it was first performed, Queen Elizabeth I herself.

*'Arise, Dissembler': Anne.* In contrast with the episodes that remain unstaged, Shakespeare introduces a number of scenes that, though critical for his dramatization, have little or no place in the historical sources, and that add areas of experience that are virtually irrelevant to the historical chronicles. The first is 1.2, in which Richard seduces Anne.

As Mistress Shore never appears in the play, her affairs with the King and Hastings are of momentary concern. There is only one character in *Richard III* who is clearly affected by sexual desire during the course of the action, and she, Anne, dies as a result. *Richard III* 'means nothing without love' declared the Romanian dramaturge Mihai Maniutiu.[1] It is certainly true that other figures

---

[1] Programme note, *Richard III*, Manchester City of Drama tour (1994).

are attracted to Richard even as he repels and frightens them. Only Margaret maintains a consistent hostility whenever she appears, and in Maniutiu's production even the exchanges between these two became 'raunchy flirtation' driven by mutual sexual fascination. More obviously in accord with the letter of the text, and more widely accepted in performance, the Queen too might discover in 4.4 some of the sexual attraction that lures Anne to him. The young princes are perhaps anxiously over-eager to play teasing nephews. Amongst the men, Clarence repeatedly asserts that Richard loves him, and even in the dream that potentially reveals his brother's intention to kill him Clarence benignly revises the murderous blow into an accident:

> Methought that Gloucester stumbled, and in stumbling
> Struck me, that sought to stay him, overboard.
>
> (1.4.17–18)

Hastings too walks into his entrapment secure in what he thinks is Richard's friendship. Buckingham enters into conspiratorial intimacy with him.

So although Richard is deeply unlovable, almost everyone expresses emotional need for him. Much of this may be interpreted as attempts to ward off and deny the Richard who is feared, much as the Prince wards off his fear of the Tower by making it a containable object of curiosity and conversation. To have Richard as friend is to feel safe. And the audience too feels specially favoured by his confidences, enjoying the security of standing beyond the stage-tyrant's reach. There is no escape, however, from the paradox of self-delusion, a state of mind that Richard engenders in Anne, in England, and in the audience as well. The fear of what Richard is prompts the semblance of love for Richard as he pretends to be. Anne is not unique. All Richard's victims are victims of seduction of one kind or another. Though many have guilts or vices—Clarence's perfidious past, Hastings's opportunistic glee at the executions in Pomfret—they scarcely deserve their fates. Yet they share a more ordinary culpability, that of shutting down any awareness they might have of the tyrant's magnitude of crime and accepting the flattering delusion that things can be all right.

Richard's seduction of Anne during the funeral procession of her father-in-law is at once a mannered set piece that explores the meaning of verbal and physical acts of figuration and a sustained moment of high drama. The episode has no visible consequence whatsoever for his ambitions to the crown. Instead it serves as a key exposition of Richard's charismatic charm, establishing that the audience is complicit with him just as much as Anne. Whether one considers Anne's position as close relative of two men murdered by Richard, the seeming inopportunity of the moment, or the physical disadvantages that Richard in the previous scene has declared to exclude him from success in love, he would seem to be attempting the impossible. In terms of his appeal to the audience, the sheer audacity of the attempt turns Richard's obstacles to advantage, challenging the audience's sense of ethical judgement.

In his most notorious work, *The Prince*, Niccolò Machiavelli wrote: 'I hold strongly to this: that it is better to be impetuous than circumspect; because fortune is a woman and if she is to be submissive it is necessary to beat and coerce her.'[1] Shakespeare's Richard absorbs a similar misogynist logic, and identifies Anne as the touchstone of his fortune. She presents a challenge so severe that his conquest will act as a passport to more general success.

Richard's achievement strains credulity, but it is a commonplace that roused emotions are unstable and capable of sudden shifts from one feeling to another. Anne, like the audience, is susceptible to the perverse erotic charm of theatre, notwithstanding the presence of Henry's corpse (fig. 2). The protestations of love as a Petrarchan and quasi-religious form of devotion, if considered in their own right, simply lack credibility. Richard's explanation, that the aggression was an effect of his love, might seem scandalously transparent. But he depends on neither poetic cliché nor cool reason. He plays on her contempt, he exploits a vulnerability that is social as well as emotional, and so lures her into a knowing suspension of disbelief in his implausible arguments. The outcome is that violence, seductively transformed into a trope of courtship and eroticism, is woven into the very bond that promises love and safety.

Anne's vehement hate before she capitulates is expressed in the crudely physical gesture of spitting. As a shockingly unexpected

---

[1] Niccolò Machiavelli, *The Prince* (1514), trans. George Bull (Harmondsworth, 1961), p. 133.

2. Richard (David Troughton) and Anne ( Jennifer Ehle), the shroud
of Henry VI behind, RSC, 1995.

ejaculation from the body, the action correlates with the unnatural bleeding of the wounds in Henry's corpse. One of the few
other characters to be spat at in Shakespeare's plays is Shylock,
where it is an expression of racist contempt. Even that incident is
related, not staged, and the spitter in question is a mercantile man.
The action of an aristocratic woman spitting at a social equal or superior is a forceful transgression of social decorum. She is in a state
where physical acts normally unthinkable are actually done.
Antony Sher as Richard wrested her meanings from her, attribut-
ing an unintended sexual significance to the gesture by lascivi-
ously running his finger through the saliva on his cheek,
transferring it to her face, and continuing the movement of his
hand down between her breasts.[1] Andrew Jarvis tasted it from his
finger on a lewdly projecting tongue. These are effective gestural
summaries of Richard's appropriation of Anne's intentions and
her body.

---

[1] Hankey, p. III.

42

When Anne assumes a more decorous pride over him—'*She looks scornfully at him*' (1.2.156.1)—Richard can install her as the Petrarchan cruel lady, making literal the Petrarchan conceit that the cruel object of devotion 'kills' her suitor by her disdain. By giving Anne his sword and baring his chest to her, he manufactures sincerity, making the images invoked in his language of courtship dangerously and urgently real. He turns himself from aggressor to victim in an act of 'aggressive passivity',[1] and so Richard transfigures Anne herself.

The image of the woman holding or even lunging the sword at her suitor's breast is tainted with the violent killing that the stage picture both displaces and recollects. In this temporary mirror Anne has an illusory sexual power that disarms danger and shapes destiny. This is the fantasy to which she is subjected, and, hesitatingly, the temptation of fantasy prevails. Anne gives in to Richard, calling him 'dissembler' (1.2.170). Her chiding is that of the resentful though forgiving lover. The word accusatorily reflects back on the self-deceit of the speaker, who both sees and disregards the insincerity. Set against her earlier and justified vituperation, it is an absurdly mild rebuke, and it is mollified further by its finely ingrained connotations of both acting and courtship. Nothing is dissembled more than Richard's empowerment of her so that she can exercise mercy and say 'Arise, dissembler'.

The sword withheld at the naked breast very quickly transforms into the ring placed on the finger. We might be reminded of how as a symbol of the sexual act the gift of a ring from man to woman in betrothal reverses the gender roles: the empty circle is the man's gift that encloses the woman's finger. The male/female configuration is flipped back again in Richard's commentary: 'Look how this ring encompasseth thy finger, | Even so thy breast encloseth my poor heart' (1.2.189–90).[2] As John Webster suggested in presenting the Duchess of Malfi's betrothal involving a fateful giving of a ring some two decades later, to enter such a relationship can 'sign your *Quietus est*'.[3]

---

[1] Howard and Rackin, p. 109.

[2] The image is an extreme and insincere Petrarchan conceit, but it does happen to exemplify a fantasy of prenatal engulfment by the female that Richard expresses elsewhere too.

[3] John Webster, *The Duchess of Malfi*, ed. John Russell Brown (1964), 1.1.464.

Following the ring ceremony, Richard assumes an abrupt patriarchal authority, and the erotic tension is dispersed. In his soliloquy at the end of 1.2 Richard snaps out of what remains of his
solicitous attitude, revealing his contempt for Anne, and acknow-
ledging his lack of libidinal investment in her: 'I'll have her, but I
will not keep her long' (1.2.215). Audiences can laugh at such a
moment, for the line is spoken by the cajoling, confiding Richard
who steps out of the action to address them directly. But the laugh-
ter might well be nervous or disconcerted, and Richard is most
deadly where he seems most flippant. For him, the only thing that
can be erotically charged is his own performance: his flirtation
with perversity, death, and danger, his sadism in reducing the
outraged mourner to a limp acquiescent object and a corpse for the
future.

Richard keeps her for as long as his fortune is in the ascendant.
She disappears until 4.1, her last appearance before Richard has
her killed.[1] At the moment he says 'Anne my wife hath bid the
world goodnight' (4.3.39), he has himself bid fortune goodnight.

*Prophecy of Revenge.* It is a distinctive quality of Shakespeare's
representation of reality that, though the physical and social world
is tangible and real, it is at the same time subject to intrusion and
redefinition from something the plays' characters experience as
beyond the material. For all its immediacy and solidity, the world's
epistemological foundations are shifting and insecure. When
Richard declares that he is 'determinèd to prove a villain' (1.1.30)
he seems to speak of his autonomy of will, but the words might
mean that his villainy is predetermined, an effect of destiny. The
individual events in *Richard III* are not simply events in themselves.
They are subject to prophecy, prefiguration, and repetition. They
fall within larger patterns of symbolic meaning.[2]

In the opening scenes the action seems subservient to Richard's
will. Clarence enters on cue: 'This day should Clarence closely be
mewed up | About a prophecy . . . Dive, thoughts, down to my
soul; here Clarence comes.' Lady Anne's first entry similarly follows hard on Richard's announcing his intention towards her. The
action begins to assume a dynamic that is independent of Richard

---

[1] But see headnote to 4.2.

[2] Compare Kristian Smidt, *Unconformities in Shakespeare's History Plays* (1982),
pp. 53–71.

only in 1.3, when we are suddenly in the thick of court factions. The contrast between 1.2 and 1.3 is clear. In the wooing scene Richard develops plans he has announced in advance, and so takes control over what seem to be the last remnants of the house of Lancaster, the corpse of the king and its solitary mourner. In 1.3 the Yorkists and the Greys are busy squabbling over the present and the immediate future. Richard surprises and confuses us too with his disruptive and sudden entry, 'They do me wrong and I will not endure it'. For the first time Richard's plots are beyond our immediate knowing. But no sooner has Richard stamped his fractious authority on the scene than Margaret enters, reframing the scene within a perspective that is far from that of Richard's choosing. Like Anne, she belongs to the house of Lancaster and comes into the play burdened with grievance. In other ways they will decisively contrast.

Even an audience member familiar with the chronicles might not know who this alien figure is, for Margaret had died in France. The play has already led us to assume her absence, for in 1.2 only Anne attends the corpse of Margaret's husband. Her presence is both ahistorical and ghostly. It is an extreme paradox that this figure, a fictive intrusion on the historical events, should be the guarantor of Tudor ideology and indeed of history itself. Because she preserves the past and makes it actively meaningful during the course of the play, she in effect preserves the future. Her interventions ensure that Richard's wrongdoings are remembered and avenged, and so ensure that the Tudor dynasty will finally be installed.

From the outset she cryptically defines herself in relation to past events that no one else wishes to remember. To the Queen she says, 'Thy honour, state, and seat is due to me' (1.3.112), and to Richard,

> Thou slewest my husband Henry in the Tower,
> And Edward, my poor son, at Tewkesbury.
>
> (1.3.119–20)

In winning the hand of Anne, Richard has not quite eliminated the past, nor mastered the future.

Margaret might appear to be a pathetic war victim in hostile surroundings, someone who needs to believe that God, if only God, will hear, understand, and respond to her laments. Her belief in the efficacy of cursing might be evidence of crazed desperation. Yet her curses relate very closely to what will happen. The implications are unnerving. She sees Richard as a 'cacodemon' from hell (1.3.143–4), yet it is he who will fulfil her petition to God for vengeance against all the others. To the Protestant theologian Calvin 'it is no absurdity that one self act be ascribed to God, to Satan, and to man' (*Institution*, 2.4.2). There is no question of conspiracy; rather, there are different levels of explanation. Calvin recognized the challenge to common sense, admitting that 'the sense of the flesh scarcely conceiveth how he [God] working by them [Satan and the reprobate] should not gather some spot of their fault' (1.18.1). Understanding God's righteousness in inflicting natural disasters posed similar challenges. *Richard III* was probably written just before or during one of the worst outbreaks of the plague in Elizabethan London. Confronted with arbitrary suffering and death, potentially evidence of a cruel God, the pious could respond only by seeing plague as evidence of God's wrath at the depravity of the society upon whom he unleashes plague as just punishment.

As Margaret asserts that there is a machinery of divine retribution, Richard attempts to puncture such claims as mere rhetoric. Indeed, he takes the offensive, shifting the blame for Queen Margaret's misfortunes away from the immediate perpetrators: 'And God, not we, hath plagued thy bloody deed' (1.3.178). The piety is a barefaced use of religion for political ends. More subtly, it anticipates and compromises Margaret's attempts to enlist God on her side. Richard identifies Margaret as a 'wrinkled witch' (1.3.164), a monstrously cruel woman without pity for children, cursed by the patriarch of the York family, and the victim of God's wrath. He succeeds in rallying the court factions against her:

> HASTINGS (*to Margaret*)
>
> O, 'twas the foulest deed to slay that babe,
>
> And the most merciless that e'er was heard of.
>
> RIVERS (*to Margaret*)
>
> Tyrants themselves wept when it was reported.
>
> DORSET [GREY] (*to Margaret*)
>
> No man but prophesied revenge for it.
>
> BUCKINGHAM (*to Margaret*)
>
> Northumberland, then present, wept to see it.
>
> (1.3.180–4)

3. Hog and hag: Simon Russell Beale as Richard exchanges glares
with Cherry Morris as Queen Margaret, RSC, 1992.

These accusations imply that it is Margaret rather than Richard
who is the unnatural and cruel tyrant whose overthrow is anticipated in curses and prophecies. For a moment Margaret and
Richard seem similar, caught in the symmetries of killing and
counter-killing, rhetoric and counter-rhetoric, curse and counter-
curse, patterns that typify the Henry VI plays. She has fallen prey
to the curses poured on her when she tormented and killed
Richard's father; her own curses will ruin him. The 'hateful, withered hag' fights it out verbally with the 'elvish-marked, abortive
rooting-hog' (1.3.212, 225; see fig. 3). Hog and hag both belong
to a frightening supernatural twilight. Richard as much as
Margaret is 'hateful' and 'withered', and it is even possible to see a
symbiotic alliance between them. But politically at least Margaret
is a spent force. Only a new tyrant can be subject to new curses and
prophecies. The roles are rapidly demarcated along the lines of
gender, with Richard as the aggressor and Margaret as the female
voice of lamentation, curse, and prophecy.

The anti-Richard play has its origin here in 1.3 with Margaret's
curses. Their rhetorical power depends on the comprehensiveness
with which every person is caught within the mode of subjunctive

petition for death. Margaret comes as it were from beyond the grave, breathing death on the living. Richard is last in her catalogue, and is cursed most fully. Yet this final catalogue of imprecation remains incomplete, for Richard returns her insults on the speaker, interrupting her '. . . thou detested—' with 'Margaret' (1.3.230–1). It is a childishly glib intervention, but it unseats the speaker. Can curses pierce the clouds if they are so easily bounced back by the human respondent?

In fact their potency as predictions cannot be deflected. Richard shows no sign of caring that the machinations by which he kills Rivers, Vaughan, Grey, Hastings, and Buckingham enact not only his own programme but also Margaret's. By the logic that they die, so will he. We should probably understand that the drowning of Clarence brings about the King's death, and certainly the murder of the young princes causes the state of sorrow that Margaret so particularly describes as the property of their mother the Queen. The play, in particular the action that Richard orchestrates, is an almost comprehensive enactment of Margaret's prophecy, as was made particularly clear in Sam Mendes's production of 1992, in which Cherry Morris as Margaret was allowed to reappear hauntingly as each of Richard's victims went off to his death. Richard's interruption of Margaret's curse by replacing his name with hers implies that he can evade the larger syntax of prophecy with its final term 'Richard'. But by 4.2, the scene after his coronation, he is muttering nervously about the 'Rougemont' prophecy (ll. 103–7). Like Henry VI's more formal prophecy, it might mean Richmond will be king: 'perhaps, perhaps' (l. 99).

*Unquiet Slumbers.* From Clarence to the Grey faction to Hastings to the young princes to Buckingham, Richard's victims process from confinement to the grave. The staged episodes all have relevance, indirectly, to the episode Shakespeare does not put on stage at all, the murder of the young princes. Repeatedly the audience sees what it is like to be a victim of abusive political power in a fragile interim before death, when the order has been given but the execution has yet to come. The depiction of Clarence's death in 1.4 gives particularly full amplitude to a Christian spiritual area of experience that can then be given more summary presentation later on. It allows those later and shorter episodes to resonate with understated implication.

Clarence dreams an imaginary version of his death, awakes to tell his dream, sleeps, and then awakes to face death itself, as though the whole sequence were an inescapable nightmare. His account of his dream is a richly intertextual passage, with echoes in its phrasing of journeys to the underworld in Virgil, Seneca, the Englished Seneca of Thomas Sackville, in his additions to *Mirror for Magistrates*, and Thomas Kyd, in *The Spanish Tragedy*. These are interwoven with recollections of drownings at sea in Ovid and the Cave of Mammon in Spenser's *Faerie Queene*.[1] There are also biblical allusions and echoes of Marlowe. Clarence's identification of the 'grim ferryman' Charon as a figure 'which poets write of' (1.4.43) affirms the allusive quality of the episode, and is in itself a formulaic literary tag. The very text dreams beyond itself. Harold Brooks writes of 'a molten confluence of influences fusing together at high temperature and pressure of creative imagination, to yield the most eloquent poetry in the play'.[2] At some overarching level the play is diversifying its status as a retold myth of English political nationhood, claiming its part in a new English vernacular literature that could comfortably assimilate the classical influence. The Plantagenet duke becomes a consciousness through which a poetic, visionary, and primarily pagan conception of death is transmitted to the audience of the popular theatre.

But it is the imaginative force of Clarence's account of his dream that is of most immediate impact. There is dream within dream, death within death, as the man about to die both in reality and in his dream sees the fantastical vision of those already dead mocked by the artificial life of glittering gems. Shakespeare's debt to Spenser's Cave of Mammon might alert us to the possibilities of moralizing the vision as an emblem of the vanity of earthly acquisitions, including power. It should also suggest that the vision is grotesque, not only as usually understood today, but also in an etymological sense of the word that relates it to the idea of a grotto or artificially ornamented cave. The dream goes on to become a vision of the death agony itself, and then goes on further as it is 'lengthened after life' (1.4.40). The drowning now alters to the 'tempest to my soul', and, in a very dreamlike transition, the

[1] Brooks, 'Antecedents', pp. 148–50.
[2] Brooks, 'Antecedents', p. 150. See Commentary to 1.4.9–19, 25, 41–8, etc.

underwater setting is transformed into a journey over the surface of the 'melancholy flood' (1.4.41–2). If this recalls Clarence's imagined escape from England in the opening of the dream, his companion Richard has now been translated into Charon, the Virgilian 'grim ferryman' who takes Clarence to the kingdom of perpetual night. Here the ghosts of Warwick and Edward of Lancaster confront Clarence before the tormenting fiends seize on him. The ghosts are a sharp anticipation of ghosts that later visit Richard as he confronts his imminent death.

The only sustained passage of prose occurs in the Executioners' dialogue as Clarence once more sleeps, a passage of grim humour shedding a grotesque but moralized light on death from the point of view of its agents. There are analogues such as the semi-comic torturers of Christ in medieval pageant plays such as the Wakefield 'Coliphizacio',[1] but in such episodes the range of tone and subjective experience is, by virtue of the dramatic form, much narrower. As with the Porter scene that unexpectedly disrupts the brooding intensity after Duncan's murder in *Macbeth*, the comedy is far more complex than light relief. In this case the episode builds tension, and it develops the theme of conscience in a different key. Both here and in Tyrrell's account of the killing of the princes, Shakespeare contrasts Richard's radical amorality with the 'dregs of conscience' that remain in his henchmen. Conscience is as yet inexpressible in Richard's mind, though it will have its day after he is confronted by the ghosts of Clarence, the princes, and all the rest.

Much of the comedy lies in illogical shifts between a very literal Christianity learnt from the pulpit and the grim materialism of the needy:

> SECOND EXECUTIONER  I pray thee, stay a while; I hope my
> holy humour will change, 'twas wont to hold me but
> while one would tell twenty.
>> [*They wait*]
> FIRST EXECUTIONER  How dost thou feel thyself now?
> SECOND EXECUTIONER  Faith, some certain dregs of con-
> science are yet within me.
> FIRST EXECUTIONER  Remember our reward when the deed is
> done.

[1]  *The Wakefield Pageants in the Towneley Cycle*, ed. A. C. Cawley (Manchester, 1958), pp. 78–90.

SECOND EXECUTIONER  Zounds, he dies. I had forgot the
        reward.
FIRST EXECUTIONER  Where is thy conscience now?
SECOND EXECUTIONER  In the Duke of Gloucester's purse.
                                    (1.4.106–17)

Conscience is absurdly alienable from the person. It is materialized
as the equivalent of the drainable dregs of a barrel, or coins that
can be enclosed in someone's purse. It is like a spirit or demon that
can afflict a person unless it is turned away or safely contained elsewhere. One moment it is conscience who is 'at my elbow persuading me not to kill the Duke'; the next moment it is the Duke
himself. The Executioners and Clarence are in effect the voice of
each other's conscience.

Accepting that the King has ordered his execution, Clarence
argues that God 'holds vengeance in his hands | To hurl upon their
heads that break his law' (ll. 180–1), recalling God's words in
Deuteronomy 32: 35, 'Vengeance and recompense are mine'. Even
the 'Homily against Disobedience' advised that rulers should
be disobeyed 'if they would command us to do anything contrary to
God's commandments'.[1] Clarence has a strong and simple case,
but he is not well placed to urge it. In the Executioners' account,
his guilt is twofold. He is a perjured turncoat who betrayed
his brother Edward by swearing an oath of allegiance to the
Lancastrians, and then reverted to the Yorkist cause. Clarence's
second guilt puts him in line with his brother from the beginning,
for both of them were implicated in butchering Edward of Lancaster
at Tewkesbury. Thus Clarence, though in other circumstances he
broke his loyalty, went along with a command that was against
God's laws. One 'bloody minister' (1.4.200) can scarcely argue
his case against another on the basis of the divine injunction.

When the truth is declared Clarence realizes that it is not King
Edward who has arranged the killing but his other, more trusted,
brother Richard. The excuse that 'he that hath commanded is the
King' (1.4.175) collapses. But if the debate on disobeying royal
command is redundant in relation to the Executioners, it raises
the spectre of Richard in authority as king: what then would be the
case? Principled disobedience is hard to find in the world ruled

---

[1] *Certain Sermons or Homilies (1547), and A Homily against Disobedience and
Wilful Rebellion (1570)*, ed. Ronald B. Bond (Toronto and London, 1987), p. 167.

by dagger and purse. Moreover, the debate in 1.4 and the Homily both fail to provide a rationale for moving beyond disobedience to something that will materialize at the end of the play, forcible resistance and rebellion. There is no vindication of Richmond in prospect here.

Much is at stake in the debate, but nothing can detract from the foreground: the sense of a human existence, a man imprisoned, helpless, and struggling towards knowledge of what is most to be feared. The dream and the mock-trial offer both premonition and false hope. In theory at least a dreamer can awaken from nightmares; in theory an accused can be acquitted if innocent. It is not so in the world of terror. Here the riches of life's experience lie as relics amongst dead men's skulls. The murderer's blow and death by drowning are implacable and close, despite the momentary grotesque richness and grotesque comedy of the interim.

The word 'dream' and its cognates appear more often in *Richard III* than any other Shakespeare play.[1] There are the prophetic 'dreams' that Richard unleashes on the King in 1.1, the butcheries that exclusively occupy Richard's dreams according to Anne in 1.2, the tormenting dreams of devils Margaret prophesies for Richard in 1.3 that are actualized in Anne's account in 4.1, Clarence's dream of drowning in 1.4, Stanley's emblematic vision of the boar razing his helm relayed to Hastings in 3.2 and mentioned again in 3.4, the Queen's reduction to 'A dream of which thou wert a breath, a bubble' (4.4.83), and Richard and Richmond's visions of the ghosts in 5.4, these probably the 'babbling dreams' Richard attempts to dismiss at 5.5.37. Though none of them is sweet, these dreams signify in a variety of ways, sometimes indeterminately. Some are prophetic, some reflect the dreamer's state of being; sometimes there is little distinction.

The dreams that have specific content are those of Clarence, Stanley, Richard, and Richmond. Stanley's is told indirectly by a messenger, and is no more than a single image. Hastings, when told of Stanley's dream, cannot see or accept its implication, preferring, like Clarence, to be lulled by another kind of illusion. In what they express and what they cannot express, dreams can be

---

[1] Twenty-five occurrences in dialogue, plus one stage direction. The next play is *Midsummer Night's Dream*, with sixteen occurrences (a lower count, though an admittedly higher frequency, as it is a shorter play).

understood as expressions within the individual consciousness of the effect of political violence. They are expressions of political suffering—and even, in Richmond's dream, of resistance.

Details such as Stanley's dream, Hastings's coincidental meeting with the Pursuivant he previously encountered when going to the Tower under arrest, and his later recollection of his horse presciently stumbling on his way to the Tower, anticipate the omens of Caesar's fall in *Julius Caesar*. Hastings, like Caesar, is fed knowledge he chooses to reject; he leaves home and walks to his doom in voluntary ignorance. The imaginative experience of those facing entrapment, arrest, or murder by politicians and their henchmen, or betrayal by patrons in high office, would have registered in late Elizabethan London as much as a modern totalitarian state. In the play, dreams and omens represent the point at which nothing less than reality impinges on the life we think we lead.

*Upon Record*. In 3.1 Prince Edward formally enters the capital city as king-to-be. It is his first and last scene, unless one counts his reappearance after death as a ghost. The overall movement of the scene is to conduct him to join his brother in the city's oldest and most oppressive building, the Tower. It is a moment of hollow welcoming and contrived political manoeuvre. The princes themselves are not the innocent babes depicted by Tyrrell after they are murdered, but adolescents who are outstripping childhood and, in a vulnerable, gangly way, beginning to confront those who have control over them. There is a stage tradition going back as far as Colley Cibber's 1699 adaptation of the Duke of York or both princes being performed by women; indeed in the Victorian period the practice was invariable, and it continued into Frank Benson's 1910 film (fig. 6). George Bernard Shaw complained about the role of Prince Edward being taken in Henry Irving's revival by an assertive actress, Lena Ashwell: 'he [Richard] is obviously addressing a fine young woman . . . who treads the boards with no little authority and assurance as one of the younger generation knocking vigorously at the door'.[1] Perhaps that was the point. Perhaps the surprise arose because audiences had been brought up on

---

[1] George Bernard Shaw, in *Shaw on Shakespeare*, ed. Edwin Wilson (1962), p. 168.

Cibber's adaptation in which the princes are more simply pathetic figures.

What the Victorian stage did not reflect was the requirement in the Elizabethan theatre whereby the princes would be played by the same actors, boys, as some of the women. Mendes's 1992 production brought together the two traditions by having actresses double the princes with two of the female roles: Annabelle Apsion played both the Duke of York and Anne, whilst Kate Duchêne doubled Prince Edward and the Queen. Such an arrangement can inconspicuously bond the community of Richard's victims.

The princes are presciently mindful of their uncle. In 2.4 the Duke of York remembers Richard correlating physical growth and moral worth, 'Small herbs have grace; gross weeds grow apace' (2.4.13), an ironic variation on Richard's attitude to his own warped body, as his mother's comment makes clear:

> He was the wretched'st thing when he was young,
> So long a-growing and so leisurely
> That if this were a true rule he should be gracious.
>
> (2.4.18–20)

But the received memory of Richard's infancy suggests otherwise:

> Marry, they say my uncle grew so fast
> That he could gnaw a crust at two hours old.
> 'Twas full two years ere I could get a tooth.
> Grannam, this would have been a biting jest.
>
> (2.4.27–30)

Young York discloses Richard as the gross weed, as the infant with teeth, and then in 3.1 as the Vice with his hand on his dagger, as the grotesque hunchback, all these being the trademarks of the Richard whose picture departs from verisimilitude to join with political mythology. He imagines himself as the ape on the shoulder-saddle of Richard as the lopsided showman:

> Uncle, my brother mocks both you and me.
> Because that I am little, like an ape,
> He thinks that you should bear me on your shoulders.
>
> (3.1.129–31)

This can be a painful moment for Richard, and a correspondingly dangerous one for the future of his young adversary. In Sam

Mendes's 1992 RSC production, York climbed up on Richard's shoulders. Henry Irving as Richard responded to the quip with a silent glare of concentrated hatred, and John Wood lunged murderously at a York who was parodying his gait. York's mock might suggest that he is a diminutive version of his uncle, and when Buckingham notes his 'sharp, provided wit' (3.1.132) he confirms that they share some qualities. The audience knows that Young York will never grow up to be his father or his uncle. But though Richard can do away with the princes, he cannot do away with the hunch that symbolizes his criminality in that act.

York's elder brother shows a more intellectual precocity, appearing as a ruler in the making who is educating himself, with a little ostentation, into a sense of his own place in history. He knows something about the past of London's main edifice representing coercive rule. It is a building he should ultimately control as king, but, reflecting his lack of real power, he has been consigned into it against his will—'For your best health and recreation', as Richard reassures him. His glance back in time to the founding of the Tower by Julius Caesar bears comparison with metatheatrical moments such as Shakespeare's glance forward in time from the period of Julius Caesar itself,

> How many ages hence
> Shall this our lofty scene be acted over,
> In states unborn and accents yet unknown!
> (*Julius Caesar* 3.1.112–14)

Cassius refers directly to the way he and his fellow conspirators are making history by killing Caesar. More allusively, when the Prince hails the originatory moment of the Tower he prompts us to remember that an edifice bears the memory of the events that have happened in it. We might reflect that he is being literally, physically placed within the civic history and history of oppression associated with the Tower. It is not after all a monument like the bruised armour Richard describes as disarmedly hanging on the walls,[1] for its malign potency continues.

---

[1] Compare Sigmund Freud's commentary on the monuments of London as 'mnemic symbols', in 'Five Lectures in Psycho-Analysis', in *The Standard Edition of the Complete Psychological Works*, ed. James Strachey *et al.*, 24 vols. (1953–74), xi. 16–17.

It is relevant too that the Prince's own concerns with recuperating the classical past, interrogating documentary evidence, and establishing a polity based on scholarly learning identify him as a humanist in the tradition-to-be of More himself—the More of *Utopia* with its carefully regulated dispersal of power as well as the More of *The History of Richard III*. From this point of view, Richard's assassination of the Princes delays the emergence of humanist culture itself. Richard's England is no place for Erasmus, whose visits to England are celebrated in *Sir Thomas More*, a play written at about the same time as Shakespeare's *Richard III*, and perhaps commissioned by Lord Strange's Men.[1] Humanist culture might seem one way in which the Tudor regime ushered in with Richmond's victory contrasts with the twilight medieval past. Here again, though, it might be remembered that More himself would suffer imprisonment in the Tower and execution at the hands of Henry VIII, epitome of the Tudor king.

The Prince has managed to pick up on a topical controversy about the past of the building in which he is about to be incarcerated and destroyed, as though the knowledge he has acquired might offer some purchase over the place and its ability to do harm. Yet the attempt to ward off the ominous presence of the Tower by positioning it as an object of knowledge is undermined by the very uncertainty to which the Prince refers. Interrogation of the truth about legendary figures such as Julius Caesar is symptomatic of an age witnessing the growth of antiquarian historical study, to whom oral tradition was no longer straightforwardly acceptable. The issue in question, whether Julius Caesar's building of the Tower is a matter of record or legend, was debated at the time Shakespeare was writing *Richard III* by that industrious recorder of London's past and England's, John Stow. In the 1592 edition of his *Annals of England*, Stow remarks as follows: 'John Lydgate, John Rous, and others write that Julius Caesar builded in this land the castles of Dover, of Canterbury, Rochester, and the Tower of London; but it is not like that Caesar remained any such time here, neither do the Roman histories make mention thereof' (B3$^v$).

---

[1] The play was written by Anthony Munday, probably with Henry Chettle. A passage in it influences a passage in *Richard III*, or vice versa: see Commentary to 1.4.2–65. Shakespeare helped revise *Sir Thomas More* if, as many scholars believe, the 'Hand D' additions to the manuscript are his, but the revisions may have been a decade later (see Howard-Hill).

The note of scepticism corrects Stow's own earlier naivety, for in his *Summary of English Chronicles* of 1565 and his *Chronicles of England* of 1580 he transmits the account of Caesar building the Tower without the qualification 'but it is not like . . .', as if it were undisputed.[1] The Prince's question as to whether it is recorded or reported history seems to show Shakespeare's knowledge of Stow's newly acquired rigour, whether directly or by report. Buckingham assures the Prince that Caesar's building of the Tower is 'Upon record'. No such record exists, so the Prince is suitably dissatisfied with the answer. Though he does not challenge Buckingham's supposedly superior knowledge, he continues to talk on the supposition that, as is the case, the records from the Roman period are silent on the matter:

> But say, my lord, it were not registered,
> Methinks the truth should live from age to age,
> As 'twere retailed to all posterity,
> Even to the general all-ending day.
>
> (3.1.75–8)

The principle is exactly that attributed to Caesar for his edifications in the 1565 *Summary*, 'for a perpetual memory, to put his name in remembrance' (C3$^v$). For the Prince, the absence of a record does not mean the absence of a truth.

As Hammond notes, similar questions surround the play's own historical foundations. After all, Stow questions the authority of Rous, a determined vilifier of Richard whose manuscript *Historia Regum Angliae* was a major written source for More's *History*. In the play, the Prince's comments bring into close association the ideas that 'succeeding ages have re-edified' the Tower and that 'truth should live from age to age' (3.1.71, 76). The processes are correlated through the verb 're-edify', as 'edify' can and could mean 'to give instruction'. The truth, like the building itself, can be re-edified 'from age to age'. And, to acknowledge again the interweaving of memory and document, the image of re-edification is conspicuously apt in relation to the retrospective retelling of Richard's life by More, in the chronicles, and in the play itself.

This idea of re-edified knowledge applies pre-eminently to

---

[1] Stow had edited one of his sources of information, Lydgate's *Serpent of Division* (1559). Lydgate uses the verb 'edified', which survives in Stow's *Summary* in the same passage to describe the building of Chichester.

Richard's responsibility for the two Princes' deaths. The Prince's seemingly intuitive wisdom carries with it an implication that is, presumably, beyond his conscious knowledge. When the Princes are murdered, Richard will silence the historical record, but he cannot silence the oral record that will have the story 'retailed to all posterity'. Richard himself forces the issue by responding with the grimly joking aside 'So wise so young, they say, do never live long' (3.1.79), as if the principle of truth itself could be killed. By appealing to proverbial oral wisdom, 'they say', he unwittingly admits, however, that shared knowledge is not so easily silenced. It is one of those moments when the play has the last say over Richard himself. The very act of retelling or retailing the events of his life, as the play does, testifies that the murders will stimulate rather than silence his notoriety.

Ironically, John Stow, the touchstone for documented information about the Tower, was himself responsible for the transmission of an oral tradition concerning Richard III that was far more favourable than the chronicle account from More that he himself retails in print. As D. R. Woolf records, 'Sir George Buck, whose dogged attempt to rescue the character of Richard III from a century of Tudor vilification was published only several years after his death, and even then in a bowdlerized, watered-down form, based his case not only on scrupulous scholarship but on traditions. Much of his information came orally from the octogenarian John Stow, who had himself spoken in the mid-sixteenth century with old men who recalled Richard in a favourable light.'[1] Might Shakespeare have been aware that what Stow said about Richard on record differed from the inadmissible accounts he later retailed to Buck? That is conjecture, but a wider cultural anxiety about the foundations of historical knowledge, specifically knowledge relating to *these* events, is clearly feeding into the play and posing questions as to the security of documented historical truth.

The concern with absent record is balanced out when the play considers too what is the truth in the presence of documentation. The quasi-judicial murder of Hastings becomes a matter of falsified record. A little scene introducing a new character specially makes the point. In so far as he is simply a copyist, the Scrivener in 3.6 is

[1] D. R. Woolf, 'The "Common Voice": History, Folklore and Oral Tradition in Early Modern England', in *Past and Present*, 120 (1988), 26–52, p. 37.

a nonentity. He acquires status as a contestatory voice behind the official declaration whose personal knowledge, like Stow's, conflicts with the document he has prepared. He is indignant but self-repressing, aware that the mechanics of repression flow directly and traumatically from politics to the inward experience of the divided self.

The Scrivener explains to the audience that Richard's henchman Catesby brought him a legal indictment of Hastings 'yesternight' and it has taken him eleven hours overnight for him to produce the copy in the 'set hand' of an official legal document. He infers that the 'precedent' from which he copied must have taken just as long to write. As Hastings was alive and unaccused just five hours ago, Catesby, or whoever wrote the original, must have begun penning the account of his execution and the reasons for it more than seventeen hours before Hastings was executed.

The Scrivener's speech is a protesting meditation on the manuscript he is carrying, on its position within a historical sequence of events and its function as a documentary falsification of those events. His words highlight the ironies of the situation. An 'indictment' (3.6.1) would usually be an accusation that would lead to trial by a jury, but in this case it is clearly a proclamation issued after Hastings's execution as a justification for what has already happened. In the sequence of things it has slipped from pre-trial to post-execution. When he draws attention to how the 'sequel' hangs together (3.6.4), the Scrivener's unusual choice of term draws attention to the lack of due order in the events as they have happened: this is a sequence without proper sequels. The bringing together of the scrivening terms 'fairly' and 'engrossed' at 3.6.2 brings out their moral connotation. This becomes even clearer when the Scrivener asks, 'Why, who's so gross | That cannot see this palpable device?' (3.6.10–11). Richard earlier pointed out that 'gross' weeds grow apace. Here the large and elaborate 'gross' handwriting, part of the manuscript's character as a 'fair' legal document, draws attention to the palpable device that it tries to pass off. The truth of the matter, like the building of the Tower, is not on record. Indeed it cannot even be spoken of.

However, it can be 'seen in thought' (3.6.14). The play's very existence once again testifies to the durability and final prevailing of this kind of memory, at least when it can be translated into words by those who believe they have nothing further to lose. The critique of textual record and the vindication of thought and memory are exactly appropriate to a stage work that breaks free from chronicled history, creates the illusion of events re-membered, and depends on the actors' memories as the conduit from script to audience.

*Woe's Scene.* The play is punctuated by successive scenes, beginning with the killing of Clarence, that show Richard's victims just before their deaths. In these claustrophobic episodes the audience itself bears witness, and is the most immediate and effective vehicle of memory. Each death is private but monumentalized. The scenes show the living, sentient, aware person, and the person is set within an emblematically moralized frame. These are portraits in a gallery of the missing that moves through dramatic time. Sam Mendes's production made the point effectively by having each executioner make the same gesture of lowering his hand in front of the victim's face to represent his death. A choric Margaret (Medea Chakhava) evidently performed a similar gesture on the victims in Robert Sturua's production some thirteen years earlier. The ghost scene will later compress this procession into a single dramatic event. Meanwhile, as the executions take place, individuation of the victims is held in check by a growing sense of echo and repetition between their situations and between their belated condemnations of Richard.

Something more effectual emerges in the second and final scene where Margaret appears, 4.4. In her soliloquy that begins the scene there are specific echoes of Richard's soliloquy at the beginning of the play, not least in their shared theatrical vocabulary. Richard's 'inductious' plots set the cycle of murders in motion;[1] Margaret reformulates the murders themselves as an 'induction' to the tragedy of Richard's fall.[2] From this point, Margaret as a figure of Nemesis will preside over the action, in spirit at least. Despite the rhetorical language and the abstract frame of reference, it is Margaret and the other women rather than the men who are attuned to the reality of the larger historical process. Indeed the

---

[1] On the reading 'inductious', see Appendix D, Note 4.

[2] A later play with a similar structure is Henry Chettle's *Tragedy of Hoffman* (1602–3), where the first revenge sequence begins with Hoffman's opening soliloquy and the counter-revenge begins two-thirds of the way through the play with the entry of Martha, the widowed Duchess.

loaded patterning of the rhetoric is, in line with classical tradition, a kind of artificial memory that signifies the retention of historical knowledge.[1] The women unflinchingly see the past and the future, and construct choric narratives that make the past and the future manifest. Shakespeare empowers them as chroniclers, the voices of those who understand and know. They apprehend meaning in the dismal chaos of the moment. Through them the tragic complexion becomes bifocal. There is the tragedy of Richard, but also there is tragedy as a theatrical experience that moves the audience towards grief because of his deeds. These women are a stage audience: witnesses, interpreters, and, in contrast with Anne, points of resistance to the seductive masculine energies of Richard.[2]

Margaret knows exactly where the tragedy is going. Richard's latest murders offer her the opportunity for grim triumph over him. They are inexcusable even to someone who welcomes vicarious vengeance on behalf of the Lancastrians, and the scene shows how the Princes' deaths bring an unpredictable alignment between the representative mother figures of Lancaster, York, and the Greys. Having presided over this new configuration, Margaret can disappear for good. The ghosts of the dead will later follow the women's example, aligning themselves in their cry of outrage against Richard, calling on him to despair and die.

This magniloquent scene 4.4 is significantly shorter in Q1 than in F,[3] and in the vast majority of productions it is shorter still. Arguably the full weight of at least the Quarto version is needed, in that too much further diminishment of Margaret's role and the Queen's trenchant verbal resistance leaves Richard without any significant opposition. The thin presentation of 'shallow Richmond' (5.4.198) in Act 5 finds compensation in the almost excessive and static lamentation of 4.4. Richmond is the effect. The

[1] On Renaissance memory machines and their antecedents in classical rhetoric, see Frances A. Yates, *The Art of Memory* (1966).
[2] Howard and Rackin argue that the women are subordinated to Richmond's patriarchal agenda (pp. 113–18). I suggest, less retrospectively and more with a sense of the play as it develops in action, that Richmond is virtually a mere outcome of the feminized process, an agent for the voice of motherhood and a future king whose wife will carry the stronger right to the throne. Richmond's mother is mentioned long before he is (1.3.20), and the first mention of him identifies him as a figure free of Margaret's curse on the Queen as a mother whose name is ominous to children (4.1.34–42).
[3] See Appendix A for the Folio-only material.

cause and meaning can be seen to lie in the interstices between political and military reality, in Richard's confrontation with the women.

Barber and Wheeler suggest that in the web of curses 'verbal play releases and seems to confirm aggression and destruction by uncanny power, suggesting an under-the-surface or enveloping force beyond the control of will and executive intelligence'.[1] The challenges for performers are to find a dramaturgical style that will allow the opening episode of 4.4 to give expression to this power, to recognize the simultaneous ugliness and necessity of retribution, and to allow the humanity of the women's suffering its place too.

An effect of tableau is indicated by the simple device of having at least two of the three women sit on the ground.[2] They are at once stationary, abjected, and placed in choric equivalence one to another. As mourners, they will wear black. The repetition of names, at its most extreme in ll. 37–43, can resound impressively if the play is performed as the last of a cycle, as in Peter Hall's production, where one reviewer thought the passage particularly effective because the dead were remembered by the audience too.[3] In a free-standing *Richard III* Margaret will be more of an inexplicable outsider, an ironic contaminator of the play's world. Many of the dead will not be remembered by an audience which has not seen the Henry VI plays, and there will be relatively little sense that the rhetoric matches a momentous reality spanning a large sequence of history. In this situation the incantatory quality of the women's patterned repetition of names of the dead is just as much to the point as the specific people and events mentioned. The circumstance that three victims happen to have been called Edward allows the word 'Edward' to become in itself a token in the female memory of kinship, princeliness, and loss. Facts and discriminations are levelled out, for, as Margaret prophesies, they share victims who have suffered 'like' untimely violence (1.3.198) just as they have the like names. This is memory at its most selective. It foregrounds the figuration of grief as an emotional artifice over the

---

[1] Barber and Wheeler, p. 107.

[2] Margaret might sit on the throne (see Commentary, headnote to 4.4, and 4.4.455.2 n.) or remain standing.

[3] Hankey, p. 213, citing *Financial Times*, 13 January 1964.

events that gave rise to it. It bleeds away the actual detail of narrative to reveal a skeletonic poetic structure of willed similarities.

In some stage performances—Bill Alexander's was an example—the 'three queens' all remain on stage to confront Richard. Three can be a portentous number, and to a modern audience the visual echo of the three witches meeting Macbeth and Banquo might make its own point. The early texts are clear, however: Margaret leaves before Richard enters. The effect is to put her beyond reach of his insult and insinuation. As elsewhere, Richard's entry is disruptive. He arrives in military haste with drums and trumpets. He will sneer at his mother, and he will seduce the Queen, as he thinks, into promoting the marriage he intends to the Lady Elizabeth. But this time he will not be able to confute Margaret's rhetoric with cheap interruption. Her encounter with Richard's mother and the Queen has achieved its effect, which is to forge the matriarchal commonality of grief that binds these women, and ultimately almost everyone else, against Richard. She has taught the Queen, furthermore, that she has become a second Queen Margaret, 'For queen, a very caitiff crowned with care' (4.4.95). This new caitiff must learn, like her, to curse. That is Margaret's final exit. The rest of the scene will provide fitting final exits for the other two women, and will intimate that Anne has already made hers.

Richard attempts to deal with his mother and the young Princes' mother by drowning out their accusations with trumpets and drums. Just as he seems about to march away, he instead implores the women to 'be patient and entreat me fair' (4.4.145), and so he enters into the endgame in his relationship with his mother. The Duchess of York exists primarily so that she can definitively reject him in this scene. Before she curses Richard and invokes a bloody death for him, she sketches the life-history of a son offensively violent and unlovable from his birth onwards (4.4.160–4). In many stage productions Richard becomes childish in this exchange. Though the use of a drum to drown out intercession has classical precedent, as a response to one's mother it is purely infantile. Richard is given no verbal response to his mother's curse, but in some productions he appears shaken.[1]

The imagery of the scene develops the Duchess's earlier description of her womb as 'the bed of death' (4.1.49) and Margaret's

---

[1] See below, pp. 108–9, on Troughton's interpretation.

account of Richard as a 'hell-hound' crept from 'the kennel of thy womb' (4.4.44–5).[1] She cannot retrospectively make the womb a 'bed of death' to Richard himself, but her curse as mother can perhaps be equivalent:

> KING RICHARD
> Who intercepts my expedition?
> DUCHESS OF YORK
> A she that might have intercepted thee
> By strangling thee in her accursèd womb . . .
>
> Thou cam'st on earth to make the earth my hell.
>
> Therefore take with thee my most heavy curse,
> Which in the day of battle tire thee more
> Than all the complete armour that thou wear'st.
>
> Bloody thou art, bloody will be thy end.
>                     (4.4.130–2, 159, 177–9, 184)

After this desertion, Richard solicits the Queen for the hand of her daughter Lady Elizabeth in order to consolidate his right to the throne. It is a long exchange, and the Queen proves a fierce debater, suggesting that there is more to her than the vapid, suffering 'Poor painted queen' of Margaret's account (1.3.241).[2] She drives Richard round in circles, making him return to repeat almost the same protestation he had uttered over a hundred lines earlier (see 4.4.211–12 and 317–19). What breaks the deadlock is Richard's urging of necessity, with an implied threat:

> Without her follows to this land and me,
> To thee, herself, and many a Christian soul,
> Sad desolation, ruin, and decay.
> It cannot be avoided but by this,
> It will not be avoided but by this.
> Therefore good mother—I must call you so . . .
>                     (4.4.327–32)

---

[1] Like 'dream', the word 'womb' appears more often in *Richard III* than any other Shakespeare play. On every occasion it is in connection with Richard, and that connection gives the word a strong negative connotation.

[2] Hassel, 'Context', p. 636, approves of Frances Tomelty's portrayal of the Queen as 'a tough, smart, skeptical, worldly woman' in Alexander's production, and cites reviews of other productions where she has proved 'a strong adversary' (n. 31). In Al Pacino's film *Looking for Richard* (1996), the actor playing the Queen, Penelope Allen, argues keenly for presenting her thus.

A short passage of stichomythia follows this speech, reminiscent of Richard's seduction of Anne in 1.2. The exchange takes on a bizarre erotic coloration as Richard attempts to turn the woman on stage, already his sister-in-law, into a new mother figure.[1] Not long after addressing the words 'good mother' to the Duchess he is (in Q1) using the same phrase to the Queen. Despite his political aim, there are hints now that his earlier claims to self-fashioning might have been played out against a then invisible background of maternal dependency. It is only after rejection (by the Queen as well as his mother) that he can be existentially perturbed by the thought that 'There is no creature loves me' (5.4.179). His attempt to stave off this conclusion takes him through a contorted vision in which his offspring will bring his dead victims back to life:

> THE QUEEN
> But thou didst kill my children.
> KING RICHARD
> But in your daughter's womb I bury them,
> Where in that nest of spicery they shall breed
> Selves of themselves, to your recomforture.
>
> (4.4.342–5)

The reference to the passive and sacrificially nurturing 'nest of spicery' invokes the legend of the Phoenix that dies by burning its nest, to be reborn in the ashes. The imagined act of sexual ingression supposedly compensates for the act of murder. In fancying that his own children might be new selves for his dead victims, by implication he proposes that he too can be re-mothered, by Lady Elizabeth the daughter as well as her mother. When he invokes the Phoenix he brings to mind new birth as resurrection and spiritual salvation. This is a desperate hope indeed. Moreover, from the Queen's point of view, nothing could be less plausible than the suggestion that this re-fathering of the children on their sister might transmute infanticide into a happy outcome. She may well take refuge in evasions and make her escape, though in some productions the eroticized intensity of Richard's language at last mesmerizes and subdues her. However enigmatic the Queen's response, the audience knows that it will be his rival Richmond who will breed new princes by marrying Elizabeth.

[1] As noted by Hodgdon, pp. 104–11.

In 4.4 we therefore see a new version of 'Love forswore me in my mother's womb'. As a consequence of his acts, women representing the gynocratic powers of motherhood, sexual love, and hope of dynastic succession forsake Richard. Something similar happens in *King John* at virtually the same stage in the action: in a single speech John hears that both his mother Eleanor and his sister-in-law Constance are dead (4.2.119–24). The concluding scenes of both plays are exclusively male.[1] In *King John*, however, there is no dynastic consequence, for a son mysteriously materializes in the final scene. For Richard the desertion is absolute. It is Richard's rejection by his mother that causes his overthrow from a psychological standpoint, and it is the Queen's off-stage resistance to Richard that secures the political outcome. She transfers her allegiance and her daughter to Richmond. She will be his 'mother',[2] and the conditions are ripe for him finally to come into being as a dramatic character.

*Conscience.* Richard first mentions Richmond by referring to two prophecies. One of them is about the castle called Rougemont, whose name Richard now imagines to be a bardic pun on 'Richmond'. If such puns indeed mean anything, we might be disconcerted by the similarity between 'Richmond' and 'Richard' itself, as though Richmond were a kind of doppelgänger. They compete for both the hand of Lady Elizabeth and the crown itself. The whole of Act 5 is arranged as a series of episodes contrasting the two 'Rich...d's, the present and future kings. Throughout, Richard has been associated with the inhuman, with the bestial and monstrous. He is a dog, a hell-hound, a charnel-cur, a hedgehog, an abortive rooting hog, a bloody boar. Richmond, in contrast with Richard, is associated with calm, goodness, and blessing. He is less vital and personable than Richard: he can be metallic and icy, or a calmly militant angel. In Alexander's production, Christopher Ravenscroft played him 'humane, thoughtful, reaching out with love'.[3] His conversation flows unperturbed, more a form of quiet leadership than personal interaction. This effacing self-assurance acquires value because it represents what Richard is not.

---

[1] Compare also Portia's reported death and the all-male end of *Julius Caesar*.

[2] As Richard recognizes in the 'Freudian slip' of 5.5.53: see Commentary.

[3] Hassel, 'Context', p. 638.

The ghost scene bears witness to a disintegration of self—that is to say, of Richard's earlier self, the figure of unquenchable exteriorization, the man of wit and will. By a horrible irony, the self that now emerges is that of Christian polemics: the renegade soul seeing itself as in a mirror and despairing at what it sees. Now he is beyond cheering; wine, a white horse, and sound staves will do little for him, and his death might be, as several productions have suggested, a form of suicide. Alan Bates's Richard gave Richmond his dagger so he could kill him.

Perhaps surprisingly, Shakespeare keeps his presentation of Richard at a distance from the forms of subjectivity that were available to him even early in his career as dramatist. More's account provided plenty of hints that Richard was an ambitious villain tormented by bad conscience. In this respect Shakespeare's Richard subtly parts from Sir Thomas More's. It is distinct too from Colley Cibber's later Richard. Nor is Richard akin to Shakespeare's own conscience-plagued tyrant, Macbeth.[1] The play insists from early on, in its representation of other figures such as Clarence, that a more inwardly and spiritual sense of being is possible, but for most of the play it is not so for Richard. At least until he is king, his temperament is buoyant and sanguine. Even Richard's self-perceptions are so ironic and bemused that it is impossible to secure from them a residue of safe and serious content. His character is performative and phenomenological. Through that gambit Shakespeare hints at the experience of inner self behind the mask. This indirect, elusive, and unverifiable depiction of subjectivity is a technique to which he would return in presenting other role-playing figures, such as Rosalind in *As You Like It*, and Hamlet. But the hints from Richard are not reassuring. We may wonder whether the startling outwardly figure is of the same order of humanity as, for example, his brother Clarence.

But Richard does eventually wake up in his sleep and discover that, after all, he too partook of humanity as others experienced it. It could even be argued that the entire play's vantage point is that of Richard on the eve of the battle, a Richard on the point of death who meditates on the sequence that has brought him to where he

---

[1] Nevertheless, *Richard III* is an important precursor of *Macbeth*. Comparison of Richard and Macbeth played a central part in the development of eighteenth-century character criticism; see Joseph W. Donohue, *Dramatic Character in the English Romantic Age* (Princeton, 1970), pp. 189–215.

is. By the end, the carefully patterned repetitions, implausible in themselves, might be understood as a retrospective narrative of self. After all, the ghosts are a condensed recapitulation of the longer story. If the viewpoint is Richard's, we might better understand why the logically absent Margaret is actually present in the play, why it can be coherent for Richmond, as an element in Richard's own account, to have a simultaneous dream in which he is simultaneously visited by the ghosts, and why the material world and the otherworld seem perfectly conjoined against Richard. To develop the speculative view that a subjectively based reading would be available to the early audiences, one might invoke Elizabethan forms of writing such as lamentation, complaint, spiritual autobiography, repentance, and deathbed meditation. For an audience familiar with the story, the play might be experienced as a horrible and remorselessly patterned unfolding of events that reached towards a moment of nemesis as well as a moment of triumph.

What Richard experiences after his nightmare of the ghosts is loss of grace, and in this the play is theologically orthodox. Richard is a sinner who knows himself as such and who cannot repent. Without grace there is no essential self: 'I myself | Find in myself no pity to myself' (5.4.181–2; see Commentary). His dialogue with himself grows from the premiss that 'There's none else by' (5.4.161): specifically, no murderer about to kill him. He realizes that this is untrue, for spiritual despair makes him potentially his own self-assassin. John Donne wrote that 'It is a fearful thing to fall into the hands of the living God; but to fall out of the hands of the living God is a horror beyond our expression, beyond our imagination.'[1] In Christian thought reaching back to St Augustine, the spiritual self finds validation in the knowledge of God's love. The consequences could be dire for those, following Calvinist assumptions, whose knowledge of God depended in the first place on interrogating the inner self. At worst, awareness of self could be experienced as rupture, the pain of exclusion from God.[2]

After his call 'Have mercy, Jesu' uttered in sleep, Richard's dialogue with himself is pointed in its failure to mention God as the

[1] John Donne, *Sermons*, ed. George R. Potter and Evelyn M. Simpson, 10 vols. (Berkeley, 1953–62), v. 266.

[2] Stachniewski, p. 70.

ultimate source of love and affinity. God speaks his judgement through the courtroom of Richard's conscience, which anticipates the Last Judgement itself, but in so doing actually signifies his absence. The absent God has left a record of his departure in the form of a morally aware self, and that self now joins with his victims in seeking his death. Richard has attempted to fabricate himself as an autonomous being, but his recognition of conscience is a discovery that he has done so within a larger scheme of creation.

Richard fended off any responsibility for his own actions for as long as he could blame himself on his ontological beginnings, and hence on his mother. Her rejection of him signifies not only that humanity as a whole has turned against him, but also that he must take new account of himself. Before, his self-awareness fed on the death of others, specifically those within the bonds of kinship. Now there is a vacuum of otherness of every kind. Richard's annihilation of form, kinship, and law has turned back on him.[1] 'Richard loves Richard' is a last-ditch gesture towards self-engendering through a narcissistic embrace of self, as well as a sad parody of God's love for humanity.

On the page Richard's soliloquy after his dream can seem disjointed and without eloquence, but as a script for performance its fragmentation is the whole point. In performance it can be and often has been the apex of the entire play. The speech occupies the space between what is no ordinary dream and the waking world of the battlefield. Though Richard revives impressively to fight his last battle, the speech is spiritually *in extremis*, poised between life and death. It is the critical moment in the play as a tragedy, as Richard attains theology by knowing of God's absence, and attains ironic self-awareness by seeing lost possibilities for selfhood.

*Succeeding Ages*. He is a figure about to die, and Richmond a figure ready to succeed. Shakespeare's dramatic elaborations on his sources throughout the play converge with historical hindsight in making this a certainty. Before the battle Richard is brave, monstrously: 'A thousand hearts are great within my bosom' (5.5.76). Off stage, in the battle itself, he 'enacts more wonders than a man' (5.6.2) as he kills phantom Richmonds who are really other

[1] See William C. Carroll, 'Desacralization and Succession in *Richard III*', *Deutsche Shakespeare-Gesellschaft West, Jahrbuch 1991*, 82–96.

soldiers in disguise.¹ In Cibber's version especially, he can face Richmond heroically, even if that means enlisting on his side the ghosts that haunted him. Edmund Kean, playing Cibber's 'aspiring soul' for full, 'fought like one drunk with wounds: and the attitude in which he stands with his hands stretched out, after his sword is taken from him, had a preternatural and terrific grandeur, as if his will could not be disarmed, and the very phantoms of his despair had a withering power'.² Yet a staging of the combat that reflects Richard's mortal and spiritual desperation in Shakespeare's text might find his will finally disarmed. Sher's stooped Richard looked unable to fight; Richmond approached him ceremonially from behind and thrust his sword down on him.

Richmond's final speech is usually considered to be persuasive to the audience and sincere, though Wilbur Sanders calls it 'a pious shell and a hard core of prudential self-interest'.³ He also remarks that it is 'tenuously integrated' with the rest of the play.⁴ Is it, as in Bogdanov's production, a smooth exercise in public relations, scarcely ruffled by the darkly ambiguous and repeated injunction 'Let them not live'? Is it irrelevant because dissociated from the areas of emotional involvement that have typified the play? Or is this seedling of civic peace exactly what is most needed after Richard's manic and Herculean wrenching of England? At all events, by the end of the play Richmond is, as it were, remembering the future, speaking with the inflections of Elizabethan polity. The 1559 pageant celebrating the coronation of Queen Elizabeth had established the connection between the two new reigns at the earliest opportunity. Its theme, 'Unity', referred specifically to a concord aimed at healing the strife between church reformers and Catholics. The pageant stage was decorated with red and white roses illustrating 'The Uniting of the Two Houses of Lancaster and York', and the narrator, a child, petitioned that:

---

¹ See 5.6.11. This detail, not in the sources, gives Richmond a touch of the Machiavel, though the role-playing works on the opposite principle to his opponent's earlier single-handed performance of many roles.

² William Hazlitt (1820), in Bate, ed., *Romantics*, p. 510.

³ Wilbur Sanders, *The Dramatist and the Received Idea* (Cambridge, 1968), p. 73.

⁴ A reader who considers it important to uphold the speech's detachment from the rest of the play may wish to reject the editorial emendation at 5.7.28.

> Therefore, as civil war and shed of blood did cease
> When these two houses were united into one,
> So now, that jar shall stint and quietness increase,
> We trust, O noble Queen, thou wilt be cause alone.[1]

As the pageant looks to the past, Richmond's speech looks towards the original audiences' present, which has been made possible by his own impending marriage to an earlier Elizabeth. He himself has been all along a product of Elizabethan hindsight. This is a strong closure, to the tetralogy as well as the play, because it confirms an effective alignment between the projection forwards and the projection back in time. In contrast with the coronation pageant, where a child could usher in a new age even as it speaks of the past, Shakespeare's play is locked into a circular dialogue between the past it depicts and its own present moment, for by then Queen Elizabeth was without an heir and long past childbearing.

The play as a whole perhaps presents a conflict between what Richard P. Wheeler calls 'a redemptive destiny' that 'makes history sacred' and a profane history in which Richard's 'terrible presence is a source of fascination'.[2] At narrative and thematic levels, the sacralizing myth prevails, and the play accords with Walter Benjamin's enigmatic thesis: 'As flowers turn toward the sun, by dint of a secret heliotropism the past strives to turn toward that sun which is rising in the sky of history.'[3] In terms of the play's emotional impact, the effect might be otherwise. For in the conflict between the singular and the dispersed, between the demotic and the formal, between charismatic evil and bland virtue, the singular, the demotic, and the charismatic are likely to work theatrically in Richard's favour.

The reader's play of the mind might be able both to celebrate Richard as a creature of the theatre and to denounce him as an actor in an imagined political world. It might, correspondingly, both trace the 'secret heliotropism' of retelling the past so as to vindicate the present, and find in Richard an explosive figure whose very theatricality reveals the artifice and gives away the secret. As

---

[1] *The Passage of our most Dread Sovereign Lady Queen Elizabeth through the City of London to Westminster, the Day before her Coronation* (1558 [1559]), sig. B1.

[2] Richard P. Wheeler, 'History, Character and Conscience in *Richard III*', *Comparative Drama*, 5 (1971), 301–21; pp. 303, 304.

[3] Walter Benjamin, 'Theses on the Philosophy of History', written 1940, in *Illuminations*, trans. Harry Zohn, ed. Hannah Arendt (New York, 1968), p. 255.

a whole, these are extravagant expectations to have of any one production. But theatre has its own purposes. For the very reason that stage performance is capable of challenging and reshaping our understanding of the play, the practices of theatre cannot be bound by prior assumptions as to the text's potential, let alone one editor's summary of it.

## On Stage

The first phase in the history of performance of *Richard III* belongs to the actor who made the role famous in Shakespeare's time, Richard Burbage. The second is summarized in the name Colley Cibber. His adaptation was the means whereby the play acquired a new semantics that survived the rejection of Cibber's text: Cibber's influence found apotheosis and eclipse in the spectacular melodramatic stagings of the late Victorian theatre. Subsequently, a third phase began as the modern theatre discovered its own ways of rewriting Shakespeare using the vocabularies of symbolism and expressionism, and, later, Brechtian theatre and postmodernism. These techniques have been used to bring out meanings that actors and directors have considered implicit in or usefully built upon the play, usually at the cost, again, of altering and manipulating the text itself, often in a radical way. Words such as 'innovation' and 'distortion' can be different ways of describing the same thing, and the experiments of the twentieth century were as localized to their period as Cibber's adaptation. Cibber too was drawing out and adding to meanings implicit in Shakespeare's text. His version, articulated just before the War of Spanish Succession, challenged by Romantic radicals, dominant until the period of revolutionary nationalism in Europe, and vestigially surviving until after the Second World War, has a history that runs in loose parallel to the ascendancy and decline of the British empire. Modern productions often engage with social and political ideas more directly, but what they share with the Cibber tradition is a commitment to make the play speak to the times. The play is neither a fixed cultural icon nor an empty space. The present finds its meanings in dialogue with the past.

The history of *Richard III* on the stage is exceptionally rich, and for the most part it is richly documented.[1] The following account

---

[1] The fullest accounts are by Hankey and Colley. See also Richmond.

is, necessarily, selective. It attempts to locate turning points in the representation of the play and its leading role, and to relate them, if only with brief touches, to the cultural context in which they appeared. Some excellent productions fall short of redefining the play, and can pass unnoticed in the present brief survey. What matters are the new ways of conceptualizing the play in relation to the present moment of a production. I therefore lean towards productions that deviate some way, or even considerably, from the texts as originally written, modified, and printed in the Shakespearian period. At the same time it remains important that the productions surveyed are effective in communicating something implicit or explicit in what I refer to, less protectively than the phrase might sound, as 'Shakespeare's play'.

*Burbage and Others*. *Richard III* probably relied heavily on the skills of a single actor, Burbage.[1] There was the precedent of Marlowe's dependence on Alleyn in a series of plays beginning with the two parts of *Tamburlaine the Great* (1587). This work established Marlowe as a famous dramatist to the extent that the name Tamburlaine could be used to invoke Marlowe himself.[2] It established Alleyn, too, as an actor of heroically large-scale roles. Alleyn's role of Barabas was even longer, and is the only extant part written before Richard that compares in its line-count.[3] *Richard III* did much the same for Shakespeare and Burbage. He was the actor who a few years later would play Hamlet, the only Shakespearian role longer than Richard, and the one most closely comparable for its demands on the player by way of dexterity, actorliness, and sheer endurance. If Shakespeare was writing with Burbage in mind from the beginning, he would have been responding to qualities that set him apart from the more rhetorical Alleyn as an actor whose roles 'give little sense of the ebbs and flows of a character's

[1] Burbage may already have played Richard Duke of Gloucester in *Richard Duke of York*.

[2] In 1592 racist anti-alien verses signed '*per* Tamberlaine' were posted on the yard-wall of the Dutch Church. The words were taken to mean 'by Marlowe'.

[3] Barabas: 1,138 lines; Richard (Folio): 1,145 lines; Richard (Quarto): 1,070 lines. Roles of over 800 lines in public theatre plays are listed by Scott McMillin, in '*The Book of Sir Thomas More*: Dates and Acting Companies', in Howard-Hill, pp. 57–76 (pp. 62–3). McMillin notes that almost all such roles were played by Alleyn or Burbage.

consciousness'.[1] Both Shakespeare and Burbage were already established in their professions, but neither had made an individual
mark of such unignorable distinction. The relatively small cast
needed to perform the play is a consequence of Richard's part ab-
sorbing a large number of lines. The action is closely centred on a
single figure. Almost everyone relates directly to Richard. There is
a single plot line, and it is his.

The diarist John Manningham tells a scurrilous story that implies an alliance and rivalry between the dramatist and the lead
actor of *Richard III*. In 1602 Manningham noted that:

Upon a time when Burbage played Richard III there was a citizen grew so
far in liking with him that before she went from the play she appointed him
to come that night unto her by the name of Richard the Third. Shakespeare, overhearing their conclusion, went before, was entertained, and
at his game ere Burbage came. Then message being brought that Richard
the Third was at the door, Shakespeare caused return to be made that
William the Conqueror was before Richard the Third. Shakespeare's
name William.[2]

This anecdote can be read in more than one way. It is, in part, an
eroticized narrative of the dramatic process in which the auditor is
defined in a stereotypically passive female role. The term 'citizen',
often presumptively male, translates the predominantly male audience into a person who for the purpose of the story is a woman.
Shakespeare proves to be a more effective role-player and more re-
sourceful opportunist than the actor. If Burbage is Richard, his ancestor conquering William has to be before Richard. Yet if writing
precedes acting, the actor is crucially important too, for without
him the dramatist would not have met his audience; in this respect
the actor comes before the dramatist who writes for him. These
glosses on Manningham have a general pertinence to the business
of theatre, but it seems no accident that the story itself finds its
focus on the play where the fortunes of one actor and one dramatist
so intensely combined.

If Richard is the protagonist, the antagonist is a collective entity.
The parts are carefully arranged to enable *Richard III* to be

[1] Michael Hattaway, *Elizabethan Popular Theatre* (1982), p. 91.
[2] Chambers, *William Shakespeare*, 2 vols. (Oxford, 1930), ii. 212. Roslyn Lander
Knutson notes that William the Conqueror was a part in the play *Fair Em*, and that
Shakespeare might have played it; see *The Repertory of Shakespeare's Company
1594–1623* (Fayetteville, 1991), p. 59.

performed by a small to average-sized theatre company,[1] and they make few out-of-the-ordinary demands on the actors. There is no need to suppose that Q1's economy in this respect shows that it was prepared especially for touring the provinces, for the main elements in the doubling pattern are already apparent in F, and the adjustments between them are reasonably routine.

The Quarto text certainly saves on one boy actor by switching around the order in which the boy ghosts enter to haunt Richard and commend Richmond on the eve of the battle. Exactly how many boys would have been required to stage this version is hard to say, because one cannot rule out the possibility that old women such as Margaret and the Duchess of York would have been performed by adult men. Q1's adjustment to the point in the procession of ghosts for the two young Princes prevents their exit from falling immediately before Anne enters. One of them, perhaps Prince Edward as the elder of the two, must have doubled with Anne, and the disposition of roles in earlier scenes confirms this as probable. Anne does not dwindle from the action after 1.2 in order to meet the demands of doubling. But the impression that the plot line involving Anne fades away unsatisfactorily perhaps takes too literal a reading of her role. Emblematically speaking, she might be said to 'become' one of the young Princes, and the doubling enacts this transformation. The play encourages us to view their fates as equivalent in other ways. Anne, like the young Princes, is mistrustful of Richard. Yet, unable to resist being delivered into his hands, she too becomes his innocent victim as a direct result of becoming his dependant. The Princes die off stage at the same time as her death. Anne's seduction prefigures the political fortunes of England itself as they later unfold. The unity conferred by the actor's body and person might have made this more apparent.

Amongst the adult actors, Derby would conveniently have

[1] By the reckoning of T. J. King, in *Casting Shakespeare's Plays* (Cambridge, 1992), 95 per cent of the lines in either Q or F could be played by eleven men and six boys (p. 80; Tables 36 and 37). For Q1, Karl P. Wentersdorf calculates eleven men and four boys plus mutes: 'The Repertory and Size of Pembroke's Company', *Theatre Annual*, 33 (1977), 71–85; p. 80. Davison reckons ten men and two boys (p. 17), assuming that the Duchess of York and Margaret would have been played by men. By my own calculations, with a tight and unforgiving distribution of roles, and assuming (a) women were played by boys and (b) 'Grey' and 'Dorset' were a single role in the early scenes (see Appendix D, Note 3), all the speaking parts in Q could be taken by nine men and four boys.

doubled with Clarence. An interesting complication arises in the roles of the Queen's sons Dorset and Grey. Historically they are separate figures, though they shared the surname Grey. In the play they are treated as two figures only after Grey is arrested and taken to Pomfret. Before Dorset brings the Queen news of Grey's arrest the two names seem to refer to a single figure. In F there is some confusion on this point, though the evidence for 'Grey' and 'Dorset' representing one figure in the early scenes outweighs the evidence for seeing them as separate. Q1 resolves the difficulty in the less obvious direction: instead of separating the figures out, it establishes with greater consistency that they are one and the same person in the early scenes. The instability here is not strictly speaking a mere question of doubling. Once it was affirmed, in 2.4, that there were in fact two roles, doubling of a more routine kind was no doubt followed. Before that, there was, apparently, only one role.

Perhaps expediency dictated this outcome, for the scene-break at the beginning of 2.1, where Dorset/Grey enters, is one of the tightest pressure-points on the cast for the number of adult actors it requires. The effect is, however, consistent with other elements that might be called uncanny. After Dorset's news of Grey's arrest, Grey appears only twice, first in 3.3, where he is taken to execution at Pomfret, and then when he returns as a ghost to haunt Richard and offer Richmond valediction. Meanwhile Dorset has fled to join Richmond. In the Quarto it is never specified that he returns to the stage, but Dorset's name returns to haunt Richard in a different way towards the end of 4.4. Richard is defeated psychologically by the absent living and the present dead as much as by Richmond himself. These two aspects of the original Grey/Dorset are strangely complementary.

*Elizabethan Staging.* In contrast with plays such as, for example, *Titus Andronicus* or *Romeo and Juliet*, *Richard III* is relatively straightforward to stage. This is in some ways unexceptional. For instance, before the Rose was remodelled in 1592, playhouses were probably not equipped with trapdoors or equipment for a descent from the 'heavens'.[1] Moreover, the play makes no use of a

[1] Glynne Wickham, '"Heavens", Machinery, and Pillars in the Theatre and Other Early Playhouses', in *The First Public Playhouse: The Theatre in Shoreditch*, ed. Herbert Berry (Montreal, 1979), pp. 1–15.

feature that would have been available in the public playhouses, the 'inner' acting area behind central curtains. It does require that in 3.7 Richard and his attendant bishops appear '*aloft*'; that is to say in the upper acting space formed by the continuation of the first gallery above the tiring-house wall at the rear of the stage. When Richard and Richmond sleep in their tents, the tents appear to be movable structures, erected like real tents but by actors playing soldiers.[1] Other properties amount to little more than a bench or couch on which Clarence can lie, a table for the council scene, and a throne, along with costumes and weapons. *Richard III* would have been performable at the Theatre or the Rose in London, or on provincial tour.

On tour, the local conditions would have varied, but the simplicity of staging requirements would have enabled the play to be put on with little modification. A touring troupe might have been smaller than a London company at full strength,[2] and if so the play's efficient crafting in terms of the possibilities it offers for doubling actors' roles would have made it attractive for taking on the road. *Richard III* is an intensely London-based play, and to provincial audiences the spectacle of a London company performing it would have confirmed the city's significance as the historical and present-day metropolitan centre of the country. On the other hand, the defining events in Act 5 involve travel across Wales and the English shires. The players, journeying with their cartload of tents, weapons, halberds, and old armour, would have shown some affinity with the soldiers they played.

The comments that follow relate to London amphitheatre playhouses such as the Theatre, where the play would have been seen on a large thrust stage. Entries and exits would be through doors in the rear stage wall. It remains uncertain whether there would have been two or three doors in the early theatres. During the post-coronation scene, 4.2, a throne would be set forth against the middle of the rear wall. If a third door were available between the other two, the throne would have been pushed on to the stage through it. The third door, if there were one, may have been curtained off, its use held in reserve for moments when it would acquire a symbolic significance. A possible example is the final scene. Just before

---

[1] For discussion of the staging, see Commentary to 5.3.1.1.

[2] For the uncertainty on this matter compare Gurr, pp. 40–4, with Peter H. Greenfield, 'Touring', in Cox and Kastan, pp. 251–68 (p. 264).

it, Richard and Richmond meet in battle, and so they evidently enter through the left and right doors. Richmond kills Richard, and leaves the stage, presumably by the same door at which he entered. He immediately comes back on stage in a ceremonial entry marking his victory and the anticipated union of the houses of York and Lancaster. If a third door were available, this would have been a good time to use it. There is an earlier opportunity for symbolic use of a third door in 1.3. After separate entries for the Queen and her faction, and then Richard and Hastings, finally Margaret appears on stage. She is clearly dissociated from both groups, supposedly banished, and a haunting reminder of former conflict and killing; she comes into the play unexpectedly and as from nowhere. Entry through a middle door would clarify her isolated status in this her first entry, and it would usefully define her role as an arbiter of fate. The device could be repeated when she returns at the beginning of 4.4, witnessing the induction to Richard's final fall. It would be dramatically coherent for the use of a third door to enable a visual connection between Margaret and triumphant Richmond.

For most of the action the logic of entrances and exits by two doors probably prevailed, whether out of necessity or not. In the first scene, the action generates temporary and redefinable associations between a door and a place (the Tower), a state of being (enclosure and death), or a character (Richard). Richard enters from court; Clarence could come from the same direction but exit by the other door to the Tower, then Hastings would make the same passage across the stage in the opposite direction. In 1.2 Anne and the funeral cortège might enter from the 'Tower' door, as did Hastings. The off-stage location is now St Paul's Cathedral, but as Richard murdered the dead Henry VI in the Tower there would be a symbolic logic to the corpse entering from the door associated with his place of death. Richard would meet the procession from the same door as that by which he entered before. Towards the end of the scene he 'captures' both Anne and the funeral procession, but sends them in different directions. He will first follow the corpse, but Anne awaits him at his house. Is this a case where a third door would have been used, or does the logic shaping the identity of real and symbolic spaces temporarily fade? The situation remains unclear.

Early playhouses such as the Theatre and its successor the Globe would have made little use of stage scenery. The rear wall could represent an inside or outside wall of the Tower, or of any other building. An emblematic highlighting of spaces and objects is more readily achieved on a stage without scenery. A costume or a property can become the object of intense visual focus. In 1.2, for example, the halberds are not just there as medieval scene-setting; they are deployed as objects through which confrontation is staged. When they cease to debar the outsider Richard from Anne and the funeral cortège, he passes into a protected space. That invasion is comparable with the puncturing of the bodies of Prince Edward and King Henry, and anticipates Richard's surgical cuts into Anne's self-possession. Later in the scene, there is intense interplay between Anne and Richard using his sword and then the ring that he gives her. The sexual symbolism of the object relates immediately to the psychological tension of the verbal exchange.

Much would have depended too on the lavishness and choice of stage costumes. In the Elizabethan theatre, royalty and high nobility looked the parts. Mourners would be marked out by black costumes. As in Hall's account, the funeral procession in 1.2 would probably have been meagre, allowing fullest concentration on the corpse and its vulnerable mourner. Richard's no doubt less sober outfit would have marked him off as an outsider to the funeral procession. In the following scene, this emphasis on the interrupting figure through a contrast in costuming would have played the opposite way. Margaret would have appeared in black, an outsider to the Yorkist courtiers. Later, in 4.2, when the opening stage direction calls for the courtiers to enter to the sound of trumpets '*in pomp*' after Richard's coronation, there is opportunity for pageantry with a massed display of the best apparel as the actors process over the stage. It is the only moment of its kind in the play, and is rapidly punctured by Richard's first words, 'Stand all apart', and the unregal mutterings that follow. After a short scene Margaret enters, followed by the Duchess of York and the Queen, all of them presumably dressed in black. The latter two confront a Richard bristling with the paraphernalia of war. His military expedition is on the move with banners and drums. This is spectacle of a different kind, but the spectacle is never neutral, never merely visual. In this scene there is something self-parodic about Richard's part in it, and the episode is another example, following the pattern of 1.2 and 1.3, of confrontation between the mourner and the perpetrator of crime.

Nothing is more typical of Richard than his puncturing of ceremony, his disruption and distortion of formal rhetoric, his disrespect for convention, and his attrition of order in all its aspects. His entrances are violent; he interrupts speakers with deflating irony. These characteristics would have made clear his affinity with the Vice (see above, pp. 30–2). Above all, he speaks directly to the stage audience and connives with them. For these purposes he might have come to the edge of the stage, the liminal space between the play in performance and the audience that was traditionally reserved for the Vice. The conventions of Elizabethan theatre enable the energy of the role, providing the opportunity for Richard to break through the play's fiction and revitalize his special relationship with the audience. It has been suggested that his disruptive, restless, and demotic mobility of language and body represents the seething dynamic of early capitalism, born before its time with its teeth ready formed and struggling towards the dominance it would later enjoy.[1] It is not the purpose of the present account to depict the stage history of Richard as an allegory of the development of bourgeois man over the course of three centuries, though no doubt such an account could be constructed. Always, the middle term standing between Richard and the socio-economic order of a given time is the theatre, and Richard certainly represents principles of energy, vitality, dissimulation, seduction, and aggression typical of theatre, both as it is loved and as it might be feared.

*Early Revivals.* Some of the leading actors in Strange's Men and Pembroke's Men, including Shakespeare and Burbage, moved on directly or indirectly to the Lord Chamberlain's company, which began playing in June 1594. The new company came into possession of Shakespeare's earlier plays, at least those that are extant, including *Richard III*. Revivals probably followed. When a manuscript was eventually sold to the stationer Andrew Wise for publication in 1597, it came from this, the company in which Shakespeare had become a leading actor and sharer. The title-page tells us that the text is given 'as it hath been lately acted' by them. *Richard III* proved exceptionally popular as a reading text, with two reprints during the reign of Elizabeth, a further three before the appearance of the 1623 Folio, and two more thereafter.

[1]  Paul N. Siegel, *The Gathering Storm* (1992), pp. 85–92.

The play was well remembered. When Francis Meres in *Palladis Tamia* of 1598 mentioned *Richard III* amongst Shakespeare plays, he might have been recalling the revival mentioned on the title-page of the First Quarto, as might John Marston when in the same year he parodied the famous line in 'A man, a man, a kingdom for a man!'[1] There are five quotations from it in the anthology *England's Parnassus* (1600). About a year later John Manningham recorded the anecdote about Burbage playing the lead role, and one of the Cambridge *Parnassus* plays represented Burbage encouraging the student Philomusus to recite the opening lines. These last responses affirm Burbage's strong association with the role.

So the play seems to have remained popular on stage after the turn of the century. Later revivals would probably have been at the indoor Blackfriars theatre, though the Globe continued to be used as well. The Folio's act breaks, perpetuated in all subsequent editions, might reflect the intervals observed in the indoor theatres for the trimming of the candles. Hankey notes that in these conditions 'the close atmosphere, the smaller audience, the candles . . . would have emphasized all that was sinister' (p. 15). Richard would have found affinity with the vindictive villains of Jacobean tragedy such as Thomas Middleton's Vindice in *The Revenger's Tragedy* and John Webster's Flamineo in *The White Devil*.

Burbage died in 1619, and in Middleton's 'Funeral Elegy' on his death it is predicted that 'Crookback, as befits, shall cease to live'. Richard Corbet echoed the thought in his narrative poem describing his travels through England, 'Iter Boreale' (published in 1647). He relates how his guide at Bosworth Field 'mistook a player for a king':

> For when he would have said 'King Richard died',
> And called 'A horse! a horse!' he 'Burbage' cried.[2]

Crookback did not cease to live, but certainly suffered a decline. On 16 or 17 November 1633 the King's Men performed *Richard III* before King Charles and Queen Henrietta Maria at St James's Palace. In his office book, the Master of the Revels, Sir Henry Herbert, noted that this was 'the first play the Queen saw since her

[1] *Scourge of Villainy*, 1598. Marston recycled the parody in his contribution to *Eastward Ho!* (1605), and in *Parasitaster* (1606) and *What you Will* (1607). For these and other echoes, see C. M. Ingleby, *The Shakspere Allusion-Book*, 2 vols. (1932).
[2] In *Certain Elegant Poems* (1647), p. 12.

majesty's delivery of the Duke of York'.[1] Herbert's is the only definite record of a performance before the theatres were closed for the duration of the Civil Wars and the Interregnum. John Ford's *Perkin Warbeck* was published the year after this revival, in 1634.[2] In it, Warbeck claims the throne on the basis that he is the Duke of York who was supposedly murdered at Richard's instigation. If, as is probable, *Perkin Warbeck* was performed in the early 1630s, it might have provoked a new interest in Shakespeare's play.

After the theatres reopened, *Richard III* was assigned to the King's Company under Thomas Killigrew.[3] It was revived in the early 1660s. A new Prologue, later printed in *Covent Garden Drollery* (1672), implies that the play is about the recent events. A period of tyranny when Fortune will 'seem to eclipse the lustre of a crown', as though Richard were Oliver Cromwell, leads on to the restoration of legitimate monarchy.[4]

From the Restoration on, *Richard III* would have played on a stage furnished with a proscenium arch and decorated with scenery; women rather than boys would have taken the women's roles. Shakespeare's play was probably by this time showing its age. John Caryll, basing his *The English Princess* (1666) on the events surrounding the Battle of Bosworth, made a fresh start, returning, in the words of the Prologue, 'to plain Holinshed and downright Stow'. Caryll takes Lady Elizabeth as the central figure, making the plot hinge on her choice between virtuous Richmond and a luridly villainous Richard. When Shakespeare's play was revived by the combined King's and Duke's company at the theatre in Drury Lane in around 1690, the principal role was taken not by the King's Company's leading actor, Thomas Betterton, who was content with King Edward, but instead by a specialist in villains, Samuel Sandford.[5]

Colley Cibber admired Sandford's 'uncouth stateliness in his motion and sullen pride of speech'.[6] His adaptation, though in the

[1] Chambers, *William Shakespeare*, ii. 352.

[2] The date of performance is unknown. Gerald Eades Bentley places it '1622–32?', in *The Jacobean and Caroline Stage*, 7 vols. (Oxford, 1941–68), iii. 454.

[3] Allardyce Nicoll, *A History of English Drama 1660–1900*, vol. 1, *Restoration Drama 1660–1700* (Cambridge, 1952), pp. 353–4.

[4] Michael Dobson, *The Making of the National Poet* (Oxford, 1992), pp. 26–7.

[5] Montague Summers, *The Playhouse of Pepys* (1935), pp. 224–5; John Dover Wilson, ed., p. xlviii. Mrs Betterton appeared as the Duchess of York, and Mrs Bracegirdle as Anne.

[6] Cibber, *Apology*, p. 144.

event performed by Cibber himself, was initially conceived with Sandford in mind. Richard's mercurial qualities seem to have vanished already in Sandford. Perhaps a post-Cromwellian theatre audience, accustomed to reading plays by the light of contemporary politics, found it difficult to accept a regicidal ruler who was also, in line with the spirit of Restoration culture, a cynic and a wit. The change in staging conditions must have contributed too. The conflict between tyrant and wit is managed in the Shakespearian play by making full use of a platform stage that allowed the actor to walk forward and out of the theatrical illusion and address the audience directly. Perhaps these characteristics made adaptation particularly necessary. Richard needed stabilizing and consolidating within the new dramaturgy before he could re-emerge as one of the most vital figures on the English stage.

*Cibber's Adaptation.* Colley Cibber's adaptation of *Richard III*, first seen at Drury Lane in 1699 and published the following year, was the basis for all performances in the eighteenth century. Its hegemony was unchallenged until 1821, and it was only in the closing decades of the nineteenth century that Shakespeare's text became preferred. As Stanley Wells points out, Cibber's adaptation had been 'for a couple of centuries probably the most popular play on the English stage'.[1]

Though often mocked both in his own time and more recently for his crudely melodramatic style, Cibber had a shrewd understanding of theatrical art. His changes respond to some of the difficulties perceived in Shakespeare's play by Cibber as an actor-playwright working at the end of the seventeenth century. First there was the question of length: Cibber's redaction was above all a reduction, and came in at not much over a half the length of the Folio text. But Cibber was also a radical reconstructor, freshly composing over half of his text. He took less than eight hundred lines from *Richard III*, splicing in another two hundred from other Shakespeare plays.[2] Cibber seems to have been proud of his work as a collage of Shakespeare's script and his own. In the printed text, as he explains in the Preface, 'I have caused those [lines] that are entirely Shakespeare's to be printed in this

[1]  Stanley Wells, 'Television Shakespeare', *SQ* 33 (1982), 261–73 (p. 266).
[2]  Tabulated by H. H. Furness, New Variorum edn. (Philadelphia, 1908), p. 604.

*italic character*, and those lines with this mark (') before 'em are generally his thoughts, in the best dress I could afford 'em.' The text is therefore designed to show off the extent to which Cibber's adaptation is an independent piece of work even as it is an inter-mingling of different 'thoughts'.

Shakespeare had staged the early career of Richard in *Richard Duke of York*, the last play of the Henry VI trilogy, so that the sequel had to begin at a mid-point in Richard's rise to power. The subtle structure of *Richard III* itself makes a fine art of this necessity. Yet for those members of the audience who were unfamiliar with the preceding events the action could be perplexing. By Cibber's time the foundation of the Tudor dynasty was no longer of pressing con-cern, and the Henry VI plays were unfamiliar to the theatre-going public. Cibber's first Act, which he called 'the best Act in the whole', showed the main events in Richard's early career of vil-lainy, and was almost entirely of his own invention. He was piqued to find that the stage licenser forbade performance of this opening section because he thought that the representation of Henry VI would elicit sympathy for the deposed and recently deceased James II.

Cibber presents Henry VI mourning for the murder of his son Edward at Tewkesbury. Richard later enters to give a truncated version of his original opening soliloquy, beginning 'Now are our brows bound with victorious wreaths'. This leads on to a scene based on 5.6 in *Richard Duke of York* in which Richard kills King Henry. Act 2 shows the seduction of Anne, followed by a largely invented court scene. Act 3 gives abbreviated versions of Prince Edward's welcome to London and Richard's persuasion of the London citizens, separated by a scene in which Anne laments her new husband Richard's hatred towards her (with '*Song here*' and lines from Henry IV's invocation of sleep in *2 Henry IV* 3.1). Act 4 corresponds roughly to Shakespeare's Act 4, but is shorter, and omits the lamentation of the women in 4.4. A brief scene unique to the first edition of 1700 and probably abandoned on stage well be-fore 1718 displays, with '*The stage darkened*', the critical incident Shakespeare withheld from view, the murder of the princes in the Tower.[1] Act 5 is a shortened rewriting of Shakespeare's Act 5,

---

[1] The omission is probably connected with the mechanics of staging. See Albert E. Kalson, 'Colley Cibber's Alteration of Shakespeare's *Richard III*', unpublished Ph.D. dissertation, University of Birmingham, 1964, pp. 104–5.

with the striking rationalization that the ghosts appear to Richard only, and not to Richmond. Lines from other Shakespeare plays include a passage based on *Henry V* spoken by Richard before seeing the ghosts; it begins 'The hum of either army stilly sounds'. The ghosts appear as a single group to Richard, but Richmond is not on stage. After the ghosts, the section of Richard's last soliloquy in which he enters into dialogue with himself is cut, and in a famous passage Cibber spells out very clearly how Richard puts the ghosts behind him:

> Perish that thought. No, never be it said
> That fate itself could awe the soul of Richard.
> Hence, babbling dreams, you threaten here in vain.
> Conscience, avaunt! Richard's himself again.

That is more resolute, and less of a public façade, than the equivalent lines in Shakespeare's play (5.5.37–40). In Cibber's version Richard is most 'himself' at the end of the play as a fiery and defiant man of the battlefield, a change of emphasis that would be crucial for the success of actors such as Garrick.

Cibber's reshaping is carefully deliberated, and has clear consequences. The complete removal of Queen Margaret has been followed in more recent times in, for example, Olivier's film and Alexander's touring production. It makes the play's action less supernaturally fated and more rational in its premisses. The scenes showing the murder of Clarence and the entrapment of Hastings vanish. Cibber consigns Buckingham to execution in a casually peremptory line 'Off with his head! So much for Buckingham'; the line was so deeply entrenched in acting tradition that (like 'Richard's himself again') it survived into twentieth-century performances including Olivier's film version. But the scenes that in Shakespeare's play focus the audience's attention on the successive deaths of Clarence, Rivers, Grey, Vaughan, Hastings, and finally Buckingham himself are all absent. The only ghosts that haunt Richard are those of Henry VI, the two young princes, and Anne.

Richard is therefore pitted against a smaller range of innocent victims whose pasts have been wiped clean. Stanley is a moral commentator who guides the audience's responses throughout. The role of Anne is enhanced in pathos, but to demonstrate Richard's bullying rather than to create an effective role in its own right. In 1776 a young Sarah Siddons failed in it. As Hankey points out, the

4. William Hogarth, *Mr Garrick in the Character of Richard III*.

elimination of characters with whom Richard interacts narrows the range of his field of action: 'He can no longer play games with the queen and her faction . . . He cannot piously pity Margaret, or lay his trap for Hastings' (p. 23). Richard's actions as a man are more muscular; in the later acts he is less unnerved and fragmented. Cibber shifts the emphasis of the role away from virtuosity and wit. He sets in place a more stable subjectivity but a more plainly unpleasant villain, adding seven soliloquies in which Richard explains his plots and resists Conscience in the name of Ambition.

As a self-contained dramatic unit, the adaptation makes more immediate sense than the original on which it is based. It hinges on two on-stage murder scenes and the ghost scene. Both murders take place in a bedchamber, with the victims initially sleeping. In the ghost scene Richard sleeps on his couch, probably on the same area of the stage. Indeed the tent drapes with the couch within—a substantial piece of furniture heavy with bedcovers in Hogarth's depiction of Garrick at this moment (fig. 4)—would surely have acted as a reminder of the bedchamber itself. The on-stage theatrical representation of troubled sleep broken by sudden awakenings and ensuing death acts as a strong unifying principle.

*Cibber to Shakespeare, Garrick to Irving.* In 1741, David Garrick, playing at the obscure London theatre of Goodman's Fields, revolutionized Shakespearian acting and launched one of the most famous careers in the history of English theatre with his Richard in Cibber's version. An ageing Cibber was able to comment with envy and reluctant admiration, 'The young fellow is clever'. The novelty of Garrick's acting technique depended on its rejection of more mechanically rhetorical methods in favour of an avidly extroverted and yet relaxed psychological naturalism.[1] The melodramatic gestures such as those recorded in Hogarth's painting have elements of both formulaic artifice and emotional immediacy. In action they would have been transformed from the frozen posture by the mobility of face and gesture for which Garrick was famous. His insistence on the contiguity between the imagined mind of the character and the performance of the actor was the source of the interpretative energy that amazed his audiences. In 1772 Fanny Burney described the effect of Garrick's performance in Gothic terms of praise as 'sublimely horrible'.[2] That complexity of response is in line with Garrick's more or less conscious application of the Scottish Enlightenment philosophical principle of 'sympathetic imagination', whereby 'the imagination through attendant emotional sensitivity, succeeds in identifying itself with the object of its attention, and consequently enters with almost intuitive force into the distinctive character of the object'.[3] For a later generation of Romantic critics such as William Hazlitt, Shakespeare would provide the finest example of the sympathetic imagination. Paradoxically, Garrick's revolution, whilst entrenching Cibber's version as the standard performance text, also set new parameters for what the acting of Shakespeare would entail.

---

[1] Donohue, pp. 216–42 (see p. 67 n. 1); George Winchester Stone, Jr., and George M. Kahrl, *David Garrick: A Critical Biography* (Carbondale, 1979), pp. 23–51.

[2] Frances Burney, *Early Diary*, ed. Annie Raine Ellis, 2 vols. (1913), i. 186.

[3] Stone and Kahrl, p. 37, quoting Earl R. Wasserman. Compare Johnson, speaking to Kemble: 'Are you, sir, one of those enthusiasts who believe yourself transformed into the very character you represent?', to which Kemble answered 'that he had never felt so strong a persuasion himself'. Johnson went on to cite Garrick as an example (Boswell, p. 1252).

John Philip Kemble and George Frederick Cooke developed contrasting acting styles that survived into the massive rebuilt theatres
of the early nineteenth century. Playing at both the old Drury
Lane before it burned and in the new theatre of the same name,
Kemble presented Richard in an aristocratic, statuesque, carefully
nuanced performance of 'iron and undeviating austerity'.[1] The
architect and antiquarian William Capon designed scenery for the
large flats against which Kemble played on the enlarged Drury
Lane stage in 1811. The flat of the Tower of London reconstructed
its appearance in the period, and chamber wings attempted to
show architecture in genuine medieval pointed style. It was the
first such attempt at scenic accuracy. Meanwhile Covent Garden
offered the inelegant and unaristocratic Cooke. Charles Lamb denounced him for indulging in 'the coarse, taunting humour, and
clumsy merriment, of a low-minded assassin'.[2] Macready was a
touch more sympathetic: 'Cooke's varieties of tone seemed limited
to a loud harsh croak descending to the lowest audible murmur;
but there was such significance in each inflexion, look, and gesture, and such impressive earnestness in his whole bearing, that
he compelled your interest and attention.'[3]

Once Coleridge, in his lectures delivered in about 1808, had defined Shakespeare as a Proteus, and Hazlitt had influentially at-
tacked Cibber's text as a 'miserable medley',[4] the agenda was set
for the eventual return of Shakespeare's self-declared Protean
character to the stage. The moment seems propitious, but in the
event compromise prevailed. Hazlitt and Lamb agreed that Edmund
Kean's performance showed a convincing new rapprochement
between the text of Cibber and the spirit of Shakespeare. By the
emerging Romantic consensus, Shakespeare's Richard could be
admired as a figure of 'daring and comprehensive intelligence,
which seizes its objects with the grasp of a giant'.[5] It was most nearly
realized in Kean's stormy, improvisational, and mood-switching

[1] Anon., *Remarks on the Character of Richard the Third as Played by Cooke and Kemble* (1801), p. 11.

[2] Bate, ed., *Romantics*, p. 503.

[3] W. C. Macready, *Reminiscences, and Selections from his Diaries and Letters*, 2 vols. (1875), i. 66.

[4] William Hazlitt, *Characters of Shakespear's Plays* (1817; repr. 1916), p. 176.

[5] Thomas Barnes, in *The Examiner*, 27 February 1814, quoted in Donohue, *Dramatic Character*, p. 319.

5. *Mr Kean in 'Richard the Third'*, C. Turner after
J. J. Halls.

rendition of Cibber's text. Kean could be seductively intense, as
J. J. Halls's Byronic depiction of him suggests (fig. 5).[1]

The financial success of Kean's *Richard III* induced the populist
Coburg Theatre to stage the play in 1820. The Coburg held no patent
for playing 'Shakespeare' as performed, but, as 'Shakespeare' was in
this case Cibber, they got round their exclusion by basing their production on the actual Shakespeare text. This early restoration was
compromised by a deliberately melodramatic and pantomimic style.[2]

---

[1] William Hazlitt wrote a compelling account of Kean in *A View of the English
Stage* (1818), reprinted in Bate, ed., *Romantics*, pp. 507–10. See p. 70 for part of it.
[2] Jonathan Bate, 'The Romantic Stage', in *Shakespeare: An Illustrated Stage
History*, ed. Bate and Russell Jackson (Oxford, 1996), pp. 92–111 (p. 110).

A more thoughtful advocacy came in Thomas Bridgman's synthesis of the two texts which was published in the same year. It sought to bridge the gap between the playability of Cibber and the aesthetic superiority of Shakespeare, but it was not brought to the stage.[1]

William Macready's return 'to the true source of inspiration' for his 1821 revival of *Richard III* was similarly a mixture of both versions.[2] Many of Cibber's cuts remained in place, as did his introduction of passages from *Richard Duke of York*. Macready admitted to retaining 'in deference to the taste of the times' lines from Cibber that he nevertheless dismissed as 'claptraps' and 'bombast'. His attitude was still that of the actor-manager hanging on to the strong playing points of Richard's role in the Cibber text. He restored Shakespeare selectively. In his Preface to the printed edition of his version, Macready asserted that his 'sole object' was 'To restore *the character of Richard* and *the language of Shakespeare* to the stage . . . no incident whatsoever, bearing upon the character of Richard, is withheld from the audience'.[3] The corollary is that Margaret, Hastings, and Clarence were introduced only for the opportunities they offered Richard, not as significant dramatic roles in themselves. Margaret's role in particular remained severely curtailed. Macready made the tent scene and Richard's death the key points of his performance, and that too reflects the spirit of Cibber. Still, the view of Richard was distinctively Romantic. Macready sought to rehabilitate 'that "alacrity and mirth of mind" instanced by More', and he followed Lamb in noting Richard's 'rich intellect . . . his wit, his resources, his buoyant spirits, his vast knowledge, and insight into character'.[4] The audience's response to the usually unperformed roles of Clarence and Margaret was largely favourable, but the production as a whole met with a lukewarm response. Macready allowed it to play one more time before closing it. The experiment was over, but only temporarily. Early in his career Samuel Phelps worked with Macready, and when he prepared *Richard III* for the new Sadler's Wells Theatre in 1845 he went far beyond Macready in using Shakespeare's text.

[1]  Thomas Bridgman, *King Richard III* (1820), ed. Albert E. Kalson (1971).

[2]  Macready, *Reminiscences*, i. 224.

[3]  Macready, *King Richard III* (1821), ed. Albert E. Kalson (1970), 'Preface', p. iii.

[4]  Macready, 'Preface', p. vi, quoting Lamb, 'On the Tragedies of Shakespeare', reprinted in Bate, ed., *Romantics*, p. 121. 'Alacrity and mirth of mind' in contrast with Kean's moodily sinister Richard had already characterized his successful performance of Cibber's Richard in 1818.

However, it was Charles Kean's performances of Cibber that
dominated the London stage in the mid-century. His acting style
was more restrained than that of his father. He encouraged a
strong ensemble of rigorously rehearsed actors, and his staging
evolved progressively towards the spectacular. The 1854 production at the Princess's Theatre boasted realistic arches and towers
in 4.4, and in Act 5 soldiers in suits of steel armour with decorated
surcoats and armorial bearings crossed a substantial bridge.[1]
Meanwhile, burlesques based on Cibber's play prospered.[2] So did
lowbrow productions, and the German novelist Theodor Fontane
left memorable comments on two of them.[3] At Philip Astley's
circus in Southwark he found *Richard III* staged by actors on horse-
back: 'As a Berlin critic went so far in his enthusiasm for Elssler or
Taglione as to employ the dubious expression, "She dances
Goethe", I can feel safer in allowing myself to declare that at Astley's they *ride* Shakespeare.' He added by way of explanation that
this obsession with horses 'is expressive of a national tendency'.
Fontane also saw *Richard III* in Dean Street, Soho, 'at an exceptionally reasonable price'. Entr'acte music included 'The Rat-
catcher's Polka' and the 'Alma Quadrille'. Richard, seen here and
elsewhere in England as 'a tormentor, a villain and a blackguard in
the "family circle" as well, beating his wife', was played by an
actor 'not an inch of a king, and six feet of journeyman butcher'.

The German Romantic theatre was untrammelled by English
stage tradition. Productions of *Richard III* at the Dresden Court
Theatre in the 1850s simply worked from the Schlegel–Tieck
translation of 1810, and so unostentatiously banished the Cibber
version that continued to play on the English and American stage.[4]
In contrast with usual Anglophone practice, the roles of actor and

[1] Colley, pp. 89–91.

[2] For examples and discussion of burlesques, see *Shakespeare Burlesques*, ed.
Stanley Wells, 5 vols. (1977–8).

[3] Theodor Fontane, *Shakespeare in the London Theatre, 1855–58*, trans. and ed.
Russell Jackson (1999), pp. 9–16. I am grateful to Jackson for making his translation available in advance of publication.

[4] *Richard III* was not performed in nineteenth-century France, though in 1781
Firmain de Rozoi began a tradition of writing plays loosely based on it. Népomucène
Lemercier's 1824 play adapted from Shakespeare's *Richard III* and from Nicholas
Rowe's *Jane Shore* (1714) aspired to make Shakespeare 'supportable au goût noble
et délicat du publique français'. For a stage history of *Richard III* in France see
Fortunato Israel, '*Richard III* sur la scène française', in *Le Tyran*, ed. Dominique
Goy-Blanquet (Amiens, 1990), pp. 151–62.

director-manager were separate; Ludwig Tieck himself was
dramaturge to Bogumil Dawison's Richard III. Audiences would
have heard a relatively full text, and witnessed a virtuoso,
variable Richard. The acting might have been reminiscent of
Edmund Kean, whom Tieck had seen perform the role in London.
Dawison would presumably have avoided what Tieck called the
'stupid dumb-show'[1] that he noted in Kean's awakening from the
dream, conventionally a protracted high-point of Cibber's version.
It may be that Henrik Ibsen saw Dawison as Richard and as Hamlet. These examples of an actor playing with the role may therefore
have influenced Ibsen's mature dramaturgy in plays such as *Peer
Gynt* (1867).[2]

*Richard III* was first taken to America by Cooke in 1810. Ten
years later Edmund Kean followed. In 1821 Junius Brutus Booth, a
British actor heavily influenced by Kean's style, emigrated and established in America some of the traditions of the London stage.
William Winter noted how Booth's performance of Richard
evolved through the play from watchful craftiness, to fury and
scorn as king, to 'a whirlwind' on the field of battle.[3] Booth initiated a physical style of acting that was taken still further in the
American nineteenth-century theatre by Edwin Forrest. Forrest
rejected the hunched villain, rendering the part with a rough and
primitive energy directed against the enervated English courtiers.
Booth's son Edwin concentrated himself on a 'deftly ingratiating'
Richard 'whose contrasting wickedness was so frank, entire, and
cheerfully sinister as to be literally diabolical'.[4] Beneath the demon-
iac figure was a man of pained conscience. Like his father,
Booth wore no hump and walked without a limp. Asked to compare his own acting with his father's, he said 'I think I must be
somewhat quieter'.[5] It was that calm professionalism that perhaps
drew him away from Cibber and led him, in 1868, to declare that
'in my devotion to the sacred text . . . I intend restoring . . . the
unadulterated . . . *Richard III*'.[6] By the time he did so, in 1878,[7]

[1] Harold Newcomb Hillebrand, *Edmund Kean* (New York, 1933), p. 337.

[2] Inga-Stina Ewbank, 'European Cross-Currents', in *Shakespeare: An Illustrated
Stage History*, pp. 128–38 (p. 135).

[3] William Winter, *Shakespeare on the Stage* (1912), pp. 99–101.

[4] Winter, p. 108.     [5] Colley, p. 107.

[6] Grossman, pp. 176–7, quoted in Colley, p. 107.

[7] Winter, p. 108, misdates 1876.

Henry Irving, performing at the Lyceum in London, had beaten him to it.

Irving's return to Shakespeare aimed to rescue the play from 'the taste of a succeeding generation'.[1] His productions of 1877 and 1896, separated by almost twenty years, presented contrasting Richards. The first was a man isolated by his deformity and driven by what Irving described as 'youthful audacity'.[2] The later Richard was, more than the actor himself, an older figure. He had 'outlived all pleasures but the intellectual one of doing evil superbly'.[3] Shaw described the end of the production, not uncritically, as 'pathetically sublime'.[4] 'A horse! a horse! my kingdom for a horse!' was the final line, followed only by the action in which Richard is killed.

Especially in the later production, Irving built on Charles Kean's example of turning the stage into a scene of operatic splendour that seemed to be literally inhabited by the persons in the play. Irving's pictorial stage, like his acceptance of Shakespeare's text, appealed to a newly respectable and educated middle-class audience. The scenery connected them with an idealized vision of early English history, just as the text connected them with the national poet. Irving perfected the stage as picture-frame, and was the first manager to cover the house lights during performance. Within the illuminated frame the focus remained firmly on Richard, whether audacious or inhumanly evil.

Despite restoring the text, Irving retained some elements of the Cibber tradition, such as the appearance of the ghosts to Richard but not Richmond. In America that tradition remained strong well into the twentieth century, despite Edwin Booth's efforts to reinstate Shakespeare.[5] Cibber's text informed early silent films such as J. Stuart Blackton's ten-minute 1908 Vitagraph. In England, the 1910 Co-operative film with Frank Benson followed Benson's eclectic stage version. Its fixed-frame tableaux filmed in the

---

[1] *Shakespeare's King Richard III: Arranged for the Stage Exclusively from the Author's Text by Henry Irving* [1877].

[2] Alan Hughes, *Henry Irving, Shakespearean* (Cambridge, 1981), p. 154.

[3] Hughes, p. 154.

[4] *Shaw on Shakespeare*, p. 164. Shaw wanted a more fiery and Nietzschean Richard.

[5] Arthur Colby Sprague was witness to a performance of Cibber in Boston in 1930: see his *Shakespeare's Histories* (Glasgow, 1964), pp. 132–3.

6. Frank Benson as Richard, with nephews (Miss A. P. Nicholson and Miss Molly Terraine), Memorial Theatre, Stratford-upon-Avon, evidently photographed during filming, 1910.

Stratford-upon-Avon Memorial Theatre offer valuable insights into late Victorian stage productions once allowance is made for the silent film medium (fig. 6).[1] A longer 1912 American silent film of *Richard III* with Frederick B. Warde as Richard is similarly closer in structure to Cibber than to Shakespeare, even though the pro-Shakespearian Booth had trained Warde. Despite its greater assurance as a film work, its melodramatic acting against pseudo-medieval sets retains the hallmarks of the popular nineteenth-century tradition.[2]

Today Cibber's text still offers an important model in that it initiates cuts and alterations some of which remain widely copied. Perhaps more important, Cibber embodies a vigorous and populist

[1] For accounts of early films, see Robert Hamilton Ball, *Shakespeare on Silent Film* (1968). For documentation of film versions generally, see Kenneth S. Rothwell and Annabelle Henkin Melzer, *Shakespeare on Screen* (1990). The Benson film is reproduced on the video *Silent Shakespeare* (British Film Institute, 1999). One genuinely filmic effect is the fading from one ghost to another in the ghost scene.

[2] Margaret A. Varnell, 'A Note on *Richard III* (1912)', *Post Script*, 17.1 (Fall 1997), 88–90. The film was rediscovered and screened by the American Film Institute in 1996 (*Los Angeles Times*, 31 August 1996). *Richard III* was also quickly on television. A 1937 BBC broadcast of Richard wooing Anne was one of the earliest transmissions of Shakespeare.

vision of the play that still endures. Olivier's film version, with its antecedents in Irving and Warde, acts as a channel whereby some of Cibber's decisions have been transmitted to more recent performers. Olivier too cut the role of Margaret and absorbed material from *Richard Duke of York* into the script. He too made Richard finally resolute with Cibber's line 'Richard's himself again'. Of course the Richard who says this line is not himself as Shakespeare wrote him. The irony has not escaped Scott Colley, whose stage history of Richard takes this quotation as its title.

*Modernism and After.* Edwin Booth's naturalistically presented and introspective Richard influenced Richard Mansfield, who emphasized Richard as a human rather than a monster. He traced his maturation from impulsive youth at Tewkesbury towards gloomy age at Bosworth. John Barrymore on Broadway in 1920 at once heightened the titanic scale of the role and established an even more clearly defined psychological interpretation. He prepared for the role through intensive coaching by Margaret Carrington, who trained him to adopt a vocal style that would bridge the usual gap between artificial 'Shakespearian' and 'natural' acting.[1] His director, Arthur Hopkins, was widely read in Sigmund Freud's writings, and was fully aware of their significance to the modern theatre. Hopkins probably responded to Freud's specific comments on Shakespeare's Richard as an example of individuals who are conscious from infancy of an 'unjust disadvantage'. Freud had noted that Richard's predicament allows the audience to have 'a secret background of sympathy' with him, because he expresses 'an enormous magnification of something we find in ourselves as well . . . we all demand reparation for early wounds to our narcissism, our self-love'.[2]

Barrymore, who himself had a taste for the macabre, was not the last Richard to find inspiration from watching one of the creatures to whom Richard is compared in the play. In his case it was the bottled spider, identified with a red tarantula he saw in the Bronx Zoo, 'peculiarly sinister and evil looking; the personification of a

[1] Michael A. Morrison, *John Barrymore, Shakespearean Actor* (Cambridge, 1997), p. 79.
[2] Sigmund Freud, 'Some Character-Types Met with in Psychoanalytic Work' (1916), in *The Standard Edition of the Complete Psychological Works*, ed. James Strachey *et al.*, 24 vols. (1953–74), xiv. 309–33.

crawling power'.[1] In performance Barrymore disguised Richard's evil with bright bursts of orange and scarlet costume, a heroic outer demeanour, and athletic movements. This extroversion did not hide his malice, and a Hamlet-like intelligence was also apparent, eventually suffering under its self-imposed pressure. Reviewers noted that Barrymore's Richard was 'on the rising crest of good fortune' and 'in the best of spirits' when wooing Anne.[2] But, by the encounter with his mother in 4.4 or before, streaks of madness marked the onset of mental disintegration. In the final battle he was powerless and infuriated—a far cry from the Cibber tradition. In the accounts of Barrymore's Richard one senses the possibility that the alignment between the actor's own attempt to seize the audience's attention and the political ambitions of the Richard he plays might be dissociated. Barrymore's success as an actor lay partly in communicating Richard's final disintegration and incapacity.

The psychological acuity of Barrymore's account contrasts with Leopold Jessner's production of the same year at the Staatliches Schauspielhaus in Berlin, the first attempt to relate *Richard III* to modern politics. Jessner and his Richard, Fritz Kortner, responded to the audience's immediate knowledge of the attempts by both Marxists and right-wing Prussian Junkers to overthrow the fledgling Weimar regime. They enlisted the play to the defence of republican democracy, conceiving of theatre as 'political in the wider, philosophical sense, roughly in the way the theatre of the Greeks was religious in the philosophical sense'.[3] The staging was symbolist. A hallmark of Jessner productions, a large set of stairs, dominated the set once Richard became king. These stairs recall, perhaps, the image of the steps up Fortune's hill in *Timon of Athens*. From its heights Fortune eventually 'Spurns down her late belovèd . . . The foot above the head' (*Timon* 1.1.86–95). In Jessner's theatre the mechanism by which the protagonist ascended and was spurned down had become not fortune but power.

Kortner's acting consistently eschewed naturalism (fig. 7). According to Robert Speaight, 'Richard reminded people of a humped toad, a grinning Japanese mask, or Rodin's Balzac.'[4] He was

[1] John Barrymore, *Confessions of an Actor* (1926), p. 99.

[2] Colley, p. 155.

[3] Jessner, quoted by William Grange, 'Shakespeare in the Weimar Republic', *Theatre Survey*, 28 (1987), 89–100; p. 93.

[4] Robert Speaight, *Shakespeare on the Stage* (1973), p. 210.

7. Fritz Kortner's expressionist Richard, Berlin, 1920.

dressed in black, his pale face against a black curtain for his first
soliloquy. Jessner's *Richard III* anticipated the theatre of Bertolt
Brecht, and indeed provided a model for his study of dictatorship,
*The Resistible Rise of Arturo Ui* (1957). Like Brecht, Jessner laid bare
the historical process rather than portraying the events. His production emphasized the medium of language itself rather than using
language as expressive of character. Kortner's delivery switched
between the incredibly rapid and the deliberately slow, building
what one critic described as 'cathedrals of words'.[1] The violence
was abstracted. It was enough to point a dagger towards Clarence.
Instead of being killed in stage battle, Richard fell slowly down the

[1]  Hortmann, p. 62.

emblematic steps, towards armies emblematically swathed in red and white, whilst off stage the kettledrums beat.

Jessner's rejection of pictorial stage-sets and adoption of expressionist lighting effects was followed through in England by Terence Gray at the Cambridge Festival Theatre. The set for his 1926 *Richard III* centred on an arrangement of cubes built into abstract architectural shapes. It was mounted on a turntable so as to provide 'a versatile sequence of playing spaces'.[1] Properties were minimal. Lighting picked out characters in conflict and, notably in the ghost scene, projected huge shadows. The production stands out in a period when ranting Richards on scenic sets continued to dominate the theatres of Stratford-upon-Avon, London, and New York.

Mid-century productions began to echo Jessner's reinvigoration of the play as a political drama, pitting a totalitarian Richard against the ideals of modern democracy. In Jürgen Fehling's risk-taking 1937 production in Nazi Berlin, Werner Krauss 'took a devilish pleasure in turning the last scion of the house of York into a likeness of the club-footed Minister of Propaganda [Joseph Goebbels] with all his lies, treacheries and womanizing'.[2] In this context the Scrivener's scene, with its exposure of the use of spurious documentation to legalize butchery and its comment on the censorship of political expression ('who's so bold but says he sees it not?'), became heavily loaded. The speech was addressed directly to the audience, and produced a stunning outwardly referential lead-in to the interval.

Not surprisingly, parodies of fascism were particularly in evidence in English productions immediately prior to and during the Second World War: John Laurie at Stratford-upon-Avon in 1939; Donald Wolfit at the London Strand in 1942 in an exaggerated performance that consciously mimicked the Führer; and Laurence Olivier, whose landmark interpretation opened at the New Theatre in 1944. As Olivier himself put it, 'One had Hitler over the way, one was playing it definitely as a paranoiac.'[3]

The nonchalance and the shift from political history to personality are both telling. As a response to the enormity of Fascist political evil as it was being revealed to the English public, Olivier's

[1] Dennis Kennedy, *Looking at Shakespeare* (Cambridge, 1993), p. 115.
[2] John Newmark, quoted in Hortmann, p. 137.
[3] Hal Burton, ed., *Great Acting* (1967), p. 24.

8. Laurence Olivier as Richard, with Joyce Redman
as Lady Anne, Old Vic, *c.*1944.

production was euphemistic. Like the other English Richards of
the period, his performance technique owed little to the Jessner
experiment.[1] Olivier consciously hearkened back to Irving and
Cibber. Above all else he delivered the role and made it riveting to
watch, grabbing the limelight with a hawk-like Richard who was
both menacing and self-parodically humorous (fig. 8). For Harold
Hobson and others, Olivier's Richard parted from his Cibberian
forebears in that he had no inwardness.[2] His evil was icy, impene-
trable, and exhilarating. The pleasure lay in 'watching Olivier the

[1] Both productions, however, used the device of the menacing shadow at the
end of 1.2.
[2] Richmond, p. 57.

consummate actor play Richard the consummate actor'.[1] James Agate was offended by the way Olivier broke the theatrical illusion by stepping out of the picture.[2] The trait was consonant with the Elizabethan Vice, even though the post-Elizabethan proscenium arch was firmly in place.

Olivier played the role over a period of five years. He performed in London, toured Europe, Australia, and New Zealand, and visited New York. His supporting actors were the best of the period— Sybil Thorndike as Margaret, Ralph Richardson as Buckingham, Joyce Redman and later Vivien Leigh as Anne. The 1955 film brought in John Gielgud as Clarence; Claire Bloom now played Anne. Olivier made innovative use of the film camera, especially for the soliloquies, where Richard addressed it with casual and conniving cynicism as though it were a confidant. The influence of Olivier on audiences worldwide can scarcely be overstated. His film still generates a strong set of expectations as to how the role of Richard should be played.

Meanwhile, 1953 saw two productions that turned away from the practice of playing a melodramatic Richard against a background of medieval stage scenery. At Stratford-upon-Avon, Glen Byam Shaw presented a smooth production on a simple stage, restoring many of the Shakespearian contours that were regularly cut. Marius Goring's performance as Richard was thoughtful and detailed: to some it seemed slight beside Olivier, to others, subtly convincing. Hugh M. Richmond sees the production as representing a key moment in the recovery of a more truly Shakespearian *Richard III* (pp. 64–8). Across the Atlantic, Tyrone Guthrie produced *Richard III* as part of the opening season of the Shakespearean Festival Theatre at Stratford, Ontario, with Alec Guinness playing Richard. Where Garrick over two hundred years earlier had played Richard as an opportunity for the virtuoso actor, Guthrie's innovation was to pull the emphasis away from Richard and use the play as a showpiece for a theatre so new that it was temporarily roofed with canvas. Tanya Moiseiwitsch designed the stage, which was a multi-level variant on the open stage of the Elizabethan theatre. Guthrie's production was meticulously planned as a theatrical event, spectacle being provided through costumes,

---

[1] Jack Jorgens, *Shakespeare on Film* (Bloomington, Ind., and London, 1977), p. 142.

[2] *Sunday Times*, 17 September 1944.

banners, and the imaginative positioning of actors in the three-dimensional stage space. Colley describes Guthrie's rendition of the play as 'a ritualistic pageant of a scapegoat Devil-King' (p. 186). Guinness played with a light touch that allowed space for other performances, such as Irene Worth as Margaret, to make a strong impression. Stylized episodes such as the cursing queens in 4.4 and the clustering ghosts in Act 5 became key moments.

Christopher Plummer gave the performance that was most widely celebrated as breaking with Olivier's presentation of Richard at the Royal Shakespeare Theatre, Stratford-upon-Avon, in 1961. Richard looked malignant, but his speech was controlled and reasonable. To Harold Hobson, he 'does not want to be king; he does not wish to be married. What he does wish is to prove that the crown is his if he wants it, and that he can marry who he chooses. There is a sadness in his setting about achieving both these objects in the most difficult way possible, just as there is bitterness in his rapid wearying of them when he has got them. This is a subtler Richard than we have grown accustomed to.'[1]

Plummer's Richard, like Barrymore's, was a psychological study of a man streaked with neurosis. But once again, a heavily contrasting political reading was about to emerge. It came from the RSC in 1963–4, in the shape of Peter Hall and John Barton's *The Wars of the Roses*, where an adapted version of *Richard III* followed a two-play rendition of the Henry VI trilogy.[2] This sequence was expanded in the second season to include the 'Second Tetralogy', which shows the events leading to the reign of Henry VI. The project was immediately acclaimed as one of the most monumental and significant treatments of Shakespeare ever. It generated an epic sense of history as a horrific process. Richard's deeds, far from appearing as gratuitous crimes, were the final retributive throes of a sequence of events starting far back in the murder of Richard II. Hall was influenced by Jan Kott's *Shakespeare Our Contemporary*. Kott had read the history plays with reference to Jessner's production of *Richard III*, seeing his staircase as representative of Shakespeare's 'Grand Mechanism' of history; Richard III was the Mechanism's 'mastermind', its 'will and awareness'.[3] Hall

---

[1] Harold Hobson, in *Sunday Times*, 28 May 1961, quoted in Richmond, p. 70.

[2] The playscript of *The Wars of the Roses* was published in 1970.

[3] Jan Kott, *Shakespeare Our Contemporary*, trans. Boleslaw Taborski (1965), pp. 32, 35. Hodgdon suggests a contradiction in the production between this

in turn, in his programme note, cited Kott's vision of the 'Grand Mechanism', revealing that he had read Kott's book in proof 'as I travelled to Stratford for the first rehearsal of *The Wars of the Roses*'.[1]

*Richard III* was staged on a metallic set. In the opening scenes the heads of those executed earlier in the trilogy were displayed on spikes on the walls, and Clarence was unapologetically drowned on stage. Ian Holm performed Richard as a product of a violent culture, almost childlike in himself, 'clearly mad to the audience, utterly sane to his contemporaries'.[2] Here too Kott influenced Hall, though now the point of reference was the performance of Jacek Woszczerowicz at the Ateneum Theatre, Warsaw, in 1960. Woszczerowicz, like Holm, was smaller than the other actors.[3] He was, Kott claimed, 'the first to build up Richard's part with all the means available to a comic actor', a super-clown (p. 45). Kott propounded that 'Richard is impersonal like history itself. He is the consciousness and mastermind of the Grand Mechanism. He puts in motion the roller of history, and later is crushed by it. Psychology does not apply to him. He is just history, one of its ever-repeating chapters. He has no face.' Yet at the end of the play, in Woszczerowicz's performance, 'He is not laughing any more. He is just a heavy, misshapen dwarf. Soon he will be butchered like a pig' (pp. 46–7). Holm's performance was less idiosyncratically anti-human, and indeed he used to advantage the rare opportunity to develop the role over the course of two plays. But he too showed Richard as a person trapped in an impersonal function much larger than himself.

The moralizer of the Mechanism in the *Richard III* of *The Wars of the Roses* was Queen Margaret, who, despite some of the customary trimming of her role, still managed to emerge in this production as a significant tragic figure in her own right. As with Richard, the epic scale of the trilogy lent stature to the role. Her

radical-modernist influence and a more reassuring and idealizing vision based on Tillyard (p. 118).

[1] Barton and Hall, *Wars of the Roses*, p. xi. The date was 25 April 1963 (Richard Pearson, *A Band of Arrogant and United Heroes* (1990), pp. 23–7), a year before publication of the Polish original and two years before publication of the English translation. A version of Kott's chapter on the 'Grand Mechanism' titled 'Shakespeare contemporain' had appeared earlier in *Les Temps Modernes*, 155 (1959), 1095–1130, but it lacked the book's reference to Jessner; the French version of the book (*Shakespeare notre contemporain*) was published in 1963.

[2] Roger Gellert, quoted in Hankey, p. 72.

[3] Other notable Richards who were short in height include Garrick and Sher.

grievances were actual and known to the audience, not least because she was the only character from the first play of the Hall–Barton trilogy to survive through to *Richard III*. Peggy Ashcroft played her, stranded from a former time, as 'not merely indignant, but profoundly, incurably unhappy'.[1] She had visibly aged from the young and beautiful bride of Henry VI to a wretched and destructive old woman.

*The Wars of the Roses* stands at the head of a tradition of productions influenced by Kott and so, indirectly, by the theatre of central Europe. Yet Hankey argues that performances such as those of Holm, and Alan Bates in John Hirsch's Stratford, Ontario, production of 1967, retained strong elements of naturalistic acting despite their debt to the theatre of impersonality (p. 74). The emphasis lay on contemporary styles for performing the play as a received text rather than reworkings of the play to new ends entirely. Meanwhile, Terry Hands's 1970 Stratford-upon-Avon production was characterized by a Kott-like emphasis on senseless atrocity and a 'Marat-Sade madness'.[2] Norman Rodway played an albino blond and heavily hunchbacked Richard who was agile, extreme, and clearly insane. He also suffered pain, as became evident when he commanded onlookers to turn their backs whilst his body was racked with physical convulsions.

A more immediate impact than Jessner or Woszczerowicz was made by another major foreign-language production that wrested the Shakespeare text to make a compelling and influential piece of modern theatre. This time the production was seen in Britain. The Rustaveli Company of Tbilisi, Georgia, staged *Richard III* at the Rustaveli Theatre and at various other European venues including the Royal Lyceum in Edinburgh (1979) and the Roundhouse in London (1980).[3] Director Robert Sturua's theatrical techniques were Brechtian, modified by the concepts of the carnival and the grotesque as set out by Mikhail Bakhtin. As Woszczerowicz deflated Tudor seriousness with techniques going back to Commedia dell'Arte, Sturua reached back to medieval and Rabelaisian techniques of subversive mocking. In doing so he brought Bakhtin's

---

[1] Speaight, p. 287.

[2] D. A. N. Jones, quoted in Colley, p. 204.

[3] A videotape of the production was shown at the World Shakespeare Congress, Stratford-upon-Avon, 1981: see Rothwell and Melzer, pp. 243–4.

concepts in action to British audiences some five years before Katerina Clark and Michael Holquist's influential study of the philosopher and theorist.[1]

Sturua structured his production in three parts, ending with Edward's death, Richard's coronation, and Richmond's victory. The set could evoke 'a Bosch landscape of Hellish characters, a circus for freak shows, and the Last Judgement'.[2] Queen Margaret acted as a Chorus-prompter, both introducing and directing the action from the beginning. Ramaz Chkhikvadze played a squat-faced Richard, a mesmerizing figure of magnetic presence and violently changing moods. To one reviewer, 'grotesque and satanic at once, he suggests simultaneously the cosmic clown and the disintegrating psychopath'.[3] Changes of costume from Victorian cape to Napoleonic raincoat to Wehrmacht black leather suggested that he represented the recurrent presence of such figures in human history.

The vitality of *Richard III* to the late twentieth-century imagination was shown in the series of impressive and distinctive stage and film versions that emerged refreshingly unhampered by the pre-existing weight of performance tradition. Olivier's intellectual concentration on the role of Richard, Hall's epic politicization, and Sturua's savage nihilism map out a large interpretive territory, but the performances of Sher, McKellen, Jarvis, Beale, and Troughton have both remapped and extended our understanding of the play.

Sher's was a performance of the body. His hunched figure was supported on long crutches, which became an extension of his spiderish being (fig. 9). The opening lines remained quiet, almost sweet. At 'But I, that am not shaped . . .' his body erupted forwards on the crutches with unexpected energy and violence. R. Chris Hassel lists some details of Sher's fearsomely virtuoso deployment of the crutches: 'They are effective weapons against the guard of Henry's corpse. They punctuate Richard's use of obscene innuendo, as when he grinds them together on the line "Naught to do with Mistress Shore?" They find their seductive way between Lady Anne's legs. They crash the table with intimidating power as

[1] Katerina Clark and Michael Holquist, *Mikhail Bakhtin* (Cambridge, Mass., and London, 1984).

[2] Marie Tarsitano, 'Sturua's Georgian *Richard III*', *Theatre History Studies*, 9 (1989), 69–76; p. 72.

[3] David Lang, quoted in Tarsitano, p. 72.

9. Antony Sher as Richard, RSC, 1984.

Sher pronounces Hastings' sentence of death. As two mandibles, they saw back and forth on Hastings' doomed neck . . .'[1]

Sher acted a Richard who was charismatic, grotesque, and often funny. Yet the production made light neither of Richard nor of the play as a tragedy. For Sher, the humour was defensive, a way of avoiding pain. A tableau before the interval showing his coronation turned the ceremony into a disclosure of the source of malevolence and suffering. Sher slipped off his robe for his body to be anointed, revealing a naked and hideously mounded back. This Richard became less effectual as the play developed. When he

[1] Hassel, 'Context', p. 632.

achieved the throne he lost his crutches, and with them his confidence and mobility. The throne became a litter in which attendants carried him. At the end he was incapable of fighting, and resigned himself to ritualistic execution by Richmond.

There was a tension throughout the enactment between Richard's initially explosive physical presence and the inevitability of his downfall. Alexander's production was seen as unusually well balanced, with strong performances from the women and full weight given to the prophecies and the ghosts.[1] Patricia Routledge as Margaret competed effectively with Richard, convincing the audience that the play showed a ritualistic purgation of evil.[2] Barbara Hodgdon has suggestively remarked that the presence of the women in Act 4 set a frame round Richard that formed 'a womb which unmothers him to remother England' (p. 107).

The reminders of the play's affinities with classical tragedy articulated in Antony Hammond's introduction to his Arden edition of 1981 had been read and taken seriously. And the production itself was notable for its impact on the academic study of Shakespeare in performance. The widespread reviews and Sher's own intriguing diary of his preparation for the role in *Year of the King* (1985) were soon supplemented by two articles in a special issue of *Shakespeare Quarterly* devoted to 'Reviewing Shakespeare',[3] and subsequently by the sophisticated theorization of this and other performances in Hodgdon's *The End Crowns All* (1991).

Alexander had rejected the brutalist sets introduced by Hall and Barton in favour of a detailed neo-Victorian imitation of medieval architecture. Elsewhere, the determination to modernize the setting and politics of Shakespeare's play remained, and found new expressions. In Michael Bogdanov's 1988–9 contemporary-style computer-age production of a re-adapted *Wars of the Roses* trilogy, *Richard III* began with a cocktail party in which a presenter introduced the main characters to the audience (see Appendix F).[4] Andrew Jarvis played Richard as a yuppie with shaved head and pinstriped suit. Menacing and slightly crazed, his eyes goggling, he made sudden switches of intonation and absurdly overstated

[1] Hassel, 'Context', p. 642.

[2] Roger Warren, 'Shakespeare at Stratford-upon-Avon', *SQ* 36 (1985), 79–87; p. 82.

[3] S. P. Cerasano, 'Churls Just Wanna Have Fun', *SQ* 36 (1985), 618–29; Hassel, 'Context'.

[4] A video of the production was issued in 1990.

gestures. This Richard's self-projection was flippant at first, tren-
chantly determined later, but the ghosts finally broke him. As if to
signal that his will no longer imposed itself on the action, the battle
was fought in anachronistic medieval armour with Richard in
black and Richmond in gold. It anticipates, one surmises, the
iconography of the victor. As Richmond stabbed into Richard's
hump with Richard's own dagger, the audience heard the death-
cry of a boar. The performance ended with Richmond as king
making a televised address to the nation.

Ian McKellen's granitic performances on the stage (directed by
Richard Eyre, 1990) and film (directed by Richard Loncraine,
1995) looked back to Britain of the 1930s, showing the rise of a military dictator through the complicity of a decadent ruling class. If
this Richard was reminiscent of the fascist leader Sir Oswald
Mosley, his centrality to aristocratic and political life also invoked
the pro-fascist sympathies of the English royal family in the thir-
ties. Eyre's stage version used minimal and symptomatic stage
properties; for the Princes' arrival in London there were train
noises off stage and a model train-set on stage. Properties were designed to indicate both a period setting and a timeless mythological
landscape.[1] In contrast, the film was monumentally realistic in its
visual depiction of the social fabric, architecture, and technology
of war of the 1930s, making cleverly disjunctive use of Shakespeare's language as a counterpoint to the setting. The scene locations play both with and against the connotations of the imagery.
The first few lines of Richard's opening soliloquy are delivered as a
political speech at a victory ball. Where Jarvis had closed a curtain
on the courtiers' party to isolate Richard for the second part of his
opening speech ('But I that am not shaped for sportive tricks'),
Loncraine switched McKellen from the ball to a urinal for his mut-
tered continuation. McKellen goes on to woo Anne with cold coer-
cion in a morgue, and soon afterwards she degenerates into a
disregarded heroin addict. Clarence relates his dream of drowning
from a 'circular slab of concrete ringed with sluggish water',
which was 'the centre of a disused gasometer',[2] and dies drowned
in an enamel bathtub. A wasteland of railway lines and bulldozed
rubble backed by heavy industrial plant represents the battlefield.

[1] Richard Eyre, 'On Directing *Richard III*', in *Le Tyran*, pp. 133–9 (p. 135).
[2] Ian McKellen, with Richard Loncraine, *William Shakespeare's 'Richard III'*
(1996), p. 98.

10. David Troughton's Richard as court jester, RSC, 1995.

McKellen's Richard is relentless and without love or charm; his connivances with the camera are at once repulsive and amusing. Yet those glances can be read as a communication between Richard and the film itself, which, despite the thuggery with which it deals, has wit and poise.

Sam Mendes's 1992 production at the studio Other Place in Stratford-upon-Avon was praised for its intelligent grasp of the play's structure and for convincing performances by most of the players. Simon Russell Beale as Richard was lumpish in appearance and slightly camp in manner. His seduction of Anne involved a strenuous piece of acting whose success surprised even Richard himself. The submerged brutal intelligence that surfaced in asides to the audience made him almost unstoppable, and in the battle it was only his discomfiture at seeing Margaret make a haunting appearance that prevented him from hacking Richmond down.

A more vulnerable Richard was evident in David Troughton's performance at the Royal Shakespeare Theatre in 1995. He wore a jester's outfit for the opening soliloquy and carried a bauble with a double head, an effigy of Troughton on one side and a skull on the other (fig. 10). Elsewhere he looked like an unsocialized schoolboy in his short trousers, an awkward and overgrown version of the young princes, who, following nineteenth-century tradition, were played by women. His courtship of Anne was for real, though the nature of Richard's need was most clearly suggested when he played the sulky child in asking her 'Bid me farewell'. She indulged him as 'a benignly mocking mother' with ''Tis more than you deserve.'[1] In contrast, his mother's farewell to him in 4.4 became a fearsome curse as Richard lay awkwardly with his head on her lap seeking blessing. The moment was horrifying and decisive. This Richard was heading towards a particular despair. It entailed realizing that behind his infantile ambitions and clownish charades there lay no meaningful connection with the world: that is, with the world of the play. At the end of the play no fighting took place. Instead, Richard delivered a speech (based on the soliloquy in *Richard Duke of York*) to a gallery of ghosts, just as he had delivered his opening soliloquy to a gallery of courtiers. He then gave up, to become a sardonic, disillusioned audience to Richmond's final victory-speech.

Perhaps the most intriguing late twentieth-century American response to *Richard III* came not in a performance as such, but in a film about the filming of a performance. Al Pacino played Richard and played himself playing Richard; *Looking for Richard* (1996) was also directed by him.[2] Pacino's aim was to wrest the play from academe and relate its vitality as theatre to the vibrant energies of contemporary city life. Pacino is most memorable as the streetwise actor with reversed baseball hat who paces New York seeking to trace Shakespeare's presence in the cultural landscape by interviewing people on the sidewalks. Mobile, demotic, witty, and controlling, he shows some affinities with the character for whom he is searching. Yet the scenes enacted from *Richard III*, with Pacino lurking in the shadows of stylistically old-world monastic architecture, are curiously stilted. It is as though the hand of tradition lies, after all, heavily on his shoulder. His scenes lack the pace, nerve, and self-confidence of, for example, the populist and unpretentiously convincing English touring production by Barrie Rutter's

---

[1] Peter Holland, 'Shakespeare Performances in England, 1994–1995', in *Shakespeare Survey 49* (1996), 235–67; p. 258.

[2] See Margaret A. Varnell, '*Looking for Richard*', *Shakespeare Bulletin*, 15.1 (Winter 1997), 35–6. Pacino had previously played Richard on stage in 1973 and 1979.

Northern Broadsides company, in which the actors made Shakespeare familiar by adapting his language to the inflexions of their own predominantly Yorkshire dialects.

Though the energy of performative reinvention seems to have proved elusive, Pacino's premisses were surely right. *Richard III* can, as McKellen demonstrated, successfully translate into film (and also, as the BBC 'Animated Tales' version of 1994 demonstrated, into film animation for television).[1] The political and social preoccupations of modern life can, as the English Stage Company and others proved, successfully be grafted on to it. For these things to happen, the anxieties of theatrical influence have to be overcome. In this Antony Sher showed the way, haunted as he was by his memories of Olivier and Chkhikvadze before he sketched out the distinctive contours of his own Richard. Past productions might properly be hung up for monuments, but the space of performance itself needs to be free.

## *In Print*

This section reviews the early printed texts of *Richard III* and their value for a modern printed edition. As compared with the play in performance, the play as a text on the page is relatively fixed. Yet printed books too are representations of the play rather than the thing itself, and there is a real sense in which the play can exist only in representations of it. Even the lost early manuscripts of *Richard III* would offer not so much 'the play' as versions of it. This is all the more true of the editions that appeared in print between 1597 and 1623, including the 1597 First Quarto and the 1623 Folio which are the significant editions by which we know the play. It is these two texts, Q1 and F, that form the basis of the editions used by almost all readers. What sets them apart from the quarto reprints is that Q1 was printed directly from a previously unpublished manuscript and F was printed with detailed reference to another such manuscript. The quality and editorial value of the two substantive texts depend on the characteristics of these manuscripts, and, to a lesser extent, on the use made of them in the printing houses.

[1] See Laurie E. Osborne, 'Mixing Media in Shakespeare', *Post Script*, 17.2 (Spring 1998), 73–89; pp. 82–5.

*The First Quarto*. Before 1597 only three Shakespeare plays had appeared in print, John Danter's edition of *Titus Andronicus* (1594) and Thomas Millington's editions of *The Contention* (1594) and *Richard Duke of York* (1595). The latter two are shorter and heavily variant versions of the plays later published in the First Folio as the second and third parts of *Henry VI*. It might not be an accident that two plays handed over to the stationers in 1597 were both, like *Henry VI*, history plays. One of them, *Richard II*, was a relatively recent work depicting events some time before the reign of Henry VI. The other play, *Richard III*, brought the events of *Henry VI* to a close. It is doubtful whether either play had lost its appeal in the theatre. Shakespeare was currently engaged above all in writing the two parts of *Henry IV* with a view eventually to completing what we now call the Second Tetralogy. It therefore looks as though the Chamberlain's Men were advertising their principal dramatist's specialization in writing history plays.[1]

Nevertheless, they found a new publisher in Andrew Wise, who a year later went on to issue reprints of both plays as well as the first edition of *1 Henry IV*.[2] Wise entered *Richard III* in the Register of the Stationers' Company to secure his entitlement on 20 October 1597:

> Andrew Wise / Entred for his copie vnder thand*es* of
> m$^r$ Barlowe, and m$^r$ warden
> Man./ The tragedie of kinge
> Richard the Third w$^{th}$ the
> death of the duke of Clarence

These words testify that *Richard III* passed through three stages for the securing and recording of permission to print, each of which would have entailed a separate fee from Wise: *authorization* by the ecclesiastical authorities, *licence* by the Stationers' Company, and *entrance* of these forms of approval in the Stationers' Register itself.[3] Thomas Man licensed the text for printing as a warden of the Stationers' Company. William Barlow was the chaplain to John

---

[1] It should be noted too that the company released its manuscripts at a time of crisis for the theatres. In July 1597 the Privy Council had acceded to a petition of the City of London by ordering that all purpose-built theatres should be demolished.

[2] *1 Henry IV* was entered in the Stationers' Register on 25 February 1598. The first edition is now lost except for a single sheet of a single copy. The play was reprinted within the year.

[3] For a reassessment of these procedures, see Peter W. M. Blayney, 'The Publication of Playbooks', in Cox and Kastan, pp. 383–422.

Whitgift, the Archbishop of Canterbury. The Church had jurisdiction over the printing and publishing industry, and in this case the ecclesiastical authorities reviewed the book, probably for the simple reason that it dealt with potentially contentious political affairs.[1] By 1596, the year before Q1 was published, only 40 per cent of all books entered in the Register were officially authorized, but books dealing with political and religious matters nearly always went to the Church authorities. Curiously, *Richard II* was able to get by with allowance from the Stationers' Company alone, despite its treatment of equally or more contentious historical matters. It is the case of *Richard II* rather than *Richard III* that is a little surprising, not least because Q1 *Richard II* seems to have been censored by removal of the deposition scene. For *Richard III*, the circumstances of publication are spotlessly regular.

The text was subsequently printed in the 1597 edition referred to as Q1, of which five copies now survive.[2] Twelve sheets make up the book, each normally of four leaves. The sheets are identified by letters running from A to M; as 'I' and 'J' were undifferentiated there is no sheet J. Signatures printed at the foot of the first page of each sheet name the sheet by its letter; those at the foot of the third and fifth pages identify the sheet by letter and the leaf by number.[3] A1 is the title-page; the verso is blank. The play occupies A2 to M3. In extant copies the inferably blank M4 is missing. The imprint on the title-page (fig. 11) tells us that the text was 'Printed by Valentine Sims', but this statement needs qualifying. Simmes printed the first seven sheets, those signed A–G (up to 3.7.48). The remainder, sheets H–M, were handed over to Peter Short, perhaps to speed up the printing process.[4] The effect of the change of printer is not immediately obvious, but analysis of the type has revealed

[1] Davison, p. 11, suggests that authorization was obtained because the manuscript lacked a licence to perform from the Master of the Revels. But referral to the Church authorities was routine for works on political matters, and a licence for performance was not acceptable for the press (Blayney, p. 397).

[2] British Library, Huth 47; Bodleian, Malone 37–Arch. G. d. 44 (seven missing leaves made up from a copy of Q2); Huntington, HEH 69350; Folger; Elizabethan Club, Yale, C. 39. i. 14 (four half-sheets making up sheets C and D). For press correction, see Q1 collation to 1.1.44 (A2$^v$), 2.1.5 (D3$^v$), 5.3.10 (L2), 5.4.82 (L3$^v$), 5.5.5 (M2), and 5.5.16.1 (M2). For details of extant copies of all early quartos and full collation of variants, see Kristian Smidt, ed., *The Tragedy of King Richard the Third: Parallel Texts of the First Quarto and the First Folio with Variants of the Early Quartos* (Oslo and New York, 1969).

[3] Exceptions are A1 (unsigned, as was common on title-pages) and L4 (signed).

[4] W. W. Greg, ed., *Richard III, 1597* (Oxford, 1959), p. v.

# THE TRAGEDY OF
King Richard the third.

Containing,
His treacherous Plots againſt his brother Clarence:
the pittiefull murther of his iunocent nephewes:
his tyrannicall vſurpation: with the whole courſe
of his deteſted life, and moſt deſerued death.

## As it hath beene lately Acted by the
Right honourable the Lord Chamber-
laine his ſeruants.

AT LONDON
Printed by Valentine Sims, for Andrew Wiſe,
dwelling in Paules Chuch-yard, at the
Signe of the Angell.
1597.

11. The 1597 First Quarto's title-page: Bodleian,
Arch. G. d. 44.

beyond doubt that the second part of the book was printed in
Short's shop. One can go some way further so as to distinguish between the contributions of different compositors. MacD. P. Jackson
identified two compositors in Short's section, though his conclusions have been questioned by Susan Zimmerman.[1] It is generally
agreed that at least part of Simmes's section was set by a compositor detected in other play quartos printed in Simmes's shop and

---

[1] See MacD. P. Jackson, 'Two Shakespeare Quartos: *Richard III* (1597) and
*1 Henry IV* (1598)', *Studies in Bibliography*, 35 (1982), 173–90; Susan Zimmerman,
'The Uses of Headlines: Peter Short's Shakespearian Quartos *1 Henry IV* and *Richard
III*', *The Library*, VI, 7 (1985), 218–55.

labelled as 'A'.[1] However, there are suspicions that Compositor A was assisted by another workman.[2]

The composed type was assembled in pages, and the pages placed and wedged together as 'formes' that would go through the press together to print one side of a sheet. As usual in quarto format, the first, fourth, fifth, and eighth pages of the sheet made up the outer forme; the second, third, sixth, and seventh pages made up the inner forme. The pages of each forme were supplied with running headlines so as to read '*The Tragedy*' on the left-hand page of an opening and '*of Richard the third*' on the right. The running headlines and wooden blocks and wedges locking the pages of type together, known as the skeleton forme, could be re-used from one forme to another. In Simmes's section, a single set was used for the printing of all the formes. In Short's section two skeletons were used.[3] One skeleton was used to impose sheets H and K, and outer forme M. The other was used to impose sheets I and L, and inner forme M. This pattern is such that the final sheet M was the only sheet in the entire book where a different skeleton was used for each of the two formes.

There are implications for the sequence of the compositors' work. Setting M aside, the compositors in both shops laid out the print for each forme within the same skeleton. Consequently, they would probably have needed to complete a forme at a time rather than setting the text continuously. If the compositor began on the 'outer' forme with the first page of a sheet, he would have proceeded to the fourth, fifth, and eighth pages so as to make up the forme. Only then would he have returned to set the pages that would be printed on the other side of the sheet. In order for this to happen, the printers' copy would need to be marked so as to indicate exactly where the page breaks would fall. This would need to be done carefully, for there are few variations on the standard number of type-lines per page, and the common practice of leaving

[1] Alan E. Craven, 'Simmes' Compositor A and Five Shakespeare Quartos', *Studies in Bibliography*, 26 (1973), 37–60, following W. Craig Ferguson's identification of the compositor in 'The Compositors of *Henry IV, Part 2, Much Ado About Nothing, The Shoemakers' Holiday*, and *The First Part of the Contention*', *Studies in Bibliography*, 13 (1960), 19–29.

[2] Jackson, pp. 178–9, demonstrates a significant alternation of 'o' and 'oh' spellings. As he finds no other indication of compositorial differences, he suggests variation in the copy. Gary Taylor and John Jowett, *Shakespeare Reshaped 1606–23* (Oxford, 1993), 248–50, incline more towards compositorial variation, but regard the matter as unresolved.

[3] Jackson, p. 176.

a variable amount of space above and/or below a stage direction was almost entirely avoided.[1] In Simmes's section especially, space was tight. Many stage directions are printed to the right of the verse-lines. This feature may by and large reflect the copy,[2] though the compositors might have responded to the manuscript layout flexibly so as to help them keep to the casting-off marks. The habit of printing a short part-line on the same line of type as the last words of the previous speech, found especially in Simmes's section, is more likely to have been introduced by the printers. It is possible too that they went so far as to omit some stage directions, as might possibly be indicated by the introduction of new stage directions in Q3 (see following paragraphs). Towards the end of the book the pressure on space slackens. For example, mid-scene entries are set to the right in Short's section up to the verso of I2, but thereafter are almost always centred. Jackson conjectures a change in the character of the copy (pp. 177–8), but a recalculation of the casting-off to make more efficient use of the final leaves is as likely. The verso of M3 just has room for '*FINIS.*' and a printer's ornament.

*Quarto Reprints.* Each of the quartos intervening between Q1 and F was printed from its immediate predecessor, except that sheets C and E–M of Q5 were printed from Q3.[3] These reprints tell us clearly that for the readers of Shakespeare's time *Richard III* was one of his most popular plays. Only *1 Henry IV* was reprinted as often. As textual evidence the derivative quartos usually have limited value, and there is a clear tendency for errors to accumulate from one edition to the next. The first two reprints, however, make limited textual changes that are of some consequence. Q2 1598, printed by Thomas Creede for Wise, along with Wise's 1598 reprint of *Richard II* and the 1598 Quarto of *Love's Labour's Lost*, are the first extant printed play texts to name Shakespeare on the title-page. Q2 includes two lines not printed in Q1.[4] This addition might

---

[1] Overlength pages are D3[v] and E1[v], where there is text on the catchword line, and I2[v]. Spaced stage directions appear on A2, where Richard's initial entry has an ornament above it and a blank line immediately above and below it, and M1.

[2] For example, at 1.1.41 (Simmes) and 4.2.2 (Short) the verse-line is split on to a second type-line to allow space to the right for a stage direction; no space is saved.

[3] W. W. Greg, '*Richard III*—Q5 (1612)', *The Library*, IV, 17 (1936), 88–97. See also Hammond, pp. 30–1.

[4] See Commentary to 1.1.102. The lines, on A2, are accommodated by introducing a turn-up and printing on the catchword line, both on the verso.

indicate that the printer's copy for Q1 was consulted here, presumably by Wise.

Q3 (1603) certainly received some light editing. The claim introduced on the title-page to the effect that the text has been 'Newly augmented' is misleading, for there is no new dialogue, but the text does introduce some new stage directions. Of these, the most striking are '*Cla. awaketh.*' (1.4.146.1), '*Exit Car. & Hast.*' (3.1.60.1), the addition of '*to L. Hastings*' after '*Enter Catesby*' (3.2.32.2), '*Exit L. Standley, & Cat.*' (3.2.94.1),[1] '*Exit. Pur.*' (3.2.106), addition of '*of the Tower*' after '*Enter Lieutenant*' (4.1.6.1), '*Exit Dar.*' (4.4.415). Some details, such as the inclusion of Catesby in its exit at 3.2.94.1, are not obvious from the text. The termination of '*awaketh*' is consistent with the seven '*-eth*' verbs in the stage directions of Q1. Q3 also brings in just a few convincing corrections of errors in dialogue and speech-prefixes that are not evident at first sight.[2] Alert to the ambiguity of the stage directions '*to Ri.*' in the ghost scene, it introduces '*K.*' for 'king' to establish that the addressee is Richard, not Richmond.

These alterations seem consistent with the added lines of dialogue in Q2 in suggesting that Wise on both occasions might have referred to his manuscript before proceeding with the reprint.[3] On the other hand, Q3 makes another innovation which, though it looks authoritative, might have come from another source. It switches the order in which the ghosts appear in 5.4 so that it more closely accords with the order in which the figures died. The arrangement in Q1 probably reflects actual stage practice. It allows one of the boy actors who played the young princes to return as the ghost of Anne. The revision in Q3 could have arisen because, for example, the manuscript followed the Q3 arrangement whilst marking a transposition that was ambiguously indicated or optional; or because Wise became aware that the staging had been altered; or because Shakespeare himself demanded the change

---

[1] For the spelling, compare Q1's 'Standlie' at 5.5.19. ('Standley' is also the usual spelling in *True Tragedy*.)

[2] As an example of potentially authoritative correction, at 2.3.17 Henry VI's age at his coronation is given as 'ix. moneths' in Q1, 'xi. moneths' in Q2, and 'nine moneths' in Q3. See also 1.1.40, 1.3.33, and 4.4.343. Speech-prefixes are corrected at 3.4.6, 3.5.51, and 5.4.118.

[3] Wise was the legal owner of the manuscript, and it would have held the authorization and licence. For extant examples, see Peter W. M. Blayney, *The Texts of 'King Lear' and their Origins*, vol. 1, *Nicholas Okes and the First Quarto* (Cambridge, 1982), pp. 260, 270.

even though it was out of line with stage practice. This uncertainty influences our understanding of other apparently authoritative alterations in Q3. It becomes impossible to be sure whether they derive from the manuscript or whether they were independently initiated by the theatre company. What does seem clear is that, in either case, Q3 can sometimes be a valuable source for corrections and alternative readings in the speech-prefixes and stage directions, and very occasionally in the dialogue too.

There are other expansions and corrections in Q3's stage directions, and a tendency to print Q1–2's marginal directions on a separate type-line. These changes are accommodated by increasing the number of type-lines per page, with the further result that the play occupies one leaf of paper less and a half-sheet of paper is saved. The overall improvement in the substance and spacing of the stage directions indicates a minor uplift in the cultural status of the text.

Q3 was the last quarto issued by Wise. On 25 June 1603 the titles to *Richard III*, *Richard II*, and *1 Henry IV* were transferred in the Stationers' Register from Wise to Matthew Law. Subsequent quartos of 1605 (Q4), 1612 (Q5), and 1622 (Q6) were issued as 'to be sold by' Law. Creede printed all but Q6, which came from the shop of Thomas Purfoot. Q5 deserves mention for updating the theatrical information given on the title-page by correcting the named acting company from the Lord Chamberlain's Servants to the King's Majesty's Servants. The rewording reflects the change in the name of Shakespeare's company in 1603. It may not bear witness to a revival under the new name, as it is anticipated in the Stationers' Register note that the plays transferred to Law were 'all kinges'. Following Wise's precedent, Law tended to reprint his three Shakespeare history plays in groups: *1 Henry IV* and *Richard III* in 1604–5, *Richard II* and *1 Henry IV* in 1608, all three plays in 1612–15, and *Richard III* and *1 Henry IV* in 1622. The 1622 books might have been issued in the knowledge that Shakespeare's plays would soon be available in the Folio, though yet further quartos of *Richard III* were to appear in 1629 (Q7) and 1634 (Q8).

For early seventeenth-century readers, and perhaps playgoers too, the trio of plays issued by Wise then Law would have made up the core of Shakespeare's output as a writer of history plays. In 1619 Thomas Pavier began to fill the gaps with reprints of *The Contention*, *Richard Duke of York*, and *Henry V*. But it was left to the stationers who issued the First Folio, Isaac Jaggard and Edward Blount, to string *Richard III* within a sequence of ten histories.

*The Folio.* The printing of the First Folio was a large-scale undertaking. Its publication established Shakespeare as a prestigious writer, and gave enduring definition to the canon of his dramatic works. In F the play was placed towards the end of the Histories section, as was determined by the order of historical chronology followed in the section. So *3 Henry VI* comes immediately before it. After it is the late play *Henry VIII.*[1] The first two leaves of *Richard III* occupy the end of the quire signed 'q', the remaining four leaves of which contain the end of *3 Henry VI*. Quires r and s are taken up entirely with *Richard III*, and the end of the play is printed on the first two leaves of quire t. Each quire comprises six leaves (three sheets folded together), so *Richard III* occupies sixteen leaves, or thirty-two pages. The pages are large and each contains two columns, giving typically over 120 lines per page. Two compositors, who are identified as 'A' and 'B', set the type.[2] As was usual, they worked outwards from the middle of each quire, sometimes setting alongside each other, sometimes alone. Between quires s and t, at 5.3.16, there was a major break on *Richard III* while work began on the Tragedies section of the volume.

The compositors followed mixed printed quarto copy, which evidently alternated between Q3 and Q6. The division in the use of these books seems to have been determined by the quarto page-breaks, the anticipated Folio page-breaks, and the need to interleave manuscript

---

[1] Modern criticism often sees *Henry VIII* as standing apart from the two 'tetralogies', though by representing the king who was Richmond's son and Queen Elizabeth's father the play forms a bridge from the period of the earlier histories towards the present time of the Jacobean audience.

[2] Their contributions were as follows:

| B to: | | A to: | |
|---|---|---|---|
| 'blood than his or thine', 1.3.126 | | | 'scarce current', 1.3.256 |
| 'and thank you all', 3.1.19 | | | 'piteous massacre', 4.3.2 |
| 'changing woman', 4.4.350 | | | 'Earl of Richmond', 4.4.449 |
| End | | | |

For further details of the printing process, see Charlton Hinman, *The Printing and Proof-Reading of the First Folio of Shakespeare*, 2 vols. (Oxford, 1963), ii. 113–27 and 220–5. His conclusions for the pages of *Richard III* are not modified by more recent compositor study. Substantive press variants recorded by Hinman are:
1.3.344 RICHARD DUKE OF GLOUCESTER] *Riu.* F (Folger 67); *Ric.* F (others) 1.4.0.1 *Enter . . . Brakenbury*] *not in* F (Folger 67); *Enter Clarence and Keeper.* F (others)     4.4.274 and] end F (Folger 11, 33, 78); and F (others)     4.5.4 off] oft F (Folger 33, 66); off F (others)     5.3.13 want] went F (Folger 33 and 36); want F (others)

passages that were not printed in the quartos.[1] The presence of these passages is unequivocal evidence that a manuscript was available to the printers that differed substantially from the copy for Q1.[2] It is clearly the source for hundreds of variant readings introduced into the dialogue and stage directions, and probably for the act and scene divisions that punctuate what in the quartos was a continuous text. The annotations also introduced numerous changes that restore Q1 where the derivative quartos had introduced error (see Appendix B). These readings give an active indication of the extent to which the printers' copies for Q1 and F were in agreement, as the agreement cannot have been caused by the Folio compositors following printed copy. They also testify to the general thoroughness of the annotation. There are, however, sections that benefited minimally from annotation: 3.1.0.1–148, and 5.4.28 onwards.[3] Setting aside these sections, and notwithstanding the areas of consistency with Q1, F modifies the quarto copy sufficiently thoroughly for it to assume the substantive features of an independent version of the play.

Complicating *Richard III*'s appearance in the Histories section are its identifications of the play. Both in the table of contents and in the running titles, it is 'The Life and Death of Richard the Third'. This formula, though also used for *King John*, *Richard II*, *Henry V*, and *Henry VIII*, suggests a biographical slant on the representation of history. However, F's head-title describes the play as 'The Tragedy of Richard the Third: with the Landing of Earle Richmond, and the Battell at Bosworth Field'. Though the Folio editors made no change to their printed copy with respect to the description of the play as a tragedy, they abandoned the biographical trappings of Q1's title. In their place they introduced a summary of the key events that set the Tudors in power. It is the only time F names a battle in a play title.

*Quarto and Folio Compared*. Little could be gleaned as to the character of the immediately underlying manuscripts without comparing Q1 and F with each other. Comparison is revealing, though it does not reveal manuscripts that conform in any straightforward way with the standard classifications of documents under headings

[1] Taylor, in *Textual Companion*, pp. 229–30, building on J. K. Walton, *The Copy for the Folio Text of 'Richard III'* (Auckland, 1955), pp. 11–60.

[2] The passages are reproduced in edited form in Appendix A.

[3] Walton, pp. 97–126.

such as 'foul papers' or 'prompt books'.[1] For brevity I will refer to these elusive lost documents as 'MSQ' and 'MSF'. The most import-ant statement to make about them is that, notwithstanding the dates of publication of Q1 and F, it is MSF that represents the earlier version of the play. It probably derives from a manuscript that had not yet reached the theatre.

In summary, the reasons for considering that MSQ was the later and more performance-oriented text are as follows.[2] First, Q1 pre-sents an exceptionally long play in its own right, having more lines to it than any play previously published. Anyone seeking to prepare this script for the stage by altering the text would be looking to make cuts. The Folio text, however, is about two hundred lines longer still. F lacks one passage of substance, but that passage, the 'clock' dialogue between Richard and Buckingham in 4.2, is dramatically incisive.[3] As for the material unique to F, if one sets aside, as a rule of thumb, single and double verse-lines that might have been lost from Q1 through eyeskip, the remaining passages tend to be wordy and repetitious. The two longest Folio-only passages occur in 4.4, an extended scene that has probably attracted more cutting in the history of the play in performance than any other part.

How these passages as a whole could have been introduced into the Folio text through a strategy of revision is hard to imagine, but it makes obvious sense for them to have been deleted from the Quarto text as the play was prepared for the stage. In this respect they are comparable with the cuts in Folio *Hamlet*, where there is no question of the direction of influence between it and the Second Quarto; recent editors have praised the reshaping of *Hamlet* for its theatrical and even literary cogency.[4] Two passages not in Quarto *Richard III* would seem to be clear examples of dramatic streamlin-ing as the play moves towards the practical requirements of the stage. In 3.5 F has an address to Lovel, who appears nowhere in Q1; the lines are omitted in Q1. Similarly absent is F's introduction in 4.1 of Clarence's daughter, whose appearance here would neces-sitate an extra boy actor. This latter change accords with a

[1] 'Prompt book' has been the standard but anachronistic term for the com-pany's official script bearing the licence to perform. Elsewhere I generally prefer the term 'playbook'.

[2] This paragraph is based on John Jowett, '*Richard III* and the Perplexities of Editing', *TEXT*, 11 (1998), 224–45 (pp. 225–7).

[3] See Commentary to 4.2.99–118.

[4] For example G. R. Hibbard's edition of *Hamlet* (Oxford, 1987), pp. 104–10.

transposition in the order of the ghosts in Act 5 that, if the change
originates in the Quarto text, once again enables the play to be
performed with four boys.[1] Another cut in Q1 helps to make the
play stand more independent of the *Henry VI* trilogy. The Folio-
only passage in question, in 1.2, describes the murder of Rutland,
an event enacted in *Richard Duke of York (3 Henry VI)*. The play is
far more likely to have grown towards greater independence of the
events in the Henry VI plays. This would be all the more true if the
popularity of *Richard III* outlived that of its predecessors.

Q1 also offers a more streamlined account of the action by reducing the number of persons represented. The Keeper of the Tower,
the Archbishop, and the Messenger of 2.4, Lovel, the Sheriff, and
Surrey are assimilated respectively to Brakenbury, the Cardinal,
Dorset, Catesby, Ratcliffe, and Catesby. There is little gain in terms
of the number of actors required. The gain is in dramatic intelligibility, and it is achieved at the expense of historical accuracy.

Similarly, whether authorially or non-authorially altered, the
play is likely to have grown towards greater independence of the
source materials rather than to have become increasingly close to
them. Steven Urkowitz points to one passage where it is indeed Q1
that is closer to the sources,[2] and there are other such details that
prevent us from placing an unambiguous one-way arrow on the
direction of immediacy; these cases are, however, outweighed by
the cases where it is F that shows greater proximity. A striking instance can be found in the roles of Ratcliffe and Catesby. Some of
the business undertaken by Ratcliffe in both the chronicles and F,
such as the arrest of Hastings in the Council chamber, is transferred in Q1 to Catesby. The rearrangement does not, on the face of
it, save an actor, nor can it reflect confusion between roles played
by the same actor, but it may nonetheless have been made for reasons of theatrical contingency. Finally, F has a few characteristics
of an unperfected authorial draft that are resolved in Q1. The best
examples are the 'ghosts' Woodville and Scales. Historically, these
names were alternative titles for Rivers. Shakespeare, in writing
1.3 as it stands in F, seems to have initially been confused by the

[1] These counts assume that all women's parts were played by boys. The count
would be modified if, for example, a man played the old Duchess of York. But an
extra boy actor would be required for Clarence's daughter and one of the boy-ghosts
in Q all the same.

[2] Steven Urkowitz, 'Reconsidering the Relationship of Quarto and Folio Texts of
*Richard III*', *English Literary Renaissance*, 16 (1986), 442–66.

punctuation in Hall's *Union* into thinking that they were separate figures. The error is corrected in QI. So QI is, as compared with F, more independent of the Henry VI plays, more theatrical, and more distant from the historical chronicles on which the play is based. In all three respects it has a strong claim to be a derivative version.

Though MSF seems to have retained a few features consonant with an authorial draft, it was probably a copy of such a document rather than the document itself. Authorial confusions and inconsistencies are not generally typical of it; on the whole it is a well-ordered text. Some minor lexical preferences depart from Shakespeare's habits, and indeed in some such respects (though not on the whole) QI is closer to what we would expect of Shakespeare than is F.[1] The manuscript may indeed have been divided between more than one scribe.[2] The provision of act and scene headings and some occasional expurgation of profanity are further signs that MSF was a tidied-up transcript. These features might indicate annotation in anticipation of transcription for a new mid-Jacobean prompt book that would have conformed with the 1606 requirements for a script clean of profanity and would have allowed for act intervals in a private hall theatre, though the inference is far from secure. There are also a few variants that look like misreadings,[3] though these might have been introduced by the annotator preparing the Folio copy, and so were not necessarily present in MSF itself. Taylor proposes that MSF was a transcript prepared for a patron, and it is hard to resist adding that one such possible figure is Henry Herbert, second Earl of Pembroke and patron of Pembroke's Men, whose sons were dedicatees of the Folio.[4]

In one respect at least QI does not conform to usual expectations of a theatre company's official 'playbook' or 'prompt book'. The stage directions, certainly as compared with those in F, are clipped and somewhat deficient. There are, for example, a number of

[1] E. A. J. Honigmann, 'The Text of *Richard III*', *Theatre Research*, 7 (1965), 48–55, cites QI 'yea' for F 'ay' and QI 'pray thee' for F 'prithee'. Jonathan Hope, in an unpublished paper presented at a seminar at the International Shakespeare Conference, Stratford-upon-Avon, 1996, cites QI 'that' for F 'which'.

[2] Hope, pp. 7–10.     [3] Taylor, in *Textual Companion*, p. 230.

[4] Michael Brennan, in *Literary Patronage in the English Renaissance* (1988), points out that William Herbert, third Earl of Pembroke, was a close acquaintance of Burbage. After his death in 1619 he refrained from seeing a play at court 'which I, being tender-hearted, could not endure to see so soon after the loss of my old acquaintance Burbage' (p. 140).

missing exits, and in entrance directions a peremptory '*&c.*' is
sometimes the only indication of a number of speakers. Two considerations urge caution in reaching too firm a conclusion against
MSQ's utility in the theatre. First, the printing of Q1 is unusually
cramped. As is exemplified in fig. 12, many stage directions are
forced into the space to the right of verse dialogue rather than oc-
cupying type-lines of their own. In these circumstances it is possible that the compositors ignored certain kinds of annotation in the
manuscript. Secondly, it is now understood that earlier scholars
advanced a description of prompt books that was too narrow and
prescriptive.[1] These considerations at least lessen the perceived distance between MSQ and a playbook. It remains plausible that MSQ
was not a playbook after all, if only because the Chamberlain's
Men would probably have been reluctant to hand over to the stationers the document containing their licence to perform the play.
Just as MSF would seem to derive from an authorial draft, MSQ
might derive from a playbook. Nevertheless, one cannot exclude
the possibility that MSQ was an early playbook that by 1597 had
been superseded.

These speculations do not exclude the usual diagnosis of MSQ,
which is that it is based on a reconstruction of the play put together
by the actors of the Lord Chamberlain's Men. The hypothesis of
memorial transmission was stated in fullest detail by David Patrick
and endorsed by W. W. Greg.[2] Kristian Smidt, the one critic who
challenged Patrick's hypothesis, later modified his views so as to
admit a significant memorial element in Q1.[3] By the time of
Hammond's Arden 2 edition (1981) it had become a matter of consensus that the Chamberlain's Men had reconstructed the text
jointly when they found themselves on tour without their playbook. Further elaboration came in Peter Davison's 1996 edition of
the Quarto text.

Some recent studies have become sceptical as to whether memorial reconstruction can be safely demonstrated even in some of the
more radically altered 'bad' quartos. Despite the work of Patrick

[1] William B. Long, 'Stage-Directions: A Misinterpreted Factor in Determining
Textual Provenance', *TEXT*, 2 (1985), 121–37.

[2] David Lyall Patrick, *The Textual History of 'Richard III'* (1936); reviewed and
endorsed by W. W. Greg, in *The Library*, IV, 19 (1938–9), 118–20.

[3] Kristian Smidt, *Iniurious Imposters and 'Richard III'* (Oslo and New York,
1964); *Memorial Transmission and Quarto Copy in 'Richard III'* (Oslo and New York,
1970).

and others, the evidence with respect to Q1 *Richard III*, which was always admitted to be a 'doubtful' text or a remarkably good reconstruction, is far from compelling. Even if one addresses the question in terms of the balance of probability without imposing the onus of proof in any direction, my own provisional conclusion would be that Q1 was probably not reconstructed by actors on tour. Of course if it had been put together in this way, it would have peculiar value as a record of what was actually performed. But it seems more likely that the characteristics unique to Q1 were introduced through transcription and adaptation in the professional theatre.

A highly variant passage (3.2.106–10) shows the deficiency of memorial reconstruction as a general explanation at a point where it might be expected to be most effective.[1] F has:

> *Enter a Priest.*
> *Priest.* Well met, my Lord, I am glad to see your Honor.
> *Hast.* I thanke thee, good Sir *Iohn*, with all my heart.
> I am in your debt, for your last Exercise:
> Come the next Sabboth, and I will content you.
> *Priest.* Ile wait vpon your Lordship.
> *Enter Buckingham.*
> *Buc.* What, talking with a Priest, Lord Chamberlaine?
> Your friends at Pomfret, they doe need the Priest,
>
> (TLN 1912–21)[2]

Q1 varies the passage to read:

> *Hast.* What Sir Iohn, you are wel met, *(Enter a priest.*
> I am beholding to you for your last daies exercise:
> Come the next sabaoth and I will content you. *He whis-*
> *Enter Buckingham.* *(pers in his eare.*
> *Buc.* How now Lo: Chamberlaine, what talking with a
> Your friends at Pomfret they doe need the priest (priest,
>
> (F4$^v$)

The texts suddenly lurch into this instability in relation to each other, for in most of the scene they are in much closer general

---

[1] My discussion here follows Jowett, 'Perplexities', pp. 229–31.

[2] TLNs (through line numbers) from *The Norton Facsimile: The First Folio of Shakespeare*, ed. Charlton Hinman (New York and London, 1968).

conformity. There is a wider tendency for textual variation to intensify around short exchanges involving exits or entrances, moments when there is a marked interdependence between actors. In the passage, both speakers have lines that vary between Q1 and F. Both use hexameters in Q1, a puzzling characteristic for the two actors to share if, as is argued, they both transmitted their own parts; Hastings also has a seven-foot line. Q1 is characterized by its redistribution of idiomatic familiarities from one role to another. Most notably, when Hastings greets the Priest his opening 'What' anticipates Buckingham's greeting of him, but in Q1 Buckingham's 'what' is displaced to the middle of the line, thus avoiding obvious repetition. Q1 is not a garbled recollection of F. Indeed actors would have difficulty in playing a passage if the recollection of one of them as to who should say what (for example, who should speak first when the Priest enters) was at variance with the script they were performing. It might reasonably be inferred that the Quarto reflects performance accurately.

Of course, performance may itself have developed away from the written script in such details, but there are signs that the dialogue has been consciously modified. Though they do not save on the number of actors needed to perform the play, the Quarto's suddenly active changes seem to be directed at saving a minor speaking role and adjusting the dynamic of the exchange. The loss of the Priest's lines is of comparatively little consequence, and the adjustments are responsive and delicate. Editors usually import Q1's direction for whispering into their Folio-based texts, but arguably Q1 and F deal with the staging differently. In F alone Buckingham finds Hastings and the Priest parting separate ways; in Q1 alone he catches them whispering. Therefore the stage direction is an alternative to the Priest's 'Ile wait vpon your Lordship', not a prelude to it; the whispering business compensates for the Priest's silence. Buckingham's 'How now', though dismissable as redundant padding, is evidently part of the same alteration: Buckingham is made more insistent because he is interrupting a more private conversation. The presence of a 'theatrical' change (deletion of the Priest's speaking role, introduction of the whispering) seems connected with the verbal instability of the dialogue down to its fine detail. The outcome is less literary, in so far as metre is a literary quality, but it presents a cleaner playing text. Q1 offers a different version, not a misrepresentation of the same version.

It is true that in some cases the alterations have been effected clumsily. This seems to be especially the case in Buckingham's role.[1] A number of short passages in his speeches have been altered verbally, slightly shortened, and metrically disrupted. Such changes are not incompatible with adaptation, though the concentration of such passages in one role is, in itself, more compatible with lapse of memory on the part of one actor. However, the main criterion here is again disruption of metre, and the inference from it is far from conclusive. There is only one passage, spoken by the Queen at 4.4.251–3, that seems to have become incoherent beyond the everyday errors of misreading and substitution. Even here inattentive adaptation is possible, not least because the deletion of the reference to Rutland's murder and Margaret's tormenting of the Duke of York is consistent with a similar and more extensive cut after 1.2.152 (Appendix A, Passage A).

A few single-word variants show distinctive traits of memorial slips as they are usually understood. Take, for example, Q1's 'laid in darkenes' as against F's 'cast in darknesse' at 1.3.327 (C3ᵛ; TLN 803). Q1's verb 'laid' is more passive and more commonplace. It also enfeebles the biblical echo (see Commentary). Moreover, it repeats the verb from the previous line, 'I lay vnto the grieuous charge of others'. This internal echo both weakens the Quarto text and suggests a possible explanation for it. Q1's 'laid' could be a memorial error influenced by 'lay', and in this edition it is corrected to the Folio reading.

As variants like this accumulate, a memorial intervention becomes increasingly likely. There are a number of other such examples, though few in which the mechanics of error and the preferability of the Folio reading are so well defined. An important difference should be observed between recognizing local effects of memorial lapse that could result from the carelessness of a scribe or compositor and instituting a full-blown theory of reconstruction by actors. Every act of transcription is an act of memory, and in particular a scribe responsible for adapting the text would not have been rigorously committed to textual preservation.

There is in fact some evidence for non-memorial continuity in the transmission of the text. This is to be found principally in the stage directions and speech-prefixes. Where stage directions vary

---

[1] See Appendix C, where examples of mislineation in the role are identified.

enough to confirm that F's wording reflects MSF, some distinctive details are shared. For example, at 1.2.142 Q1 reads '*Shee spitteth at him.*' and F reads '*Spits at him.*'; at 1.2.168 Q1's '*Here she lets fall | the sword.*' is echoed in F's '*She fals the Sword.*'; after 1.4.82 Q1's '*He readeth it.*' is picked up in F's '*Reads.*', and so on. The variation in details such as the form of the verbs 'spit', 'fall', and 'read' indicates that F's reading comes from MSF, not the quarto copy, whilst the presence of these distinctive directions and the specific detail of the verbs themselves would not be expected to survive memorial transmission. There is a similar concurrence with variation to be found in the forms of reference to Lord Stanley, Earl of Derby (see Appendix D, Note 2). Some of these details could conceivably have been transmitted alongside memorial reconstruction by actors if they had access to a manuscript 'plot' outlining the stage action, but this seems unlikely; the evidence undermines confidence in the memorial hypothesis still further.

Precise diagnosis of the origin of Q1 may prove impossible. Fixed categories such as 'playbook' or 'memorial reconstruction' are of little help. But the text is more plausibly designated 'theatrical' than 'memorial', and most of its theatricality seems intentional and constructive. I would posit that Q1 was given its distinct form by an adapting theatrical scribe, with some contribution at some point from Shakespeare as reviser. There may have been some form of input from other theatrical personnel too.[1]

*Editorial Issues.* Put simply, editing entails establishing the most authoritative source text and following it. Beyond this, it entails making certain kinds of alteration to the text on the basis that this document, from the viewpoint of the modern reader, is obfuscatory, misleading, or wrong. In the present edition, such alterations include correction of error, modernization of Elizabethan spelling, stabilization of stage directions, and so on, as discussed in 'Editorial Procedures'. The general appearance of Q1, which is followed in this edition, can be studied in fig. 12. As can be seen from the illustration (compare 2.2.77–2.3.28), the aim of the edition is not in any simple sense to reproduce that text as a printed document.

---

[1] In an unpublished paper given at the conference 'Material Shakespeare' at the University of Queensland, 1998, Adrian Kiernander similarly argued that Q1 is conditioned to the theatre in respectable ways, suggestively conjecturing that dictation by actors may have given the text some of its characteristics.

*The Tragedy*

*Ambo.* Was neuer Orphanes had a dearer losse,
*Du.* Was neuer mother had a dearer losse:
Alas I am the mother of these mones,
Their woes are parceld, mine are generall:
She for Edward weepes, and so doe I:
I for a Clarence weepe, so doth not she:
These babes for Clarence weepe, and so doe I:
I for an Edward weepe, so doe not they.
Alas, you three on me threefold distrest,
Poure all your teares, I am your sorrowes nurse,
And I will pamper it with lamentations. *Enter Glocest.*
*Gl.* Madame haue comfort, al of vs haue cause, *with others.*
To waile the dimming of our shining starre:
But none can cure their harmes by wailing them,
Madame my mother, I doe crie you mercy,
I did not see your Grace, humbly on my knee
I craue your blessing.
*Du.* God blesse thee, and put meekenes in thy minde,
Loue, charity, obedience, and true duety.
*Glo.* Amen, and make me die a good old man,
Thats the butt end of a mothers blessing:
I maruell why her Grace did leaue it out.
*Buck.* You cloudy Princes, and hart-sorrowing peeres
That beare this mutuall heauy lode of moane:
Now cheare each other, in each others loue:
Though we haue spent our haruest of this King,
We are to reape the haruest of his sonne:
The broken rancour of your high swolne hearts,
But lately splinterd, knit, and ioynd togeather,
Must gently be preseru'd, cherisht and kept,
Me seemeth good that with some little traine,
Forthwith from Ludlow the yong Prince be fetcht
Hither to London, to be crownd our King.
*Glo.* Then be it so, and go we to determine.
Who they shalbe that straight shall post to Ludlow:
Madame, and you my mother will you go,
To giue your censures in this waighty busines,
*Ans.* With all our hearts. *Exeunt man, Glo. Buck.*
*Buck.*

*of Richard the third.*

*Buck.* My Lord who euer iournies to the Prince,
For Gods sake let not vs two stay behinde:
For by the way Ile sort occasion,
As index to the story we late talkt of,
To part the Queenes proud kindred from the King.
*Glo.* My other selfe, my counsels consistory:
My Oracle, my Prophet, my deare Cosen:
I like a childe will go by thy direction:
Towards Ludlow then, for we will not stay behinde.
*Enter two Citizens.*
1 *Cit.* Neighbour well met, whither away so fast?
2 *Cit.* I promise you, I scarcely know my selfe.
1 Heare you the newes abroad?
2 I, that the King is dead.
1 Bad newes birlady, seldome comes the better,
I feare, I feare, twill prooue a troublous world. *Ent. ano-*
3 *Cit.* Good morrow neighbours. *ther Cit.*
Doth this newes hold of good King Edwards death?
1 It doth. 3 Then masters looke to see a troublous world
2 No no, by Gods good grace his sonne shall raigne.
3 Woe to that land thats gouernd by a childe.
2 In him there is a hope of gouernement,
That in his nonage counsell vnder him,
And in his full and ripened yeres himselfe,
No doubt shall then, and till then gouerns we'l,
1 So stoode the state when Harry the sixe
Was crownd at Paris, but at ix. moneths olde,
3 Stoode the state so? no good my friend not so,
For then this land was famously enricht
With pollitike graue counsell: then the King
Had vertuous Vnckles to protect his Grace,
2 So hath this, both by the father and mother.
3 Better it were they all came by the father,
Or by the father there were none at all:
For emulation now, who shall be neerest:
Will touch vs all too neare, if God preuent not,
Oh full of danger is the Duke of Glocester,
And the Queenes kindred hauty and proud,
E 3                                                      And

12. Two adjacent pages from the 1597 First Quarto: Bodleian, Arch. G. d. 44, sigs. E2ᵛ-3.

For this, there is no substitute for the original book itself or a photofacsimile edition of it. The reader is recommended to study Q1 in *Richard III* as edited by W. W. Greg in the Shakespeare Quarto Facsimiles series (1959), or in *Shakespeare's Plays in Quarto*, edited by M. J. B. Allen and Kenneth Muir (1981). The 1623 Folio text can be examined in *The Norton Facsimile: The First Folio of Shakespeare*, edited by Charlton Hinman (1968).

Earlier editors were concerned almost exclusively with recovering the text as Shakespeare wrote it or, more problematically, in the form he intended it to assume. The great bibliographer W. W. Greg, for example, defined the ideal text from an editor's point of view as one reflecting '*a fair copy, made by the author himself*'. One problem with such a definition is that it cannot take positive account of the changes that would regularly take place in order to bring the play to performance. They will be rejected as corruptions. The Oxford Shakespeare *Complete Works* played a significant part in challenging this perception, arguing that the play found its completion in the theatre. Shakespeare was writing primarily with performance in mind, and pragmatic adjustments for the stage fulfil this aim even if they were not literally made by Shakespeare himself.

Other considerations take us further down this road. The dramatist in the early modern theatre was not a self-determining agent in his own right. He worked in co-operation with the acting company from the beginning, and it was the company that usually had proprietorial control over the manuscript. They commissioned it and came to own it. When a play appeared in print the company is named as the source for the play far more often than the author. Such is the case with Q1 *Richard III*, where the Lord Chamberlain's Servants are mentioned on the title-page but the dramatist is not. There is a logic to presenting a performance text without reference to the interests of the author.

If that logic is pursued remorselessly, it ceases to matter whether the words or meanings were coarsened as the play pursued its career on the stage. When performance is all that counts, there remains no reason for preferring a version of the play performed by a company in which Shakespeare acted over a heavily altered version put on by another company. If we have found a way of valuing a relatively short, vigorous, and crude version such as Q1 *Hamlet* over the longer and more refined version with which readers are familiar, we have lost a criterion by which to select the most valuable single text for a modern reader, and we have lost a principle whereby to uphold the play as an intricate, deliberated, and scripted work of literature.

These are matters of choice rather than law. The editorial perspective is particularly critical in the difficult case of *Richard III*, where neither Q1 nor F presents an entirely satisfactory basis for an edition. The tendency in the past has been to denigrate Q1 as a text of compromised authority and so to favour F. But that prioritization has been made on two bases that must be questioned. The first is that the theatrical text is less authoritative than the more purely authorial text even if it comes from Shakespeare's theatre. This view is rejected in the Oxford *Complete Works* editing of *Richard III*, but the second basis remains. It is the hypothesis of systematic memorial reconstruction, which is, to say the least, contestable in the form in which it is usually given.

In following Q1 in this edition, I have taken the view that the text has high theatrical authority. Authorial authority matters too, and it is somewhat compromised. But it is compromised only to an extent that can be expected in the relatively fluid conditions of the early 1590s, at a time when Shakespeare was not a sharer in his company and lacked the authorial prestige that he was beginning to acquire by the end of the decade. Q1 largely retains authorial texture. It has gained theatrical experience, and although it is very much to be doubted that Shakespeare was directly responsible for many of the changes, he is obviously one of the people who could have been involved in adjusting the text for theatrical needs. Q1 indeed has a number of verbal variants that are superior to the Folio readings and which might reflect authorial revision as part of the larger process of adaptation.

It should be emphasized that there are unignorable disadvantages in selecting Q1 as control text. But if one is seriously interested in the play as a theatrical phenomenon there is a strong incentive for dealing with Q1's marked deficiencies editorially and for accepting its slighter blemishes into the edited text. After all, F too has limitations, not only on account of its representing the play before it was completed for the stage. *Richard III* in F is a highly complex and synthetic textual object containing accrued error from the quartos, Folio compositors' mistakes, scribal characteristics from the manuscript consulted, and characteristics deriving from the transcription of readings from manuscript to printed copy. The mistakes it inherits from the derivative quarto copy can be stripped away editorially with reference to Q1, but nothing can be done about the sections where the annotation from the manuscript either became sporadic or stopped entirely. The integrity of the version represented in the manuscript available to the printers is distinctly compromised.

Most of the cuts in Q1, major and minor, can be afforded coherent theatrical or authorial explanations.[1] One can see, for

---

[1] For a suggestive account of the Folio-only passages in relation to the play's politics, see Kaegi.

instance, cuts that clarify staging (Appendix A, Passages D, F, G, J), that reduce the amount of reference to historical persons and to events outside the play's action (Passages A, H), that cut back on Richard's more extravagant and lengthy oratory (Passages A, I, M), and that remove purposeless repetition (Passage H). Almost half the lines are taken from 4.4, a long scene (the play's longest), and one in which very little happens by way of action. The cuts in the Queen's lines in 4.4 are connected with the loss of her speech at the end of 4.1, and the more extensive pruning of Richard's persuasions runs in parallel with a similar cut to his seduction of Anne in 1.2. A persistent theme running through the deleted passages is the begetting, presence, or killing of children. These passages are significant to a reading of the play that stresses its moments of pathos, as are the deleted lines in which the speaker utters prophecy or prays for a merciful outcome (Passages B, C, F, K). From another point of view these passages clog the play with senti-
ment and slow its action.

In contrast, some Quarto omissions of single verse-lines, or of two part-lines in a sequence of speeches alternating between two characters, are unequivocal losses to the effectiveness of the passage. These can all be explained as mistakes in the printing house; eyeskip is usually plausible. Moreover, as has been suggested, Q1 is generally a very crowded text.

One of the consequences of following Q1 is that the editorial process becomes less stable. If the author cannot be invoked as sole arbiter, the cut-off point between what is treated as acceptable variation and what is treated as corruption or error becomes harder to define. Despite its legitimacy as a version of the play, Q1 is prone to error of various kinds. As has been seen, readings in Q1 can sometimes merit emendation even when they make sense, on the basis that the text has deteriorated in the process of transmission. Most of the emendations in this edition adopt readings found in F, but many are readings that first appeared in other quarto editions, and corrected what the play's early printers saw as self-evident error. Sometimes the difference between true Q1/F variants can be illuminating in itself. Very often the arguments that can be marshalled in defence of one reading can, with limited ingenuity, be matched by corresponding arguments in favour of its opposite. Though many variants call out for editorial comment, I have tried to prevent the Commentary becoming a battleground between Q1 and F, and to recognize that many alternative readings can legitimately coexist.

In such cases, of course, the reading of the control text, Q1, prevails. The result of editing the play from Q1 is a theatrically cleaner and more intelligible text with fewer dramatic roles, less repetition between speeches, and less reference to historical events that might puzzle the audience—or the reader for that matter. In contrast with most of the 'short' quartos of Shakespeare plays, virtually all the aesthetic richness and complexity of the original is preserved, and what emerges is a subtly different reading of the play. The emphasis is shifted away from a melodrama crowning a historical sequence sustained by a sense of fate and an appeal to pathos, towards a more secular, free-standing, and psycho-political drama about Richard's rise and fall in relation to a more narrowly prescribed group of other characters. Quarto *Richard III* is breaking free from the *Henry VI* trilogy. By 1597 the play had already achieved on the stage a resilient independence that would endure.

# EDITORIAL PROCEDURES

THIS is a critical edition which presents the text with modernized spelling and punctuation; the layout is regularized, and stage directions are expanded to give consistency and clarity to the stage action. For reasons explained in the Introduction, the present edition is based on the First Quarto of 1597 (Q1). Some impression of the relationship between the 1597 edition and the present edited text may be obtained by comparing the pages shown in fig. 12 with the equivalent edited text at 2.2.77–2.3.28. The edition follows the general procedures compiled by Stanley Wells for the Oxford Shakespeare series.[1] The main innovation relating to the design of the edition is the division of the collation line into two separate listings that relate to Q1 and F. The separation is intended to simplify documentation that for this play is intrinsically complex. For the same reason, listings of changes to the Q1 lineation, and of readings altered in quarto reprints and restored to the Q1 reading in F, are printed as appendices.

*Special Uses of the Folio Text.* Apart from correction of Q1 error, readings from the 1623 Folio (F) are accepted in the following situations:

(a) For convenience of reference, though original performances would almost certainly have been without act breaks, the text is divided into acts and scenes in the familiar way. F is the source for all act divisions and most scene divisions (see Appendix D, Note 1).
(b) Folio stage directions often provide essential information that is required for the purposes of a modern edition but that is absent in Q1. The wording of Q1 has been followed in the first instance, but, in the absence of indications that F represents an alternative staging, F has been allowed to supplement Q1's information. Where there is doubt as to whether F offers a supplement or an alternative, its reading, if accepted, has been placed in 'broken' brackets, as is the case with other contentious stage directions.
(c) F preserves some metrical elisions that are absent from Q1.

---

[1] For a summary, see Gary Taylor's edition of *Henry V* in the series (1982), pp. 75–81.

These have relevance to both the text as Shakespeare wrote it and the text as spoken in the theatre, and accordingly have been accepted into this edition.[1]

*Collations.* The first sequence between text and commentary records departures from Q1. The second sequence records the readings from F that have not been adopted in the text. Significant emendations accepted or conjectured by other editors but rejected in this edition are mentioned in the Commentary. The Commentary also discusses some of the more significant readings in F. Though most of the Q1/F variants make little difference to the substance of the text, most Folio readings can be considered as valid alternative readings.

In the 'F' collation, Folio readings originating in the quarto reprints are systematically recorded only as far as the copy for F in the passage in question, whether it be Q3 or Q6.[2] Readings can be assumed to be reproduced from one edition to another up to and including the Folio unless otherwise stated.

However, in the 'Q1' collation F is explicitly confirmed as following a quarto reading where it does so. An exception to this occurs in passages where F reprints the quarto copy without evident reference to the manuscript (see above, p. 119); here F is not automatically recorded.

The forms adopted in the Quarto collation include the following:

1.1.40 murderer] Q3, F; murtherers Q1     'Murderer' is initiated in Q3 and into F, correcting the Q1 plural 'murtherers'.

2.3.0.1 *meeting*] *not in* Q1. Compare F.     The information as to staging (or a significant part of it) comes from F, but, as the form of the direction follows Q1, F's wording is different. F is recorded in the Folio collation.

---

[1] Though Q1, like other early texts, uses contracted spellings such as 'crown'd' or 'rulde' for non-syllabic '-ed', it does not consistently reserve '-ed' terminations for syllabic '-ed' ('-èd'). Editorial interpretation of Q1 '-ed' as non-syllabic (hence unaccented) is not generally recorded. Similarly with 'doest' (Q1's usual spelling of 'dost'), etc.

[2] See Appendix B for the posited division of Folio copy between Q3 and Q6.

| | |
|---|---|
| 2.3.43 see‿] ~. | Significant misprints and incidentals are recorded except where punctuation is deficient at the end of a speech. No authority is cited for the correction. Here, the caret (‿) signals the absence of punctuation. The swung dash (~) signals that the word is the same, and so that the punctuation is what is being recorded. |
| 2.4.35 parlous] perilous | Notes such as this record ambiguous and contentious modernizations. 'Perilous' is taken to be a spelling of 'parlous'. It is recorded because there is an editorial choice between printing 'parlous' or 'perilous'. As the alteration is to the form of the word rather than the word itself, no independent source for 'parlous' is cited.[1] |

*Stage Directions.* As elsewhere in this series, 'broken' brackets are placed around stage directions that are regarded as significantly disputable. Accordingly, editorial emendations of stage directions are not automatically bracketed. Instead, they are recorded in the 'Q1' collation, as with other emendations. With directions of the kind '*to Margaret*' and '*aside*' printed after the speech-prefix, the assumption works the other way. These directions are in general editorial. In the exceptional cases in the ghost scene where the early texts have such directions, the fact is recorded.

### Abbreviations and References

Quotations from sources in old spelling are modernized. In quoting the chronicles, Holinshed has been followed, except where there is specific evidence for Shakespeare consulting Hall. Shakespeare plays

---

[1] For the principles of modernization, see Stanley Wells and Gary Taylor, *Modernizing Shakespeare's Spelling, with Three Studies in the Text of 'Henry V'* (Oxford, 1979); Stanley Wells, *Re-Editing Shakespeare for the Modern Reader* (Oxford, 1984).

other than *Richard III* are quoted from the Oxford *Complete Works* (1986). Biblical quotations are from the Geneva Bible unless otherwise stated. Place of publication is London unless otherwise stated.

EDITIONS OF 'RICHARD III' AND SHAKESPEARE

| | |
|---|---|
| Q1 | *The Tragedy of King Richard the Third* (1597) |
| Q2 | *The Tragedy of King Richard the Third* (1598) |
| Q3 | *The Tragedy of King Richard the Third* (1602) |
| Q4 | *The Tragedy of King Richard the Third* (1605) |
| Q5 | *The Tragedy of King Richard the Third* (1612) |
| Q6 | *The Tragedy of King Richard the Third* (1622) |
| Q7 | *The Tragedy of King Richard the Third* (1629) |
| Q8 | *The Tragedy of King Richard the Third* (1634) |
| F, F1 | *Comedies, Histories, and Tragedies* (The First Folio, 1623) |
| F2 | *Comedies, Histories, and Tragedies* (The Second Folio, 1632) |
| F3 | *Comedies, Histories, and Tragedies* (The Third Folio, 1663–4) |
| F4 | *Comedies, Histories, and Tragedies* (The Fourth Folio, 1685) |
| Alexander | Peter Alexander, *Complete Works* (1951) |
| Bate, ed., *Titus* | Jonathan Bate, *Titus Andronicus* (1995) |
| Bevington | David Bevington, *Complete Works* (Glenview, Ill., 1973) |
| Cambridge | W. G. Clark and W. A. Wright, *Works*, 9 vols. (Cambridge, 1863–6) |
| Capell | Edward Capell, *Comedies, Histories, and Tragedies*, 10 vols. (1767–8) |
| Cibber | Colley Cibber, *The Tragical History of King Richard III* (*c*.1700) |
| Collier 1853 | John Payne Collier, *Plays*, 2nd edn. (1853) |
| Craig | W. J. Craig, *Complete Works* (Oxford, 1891) |
| Davison | Peter Davison, *The First Quarto of King Richard III* (Cambridge, 1996) |
| Eccles | Mark Eccles, *The Tragedy of Richard the Third* (New York and London, 1964) |
| Hammond | Antony Hammond, *King Richard III* (1981) |
| Hanmer | Thomas Hanmer, *Works*, 6 vols. (Oxford, 1743–4) |

| | |
|---|---|
| Honigmann | E. A. J. Honigmann, *King Richard the Third* (Harmondsworth, 1968) |
| Johnson | Samuel Johnson, *Plays*, 8 vols. (1765) |
| Macready | William Charles Macready, *The Life and Death of King Richard III* (1821) |
| Malone | Edmond Malone, *Plays and Poems*, 10 vols. (1790) |
| Marshall | Henry Irving and Frank A. Marshall, *The Henry Irving Shakespeare*, 8 vols. (1887–90) |
| Oxberry | William Oxberry, *King Richard III* (1822) |
| Oxford | Stanley Wells and Gary Taylor, gen. eds., *Complete Works* (Oxford, 1986) |
| Pelican | Alfred Harbage, gen. ed., *Complete Works* (1969) |
| Pope | Alexander Pope, *Works*, 6 vols. (1723–5) |
| Riverside | G. Blakemore Evans, textual ed., *The Riverside Shakespeare* (Boston, 1974) |
| Rowe | Nicholas Rowe, *Works*, 6 vols. (1709) |
| Staunton | Howard Staunton, *Plays*, 3 vols. (1858–60) |
| Steevens | Samuel Johnson and George Steevens, *Plays*, 10 vols. (1773) |
| Theobald | Lewis Theobald, *Works*, 8 vols. (1733) |
| Thompson | A. Hamilton Thompson, *The Tragedy of King Richard the Third* (1907) |
| White | Richard Grant White, *Works*, 12 vols. (Boston, 1857–66) |
| Wilson | John Dover Wilson, *Richard III* (Cambridge, 1954) |

OTHER ABBREVIATIONS

| | |
|---|---|
| Abbott | E. A. Abbott, *A Shakespearian Grammar* (1869) |
| Articles of Religion | 'Articles of Religion', in *The Book of Common Prayer* (1571) |
| Barber and Wheeler | C. L. Barber and Richard P. Wheeler, *The Whole Journey* (Berkeley and London, 1986) |
| Bate, ed., *Romantics* | Jonathan Bate, ed., *The Romantics on Shakespeare* (Harmondsworth, 1992) |
| Brooks, 'Antecedents' | Harold Brooks, '*Richard III*: Antecedents of Clarence's Dream', *Shakespeare Survey 32* (1979), 145–50 |

| | |
|---|---|
| Calvin, *Institution* | John Calvin, *Institution of Christian Religion* [*Institutes*] (1561) |
| Capell, *Notes* | Edward Capell, *Notes and Various Readings to Shakespeare*, 3 vols. (1873) |
| Cercignani | Fausto Cercignani, *Shakespeare's Works and Elizabethan Pronunciation* (Oxford, 1981) |
| Chambers | E. K. Chambers, *William Shakespeare*, 2 vols. (Oxford, 1930) |
| Charnes | Linda Charnes, *Notorious Identity* (Cambridge, Mass., and London, 1993) |
| Chaucer | Geoffrey Chaucer, *Works*, ed. F. N. Robinson, 2nd edn. (Boston, 1957) |
| Colley | Scott Colley, *Richard's Himself Again* (New York and London, 1992) |
| *Common Prayer* | *The Book of Common Prayer*, 1559, ed. John E. Booty (Washington, DC, 1976) |
| Cox and Kastan | John D. Cox and David Scott Kastan, eds., *A New History of Early English Drama* (New York, 1997) |
| Daniel | P. A. Daniel, 'Introduction', in *'Richard the Third': The First Quarto* (Griggs Facsimiles, 1886) |
| Dent | R. W. Dent, *Shakespeare's Proverbial Language* (Berkeley and London, 1981) |
| *Edward III* | William Shakespeare, *King Edward the Third*, ed. Giorgio Melchiori (Cambridge, 1998) |
| Edwards | Thomas Edwards, *The Canons of Criticism*, 7th edn. (1765) |
| Gurr | Andrew Gurr, *The Shakespearian Playing Companies* (Oxford, 1996) |
| Hall | Edward Hall, *The Union of the Two Noble and Illustre Families of Lancaster and York*, 2nd edn. (1550; repr. Menston, 1970) |
| Hankey | Julie Hankey, *Plays in Perfomance: Richard III* (1981); 2nd edn. (Bristol, 1988) |
| Hassel, 'Context' | R. Chris Hassel, 'Context and Charisma', *Shakespeare Quarterly*, 36 (1985), 630–43 |
| Hassel, *Songs* | R. Chris Hassel, *Songs of Death: Performance, Interpretation, and the Text of 'Richard III'* (Lincoln, Neb., and London, 1987) |

| | |
|---|---|
| Heath | Benjamin Heath, *A Revisal of Shakespear's Text* (1765) |
| Hodgdon | Barbara Hodgdon, *The End Crowns All* (Princeton and Oxford, 1991) |
| Holinshed | Raphael Holinshed, *Chronicles of England, Scotland, and Ireland*, 2nd edn. (1587; repr. in 6 vols., 1808), vol. 3 |
| Honigmann, *Lost Years* | E. A. J. Honigmann, *Shakespeare: The Lost Years* (Manchester, 1985) |
| Hortmann | Wilhelm Hortmann, *Shakespeare on the German Stage: The Twentieth Century* (Cambridge, 1998) |
| Howard and Rackin | Jean E. Howard and Phyllis Rackin, *Engendering a Nation* (London and New York, 1997) |
| Howard-Hill | T. H. Howard-Hill, ed., *Shakespeare and 'Sir Thomas More'* (Cambridge, 1989) |
| *Jack Straw* | *The Life and Death of Jack Straw, 1594*, ed. Kenneth Muir, Malone Society Reprints (Oxford, 1957) |
| Jones | Emrys Jones, *The Origins of Shakespeare* (Oxford, 1977) |
| Kaegi | Ann G. Kaegi, 'Political Persuasions' (unpublished Ph.D. dissertation, University of Birmingham, 1998) |
| Kinnear | B. G. Kinnear, *Cruces Shakespearianae* (1883) |
| Kyd, *Spanish Tragedy* | Thomas Kyd, *The Spanish Tragedy*, ed. Philip Edwards (1959) |
| *Leir* | *The True Chronicle History of King Leir, 1605*, ed. W. W. Greg, Malone Society Reprints (Oxford, 1907) |
| Lyly | John Lyly, *Campaspe, Sappho and Phao*, ed. G. K. Hunter and David Bevington (Manchester, 1991) |
| Marlowe | Christopher Marlowe, *'Doctor Faustus' and Other Plays*, ed. David Bevington and Eric Rasmussen (Manchester, 1993) |
| *Metamorphoses* | Ovid, *Metamorphoses*, trans. Arthur Golding (1567), ed. John Frederick Nims (New York, 1965) |

| | |
|---|---|
| *Mirror for Magistrates* | *The Mirror for Magistrates*, ed. Lily B. Campbell (Cambridge, 1938) |
| *'Mirror', Parts Added* | John Higgins and Thomas Blenerhasset, *Parts Added to 'The Mirror for Magistrates'*, ed. Lily B. Campbell (Cambridge, 1946) |
| More | Sir Thomas More, *History of Richard III*, as reprinted in Holinshed |
| Nashe, *Have With You* | Thomas Nashe, *Have With You to Saffron Walden*, in *Works*, ed. R. B. McKerrow, 5 vols. (Oxford, 1958), vol. 3 |
| Neill | Michael Neill, 'Shakespeare's Halle of Mirrors', in *Shakespeare Studies*, 8 (1975), 99–130 |
| *OED* | *The Oxford English Dictionary*, 2nd edn., 20 vols. (Oxford, 1989) |
| Peele, *Alcazar* | George Peele, *The Battle of Alcazar, 1594*, ed. W. W. Greg, Malone Society Reprints (Oxford, 1907) |
| *Ricardus Tertius* | Thomas Legge, *Ricardus Tertius*, in *Shakespeare's Library*, ed. J. P. Collier and W. C. Hazlitt, 2nd edn., 6 vols. (1867–75), vol. 5 |
| Richmond | Hugh Richmond, *King Richard III* (Manchester, 1989) |
| Ritson | Joseph Ritson, *Remarks, Critical and Illustrative* (1783) |
| Seneca | Line references to Seneca, *Tragedies*, in Latin and trans. Frank Justus Miller, 2 vols., Loeb Classical Library (1917 and 1929) |
| Seneca, *Ten Tragedies* | Seneca, *His Ten Tragedies* (1581, repr. Amsterdam and New York, 1969) |
| Shaheen | Naseeb Shaheen, *Biblical References in Shakespeare's History Plays* (Newark, Del., and London, 1989) |
| Spenser, *Faerie Queene* | Edmund Spenser, *The Faerie Queene*, ed. J. C. Smith, 2 vols. (Oxford, 1909) |
| *SQ* | *Shakespeare Quarterly* |
| Stachniewski | John Stachniewski, *The Persecutory Imagination* (Oxford, 1991) |
| Taylor | Gary Taylor, '*Richard III*', in *Textual Companion*, pp. 228–63 |

| | |
|---|---|
| *Textual Companion* | Stanley Wells and Gary Taylor, with John Jowett and William Montgomery, *William Shakespeare: A Textual Companion* (Oxford, 1987) |
| Tilley | Morris Palmer Tilley, *A Dictionary of Proverbs in England in the Sixteenth and Seventeenth Centuries* (Ann Arbor, 1950) |
| *True Tragedy* | *The True Tragedy of Richard the Third, 1594*, ed. W. W. Greg, Malone Society Reprints (Oxford, 1929) |
| Vergil, Polydore | *Three Books of Polydore Vergil's English History . . . From an Early Translation*, ed. Henry Ellis (1844) |
| Walker, Alice | Alice Walker, *Textual Problems of the First Folio* (Cambridge, 1953) |
| Walker, W. S. | W. S. Walker, *A Critical Examination of the Text of Shakespeare*, ed. W. N. Lettsom, 3 vols. (1860) |
| Yamada | Akihiro Yamada, ed., *The First Folio of Shakespeare: A Transcript of Contemporary Marginalia in a Copy of the Kodama Memorial Library of Meisei University* (Tokyo, 1998) |

*The Tragedy of King Richard the Third*

# THE PERSONS OF THE PLAY

RICHARD DUKE OF GLOUCESTER, later KING RICHARD III

George, Duke of CLARENCE, his brother

KING Edward IV, their brother

The DUCHESS OF YORK, their mother

The QUEEN, King Edward's wife

Anthony Woodville, Lord RIVERS, her brother

Lord GREY and Marquis DORSET, the Queen's sons (treated as one figure in early scenes)

Edward, the young PRINCE of Wales ⎱ King Edward's sons
Richard, the young Duke of YORK ⎰

BOY ⎱ Clarence's children
GIRL ⎰

LADY ANNE, later ANNE DUCHESS OF GLOUCESTER, formerly betrothed to King Henry VI's son Edward

Queen MARGARET, widow of King Henry VI

William Lord HASTINGS, the Lord Chamberlain

The Duke of BUCKINGHAM

Lord STANLEY, EARL OF DERBY

The Earl of RICHMOND, his stepson

CATESBY

Sir Richard RATCLIFFE

Sir Robert BRAKENBURY, 'Keeper' (1.4) or 'LIEUTENANT' (4.1) of the Tower

Tressill and Berkeley, two GENTLEMEN attending the corpse of Henry VI

SERVANTS bearing the corpse (one speaking)

Two EXECUTIONERS

CITIZENS (three speaking in 2.3)

The CARDINAL

The Lord MAYOR of London

A PURSUIVANT called Hastings

A Priest

A SCRIVENER

Sir Thomas Vaughan

The BISHOP of Ely

A BOY, a page in King Richard's court

James TYRRELL

SIR CHRISTOPHER, chaplain of Lord Stanley's household

Three LORDS  ⎫
              ⎬ Supporters of Richmond
Sir James BLUNT ⎭

John Duke of NORFOLK, a supporter of Richard III

MESSENGERS (four in 4.4)

The GHOST of King Henry VI

The GHOST of Prince Edward, Henry VI's son

(Also the GHOSTS of persons formerly alive in the play: Clarence, Rivers, Grey, VAUGHAN, the two young princes (Prince of Wales and Duke of York), Hastings, Anne, and Buckingham)

Guards, Bishops, Lords, Soldiers, and others

There is no comparable list in early editions. The first was constructed by Rowe in 1709.

# The Tragedy of King Richard III

[1.1]     *Enter Richard Duke of Gloucester, alone*
RICHARD DUKE OF GLOUCESTER
    Now is the winter of our discontent
    Made glorious summer by this sun of York,
    And all the clouds that loured upon our house
    In the deep bosom of the ocean buried.
    Now are our brows bound with victorious wreaths,

*[handwritten annotations: Not a soliloquy but an address. The audi. etc. A perfect syllogism. A major & minor premiss & a conclusion —]*

Q:
    **Title**] THE TRAGEDY OF | King Richard the third. | Containing, | His treacherous Plots against his brother Clarence: | the pittiefull murther of his iunocent nephewes: | his tyrannicall vsurpation: with the whole course | of his detested life, and most deserued death. | As it hath beene lately Acted by the | Right honourable the Lord Chamber-|laine his seruants.
    **1.1**] Q1 *has no act and scene divisions. See Appendix B.*     0.1 *alone*] solus     1 RICHARD DUKE OF GLOUCESTER] *speech-prefix not in* Q1, F     2 sun] sonne

F:
    **Title**] The Tragedy of Richard the Third: | with the Landing of Earle Richmond, and the | Battell at Bosworth Field. *(head title)*; *The Life and Death of Richard the Third. (running titles; similarly Catalogue)*
    **1.1**] *Actus Primus. Scoena Prima.* F. *See Appendix B.*

1.1 The opening lines might suggest Richard is at Court, but from l. 41 the action seems to be located near the Tower of London.

0.1 *alone* In production, Richard's soliloquy has sometimes been addressed at least partly to a stage audience (see Illustration 8). The Quarto stage directions specify an entry alone once elsewhere: Margaret's entry '*sola*' at the beginning of 4.4.

1–31 **Now . . . days** The house of York has triumphed over the house of Lancaster at the Battle of Tewkesbury, and Edward IV is king in place of the Lancastrian Henry VI, Richard presents himself as a warrior without function in peacetime, but in *Richard Duke of York* 3.2.182–95 he declared his intention to use Machiavellian intrigue and deception to win the crown.

1–2 **Now . . . York** Recalls Sidney, *Astrophil and Stella* (first published 1591), in *Poems*, ed. W. A. Ringler (1962), 69.7–10: 'Gone is the winter of my misery. | My

spring appears; O see what here doth grow; | For Stella hath with words where faith doth shine | Of her high heart giv'n me the monarchy.' The lines were soon famous. In the Cambridge play *2 Return from Parnassus* (*c*.1601; ed. W. D. Macray (1886), 4.3.78–9), Burbage encourages the student Philomusus to recite them, which he does, with the variant 'the sonne' for Q1's 'this sonne'.

1 **discontent** Refers to cause as well as the effect, and suggests a stronger feeling (grievance) than in modern use.

2 **sun** Q1's 'sonne' is a spelling variant, though King Edward is both 'son' of Richard Duke of York and the royal 'sun' that makes summer. In *Richard Duke of York* 2.1.20–40, the vision of three suns represents the three sons of York. After this vision Edward took the sun as his emblem.

3 **our house** the family of York

4 **In . . . buried** The literal sense is 'sunk below the sea-horizon'.

147

Our bruisèd arms hung up for monuments,
Our stern alarums changed to merry meetings,
Our dreadful marches to delightful measures.
Grim-visaged war hath smoothed his wrinkled front,
And now, instead of mounting barbèd steeds                    10
To fright the souls of fearful adversaries,
He capers nimbly in a lady's chamber
To the lascivious pleasing of a lute.
But I that am not shaped for sportive tricks
Nor made to court an amorous looking-glass,                   15
I that am rudely stamped, and want love's majesty
To strut before a wanton-ambling nymph,
I that am curtailed of this fair proportion,

*Venus displaces*
*Mars!*
*—But . . .*

Q:
7 alarums] Q2, F; alarmes Q1    10 instead] in steed    11 adversaries,] ~.    13 lute] F; loue
Q1

6–13 **Our . . . lute** Recalls in particular Lyly, *Campaspe* (1584): 'Is the warlike sound of drum and trump turned to the soft noise of lyre and lute, the neighing of barbed steeds, whose loudness filled the air with terror and whose breaths dimmed the sun with smoke, converted to delicate tunes and amorous glances? . . . Remember, Alexander, thou hast a camp to govern, not a chamber' (2.2.40–5, 67–9). Richard temporarily withholds stating his mislike.

6 **bruisèd arms** Though *bruisèd* hints at limbs, the sense required is 'battered armour'. Might also suggest heraldic coats of arms (as on battered shields?).
   **for** as
7 **alarums** (a) summons to battle by drums and trumpets, (b) sudden atttacks
   **merry meetings** in contrast with *meetings* in battle
8 **marches** Suggests both the action and the accompanying drum-beat.
   **measures** Both 'stately dances' and 'melodies'.
9 **Grim-visaged war** Similarly in Sackville's 'Induction', in *Mirror for Magistrates* (ll. 386–7): 'War . . . with visage grim'.
   **front** forehead, face
10 **barbèd** wearing armour to protect breast and flank
11 **fearful** terrifying (not 'timorous')
12 **He . . . chamber** There is a sexual undercurrent: instead of *mounting* steeds, he

makes energetic rhythmic movements (*capers*) in a lady's vagina (*chamber*).
12 **He** Refers initially to war personified, hence to the warrior, hence perhaps to Edward in particular.
13 **lascivious . . . lute** *Lascivious pleasing* suggests 'pleasingly lascivious sounds'. Also, the dancing itself gives erotic pleasure, in which case the lute might be metonymic for the lady as its player. *Lute* might even, like *chamber*, be euphemistic for the female sex organs. Though Q1's 'loue' makes sense, it is almost certainly an error. Lyly refers to the lute in the passage quoted in note to ll. 6–13.
14 **But I** A strong transition in subject and tone.
   **sportive** amorous, sexual
   **tricks** ways, game-playing, dexterity
15 **an amorous looking-glass** i.e. the amorous reflection in it
16 **rudely** roughly, crudely
   **stamped** i.e. formed in the womb. Might imply 'printed', or suggest a coin stamped with a monarch's image.
   **want** lack
17 **wanton-ambling** walking with a sexy sway
18–21 **I . . . up** Recalls the self-description of the lame Roman emperor Claudius, in *The First Part of the Mirror for Magistrates* (1587), in '*Mirror*', *Parts Added*, 'Claudius Tiberius Drusus', ll. 10–11: 'Unperfect all, begun by nature, but begot | Not

Cheated of feature by dissembling nature,
Deformed, unfinished, sent before my time                                    20
Into this breathing world scarce half made up,
And that so lamely and unfashionable
That dogs bark at me as I halt by them:
Why, I in this weak-piping time of peace
Have no delight to pass away the time,                                        25
Unless to spy my shadow in the sun
And descant on mine own deformity.
And therefore, since I cannot prove a lover
To entertain these fair well-spoken days,
I am determinèd to prove a villain,                                          30
And hate the idle pleasures of these days.
Plots have I laid inductious, dangerous,
By drunken prophecies, libels, and dreams,
To set my brother Clarence and the King
In deadly hate the one against the other;                                    35
And if King Edward be as true and just
As I am subtle, false, and treacherous,
This day should Clarence closely be mewed up

Q:
29 days,] ~ .

F:
26 spy] see    32 inductious] Inductions (*from* Q3)

absolute, not well nor fully framed'.
Claudius blames Fortune. See also More
(Appendix E, Passage 1).
18 **curtailed** Literally 'docked', as of a
horse's or dog's tail. Stressed on the first
syllable.

19 **feature** good shape, comeliness of body
**dissembling** Nature cheats Richard in
that he would expect to look better than
he does and his physical desires are frustrated. The sense 'disassembling' is also
just possible.
20 **unfinished** As such, Richard has opportunity to 'make' himself.
**sent before my time** born prematurely
21 **made up** completed
22 **unfashionable** badly shaped
23 **halt** limp
24 **weak-piping** Probably suggests (a) the
cheeping of feeble chicks (*OED*, *pipe*, *v.*¹ 4;
also said contemptuously of persons,
particularly of women and children), (b)

the pipes of pastoral, as opposed to
martial, music.
27 **descant on** play an improvisatory accom-
paniment above the simple and repeated
bass theme of; hence 'sing harmoniously
about' or, more prosaically, 'comment
on'. Compare the lover and his lascivious
lute-music in l. 13.
28 **prove** show myself to be
30 **determinèd** (a) resolved, (b) preordained
32 **inductious** 'persuasive, seductive' (*OED*);
initiatory, productive. The Folio reading
'Inductions' is usually followed. See
Appendix D, Note 4.
34 **my . . . King** Richard was youngest of the
three surviving brothers.
36 **true and just** The compliment has a negative undertow: 'utterly predictable'. *True*
contrasts with Richard in the sense 'well-
proportioned'.
38 **mewed** cooped. Might apply to a trained
bird of prey, as at l. 132, or, more likely, to
poultry being fattened before slaughter.

About a prophecy which says that 'G'
Of Edward's heirs the murderer shall be.                    40
    *Enter Clarence with Brakenbury and a guard of men*
Dive, thoughts, down to my soul; here Clarence
    comes.—
Brother, good days! What means this armèd guard
That waits upon your grace?
CLARENCE                                   His majesty,
Tend'ring my person's safety, hath appointed
This conduct to convey me to the Tower.                    45
RICHARD DUKE OF GLOUCESTER
  Upon what cause?
CLARENCE                    Because my name is George.
RICHARD DUKE OF GLOUCESTER
  Alack, my lord, that fault is none of yours.
He should for that commit your godfathers.
O, belike his majesty hath some intent
That you shall be new christened in the Tower.             50
But what's the matter, Clarence, may I know?

Q:

40 murderer] Q3, F; murtherers Q1    40.1 *Enter . . . men*] *position as in* F; *right of l.* 41 Q1
*Brakenbury and*] *not in* Q1. *Compare* F.    44 Tend'ring] F; tendering Q1    44 appointed] ap-|
pointed Q1 (*Bodleian, Folger*); ap-|po nted Q1 (*British Library, Huntington*)    46 RICHARD DUKE
OF GLOUCESTER] *Glo.* Q1. *Similarly to the end of* 3.7, *except at* 3.5.51. *Compare* F.

F:

40.1 *with . . . men*] *and Brakenbury, guarded*    42 days] day    45 the Tower] th'Tower
46 RICHARD DUKE OF GLOUCESTER] *Glo.* Q1; *Rich.* F. *Similarly to the end of* 3.7, *except in*
3.1.1–148, *where* F *follows quarto copy.*    50 shall] should

39–40 **About . . . be** See note to ll. 54–9.
40.1 *Brakenbury* Sir Robert Brakenbury
    was not appointed Constable of the Tower
    until five years after Clarence was killed
    there, and in More's account held that
    post when the Princes were murdered.
    Q1's consistent form 'Brokenbury' is no
    more than a spelling variant on More's
    and F's 'Brakenberie', and is found also
    in *True Tragedy*.
42 **good days** Where F gives the conven-
    tional greeting 'good day', Q1 gives an
    ironic exclamation in response to seeing
    Clarence under guard, and sounds a vari-
    ation on Richard's criticism of 'these
    days' at l. 31. For the idiom, which com-
    positors of all the quartos accepted, com-
    pare 'I do hope good days', *Shrew*
    1.2.191.

44 **Tend'ring my person's safety** Clarence is
    ironic: the King's concern is for his own
    safety. *Safety* plays on the sense 'close
    custody'. *Conduct* (l. 45) similarly equivo-
    cates between protection and custody.
49 **O** Omitted by Pope and many subsequent
    editors as extrametrical, and suspected as
    an actor's interpolation; but compare,
    for example, 'Ha' in *Hamlet* (Q2 and F)
    2.2.578. The pretence of a thought sud-
    denly occurring seems typical of Richard.
50 **new christened** By changing his name,
    Clarence would evade the prophecy. But
    there is a sinister and ironic anticipation
    of Clarence's death by drowning in the
    butt of malmsey in 1.4, especially as
    *Mirror for Magistrates*, the closest source
    for the prophecy, has Clarence's ghost
    relate how Richard's accomplices 'in a

CLARENCE

Yea, Richard, when I know, for I protest
As yet I do not. But as I can learn,
He harkens after prophecies and dreams,     *cf. R's dreams at end*
And from the cross-row plucks the letter G,                    55
And says a wizard told him that by 'G'
His issue disinherited should be.
And for my name of George begins with G,
It follows in his thought that I am he.
These, as I learn, and such like toys as these,               60
Have moved his highness to commit me now.

RICHARD DUKE OF GLOUCESTER

Why, this it is when men are ruled by women.
'Tis not the King that sends you to the Tower;
My lady Grey his wife, Clarence, 'tis she
That tempers him to this extremity.                           65
Was it not she and that goodman of worship
Anthony Woodville, her brother there,

Q:
66 goodman] good man

F:
52 for] but    61 Have] Hath    65 tempers] tempts (*from* Q2 'tempts', Q3 'temps')    this] this
harsh    67 Woodville] *Woodeulle* (perhaps for trisyllabic 'Woodeville')

butt of malmsey standing by | New
christened me' ('Clarence', ll. 370–1).

54–9 **He . . . he** The prophecy is mentioned
by Holinshed, with the marginal note
'prophecies devilish fantasies' (p. 346),
but Shakespeare echoes the rhymes
of *Mirror for Magistrates*, 'Clarence',
181–6: 'A prophecy was found which
said a G | Of Edward's children should
destruction be. | Me to be G, because my
name was George; | My brother thought,
and therefore did me hate. | But woe be
to the wicked heads that forge | Such
doubtful dreams to breed unkind debate.'
Shakespeare adds the suggestion that
Richard contrived the prophecy. It turns
out true in that 'G' begins 'Gloucester'
(as, in More, Vaughan realizes when he is
going to his death).

55 **cross-row** alphabet (formerly prefixed
with a cross)

60 **toys** fancies

62–5 **Why . . . extremity** More suggests that
the Queen or her kindred might have

'maligned    the    King's    kindred'
(Holinshed, p. 362).

64 **My lady Grey** Richard's contemptuous
use of her title before marriage to Edward
recalls his lascivious courtship (*Richard
Duke of York* 3.2). Richard will later deny
the legitimacy of her marriage.

65 **tempers** disposes, persuades; hardens (as
of tempering steel)

66–9 **Was . . . delivered** In More the event is
unmentioned except as recalled by the
Pursuivant of the play's 3.2.

66 **goodman** 'a man of substance, not of
gentle birth' (*OED* 4); also, ironically,
'good man'
**of worship** of good repute. With the implied caveat 'but not properly of the
nobility'.

67 **Anthony . . . there** Woodville is the family name of the character later identified
as Rivers. The final syllable of l. 66 is superfluous to the metre and supplies the
missing syllable for l. 67. *Woodville* is
stressed on the second syllable, or is a tri-
syllable, as F's '*Woodeuelle*' allows.

That made him send Lord Hastings to the Tower,
From whence this present day he is delivered?
We are not safe, Clarence, we are not safe.                    70

CLARENCE

By heaven, I think there is no man is secured
But the Queen's kindred, and night-walking heralds
That trudge betwixt the King and Mistress Shore.
Heard ye not what an humble suppliant
Lord Hastings was to her for his delivery?                    75

RICHARD DUKE OF GLOUCESTER

Humbly complaining to her deity
Got my lord Chamberlain his liberty.
I'll tell you what, I think it is our way,
If we will keep in favour with the King,
To be her men and wear her livery.                    80
The jealous o'erworn widow and herself,
Since that our brother dubbed them gentlewomen,
Are mighty gossips in this monarchy.

F:
71 is secured] secure    74 ye] you    75 to her for his] for her    83 this] our

71 **By . . . secured** 'Heaven' and 'there is'
(there's) are pronounced as single
syllables.

72 **night-walking heralds** The King's messengers would have his protection, but
might still be at risk if walking by night.
In Clarence's account night-walking is,
ironically, an advantage, as the dishon-
est task affords special protection. The
heralds' officiality is undercut by both
*night-walking* and *trudge*. *Night-walker* was
a term for a thief.

73 **Mistress Shore** Later Hastings's mistress,
to his cost (3.1.182, 3.4.76–9, etc.). She
has her own 'tragedy' of 'How Shore's
wife, King Edward the Fourth's concubine, was by King Richard despoiled of all
her goods, and forced to do open
penance' in Thomas Churchyard's 1563
expansion of *Mirror for Magistrates*. She is
kept off stage by Shakespeare, though she
has been a silent presence in 3.2 and elsewhere in many productions, including
Olivier's film.
**Mistress** Equivalent to modern 'Mrs'. The
context suggests that Richard also
glances at the senses 'woman of power,
female governor', 'patroness, *deity*'

(l. 76), and 'illicit sexual partner'.

77 **lord Chamberlain** Hastings's office

80 **To . . . livery** A jibe: Mistress Shore is unlikely to have had servants in her own livery, and there is a sexual innuendo. The
clothing figure is developed in the next
line: Shore's livery is 'in favour', but the
Queen is 'o'erworn'.

81 **o'erworn** worn out, (a) sexually, (b) like
a garment

82 **dubbed them** conferred on them the rank
of. A sneer against the women's rank
and gender, as dubbing usually elevates a
man to knighthood. The Queen was already a 'gentlewoman', but it suits Richard
to lump her together with Mistress Shore.

83 **gossips** There seem to be two ideas: (a) idle
women's talk has undue political power;
(b) the Queen and Shore are *gossips* in the
sense 'godparents', which enables them
to challenge the King's authority as the
country's 'natural' parent. Richard has
already jokingly pointed out that
Clarence's name, and hence his fate, can
be laid at his godparents' door (l. 48), and
suggested that Clarence's imprisonment
on the prompting of the Queen is for him
to be 'new-christened' (l. 50).

152

BRAKENBURY

   I beseech your graces both to pardon me:

   His majesty hath straitly given in charge            85

   That no man shall have private conference,

   Of what degree soever, with his brother.

RICHARD DUKE OF GLOUCESTER

   Even so. An't please your worship Brakenbury,

   You may partake of anything we say.

   We speak no treason, man; we say the King         90

   Is wise and virtuous, and his noble Queen

   Well struck in years, fair, and not jealous.

   We say that Shore's wife hath a pretty foot,

   A cherry lip,

   A bonny eye, a passing-pleasing tongue,           95

   And that the Queen's kindred are made gentlefolks.

   How say you, sir, can you deny all this?

BRAKENBURY

   With this, my lord, myself have nought to do.

RICHARD DUKE OF GLOUCESTER

   Naught to do with Mistress Shore? I tell thee, fellow,

   He that doth naught with her, excepting one,     100

   Were best he do it secretly alone.

BRAKENBURY

   What one, my lord?

Q:
84 BRAKENBURY] *Bro.* Q1. Q1 *uses the '*o*' spelling throughout.*   88 An't] and   92 struck] stroke.
*Similarly elsewhere.*   98–100 nought . . . Naught . . . naught] Q1 *'s spellings.*   102 BRAKEN-
BURY . . . me?] Q2, F;  *not in extant copies of* Q1

F:
87 his] your   92 jealous] iealious   101 he] to

85  **straitly** strictly
87  **degree** social rank (referring back to
    'man', l. 86)
92  **Well struck in years** Richard seems to
    mean 'well preserved for her age', but
    this invented use cannot conceal the
    usual sense, 'very advanced in age'.
    **jealous** Possibly pronounced as three
    syllables: 'jealious'.
94  **cherry lip** A phrase George Gascoigne had
    earlier mocked as a Petrarchan cliché
    ('Certain Notes of Instruction', in *Posies*,
    1575).
95  **a passing-pleasing tongue** According to
    More she was 'merry in company, ready

and quick of answer, neither mute nor
full of babble, sometime taunting without displeasure [i.e. without causing of-
fence], and not without disport'
(Holinshed, p. 384).
96  **kindred** The emendation 'kin' (Marshall)
    is plausible, but produces regular scan-
    sion only if unstressed.
99  **Naught** wickedness, naughtiness. Richard
    deliberately misunderstands Brakenbury.
    Sher made obscene gestures with his
    crutches.
102  **BRAKENBURY . . . me?** This exchange was
    introduced in Q2, unless it was, by some
    expedient hard to imagine, squeezed into

RICHARD DUKE OF GLOUCESTER
       Her husband, knave. Wouldst thou betray me?

BRAKENBURY
    I beseech your grace to pardon me, and withal
    Forbear your conference with the noble Duke.

CLARENCE
    We know thy charge, Brakenbury, and will obey.          105

RICHARD DUKE OF GLOUCESTER
   ⌣ We are the Queen's abjects, and must obey.
    Brother, farewell. I will unto the King,
    And whatsoe'er you will employ me in,
   ⌣ Were it to call King Edward's widow 'sister',
    I will perform it to enfranchise you.              110
    Meantime this deep disgrace in brotherhood
    Touches me dearer than you can imagine.
      *[He embraces Clarence, weeping]*

CLARENCE
    I know it pleaseth neither of us well.

RICHARD DUKE OF GLOUCESTER
    Well, your imprisonment shall not be long.
    I will deliver you or lie for you;             115

Q:
105 CLARENCE We] Q1 (*text*), F (*Cla.* We); We Q1 (*catchword*)    obey.] ~ ,    108 whatsoe'er] F;
whatsoeuer Q1    112 dearer] OXFORD; deeper Q1, F; nearer WILSON    112.1 *He . . . weeping*]
HAMMOND; *not in* Q1, F

F:
103 I] I do    115 or] or else

a press-corrected text of Q1, copies of which no longer survive. An alteration of this order of a text with no self-evident flaw can scarcely have been made without some written or oral prompting. As the stationer Thomas Creede issued both Q1 and Q2 and would in the usual course of things have owned the manuscript, Q2 may, exceptionally, have been corrected here from the copy for Q1.

102 **betray me** i.e. trick me into accusing the King

104 **conference** conversation

106 **abjects** Literally, 'outcasts'. Richard varies the predicated word 'subjects' to suggest 'humiliated subjects'.

109 **King Edward's widow** Pointedly not 'King Edward's wife', hence Richard's supposed extreme difficulty in calling her

'sister' (i.e. sister-in-law). He might virtually insinuate 'King Edward's whore', as her widowhood pertains to another man. Some early modern theologians considered remarriage a form of infidelity, and widows were often regarded as lustful.

110 **enfranchise** free

112 **dearer** more closely; more grievously. Taylor's convincing emendation of Q1/F's 'deeper' is supported by Shakespeare's usage in *Errors* 2.2.133, 'How dearly would it touch thee to the quick', and the collocation of *deep* and *dearer* in *Richard II* 1.3.150, 'A dearer merit, not so deep a maim'.

112.1 *He . . . weeping* Hammond's editorial stage direction (anticipated in Phelps's prompt book) is suggested by 1.4.224–6.

115 **lie for you** lie in prison in place of you.

Meantime have patience.

CLARENCE                    I must perforce; farewell.

*Exit Clarence, with Brakenbury and guard*

RICHARD DUKE OF GLOUCESTER

Go tread the path that thou shalt ne'er return.

Simple plain Clarence, I do love thee so

That I will shortly send thy soul to heaven,

If heaven will take the present at our hands.                    120

But who comes here, the new-delivered Hastings?

*Enter Lord Hastings*

HASTINGS

Good time of day unto my gracious lord.

RICHARD DUKE OF GLOUCESTER

As much unto my good lord Chamberlain.

Well are you welcome to the open air.

How hath your lordship brooked imprisonment?                    125

HASTINGS

With patience, noble lord, as prisoners must;

But I shall live, my lord, to give them thanks

That were the cause of my imprisonment.

RICHARD DUKE OF GLOUCESTER

No doubt, no doubt; and so shall Clarence too,

For they that were your enemies are his,                    130

And have prevailed as much on him as you.

HASTINGS

More pity that the eagle should be mewed

While kites and buzzards prey at liberty.

Q:

116.1 *with . . . guard*] ROWE (*subs.*); *not in* Q1, F      121 Hastings] hastings

F:

124 the] this (*from* Q3)      132 eagle] Eagles      133 While] Whiles      prey] play

The quibbling sense 'tell lies on your behalf' is to the point in that he is lying *to*
Clarence.

116 **have . . . perforce** Compare proverbial
'Patience perforce' (Dent P111).

117–20 **Go . . . hands** For Richard's alleged
responsibility for Clarence's death, see
Appendix E, Passage 1.

119–20 **That . . . hands** There are ironized
connotations of religious sacrifice. Compare the Holy Communion service, 'And
here we offer and present unto thee, O

Lord, ourselves, our souls and bodies, to
be a reasonable, holy, and lively sacrifice
unto thee' (*Common Prayer*, p. 264).
Hence Richard's plural *our*.

121 **new-delivered** i.e. newly released from
prison (but an ironic parallel with 'send
thy soul to heaven', l. 119, foreshadows
Hastings's fate at Richard's hands)

132 **eagle** 'F has "Eagles" which might reasonably refer to Clarence and Hastings,
but Clarence is more properly described
as a royal bird than Hastings, and only
Clarence is now in prison' (Davison).

RICHARD DUKE OF GLOUCESTER   What news abroad?

HASTINGS

No news so bad abroad as this at home:                    135
The King is sickly, weak and melancholy,
And his physicians fear him mightily.

RICHARD DUKE OF GLOUCESTER

Now by Saint Paul, this news is bad indeed.
O, he hath kept an evil diet long,
And overmuch consumed his royal person.                    140
'Tis very grievous to be thought upon.
What, is he in his bed?

HASTINGS                          He is.

RICHARD DUKE OF GLOUCESTER

Go you before, and I will follow you.        *Exit Hastings*
He cannot live, I hope, and must not die
Till George be packed with post-haste up to heaven.        145
I'll in, to urge his hatred more to Clarence
With lies well steeled with weighty arguments;
And if I fail not in my deep intent,
Clarence hath not another day to live;
Which done, God take King Edward to his mercy              150
And leave the world for me to bustle in,
For then I'll marry Warwick's youngest daughter—
What though I killed her husband and her father?

Q:
145 post-haste] COLLIER 1853;  post horse QI, F

F:
138 Paul, this] Iohn, that     142 What,] Where ‸ (*unpunctuated in* QI)

134–42 **RICHARD . . . He is** As Hastings has
just been released from prison, it is odd
that Richard should be the questioner
and Hastings the one knowing the court
news. But ll. 138–41 are very much in
Richard's idiom, with his characteristic
oath by St Paul and other signs of pretended piety. Richard is probably playing
the worldly-innocent.

134 **abroad** at large, around. Hastings jokingly understands 'from other countries'.

137 **fear him** fear for him

138 **by Saint Paul** See note to 1.2.34.

139 **evil** Both 'damaging' and 'wicked' (see
next note).

139 **diet** Probably in the wider obsolete sense
'lifestyle', so a glance at the King's sexual excesses.

147 **steeled** edged with steel

152 **Warwick's youngest daughter** i.e. Lady
Anne

153 **I . . . father** 'Her husband' is Prince
Edward of Lancaster, Henry VI's son;
'her father' Henry VI as Anne's father-
in-law. Holinshed relates that Clarence,
Richard, Dorset, and Hastings suddenly
murdered the captured Prince Edward on
the prompting of Edward IV (p. 320; compare *Richard Duke of York* 5.5.11–40.1),
and that, 'as the constant fame ran',

The readiest way to make the wench amends
Is to become her husband and her father,                   155
The which will I—not all so much for love,
As for another secret close intent
By marrying her which I must reach unto.
But yet I run before my horse to market:
Clarence still breathes, Edward still lives and reigns.     160
When they are gone, then must I count my gains.

                                              *Exit*

[1.2]   *Enter Lady Anne in mourning, with [Servants]*
        *bearing the [open] hearse of Harry the Sixth, and*
        *[two] Gentlemen bearing halberds to guard it*

Q:

  1.2.0.1–2 *Enter . . . Sixth] Enter Lady Anne with the hearse of Harry the 6.*   0.1 *in mourning]*
*not in* Q. *Compare* F.   0.1–2 *[Servants] bearing]* This edition; *not in* Q1, F   0.2 *open]* CAPELL;
*not in* Q1, F   0.3 *[two] . . . halberds] Halberds* F; *Gentlemen bearing Halberds* CAPELL; *not in* Q1

F:

  1.2.0.1–2 *Enter . . . Sixth] Enter the Coarse of Henrie the sixt with Halberds to guard it,* | *Lady
Anne being the Mourner.*

Richard 'murdered the said King Henry with a dagger' in the Tower (p. 324; *Richard Duke of York* 5.6). Shakespeare gives Richard primary responsibility for Edward's murder (but see 1.4.186–8, where Clarence is similarly accused). The Prince's marriage to Anne, and so her mourning role as Henry's daughter, are also Shakespeare's invention, though the couple were betrothed. Abruption of family relationships and murder of the young echo throughout the play.

154  **wench** Inappropriate as reference to an aristocrat. An instance of Richard's demotic diction.
155  **and her father** i.e. the equivalent of her prospective father-in-law Henry VI as king
157  **secret close intent** 'Thus Shakespeare palms off on the audience a highly effective scene [1.2] which "does not advance the action, i.e., the career of Richard, in the least"' (Wilson, quoting C. H. Herford's edition of 1900).
159  **But yet** Richard checks his train of thought, perhaps after teasing the audience into supposing that he is about to divulge his 'intent'.
     **run . . . market** i.e. count my chickens

before they're hatched (proverbial: Dent M649)
160–1  **Clarence . . . gains** The couplet might pick up from the previous line, implying that Clarence and Edward are livestock to be sold at market for slaughter.
161.1  *Exit* In Cibber's adaptation Richard retired but remained on stage for the procession and Anne's speech, a tradition that survived the restoration of Shakespeare's text. But the exit allows the unexpected and aggressive entry after 1.2.30.
1.2  In the figurative background is St Paul's Cathedral. 'The dead corpse . . . was conveyed with bills and glaives [halberds] pompously, if you will call that a funeral pomp, from the Tower to the church of St Paul, and there laid on a bier or coffin bare-faced—the same in presence of the beholders did bleed—where it rested the space of one whole day. From thence he was carried to the Blackfriars, and bled there likewise, and on the next day after it was conveyed in a boat, without priest or clerk, torch or taper, singing or saying, unto the monastery of Chertsey, distant from London fifteen miles, and there was it first buried' (Holinshed, p. 324). Richard's seduction of Anne is not

LADY ANNE

Set down, set down your honourable load,
If honour may be shrouded in a hearse,
Whilst I a while obsequiously lament
Th'untimely fall of virtuous Lancaster.
    *The hearse is set down*
Poor key-cold figure of a holy king,             5
Pale ashes of the house of Lancaster,
Thou bloodless remnant of that royal blood,
Be it lawful that I invocate thy ghost
To hear the lamentations of poor Anne,
Wife to thy Edward, to thy slaughtered son    10
Stabbed by the selfsame hands that made these holes.
Lo, in those windows that let forth thy life

Q:

1 load] F; lo Q1; lord Q2    4 Th'untimely] F; The vntimely Q1    4.1 *The hearse is set down*]
ECCLES; *not in* Q1, F

F:

1 LADY ANNE] *Anne*.    11 hands . . . holes] hand . . . wounds    12 those] these

recorded in the chronicles, but is presented in *Ricardus Tertius*.
0.1–3 **with . . . it** Q1 specifies no attendants;
F merely has '*Halberts*'. Where Q1 describes the coffin-bearer who speaks at
l. 211 as a Servant, F has him a Gentleman. It is particularly clear in Q1 that
King Henry's funeral procession is without official pomp and ceremony—in contrast with many productions (Charles
Kean's procession included 72 people,
Olivier's had priests and Gregorian
chant). A halberdier was a member of a
civic guard. He would not, historically,
have been a gentleman, though in both
Q1 and F the Gentleman who speaks at
l. 36 nonetheless evidently does bear a
halberd. Davison notes that the Company
of Gentlemen at Arms (formed in 1539)
bore partisans, which were similar to halberds. The Gentleman is presumably one
of those Anne addresses as Tressill and
Berkeley at l. 207. These two men and
the coffin-bearers are all the attendants
the scene requires.
0.2 *hearse* coffin

2 **shrouded** hidden (and perhaps literally
'wrapped in a shroud', referring to the
corpse itself)
3 **obsequiously** as a mark of mourning

4 **Lancaster** i.e. Henry, as head of the
house of Lancaster. This way of naming
him associates Henry with the fortunes of
the dynasty.
5 **key-cold** A proverbial image. Keys would
have become cold because kept in or near
an outside door, and stayed cold because
they were large.
  **figure** model, type; effigy
6 **ashes** mortal remains (as of a saint). Also
suggests the 'house' as a building that
has been burned down (and perhaps suggests a saintly relic).
7 **Thou** See note to l. 44.
8 **Be . . . ghost** In Protestant England it was
not acceptable to invocate a saint (Articles of Religion, 22). *OED* recognizes no
use of *invocate* or *invoke* without connotations of prayer before 1602, when John
Marston used the latter to mean 'conjure
spirits of the dead', but Anne's expression suggests this sense too. Anne addresses Protestant hostilities to black
magic and Catholic ritual.
11 **hands** Compare F's 'hand'. Q1 leaves it
as yet ambiguous as to whether Anne
thinks Richard acted alone, or with King
Edward and Clarence, as the event
was staged in *Richard Duke of York*
(5.5.38–40.1).
  **holes** Compared with F's 'wounds', Q1's

I pour the helpless balm of my poor eyes.
Cursed be the hand that made these fatal holes,
Cursed be the heart that had the heart to do it.                 15
More direful hap betide that hated wretch
That makes us wretched by the death of thee
Than I can wish to adders, spiders, toads,
Or any creeping venomed thing that lives.
If ever he have child, abortive be it,                           20
Prodigious, and untimely brought to light,
Whose ugly and unnatural aspect
May fright the hopeful mother at the view.
If ever he have wife, let her be made
As miserable by the death of him                                 25
As I am made by my poor lord and thee.—

F:
14 Cursed . . . fatal holes] O cursed . . . holes    15 Cursed be] Cursed    it.] it: | Cnrsed the
Blood, that let this blood from hence:    18 adders] Wolues, to    23 view.] view, | And that be
Heyre to his vnhappinesse.    25–6 As . . . As] More . . . Then    26 poor] young

'holes' leads to a more strongly patterned
echo in l. 14, but the presence of 'fatal' at
l. 14, in Q1 but not F, prevents the repetition from becoming mechanical.

12–13 **Lo . . . eyes** Echoes the meditative practice, enacted in the Corpus Christi plays, of
contemplating the wounds of Christ.

12 **those windows** i.e. the wounds. A soul
would be thought to leave a house
through a window.

13 **helpless balm** Balm is both a preparation
for anointing the dead and a healing ointment; *helpless*, 'unavailing', suggests the
latter.

15 **do it** See F's extra line. Q1's omission
could be deliberate alteration or compositorial error. The position of F's line sheds
a little light. Logically, as Alice Walker
noted (p. 32) and Wilson accepted, the
words would be better placed before l. 15,
and it would be quite easy for an annotator's addition to have been misinserted
by the Folio compositor. However, the
correlation of 'hand' and 'heart' is itself
strong rhetorically. Perhaps, then, as F's
line convincingly fits neither position,
l. 15 was supplied in the Quarto text as a
replacement for it. In this case F should

have reverted to the original by deleting
l. 15 as well as making the insertion.

18 **adders** F instead reads 'Wolues, to'. The
variant is well explained as authorial revision from F to Q1, especially as F recalls
*Richard Duke of York* 1.4.112–13 ('wolves
of France, | Whose tongue more poisons
than the adder's tooth') and Q1 anticipates *Cymbeline* 4.2.92, 'Were it toad or
adder, spider', referring to the 'double
villain' Cloten's name).

    **spiders, toads** Both considered poisonous,
as adders indeed are.

19 **any creeping venomed thing** Compare
Genesis 1: 26: 'every creeping thing that
creepeth upon the earth' (Bishops' Bible).
'Venomed' strengthens the anticipation
of the serpent that tempted Eve and was
subsequently cursed by God.

20 **abortive** born prematurely and deformed

21 **Prodigious** born deformed, and so por-
tending evil. The play's single use of the
term glances only indirectly at Richard.
Compare 'monstrous', 3.4.75.

22 **aspect** appearance (stressed on the second syllable)

23 **view.** See F's extra line.

25 **death** Wilson unnecessarily emends to
'life', on the basis of 4.1.71–2.

Come now towards Chertsey with your holy load,
Taken from Paul's to be interrèd there;
   *[The bearers lift the hearse]*
And still as you are weary of the weight
Rest you, whiles I lament King Henry's corpse.         30
   *Enter Richard Duke of Gloucester*

RICHARD DUKE OF GLOUCESTER

Stay, you that bear the corpse, and set it down.

LADY ANNE

What black magician conjures up this fiend,
To stop devoted charitable deeds?

RICHARD DUKE OF GLOUCESTER

Villains, set down the corpse, or, by Saint Paul,
I'll make a corpse of him that disobeys.         35

GENTLEMAN

My lord, stand back and let the coffin pass.

RICHARD DUKE OF GLOUCESTER

Unmannered dog, stand thou when I command.
Advance thy halberd higher than my breast,
Or, by Saint Paul, I'll strike thee to my foot
And spurn upon thee, beggar, for thy boldness.    40
   *The hearse is set down*

---

Q:
28.1 *The . . . hearse*] CAPELL (*subs., after l.* 30); *not in* Q1, F   30.1 *Richard Duke of Gloucester*]
*Glocester*   32 LADY ANNE] *La. Similarly henceforward through the rest of the scene. Compare F.*
34 Villains] F; Villaine Q1   38 halberd] halbert   40.1 *The hearse is set down*] CAPELL (*subs.*);
*not in* Q1, F

F:
29 the] this   32 LADY ANNE] *La.* Q1; *An.* F. *Similarly through the rest of the scene.*   37 stand]
Stand'st

29 **still as** whenever. *OED*'s one example of
the idiom is dated 'a 1656'.
33 **devoted** holy
34 **by Saint Paul** In Q1 this is established at
1.1.138 as a characteristic trait of
Richard's speech. The oath 'by St Paul'
is sworn by no other character in Shakespeare, but in More Richard uses it in the
divided councils episode (hence in the
play at 3.4.81). Shakespeare may have
been prompted to name Paul in 1.2 at
least partly because Henry's body has
just been 'Taken from Paul's' (l. 28). The
present reference, by opposing the saint
to a 'black magician', may perhaps also
recall his performance of miracles at Eph-
esus including the exorcism of evil spirits
(Acts 19: 11–17), which led 'Many also of
them which used curious arts' (magic) to
abandon their practices and burn their
books.
37 **stand thou** *you* stop. F's 'Stand'st thou'
is a question: 'Do you make a stand?' The
action will vary accordingly.
38 **Advance** raise
40 **spurn upon thee** kick you contemptuously

LADY ANNE (*to Gentlemen and Servants*)

  What, do you tremble, are you all afraid?

  Alas, I blame you not, for you are mortal,

  And mortal eyes cannot endure the devil.—

  Avaunt, thou dreadful minister of hell.

  Thou hadst but power over his mortal body;      45

  His soul thou canst not have, therefore be gone.

RICHARD DUKE OF GLOUCESTER

  Sweet saint, for charity be not so curst.

LADY ANNE

  Foul devil, for God's sake, hence, and trouble us not,

  For thou hast made the happy earth thy hell:

  Filled it with cursing cries and deep exclaims.      50

  If thou delight to view thy heinous deeds,

  Behold this pattern of thy butcheries.

  O gentlemen, see, see dead Henry's wounds

  Open their congealed mouths and bleed afresh.

  Blush, blush, thou lump of foul deformity,      55

---

44 **Avaunt** In Shakespeare a particularly forceful way of saying 'Be gone!', often paired with an insult, and at *Macbeth* 3.4.92 addressed to a ghost. It would be dramatically effective for Anne to hold a cross or bible between herself and Richard to repel him as a devil. Such a property would explain why she claims to have a strength that she says mortals don't have, and would prompt Richard's response, 'Sweet saint'.

**thou** Amongst social equals 'thou' could be used as a mark of affection, as perhaps in Anne's address to Henry's corpse. In Anne's speeches to Richard it is usually a mark of contempt, though in this passage it is also right for addressing him as a 'minister of hell', as 'thou' was addressed to any supernatural being. This explanation might be extended to the corpse of Henry and his invocated ghost too. Variation between 'you' and 'thou' in Richard's speeches to Anne suggests that he flexes the social codes of address.

45–6 **Thou . . . have** 'Fear ye not them which kill the body but are not able to kill the soul; but rather fear him which is able to destroy both soul and body in hell' (Matthew 10: 28). If Richard is a 'minister of hell', he has come for Anne's soul, not Henry's.

47 **Sweet . . . curst** Implies 'don't neglect sweetness and charity as aspects of your saintliness by assuming a fervour that is in fact both shrewish ("curst", thus Q1) and damnable (cursed)'. Richard outbids Anne's scriptural reference by appealing to the greatest Christian virtue, charitable love, turning the object of 'charity' from Henry (l. 33) to himself, and the object of saintly worship from Henry to her.

48 **devil** (pronounced as one syllable)

50 **cursing** Picks up from 'cursed', l. 47.
**exclaims** outcries

52 **pattern** typifying example

53–4 **dead . . . afresh** Bleeding could have been visibly staged by the actor playing the corpse using a bladder of pig's blood. In More, Richard is not mentioned as present when the corpse bled (see headnote to scene). It was believed that a murdered body would bleed afresh in the presence of the murderer. There may be a recollection of a recently publicized case in point, where the narrator, like Anne, suggests that the murderer, like Richard, lacked the grace to blush: 'the murderer . . . being brought before the dead bodies of the children . . . the wounds began to bleed afresh'. Then 'the bodies of the children . . . suddenly received their former colour of blood, and had such a lively countenance flushing in their faces as if they had been children lying asleep,

For 'tis thy presence that exhales this blood
From cold and empty veins where no blood dwells.
Thy deed, inhuman and unnatural,
Provokes this deluge most unnatural.
O God, which this blood mad'st, revenge his death.                    60
O earth, which this blood drink'st, revenge his death.
Either heav'n with lightning strike the murd'rer dead,
Or earth gape open wide and eat him quick,
As thou dost swallow up this good king's blood
Which his hell-governed arm hath butcherèd.                           65

RICHARD DUKE OF GLOUCESTER

Lady, you know no rules of charity,
Which renders good for bad, blessings for curses.

LADY ANNE

Villain, thou knowest no law of God nor man.
No beast so fierce but knows some touch of pity.

RICHARD DUKE OF GLOUCESTER

But I know none—and therefore am no beast.                           70

Q:
58 inhuman] inhumane    60 mad'st] F; madest Q1    62 heav'n . . . murd'rer] F; heauen
. . . murtherer Q1

F:
58 deed] Deeds    68 no] nor

which indeed blushed on the murderers,
when they wanted grace to blush and be
ashamed of their own wickedness'
(*Sundry Strange and Inhuman Murders
Lately Committed* (1591), sig. A4). The
pamphlet's account of infanticide might
obtusely connect the killing of Henry
with that of the two young princes. The
bleeding may have also suggested comparison with Christ. Blood flows visibly
from the wound in Christ's side in
the Chester Mystery Cycle 'Judgement',
'Tunc emittet sanguinem de latere eius':
ed. R. M. Lumiansky and David Mills
(1974), l. 428.1.

54 **congealed** Stressed on the first syllable
(Cercignani, p. 35). Taylor, emending
'Open' to Ope', queries Cercignani, but
stress on prefixes such as 'con-' is common in Shakespeare.

55 **Blush . . . deformity** Richard's physical
appearance and moral being should
make him blush. Moreover, as a formless
lump that has not been given human
shape, he is as incapable of blushing as

lifeless clay—except by a miracle corresponding to the flow of blood in Henry's
corpse.

56 **exhales** draws out
58–9 **unnatural . . . unnatural** i.e. cruel
. . . miraculous. The repetition is explained by the shift in sense.
59 **deluge** The overstatement can be understood as a providential allusion to the
Flood in Genesis 6–9, a punishment of
'the wickedness of man'.
62 **Either** (one syllable)
63–4 **earth . . . blood** Recalls Numbers
16: 30: 'if . . . the earth open her mouth
and swallow them up . . . and they go
down quick [i.e. alive] into the pit, then
ye shall understand that these men have
provoked the Lord'.
66–7 **you . . . curses** The Christian precepts,
as for instance in Matthew 5: 44, 'Bless
them that curse you . . . ', and Romans
12: 14, 'Not rendering evil for evil . . . ',
in contrast with Anne's appeal to the
*lex talionis* of Moses.

LADY ANNE

O wonderful when devils tell the truth!

RICHARD DUKE OF GLOUCESTER

More wonderful when angels are so angry.

Vouchsafe, divine perfection of a woman,

Of these supposèd evils to give me leave

By circumstance but to acquit myself.                    75

LADY ANNE

Vouchsafe, diffused infection of a man,

For these known evils but to give me leave

By circumstance to curse thy cursèd self.

RICHARD DUKE OF GLOUCESTER

Fairer than tongue can name thee, let me have

Some patient leisure to excuse myself.                   80

LADY ANNE

Fouler than heart can think thee, thou canst make

No excuse current but to hang thyself.

RICHARD DUKE OF GLOUCESTER

By such despair I should accuse myself.

LADY ANNE

And by despairing shouldst thou stand excused,

Q:
71 truth] troth    72 angry.] ~₍ₐ₎

F:
74 evils] Crimes    76 a man] man    77 For] Of    84 shouldst] shalt

71 **O . . . truth** Proverbially, the devil sometimes tells the truth (Dent D266); i.e. he
habitually lies but tells the truth when it
suits him. Richard has done so by admitting he knows no pity so as to prove that
he is 'no beast'. Anne turns this to show
that he is no man either, but a devil.

72 **More . . . angry** Echoes the proverb
'Enough to anger a saint'.

73 **Vouchsafe . . . woman** This further invocation of Anne as a saint brings Richard
closer still to the figures of Petrarchan
courtship. Richard's flattery succeeds not
simply in itself but through antagonistic
engagement; hence the carefully patterned language.

74 **evils** one syllable. Compared with F's
'Crimes', Q1 gives a stronger contrast between 'supposèd evils' and the 'known
evils' of l. 77.

75 **circumstance** point-by-point explanation

76 **diffused** widespread (as of a disease); perhaps also 'verbose', picking up from 'By

circumstance'.

76 **infection** The sense 'disease' combines
with an implied opposite to 'perfection'.

78 **to curse** Wilson, following J. Spedding's
conjecture in 'On the Quarto and Folio of
*Richard III*', *New Shakspere Society Transac-
tions* (1875–6), emends to 't'accuse', continuing the legal imagery. But 'curse' can
be judicial in the context of an ecclesiastical
court, which might pronounce a curse of
excommunication as a punishment. The
play on slightly but significantly different
senses of a word in 'curse thy cursèd self' is
characteristic of the play's language.

80 **leisure . . . myself** opportunity to uphold
my innocence

81–2 **thou . . . thyself** i.e. the only true excuse you can make for yourself is to hang
yourself

82 **current** authentic, acceptable

83 **despair** sense of being deprived of God's
mercy. A serious sin in itself, and a condition readily leading to suicide.

For doing worthy vengeance on thyself                                85
Which didst unworthy slaughter upon others.
RICHARD DUKE OF GLOUCESTER
  Say that I slew them not.
LADY ANNE                        Why then they are not dead.
  But dead they are, and, devilish slave, by thee.
RICHARD DUKE OF GLOUCESTER
  I did not kill your husband.
LADY ANNE                        Why then he is alive.
RICHARD DUKE OF GLOUCESTER
  Nay, he is dead, and slain by Edward's hand.              90
LADY ANNE
  In thy foul throat thou liest. Queen Margaret saw
  Thy bloody falchion smoking in his blood,
  The which thou once didst bend against her breast,
  But that thy brothers beat aside the point.
RICHARD DUKE OF GLOUCESTER
  I was provokèd by her sland'rous tongue,                  95
  Which laid their guilt upon my guiltless shoulders.
LADY ANNE
  Thou wast provokèd by thy bloody mind,
  Which never dreamed on aught but butcheries.
  Didst thou not kill this king?
RICHARD DUKE OF GLOUCESTER   I grant, yea.
LADY ANNE
  Dost grant me, hedgehog? Then God grant me too          100

Q:
95 sland'rous] F; slaunderous Q1

F:
86 Which] That     87 Why . . . dead] Then say they were not slaine     90 hand] hands
92 bloody] murd'rous (*altering* Q3 'bloodly')     96 Which] That     98 Which never dreamed]
That neuer dream'st     99 yea] yea Q1; yee Q3, F (ye)

86 **unworthy** Both 'despicable' and 'unjustified'.
90 **by Edward's hand** See note to I.1.153.
91 **In . . . liest** (proverbial)
91–6 **Queen . . . shoulders** The incident is staged in *Richard Duke of York* 5.5.41–3, but is not in Holinshed.
92 **falchion** sword
  **smoking** steaming
93 **once** at once
99 **grant, yea** Honigmann's 'grant ye, yea'

combines Q1 and Q3/F. But Richard's clipped and unmetrical reply in Q1 is effective in itself. As 'yee' and 'ye' were spellings of 'yea', it is questionable whether the early texts present a true variant.
100 **hedgehog** Probably alludes to Richard's crest, the white boar. The alteration of *hog* to *hedgehog* might be because (a) the animal appears hump-backed, (b) *hedge* can be a disparaging prefix for a common or inferior creature.

Thou mayst be damnèd for that wicked deed.

O, he was gentle, mild, and virtuous.

RICHARD DUKE OF GLOUCESTER

The fitter for the King of Heaven that hath him.

LADY ANNE

He is in heaven, where thou shalt never come.

RICHARD DUKE OF GLOUCESTER

Let him thank me that holp to send him thither,                    105

For he was fitter for that place than earth.

LADY ANNE

And thou unfit for any place but hell.

RICHARD DUKE OF GLOUCESTER

Yes, one place else, if you will hear me name it.

LADY ANNE

Some dungeon.

RICHARD DUKE OF GLOUCESTER   Your bedchamber.

LADY ANNE

Ill rest betide the chamber where thou liest.                      110

RICHARD DUKE OF GLOUCESTER

So will it, madam, till I lie with you.

LADY ANNE

I hope so.

RICHARD DUKE OF GLOUCESTER

        I know so. But, gentle Lady Anne,

To leave this keen encounter of our wits

And fall somewhat into a slower method:

Q:
101 damnèd] Q3, F;  damnd Q1

F:
103 fitter] better    114 somewhat] something

103–4 **The . . . come** Probably recollects from performance lines in *Leir*: 'You are fitter for the King of Heaven' (F3, l. 1604) and 'to send us both to heaven, | Where, as I think, you never mean to come' (I4, ll. 2596–7).

105 **holp** helped

107–9 **And . . . bedchamber** Brings together symbolic locations of religion (hell), political power (the dungeon) and sex (the bedchamber). Hell could be pictured as a dungeon, and both *chamber* and *hell* can allude to the vagina. Compare *chamber* at I.I.12, the maternal womb as hell at 4.4.44–5, and as burial place at 4.4.343. The negativized and grotesquely abstracted woman's body varies, but the male body is usually Richard's.

110 **betide** befall

112 **I hope so** Assumes that she will never lie with him. Complicated by (a) dramatic irony (she *will* choose to lie with him), (b) unintended ambiguity ('I hope I will lie with you').

113–14 **To . . . method** Perhaps 'a ruse designed to lull his opponent into a false sense of security' (Kaegi, p. 95).

Is not the causer of the timeless deaths                      115
Of these Plantagenets, Henry and Edward,
As blameful as the executioner?

LADY ANNE

Thou art the cause, of most accursed effect.

RICHARD DUKE OF GLOUCESTER

Your beauty was the cause of that effect,
Your beauty, which did haunt me in my sleep            120
To undertake the death of all the world
So I might rest one hour in your sweet bosom.

LADY ANNE

If I thought that, I tell thee, homicide,
These nails should rend that beauty from my cheeks.

RICHARD DUKE OF GLOUCESTER

These eyes could never endure sweet beauty's wrack;    125
You should not blemish it if I stood by.
As all the world is cheerèd by the sun,
So I by that; it is my day, my life.

LADY ANNE

Black night o'ershade thy day, and death thy life.

RICHARD DUKE OF GLOUCESTER

Curse not thyself, fair creature, thou art both.         130

LADY ANNE

I would I were, to be revenged on thee.

RICHARD DUKE OF GLOUCESTER

It is a quarrel most unnatural
To be revenged on him that loveth you.

---

**Q:**

118 of most] This edition; and most Q1, F; of that most EDWARDS *conj.*; of that WILSON (*conj.* Walker)    126 it] F; them Q1    127 sun] sonne    129 o'ershade] F; ouershade Q1

**F:**

118 art] was't    120 which] that    122 rest] liue    124 rend] rent    125 never endure sweet] not endure yᵗ    133 you] thee

115 **timeless** untimely
117 **executioner** In two senses, both novel: (a) 'perpetrator', in contrast with *causer*, l. 115 (*OED*'s earliest example 1598); (b) 'one who puts another to death' (for which *OED* cites l. 171 as the earliest example).
118 **of** Q1/F read 'and', which prompts commentators to note that the necessary

sense 'agent' is not conveyed by *effect*.
125 **never** Pronounced 'ne'er'.
   **wrack** destruction
127–8 **As . . . life** 'A sonneteer's cliché' (Hammond, citing examples from Sidney). Compare 1.1.1–2 and note.
131 **I would I were** i.e. 'day' and 'life' as overshaded in l. 129. Richard does not pick up on the implication.

LADY ANNE

  It is a quarrel just and reasonable

  To be revenged on him that slew my husband.      135

RICHARD DUKE OF GLOUCESTER

  He that bereft thee, lady, of thy husband

  Did it to help thee to a better husband.

LADY ANNE

  His better doth not breathe upon the earth.

RICHARD DUKE OF GLOUCESTER

  Go to; he lives that loves you better than he could.

LADY ANNE

  Name him.

RICHARD DUKE OF GLOUCESTER  Plantagenet.

LADY ANNE                      Why, that was he.    140

RICHARD DUKE OF GLOUCESTER

  The selfsame name, but one of better nature.

LADY ANNE

  Where is he?

RICHARD DUKE OF GLOUCESTER  Here.

    *She spitteth at him*

                   Why dost thou spit at me?

LADY ANNE

  Would it were mortal poison for thy sake.

RICHARD DUKE OF GLOUCESTER

  Never came poison from so sweet a place.

LADY ANNE

  Never hung poison on a fouler toad.           145

  Out of my sight, thou dost infect my eyes.

RICHARD DUKE OF GLOUCESTER

  Thine eyes, sweet lady, have infected mine.

Q:
142 *She spitteth at him*] *position as in* Q2, F; *right of* 'Where is he' *in* Q1

F:
135 slew] kill'd    139 Go to; he . . . you] He . . . thee    142 *She spitteth*] *Spits*    146 my eyes] mine eyes

140 **Plantagenet** The surname is strongly associated with Richard's father Richard Duke of York in the play of that name, but owing to their shared ancestry it could be applied to Yorkists and Lancastrians alike. Richard tendentiously puts (or 'plants') himself in equivalence with Anne's Lancastrian husband and father-in-law (either of whom might be indicated in Anne's reply).

143 **mortal poison** In contrast with speech, as figurative poison, in the proverb 'to spit one's venom' (Dent V28).

147 **Thine . . . mine** Behind the Petrarchan trope lies the proverb that the gaze of a sore eye could infect a sound one (Dent E246).

LADY ANNE

Would they were basilisks to strike thee dead.

RICHARD DUKE OF GLOUCESTER

I would they were, that I might die at once,

For now they kill me with a living death.                    150

Those eyes of thine from mine have drawn salt tears,

Shamed their aspect with store of childish drops.

I never sued to friend nor enemy—

My tongue could never learn sweet soothing words—

But now thy beauty is proposed my fee                        155

My proud heart sues and prompts my tongue to speak.

  *She looks scornfully at him*

Teach not thy lips such scorn, for they were made

For kissing, lady, not for such contempt.

If thy revengeful heart cannot forgive,

Lo, here I lend thee this sharp-pointed sword,               160

  [*He kneels and presents her with his sword*]

Which if thou please to hide in this true bosom

And let the soul forth that adoreth thee,

I lay it naked to the deadly stroke

And humbly beg the death upon my knee.

  *He lays his breast open. She offers at it with his sword*

---

Q:

156.1 *She . . . him*] F;  *not in* Q1      160.1 *He . . . sword*] CAPELL (*subs.*);  *not in* Q1, F      164.1 *He . . . sword*] F (*omitting* 'it');  *not in* Q1

F:

152 aspect] Aspects      drops.] F *adds* 12 *lines. See Appendix A, Passage A.*      154 soothing words] smoothing word      157 lips . . . they were] lip . . . it was      161 bosom] brest

148 **basilisks** Legendary reptiles whose look was proverbially supposed to be fatal (Dent B99.1).

152 **aspect** Both 'appearance' and 'glance'; stressed on the second syllable.
  **drops** F here has a passage describing the deaths of young Rutland and Richard's father as occasions when his 'manly eyes did scorn an humble tear'. The lines add to the historical back-ground. They also make Richard more persuasive and apparently sincere. Cibber, and later Phelps, followed Q1's cut.

154 **soothing** flattering

155 **fee** Richard imagines himself as a lawyer.

159–68 **If . . . on** Compare Seneca, *Hercules Oetaeus*, 'My breast lies bare unto thy hand. Strike; I thy guilt forgive', and

'Th'offence I did was meant in love' (ll. 999–1001, 1015; *Ten Tragedies*, Dd 5ᵛ).

164 **the death** formal sentence of death

164.1–171 *He . . . executioner* Anne's change of heart is the turning-point of the scene. The episode has been variously augmented in the theatre. Cibber added after l. 164.1: 'What shall I say or do? Direct me, heaven. | When stones weep, sure the tears are natural, | And Heaven itself instructs us to forgive | When they do flow from a sincere repentance' (p. 14). Instead of moral reflection from Anne, Sher and Downie enacted 'a continuous piece of erotic violence' with the sword (Hankey, p. 113). My editorial directions suppose that Anne takes literally the alternatives Richard offers at

Nay, do not pause, 'twas I that killed your husband;                165
But 'twas thy beauty that provokèd me.
Nay, now dispatch, 'twas I that killed King Henry;
But 'twas thy heavenly face that set me on.
        *Here she lets fall the sword*
Take up the sword again, or take up me.

LADY ANNE
Arise, dissembler. Though I wish thy death,                170
I will not be the executioner.

RICHARD DUKE OF GLOUCESTER [*rising, and taking up the
sword*]
Then bid me kill myself, and I will do it.

LADY ANNE
I have already.

RICHARD DUKE OF GLOUCESTER  Tush, that was in thy rage.
Speak it again and, even with the word,
That hand which for thy love did kill thy love                175
Shall for thy love kill a far truer love.
To both their deaths shalt thou be accessary.

LADY ANNE  I would I knew thy heart.

Q:
172 *rising*] HAMMOND (*subs.*); *not in* Q1, F    *and taking up the sword*] OXBERRY (*subs.*); *not in* Q1, F

F:
165 'twas . . . husband] For I did kill King *Henrie*    167 killed King Henry] stabb'd yong *Edward*    168.1 *Here she lets fall*] *She fals*    171 the] thy    173 Tush, that] That    175 That] This

l. 169, and that he subsequently picks up
the sword. Neither supposition is entirely
necessary to performance.

164.1 *offers at* makes as to attack

166, 168 **provokèd me . . . set me on** Both
expressions convey an undercurrent of
sexual desire.

168 **heavenly** Compare l. 47 and note.
*Heavenly* is not a mere cliché of courtship:
Richard again transfers the attribute of
saintliness from Henry to her, just as he
transfers Edward's beauty (to which he
returns at ll. 227–32) to her in ll. 165–6.
F's variant wording instead pairs Henry
with 'thy beauty' and Edward with 'thy
Heauenly face'.

169 **Take . . . me** He confounds Anne with
options 'too antithetical' (Kaegi, p. 96).
**take up me** Perhaps a cue for Anne to
take Richard's arms to raise him. Also
'take me into your possession' (with sexual undertow), but this seems not to be

what Anne hears.

171 **executioner** The senses are as at l. 117
(see note). The sense 'perpetrator' is
more prominent with Q1's 'the executioner' than F's 'thy Executioner'.

175–6 **That . . . truer love** Continues
the play between cause ('for thy love')
and perpetration, quibbling between
*love* as emotion and as loved or loving
person.

178–188.1 **I . . . finger** The stichomythic
part-lines of three feet could be arranged
as hexameters if there were an even number of them. The first four lines form two
pairs, as the final words indicate:
*heart/tongue*; *false/true*. Here Anne has
the initiative, though the faltering is apparent and she has already slipped into
Petrarchan diction. Richard's *Say then*
(l. 183) prevents a third pairing. This
interruption coincides with the stage
action of putting up the sword. The final
four lines form strong pairings, but now

RICHARD DUKE OF GLOUCESTER  'Tis figured in my tongue.
LADY ANNE  I fear me both are false.                                    180
RICHARD DUKE OF GLOUCESTER  Then never was man true.
LADY ANNE  Well, well, put up your sword.
RICHARD DUKE OF GLOUCESTER  Say then my peace is made.
        *[He puts up his sword]*
LADY ANNE  That shall you know hereafter.
RICHARD DUKE OF GLOUCESTER  But shall I live in hope?                   185
LADY ANNE  All men I hope live so.
RICHARD DUKE OF GLOUCESTER  Vouchsafe to wear this ring.
LADY ANNE  To take is not to give.
        *[She takes the ring on her finger]*
RICHARD DUKE OF GLOUCESTER
    Look how this ring encompasseth thy finger,
    Even so thy breast encloseth my poor heart.                         190
    Wear both of them, for both of them are thine;
    And if thy poor devoted suppliant may
    But beg one favour at thy gracious hand,
    Thou dost confirm his happiness for ever.
LADY ANNE  What is it?                                                  195
RICHARD DUKE OF GLOUCESTER
    That it would please thee leave these sad designs
    To him that hath more cause to be a mourner,
    And presently repair to Crosby Place,

Q:
183.1 *He puts up his sword*] OXBERRY (*after l.* 186); *not in* Q1, F        188.1 *She . . . finger*] This edition, *following* Johnson (*She puts on the ring.*); *not in* Q1, F

F:
181 was man] Man was (*from* Q3)        184 shall you] shalt thou        187 RICHARD DUKE OF GLOUCES-
TER] Q1 (*Glo.*); *not in* F        188 LADY . . . give.] *not in* F        189 this] my        192 suppliant] Seruant
196 would please thee] may please you        197 more] most        198 Place] House

the initiative lies with Richard. Their
starting-point, 'But shall I live in hope?',
is equivalent to Anne's 'I would I knew
thy heart', and the predicated stage
business with the ring matches that with
the sword. In the modern theatre the
exchange is often given an intense sexual
physicality. The feelings so expressed are
already implicit in the dialogue.

179  **figured in** represented by
182  **Well . . . sword** The change from 'thou'
    to more respectful 'you' suggests that
    Anne's contempt has run its course.
188  **LADY . . . give.** The part-line is in Q1

only; F instead and very unexpectedly
has Anne offering the ring at l. 187.
**To . . . give** Anne denies the symbolic significance of the action. In the Solemniza-
tion of Matrimony, the bride, immediately
before taking the ring, says 'I . . . take
thee . . . to my wedded husband . . . and
thereto I give thee my troth' (*Common
Prayer*, p. 292). Downie's Anne was responding to having the ring forced on her.
189  **Look how** just as
192  **suppliant** Perhaps Richard kneels.
198  **presently** immediately. After the speech's
    deferential opening, Richard now be-
    comes brisk.

Where after I have solemnly interred
At Chertsey monastery this noble king                    200
And wet his grave with my repentant tears,
I will with all expedient duty see you.
For divers unknown reasons, I beseech you
Grant me this boon.

LADY ANNE

With all my heart, and much it joys me too              205
To see you are become so penitent.—
Tressill and Berkeley, go along with me.

RICHARD DUKE OF GLOUCESTER

Bid me farewell.

LADY ANNE                    'Tis more than you deserve.

But since you teach me how to flatter you,
Imagine I have said farewell already.                    210

*Exit with two Gentlemen*

RICHARD DUKE OF GLOUCESTER

Sirs, take up the corpse.

SERVANT                    Towards Chertsey, noble lord?

RICHARD DUKE OF GLOUCESTER

No, to Whitefriars. There attend my coming.

*Exeunt with the hearse all but Gloucester*

Q:
210.1 *with two Gentlemen*] *not in* Q1. *Compare* F.    212.1 *Exeunt . . . all but Gloucester*] *position*
*as in* F; '*Exeunt. manet Gl.*' *right of l.* 213 *in* Q1    *with the hearse*] *not in* Q1. *Compare* F.

F:
210.1 *with two Gentlemen*] *not in* Q1; *two with Anne* F    211 RICHARD . . . *corpse.*] *not in* F    SER-
VANT] Q1 (*Ser.*); *Gent.* F    212.1 *Exeunt . . . Gloucester*] *Exit Coarse*

198 **Crosby Place** Richard's house in London, in Bishopsgate Street. More records
that Richard 'kept his household' and
held one of the 'divided' council meetings
there (Holinshed, p. 379).

202 **expedient duty** dutiful haste
203 **unknown** i.e. that may not be known
by Anne. Wilson comments 'Actually
"unknown" to Shakespeare!'
207 **Tressill and Berkeley** The names, used
only here in the play, resemble those of
minor characters called Trussell and
Berkeley (spelt 'Bartley') in Marlowe's *Edward II* 5.1, where the names refer to historical figures mentioned in the chronicles.
But one cannot safely infer that Marlowe
influenced Shakespeare: (a) Marlowe's

Trussell is not named in dialogue, and (b)
the play had not been published when
Shakespeare wrote *Richard III*.
208 **'Tis** Refers to either prospering (faring
well) or receiving a farewell.
209–10 **But . . . already** An avoidance of
further contact, usually played as a means
for withdrawing or escape.
211 **RICHARD . . . corpse.** F omits. There is
probably a change of F copy from Q6 to
Q3 here. But, as the line heads a page in
both quartos, change of copy does not
readily explain the omission.
212 **Whitefriars** A priory, before Henry VIII's
dissolution. According to More, the corpse
rested not at Whitefriars but at Blackfriars.
Neither Whitefriars nor Chertsey is
mentioned again in the play.

Was ever woman in this humour wooed?
Was ever woman in this humour won?
I'll have her, but I will not keep her long.                215
What, I that killed her husband and his father,
To take her in her heart's extremest hate,
With curses in her mouth, tears in her eyes,
The bleeding witness of her hatred by,
Having God, her conscience, and these bars against me,     220
And I nothing to back my suit at all
But the plain devil and dissembling looks,
And yet to win her, all the world to nothing? Ha?
Hath she forgot already that brave prince
Edward, her lord, whom I some three months since           225
Stabbed in my angry mood at Tewkesbury?
A sweeter and a lovelier gentleman,
Framed in the prodigality of nature,
Young, valiant, wise, and no doubt right royal,
The spacious world cannot again afford.                    230
And will she yet debase her eyes on me,
That cropped the golden prime of this sweet prince
And made her widow to a woeful bed,
On me, whose all not equals Edward's moiety,
On me, that halt, and am unshapen thus?                    235

F:
219 her] my    221 nothing] no Friends    at all] withall (*from* Q3)    231 debase] abase
235 halt . . . unshapen] halts . . . mishapen

213–48 **Was . . . pass** The episode ends as it
    began at the close of 1.1, with Richard
    addressing the audience.
213–14 **Was . . . won** Couplets expressing
    similar sentiments appear also in *Titus*
    2.1.82–3 (Demetrius on Lavinia) and
    *1 Henry VI* 5.5.34–5 (Suffolk on
    Margaret). Richard's apparent surprise
    that for him too the proverb is true that
    'All women may be won' (Dent W681) is
    usually a comic moment. *Humour* is
    'mood', applying to *woman*.
215 **I'll . . . long** In defiance of the pledge in
    the marriage service 'to have and to hold
    from this day forward . . . till death us de-
    part' (*Common Prayer*, p. 292). *Have* also
    has a sexual implication.
220 **Having** Pronounced lightly to count as
    one syllable.
    **bars** obstructions; legal objections suffi-
    cient to thwart a *suit* (l. 221)

221 **nothing** Pronounced 'no thing', with
    the stress on 'thing'.
223 **all . . . nothing** Possibly proverbial
    (Dent W865.1). The idiom is of betting
    odds, as in 'three to one'.
225 **lord** husband
226 **mood** Can mean specifically 'anger'.
    **Tewkesbury** In Gloucestershire; site of
    the battle where the Lancastrians were fi-
    nally defeated. The murder was after the
    battle (see *Richard Duke of York* 5.5).
228 **in . . . nature** when nature was most
    prodigal
229 **royal** noble, munificent
230 **again** The thought has shifted as the
    sentence develops. More logically, l. 227
    might read, 'As sweet and lovely a gentle-
    man'.
232 **cropped . . . prime** As of wheat or a flower
    ripening early (*prime* = 'springtime' as
    well as 'youth') and cropped prematurely.

My dukedom to a beggarly denier,
I do mistake my person all this while.
Upon my life, she finds, although I cannot,
Myself to be a marv'lous proper man.
I'll be at charges for a looking-glass,                          240
And entertain some score or two of tailors
To study fashions to adorn my body.
Since I am crept in favour with my self
I will maintain it with some little cost.
But first I'll turn yon fellow in his grave,                     245
And then return lamenting to my love.
Shine out, fair sun—till I have bought a glass—
That I may see my shadow as I pass.

*Exit*

[1.3]    *Enter Queen, Lord Rivers, Grey [also called Marquis
          Dorset]*

RIVERS
Have patience, madam; there's no doubt his majesty
Will soon recover his accustomed health.
GREY (*to the Queen*)
In that you brook it ill, it makes him worse;

Q:
239 marv'lous] F; merueilous Q1
  1.3.3 it, ill,] ~, ~

F:
241 some] a
  1.3.0.1 *Queen*] *the Queene Mother*    0.1 *Grey*] *and Lord Gray* (*'and' from* Q3)

236 **denier** French copper coin of very small
  value. Probably pronounced as two syllables with the stress on the second.
239 **proper** handsome
240 **be at charges for** spend money on
241 **entertain** employ
243 **in . . . self** The favour comes from Anne,
  on account of ('with') Richard's physical
  'self' (Abbott 193), or self-congratulatorily
  from Richard himself. Q1's printing of
  'my selfe' as two words is here retained.
244 **some little cost** Ironic, even from a duke,
  in relation to 'some score or two of tailors'.
245 **in** into
247–8 **Shine . . . pass** In Jessner's production (and others), a footlight projected a
  huge shadow of Richard on to the rear
  stage wall.
248 **shadow** Compare 1.1.26. The shadow
  is again the sun's, but when Richard has
  bought his mirror he will see his shadow

in the sense 'reflection'.
1.3 A court scene: inferably in the Palace at
  Westminster. The scene is fictitious,
  though it mentions some historical
  events. For Grey, see note to l. 183 and
  Appendix D, Note 3.
0.1 *Queen* Q1 and F are consistent in identifying her without her Christian name, Elizabeth. She continues to be designated as
  Queen even when, after Richard becomes
  king, the title has come to mock her. F here
  uniquely calls her '*the Queene Mother*', as
  does Q1 at 4.1.0.1 ('*Quee. mother*').
  Shakespeare might be responsible for both,
  though here she is logically mother to her
  son(s) by her first husband Grey, whereas
  in 4.1 she is Queen Mother of the legitimate king, Edward. In 4.4 King Richard
  attempts to make her Queen Mother of Elizabeth as his intended second wife.
3 **brook it ill** put up with it badly

Therefore for God's sake entertain good comfort,
And cheer his grace with quick and merry words.                    5

QUEEN

If he were dead, what would betide of me?

RIVERS

No other harm but loss of such a lord.

QUEEN

The loss of such a lord includes all harm.

GREY

The heavens have blessed you with a goodly son
To be your comforter when he is gone.                              10

QUEEN

O, he is young, and his minority
Is put unto the trust of Richard Gloucester,
A man that loves not me nor none of you.

RIVERS

Is it concluded he shall be Protector?

QUEEN

It is determined, not concluded yet;                               15
But so it must be if the King miscarry.

      *Enter Buckingham, Stanley Earl of Derby*

GREY

Here come the Lords of Buckingham and Derby.

BUCKINGHAM (*to the Queen*)

Good time of day unto your royal grace.

STANLEY EARL OF DERBY (*to the Queen*)

God make your majesty joyful as you have been.

---

Q:
5 with] Q2, F;  *not in* Q1   16.1 *Stanley Earl of* ] *not in* Q1, F    19 STANLEY EARL OF DERBY] *Dar.* Q1,
F. *Similarly throughout* 1.3.

F:
5 words] eyes    6 If . . . me? *printed twice* (2 *type-lines across page-break, without second speech-
prefix*)   of] on    7 RIVERS] Q1 (*Ry.*);  *Gray.* F (*catchword and text*)    8 harm] harmes    11 O,]
Ah!    16.1 *Stanley Earl of Derby*] *and Derby*    17 come] comes (*from* Q3)    Lords] Lord

9–10  **son . . . gone** Perhaps a rhyme or near-
    rhyme (Cercignani, p. 112; compare
    *Venus and Adonis* 188–90).
14  **concluded** Presumably 'legally finalized',
    as in a will.
    **Protector** There are ironic possibilities.
    The office-title is described by Richard in
    More as 'Protector of his royal person
    and his realm' (Holinshed, p. 380).
16  **miscarry** meets his death

16.1  **Stanley Earl of Derby** 'Stanley' is
    family-name title, not a forename. His-
    torically, Lord Stanley was made Earl of
    Derby by Henry VII after the Battle of
    Bosworth. In Q1 he is called Derby in the
    dialogue of this scene only, but the stage
    directions and speech-prefixes stipulate
    Derby also in 2.1, 3.4, 4.2, and there-
    after, often in conflict with the dialogue.
    See Appendix D, Note 2.

**QUEEN**

The Countess Richmond, good my lord of Derby, 　　　20
To your good prayers will scarcely say 'Amen'.
Yet, Derby, notwithstanding she's your wife,
And loves not me, be you, good lord, assured
I hate not you for her proud arrogance.

STANLEY EARL OF DERBY

I do beseech you either not believe 　　　25
The envious slanders of her false accusers;
Or, if she be accused in true report,
Bear with her weakness, which I think proceeds
From wayward sickness, and no grounded malice.

RIVERS

Saw you the King today, my lord of Derby? 　　　30

STANLEY EARL OF DERBY

But now the Duke of Buckingham and I
Came forth from visiting his majesty.

QUEEN

What likelihood of his amendment, lords?

BUCKINGHAM

Madam, good hope; his grace speaks cheerfully.

QUEEN

God grant him health. Did you confer with him? 　　　35

BUCKINGHAM

Madam, we did. He desires to make atonement
Betwixt the Duke of Gloucester and your brothers,

Q:
22 Derby, notwithstanding] ~ , ~ ,    32 Came forth] This edition; Came Q1; Are come F
33 What] Q3, F; With Q1

F:
21 prayers] prayer    27 in] on    30 RIVERS] Q1 (*Ry.*); *Qu.* F    32 Came forth] Came Q1; Are come F    36 Madam, we did] I Madam    37–8 Betwixt . . . betwixt] Betweene . . . betweene

20 **The Countess Richmond** Margaret Beaufort, Countess Richmond, was mother by her first husband, Edmund Tudor, to Henry, Earl of Richmond, who, despite his key role in Act 5, is not directly mentioned until 4.1. The Countess's descent from Edward III was the basis of Richmond's claim to the throne, and her 'arrogance' (l. 24) must lie in her (allegedly) advancing this claim.
26 **envious** malicious
29 **wayward** obstinate, hard to cure. The at-

tribute is transferred from the woman to her sickness; in her it would be 'perversely wilful'.
36 **atonement** reconciliation
37 **your brothers** Only one brother, Rivers, is identified in the play, but Shakespeare may have thought of Woodville as a separate figure from Rivers. F lists him separately in the opening direction to 2.1, and later (2.1.65–6) has Richard address separately Lord Rivers, Lord Woodville, and Lord Scales. Like Woodville, Scales

175

And betwixt them and my lord Chamberlain,
And sent to warn them to his royal presence.

QUEEN

Would all were well; but that will never be.                    40
I fear our happiness is at the highest.

    *Enter Richard Duke of Gloucester [and Hastings]*

RICHARD DUKE OF GLOUCESTER

They do me wrong and I will not endure it.
Who are they that complains unto the King
That I, forsooth, am stern and love them not?
By holy Paul, they love his grace but lightly              45
That fill his ears with such dissentious rumours.
Because I cannot flatter and speak fair,
Smile in men's faces, smooth, deceive, and cog,
Duck with French nods and apish courtesy,
I must be held a rancorous enemy.                          50
Cannot a plain man live and think no harm,
But thus his simple truth must be abused
By silken, sly, insinuating jacks?

RIVERS

To whom in all this presence speaks your grace?

---

Q:
41.1 *Richard Duke of Gloucester*] *Glocester*    *and Hastings*] HANMER; *not in* Q1, F

F:
41 highest] height    41.1 *Richard Duke of Gloucester*] *Richard*    43 are they] is it    47 speak]
looke    53 By] With    54 RIVERS] Q1 (*Ry.*); *Grey*. F    whom] who (*altering* Q6 'home')

was an alternative name for Rivers himself. The Queen's 'brothers' are again invoked at 4.4.87 and 137. F has further
references to her 'brothers' at 1.3.67 and
4.4.301. In performance it would produce consistency to refer to one brother
only.

39 **sent to warn** sent messengers to summon
41 **happiness** good fortune, prosperity.
Richard's immediate and disruptive
entrance confirms the Queen's fear.
41.1 ***and Hastings*** Curiously, Hastings
is given an entry in neither Q1 nor F.
He could appear with Buckingham
and Stanley, allowing Richard a solo
entrance. But Richard's bluster makes the
failure to greet Hastings less conspicuous if
he enters with him.

43 **are they that complains** The apparent
lack of agreement was common (Abbott
333) but obsolescent. F 'corrects' to 'is it
that complaines' and Q8 (1634) to 'are
they that complaine'; earlier quartos accepted the idiom.
48 **smooth** flatter
   **cog** fawn, deceive
49 **French** Here, as elsewhere in Shakespeare,
associated with affected courtliness.
   **apish** fantastical; grotesquely imitative
and empty of meaning (like a trained
ape's gestures)
53 **silken** ingratiating, effeminate. And perhaps wearing silk, as a glance at the costume of those on stage.
   **jacks** knaves, scoundrels
54 **presence** company (and also 'royal
presence')

176

RICHARD DUKE OF GLOUCESTER

To thee, that hast nor honesty nor grace.                                55

When have I injured thee, when done thee wrong—

Or thee, or thee, or any of your faction?

A plague upon you all! His royal person—

Whom God preserve better than you would wish—

Cannot be quiet scarce a breathing-while                                60

But you must trouble him with lewd complaints.

QUEEN

Brother of Gloucester, you mistake the matter.

The King, of his own royal disposition,

And not provoked by any suitor else,

Aiming, belike, at your interior hatred,                                65

Which in your outward actions shows itself

Against my kindred, brother, and myself,

Makes him to send, that thereby he may gather

The ground of your ill will, and to remove it.

RICHARD DUKE OF GLOUCESTER

I cannot tell, the world is grown so bad                                70

That wrens make prey where eagles dare not perch.

Since every jack became a gentleman,

There's many a gentle person made a jack.

QUEEN

Come, come, we know your meaning, brother Gloucester.

F:
58 person] Grace    63 of] on    66 Which . . . actions] That . . . action    67 kindred, brother]
Children, Brothers    68–9 thereby . . . it] he may learne the ground ('ground' *altering* Q6
'grounds')

55 **thee** Here distinctly insulting. 'You' would be the expected polite form of address between nobles.
   **nor honesty nor grace** As qualities of the 'plain man' and the man of high birth.
57 **Or thee, or thee** Presumably Grey and Stanley, unless others are present.
60 **a breathing-while** time to get his breath back
61 **lewd** vile
63–5 **The King . . . Aiming** i.e. the fact that the King guesses . . . (Abbott 376)
68–9 **Makes . . . it** F reads 'Makes him to send, that he may learne the ground.', after which a line is probably missing—though not necessarily; Honigmann sim-

ply follows F. Editors who complement the Folio version add, for example, 'Of your ill will, and thereby to remove it' (Pope). Capell emended Q1 to read '. . . and so remove it'. This simplifies the sense, but 'so' recurs in the next line. 'To remove' might be governed by 'may', or the sense could be 'and in order to remove it'.
70 **cannot tell** don't know why
71 **wrens . . . eagles** thought of as the smallest and largest of birds
72 **every . . . gentleman** Proverbial (Dent J3).
73 **made a jack** (a) reduced to the lower classes, (b) made the 'jack' in bowls: the small target bowl that larger bowls knock out of place

177

You envy my advancement and my friends'.                    75
God grant we never may have need of you.

RICHARD DUKE OF GLOUCESTER

Meantime God grants that we have need of you.
Our brother is imprisoned by your means,
Myself disgraced, and the nobility
Held in contempt, whilst many fair promotions          80
Are daily given to ennoble those
That scarce some two days since were worth a noble.

QUEEN

By Him that raised me to this careful height
From that contented hap which I enjoyed,
I never did incense his majesty                              85
Against the Duke of Clarence, but have been
An earnest advocate to plead for him.
My lord, you do me shameful injury
Falsely to draw me in these vile suspects.

RICHARD DUKE OF GLOUCESTER

You may deny that you were not the cause                 90
Of my lord Hastings' late imprisonment?

RIVERS  She may, my lord.

RICHARD DUKE OF GLOUCESTER

She may, Lord Rivers, why, who knows not so?
She may do more, sir, than denying that.
She may help you to many fair preferments,               95
And then deny her aiding hand therein,

Q:
91 imprisonment?] ~ .

F:
77 we] I    80 whilst many fair] while great    90 cause] meane    92 lord.] Lord, for————

75  **my friends'** that of my kindred
77, 78  **we . . . Our** The plural logically needs
to include his brother Edward, the Queen's
husband.
77  **you** The sarcastic echo allows Richard
to shift from 'thou' to 'you'. When Margaret speaks, she will stand out as the
user of 'thou'.
78  **by your means** See note to 1.1.62–5.
79  **disgraced** brought into disfavour; vilified
82  **a noble** A gold coin worth one-third of a
pound (punning on *ennoble* in l. 81).
83–4  **that . . . enjoyed** Based on the proverb,

'Content is more than a kingdom' (Dent
C623).
83  **careful** full of cares
84  **hap** fortune, position in life
89  **draw me in** Either 'figure me in' or 'pull
me into'.
   **suspects** suspicions
90  **deny . . . not** A 'double negative'; the *not*
is redundant in modern English.
93–8  **may** Richard quibbles on the meaning
'justifiably can' and the original sense
'has power to'.
95  **preferments** promotions, advancements

And lay those honours on your high deserts.
What may she not? She may; yea, marry, may she.
RIVERS  What, marry, may she?
RICHARD DUKE OF GLOUCESTER
What, marry, may she? Marry with a king,                           100
A bachelor, a handsome stripling too.
Iwis your grandam had a worser match.
QUEEN
My lord of Gloucester, I have too long borne
Your blunt upbraidings and your bitter scoffs.
By heaven, I will acquaint his majesty                             105
With those gross taunts I often have endured.
I had rather be a country servant maid
Than a great queen with this condition:
To be thus taunted, scorned, and baited at.
        *Enter old Queen Margaret, [at a distance]*
Small joy have I in being England's queen.                         110
MARGARET *[aside]*
And lessened be that small, God I beseech thee.
Thy honour, state, and seat is due to me.
RICHARD DUKE OF GLOUCESTER (*to the Queen*)
What, threat you me with telling of the King?
Tell him and spare not. Look what I have said
I will avouch in presence of the King.                             115

Q:
109.1 *old*] F; *not in* Q1      *at a distance*] CAPELL; *not in* Q1, F      111 MARGARET] F (*Mar.*); *Qu. Mar.* Q1

F:
97 deserts] desert      98 yea] I      101 a] and a      106 With . . . I often] Of . . . that oft I
109 thus taunted, scorned, and baited] so baited, scorn'd, and stormed      111 thee] him
114 Tell . . . said] *not in* F      115 avouch] auouch't

98  **yea** See Appendix D, Note 5.
100  **marry . . . Marry** indeed . . . wed. She
    'may' marry, and her marriage is the
    basis for what she 'may' do.
102  **Iwis** certainly. F's 'I wis' reflects the
    common misunderstanding that *wis* was
    an archaic verb meaning 'know'.
109  **baited at** harassed
109.1  **old Queen Margaret** F's '*old*' and its
    tendency to omit an abbreviated form of
    'Queen' in speech-prefixes strengthen
    the distinction between Margaret and the
    Queen, and are followed in this edition.

109.1, 111  ***at a distance . . . aside*** Margaret is
    usually understood to comment to herself
    on the dialogue, though Davison suggests
    that it might be more dramatic for the others
    to hear but disregard her interjections.
112  **Thy** Margaret uses 'thou' for deprecatory
    asides, insults, prophecies, and curses.
    **state** estate, rank
    **seat** throne
114  **Tell . . . said** F omits the line, maintain-
    ing sense by reading 'auouch't' in the
    next line.
    **Look what** whatever

I dare adventure to be sent to th' Tower.
'Tis time to speak; my pains are quite forgot.

MARGARET [*aside*]

Out, devil, I remember them too well.
Thou slewest my husband Henry in the Tower,
And Edward, my poor son, at Tewkesbury.                    120

RICHARD DUKE OF GLOUCESTER (*to the Queen*)

Ere you were Queen, yea, or your husband King,
I was a pack-horse in his great affairs,
A weeder-out of his proud adversaries,
A liberal rewarder of his friends.
To royalize his blood, I spilt mine own.                    125

MARGARET [*aside*]

Yea, and much better blood than his or thine.

RICHARD DUKE OF GLOUCESTER (*to the Queen*)

In all which time you and your husband Grey
Were factious for the house of Lancaster.—
And, Rivers, so were you. (*To the Queen*) Was not your
    husband
In Margaret's battle at Saint Albans slain?                 130
Let me put in your minds, if yours forget,
What you have been ere now, and what you are;
Withal, what I have been, and what I am.

MARGARET [*aside*]

A murd'rous villain, and so still thou art.

RICHARD DUKE OF GLOUCESTER

Poor Clarence did forsake his father Warwick,              135
Yea, and forswore himself, which Jesu pardon—

Q:
116 I . . . Tower] F; *not in* Q1   118, 126 MARGARET] F;  *Qu. Mar.* Q1   134 MARGARET] *Qu. Ma.*
Q1;  *Q.M.* F. *Similarly to l.* 255.   murd'rous] F;  murtherous Q1

F:
118 I] I do   119 slewest] killd'st   121 yea] I   125 spilt] spent   126 Yea] I   131 yours] you
132 now] this   136 Yea] I

116  I . . . Tower Q1 omits the line, probably          sufferings he has inflicted, and (b) the
by accidental eyeskip because it and the            troubles he took when he previously went
previous line begin alike.                          to the Tower.
**adventure to be** act with risk of being      127–8 **In . . . Lancaster** Accords with the
117  **my pains** (a) his (potential) punishment     chronicles. In contrast, in *Richard Duke of*
(which *he* overlooks); or, more likely,            *York* 3.2.6–7 it is said that Grey died
(b) the efforts he went to for Edward's             fighting for the Yorkists.
sake (which *others* forget); see ll. 121–5.    130  **battle** army
Margaret turns the word to refer to (a) the     135–6  **Poor . . . himself** Clarence's change of

MARGARET [*aside*] Which God revenge.

RICHARD DUKE OF GLOUCESTER

   To fight on Edward's party for the crown;

   And for his meed, poor lord, he is mewed up.

   I would to God my heart were flint, like Edward's,        140

   Or Edward's soft and pitiful, like mine.

   I am too childish-foolish for this world.

MARGARET [*aside*]

   Hie thee to hell for shame, and leave the world,

   Thou cacodemon; there thy kingdom is.

RIVERS

   My lord of Gloucester, in those busy days        145

   Which here you urge to prove us enemies,

   We followed then our lord, our lawful king;

   So should we you if you should be our king.

RICHARD DUKE OF GLOUCESTER

   If I should be? I had rather be a pedlar.

   Far be it from my heart the thought of it.        150

QUEEN

   As little joy, my lord, as you suppose

   You should enjoy were you this country's king,

   As little joy may you suppose in me

   That I enjoy being the queen thereof.

MARGARET [*aside*]

   Ah, little joy enjoys the queen thereof,        155

   For I am she, and altogether joyless.

Q:
139 up] vppe (*damaged* 'e' *looks like* 'o')   142 childish-foolish] ~, ~   155 Ah,] A‸

F:
143 the] this   147 lawful] Soueraigne   150 of it] thereof   153 may you] you may

allegiance from his father-in-law to his brothers is presented in *Richard Duke of York* 5.1.

135 **father** father-in-law

136–7 **which . . . revenge** Echoed in Webster, *White Devil*, ed. J. R. Brown (1960), 4.2.105–6, where, to Brachiano's 'Whose death God pardon', Vittoria interjects 'Whose death God revenge | On thee'.

139 **meed** reward (with aural play on *mewed*)

140 **flint** Proverbially hard (Dent H311).

144 **cacodemon** evil demon, spirit. An unusual word, emphasizing that such demons are beyond usual experience.

149 **I had . . . pedlar** Perhaps in part a joke at Richard's own expense, comparing his hunchback to a pedlar's pack.

155 **Ah,** The alteration from Q1's 'A' is merely a modernization. Editors often emend: 'As' (Craig, conj. Heath), 'And' (White), or 'Ay,' (Hammond).

I can no longer hold me patient.
      [*Coming forward*] Hear me, you wrangling pirates,
            that fall out
In sharing that which you have pilled from me.
Which of you trembles not that looks on me?—                  160
If not that, I being queen, you bow like subjects,
Yet that, by you deposed, you quake like rebels.
      (*To Gloucester*) O gentle villain, do not turn away.

RICHARD DUKE OF GLOUCESTER
      Foul wrinkled witch, what mak'st thou in my sight?

MARGARET
      But repetition of what thou hast marred;                    165
      That will I make before I let thee go.
      A husband and a son thou owest to me;
      (*To the Queen*) And thou a kingdom; all of you allegiance.
      The sorrow that I have, by right is yours;
      And all the pleasures you usurp are mine.                   170

RICHARD DUKE OF GLOUCESTER
      The curse my noble father laid on thee
      When thou didst crown his warlike brows with paper,
      And with thy scorn drew'st rivers from his eyes,
      And then to dry them gav'st the Duke a clout
      Steeped in the faultless blood of pretty Rutland:           175
      His curses then from bitterness of soul

Q:
158 *Coming forward*] CAPELL (*subs.*);   *not in* Q1, F

F:
160 of] off   161 being] am   163 O] Ah   166 go.] goe. | *Rich*. Wert thou not banished, on
paine of death? | *Q. M*. I was: but I doe find more paine in banishment, | Then death can yeeld
me here, by my abode.   169 The] This   173 scorn] scornes

159 **pilled** pillaged
162 **by you deposed** Takes 'I' as referent, from the previous line.
163 **gentle villain** A double paradox: one is unlikely to be (a) both of high birth (*gentle*) and a bondman or servant (*villain*), or (b) both kindly and a scoundrel. Richard is both of high birth and villainous.
164 **mak'st thou** are you doing. Margaret picks up on *mak'st* in both the proverbial opposition with *marred* (Dent M48) and the idiom *make repetition* ('recite').
166 **go** See Richard's challenge and Margaret's reply in F: a strong and disruptive

reminder that Margaret historically was not in England (see note to l. 190).
171–5 **The . . . Rutland** Margaret's notorious cruelty in killing the Duke of York is staged in *Richard Duke of York* 1.4. Clifford kills the boy Rutland, York's son and Richard's brother, in the previous scene. Richard invokes infanticide to rally the Queen and her kin against Margaret, but will later commit the crime himself.
174 **clout** cloth
175 **faultless** innocent
176 **bitterness of soul** The idiom is biblical (Job 10: 1, etc.).

Denounced against thee are all fall'n upon thee,
And God, not we, hath plagued thy bloody deed.

QUEEN (*to Margaret*)

So just is God to right the innocent.

HASTINGS (*to Margaret*)

O, 'twas the foulest deed to slay that babe,                    180
And the most merciless that e'er was heard of.

RIVERS (*to Margaret*)

Tyrants themselves wept when it was reported.

DORSET [GREY] (*to Margaret*)

No man but prophesied revenge for it.

BUCKINGHAM (*to Margaret*)

Northumberland, then present, wept to see it.

MARGARET

What, were you snarling all before I came,                     185
Ready to catch each other by the throat,
And turn you all your hatred now on me?
Did York's dread curse prevail so much with heaven
That Henry's death, my lovely Edward's death,
Their kingdom's loss, my woeful banishment,                    190
Could all but answer for that peevish brat?

Q:
177 fall'n] F; fallen Q1    181 e'er] F; euer Q1    183 DORSET [GREY]] This edition; *Dors.* Q1, F.
*Similarly ll.* 254, 262.    184 BUCKINGHAM] F (*Buck.*); *Buch.* Q1

F:
191 Could] Should

178 **plagued** punished. The perpetrator, not the deed, would usually be *plagued*.
180 **babe** A rhetorical exaggeration of Rutland's youth. The same word is used of the orphaned children of Clarence at 2.2.83 and Richard's child-victims at 4.4.9 and thereafter.
183 **DORSET [GREY]** Dorset (in Q1 '*Dors.*') here and at ll. 254 and 262 seems to be the same figure as Grey. Similarly, in 2.1 the '*Dorcet*' who enters at the beginning of the scene is probably the same figure as the Lord Grey addressed at l. 65. See Appendix D, Note 3.
184 **Northumberland . . . it** Refers properly to the tormenting of York, not Rutland's murder: see *Richard Duke of York* 1.4.170–4.
185–7 **were . . . me** Based on the proverb,

'Curs fight with each other but show all their might against strangers' (Dent C917.1). As York denounced Margaret to her face as 'She-wolf of France' in his death-scene (*Richard Duke of York* 1.4.112), the reference may be to the proverb in the form 'Dogs do often fight together, yet so soon as they spy the wolf they leave their brawls and together run against the common enemy' (Charles Emanuel I, *Admonition*, trans. E. Aggas, A4; cited in Dent).
190 **banishment** Margaret's unhistorical banishment is mentioned in *Richard III* only. Historically, she spent her last years in France, where she died in 1482, a year before Edward IV's death.
191 **but answer** not fully offer recompense
**peevish** stupid

Can curses pierce the clouds and enter heaven?
Why then, give way, dull clouds, to my quick curses.
If not by war, by surfeit die your king,
As ours by murder to make him a king.                                    195
(*To the Queen*) Edward thy son, which now is Prince of
    Wales,
For Edward my son, which was Prince of Wales,
Die in his youth by like untimely violence.
Thyself a queen, for me that was a queen,
Outlive thy glory like my wretched self:                                    200
Long mayst thou live, to wail thy children's loss
And see another, as I see thee now,
Decked in thy rights, as thou art stalled in mine.
Long die thy happy days before thy death,
And after many lengthened hours of grief                                    205
Die neither mother, wife, nor England's queen.
Rivers and Dorset, you were standers-by,
And so wast thou, Lord Hastings, when my son
Was stabbed with bloody daggers. God I pray him
That none of you may live your natural age,                                    210
But by some unlooked accident cut off.

RICHARD DUKE OF GLOUCESTER

Have done thy charm, thou hateful, withered hag.

MARGARET

And leave out thee? Stay, dog, for thou shalt hear me.
If heaven have any grievous plague in store
Exceeding those that I can wish upon thee,                                    215

Q:
213 thee? Stay . . . me.] the ^ stay . . . ~ ^     214–15 If . . . Exceeding] Q1's *catchword* 'Excee-' *is
printed one line early, after l. 213.*

F:
194 If] Though    196, 197 which] that    197 my] our    201 loss] death    210 your] his

192  **curses** (in contrast with prayers)
193  **dull** dark; inactive, insensible (in contrast with *quick*, 'living, active')
194  **by surfeit . . . king** *Mirror for Magistrates* explains the cause of Edward's death: 'As needs he must, he surfeited so oft' ('Clarence', l. 338). *Surfeit* can refer to excess of food or to other self-indulgences.
203  **stalled** installed, enthroned
207  **standers-by** In Holinshed those 'that

stood by' murdered Prince Edward (p. 320; 'they that stood about' in Hall, *Edward IV*, 32ᵛ). Shakespeare distinguishes between passively guilty onlookers and participants (see note to 1.1.153).
211  **by some unlooked** i.e. *be* by some unlooked-*for*
213  **Stay** Suggests that Richard was about to leave. For a moment he is not self-willed. Compare his own 'Stay' at 1.2.31.

O let them keep it till thy sins be ripe,
And then hurl down their indignation
On thee, the troubler of the poor world's peace.
The worm of conscience still begnaw thy soul.
Thy friends suspect for traitors while thou livest,              220
And take deep traitors for thy dearest friends.
No sleep close up that deadly eye of thine,
Unless it be whilst some tormenting dream
Affrights thee with a hell of ugly devils.
Thou elvish-marked, abortive rooting-hog,              225
Thou that wast sealed in thy nativity
The slave of nature and the son of hell,
Thou slander of thy mother's heavy womb,
Thou loathèd issue of thy father's loins,
Thou rag of honour, thou detested—              230
RICHARD DUKE OF GLOUCESTER  Margaret.
MARGARET  Richard.

Q:
230 detested—] F; detested, &c. Q1

F:
220 livest] liu'st   223 whilst] while   228 mother's heavy] heauie Mothers

216 **them** i.e. the gods, 'heaven'. In *Richard II* 1.2.6–8 *heaven* is similarly taken as a plural and similarly 'Will rain hot vengeance on offenders' heads'.

219 **worm** As supposed to eat the bodies of the dead. The figurative *worm of conscience* is a pain of hell (as prompted by Isaiah 66: 24, 'their worm shall not die'; glossed in the Geneva Bible 'a continual torment of conscience, which shall ever gnaw them, and never suffer them to be at rest')—here inflicted on the living.
**still** constantly

225 **elvish-marked** Steevens refers to a belief that physical defects were left by malignant elves to mark an infant out for wicked deeds.
**rooting-hog** hog that roots up plants, hence with a hunched back. See note to 1.2.100.

226 **sealed** irrevocably confirmed by the marks on your body; virtually 'branded'

227 **The . . . hell** 'Original sin . . . is the fault and corruption of the nature of every man that naturally is engendered . . . ' (Articles of Religion, 9). Whether as

'slave of nature' (i.e. one who responds only to bestial impulse) or 'son of hell', Richard is beyond redemption from original sin through divine grace.

228 **mother's heavy womb** Thus Q1; F reads 'heauie Mothers Wombe'. The difference is one of emphasis: both readings require *heavy* to mean both 'grieving, sorrowful' and 'heavy with child'.

229 **issue . . . loins** Not biblical, but occurs in *Leir* l. 26, *Edward III* 1.1.9, and *Cymbeline* 5.6.331.

230 **rag** Probably an offcut removed to give shape to *honour* as a garment.
**detested—** Q1's 'detested, &c.' is probably a compositor's misinterpretation of a dash as meaning an unspecified continuation of the speech.

231–6 **Margaret . . . names** Richard glibly substitutes Margaret's name for his own. When Margaret corrects him, his reply 'Ha?' pretends that she is calling his name to get his attention, as her reply shows. He then turns *call* to the idiom 'call me names', suggesting that she has just denied doing so.

RICHARD DUKE OF GLOUCESTER  Ha?

MARGARET  I call thee not.

RICHARD DUKE OF GLOUCESTER

  Then I cry thee mercy, for I had thought            235

  That thou hadst called me all these bitter names.

MARGARET

  Why, so I did, but looked for no reply.

  O let me make the period to my curse.

RICHARD DUKE OF GLOUCESTER

  'Tis done by me, and ends in 'Margaret'.

QUEEN (*to Margaret*)

  Thus have you breathed your curse against yourself.    240

MARGARET

  Poor painted queen, vain flourish of my fortune,

  Why strew'st thou sugar on that bottled spider

  Whose deadly web ensnareth thee about?

  Fool, fool, thou whet'st a knife to kill thyself.

  The time will come that thou shalt wish for me       245

  To help thee curse that poisonous bunch-backed toad.

HASTINGS

  False-boding woman, end thy frantic curse,

  Lest to thy harm thou move our patience.

MARGARET

  Foul shame upon you, you have all moved mine.

RIVERS

  Were you well served, you would be taught your duty.   250

---

F:
235 Then I . . . mercy] I . . . mercie then   had thought] did thinke   245 time] day   246 that] this

235 **cry thee mercy** beg your pardon
237 **but . . . reply** i.e. she was not 'calling' him in the sense of getting his attention
238 **period** end
241 **painted queen** i.e. a feigned picture of the reality that belongs with Margaret. May also suggest that she is painted with cosmetics.
  **vain . . . fortune** empty and false embellishment of the position in life rightfully mine
242 **Why . . . spider** Might allude to the proverbial joke-advice to catch a bird by casting salt on its tail (Tilley B401): the Queen vainly thinks she is trapping the

spider that is trapping her. Also, behind the sugared spider is an allusion to the proverb 'to sugar the pill' (Dent P325), the pill here being poisonous. Compare the 'painted queen', another image of false appearance.
242 **bottled** swollen (both hunch-backed and swollen with poison). Bottles would have been rounded and made of leather.
244 **thou . . . thyself** From the proverb 'to cut one's own throat' (Dent T267.1).
246 **bunch-backed** hunch-backed
250 **served** prompted by your conscience or inclination. Margaret takes *serve* as 'treat' and 'render obedience and service'.

MARGARET

To serve me well, you all should do me duty,

Teach me to be your queen, and you my subjects.

O serve me well, and teach yourselves that duty.

DORSET [GREY]

Dispute not with her, she is lunatic.

MARGARET

Peace, master Marquis, you are malapert;                    255

Your fire-new stamp of honour is scarce current.

O that your young nobility could judge

What 'twere to lose it and be miserable.

They that stand high have many blasts to shake them,

And if they fall they dash themselves to pieces.            260

RICHARD DUKE OF GLOUCESTER

Good counsel, marry. Learn it, learn it, Marquis.

DORSET [GREY]

It toucheth you, my lord, as much as me.

RICHARD DUKE OF GLOUCESTER

Yea, and much more, but I was born so high.

Our eyrie buildeth in the cedar's top,

And dallies with the wind, and scorns the sun.              265

Q:
259 blasts] Q2, F; blast Q1

F:
262 toucheth] touches      263 Yea] I

251  **do me duty** show me reverence

255  **master Marquis** A class-conscious sneer: 'master' was the form of address to an untitled gentleman, whereas a marquis is an aristocrat ranked between duke and earl.

**you** Perhaps the polite form of address is ironic, in the manner of Richard's switch at l. 77. It similarly establishes a 'you' context for a new use of 'thou': see l. 280 and note on *thy*.

**malapert** impudent

256  **Your . . . current** Perhaps epitomizes the promoted Dorset as the newly-made metal stamp with which the documents of his new office would be endorsed; and/or pictures him as a freshly-minted coin, as in proverbial 'new out of the mint' (Dent M985).

259–60  **They . . . pieces** Proverbially, the

highest tree both abides the sharpest winds (Dent T509) and has the greatest fall (Tilley T489); and 'the higher standing, the greater fall' (Dent S823).

263  **so high** as high as I am

264  **Our . . . top** In Ezekiel 17: 3 'the great eagle' takes 'the highest branch of the cedar'. Cedars, commonly cited for their height and straightness, were, on account of Ezekiel 17, regarded as emblems of royalty (as were eagles). But it was proverbial that 'High cedars fall when low shrubs remain' (Dent C208; recalling again Ezekiel: 'I the Lord have brought down the high tree, and exalted the low tree', 17: 24).

**eyrie** brood of eagles; hence 'noble stock of children'

265  **scorns the sun** Proverbially, 'only the eagle can gaze at the sun' (Dent E3).

MARGARET

And turns the sun to shade, alas, alas!

Witness my son, now in the shade of death,

Whose bright outshining beams thy cloudy wrath

Hath in eternal darkness folded up.

Your eyrie buildeth in our eyrie's nest.                              270

O God that seest it, do not suffer it!

As it was won with blood, lost be it so.

BUCKINGHAM

Have done, for shame if not for charity.

MARGARET

Urge neither charity nor shame to me.

[*To the others*] Uncharitably with me have you dealt,          275

And shamefully by you my hopes are butchered.

My charity is outrage, life my shame;

And in my shame still live my sorrow's rage.

BUCKINGHAM  Have done.

MARGARET

ᵥ O princely Buckingham, I will kiss thy hand                      280

Q:
266, 274, 280, 287, 297 MARGARET] F (*Mar.*);  *Qu. M.* Q1

F:
266, 274, 280, 287, 297 QUEEN MARGARET] *Mar.*    272 was] is    273 Have done] Peace, peace
276 by you my hopes] my hopes (by you)    278 my shame] that shame    279 Have done]
Haue done, haue done    280 I will] Ile

266 **turns the sun** The pun on *son*, highlighted in the next line, is already
inherent: Richard's 'scorns the sun'
immediately prompts Margaret to think
of her son. *Turns* draws attention to how
Margaret 'turns' Richard's meaning.
Ritson's comment 'Her distress cannot
prevent her quibbling' misses the
obsessional quality of this language-
turning that refocuses her speech on to
the object of grief.
272 **As . . . so** 'Whoso sheddeth man's
blood, by man shall his blood be shed'
(Genesis 9: 6).
273 **BUCKINGHAM** On a plausible suggestion
by Alice Walker, some editors since Wilson have emended, taking Q1/F '*Buck.*'
as a shared error for '*Rich*'. The mock-
piety does indeed sound like Richard elsewhere, but in this scene he tends instead
to abuse Margaret, and a hint of future

alignment between Richard and Buckingham in the latter's tone would not
be amiss (compare their exchange at
ll. 295–6). Buckingham's 'Have done' at
l. 279 echoes Q1 (but not F) at l. 273, and
suggests the same speaker. To retain
Q1/F as here, one must suppose a change
of addressee after l. 274. This is not prevented by the speech's continuity on the
theme of charity and shame.
276 **my hopes** i.e. those in whom I had hope
277 **My charity** Either 'my most charitable
feeling' or 'the charity shown me'.
**outrage** fury; verbal or physical abuse
**life my shame** Either 'my shame is to be
still alive' or 'the only life allowed me is a
shameful one'.
√ 280 **princely** Buckingham was descended
from Edward III.
**thy** In contrast with her earlier disparage-
ments, she may now be using 'thou' as a

In sign of league and amity with thee.
Now fair befall thee and thy princely house!
Thy garments are not spotted with our blood,
Nor thou within the compass of my curse.

BUCKINGHAM

Nor no one here, for curses never pass                    285
The lips of those that breathe them in the air.

MARGARET

I'll not believe but they ascend the sky,
And there awake God's gentle-sleeping peace.
O Buckingham, beware of yonder dog.
Look when he fawns, he bites; and when he bites,         290
His venom tooth will rankle thee to death.
Have not to do with him, beware of him.
Sin, death, and hell have set their marks on him,
And all their ministers attend on him.

RICHARD DUKE OF GLOUCESTER

What doth she say, my lord of Buckingham?                295

BUCKINGHAM

Nothing that I respect, my gracious lord.

MARGARET

What, dost thou scorn me for my gentle counsel,
And soothe the devil that I warn thee from?
O, but remember this another day
When he shall split thy very heart with sorrow,          300
And say poor Margaret was a prophetess.

---

Q:
291 rankle] Q2, F; rackle Q1

F:
282 princely] Noble       287 I'll not believe] I will not thinke       289 beware] take heede
291 thee to] to the

monarch might speak to a loyal noble, or
in an attempt to establish informal close-
ness. The King similarly singles out Buckingham for this form of address in
2.1.29–30 and 42.

282 **fair befall** may good fortune come to
285–6 **curses . . . air** i.e. curses are unheard
by God and so are ineffectual
288 **awake . . . peace** awake God from his

gentle sleep of peace. Biblical antecedents
include Psalms 44: 23, 'Up, Lord; why
sleepest thou? Awake, and be not absent
from us for ever.'
290 **Look when** whenever
291 **venom** adjectival (see Abbott 22)
    **rankle** inflict a festering wound
292 **not** Collier's 1853 emendation 'naught'
    is plausible.
298 **soothe** humour, flatter

Live each of you the subjects of his hate,
And he to your, and all of you to God's.                    *Exit*
HASTINGS
  My hair doth stand on end to hear her curses.
RIVERS
  And so doth mine. I wonder she's at liberty.                    305
RICHARD DUKE OF GLOUCESTER
  I cannot blame her, by God's holy mother;
  She hath had too much wrong, and I repent
  My part thereof that I have done.
QUEEN
  I never did her any to my knowledge.
RICHARD DUKE OF GLOUCESTER
  But you have all the vantage of this wrong.                    310
  I was too hot to do somebody good
  That is too cold in thinking of it now.
  Marry, as for Clarence, he is well repaid;
  He is franked up to fatting for his pains.
  God pardon them that are the cause of it.                    315
RIVERS
  A virtuous and a Christian-like conclusion,
  To pray for them that have done scathe to us.
RICHARD DUKE OF GLOUCESTER [*speaks to himself*]
  So do I ever, being well advised,
  For had I cursed, now I had cursed myself.
    *Enter Catesby*

Q:
318 *speaks to himself* ] F (*after* 'advised'); *not in* Q1      319.1 *Enter Catesby*] F; *not in* Q1
321 lords] Lo:

F:
302 of his] to his   303 your] Q1; you Q3; yours F   304 HASTINGS] Q1 (*Hast.*); *Buc.* F   on]
an   305 wonder] muse why   308 done] done to her   309 QUEEN] Q1 (*Qu.*); *Mar.* F (*possibly altering* Q6 '*Hast.*', *but copy uncertain*)   310 But . . . this] Yet . . . her   315 of it] thereof

303 **your** yours
311 **somebody** i.e. the King. Richard pretends he daren't name him.
314 **franked up** shut up in a pen
    **to fatting** to be fattened (for slaughter)
316–17 **A . . . us** Compare Matthew 5: 44, 'Pray for them which hurt you and persecute you'. It is not clear whether

Rivers is pious, sarcastic at what he takes to be Richard's piety, or sceptical as to Richard's piety. 'Possibly the speech belongs to Buckingham' (Wilson).
317 **scathe** harm
318 *speaks to himself* F's direction is sometimes relocated to after 'ever'.

CATESBY

Madam, his majesty doth call for you,                          320
And for your grace, and you, my noble lords.

QUEEN

Catesby, we come. Lords, will you go with us?

RIVERS

Madam, we will attend your grace.

*Exeunt all but Richard*

RICHARD DUKE OF GLOUCESTER

I do the wrong, and first begin to brawl.
The secret mischiefs that I set abroach                        325
I lay unto the grievous charge of others.
Clarence, whom I indeed have cast in darkness,
I do beweep to many simple gulls—
Namely to Hastings, Derby, Buckingham—
And say it is the Queen and her allies                         330
That stir the King against the Duke my brother.
Now they believe me, and withal whet me
To be revenged on Rivers, Vaughan, Grey.
But then I sigh, and with a piece of scripture
Tell them that God bids us do good for evil.                   335

Q:
323. I *all but*] F; *man⟨et⟩*. Q1     324 begin] F; began Q1     brawl.] ~,     327 cast] F; laid Q1

F:
321 you] yours     noble] gracious     lords] Lo: Q1 (*ambiguous*); Lord F (*from* Q3)     322 we . . .
us] I . . . mee     323 Madam, we will attend] We wait vpon     *Richard*] *Gloster* (*altering* Q3 '*Clo*.')
327 whom] who     329 Hastings, Derby] *Derby, Hastings*     330 say it is] tell them 'tis
332 believe me] beleeue it     333 Vaughan] *Dorset*

321  **your grace** The form of address is appro-
     priate to a duke: presumably Richard,
     though Buckingham also qualifies.
     **lords** In Q1, the first of several abbrevi-
     ations 'Lo:' that require expansion in the
     plural.
324  **I . . . brawl** Proverbial (compare 'some
     complain to prevent complaint', Dent
     C579).
325  **set abroach** broach
327  **cast in darkness** Literally this means 'put
     in prison' (More uses the same verb: see
     headnote to 1. 4). But it also anticipates
     Clarence's death, and the phrase's bib-
     lical associations invoke alienation from

God after death (for instance Matthew
8: 12, 'the children of the kingdom shall
be cast out into utter darkness'). See Introduction, p. 126, on Q1's 'laid'.
328  **gulls** credulous fools
330  **allies** relatives. Stressed on the second
     syllable.
333  **Vaughan** Pronounced as two syllables.
     See Appendix D, Note 3.
334–8  **But . . . devil** Proverbially, the devil
     can cite Scripture for his purpose (Dent
     D230).
335  **God . . . evil** 'Do good to them that hate
     you' (Matthew 5: 44, and similar texts
     elsewhere in the Bible).

And thus I clothe my naked villainy
With old odd ends stol'n out of holy writ,
And seem a saint when most I play the devil.
    *Enter two Executioners*
But soft, here come my executioners.
How now, my hardy, stout-resolvèd mates?                    340
Are you now going to dispatch this deed?

EXECUTIONER

We are, my lord, and come to have the warrant,
That we may be admitted where he is.

RICHARD DUKE OF GLOUCESTER

It was well thought upon; I have it here about me.
    *He gives them the warrant*
When you have done, repair to Crosby Place.                 345
But, sirs, be sudden in the execution,
Withal obdurate. Do not hear him plead,
For Clarence is well spoken, and perhaps
May move your hearts to pity if you mark him.

EXECUTIONER

Tush, fear not, my lord, we will not stand to prate.        350
Talkers are no good doers, be assured.

Q:

338.1 *Enter two Executioners*] position as in F; *right of l.* 338 *in* Q1    two] F; *not in* Q1
344.1 *He . . . warrant*] CAPELL (*subs.*);  *not in* Q1, F

F:

337 old odd . . . out] odde old . . . forth    338.1 *Executioners*] murtherers    341 deed] thing
342, 350 EXECUTIONER] *Vil.*    344 It was well] Well    350 Tush, fear not] Tut, tut

337 **ends** (a) tags, commonplaces, (b) scraps
   of cloth
338 **seem . . . devil** The proverb 'To seem a
   saint but be a devil' (Tilley S30), complicated with the theatrical verb *play*. There
   was a proverb 'To play the devil in the
   horloge' (Dent D302), meaning to cause
   confusion in an orderly mechanism or
   system, but 'play the devil' evidently was
   not proverbial in its own right.
340 **stout-resolvèd** A compound is especially
   likely for, as W. S. Walker noted, 'Shakespeare very rarely strings together three
   adjectives without an *and*' (i. 32). A
   number of other descriptive phrases are
   helpfully construed as hyphenated com-
   pounds, for instance 'wanton-ambling'
   (1.1.17), 'weak-piping' (1.1.24),

'childish-foolish' (1.3.142), 'gallant-
springing' (1.4.201).
342, 350 **EXECUTIONER** F instead has the
   prefix '*Vil.*', for 'Villain', but neither
   Q1 nor F distinguishes between 'First' and
   'Second' Executioner, as they do in
   1.4. The First Executioner is the more
   resolute in 1.4, on which basis he might be
   given both speeches here. But there would
   be stronger irony if the Second Executioner, who says 'No, first let's reason
   with him' at 1.4.146, were to speak
   1.3.350–2.
347 **obdurate** Stressed on the second
   syllable.
350 **stand to prate** wait around gossiping
351 **Talkers . . . doers** Proverbial (Dent
   T64).

We come to use our hands, and not our tongues.

RICHARD DUKE OF GLOUCESTER

Your eyes drop millstones, when fools' eyes drop tears.
I like you, lads. About your business.                *Exeunt*

[**I.4**]   *Enter Clarence, Brakenbury*

BRAKENBURY

Why looks your grace so heavily today?

CLARENCE

O, I have past a miserable night,
So full of ugly sights, of ghastly dreams,
That, as I am a Christian-faithful man,
I would not spend another such a night                5

---

F:
352 come] go     353 drop] fall     354 business.] businesse straight. | Go, go, dispatch. | *Vil.*
We will my Noble Lord.     *Exeunt*] *not in* F
   **1.4.0.1** *Brakenbury*] *and Keeper*     1 BRAKENBURY] Q1 (*Brok.*); *Keep.* F. *Similarly to l.* 68.
3 ugly sights, of ghastly dreams] fearefull Dreames, of vgly sights

352 **to . . . tongues** Draws on the proverbial
contrast between words and deeds (Dent
W797, W820).
353 **Your eyes drop millstones** A proverbial
image of hard-heartedness (Dent M967).
**drop tears** F's 'fall Teares' merits consideration because Simmes's Compositor
A elsewhere substituted 'drop' for 'fall'
(Q2 *Richard II*, G4), but 'Fooles eyes fall
Teares' is an awkward locution and might
have been deliberately altered.
354 *Exeunt* Richard and the Executioners
probably part separate ways.
1.4 See notes to 1.1.40.1 and 50. Holinshed
merely relates that Clarence was 'cast
into the Tower, and therewith adjudged
for a traitor, and privily drowned in a butt
of malmsey' (p. 346). Brakenbury figures
prominently in More's account of the
murder of the Princes. His presence now
is ahistorical; it highlights Shakespeare's
transfer into the present invented scene of
some matters pertaining to a crucial
episode not shown on stage. Q1's text in
1.4 differs from F's in staging (see next
note) and is more than usually variant in
dialogue. A bench or couch may be
brought on stage at the beginning of the
scene for Clarence to sleep on. See note to
2.1.0.1.
0.1 *Brakenbury* F instead has an unnamed

Keeper here, and brings Brakenbury on
stage after l. 68 (with the result that he
speaks ll. 69–76 in the Keeper's presence).
Q1's arrangement does not save on
the overall count of actors needed to
perform the play, but is theatrically more
cohesive, and is commonly preferred
in performance.
1 **heavily** sorrowfully, gloomily
2–65 **O . . . me** Lady More has a similar
allegorical dream of drowning in
*Sir Thomas More*, ed. Giorgio Melchiori
(1990), 4.2.8–26. The direction of influence is uncertain, but the link between
the deaths of Sir Thomas More and
Clarence is significant in either
direction. Shakespeare might not have
been particularly mindful of classical and
medieval dream theory, but part of the
dream's potency lies in its transgression
of dream categories. Though prophetic,
it also has elements of nightmare and
apparition appropriate to *enhypnion*
(anxiety-dream based on events past and
present). For Clarence it begins as a
fantasy of escape based on an earlier
escape (see note to l. 9), but turns to
bespeak a guilty conscience and anticipate death through divine vengeance.
He fails to recognize from the dream that
Richard will cause his death.

Though 'twere to buy a world of happy days,
So full of dismal terror was the time.

BRAKENBURY

What was your dream? I long to hear you tell it.

CLARENCE

Methoughts I was embarked for Burgundy,
And in my company my brother Gloucester,                    10
Who from my cabin tempted me to walk
Upon the hatches. Thence we looked toward England,
And cited up a thousand fearful times
During the wars of York and Lancaster
That had befall'n us. As we paced along                    15
Upon the giddy footing of the hatches,
Methought that Gloucester stumbled, and in stumbling
Struck me, that sought to stay him, overboard
Into the tumbling billows of the main.

Q:

   1.4.12 hatches. Thence] ~, thence    15 befall'n] F; befallen Q1    18 sought] POPE;
thought Q1, F

F:

8 I . . . it] my Lord, I pray you tel me   9 I was embarked for] that I had broken from the Tower,
| And was embark'd to crosse to   12 Thence] There (*from* Q6)   13 fearful] heauy   17 stum-
bling] falling

5 **spend** Plays on (a) passing time, (b)
spending money.

9–19 **Methoughts . . . main.** Jones suggests
that the passage is prompted by the
drowning of the helmsman Palinurus in
*Aeneid*, Book 6. Brooks, 'Antecedents',
p. 145, compares *Metamorphoses*, 3.792
and 797–8: Acetis tells how he 'stepped |
Upon the hatches' where a ruffian gave
him 'such a churlish blow . . . That overboard he had me sent'. The connection
between the drowning of Clarence and
Palinurus may have been suggested by
the detail in Reynoldes's *Foundation of
Rhetoric* (see p. 16) that Clarence was
pitched into the butt when 'the stairs
[were] suddenly removed whereon he
stepped' (D1–1ᵛ).

9 **Methoughts . . . Burgundy** See F Collation
for F's more expansive account. The loss
of narrative connection with Clarence's
present situation in Q1 makes the dream
more dream-like and removed from time.
Readers of Holinshed would see a reference

to Clarence's past: after their father's
death Gloucester and Clarence were sent
for safety to Utrecht, where they remained
under the protection of their sister's husband, the Duke of Burgundy.

9, 23, 55 **Methoughts . . . Methought . . .
methoughts** Altered to 'Me thought'
(Q4) . . . 'Me thoughts' (F) . . . 'me
thought' (Q2, F). For the grammatically
anomalous but Shakespearian *methoughts*,
favoured independently by Q1 and F
but in different lines, compare *Merchant
of Venice* 1.3.68 and *Winter's Tale*
1.2.156.

12 **hatches** deck. Can refer to permanent or
removable planking.

13 **cited up** called to mind (*OED* 5; *OED*'s
first three examples include this and are
all from early Shakespeare)

17 **Gloucester stumbled** A naturalistic effect
of his lameness, but it is through his
moral deformity that he will in reality
strike Clarence.

18 **stay** support

19 **main** sea

Lord, Lord, methought what pain it was to drown,          20
What dreadful noise of waters in my ears,
What ugly sights of death within my eyes!
Methought I saw a thousand fearful wrecks,
Ten thousand men that fishes gnawed upon,
Wedges of gold, great anchors, heaps of pearl,          25
Inestimable stones, unvalued jewels.
Some lay in dead men's skulls, and in those holes
Where eyes did once inhabit there were crept,
As 'twere in scorn of eyes, reflecting gems,
Which wooed the slimy bottom of the deep,          30
And mocked the dead bones that lay scattered by.

BRAKENBURY

Had you such leisure in the time of death
To gaze upon the secrets of the deep?

CLARENCE

Methought I had, for still the envious flood
Kept in my soul, and would not let it forth          35
To seek the empty, vast, and wand'ring air,

Q:
32 such] sueh    36 wand'ring] F; wandering Q1

F:
20 Lord, Lord] O Lord    21 waters] water (*from* Q6)    my] mine (*from* Q2)    22 ugly sights of]
sights of vgly    my] mine (*from* Q2)    23 Methought] Me thoughts    24 Ten] A    26 jewels]
Iewels, | All scattred in the bottome of the Sea    27 those] the    30 Which] That    33 the se-
crets] these secrets          34 had, for] had, and often I did striue | To yeeld the Ghost: but
35 Kept] Stop'd    36 seek] find (*altering* Q3 'keepe')

23–31 **Methought . . . by.** In Tudor poetics,
shipwrecked riches were emblematic of
the world's vanity (Jones, pp. 209–10).
25 **anchors** The reading has been emended
'ingots' (Wilson, following Kinnear's
conjecture) or 'ouches' (i.e. jewels; Taylor, following McKerrow's suggestion).
Parallels can be found for both the emendations in source-texts for the dream
(Spenser, *Faerie Queene*, II. vii. 5, l. 6,
'ingots'; III. iv. 23, l. 5, 'ouches').
'Ingots' occurs in a passage describing
the Cave of Mammon in which 'all the
ground with skulls was scattered | And
dead men's bones'; Mammon's wealth
includes 'Great heaps of gold . . . great
ingots and . . . wedges square'. The influence is highly probable, but if gold can
be diversified as pearl (emblematic of sorrow), why not also as anchors? 'Anchors' must be judged on whether a

disruption to the list of treasures can be
tolerated. In a dream about shipwrecks,
anchors amongst the gold and pearl are
not out of place. There may be an ironic
allusion to St Paul's metaphor of hope as
the anchor of the soul (Hebrews 6: 19).
26 **unvalued** beyond valuation
**jewels** F's extra line may have been deleted
because of similar wording in ll. 30–1.
30–1 **wooed . . . mocked** 'The gems in the
skulls seemed to glance around like a
capricious lover' (Wilson).
34 **had, for** F's version (see F collation)
rather distractingly correlates having
*leisure* (l. 32) with striving to yield the
ghost. The idea in F is expressed more
strongly in ll. 37–8.
**envious flood** spiteful sea. *Flood* often
means 'tide', and might here suggest the
pressure of moving water.
36 **vast** Both 'boundless' and 'desolate'.

But smothered it within my panting bulk,
Which almost burst to belch it in the sea.

BRAKENBURY

Awaked you not with this sore agony?

CLARENCE

O no, my dream was lengthened after life.                    40
O then began the tempest to my soul,
Who passed, methought, the melancholy flood
With that grim ferryman which poets write of,
Unto the kingdom of perpetual night.
The first that there did greet my stranger-soul             45
Was my great father-in-law, renownèd Warwick,
Who cried aloud, 'What scourge for perjury
Can this dark monarchy afford false Clarence?'—
And so he vanished. Then came wand'ring by
A shadow like an angel with bright hair,                     50
Dabbled in blood, and he shrieked out aloud,

Q:
47 perjury₍ₐ₎] ~ .    50 with] F; in Q1    51 shrieked] F; squakt Q1

F:
38 Which] Who    39 with] in    40 O no] No, no    42 Who] I    43 grim] sowre    47 cried]
spake

37 **bulk** trunk of the body. The narrower
sense 'belly' anticipates *belch*, and there
is perhaps allusion also to the sense 'hold
of a ship'.

39 **agony** anguish; pangs of death

40–60 **O . . . soul** 'The power of conscience to prefigure for the sufferer both
the moment of his own death and the
accusations of the Last Judgement was
. . . well documented in the Pauline tradition of scholastic philosophy': J. S. Wilks,
*The Idea of Conscience in Renaissance
Tragedy* (1990), p. 88.

41 **then . . . soul** Echoes Marlowe, *1 Tamburlaine* 3.2.87–8: 'That sent a tempest
to my daunted thoughts | And makes my
soul divine her overthrow'.

42 **the melancholy flood** i.e. the river Styx,
crossed on the way to Hades. *Flood* is
'river', but compare l. 34. The formulaic
descriptive adjective (Latin *tristes*) would
make the allusion recognizable. It initiates a description loosely based on the
visit to the underworld in Virgil's *Aeneid*,
Book 6. The *ferryman* (l. 43), also identified allusively, was Charon.

43 **which poets write of** They include—
as well as Virgil and Dante (*Inferno*,
3.109–10)—Sackville in the Induction to
'Buckingham' in *Mirror for Magistrates*,
and Kyd in the Induction to *Spanish
Tragedy*.

44, 48 **kingdom . . . night, dark monarchy**
Senecan phrases for the underworld.
'Perpetual night' (Seneca's 'noctis aeter-
nae', *Medea*, l. 9, *Hercules Furens*, l. 610)
was proverbial for death (Dent N167.1).

46 **my . . . Warwick** Clarence married Warwick's eldest daughter Isabel.

47 **perjury** See note to 1.3.135–6. At 5.1.109
in *Richard Duke of York* Warwick calls
Clarence 'passing traitor—perjured and
unjust', echoing Holinshed, 'false and
perjured' (p. 309).

50 **shadow** ghost (of Prince Edward, whose
murder has previously been blamed on
Richard alone)

51 **shrieked** Q1 has 'squakt', a spelling of
*squeaked*. The word is possible in that
ghosts were thought to squeak, as in
*Hamlet*, Additional Passage A. 9, but
seems inappropriate here as a reference to

'Clarence is come, false, fleeting, perjured Clarence,
That stabbed me in the field by Tewkesbury.
Seize on him, Furies, take him to your torments.'
With that, methoughts a legion of foul fiends                    55
Environed me about, and howlèd in mine ears
Such hideous cries that with the very noise
I trembling waked, and for a season after
Could not believe but that I was in hell,
Such terrible impression made the dream.                          60

BRAKENBURY

No marvel, my lord, though it affrighted you.
I promise you, I am afraid to hear you tell it.

CLARENCE

O Brakenbury, I have done those things
Which now bear evidence against my soul
For Edward's sake, and see how he requites me.                    65
I pray thee, gentle keeper, stay by me.
My soul is heavy, and I fain would sleep.

BRAKENBURY

I will, my lord. God give your grace good rest.
    *Clarence sleeps*

Q:
61 lord, . . . you.] Lo: . . . ~,    68.1 *Clarence sleeps*] JOHNSON; *not in* Q1, F

F:
54 to your torments] vnto Torment    55 methoughts] me thought (*from* Q2)    56 me about] me
60 the] my    61 my lord] Lord    62 promise . . . afraid] am affraid (me thinkes)    63 O Braken-
bury] Ah Keeper, Keeper    63–4 those . . . bear] these things | (That now giue    65 me.] F *adds*
4 lines. See Appendix A, Passage B.    66 I . . . me] Keeper, I prythee sit by me a-while

loud and intelligible words rather than
gibbering. A spelling such as 'shriekt'
might be misread 'squekt'.

52 **fleeting** vacillating, fickle
53 **field** battlefield
54 **Furies** In classical myth, supernatural
female beings who avenged bloodshed.
Here conflated with 'fiends' (l. 55) who
drag the damned to the hell of Christianity.
61 **No marvel . . . though** no wonder if (despite the dream itself being a marvel).
*Marvel* was pronounced as one syllable.
66 **by me.** F has four lines in which Clarence
implores God to save his wife and children. Davison suggests that the Folio
lines shift the focus away from his pathetic isolation. They also create an ex-

pectation that Clarence's family will be
either killed by Richard or decisively
saved. His wife never appears in the play,
and historically was already dead.
Clarence's son was to be executed by
Richmond (which might have rendered
the passage impolitic). As for Clarence's
daughter, whom Richard is content to
marry off meanly, it may not be coincidence that in Q1 she disappears from 4.1
(compare Appendix A, Passage J).
67 **My soul is heavy** Echoes Christ's words
expressing his sorrow and anticipation of
death at Gethsemane (Matthew 27: 38).
**heavy** Both 'sorrowful, oppressed' and
'tired'.
68 **rest.** In F Brakenbury enters here. See
note to 1.4.0.1.

Sorrow breaks seasons and reposing hours,
Makes the night morning and the noontide night.    70
Princes have but their titles for their glories,
An outward honour for an inward toil;
And for unfelt imagination
They often feel a world of restless cares,
So that betwixt their titles and low name    75
There's nothing differs but the outward fame.
     *The Murderers (Executioners) enter*
In God's name, what are you, and how came you
     hither?
FIRST EXECUTIONER   I would speak with Clarence, and I
     came hither on my legs.
BRAKENBURY   Yea, are you so brief?    80
SECOND EXECUTIONER

O sir, it is better to be brief than tedious.—
Show him our commission; talk no more.
     *Brakenbury readeth it*

Q:

69 breaks] Q2, F; breake Q1    hours,] ~ₐ    75 name] F; names Q1    76.1 (*Executioners*)] *not in* Q1, F    78 FIRST EXECUTIONER] *Execu.*    82.1 *Brakenbury*] CAPELL; *He* Q1

F:

68.1 *Clarence sleeps*] *Enter Brakenbury the Lieutenant.*    69 Sorrow] *Bra.* Sorrow    73 imagination] Imaginations    75 betwixt] betweene    76.1 *The . . . enter*] *Enter two Murtherers.*    77 In . . . hither?] 1. *Mur.* Ho, who's heere? | *Bra.* What would'st thou Fellow? And how camm'st thou hither.    78 FIRST EXECUTIONER] *Execu.* Q1; 2. *Mur.* F    80 Yea, are you] What (*altering* Q3 'Yea are ye')    81 SECOND EXECUTIONER] Q1 (2. *Exe.*); 1. F    O . . . tedious] 'Tis better (Sir) then to be tedious (*altering* Q3 '. . . better be . . .')    82 Show him] Let him see    talk] and talke    82.1 *Brakenbury readeth it*] *Reads*

69–76 **Sorrow . . . fame** 'The speech makes a complete poem: one might call it a variant on the eight-line *strambotto* form that Wyatt practised, and its subject another variant on the Senecan dispraise of courts—one of which Wyatt himself powerfully translated' (Jones, p. 194, citing Wyatt's 'Stand whoso list upon the slipper top', published 1557).

69–70 **Sorrow . . . night** Echoes Job 17: 11–12: 'The thoughts of my heart have changed the night for the day, the light that approached for darkness'.

69 **Sorrow . . . hours** *Seasons* is the due course of time; *reposing hours* is night as the time for sleep, hence sleep itself. The sufferer of sorrow is out of accord with the rhythms of time, and suffers broken sleep.

71, 72, 73 **for . . . for . . . for** as . . . at the cost of . . . instead of

73 **unfelt imagination** i.e. thought with no impact on physical reality

76.1 **The . . . enter** There are numerous divergences of idiom between Q1 and F in the rest of the scene. In F the First Murderer enters calling 'Ho, who's heere?' Davison notes that a silent approach is more chilling.

**Executioners** This is how they are identified in Q1's speech prefixes to ll. 78 ('*Execu.*'), 80 ('*Exe.*') and 89 ('*Exe.*'), after which simple numerals '1' and '2' (or '*Am.*' for both) suffice.

78–9 **I came . . . legs** Proverbial as a self-evident reply (Dent L191).

BRAKENBURY
    I am in this commanded to deliver
    The noble Duke of Clarence to your hands.
    I will not reason what is meant hereby,                    85
    Because I will be guiltless of the meaning.
    Here are the keys, there sits the Duke asleep.
    I'll to his majesty, and certify his grace
    That thus I have resigned my charge to you.
FIRST EXECUTIONER  Do so, it is a point of wisdom.            90
                                    *Exit Brakenbury*
SECOND EXECUTIONER  What, shall I stab him as he sleeps?
FIRST EXECUTIONER  No; then he will say 'twas done cow-
    ardly when he wakes.
SECOND EXECUTIONER  When he wakes? Why, fool, he shall
    never wake till the judgement day.                         95
FIRST EXECUTIONER  Why, then he will say we stabbed him
    sleeping.
SECOND EXECUTIONER  The urging of that word 'judgement'
    hath bred a kind of remorse in me.
FIRST EXECUTIONER  What, art thou afraid?                    100
SECOND EXECUTIONER  Not to kill him, having a warrant for
    it, but to be damned for killing him, from which no war-
    rant can defend us.
FIRST EXECUTIONER  Back to the Duke of Gloucester, tell
    him so.                                                    105

Q:
90.1 *Exit Brakenbury*] not in Q1. *Compare F.*

F:
86 of] from    87 Here . . . asleep] There lies the Duke asleepe, and there the Keyes    88 his
majesty . . . grace] the King, and signifie to him    89 my charge to you] to you my charge (*al-
tering* Q3 'my place to you')    90 Do . . . wisdom] You may sir, 'tis a point of wisedome: | Far
you well    90.1 *Exit Brakenbury*] '*Exit.*' *after l.* 89    91 I] we (*from* Q3)    92 then he will]
hee'l    94 When . . . fool] Why    95 till the] vntill the great    96 he will] hee'l    101–2 war-
rant for it] Warrant    102 which] the which    103 us] me. | 1 I thought thou had'st bin reso-
lute. | 2 So I am, to let him liue    104 Back . . . tell] Ile back . . . and tell

86 **will be** desire to be (Abbott 319)
87 **Here are the keys** An iconic moment in
    that Brakenbury similarly hands over his
    keys to those about to murder the young
    princes in *True Tragedy* ll. 1203–5 and in
    Thomas Heywood's *2 Edward IV* (1592–9,
    printed 1599), sig. T1.

94 **fool** Not in F. In Q1 a possible indication
    that the parts were played by the com-
    pany's clown actors (Davison). In mod-
    ern performance too the episode has often
    been clowned.
103 **us.** F follows with an effective short
    exchange not in Q.

SECOND EXECUTIONER  I pray thee, stay a while; I hope my
    holy humour will change, 'twas wont to hold me but
    while one would tell twenty.
        [*They wait*]
FIRST EXECUTIONER  How dost thou feel thyself now?
SECOND EXECUTIONER  Faith, some certain dregs of con-          110
    science are yet within me.
FIRST EXECUTIONER  Remember our reward when the deed is
    done.
SECOND EXECUTIONER  Zounds, he dies. I had forgot the
    reward.                                                   115
FIRST EXECUTIONER  Where is thy conscience now?
SECOND EXECUTIONER  In the Duke of Gloucester's purse.
FIRST EXECUTIONER  So when he opens his purse to give us
    our reward, thy conscience flies out.
SECOND EXECUTIONER  Let it go, there's few or none will       120
    entertain it.
FIRST EXECUTIONER  How if it come to thee again?
SECOND EXECUTIONER  I'll not meddle with it, it is a danger-
    ous thing, it makes a man a coward. A man cannot steal,
    but it accuseth him; he cannot swear, but it checks him;  125
    he cannot lie with his neighbour's wife, but it detects
    him. It is a blushing, shamefaced spirit, that mutinies in

Q:

108.1 *They wait*] DAVISON (*A silence*); *not in* Q1, F; *He counts to twenty* OXFORD    127 shame-
faced] shamefast

F:

106 I . . . while] Nay, I prythee stay a little    106–7 my holy humour] this passionate humor of
mine    107 'twas] It was    108 would tell] tels    110 Faith, some] Some    112 deed is] deed's
114 Zounds] Come    116 Where is] Where's    117 In] O, in    118 So when] When    120 Let]
'Tis no matter, let    122 How] What    123–4 it is a dangerous thing, it] it    125–6 he cannot
swear . . . he cannot lie] A man cannot Sweare . . . A man cannot lye    127 It is ] 'Tis

107  **humour** mood
108  **tell** count
108.1  *They wait* The dialogue demands a
    pause. Taylor's direction for the Second
    Murder to count to twenty is perhaps
    over-specific, though Hands not only
    went so far but had the count resume at
    twenty-one after l. 111 (Hankey, p. 133).
112  **our reward** In the background is the
    Commination against Sinners: 'Cursed is
    he that taketh reward to slay the soul
    of innocent blood' (*Common Prayer*,
    p. 317). Compare note to ll. 126–7.

114  **Zounds** A particularly strong oath (liter-
    ally 'by God's wounds', referring to
    Christ's wounds on the Cross).
121  **entertain it** take it into their house-
    hold for employment. The Executioners
    allegorize conscience as a treacherous
    manservant. That he might be analogous
    to the devil as a tempter is made apparent
    at l. 133 (see note).
123–32  **I'll . . . it** Based on the proverb, 'A
    guilty conscience is a self-accuser', or
    '. . . feels continual fear' (Dent C606).
126–7  **he cannot lie . . . him** Compare the

a man's bosom. It fills one full of obstacles. It made me
once restore a purse of gold that I found. It beggars any
man that keeps it. It is turned out of all towns and cities    130
for a dangerous thing, and every man that means to live
well endeavours to trust to himself and to live without it.
FIRST EXECUTIONER  Zounds, it is even now at my elbow per-
    suading me not to kill the Duke.
SECOND EXECUTIONER  Take the devil in thy mind and believe    135
    him not. He would insinuate with thee, to make thee sigh.
FIRST EXECUTIONER  Tut, I am strong in fraud. He cannot
    prevail with me, I warrant thee.
SECOND EXECUTIONER  Spoke like a tall fellow that respects
    his reputation. Come, shall we to this gear?    140
FIRST EXECUTIONER  Take him over the costard with the hilts
    of thy sword, and then we will chop him in the malmsey
    butt in the next room.

Q:
132 trust to] Q2, F; trust to | To Q1

F:
128 one] a man    129 that] that (by chance)    130 of all] of    132 to live] liue    133 Zounds,
it is] 'Tis    136 to] but to    137–8 Tut . . . thee] I am strong fram'd, he cannot preuaile with
me    139–40 fellow . . . his] man . . . thy    140 to this gear] fall to worke    141 over] on
142 we will chop him in] throw him into

Commination against Sinners: 'Cursed is
he that lieth with his neighbour's wife'
(*Common Prayer*, p. 317).
127 **shamefaced** Q1's 'shamefast' is the earlier form; 'shamefaced', based on 'an etymological misinterpretation' (*OED*), was
becoming established as an alternative as
Shakespeare wrote, and indeed F reads
'shamefac'd'. The false etymology might
urge retention of the Quarto form, were it
not that *blushing* indicates the appearance of the *face*.

129–30 **It beggars . . . keeps it** Proverbially,
'Conscience is for beggars' (Dent C601.1).
130 **keeps** employs (see note to l. 121)
130–1 **It is . . . thing** Conscience's insecure
employment lapsing into vagabondage
perhaps intimates the social experience of
the Executioner himself.
131 **for** as being
132 **well** Equivocates between 'virtuously'
and 'prosperously, enjoyably'.
133 **at my elbow** Puts conscience in the role
of devil in the proverb 'the devil is at
one's elbow' (Dent D243.1). The Second

Executioner's reply separates the two.
Compare Thomas More, *History of the
Passion* (1534; printed 1557), l. 1315:
'We may well think that the devil is then
even busy about us, and not, as it is commonly said, at our elbow, but even at our
very heart' (cited in Dent).
136 **him** i.e. conscience
**insinuate with thee** worm his way into
your favour
137 **fraud** faithlessness. For Q1's 'strong in
fraud' F has 'strong fram'd'. Q1's reading contrasts with biblical 'strong in
faith' (Romans 4: 20, Bishops' Bible),
where the reference is to Abraham, who,
through his faith, was 'fully persuaded
that what he had promised he was able
also to perform'.
139 **tall** brave
140 **gear** business
141 **Take** strike
**costard** Humorous for 'head'. Literally, a
large kind of apple.
**hilts** handle
142 **chop him in** give him a sudden thrust
into (*OED*, chop, *v.*¹ 7, quoting this line);

201

SECOND EXECUTIONER  O, excellent device: make a sop of him!
FIRST EXECUTIONER  Hark, he stirs. Shall I strike?                    145
SECOND EXECUTIONER  No, first let's reason with him.
        *Clarence awaketh*
CLARENCE

Where art thou, keeper? Give me a cup of wine.
FIRST EXECUTIONER

You shall have wine enough, my lord, anon.
CLARENCE

In God's name, what art thou?
SECOND EXECUTIONER                    A man, as you are.
CLARENCE

But not, as I am, royal.
SECOND EXECUTIONER          Nor you, as we are, loyal.          150
CLARENCE

Thy voice is thunder, but thy looks are humble.
SECOND EXECUTIONER

My voice is now the King's, my looks mine own.
CLARENCE

How darkly and how deadly dost thou speak!
Tell me who are you, wherefore come you hither?
BOTH EXECUTIONERS

To, to, to—

Q:

146.1 *Clarence awaketh*] Q3; *not in* Q1, F    155 BOTH EXECUTIONERS] *Am⟨bo⟩. Q1. Similarly before*
'Ay' and at ll. 207 and 213.

F:

144 make] and make    145 Hark . . . strike?] Soft, he wakes. | 2 Strike.    146 SECOND EXECU-
TIONER] *From here to l. 152,* F *reverses* Q1's '1' *and* '2' (*see previous note*).    first let's] wee'l
154 Tell . . . hither] Your eyes do menace me: why looke you pale? | Who sent you hither?
Wherefore do you come

this and l. 244 are the only examples of
the sense in Shakespeare. F more mundanely but more variably has 'throw him
into' and 'drowne you in'.

142 **malmsey** strong sweet wine from Mon-
emvasia (Malvasia) in the Peloponnese,
Greece

144 **device** cunning contrivance (with a
glance at the sense 'emblematic figure':
the death emblematically fits someone
over-fond of wine)
**sop** Literally, a piece of bread dipped and
soaked in wine.

146 **No . . . him** The resolution to 'use our

hands, and not our tongues' (1.3.352) is
forgotten. See note to 1.3.342, 350.

153 **darkly** frowningly; ominously
**speak** Q1 probably omits F's further line
(see F collation) deliberately, because
(a) *look* echoes *looks*, already repeated,
(b) the implied gestural style of acting
might have been becoming old-fashioned,
or (c) the menacing expression was
incompatible with the humble looks of
l. 151 or the irresolution of l. 155. F gives
the hesitant 'To, to, to' to the Second Executioner alone, leaving it possible that
the First Executioner at least looks
menacing, an option not available in Q1.

CLARENCE        To murder me.

BOTH EXECUTIONERS            Ay.                                         155

CLARENCE

You scarcely have the hearts to tell me so,

And therefore cannot have the hearts to do it.

Wherein, my friends, have I offended you?

FIRST EXECUTIONER

Offended us you have not, but the King.

CLARENCE

I shall be reconciled to him again.                                    160

SECOND EXECUTIONER

Never, my lord; therefore prepare to die.

CLARENCE

Are you called forth from out a world of men

To slay the innocent? What is my offence?

Where are the evidence that do accuse me?

What lawful quest have given their verdict up             165

Unto the frowning judge, or who pronounced

The bitter sentence of poor Clarence' death?

Before I be convict by course of law,

To threaten me with death is most unlawful.

I charge you, as you hope to have redemption             170

By Christ's dear blood shed for our grievous sins,

That you depart and lay no hands on me.

The deed you undertake is damnable.

FIRST EXECUTIONER

What we will do, we do upon command.

SECOND EXECUTIONER

And he that hath commanded is the King.                   175

Q:
167–8 death? . . . law,] ~, . . . ~?

F:
155 BOTH EXECUTIONERS To] Q1 (*Am*. To); 2 To F    BOTH EXECUTIONERS Ay] Q1 (*Am*. I); *Both*. I,
I, F    162 called forth from out] drawne forth among    164 are . . . that do] is . . . that doth
(*altering* Q3 'are . . . to')    170–1 to . . . sins] for any goodnesse    175 the] our

162 **out** out of

164 **evidence** witnesses (a collective attract-
ing plural *are* and *do*)

165 **quest** board of inquest (another collective). *Mirror for Magistrates*, 'Clarence',
describes 'A quest to give such verdict

as they should' held against Clarence
'covertly within the Tower' (ll. 351–2);
but Clarence here implies there has been
no inquest at all.

168 **convict** convicted

170–1 **to . . . sins** F avoids profanity.

CLARENCE

    Erroneous vassal, the great King of kings  *II . i. 15*

    Hath in the tables of his law commanded

    That thou shalt do no murder, and wilt thou then

    Spurn at his edict, and fulfil a man's?

    Take heed, for he holds vengeance in his hands       180

    To hurl upon their heads that break his law.

SECOND EXECUTIONER

    And that same vengeance doth he throw on thee,

    For false forswearing, and for murder too.

    Thou didst receive the holy sacrament

    To fight in quarrel of the house of Lancaster—      185

FIRST EXECUTIONER

    And, like a traitor to the name of God,

    Didst break that vow, and with thy treacherous blade

    Unrip'st the bowels of thy sovereign's son—

SECOND EXECUTIONER

    Whom thou wert sworn to cherish and defend.

FIRST EXECUTIONER

    How canst thou urge God's dreadful law to us      190

    When thou hast broke it in so dear degree?

CLARENCE

    Alas, for whose sake did I that ill deed?

---

F:
176 vassal] Vassals   177 tables] Table   178 and wilt thou] Will you   180 hands] hand
182 throw] hurle   184–5 holy . . . in] Sacrament, to fight | In   189 wert] was't   191 so] such

176–81 **Erroneous . . . law** See Introduction, 'Unquiet Slumbers'.
176 **Erroneous vassal** The Executioner has been *Erroneous* (both 'mistaken' and 'straying from virtue') in identifying his vassalage. *Vassal* is also pejorative for someone base and abject.
    **King of kings** A formulaic way of referring to God, as in Revelation 19: 16 and elsewhere.
177 **the tables of his law** The Ten Commandments (described in Exodus 32: 15 as 'the two tables of His testimony')
178 **thou . . . murder** The sixth Commandment (Exodus 20: 13); the phrasing is that of the Catechism (Shaheen).
180–1 **Take . . . law** Echoes God's warning to leave vengeance to him: Deuteronomy

32: 35; Romans 12: 19.
181 **their heads that** the heads of those who
183 **false forswearing** Another broken Commandment. The wording recalls Matthew 5: 33: 'thou shalt not forswear thyself'.
184 **receive . . . sacrament** Receiving the sacrament at mass was a particularly solemn way of affirming an oath in pre-Protestant England.
185 **in quarrel of** for the cause of, in the dispute for
190–1 **How . . . degree** Echoes Romans 2: 21–3, 'Thou therefore which teachest another, teachest thou not thyself? . . . Thou that gloriest in the Law, through breaking the Law dishonourest thou God.'
191 **so dear** such a direful

For Edward, for my brother, for his sake.
Why, sirs, he sends ye not to murder me for this,
For in this sin he is as deep as I.                                    195
If God will be revengèd for this deed,
Take not the quarrel from his powerful arm.
He needs no indirect nor lawless course
To cut off those that have offended him.

FIRST EXECUTIONER
Who made thee then a bloody minister                                   200
When gallant-springing, brave Plantagenet,
That princely novice, was struck dead by thee?

CLARENCE
My brother's love, the devil, and my rage.

FIRST EXECUTIONER
Thy brother's love, the devil, and thy fault
Have brought us hither now to murder thee.                             205

CLARENCE
O, if you love my brother hate not me.
I am his brother, and I love him well.
If you be hired for meed, go back again,
And I will send you to my brother Gloucester,
Who will reward you better for my life                                 210
Than Edward will for tidings of my death.

F:
194 Why . . . ye] He sends you    195 this] that    196 revengèd for this] auenged for the
deed] deed, | O know you yet, he doth it publiquely    198 nor] or    204–5 the . . . brought]
our Duty, and thy Faults, | Prouoke    205 murder] slaughter    206 O, if you] If you do
208 be] are    210 will] shall

196–7 **If . . . arm** See note to ll. 180–1. 'His
    powerful arm' is independently biblical
    in idiom; compare Exodus 15: 16, 'the
    greatness of thine [God's] arm', etc.
196 **deed** See F's extra line.
197 **the quarrel** i.e. the settling of it
200 **Who . . . minister** In Romans 13: 4–6
    Paul describes one in authority as 'the
    minister of God, to take vengeance on
    him that doth evil', in contrast with
    those who damnably take the law into
    their own hands.
201 **gallant-springing** growing vigorously in
    beauty and gallantry. The suggestion of a

plant is taken up in *Plantagenet*.
202 **princely novice** beginner in knighthood
    (see *Richard Duke of York* 2.2.58–61)
203 **My brother's love** love for my brother.
    In his reply, the Executioner means 'your
    brother's (lack of) love for you'.
204 **the devil** F alters to 'our Duty'. Q1's
    reading gives an empty echoic sarcasm
    that is, however, an ironically true equivo-
    cation with the devil's name; compare
    l. 135. There may be a hint too that
    Richard is the devil.
208 **meed** reward earned dishonestly

SECOND EXECUTIONER

    You are deceived, your brother Gloucester hates you.

CLARENCE

    O no, he loves me, and he holds me dear.

    Go you to him from me—

BOTH EXECUTIONERS        Ay, so we will.

CLARENCE

    Tell him, when that our princely father York       215

    Blessed his three sons with his victorious arm

    And charged us from his soul to love each other,

    He little thought of this divided friendship.

    Bid Gloucester think of this, and he will weep.

BOTH EXECUTIONERS

    Ay, millstones, as he lessoned us to weep.       220

CLARENCE

    O do not slander him, for he is kind.

FIRST EXECUTIONER

    Right, as snow in harvest. Thou deceiv'st thyself;

    'Tis he hath sent us hither now to slaughter thee.

CLARENCE

    It cannot be, for when I parted with him

    He hugged me in his arms, and swore with sobs      225

    That he would labour my delivery.

SECOND EXECUTIONER

    Why, so he doth, now he delivers thee

    From this world's thraldom to the joys of heaven.

F:

214 BOTH EXECUTIONERS] Q1 (*Am.*); 1 F   217 And . . . other,] *not in* F   219 of] on (*from* Q6) 220 BOTH EXECUTIONERS] Q1 (*Am.*); 1 F   222 Thou deceiv'st thyself] Come, you deceiue your selfe   223 hath . . . thee] that sends vs to destroy you heere (*altering* Q2 'that sent vs hither now to murder thee')   224–5 when . . . He] he bewept my Fortune, | And   227 SECOND EXECU-TIONER] Q1 (2); 1 F   now . . . thee] when . . . you   228 world's] earths

215–17 when . . . other This supposed incident is partly reminiscent of the 'three suns' episode in *Richard Duke of York* 2.1, though there York has just been killed.
222 as snow in harvest Proverbial (Dent S590); from biblical Proverbs 25: 13. Snow in harvest would be un*kind*: (a) cruel, (b) unnatural.
225 He . . . arms Atreus similarly gives his

brother and intended victim Thyestes a hypocritical embrace (Seneca, *Thyestes*, ll. 507–11).
226 That . . . delivery Closely follows Kyd, *Spanish Tragedy* 3.7.33: 'That you would labour my delivery'. The suggestion of giving birth leads in to the Executioner's use of *deliver* with reference to death.

FIRST EXECUTIONER

  Make peace with God, for you must die, my lord.

CLARENCE

  Hast thou that holy feeling in thy soul                              230

  To counsel me to make my peace with God,

  And art thou yet to thy own soul so blind

  That thou wilt war with God by murd'ring me?

  Ah sirs, consider, he that set you on

  To do this deed will hate you for this deed.                        235

SECOND EXECUTIONER [*to First Executioner*]

  What shall we do?                        Relent, and save your souls.

FIRST EXECUTIONER

  Relent? 'Tis cowardly and womanish.

CLARENCE

  Not to relent is beastly, savage, devilish.

  [*To Second Executioner*] My friend, I spy some pity in thy

      looks.

  O, if thy eye be not a flatterer,                                        240

  Come thou on my side, and entreat for me.

  A begging prince what beggar pities not?

Q:
229 Make] Q2, F;   Makes Q1

F:
229 FIRST EXECUTIONER] Q1 (1);  2 F      230 Hast thou . . . thy soul] Haue you . . . your soules
232–3 art . . . wilt] are you yet to your owne soules so blinde, | That you will      234 Ah] O
he] they      235 for this] for the      236 souls.] F *adds* 5 *lines. See Appendix A, Passage C.*
237 'Tis] no: 'Tis      240 thy] thine

230 **Hast thou** F makes the address throughout the speech plural ('Haue you . . . in
your soules', etc.), whereas in Q1 Clarence
concentrates on the more determined
executioner.

234–5 **he . . . for this deed** Proverbially, 'A
king loves the treason but hates the traitor' (Dent K64).

236 **souls.** F has a further appeal to both
Executioners of five lines. They seem
misplaced. They might follow l. 242, to
be interrupted by F's 'Looke behinde you,
my Lord' (Knight, accidentally following
Johnson's suggestion), or l. 238 (Hammond, following Harold Jenkins's suggestion); other arrangements have been

accepted by other editors. Hammond's
version is effective in producing a strong
mid-speech turn from Clarence addressing both Executioners to confining his
appeal to the Second, but requires further
emendation of the Folio lines to make
them fit the new context. The lines, Johnson noted, 'are not necessary'.

237 **Relent . . . womanish** Proverbially, 'To
fear is womanish' (Dent W724.1).

239 *To Second Executioner* The following
address is so intently addressed to him
that Clarence gives the First Executioner
his opportunity. Clarence may physically
be attempting to draw the Second 'on my
side' when the First strikes.

**FIRST EXECUTIONER**

Ay, thus, and thus. If this will not serve,
   *He stabs him*
I'll chop thee in the malmsey butt in the next room.

                          *Exit with Clarence*

**SECOND EXECUTIONER**

A bloody deed, and desperately performed.          245
How fain, like Pilate, would I wash my hand
Of this most grievous-guilty murder done.
   *Enter First Executioner*

**FIRST EXECUTIONER**  Why dost thou not help me?
By heavens, the Duke shall know how slack thou art.

**SECOND EXECUTIONER**

I would he knew that I had saved his brother.       250
Take thou the fee, and tell him what I say,
For I repent me that the Duke is slain.         *Exit*

**FIRST EXECUTIONER**

So do not I. Go, coward as thou art.
Now must I hide his body in some hole
Until the Duke take order for his burial;       255
And when I have my meed, I must away,
For this will out, and here I must not stay.    *Exit*

Q:

244.1 *Exit*] F; *not in* Q1   *with Clarence*] STEEVENS (*subs.*); *not in* Q1, F   247.1 *Enter First Executioner*] *not in* Q1. *Compare* F.   257 *Exit*] F; *Exeunt*. Q1

F:

243–4 FIRST . . . thee] 2 Looke behinde you, my Lord. | 1 Take that, and that, if all this will not do, | Ile drowne you   243.1 *He stabs him*] *Stabs him*. (*position as in* Q)   244 in the next room] within   245 performed] dispatcht   246 hand] hands   247 grievous . . . done] greeuous murther   247.1 *Enter First Executioner*] *Enter* 1. *Murtherer*   248 Why . . . me] How now? what mean'st thou that thou help'st me not   249 heavens] Heauen (*possibly from* Q6, *but* '*Textual Companion*' *identifies* Q3 *as copy*)   thou art] you haue beene   254 Now . . . his] Well, Ile go hide the   255 Until the Duke take] Till that the Duke giue   256 must] will 257 here] then

243 **Ay, thus, and thus** In a dramatically effective moment F has the Second Executioner intervene (see Folio collation). There is a page-break in Q1 before l. 243, but the catchwords 'I I' (i.e. 'FIRST EXECUTIONER Ay') confirm that a line has not been accidentally dropped. Q1 must be accepted as having its own integrity whereby the would-be repentant fails to intervene; his role is then, perhaps, closer to that of Pilate (ll. 246–7).

244 **chop** See note to l. 142.

244.1 *with Clarence* Editors usually specify

'*with Clarence's body*', but he is probably not yet dead; 'If this will not serve' might even suggest he is still struggling. Clarence dies by drowning, as his dream prefigured.

245 **desperately** in spiritual despair; with extreme recklessness

246–7 **How . . . done** Pilate's action renouncing responsibility for Christ's fate (Matthew 27: 24) led to proverbial 'to wash one's hands of something' (Dent H122).

257 **this will out** Proverbially, 'murder will out' (Dent M1315).

[2.1]    [*Flourish.*] *Enter King, sick, Queen, Hastings,*
         *Rivers, Dorset, Buckingham, and others*

KING

So, now I have done a good day's work.
You peers, continue this united league.
I every day expect an embassage
From my Redeemer to redeem me hence,
And now in peace my soul shall part to heaven                5
Since I have set my friends at peace on earth.
Rivers and Hastings, take each other's hand.
Dissemble not your hatred, swear your love.

RIVERS

By heaven, my heart is purged from grudging hate,
And with my hand I seal my true heart's love.               10
    *He gives Hastings his hand*

---

Q:
    **2.1.0.1** *Flourish.*] F; *not in* Q1        *sick*] F; *not in* Q1     0.1–2 *Hastings . . . others*] *Hastings,*
*Ryuers, Dorcet, &c* Q1; *Rivers, Dorset, Buckingham, Hastings, Grey, and Others* CAPELL.. *Compare*
F.        5 to] Q1 (*Bodleian, Folger, Yale*), Q2, F; *from* Q1 (*British Library, Huntington*)        10.1 *He*
. . . *hand*] RIVERSIDE ('*Takes Hastings' hand' after l.* 9); *not in* Q1, F

F:
    **2.1.0.1–2** *Enter . . . others*] *Flourish.* | *Enter the King sicke, the Queene, Lord Marquesse* |
*Dorset, Riuers, Hastings, Catesby,* | *Buckingham, Wooduill.* ('*Dorset' not in* Q3)        1 So, now I
have] Why so: now haue I        5 now in] more to        6 set] made        7 Rivers and Hastings] *Dorset*
*and Riuers*        9 heart] soule

---

**2.1** The preceding murder of Clarence lends ominous irony to talk of peace and 'a good day's work' (l. 1). The King's deathbed attempt to reconcile enemies, especially Dorset and Hastings, is related in detail by More; it led to 'A counterfeit and pretended reconcilement' (Holinshed, pp. 363–5 and marginal note). Buckingham and Richard are not mentioned (Richard is present but silent in *True Tragedy*). Clarence died five or six years earlier. According to Holinshed, afterwards the King 'much did both lament his infortunate chance and repent his sudden execution; inasmuch that when any person sued to him for the pardon of malefactors condemned to death, he would accustomably say and openly speak, "O infortunate brother, for whose life not one would make suit!"' (p. 346). Shakespeare's compression of time makes Richard responsible for the King's death.

**0.1** *Enter King, sick* If Clarence slept on a couch in 1.4, the same property could serve as a sickbed for the King. This would visually reinforce the brothers' shared proximity to death. A couch might even occupy the same stage-space as King Henry's coffin in 1.2.

**0.2** *Dorset* In this scene, as in 1.3, Dorset and Grey seem to be alternative titles for the same figure, 'Grey' being the family name preserved as a title.

**1–6** *So . . . earth* The opening lines intermix the languages of diplomacy and Christian doctrine. The doctrinal reference in *good day's work* is to salvation through good works. *Embassage* (l. 3) extends a diplomatic term to spiritual affairs. Christ as *Redeemer* both ensures forgiveness of sins and will deliver the King from bondage on earth. *Peace* is both spiritual (l. 5) and socio-political (l. 6). Christ's 'Blessed are the peacemakers' underlies the speech, and also ll. 49–51.

**8** **Dissemble not your hatred** don't make an empty gesture that conceals hatred

HASTINGS

So thrive I as I truly swear the like.

KING

Take heed you dally not before your king,
Lest he that is the supreme King of kings          *I . iv. 177*
Confound your hidden falsehood and award
Either of you to be the other's end.                                                15

HASTINGS

So prosper I as I swear perfect love.

RIVERS

And I as I love Hastings with my heart.

KING

Madam, yourself are not exempt in this;
Nor your son Dorset; Buckingham, nor you.
You have been factious one against the other.                        20
Wife, love Lord Hastings, let him kiss your hand,
And what you do, do it unfeignedly.

QUEEN (*giving Hastings her hand to kiss*)

Here, Hastings, I will never more remember
Our former hatred, so thrive I and mine.

KING

Dorset, embrace him. Hastings, love Lord Marquis.                    25

DORSET

This interchange of love, I here protest,
Upon my part shall be unviolable.

HASTINGS   And so swear I, my lord.

    *Dorset and Hastings embrace*

Q:

17 Hastings] hastings     23 *giving . . . kiss*] RIVERSIDE (*subs.*); *not in* Q1, F     25 KING . . . Marquis] F (*as 2 lines*: him |); *not in* Q1     28.1 *Dorset . . . embrace*] CAPELL (*subs.*); *not in* Q1, F

F:

18 are . . . in] is . . . from     19 your] you     23 Here] There     27 unviolable] inuiolable
28 I, my lord] I

11 **So thrive I** *Thrive* is subjunctive: 'may thrive'. This and similar protestations foreshadow future events with double-edged dramatic irony: Hastings, Rivers (l. 17), the Queen and her family (l. 24), and Buckingham (ll. 32–40) will not thrive, though it is already too late for

their sincerity or lack of it to make much difference.

14 **award** sentence, appoint
25 **KING . . . Marquis.** The line's absence from Q1 can perhaps be explained as compositor's eyeskip from 'Dorset' to the speech-prefix for the next line.

KING

    Now princely Buckingham, seal thou this league

    With thy embracements to my wife's allies,          30

    And make me happy in your unity.

BUCKINGHAM (*to the Queen*)

    Whenever Buckingham doth turn his hate

    On you or yours, but with all duteous love

    Doth cherish you and yours, God punish me

    With hate in those where I expect most love;      35

    When I have most need to employ a friend,

    And most assurèd that he is a friend,

    Deep, hollow, treacherous, and full of guile

    Be he unto me. This do I beg of God

    When I am cold in zeal to you or yours.          40

      [*He embraces Rivers and Dorset*]

KING

    A pleasing cordial, princely Buckingham,

    Is this thy vow unto my sickly heart.

    There wanteth now our brother Gloucester here

    To make the perfect period of this peace.

      *Enter Richard Duke of Gloucester*

BUCKINGHAM

    And in good time here comes the noble Duke.      45

---

Q:
30 wife's] wiues     40.1 *He . . . Dorset*] *not in* Q1. *Compare F.*     44.1 *Richard Duke of Gloucester*] *Glocest.*

F:
33 On you or yours] Vpon your Grace     39 God] heauen     40 zeal] loue     40.1 *He . . . Dorset*] *Embrace*     44 perfect] blessed     44.1 *Enter . . . Gloucester*] *Enter Ratcliffe, and Gloster. (after l. 45)*     45 the noble Duke] Sir *Richard Ratcliffe*, and the Duke

30 **allies** kindred (and thereby political allies)

33 **On you or yours** In Q1, Buckingham's repetition of this phrase and avoidance of F's dutiful 'your Grace' make him more obviously insincere.

33–4 **but with . . . Doth cherish** and does not cherish you with all duteous love. The syntax is perhaps treacherously ambiguous. See Abbott 125.

34–9 **God . . . me** Anticipates his league with Richard.

38 **Deep** profound in craft

40 **zeal** ardent love, devotion

41 **cordial** In the literal sense of a medicine restorative to the heart.

43–4 **There . . . peace** And Richard arrives pointedly on cue with friendly greetings. Compare his unexpected entrance at 1.3.41.1 and the Queen's unaware cue for it. Richard's appearance is also unexpected in that he plays no part in this reconciliation in the chronicles.

43 **wanteth** is needed, is missing

44 **perfect period** full completion

RICHARD DUKE OF GLOUCESTER

    Good morrow to my sovereign King and Queen;

    And princely peers, a happy time of day.

KING

    Happy indeed as we have spent the day.

    Brother, we have done deeds of charity:

    Made peace of enmity, fair love of hate,            50

    Between these swelling wrong-incensèd peers.

RICHARD DUKE OF GLOUCESTER

    A blessèd labour, my most sovereign liege.

    Amongst this princely heap if any here

    By false intelligence or wrong surmise

    Hold me a foe, if I unwittingly or in my rage       55

    Have aught committed that is hardly borne

    By any in this presence, I desire

    To reconcile me to his friendly peace.

    'Tis death to me to be at enmity. *[ How right he is? ]*

    I hate it, and desire all good men's love.           60

    First, madam, I entreat true peace of you,

    Which I will purchase with my duteous service;

    Of you, my noble cousin Buckingham,

    If ever any grudge were lodged between us;

    Of you, Lord Rivers, and Lord Grey, of you,      65

    That all without desert have frowned on me;

    Dukes, earls, lords, gentlemen—indeed of all.

    I do not know that Englishman alive

    With whom my soul is any jot at odds

    More than the infant that is born tonight.        70

  ✓ I thank my God for my humility. ¦

F:

49 Brother] Gloster    52 liege] Lord    53 Amongst] Among    55 unwittingly] vnwillingly
57 By] To    65 Lord Rivers . . . you] and you, Lord *Riuers* and of *Dorset*    66 me] me: | Of you
Lord *Wooduill*, and Lord *Scales* of you

47 **a happy time of day** Perhaps simply a
  cheerful salutation. The King takes *happy*
  to mean 'blessed'.

49–51 **we . . . peers** See note to ll. 1–6.

51 **swelling** haughty, overweening. *Swelling
  wrong-incensèd* also suggests 'swollen with
  wrongfully provoked anger'.

53 **heap** large gathering. 'It is scarcely possible
  to doubt the deflationary overtones of the
  term applied to such a group' (Hammond).

54 **intelligence** secret information (as from
  spies)

56 **hardly** with difficulty, resentfully

62 **purchase** bring about

65 **Of . . . of you** See Appendix D, Note 3.
  **Lord Grey** See note on '*Dorset*', l. 0.2.

66 **all without desert** entirely without my
  deserving it

71 **I . . . humility** 'perhaps an aside'
  (Honigmann)

QUEEN

    A holy day shall this be kept hereafter.

    I would to God all strifes were well compounded.

    My sovereign liege, I do beseech your majesty

    To take our brother Clarence to your grace.         75

RICHARD DUKE OF GLOUCESTER

    Why, madam, have I offered love for this,

    To be so flouted in this royal presence?

    Who knows not that the noble Duke is dead?

        *They all start*

    You do him injury to scorn his corpse.

RIVERS

    Who knows not he is dead? Who knows he is?      80

QUEEN

    All-seeing heaven, what a world is this!

BUCKINGHAM

    Look I so pale, Lord Dorset, as the rest?

DORSET

    Ay, my good lord, and no one in this presence

    But his red colour hath forsook his cheeks.

KING

    Is Clarence dead? The order was reversed.       85

RICHARD DUKE OF GLOUCESTER

    But he, poor soul, by your first order died,

    And that a wing-led Mercury did bear.

    Some tardy cripple bore the countermand,

    That came too lag to see him burièd.

Q:
77 so flouted] F;  thus scorned Q1     78.1 *They all start*] F;  *not in* Q1

F:
74 liege . . . majesty] Lord . . . Highnesse     78 noble] gentle     80 RIVERS] Q1 (*Ryu.*);  *King.* F
83 one in this] man in the     86 soul] man     87 wing-led] Q1 (wingled);  winged Q2, F
88 bore] bare

73 **well** as well
    **compounded** settled
75 **to your grace** into your favour
77 **so flouted** Q1's 'thus scorned' is a weak
    anticipation of 'scorn' in l. 79.
80 RIVERS F has '*King.*'. The variant prob-
    ably results from revision (see Appendix D,
    Note 3), though a misreading in either dir-
    ection ('Kin'/'Riu') cannot be ruled out.
81 **what . . . this** Proverbial (Dent W889.1).
83 **no one** i.e. there is no one

84 **But . . . hath** whose red colour has not
85–9 **The . . . burièd** Shakespeare invents
    these details. 'Some tardy cripple' sounds
    like Richard: perhaps a self-depreciatory
    joke with the audience.
87 **wing-led Mercury** i.e. speedy messenger.
    Mercury, messenger of the Roman gods,
    wore winged sandals. The unusual com-
    pound *wing-led* occurs also at *Cymbeline*
    2.4.24.
89 **lag** laggingly

God grant that some less noble and less loyal,
Nearer in bloody thoughts, but not in blood,
Deserve not worse than wretched Clarence did,
And yet go current from suspicion.

*Enter Stanley Earl of Derby*

STANLEY EARL OF DERBY (*kneeling*)

A boon, my sovereign, for my service done.

KING

I pray thee, peace. My soul is full of sorrow.            95

STANLEY EARL OF DERBY

I will not rise unless your highness grant.

KING

Then speak at once. What is it thou demand'st?

STANLEY EARL OF DERBY [*rising*]

✓The forfeit, sovereign, of my servant's life,
Who slew today a riotous gentleman
Lately attendant on the Duke of Norfolk.                  100

KING

Have I a tongue to doom my brother's death,
And shall the same give pardon to a slave?
My brother slew no man; his fault was thought;
And yet his punishment was cruel death.
Who sued to me for him? Who, in my rage,                  105
Kneeled at my feet and bade me be advised?
Who spake of brotherhood? Who of love?
Who told me how the poor soul did forsake

Q:
91 blood] Q2, F; blond Q1      93.1 *Stanley Earl of Derby*] *Darby*      94 STANLEY EARL OF DERBY]
*Dar.* Q1, F. *Similarly throughout* 2.1.      kneeling] *not in* Q1, F      98 rising] *not in* Q1, F

F:
91 but] and      93.1 *Stanley Earl of Derby*] *Earle of Derby*      95 pray thee] prethee      96 grant]
heare me      97 speak . . . demand'st] say . . . requests      102 the same] that tongue      103 slew]
kill'd      104 cruel] bitter      105 rage] wrath      106 at . . . bade] and . . . bid      107 Who spake
. . . Who] Who spoke . . . who spoke

91 **Nearer . . . blood** i.e. closer to having
bloody thoughts but less closely related to
the King. Varies the proverb 'The nearer
in kin, the less in kindness' (Tilley K38).
93 **go . . . suspicion** i.e. be accepted as free
from suspicion. Alludes to unadulterated
coinage.
94–102 STANLEY . . . **slave?** Resembles *Spanish Tragedy* 3.13, where 'The humble
supplication | Of Don Bazulto for his

murdered son' intensifies Hieronimo's
grief for his own son's death.
✓98 **The forfeit** Stanley is asking for what is
legally forfeit to be redeemed.
102 **the same** F's 'that tongue' might be
preferred.
103 **his fault was thought** As distinct from
deed. Proverbially, 'Thought is free' (Dent
T244).
106 **be advised** take advice, reconsider

The mighty Warwick, and did fight for me?
Who told me, in the field by Tewkesbury 110
When Oxford had me down, he rescued me,
And said, 'Dear brother, live, and be a king'?
Who told me, when we both lay in the field
Frozen almost to death, how he did lap me
Even in his own garments, and gave himself 115
All thin and naked to the numb-cold night?
All this from my remembrance brutish wrath
Sinfully plucked, and not a man of you
Had so much grace to put it in my mind.
But when your carters or your waiting-vassals 120
Have done a drunken slaughter, and defaced
The precious image of our dear Redeemer,
You straight are on your knees for 'Pardon, pardon'.
And I, unjustly too, must grant it you.
But for my brother not a man would speak, 125
Nor I, ungracious, speak unto myself
For him, poor soul. The proudest of you all
Have been beholden to him in his life,
Yet none of you would once plead for his life.
O God, I fear thy justice will take hold 130
On me and you, and mine and yours, for this.
Come, Hastings, help me to my closet. O, poor
  Clarence!

*Exeunt some with King and Queen;*
*Gloucester, [Buckingham, and others] remain*

Q:
118 plucked] Q2, F; puckt Q1    128 beholden] beholding. *Similarly at* 3.1.107 *and* 3.2.107.
132.1 *Exeunt . . . Queen*] F; *Exit.* Q1    132.2 *Gloucester . . . remain*] This edition; *not in* Q1, F

F:
110 by] at    115 own garments] Garments (*altering* Q6, 'owne armes')    gave] did giue
129 plead] begge    132 O] Ah

110–12 **in . . . king** Shakespeare evidently
  invented this incident.
114 **lap** wrap
116 **thin** thinly clad
122 **The . . . Redeemer** i.e. a man, as made
  in God's image (Genesis 1: 27). But 'our
  dear Redeemer' specifically invokes Christ,
  presumably because Christ taught that
  one should love one's neighbour, and
  turn the other cheek when offered an

affront. Compare Calvin, *Institution*,
  2.8.40: 'unless we well defile the image of
  God, we must have care to touch no man
  none otherwise than as a sacred thing'.
130–1 **thy . . . you** The address turns from
  God (second person singular) to the assembled company (plural).
132 **Hastings** Called on as Lord Chamberlain.
  **closet** private apartment
132.2 *Buckingham, and others* In F

RICHARD DUKE OF GLOUCESTER

This is the fruit of rashness. Marked you not
How that the guilty kindred of the Queen
Looked pale when they did hear of Clarence' death?　　　135
O, they did urge it still unto the King.
God will revenge it. But come, let's in
To comfort Edward with our company.　　　　*Exeunt*

[**2.2**]　*Enter the old Duchess of York, with Clarence's*
　　　　*children: a Boy and a Girl*

BOY

Tell me, good grannam, is our father dead?

DUCHESS OF YORK　No, boy.

BOY

Why do you wring your hands and beat your breast,
And cry, 'O Clarence, my unhappy son'?

GIRL

Why do you look on us and shake your head,　　　　5

Q:

　**2.2.0.1–2** *Enter . . . Girl*] *Enter Dutches of Yorke, with Clarence Children.*　**2** DUCHESS OF YORK]
*Dut.* QI. *In speech-prefixes she is given the further abbreviation 'yor.' only at* 4.1.18, 48, *and* 87.

F:

133 fruit] fruits　　137 But come, let's in] Come Lords will you go　　138 company.] company. |
*Buc.* We wait vpon your Grace.

　**2.2.0.1–2** *Enter . . . Girl*] *Enter the old Dutchesse of Yorke, with the two | children of Clarence.*
1 BOY Tell me, good grannam] *Edw.* Good Grandam tell vs　　3 BOY . . . you wring your hands]
*Daugh. . . . . weepe so oft.* F2 *reintroduces* 'you' *before* 'weepe'.　　5 GIRL] *Boy.*

Buckingham remains, for he has a part-
line of speech; he is not Richard's only
hearer, for at l. 137 he addresses 'Lords'.
In Q1 the following speech offers an
opportunity for a limited early complicity
between Richard and Buckingham, but
Richard's hypocritical piety makes it
plausible that he is speaking to a larger
audience: perhaps also Hastings and/or
Stanley. See note to 2.2.87.1.

136 **still** constantly

**2.2** Another court scene; without basis in
the chronicles (but see note to ll. 107–9).
In *True Tragedy* the Queen is similarly
comforted by her children after the death
of Edward. By switching to Clarence's
children Shakespeare's play again deals

allusively and by proxy with matters concerning the young princes (see headnote
to 1.4). In the Elizabethan theatre the
two pairs of children might have been
played by the same pair of boy actors.
Clarence's children were closer in line of
succession than Richard, but the play
makes no direct reference to the point.

1–87 **BOY . . . lamentations** The episode is
often severely shortened in performance,
and is shorter in Q1 than F (see note to
l. 33). Early restorers of Shakespeare's
text to the stage such as Edwin Booth,
Phelps, and Irving followed Q1's cut.

1 **grannam** A colloquial pronunciation of
'grandam'. Q1 *Richard III* provides *OED*'s
earliest illustration. F normalizes to
'Grandam'.

And call us wretches, orphans, castaways,
If that our noble father be alive?

DUCHESS OF YORK

My pretty cousins, you mistake me much.
I do lament the sickness of the King,
As loath to lose him, not your father's death.            10
It were lost labour to weep for one that's lost.

BOY

Then, grannam, you conclude that he is dead.
The King my uncle is to blame for this.
God will revenge it, whom I will importune
With daily prayers, all to that effect.                   15

DUCHESS OF YORK

Peace, children, peace. The King doth love you well.
Incapable and shallow innocents,
You cannot guess who caused your father's death.

BOY

Grannam, we can; for my good uncle Gloucester
Told me the King, provokèd by the Queen,                  20
Devised impeachments to imprison him.
And when he told me so, he wept,
And hugged me in his arm, and kindly kissed my cheek,
And bade me rely on him as in my father,
And he would love me dearly as his child.                 25

DUCHESS OF YORK

O that deceit should steal such gentle shapes,

Q:
23 cheek] Q2 (cheeke); checke Q1

F:
6 wretches, orphans] Orphans, Wretches    7 be] were    8 much] both    11 labour to weep
for] sorrow to waile    12 grannam, you conclude that] you conclude, (my Grandam)    13 my
. . . this] mine . . . it    15 daily] earnest    effect.] effect. | *Daugh.* And so will I.    19 Grannam]
Grandam. *Similarly l.* 30 *and in* 2.4.    20 provokèd] prouok'd to it    22 he told] my Vnckle
told    23 hugged me in his arm] pittied me    24 And bade . . . in] Bad . . . on    25 his] a
26 O . . . shapes] Ah . . . shape

6 **castaways** The word is entirely literal. *OED* does not record the seafaring sense before 1799.
8 **cousins** Commonly applied to various relatives.
10 **As** being
11 **It . . . that's lost** Compare the proverb, 'For a lost thing care not' (Dent T127).
12 **conclude** end up saying; demonstrate

13 **to blame** Q1's 'too blame' combines the senses 'to blame' and 'too blameworthy'.
17 **Incapable** unsusceptible
23 **kindly** with familial affection
26–7 **O . . . guile** The lines play on the theatrical senses of *shape* (role, guise) and *visor* (mask). *Deceit* and Q1's *guile* suggest morality-play figures, as does F's *vice*.

And with a virtuous visor hide foul guile!
He is my son; yea, and therein my shame;
Yet from my dugs he drew not this deceit.

BOY

Think you my uncle did dissemble, grannam?                    30

DUCHESS OF YORK   Ay, boy.

BOY

I cannot think it.

      *[Wailing within]*

            Hark, what noise is this?

    *Enter the Queen [with her hair about her ears]*

QUEEN

O who shall hinder me to wail and weep,
To chide my fortune and torment myself?
I'll join with black despair against my soul,                 35
And to myself become an enemy.

DUCHESS OF YORK

What means this scene of rude impatience?

QUEEN

To mark an act of tragic violence.
Edward, my lord, your son, our king, is dead.
Why grow the branches, now the root is withered?             40
Why wither not the leaves, the sap being gone?

Q:

27 visor] visard      32 *Wailing within*] This edition;   *not in* Q1, F      32.1 *with . . . ears*] *not in* Q1.
*Compare F.*      38 mark] WILSON *(conj.* Maxwell);   make Q1, F

F:

27 foul guile] deepe vice      28 yea] I      32.1 *with . . . ears*] *with her haire about her ears,* | *Riuers*
*& Dorset after her*      33 O who] Ah! who (Q3 'Wh Who', Q5a 'Whoy', Q5b *and* Q6 'Who'; F *copy*
Q6)      39 your] thy      40 now the root is withered] when the Roote is gone      41 the sap being
gone] that want their sap

29 **from . . . deceit** From the proverb 'He
sucked evil from the dug' (Dent E198).

32 *Wailing within* The Boy evidently hears
the Queen's lamentations.

32.1 **with . . . ears** This detail comes from F.
A woman's unbound hair was, by theatrical convention, a sign of uncontrolled
grief or madness.

33 **who shall hinder me** In F Rivers and
Dorset follow the Queen on stage, and
they have speeches offering comfort to the
Queen after l. 87. Q1 keeps this part of the
scene confined to women and children.

36 **to . . . enemy** implying suicide (compare
1.2.82–3)

37 **scene** In the theatrical sense, which the
Queen develops in the following line.
**rude** harsh, unrestrained, disorderly

38 **mark** Q1 reads 'make', which makes
little sense as the *act* is presumably the
King's death.
**act** (a) event, (b) theatrical action

39 **lord** husband

40–1 **Why . . . gone** Echoes John 15: 4–5:
'The branch cannot bear fruit of itself
except it abide in the vine . . . He is cast
forth as a branch, and withereth.' As
compared with F, Q1 is more formally
patterned: 'grow . . . withered | wither
. . . gone'.

If you will live, lament; if die, be brief,
That our swift-wingèd souls may catch the King's,
Or like obedient subjects follow him
To his new kingdom of perpetual rest.     45
DUCHESS OF YORK
Ah, so much interest have I in thy sorrow
As I had title in thy noble husband.
I have bewept a worthy husband's death
And lived by looking on his images,
But now two mirrors of his princely semblance     50
Are cracked in pieces by malignant death,
And I for comfort have but one false glass,
√ Which grieves me when I see my shame in him.
Thou art a widow, yet thou art a mother
And hast the comfort of thy children left thee;     55
But death hath snatched my children from mine arms
And plucked two crutches from my feeble limbs,
Edward and Clarence. O, what cause have I,
Thine being but a moiety of my grief,
To overgo thy plaints and drown thy cries!     60
BOY (*to the Queen*)
Good aunt, you wept not for our father's death.
How can we aid you with our kindred tears?
GIRL (*to the Queen*)
Our fatherless distress was left unmoaned.
Your widow's dolours likewise be unwept.
QUEEN
Give me no help in lamentation.     65
I am not barren to bring forth complaints.

Q:
59 Thine‸] F; Then, Q1     a] F; *not in* Q1     62 kindred] F; kindreds Q1     66 complaints] F;
laments Q1

F:
45 perpetual rest] nere-changing night     46 have I] haue     49 by] with     53 Which] That
55 left thee] left     56 children] Husband     57 limbs] hands     58 Edward and Clarence]
*Clarence,* and *Edward*     59 grief] moane (*altering* Q6 'selfe')     60 plaints] woes     61 Good] Ah
63 GIRL] *Daugh.*     64 widow's dolours] widdow-dolour

46 **interest** right to share, entitlement
48–53 **I . . . him** The Duchess does not
appear in *Richard Duke of York.*
49 **his images** i.e. his sons
√52 **false glass** Richard gives a distorted image
of his father.

64 **be** let [them] be (subjunctive)
66 **barren to** i.e. so barren as to be unable to
**complaints** Q1's 'laments' seems influenced by 'lamentation', giving a weak
near-repetition.

All springs reduce their currents to mine eyes,
That I, being governed by the wat'ry moon,
May send forth plenteous tears to drown the world.
O for my husband, for my dear lord Edward!                    70
BOTH CHILDREN
O for our father, for our dear lord Clarence!
DUCHESS OF YORK
Alas for both, both mine Edward and Clarence!
QUEEN
What stay had I but Edward? And he is gone.
BOTH CHILDREN
What stay had we but Clarence? And he is gone.
DUCHESS OF YORK
What stays had I but they? And they are gone.                75
QUEEN
Was never widow had so dear a loss.
BOTH CHILDREN
Was never orphans had a dearer loss.
DUCHESS OF YORK
Was never mother had a dearer loss.
Alas, I am the mother of these moans.
Their woes are parcelled, mine are general.                   80
She for an Edward weeps, and so do I;

Q:
68 moon] F; moane Q1    70 dear] F; eire Q1; heire Q3    71 BOTH CHILDREN] *Ambo. Similarly*
*ll.* 74 (*Am.*) *and* 77.    81 an] F; *not in* Q1

F:
70, 71 O . . . O] Ah . . . Ah    71, 77 BOTH CHILDREN] Q1 (*Ambo.*), F (*Chil.*)    73 he is] hee's (*altering* Q6 'is he')    74 BOTH CHILDREN] Q1 (*Am.*), F (*Chil.*)    he is] he's (*altering* Q6 'is he')
77 Was . . . a dearer] Were . . . so deere a    78 a dearer] so deere a    79 moans] Greefes
80 mine are] mine is

67 **reduce** bring together
68–9 **That . . . world** The Queen figures herself
as a gathering of all the waters in the world.
If she is simply a sea, the inundation caused
by the moon is tidal. But 'plenteous tears'
also suggests rain, as in *Dream* 2.1.103–4,
where 'the moon, the governess of floods, |
Pale in her anger, washes all the air'. In either case the Queen extravagantly anticipates a second Deluge. In the context of 'not
barren' (l. 66) and the Queen's desire to
'send forth' tears, there seems to be a fur-

ther reference to her menstrual cycle as
'governed by the wat'ry moon'.
68 **moon** Q1's 'moane' could simply result
from an ambiguous copy spelling such as
'mone', perhaps assisted by context.
That there was aural play betwen *moon*
and *moan* is not impossible.
73 **stay** support
76 **Was never** there was never. The construction is Spenserian (*Faerie Queene*
I. ii. 23, etc.).
80 **parcelled** divided between them

I for a Clarence weep, so doth not she.

These babes for Clarence weep, and so do I;

I for an Edward weep, so do not they.

Alas, you three on me, threefold distressed,                              85

Pour all your tears. I am your sorrow's nurse,

And I will pamper it with lamentations.

> *Enter Richard Duke of Gloucester with Buckingham*
> *and others*

RICHARD DUKE OF GLOUCESTER (*to the Queen*)

Sister, have comfort. All of us have cause

To wail the dimming of our shining star,

But none can cure their harms by wailing them.—                          90

Madam my mother, I do cry you mercy,

I did not see your grace. Humbly on my knee

I crave your blessing.

DUCHESS OF YORK

God bless thee, and put meekness in thy mind,

Love, charity, obedience, and true duty.                                 95

RICHARD DUKE OF GLOUCESTER

Amen. [*Aside*] And make me die a good old man: |

Q:

87.1–2 *Richard . . . others*] Glocest. | *with others*     88 Sister] F; Madame Q1

F:

82 weep] weepes     83–4 and . . . Edward weep] *not in* F     87 lamentations.] Lamentation. (*followed by* 12 *lines not in* Q1. *See Appendix A, Passage D.*)     87.1–2 *Richard . . . others*] *Richard, Buckingham, Derbie, Ha-*|*stings, and Ratcliffe*     90 cure their] helpe our     94 mind] breast

87 **lamentations.** F has a passage not in Q1: see note to l. 33.

87.2 **others** They should include some of the lords who appeared in 2.1. F specifies Stanley, Hastings, and Ratcliffe, the last of whom in F also enters with Richard in 2.1. In Q1 Ratcliffe makes no appearance before 3.3. Richard, Buckingham, Stanley, and Hastings might constitute the same group that remained on stage at the end of 2.1. There could, then, be a repeated stage grouping of the King's relatives and the old aristocracy. Hastings, Buckingham, and Stanley later come into conflict with Richard one by one. The opposing matriarchal group of the Queen and her allies will eventually encompass almost all, as it becomes redefined to include Richard's victims.

88 **Sister, have comfort** Cibber had Richard come forward '*weeping*'. Edmund Kean took out a handkerchief just before ad-

vancing (Hankey, p. 147).

88 **Sister** Richard cloyingly fulfils his mock-extravagant offer to 'call King Edward's widow "sister"' (1.1.109). Q1's neutral 'Madame' seems to anticipate l. 91.

89 **the . . . star** Suggests the fading and decline in astrological influence of a planet.

90 **none . . . them** Based on proverbial 'What can't be cured must be endured' (Dent C922). Margaret in *Richard Duke of York* 5.4.37–8 and Barabas in Marlowe's *Jew of Malta* 1.2.237–8 both point out the uselessness of lamentation.

91 **cry you mercy** beg your pardon

94–8 **God . . . out** The phrasing and sardonic tone resemble *Titus* 4.2.43–4, where Chiron describes his brother's desire for a thousand Roman dames to rape as 'A charitable wish, and full of love', and Aaron comments 'Here lacks but your mother for to say amen'.

96 **Amen** Might also be aside.

That's the butt-end of a mother's blessing.
I marvel why her grace did leave it out.

BUCKINGHAM

You cloudy princes and heart-sorrowing peers
That bear this mutual heavy load of moan,                    100
Now cheer each other in each other's love.
Though we have spent our harvest of this king,
We are to reap the harvest of his son.
The broken rancour of your high-swoll'n hearts,
But lately splinted, knit, and joined together,             105
Must gently be preserved, cherished and kept.
Meseemeth good that with some little train
Forthwith from Ludlow the young Prince be fetched
Hither to London to be crowned our king.

RICHARD DUKE OF GLOUCESTER

Then be it so; and go we to determine                        110

Q:
105 splinted] Q1 (splinterd), Q2 (splinted), F (splinter'd)    joined together] Q2, F; ioynd
etogether Q1

F:
97 That's] That is    98 why] that    100 mutual heavy] heauie mutuall    104 hearts] hates
108 fetched] fet    109 king.] F *adds* 18 *lines. See Appendix A, Passage E.*

97 **butt-end** (a) blunt end, (b) dregs. *OED* cites this as the earliest figurative use of the phrase, and glosses 'The mere concluding part; the "fag end"'. *OED* associates it with *butt*, *sb.³*, 'the thicker end of anything, *esp.* of a tool or weapon'; however *butt*, *sb.²*, 'cask, barrel' is also possible, as *OED*'s gloss itself suggests.

99 **cloudy** gloomy, sullen

100 **moan** grief

103 **his son** The plot to detain and eventually kill Edward's two sons is initiated while Clarence's two orphaned children are on stage. Sher, pretending no interest in Buckingham's speech, sat with an arm and crutch round each child's shoulder.

104–6 **The . . . kept** A conspicuously mixed metaphor. Primarily an image of a broken limb that has recently been set and healed; it is the healing that 'Must gently be preserved'. Also with suggestions of (a) a festering swelling that has been lanced (*broken*) and dressed to heal the wound (by this reading the breaking is part of the curing), and (b) in l. 104, a pasture overgrown with weeds (*rancour* as 'rank vegetation') that has now been ploughed up

(*broken*). See Appendix D, Note 6.

104 **The . . . hearts** Compare 'To show the rancour of their high-swoll'n hearts', in *Edward III* 3.1.131. This, *1 Henry VI* 3.1.26, and *Titus* 5.3.13 support Q1 'hearts' against F 'hates'.

105 **splinted** Q1 and F read 'splintered'; the intermediate quartos have 'splinted'. In a modern-spelling edition Q1's form is misleading, and I follow Taylor in taking it as no more than a spelling variant.

107–9 **Meseemeth . . . king** Buckingham is enabling Richard's plans, as is confirmed in ll. 115–23. In More, Richard secretly persuades the Queen on this course; *True Tragedy* Sc. 3 shows Buckingham proposing it to Richard.

108 **Ludlow** A castle in Shropshire and stronghold for English control over Wales. Historically, Edward, as Prince of Wales, had been sent there by his father to exercise royal authority.

109 **king.** F prints a passage in which Buckingham explains to Rivers why a small train is desirable. In F, Richard's 'Then be it so' (l. 110) is consensual; in Q1 it is coercive.

Who they shall be that straight shall post to Ludlow.
Madam, and you my mother, will you go
To give your censures in this weighty business?
QUEEN *and* DUCHESS OF YORK   With all our hearts.

                       *Exeunt all but Gloucester, Buckingham*

BUCKINGHAM
  My lord, whoever journeys to the Prince,                               115
  For God's sake let not us two stay behind;
  For by the way I'll sort occasion,
  As index to the story we late talked of,
  To part the Queen's proud kindred from the King.
RICHARD DUKE OF GLOUCESTER
  My other self, my counsel's consistory,                                 120
  My oracle, my prophet, my dear cousin!
  I like a child will go by thy direction.
  Towards Ludlow, then, for we'll not stay behind.

                                      *Exeunt*

Q:
114 QUEEN *and* DUCHESS OF YORK] CAMBRIDGE; *Ans.* Q1; *line not in* F   114.1 *all but] man⟨ent⟩.*
123 we'll] F;   we will Q1   *Exeunt*] F;   *not in* Q1

F:
111 Ludlow] London   112 mother] Sister   113–14 weighty . . . hearts] businesse
114.1 *Gloucester, Buckingham*] Buckingham, *and* Richard   116 God's . . . behind] God . . . at
home   119 King] Prince   122 like] as   123 Towards Ludlow] Toward London

113 **censures** opinions
114 **QUEEN . . . YORK** Q1's '*Ans.*' may per
    haps be for 'Answer', or an error for
    '*Amb.*', i.e. '*Ambo*', Latin for 'both'.
117 **by** on
    **sort** find, contrive
118 **index** preface, prologue
119 **King** Q1 here strikingly and unusually
    refers to the Prince as King. Though
    never crowned, he is recognized as King
    Edward V in Hall and Holinshed, and his
    reign is accorded a separate chapter. Still,
    Buckingham seems to be looking for
    ward, wishing to prevent the young
    King-to-be from becoming a pawn of his
    mother's family. The echo between '*kin*
    dred' and '*King*' is significant, and 'King'
    feeds into Richard's wordplay between
    'counsel' and 'council'. Richard pushes
    the analogy between the two potential
    kings-to-be further when he says he too is

'like a child' (l. 122).
120 **My other self** Proverbial ('A friend is
    another self', Dent F696). From Aristotle,
    and popularized in Erasmus' account of
    Alexander's friendship with Hephaestion:
    '*amicus alter ipse*, that is, two friends are
    one soul and one body' (*Apophthegms*,
    trans. Nicholas Udall, 1542, 207$^v$). Eras
    mus says, 'Hephaestion was so highly in
    favour with Alexander that he called him
    *alter se*, the second Alexander, and used
    him as familiarly as his own self, hiding
    from him none of all his secrets', noting
    an incident in which he warned him 'to
    keep his counsel secret' (187–187$^v$; com
    pare l. 121). For the echo of Marlowe's
    *Jew of Malta*, see Introduction, 'Barabas
    and the Vice'.
    **counsel's** innermost thoughts'. With a
    pun on *council's*: see following note.
    **consistory** council-chamber

**[2.3]**    *Enter two Citizens, meeting*

FIRST CITIZEN

Neighbour, well met. Whither away so fast?

SECOND CITIZEN

I promise you, I scarcely know myself.

FIRST CITIZEN

Hear you the news abroad?

SECOND CITIZEN                        Ay, that the King is dead.

FIRST CITIZEN

Bad news, by'r Lady; seldom comes the better.

I fear, I fear 'twill prove a troublous world.                          5

> *Enter another Citizen*

THIRD CITIZEN   Good morrow, neighbours.

Doth this news hold of good King Edward's death?

FIRST CITIZEN   It doth.

THIRD CITIZEN

Then, masters, look to see a troublous world.

SECOND CITIZEN

No, no; by God's good grace his son shall reign.                          10

Q:

   **2.3.0.1** *meeting*] *not in* Q1. *Compare F*.    **10** SECOND CITIZEN] This edition; 1 (*i.e. First Citizen*) Q1, F

F:

   **2.3.0.1** *Enter . . . meeting*] *Enter one Citizen at one doore, and another at* | *the other*.    **1** Neighbour, well met] Good morrow Neighbour    **3** FIRST CITIZEN *not in* F    **3** Ay] Yes    **3–4** SECOND CITIZEN . . . FIRST CITIZEN] Q1 (2 . . . 1); 1. . . . 2: F    **4** Bad] Ill    **5** troublous] giddy (*altering* Q2 'troublesome')    **6–7** Good . . . this] Neighbours, God speed. | 1. Giue you good morrow sir. | 3. Doth the    **8** FIRST CITIZEN It doth] Q1 (1 It doth.); 2. I sir, it is too true, God helpe the while F

**2.3** A street scene in London. It establishes for the first time that political events are playing before a wider audience than the court. More records: 'Yet began there . . . some manner of muttering among the people as though all should not long be well, though they neither wist what they feared nor wherefore; were it that before such great things men's hearts of a secret instinct of nature misgive them, as the sea without wind swelleth of himself sometime before a tempest' (Holinshed, p. 379).

**3** **abroad** that's going round

**4** **by'r Lady** An oath by the Virgin Mary (compare 3.7.2).

   **seldom comes the better** things seldom improve. A proverb (Dent B332) associated particularly with the fear that worse

is to come after a person in authority dies.

**5, 9** **troublous** F avoids repetition by reading 'giddy' at l. 5. I resist emendation because F and Q1 are considerably variant in this passage. The hint of the uncanny in Q1's repetition helps give prophetic force to a dialogue based on homely wisdoms.

**9** **masters** Here a term of address between 'freed' artisans (members of trade guilds).

**10** SECOND CITIZEN Q1 and F attribute this line to the First Citizen, but in Q1 in the following lines it is consistently the Second Citizen who is the optimist and the First Citizen remains doubtful or pessimistic. The characterization is less clear-cut in F: though Q1 and F agree that the Second Citizen says ll. 12–15, F gives the other hopeful speech, l. 22, to the First.

**THIRD CITIZEN**

Woe to that land that's governed by a child.

**SECOND CITIZEN**

In him there is a hope of government:

That in his nonage council under him,

And in his full and ripened years himself,

No doubt shall then, and till then, govern well.                    15

**FIRST CITIZEN**

So stood the state when Harry the Sixth

Was crowned at Paris but at nine months old.

**THIRD CITIZEN**

Stood the state so? No, good my friend, not so;

For then this land was famously enriched

With politic grave counsel, then the King                           20

Had virtuous uncles to protect his grace.

**SECOND CITIZEN**

So hath this, both by the father and mother.

**THIRD CITIZEN**

Better it were they all came by the father

Or by the father there were none at all;

For emulation now who shall be nearest                              25

Will touch us all too near, if God prevent not.

O full of danger is the Duke of Gloucester,

F:
13 That] Which    16 Harry] *Henry*    17 at Paris] in Paris    18 good . . . so] no, good friends,
God wot    22 SECOND CITIZEN So] Q1 (2 So);  1. Why so F    22, 23, 24 the . . . the . . . the] his
. . . his . . . his    25 now who shall] who shall now

11 **Woe . . . child** Proverbial (Dent W600).
Derives from Ecclesiastes 10: 16, 'Woe to
thee, O land, when thy king is a child', in
this case probably by way of More, who has
Buckingham use the phrase twice, though
the text was also familiar from the Homily
against Disobedience. Exeter expresses a
similar thought in *1 Henry VI* 4.1.192,
''Tis much when sceptres are in children's
hands'. The analogy with Henry VI is developed in the following lines.
12 **government** good rule
13 **That** i.e. a hope that (or 'with the result
that')
**nonage** youth, minority

15 **then, and till then** Reverses the sequence
as given in the previous lines.
20 **politic** sagacious, learned in political
science. But the sense 'unscrupulously
scheming', if unintended by the Citizen,
offers a relevant qualification, as the
events of *1 Henry VI* and *The Contention*
show.
21 **uncles** i.e. the Dukes of Gloucester and
Bedford, and Henry VI's great-uncle the
Bishop of Winchester
25 **emulation** contention
**nearest** Poised between 'most closely related' and 'most influential'. In l. 26,
*near* is 'closely'.

And the Queen's kindred haught and proud.
An were they to be ruled, and not to rule,
This sickly land might solace as before.                                    30
SECOND CITIZEN
Come, come, we fear the worst. All shall be well.
THIRD CITIZEN
When clouds appear, wise men put on their cloaks.
When great leaves fall, the winter is at hand.
When the sun sets, who doth not look for night?
Untimely storms make men expect a dearth.                                   35
All may be well; but if God sort it so,
'Tis more than we deserve, or I expect.
FIRST CITIZEN
Truly, the souls of men are full of dread.
Ye cannot, almost, reason with a man
That looks not heavily and full of fear.                                    40
THIRD CITIZEN
Before the times of change still is it so.
By a divine instinct men's minds mistrust
Ensuing dangers, as by proof we see
The waters swell before a boist'rous storm;
But leave it all to God. Whither away?                                      45
SECOND CITIZEN  We are sent for to the Justice.

Q:
28 haught] F; hauty Q1    29 An] And    38 dread] Q3; bread Q1; feare F    43 see̩] ~.

F:
28 kindred haught] kindred hauty Q1; Sons, and Brothers, haught F    31 SECOND CITIZEN] Q1
(2); 1. F    shall be] will be    32 appear] are seen    33 the] then    35 make] makes
38 FIRST CITIZEN] Q1 (1); 2. F    souls] hearts    dread] Q3; bread Q1; feare F    39 Ye cannot,
almost, reason] You cannot reason (almost)    40 fear] dread    41 times] dayes    43 Ensuing]
Q1, F (*catchword*); Pursuing F (*text*)    dangers] danger    44 waters] Water    46 We are . . .
Justice] Marry, we were . . . Iustices

28  **kindred haught** Q1 has unmetrical 'kin-
    dred hauty'; F has 'Sons, and Brothers,
    haught'. The present emendation gives a
    metrically acceptable four-foot line, assum-
    ing 'haute' misread from the commoner di-
    syllabic form 'hautie'. Capell's suggestion
    'hautie are' would fill the line to a penta-
    meter, but is less terse and admits three
    instances of 'to be' in three lines.
29  **An were they** if indeed they were (Abbott
    105)
30  **solace** take comfort, be happy
31  **we . . . well** From the proverb 'It is good

to fear the worst' (Dent W912).
32–5  **When . . . dearth** These are common-
    place truisms rather than recognized
    proverbs.
36  **sort** arrange, ordain
39  **cannot, almost,** can scarcely (Abbott 29)
41–4  **Before . . . storm** See headnote to 2.3.
42  **instinct** (stressed on the second syllable)
    **mistrust** apprehensively anticipate
43  **proof** knowledge from experience
46  **We . . . Justice** The purpose of this sum-
    mons is not clear. It might hint at the
    arming or mustering of militia, or merely

THIRD CITIZEN

And so was I. I'll bear you company.            *Exeunt*

[**2.4**]    *Enter Cardinal, Duchess of York, Queen, young York*

CARDINAL

Last night, I hear, they lay at Northampton.

At Stony Stratford will they rest tonight.

Tomorrow or next day they will be here.

DUCHESS OF YORK

I long with all my heart to see the Prince.

I hope he is much grown since last I saw him.            5

QUEEN

But I hear no; they say my son of York

Hath almost overta'en him in his growth.

YOUNG YORK

Ay, mother, but I would not have it so.

DUCHESS OF YORK

Why, my young cousin? It is good to grow.

YOUNG YORK

Grandam, one night as we did sit at supper,            10

My uncle Rivers talked how I did grow

Q:

2.4.2 rest] F; be Q1      8 YOUNG YORK] *Yor. Similarly throughout 2.4 and 3.1.*

F:

2.4.0.1 *Cardinal . . . young York*] Arch-bishop, *yong Yorke, the Queene,* | *and the Dutchesse*
1 CARDINAL] Q1 (*Car.*); *Arch.* F. *Similarly throughout scene.*      hear] heard (*from* Q3)
1–2 Northampton . . . Stony Stratford] Stony Stratford . . . Northampton      2 will they] they do
7 Hath] Ha's      9 young] good

associate the Citizens with the administration of justice.

**2.4** Location: the Court.

0.1 *Cardinal* He would be identified on stage
by scarlet cassock and Cardinal's cap.
See Appendix D, Note 7.

1–2 **Northampton . . . Stony Stratford** Situ-
ated 18 km (12 miles) apart on the road
from Ludlow and the Midlands to London. More's account explains that the
Prince went ahead of Rivers to Stony
Stratford; Richard and Buckingham arrested Rivers at Northampton, met the
Prince at Stony Stratford, where Grey
and Vaughan were detained, then they

brought the Prince back north to
Northampton. River, Grey and Vaughan
were dispatched to Pontefract (Pomfret)
for execution; the journey to London
then resumed with the Prince's new es-
cort. F follows More by naming Stony
Stratford first, which makes little sense in
the absence of further explanation. The
scene's references to these key events
are sparse, and they need to be clear. Q1
probably represents a revision away
from the source material and towards
intelligibility.

1 **they** Members of the 'little train' accompanying the Prince are not identified until
news of their arrest at ll. 44–5.

More than my brother. 'Ay,' quoth my nuncle
    Gloucester,
'Small herbs have grace; gross weeds grow apace.'
And since, methinks, I would not grow so fast,
Because sweet flow'rs are slow, and weeds make haste.          15

DUCHESS OF YORK

Good faith, good faith, the saying did not hold
 In him that did object the same to thee.
He was the wretched'st thing when he was young,
So long a-growing and so leisurely
That if this were a true rule he should be gracious.          20

CARDINAL

Why, madam, so no doubt he is.

DUCHESS OF YORK

I hope so too, but yet let mothers doubt.

YOUNG YORK

Now by my troth, if I had been remembered,
I could have given my uncle's grace a flout
That nearer touched his growth than he did mine.          25

DUCHESS OF YORK

How, my pretty York? I pray thee, let me hear it.

YOUNG YORK

Marry, they say my uncle grew so fast
That he could gnaw a crust at two hours old.

---

Q:

12 nuncle] Q2; Nnckle Q1; Vnkle F    13 gross] OXFORD; great Q1, F; ill WILSON (*conj.* Maxwell)    15 flow'rs] F; flowers Q1    22 yet] Q2, F; yer Q1    25 That] This edition; That should haue Q1. F *rephrases.*

F:

13 grow] do grow    20 this were a true rule] his rule were true (*altering* Q3 'this were a rule')    21 CARDINAL . . . is] *Yor.* And so no doubt he is, my gracious Madam    22 so too] he is    25 That . . . mine] To touch his growth, neerer then he toucht mine (*compare* Q1)    26 pretty] yong    26, 31 pray thee . . . pray thee] prythee . . . prythee

---

12 **nuncle** A childish and/or affectionate variant of 'uncle', assimilating 'n' from 'mine' (but Q1's 'Nnckle' could alternatively be corrected to F's 'Vnkle').

13 **Small herbs have grace** Perhaps calls to mind 'herb of grace' or rue, known for its beneficial medicinal properties (*grace* meaning 'virtuous properties'), but also associated with *rue* as sorrow.
   **gross . . . apace** Proverbial (Dent W232). Q1's epithet is 'great', but 'gross' (i.e. coarse) is closer to the proverb, which has

'ill', and to 'idle' at 3.1.103. Because 'gross' is antithetical with 'have grace' it also allows the line a chiastic structure (small plants have grace: graceless plants grow big).

13 **apace** quickly

17 **object** urge

23 **been remembered** remembered

27–8 **they . . . old** A variation on More's report that Richard was born 'not untoothed', which he admits might be what 'men of hatred report above the truth' (Holinshed, p. 362).

'Twas full two years ere I could get a tooth.
Grannam, this would have been a biting jest.                    30

DUCHESS OF YORK
I pray thee, pretty York, who told thee so?

YOUNG YORK  Grannam, his nurse.

DUCHESS OF YORK
His nurse? Why, she was dead ere thou wert born.

YOUNG YORK
If 'twere not she, I cannot tell who told me.

QUEEN
A parlous boy. Go to, you are too shrewd.                       35

CARDINAL
Good madam, be not angry with the child.

QUEEN  Pitchers have ears.

*Enter Dorset*

CARDINAL
Here comes your son, Lord Marquis Dorset.
What news, Lord Marquis?

DORSET
Such news, my lord, as grieves me to unfold.                    40

QUEEN  How fares the Prince?

DORSET  Well, madam, and in health.

DUCHESS OF YORK  What is thy news then?

DORSET
Lord Rivers and Lord Grey are sent to Pomfret,
With them Sir Thomas Vaughan, prisoners.                        45

Q:
30 been] heene    35 parlous] perilous    38 Marquis] M.

F:
31 so] this    33 wert] wast    36 CARDINAL] *Dut.*    37.1 *Dorset] a Messenger*    38–9 your . . .
Marquis?] a Messenger: What Newes?    40 DORSET] Q1 (*Dor.*); *Mes.* F. *Similarly throughout rest of
scene.*    unfold] report    41 fares] doth    43 news then] Newes    45 With] and with (*dividing
after 'Grey' and* 'them')

30 **biting** (a) sharp, (b) about biting with
teeth. For Richard as biter, see l. 53, and
4.4.44–9 and note to 4.4.46.
35 **parlous** clever, precocious, naughty
**shrewd** mischievous, sharp-tongued
37 **Pitchers have ears** Proverbial (Dent
P363); compare 'walls have ears', etc.
Suggested by the pair of handles on pitchers, thought of as resembling ears.
37.1 *Dorset* F instead has an anonymous
Messenger. See Appendix D, Note 3. Q1's

variants reflect the alteration to Dorset: he
offers genteelly to 'unfold' news rather
than 'report' it (l. 40); he acknowledges
his mother by addressing 'my gracious
lady' where in F 'my gracious Lord' is addressed to the Archbishop (l. 51); and the
Queen answers her son by referring to 'our
house' rather than 'my House' (l. 52).
44–5 **Lord Rivers . . . prisoners** See second
note to ll. 1–2.
44 **Lord Grey** From now on Grey and Dorset

229

DUCHESS OF YORK  Who hath committed them?
DORSET

   The mighty dukes, Gloucester and Buckingham.
CARDINAL  For what offence?
DORSET

   The sum of all I can, I have disclosed.

   (*To the Queen*) Why or for what these nobles were
      committed                                                                    50

   Is all unknown to me, my gracious lady.
QUEEN

   Ay me, I see the downfall of our house.

   The tiger now hath seized the gentle hind.

   Insulting tyranny begins to jet

   Upon the innocent and aweless throne.                         55

   Welcome, destruction, death, and massacre.

   I see, as in a map, the end of all.
DUCHESS OF YORK

   Accursèd and unquiet wrangling days!

   How many of you have mine eyes beheld?

   My husband lost his life to get the crown,              60

   And often up and down my sons were tossed

   For me to joy and weep their gain and loss;

   And being seated, and domestic broils

   Clean overblown, themselves the conquerors

   Make war upon themselves, blood against blood,       65

   Self against self. O preposterous

**Q:**
55 aweless] F;  lawlesse Q1     64 overblown, themselves$_\wedge$] Q2, F;  $\sim_\wedge \sim$, Q1

**F:**
50 these] the     51 lady] Lord     52 downfall of our] ruine of my     56 death] Blood     65 upon themselves] vpon themselues, Brother to Brother

are clearly defined as two separate brothers.

44 **Pomfret** A castle in Yorkshire. *Pomfret* is a disyllabic form of 'Pontefract'.

49 **can** have knowledge of (Abbott 307)
50 **Why or for what** '*Why*, perhaps, refers to the past cause, *for what* to the future object' (Abbott 75).
54 **Insulting** exulting, scornfully triumphing **jet** (a) encroach (as best fits 'Upon'), (b) strut, swagger (taking up the personification in 'Insulting tyranny')

55 **aweless** inspiring no awe. The line provides the first of just two illustrations of the sense in *OED*. Q1's 'lawlesse' has never been adopted since F emended it, and is perhaps a conscious but misguided attempt to correct the unfamiliar.
63 **seated** installed in power, settled
64 **overblown** blown away
66 **preposterous** contrary to the natural order of things. Probably pronounced as four syllables, so that the metrical licence is a missing unstressed syllable at the caesura.

And frantic outrage, end thy damnèd spleen,

Or let me die, to look on death no more.

QUEEN (*to young York*)

Come, come, my boy, we will to sanctuary.

DUCHESS OF YORK  I'll go along with you.                    70

QUEEN  You have no cause.

CARDINAL  My gracious lady, go,

And thither bear your treasure and your goods.

For my part, I'll resign unto your grace

✓The seal I keep; and so betide to me                      75

As well I tender you and all of yours.

Come, I'll conduct you to the sanctuary.        *Exeunt*


[3.1]     *The trumpets sound. Enter young Prince, Richard*
          *Duke of Gloucester, the Duke of Buckingham,*
          *Cardinal, [Stanley Earl of Derby, Catesby], and others*

Q:

   3.1.0.1–3 *Richard . . . others*] *the Dukes of Glo-|cester, and Buckingham, Cardinall, &c.*
0.3 *Stanley Earl of Derby*] OXFORD (*conj.* Proudfoot; *similarly* Cibber); *not in* Q1     *Catesby*]
CAPELL; *not in* Q1     *and others*] &c.

F:

68 death] earth     69 sanctuary.] Sanctuary. | Madam, farwell.     70 I'll go along] Stay, I
will go     77 Come] Go

   3.1.0.1–3 *Richard . . . others*] *the Dukes of Glocester, and Buckingham,* | *Lord Cardinall, with*
*others*

67 **outrage** violent conduct
  **spleen** malice
69 **sanctuary** The cathedral precincts at
  Westminster provided a refuge for those
  pursued by the law.
70 **DUCHESS . . . you** A surprising and symptomatic decision, anticipating her renun-
  ciation of her son in 4.4 (Kaegi, p. 132).
74–5 **For . . . keep** The equivalent figure in
  More, Archbishop Rotherham, says,
  'And here is the Great Seal, which in likewise as that noble prince your husband
  delivered it unto me, so here I deliver it
  unto you, to the use and behoof of your
  son' (Holinshed, p. 368). As the Great
  Seal was used to authenticate royal documents, this intervention is 'an illegal and
  politically extreme act' (Hammond).
76 **As well** in accordance with how well
3.1.0.1–3 **The . . . others** In More's account, Richard 'bare him in open sight so
  reverently to the Prince, with all semblance of lowliness' (Holinshed, p. 369).
  More relates the political manoeuvrings

at some length (see notes to ll. 23.1,
35–6, 44–56, and 55–6). The dialogue
between Richard and the princes is fictional. On the stage, possibly the Prince,
Richard, and Buckingham enter at one
door, the rest at another. A ceremonious
royal entry would briefly delay the Cardinal's appearance and so avoid an
immediate re-entry after 2.4, which was
not usually permitted in the Elizabethan
theatre (see Appendix D, Note 7). Though
Charles Kean seized the opportunity for
pageantry, the welcoming party may
look conspicuously thin, as the Prince's
comments at l. 6 and ll. 20–4 suggest.
His travelling escorts have to double as
his welcomers, perhaps in an obviously
stage-managed way. The scene is tensely
strung between formality and informal-
ity, planned event and happenstance, political action and domestic banter.
0.3 *Stanley Earl of Derby* Not mentioned in
  Q1 or F here. They provide an exit for
  Dorset at l. 149.1, but Dorset's presence

BUCKINGHAM

Welcome, sweet Prince, to London, to your chamber.

RICHARD DUKE OF GLOUCESTER (*to the Prince*)

Welcome, dear cousin, my thoughts' sovereign.

The weary way hath made you melancholy.

PRINCE

No, uncle, but our crosses on the way

Have made it tedious, wearisome, and heavy.                      5

I want more uncles here to welcome me.

RICHARD DUKE OF GLOUCESTER

Sweet Prince, the untainted virtue of your years

Hath not yet dived into the world's deceit;

Nor more can you distinguish of a man

Than of his outward show, which God He knows          10

Seldom or never jumpeth with the heart.

Those uncles which you want were dangerous.

Your grace attended to their sugared words,

But looked not on the poison of their hearts.

God keep you from them, and from such false friends.    15

PRINCE

God keep me from false friends, but they were none.

RICHARD DUKE OF GLOUCESTER

My lord the Mayor of London comes to greet you.

*Enter Lord Mayor*

F:

9 Nor] No

in Q1 at the end of 2.4 suggests that he is
not present at the beginning of 3.1. Cibber includes Stanley, but is probably expanding the role rather than responding
to the textual difficulty. Richard Proudfoot, as recorded in *Textual Companion*,
suggests confusion between '*Der*.' (Derby)
and '*Dor*.' behind Q1's exit.

0.3 *Catesby* His entry is not in Q1 or F
(which here lacks independent authority), but he may be amongst the unnamed others. Alternatively, (a) entry
with Hastings would single him out as his
supposed friend, or (b) entry when first
summoned at l. 156 would reserve his
presence for the exchange in which he actively takes part.

1 **chamber** royal capital. The term appears in
a marginal note in Holinshed: 'London,

the King's especial chamber' (p. 392).

2 **my thoughts' sovereign** chief of all my
thoughts. 'With sinister implication'
(Honigmann), as well as play on the
Prince's actual status.

4 **crosses** difficulties, thwartings. Referring
specifically to the events at Northampton,
hence 'I want more uncles' (l. 6). Also,
with possible reference to Christ bearing
his cross on the way to crucifixion.

6 **want** lack

9–11 **Nor . . . heart** Echoes 1 Samuel 16: 7,
'For man looketh on the outward appearance, but the Lord beholdeth the heart'.

9–10 **of . . . of** about . . . in relation to

10, 26 **God He knows** God knows

11 **jumpeth** accords

13–14 **Your . . . hearts** Compare 1.3.242–3
and notes.

17.1 *Lord Mayor* He may be attended, as

232

LORD MAYOR (*to the Prince*)
    God bless your grace with health and happy days.
PRINCE
    I thank you, good my lord, and thank you all.
    I thought my mother and my brother York                    20
    Would long ere this have met us on the way.
    Fie, what a slug is Hastings that he hastes not
    To tell us whether they will come or no.
        *Enter Lord Hastings*
BUCKINGHAM
    And in good time here comes the sweating lord.
PRINCE
    Welcome, my lord. What, will our mother come?              25
HASTINGS
    On what occasion, God He knows, not I,
    The Queen your mother and your brother York
    Have taken sanctuary. The tender Prince
    Would fain have come with me to meet your grace,
    But by his mother was perforce withheld.                   30
BUCKINGHAM
    Fie, what an indirect and peevish course
    Is this of hers! Lord Cardinal, will your grace
    Persuade the Queen to send the Duke of York
    Unto his princely brother presently?
    If she deny, Lord Hastings, go with him,                   35
    And from her jealous arms pluck him perforce.

Q:
22 hastes] OXFORD;  comes Q1

'and thank you all' (l. 19) might suggest.
It is unclear when he exits; see note to
'*Mayor*', l. 149.1.

22  **hastes** Taylor's emendation gives a pun
    on Hastings's name and avoids 'come(s)'
    three times in as many lines.
23.1  ***Enter Lord Hastings*** In More, Hastings
    plays no part in this episode and the Car-
    dinal, as one 'in favour and credence
    with her', goes to the Queen alone
    (Holinshed, p. 370). Hastings's involve-
    ment shows Buckingham and Richard
    adopting a more aggressive stance, as
    does the explicit threat of violence and
    avoidance of Buckingham's sophistic
    argument in More about the Prince's

own best interest at l. 36. Cibber omitted
the episode to l. 60, playing down both
Buckingham's role and the cruel off-
stage events.
24  **And . . . lord** 'Sweating' might indicate a
    patronising and jocular response to the
    Prince. It corrects 'slug', l. 22, but the
    terms together suggest someone unctu-
    ous if not fat.
31  **indirect** wrong
35–6  **If . . . perforce** Compare More, 'if
    she be percase so obstinate . . . then shall
    we by mine advice by the King's author-
    ity fetch him [the Duke] out of that
    prison' (Holinshed, p. 370). See note to
    l. 23.1.
36  **jealous** suspicious

CARDINAL
My lord of Buckingham, if my weak oratory
Can from his mother win the Duke of York,
Anon expect him here. But if she be obdurate
To mild entreaties, God in heaven forbid      40
We should infringe the holy privilege
Of blessèd sanctuary. Not for all this land
Would I be guilty of so deep a sin.

BUCKINGHAM
You are too senseless-obstinate, my lord,
Too ceremonious and traditional.      45
Weigh it but with the grossness of this age,
You break not sanctuary in seizing him.
The benefit thereof is always granted
To those whose dealings have deserved the place,
And those who have the wit to claim the place.      50
This prince hath neither claimed it nor deserved it,
And therefore, in mine opinion, cannot have it.
Then taking him from thence that is not there,
You break no privilege nor charter there.
Oft have I heard of sanctuary men,      55
But sanctuary children ne'er till now.

Q:
56 ne'er] F; neuer Q1

F:
40 God in heaven] God (*from* Q3)     43 deep] great (*from* Q3)

40–2 **God . . . sanctuary** From More: 'God forbid that any man should, for any thing earthly, enterprise to break the immunity and liberty of the sacred sanctuary' (Holinshed, p. 371).
41 **holy** Taylor emends to 'sacred', the reading in the sources.
44–56 **You . . . now** From Buckingham's long disquisition on sanctuaries in More.
44 **senseless-obstinate** irrationally inflexible
45 **ceremonious and traditional** Buckingham, drawing on anti-Catholic polemics, reinforces his point by using modern, post-reformation words. *OED*'s first example of *ceremonious* is in 1553; it cites only two examples before *Richard III*, and only one for the relevant sense 5. The line is the

earliest known use of *traditional*.
46 **Weigh it but with** if only you consider it in accordance with
50 **wit** intelligence, prudence (implying 'intellectual maturity')
53 **is not there** A philosophical nicety: the Duke is in the place of sanctuary but not in a state of sanctuary.
54 **charter** immunity by royal charter
**there** by that. The repetition of the line's terminal word continues the pattern of ll. 49–52, and has become a mark of Buckingham's speciousness.
55–6 **Oft . . . now** Closely based on More: 'And verily I have often heard of sanctuary men, but I never heard erst of sanctuary children' (Holinshed, p. 373).

CARDINAL

My lord, you shall o'errule my mind for once.

Come on, Lord Hastings, will you go with me?

HASTINGS  I go, my lord.

PRINCE

Good lords, make all the speedy haste you may.                     60

                          *Exeunt Cardinal and Hastings*

Say, uncle Gloucester, if our brother come

Where shall we sojourn till our coronation?

RICHARD DUKE OF GLOUCESTER

Where it seems best unto your royal self.

If I may counsel you, some day or two

Your highness shall repose you at the Tower;                       65

Then where you please and shall be thought most fit

For your best health and recreation.

PRINCE

I do not like the Tower of any place.

*(To Buckingham)* Did Julius Caesar build that place, my lord?

BUCKINGHAM

He did, my gracious lord, begin that place,                        70

Which since succeeding ages have re-edified.

PRINCE

Is it upon record, or else reported

Successively from age to age he built it?

BUCKINGHAM

Upon record, my gracious lord.

PRINCE

But say, my lord, it were not registered,                          75

Methinks the truth should live from age to age,

---

Q:

57 o'errule] F;  ouerrule Q1    60.1 *Exeunt Cardinal and Hastings*] Q3, F ('*Exit* . . .'; *after l.* 59);
*not in* Q1. *Position as in* CAMBRIDGE

F:

63 seems] think'st (*from* Q3)

68  **of any place** of all places                      Tower.
69–78 **Did . . . day** A summary of 'The      72 **record** (stressed on the second syllable)
    Coming of Julius Caesar into Britain' im-   74 **lord** Taylor emends to 'liege' to avoid
    mediately  follows  a  summary  of              Buckingham's self-repetition and the
    Richard's career as models of historical       jingle in the line, but these features might
    narration in Reynoldes's *Foundation of*        lend an effective note of self-parody to
    *Rhetoric*, D2 (see p. 16). But Reynoldes        Buckingham's deference.
    does not refer to the building of the      75 **registered** recorded

As 'twere retailed to all posterity,
Even to the general all-ending day.

RICHARD DUKE OF GLOUCESTER (*aside*)

So wise so young, they say, do never live long.

PRINCE  What say you, uncle?                                         80

RICHARD DUKE OF GLOUCESTER

I say, 'Without characters fame lives long'.
(*Aside*) Thus like the formal Vice Iniquity,
I moralize two meanings in one word.

PRINCE

That Julius Caesar was a famous man.
With what his valour did enrich his wit,                             85
His wit set down, to make his valour live.
Death makes no conquest of this conqueror,
For now he lives in fame, though not in life.
I'll tell you what, my cousin Buckingham.

BUCKINGHAM  What, my gracious lord?                                  90

Q:
86 valour] valure

F:
78 all-ending] ending (*from* Q2)     87 this] his (*from* Q2)

77 **retailed** OED's earliest instance of the
sense 'told over again'. The required
stress on the second syllable opens the
possibility that it assimilates *retell*. OED's
earliest example of *retell* is from Gabriel
Harvey in 1593, though there is an earlier example in Thomas Thomas's Latin–
English dictionary of 1587. Christine
Buckley privately suggests that here and
in Additional Passage G.48 Shakespeare
might also be using *retail* as equivalent to
*entail*, 'irrevocably bestow'.

79 **So . . . long** Proverbial (Dent L384, 'Too
soon wise to live long').
**never** Pronounced 'ne'er'.

81 **Without . . . long** In contrast with *Measure* 5.1.11–13, where 'characters of
brass' provide 'A forted residence 'gainst
the tooth of time | And razure of oblivion'.
**characters** written records. Stressed on
the second syllable.

82 **formal** conventional. As an 'informal'
Vice figure, Richard can reproduce its
conventional devices, but he does so by

exerting an imitative skill of his own.

82 **Vice** The conventional Vice figure of the
medieval stage (see Introduction).

83 **I . . . word** I find two (contradictory)
moral meanings in one utterance (as
though the *word* were from the Bible and
the moralization were biblical exegesis).
A reductive gloss 'equivocate' would
apply equally to what Richard has said to
the Prince, and to a characteristic of the
Vice figure, and to Richard's subtly misleading account to the audience of what
he has just done.

85 **With . . . wit** whatever his valour enriched his wit with (i.e. the resulting military actions). The syntax is irregular, but
more on account of the position of 'With'
than the sense of 'what' ('a curious use',
Abbott 252). *Wit* is 'intellect'. Taylor
emends to '. . . t'enrich', and another pos-
sibility is 'man, | Who what his valour
did—enrich his wit—', but neither solu-
tion leaves the sentence entirely clear.

86 **set down** put in writing

PRINCE

  An if I live until I be a man,

  I'll win our ancient right in France again,

  Or die a soldier as I lived a king.

RICHARD DUKE OF GLOUCESTER (*aside*)

  Short summers lightly have a forward spring.

    *Enter young York, Hastings, Cardinal*

BUCKINGHAM

  Now in good time here comes the Duke of York.                    95

PRINCE

  Richard of York, how fares our loving brother?

YOUNG YORK

  Well, my dread lord—so must I call you now.

PRINCE

  Ay, brother, to our grief, as it is yours.

  Too late he died that might have kept that title,

  Which by his death hath lost much majesty.                    100

RICHARD DUKE OF GLOUCESTER

  How fares our cousin, noble lord of York?

YOUNG YORK

  I thank you, gentle uncle. O my lord,

  You said that idle weeds are fast in growth;

  The Prince my brother hath outgrown me far.

RICHARD DUKE OF GLOUCESTER

  He hath, my lord.

YOUNG YORK      And therefore is he idle?                    105

RICHARD DUKE OF GLOUCESTER

  O my fair cousin, I must not say so.

F:

94.1 Cardinal] *and Cardinall*     96 loving] *Noble (from* Q2*)*     97 dread] *deare (from* Q3*)*

92 **our ancient right** English claims to territories in France went back to the installation of the Norman kings in England in 1066 and Henry Plantagenet's marriage to Eleanor of Aquitaine in 1152.

94 **Short . . . spring** Adapts the proverb 'Sharp frosts bite forward springs' (Tilley F774). Richard affirms that the Prince is indeed set to die young if when he grows up he pursues his present military aims, but the echoed proverb suggests a more immediate fate.

94 **lightly** commonly
**forward** (a) early, (b) pert

96 **our loving brother** The Prince assumes the formality of a king—entirely seriously, to judge by the 'royal' plural again at l. 98.

99 **late** recently
**that might** who wishedly would

103 **idle** useless. The sense 'foolish, silly' also comes in view at l. 105.

106 **fair** fine. Slyly insinuates that the taller 'cousin' might be the opposite; compare 'gross', 2.4.13.

237

YOUNG YORK

    Then he is more beholden to you than I.

RICHARD DUKE OF GLOUCESTER

    He may command me as my sovereign,

    But you have power in me as in a kinsman.

YOUNG YORK

    I pray you, uncle, give me this dagger.        110

RICHARD DUKE OF GLOUCESTER

    My dagger, little cousin? With all my heart.

PRINCE  A beggar, brother?

YOUNG YORK

    Of my kind uncle that I know will give,

    And being but a toy, which is no grief to give.

RICHARD DUKE OF GLOUCESTER

    A greater gift than that I'll give my cousin.        115

YOUNG YORK

    A greater gift? O, that's the sword to it.

RICHARD DUKE OF GLOUCESTER

    Ay, gentle cousin, were it light enough.

Q:
111 With all] withall

109 **as in** in that I am
110 **I . . . dagger** Metrically deficient. Taylor emends *give* to *render*.
111 **My dagger** The dagger of the medieval Vice was well known as a theatre prop. More describes Richard after the murder of the princes as 'his hand ever upon his dagger' (Holinshed, p. 403). Holinshed later amplifies: 'the dagger which he ware he would, when he studied, with his hand pluck up and down in the sheath to the midst, never drawing it fully out' (p. 447). Samuel Rowlands wrote of gallants who 'like Richard the usurper swagger, | That had his hand continual on his dagger', in *The Letting of Humours' Blood in the Head-Vein* (1600), A2. Though Rowlands might have been recalling the chronicles, the quirk may have featured prominently in early stage performance: see A. C. Dessen, *Shakespeare and the Late Moral Plays* (1986), p. 42. The Ricardian villain Orante in Thomas Killigrew's *Cicilia and Clorinda* (1649) appears '*crooked and*

*ugly, with a dagger by his side'*. Later, Booth's Richard, evidently following stage tradition, 'had the habit of sheathing and unsheathing a dagger': William Winter, *Life and Art of Edwin Booth* (1893), p. 214.
111 **With all my heart** A loaded line: Richard wishes with all his heart that the dagger were in York's heart.
    **With all** Q1's 'withall' might alternatively be modernized *withal*, 'along with'.
113–14 **Of . . . to give** Compressed syntax; one should understand 'will give [it]' ('it' avoided to concord with the following line) or 'And [it] being'.
114 **toy** (a) trifle, (b) plaything. The childish play foreshadows the later and deadly 'greater gift' as Richard means it.
    **grief** hardship
116 **to it** that goes with it
117 **light** In terms of weight, but also in contrast with the figuratively 'heavy' deed Richard has in mind. York turns the word to mean 'cheap' (*OED* 13b).

YOUNG YORK

    O, then I see you will part but with light gifts.

    In weightier things you'll say a beggar nay.

RICHARD DUKE OF GLOUCESTER

    It is too heavy for your grace to wear.                    120

YOUNG YORK

    I'd weigh it lightly were it heavier.

RICHARD DUKE OF GLOUCESTER

    What, would you have my weapon, little lord?

YOUNG YORK

    I would, that I might thank you as you call me.

RICHARD DUKE OF GLOUCESTER  How?

YOUNG YORK  Little.                                             125

PRINCE

    My lord of York will still be cross in talk.

    Uncle, your grace knows how to bear with him.

YOUNG YORK

    You mean to bear me, not to bear with me.

    Uncle, my brother mocks both you and me.

    Because that I am little, like an ape,                     130

    He thinks that you should bear me on your shoulders.

BUCKINGHAM [*aside to Hastings*]

    With what a sharp, provided wit he reasons!

    To mitigate the scorn he gives his uncle

    He prettily and aptly taunts himself.

    So cunning and so young is wonderful.                      135

Q:
121 I'd] HANMER; I Q1

F:
120 heavy] weightie (*from* Q2)    123 as] as, as, (*from* Q3)

121 **weigh it lightly** (a) find it light in weight, (b) not think much of it
**were it** even if it were
126 **cross** contrarious. And gives in conjunction with 'bear' in l. 5 a possible allusion to Luke 14: 27, 'Whosoever doth not bear his cross'. See note to l. 4.
130–1 **Because . . . shoulders** Showmen or professional fools with trained apes apparently carried them on a shoulder-saddle that made the bearer look hunchbacked. York's mockery of Richard's disfigurement gives the actor a good opportunity for non-verbal response. In Baliol Holloway's performance 'it was the only time one felt pity for him' (*Times*, 27 January 1927, quoted in Hankey, p. 163).
132 **sharp, provided wit** It might be relevant that Polydore Vergil describes Richard as having 'a sharp wit, provident and subtle' (p. 227), though there is no evidence that Shakespeare knew the original in Latin or the abridged manuscript translation.
**provided** in a state of readiness
134 **prettily** ingeniously, cutely
135 **cunning** clever (but also 'crafty')

239

RICHARD DUKE OF GLOUCESTER (*to the Prince*)

　My lord, will't please you pass along,

　Myself and my good cousin Buckingham

　Will to your mother, to entreat of her

　To meet you at the Tower and welcome you.

YOUNG YORK (*to the Prince*)

　What, will you go unto the Tower, my lord?　　　　　140

PRINCE

　My lord Protector needs will have it so.

YOUNG YORK

　I shall not sleep in quiet at the Tower.

RICHARD DUKE OF GLOUCESTER　Why, what should you fear?

YOUNG YORK

　Marry, my uncle Clarence' angry ghost.

　My grannam told me he was murdered there.　　　　145

PRINCE

　I fear no uncles dead.

RICHARD DUKE OF GLOUCESTER　Nor none that live, I hope.

PRINCE

　An if they live, I hope I need not fear.

　(*To young York*) But come, my lord. With a heavy heart

　Thinking on them, go I unto the Tower.

　　　　　　[*A sennet.*] *Exeunt Prince, York, Hastings, Cardinal,*

　　　　　　[*Stanley Earl of Derby, Mayor, and others*]; *Richard,*

　　　　　　　　　　　　　*Buckingham, and Catesby remain*

BUCKINGHAM

　Think you, my lord, this little prating York　　　　150

　Was not incensèd by his subtle mother

　To taunt and scorn you thus opprobriously?

Q:
136 will't] wilt　　149.1 *A sennet.*] F; *not in* Q1　*Cardinal*] HANMER (*subs.*); *not in* Q1, F
149.2 *Stanley Earl of Derby*] OXFORD (*conj.* Proudfoot); *Dors.* Q1; *and Dorset* F　*Mayor, and others*] *not in* Q1, F　149.2–3 *Richard . . . remain*] *manet. Rich. Buck.*　149.3 *and Catesby*] F; *not in* Q1

F:
141 needs will] will (*from* Q2)　148 With] and with

140 **What,** Might instead be read without the comma, as in Q1, meaning 'why' (compare Abbott 253).
141 **My lord Protector** See 1.3.14 and note.
149.1 *sennet* blast of trumpets
149.2 *Mayor* Q1 provides no exit for him. Capell supplied one at l. 19, after a per-

functory appearance. The Mayor's continued presence puts more at stake in the debate on sanctuary and the exchanges between Richard and the Prince; and it connects with the city concern in 3.5 and 3.7.
151 **incensèd** incited, instructed

RICHARD DUKE OF GLOUCESTER

No doubt, no doubt. O, 'tis a parlous boy,

Bold, quick, ingenious, forward, capable.

He is all the mother's, from the top to toe.                    155

BUCKINGHAM

Well, let them rest.—Come hither, Catesby. Thou art
        sworn

As deeply to effect what we intend

As closely to conceal what we impart.

Thou knowest our reasons urged upon the way.

What think'st thou? Is it not an easy matter                   160

To make William Lord Hastings of our mind

For the instalment of this noble duke   Richard

In the seat royal of this famous isle?

CATESBY

He for his father's sake so loves the Prince

That he will not be won to aught against him.                  165

BUCKINGHAM

What think'st thou then of Stanley, what will he?

CATESBY

He will do all in all as Hastings doth.

BUCKINGHAM  Well then, no more but this:

Go, gentle Catesby, and as it were afar off,

Sound thou Lord Hastings, how he stands affected              170

Unto our purpose. If he be tractable,

Q:
153 parlous] perillous     160, 166 think'st] F; thinkest Q1     171 tractable] F (*with further variants*); willing Q1

F:
166 what will] Will not     169 afar] farre     170 stands] doth stand (*dividing ll.* 170–1 *after 'Hastings' and* 'purpose')     171 Unto] to     If he be tractable] if he be willing Q1; And summon him to morrow to the Tower, | To sit about the Coronation. | If thou do'st finde him tractable to us F

153 **parlous** Compare 2.4.35 and note.
154 **quick** lively
   **ingenious** able, intelligent
   **capable** able, gifted
155 **all the mother's** Richard means 'entirely of his mother's disposition', but perhaps also 'entirely manipulated by his mother'. The joke might be ironic, implying that such a dull woman could scarcely produce or incite such intelligence and manly ability.
156 **Well . . . Catesby** As towards the end of

2.2, Buckingham takes the initiative in the political intrigue. Sher came to see Buckingham as 'a classy theatrical agent' (*Times*, 29 July 1986).
163 **the seat royal** The phrase is from Hall's account of Richard being proclaimed king (*Richard III*, 1).
164 **his** i.e. the Prince's
170–1 **affected | Unto** disposed towards
171 **tractable** Q1's 'willing' is both commonplace in sense and irregular in metre.

Encourage him, and show him all our reasons.
If he be leaden, icy-cold, unwilling,
Be thou so too, and so break off your talk,
And give us notice of his inclination.                              175
For we tomorrow hold divided councils,
Wherein thyself shalt highly be employed.

RICHARD DUKE OF GLOUCESTER
Commend me to Lord William; tell him, Catesby,
His ancient knot of dangerous adversaries
Tomorrow are let blood at Pomfret Castle,                           180
And bid my friend for joy of this good news
Give Mistress Shore one gentle kiss the more.

BUCKINGHAM
Good Catesby, go effect this business soundly.

CATESBY
My good lords both, with all the heed I may.

RICHARD DUKE OF GLOUCESTER
Shall we hear from you, Catesby, ere we sleep?                       185
CATESBY You shall, my lord.

RICHARD DUKE OF GLOUCESTER
At Crosby Place, there shall you find us both.

                                              *Exit Catesby*

BUCKINGHAM
Now, my lord, what shall we do if we perceive
William Lord Hastings will not yield to our complots?

Q:
183 go] F; *not in* Q1   184 lords] Lo:   187.1 *Exit Catesby*] Q3, F; *not in* Q1

F:
172 show] tell   174 your] the   181 friend] Lord   184 may] can   187 Place] House
189 William Lord] Lord

As an error, it may be memorial, or substitution of synonyms under the influence
of 'vnwilling' in the same position two
lines below. F's reading comes in a variant passage reading, 'And summon him
to morrow to the Tower, | To sit about
the Coronation. | If thou do'st finde him
tractable to vs'. Q1's cut removes an inconsistency: Catesby does not summon
Hastings to the Tower.

176 **divided councils** According to More,
while the council shown in 3.4 met to determine arrangements for the coronation
of the Prince, 'as fast were they in an-

other place contriving the contrary, and
to make the Protector king' (Holinshed,
p. 379). For 'another place' Hall reads
'Crosby's place'.

179 **knot** closely-tied group. With a possible
pun on 'swelling, tumour', as a medical
figure continued in *are let blood*.

180 **are let blood** are to bleed surgically
(euphemistic)

185–6 RICHARD . . . **lord**. See Appendix D,
Note 8.

188 **Now** Extrametrical. Retained in F, but
omitted by Pope and some subsequent
editors.

RICHARD DUKE OF GLOUCESTER

  Chop off his head, man. Somewhat we will do.     190

  And look when I am King, claim thou of me

  The earldom of Hereford and the movables

  Whereof the King my brother stood possessed.

BUCKINGHAM

  I'll claim that promise at your grace's hands.

RICHARD DUKE OF GLOUCESTER

  And look to have it yielded with all willingness.    195

  Come, let us sup betimes, that afterwards

  We may digest our complots in some form.    *Exeunt*

[*To claim is not necessarily to get!*]

[3.2]   *Enter a Messenger to the door of Lord Hastings*

MESSENGER (*knocking*)  What ho, my lord!

HASTINGS (*within*)  Who knocks at the door?

Q:

    **3.2**.0.1 *the door of Lord*] F; *Lord* Q1   1 *knocking*] WILSON (*subs.*); *not in* Q1, F   2 *within*] THOMPSON; *not in* Q1, F

F:

190 head, man. Somewhat we will do] Head: | Something wee will determine   192 and] and all   193 stood] was   194 hands] hand   195 willingness] kindnesse

    **3.2**.0.1 *of Lord*] *of*   1 What ho] My Lord   2 knocks at the door] knockes

190 **Somewhat we will do** In Q1 the tone remains nonchalantly brutal. F omits 'man' and reads 'Something wee will determine': more formal and serious.

191–3 **And . . . possessed** Follows More, where in return for help in making him king Richard promised Buckingham 'quiet possession of the earldom of Hereford, which he claimed as his inheritance' and 'a great quantity of the King's treasure and of his household stuff' (Holinshed, p. 378). The earldom of Hereford had passed into the hands of the King. In the play, the *movables* are probably merely those that relate to the earldom. The term in civil law contrasted with 'heritable' land and buildings (i.e. automatically inherited as part of the estate); thus *earldom* and *movables* are complementary, and *stood possessed* refers to both.

191 **look when** as soon as. With a suggestion of 'expect when', as with *look* at l. 195, but this sense strains the syntax.

192 **Hereford** Regularly pronounced as two syllables.

196 **sup betimes** eat supper early (leading to a quip on *digest*, l. 197)

197 **complots** plots

3.2, 3.4–6 These scenes are based on a continuous section in More's narrative. See Appendix E.

3.2 Hastings might begin the scene in nightclothes. In many productions he dresses during the scene; in some he has been accompanied by Mistress Shore. But the action evidently begins outside his house, and towards the end (by when several hours seem to have elapsed) Hastings might be on his way to the council in the Tower, meeting acquaintances casually in the street (as in equivalent source passages: see notes to ll. 93.1–106 and 109–11). The Pursuivant and Priest are, by dramatic irony, reminders of arrest and execution to come. The other encounters are symmetrical: Stanley's servant, Buckingham's spy, Stanley, Buckingham. Though little happens, the scene is an emblematic distillation of the entire Hastings plot.

0.1–32 *Enter . . . Exit* Develops a paragraph in More, placed after the account of Hastings's arrest and execution.

MESSENGER  A messenger from the Lord Stanley.
    *Enter Lord Hastings*
HASTINGS
    What's o'clock?
MESSENGER                    Upon the stroke of four.
HASTINGS
    Cannot thy master sleep these tedious nights?        5
MESSENGER
    So it should seem by that I have to say.
    First, he commends him to your noble lordship.
HASTINGS
    And then?
MESSENGER  And then he sends you word
    He dreamt tonight the boar had razed his helm. ✔
    Besides, he says there are two councils held,        10
    And that may be determined at the one
    Which may make you and him to rue at th'other.
    Therefore he sends to know your lordship's pleasure:
    If presently you will take horse with him
    And with all speed post into the north        15
    To shun the danger that his soul divines.
HASTINGS
    Go, fellow, go, return unto thy lord.
    Bid him not fear the separated councils.
    His honour and myself are at the one,

---

Q:
9 boar] Q6, F;  beare Q1    12 th'] F;  'the Q1

F:
3 A messenger] One    3.1 *Enter Lord Hastings] after l.* 4    4 What's] What is't    5 thy master]
my Lord *Stanley*    6 should seem] appeares    7 lordship] selfe    8 And then?] What then?
8–9 And then he . . . tonight] Then certifies your Lordship, that this Night | He dreamt
9 razed] rased off    10 held] kept    14 presently you will] you will presently    15 into] with
him toward    18 councils] Councell

0.1 *Enter . . . Hastings* The Messenger
   enters at one door and knocks at another,
   the door of Hastings's house. He might
   carry a lantern as an indication that it is
   night.

9 **the boar** Emblematic of Richard (see note
   to 1.2.100).
✔ **razed his helm** slashed his helmet. By
   More's account of the dream (recalled

after Hastings's execution), 'a boar with
his tusks so razed them both [Stanley and
Hastings] by the heads that the blood ran
about both their shoulders' (Holinshed,
p. 381). There may also be a suggestion of
*razed* as 'pulled off'. See Appendix D,
Note 9.

10 **two councils** The 'divided councils' of
   3.1.176 (see note).

14 **presently** immediately

And at the other is my servant Catesby,                    20
Where nothing can proceed that toucheth us
Whereof I shall not have intelligence.
Tell him his fears are shallow, wanting instance;
And for his dreams, I wonder he's so fond
To trust the mock'ry of unquiet slumbers.    *Ho hubris*    25
To fly the boar before the boar pursues us
Were to incense the boar to follow us
And make pursuit where he did mean no chase.
Go, bid thy master rise and come to me,
And we will both together to the Tower,                    30
Where he shall see the boar will use us kindly.

MESSENGER
My gracious lord, I'll tell him what you say.        *Exit*
        *Enter Catesby*

CATESBY
Many good morrows to my noble lord.

HASTINGS
Good morrow, Catesby. You are early stirring.
What news, what news in this our tott'ring state?        35

CATESBY
It is a reeling world indeed, my lord,
And I believe 'twill never stand upright
Till Richard wear the garland of the realm.

Q:
24 he's] F;  he is Q1    25 mock'ry] F;  mockery Q1    32 *Exit*] F;  *not in* Q1    35 tott'ring] F;
tottering Q1    37 'twill] Q3;  it will Q1

F:
20 servant] good friend    23 wanting] without    24 fond] simple    26 pursues us] pursues
(*altering* Q3 'pursue vs')    32 My gracious lord, I'll] Ile goe, my Lord, and    37 'twill] will

20 **my servant** More describes Catesby as 'of
his near secret counsel, and whom he
very familiarly used, and in his most
weighty matters put no man in so special
trust'; he 'was a man well learned in the
laws of this land, and by the special
favour of the Lord Chamberlain in good
authority, and much rule bare in all the
county of Leicester where the Lord Chamberlain's power chiefly lay' (Holinshed,
p. 379).
21 **toucheth** relates to

22 **intelligence** secret information
23 **wanting instance** lacking evidence
25 **mock'ry** Suggests an enactment both
deriding and unreal.
27 **Were** would be
32.1 *Enter Catesby* Q3 adds '*to L. Hastings*',
repeating the formula of the scene's
opening direction. This might suggest
that Hastings retreats to the door by which
he entered before Catesby comes to him.
37 **'twill** Q3's alteration establishes the
metre.

HASTINGS

How? 'Wear the garland'? Dost thou mean the crown?

CATESBY  Ay, my good lord.                                    40

HASTINGS

I'll have this crown of mine cut from my shoulders

Ere I will see the crown so foul misplaced.

But canst thou guess that he doth aim at it?

CATESBY

Ay, on my life, my lord, and hopes to find you forward

Upon his party for the gain thereof.                          45

And thereupon he sends you this good news:

That this same very day your enemies,

The kindred of the Queen, must die at Pomfret.

HASTINGS

Indeed I am no mourner for that news,

Because they have been still mine enemies;                    50

But that I'll give my voice on Richard's side,

To bar my master's heirs in true descent,

God knows I will not do it, to the death.

CATESBY

God keep your lordship in that gracious mind.

HASTINGS

But I shall laugh at this a twelvemonth hence,                55

That they who brought me in my master's hate,

I live to look upon their tragedy.

I tell thee, Catesby.

CATESBY  What, my lord?

HASTINGS  Ere a fortnight make me elder                        60

I'll send some packing that yet think not on it.

CATESBY

'Tis a vile thing to die, my gracious lord,

When men are unprepared and look not for it.

Q:
44 Ay, on] F; Vpon Q1

F:
42 Ere I will] Before Ile    44 life, my lord] life    50 mine enemies] my aduersaries    56 who]
which    58–60 I . . . Ere] Well *Catesby*, ere    60 elder] older    61 on it] on't

41–2 **I'll . . . misplaced** The quibble on
  *crown* leads to a slight glance at Richard's
  appearance.
44 **Ay, on** Q1's 'Vpon' gives implausible repetition in ll. 44–6, and seems caught from

the following line.
52, 56 **my master's** Refers to the dead Edward IV. Richard mocks this turn of
  phrase at 3.4.44.
56 **in** into

HASTINGS

O, monstrous, monstrous. And so falls it out

With Rivers, Vaughan, Grey; and so 'twill do                65

With some men else who think themselves as safe

As thou and I, who as thou knowest are dear

To princely Richard and to Buckingham.

CATESBY

The princes both make high account of you—

(*Aside*) For they account his head upon the Bridge.        70

HASTINGS

I know they do, and I have well deserved it.

    *Enter Lord Stanley Earl of Derby*

What, my lord, where is your boar-spear, man?

Fear you the boar, and go so unprovided?

STANLEY EARL OF DERBY

My lord, good morrow.—Good morrow, Catesby.—

You may jest on, but, by the holy rood,                    75

I do not like these several councils, I.

HASTINGS

My lord, I hold my life as dear as you do yours,

And never in my life, I do protest,

Was it more precious to me than 'tis now.

Think you, but that I know our state secure,               80

I would be so triumphant as I am?

STANLEY EARL OF DERBY

The lords at Pomfret when they rode from London

Were jocund, and supposed their states was sure,

And they indeed had no cause to mistrust;

But yet you see how soon the day o'ercast.                 85

Q:
71.1 *Earl of Derby*] not in Q1, F    74 EARL OF DERBY] *not in* Q1, F. *Similarly at ll. 82 and 91.*
75 rood,] ~.   79 'tis] F; it is Q1   85 o'ercast] F; ouercast Q1

F:
66 who] that   72 What, my lord] Come on, come on   77 as you do] as   78 life] dayes
79 more . . . than] so . . . as   83 was] were

69–70 **The . . . Bridge** The heads of executed felons were displayed on poles, literally 'high', on London Bridge.
75 **the holy rood** the cross on which Christ was crucified
76 **several** separate

77 **as you do yours** Hammond, working from F's 'as yours', emends 'as you'.
83 **was** F corrects 'were'. As the derivative quarto compositors found no fault, Q1's reading is retained as an acceptable grammatical licence.

This sudden scab of rancour I misdoubt.

Pray God, I say, I prove a needless coward.

But come, my lord, shall we to the Tower?

HASTINGS

I go. But stay; hear you not the news?

This day those men you talked of are beheaded.                    90

STANLEY EARL OF DERBY

They for their truth might better wear their heads

Than some that have accused them wear their hats.

But come, my lord, let us away.

    *Enter a Pursuivant, [also called] Hastings*

HASTINGS

Go you before, I'll follow presently.

                *Exeunt Lord Stanley and Catesby*

Well met, Hastings. How goes the world with thee?                    95

PURSUIVANT

The better that it please your lordship to ask.

HASTINGS

I tell thee, fellow, 'tis better with me now

Than when I met thee last where now we meet.

Then was I going prisoner to the Tower

Q:

93.1 *a . . . Hastings*] *Hastin. a Purssuant*    94.1 *Exeunt . . . Catesby*] Q3 (*subs., after l. 93*), F
(*subs., after l. 94*); *not in* Q1    95 Well] *Hast.* Well    96 lordship] Lo:    97 now‸] ~ .

F:

86 scab] stab    88 But . . . Tower?] What, shall we toward the Tower? the day is spent.
89–90 I . . . men] Come, come, haue with you: | Wot you what, my Lord, | To day the Lords
90 talked] talke (*from* Q3)    93 let us] let's    93.1 *a . . . Hastings*] *a Pursuiuant*    94 you . . .
follow presently] on . . . talke with this good fellow    94.1 *Exeunt*] *Exit*    95 Well met, Hast-
ings] How now, Sirrha    96 it please your lordship] your Lordship please (*altering* Q3 'it please
your good Lordship')    97 fellow] man    98 I met thee] thou met'st me

86    **scab** irritable skin-rash; hence 'outbreak'.
'Applied to moral or spiritual disease'
(*OED* 1b). F's 'stab' gives more obvious
sense to the modern reader, but there is
a suggestive similarity between the
suddenly overcast sky and the sudden outbreak of skin disease.
    **misdoubt** mistrust, suspect

91    **truth** loyalty

92    **wear their hats** as symbols of their official
positions? Evidently a glance specifically
at Richard and his office of Protector.

93.1–106    *Enter . . . Exit* In More, this incident takes place outside the Tower, 'so
near the place where his head was off
soon after' (Holinshed, p. 382). In the
play, this self-contained episode emphasizes Hastings's carefree and celebratory
frame of mind, in contrast with his previous meeting with the Pursuivant (see
note to l. 99). F does not identify the Pursuivant as another Hastings.

93.1    **Pursuivant** Probably here an officer
who executed warrants and made arrests.
See following note.

99    **Then . . . Tower** *Then* is in contrast with
now, when he returns as a member of the
council. It might be implied that the
Pursuivant delivered the warrant for
Hastings's arrest. This would heighten
his present complacency, and the irony
of it.

By the suggestion of the Queen's allies;     100
But now, I tell thee—keep it to thyself—
This day those enemies are put to death,
And I in better state than e'er I was.

PURSUIVANT

God hold it to your honour's good content.

HASTINGS

Gramercy, Hastings. Hold, spend thou that.     105
> *He gives him his purse*

PURSUIVANT

God save your lordship.          *Exit*
> *Enter a priest*

HASTINGS          What, Sir John! You are well met.
I am beholden to you for your last day's exercise.
Come the next sabbath and I will content you.
> *He whispers in his ear.*
> *Enter Buckingham*

BUCKINGHAM

How now, Lord Chamberlain, what, talking with a
    priest?
Your friends at Pomfret, they do need the priest.     110
Your honour hath no shriving work in hand.

HASTINGS

Good faith, and when I met this holy man

---

Q:

103 e'er] F; euer Q1     106 *Exit*] Q3 (*Exit Pur.*), F (*Exit Pusuiuant.*); *not in* Q1     *Enter a priest*] *position as in* Q3, F; *bracketed as turn-over after* 'met' *in* Q1

F:

105 Hastings . . . that] fellow: there, drinke that for me     105.1 *He gives*] *Throwes him*
106 God save your lordship] I thanke your Honor     106–7 HASTINGS . . . to you] *Priest*. Well met, my Lord, I am glad to see your Honor. | *Hast*. I thanke thee, good Sir *Iohn*, with all my heart. | I am in your debt     107 last day's] last     108 you.] you. | *Priest*. Ile wait vpon your Lordship.     108.1 *He . . . ear*] *not in* F     109 How . . . priest] What, talking with a Priest, Lord Chamberlaine

100 **suggestion** instigation
103 **state** fortune, prosperity
104 **hold** maintain
105 **Gramercy** (anglicization of Old French *grant merci*, 'great thanks')
105.1 *He . . . purse* In F he throws the purse. In Q1 Hastings is physically closer to his companion both here and in whispering to the Priest.
106 **Sir John** A conventional title and name

for a priest.
107–8 **I . . . you** An apology for absence last Sunday (when Hastings was still in prison) and a promise to attend next Sunday (by which time he will be dead).
107 **exercise** religious service, preaching
109–11 **How . . . hand** Closely based on More (Holinshed, p. 382; see Appendix E).
111 **shriving work** task of confession

Those men you talk of came into my mind.
What, go you to the Tower, my lord?

BUCKINGHAM

I do, but long I shall not stay.                                                    115

I shall return before your lordship thence.

HASTINGS

'Tis like enough, for I stay dinner there.

BUCKINGHAM (*aside*)

And supper too, although thou know'st it not.—
Come, shall we go along?                                         *Exeunt*

[3.3]    *Enter Sir Richard Ratcliffe and a guard, with the lords*
         *Rivers, Grey, and Vaughan, prisoners*

RATCLIFFE  Come, bring forth the prisoners.

RIVERS

Sir Richard Ratcliffe, let me tell thee this:
Today shalt thou behold a subject die
For truth, for duty, and for loyalty.

GREY (*to Ratcliffe*)

God keep the Prince from all the pack of you!                     5
A knot you are of damnèd bloodsuckers.

Q:

118 know'st] Q3, F;  knowest Q1

   3.3.0.1 *Richard*] Q2, F;  *Rickard* Q1      *Ratcliffe*] *Ratliffe* Q1. *Similarly at* 3.3.1 (*speech prefix*
'*Ratl.*'), 3.3.2, 5.4.45, 5.4.57, *and* 5.4.57.1.      *and a guard*] *not in* Q1. *Compare F.*      *lords*] Lo:

F:

113 Those] The      114 to the Tower, my lord] toward the Tower      115 I . . . stay] I doe, my
Lord, but long I cannot stay there      117 'Tis] Nay      119 shall we go along?] will you goe? |
*Hast.* Ile wait vpon your Lordship

   3.3.0.1–2 *and a . . . prisoners*] *with Halberds, carrying | the Nobles to death at Pomfret*      1 RAT-
CLIFFE . . . prisoners.] *not in* F      5 keep] blesse      6 bloodsuckers.] Blood-suckers. | *Vaugh.* You
liue, that shall cry woe for this heereafter. | *Rat.* Dispatch, the limit of your Liues is out. (*Com-
pare l.* 21.)

118  **and supper too** Ironic: Hastings will not
       even live to eat dinner.

3.3  'Now was it so devised by the Protector
       and his council that the self day in which
       the Lord Chamberlain was beheaded in the
       Tower of London, and about the selfsame
       hour, was there, not without his assent,
       beheaded at Pomfret the foreremembered
       lords and knights that were taken from the
       King at Northampton and Stony Stratford,
       which thing was done in the presence and
       by the order of Sir Richard Ratcliffe,
       knight, whose service the Protector spe-
       cially used in that council, and in the exe-
       cution of such lawless enterprises, as a
       man that had been long secret with him,
       having experience of the world and a
       shrewd wit, short and rude in speech,
       rough and boisterous of behaviour, bold in
       mischief, as far from pity as from all fear of
       God' (More, in Holinshed, p. 385). The ini-
       tial sense of location depends on the audi-
       ence recognizing Rivers and Grey, but
       Pomfret is soon named (l. 7). Apart from
       this short scene, the first four acts are con-
       fined entirely to Westminster and London.
       Pomfret is a Yorkshire counterpart to the
       Tower.

RIVERS

   O Pomfret, Pomfret, O thou bloody prison,

   Fatal and ominous to noble peers!

   Within the guilty closure of thy walls

   Richard the Second here was hacked to death;   *Not really*   10

   And, for more slander to thy dismal soul,

   We give thee up our guiltless bloods to drink.

GREY

   Now Margaret's curse is fall'n upon our heads,

   For standing by when Richard stabbed her son.

RIVERS

   Then cursed she Hastings, then cursed she Buckingham,   15

   Then cursed she Richard. O remember, God,

   To hear her prayers for them as now for us;

   And for my sister and her princely sons,

   Be satisfied, dear God, with our true bloods,

   Which, as thou knowest, unjustly must be spilt.   20

RATCLIFFE

   Come, come, dispatch. The limit of your lives is out.

RIVERS

   Come, Grey; come Vaughan; let us all embrace,

   And take our leave until we meet in heaven.     *Exeunt*

[3.4]     *Enter the lords to council: [Hastings, Buckingham,*
     *Stanley Earl of Derby, Bishop of Ely. They sit]*
     *at a table*

Q:
10 Richard] Richatd   18 sons] F; sonne Q1   21 lives] Q3, F; linea Q1; lines Q2
   3.4.0.1–2 *Hastings . . . Ely*] This edition; *not in* Q1; *Stanley, Hastings, Buckingham, Bishop of Ely, and Others* CAPELL. *Compare F.*   0.2–3 *They sit] at a table*] F (*at a Table*); *not in* Q1

F:
11 soul] Seat   12 thee up . . . bloods] to thee . . . blood   13 heads] Heads, | When shee exclaim'd on *Hastings*, you, and I   15–16 Hastings . . . Richard] *Richard . . . Hastings*   17 prayers] prayer   19 bloods] blood   21 Come . . . out] Make haste, the houre of death is expiate   22 all] here   23 And . . . meet] Farewell, vntill we meet againe
   3.4.0.1–2 *Hastings . . . Ely*] *Buckingham, Darby, Hastings, Bishop of Ely, | Norfolke, Ratcliffe, Louell, with others*

11 **soul** The castle is personified: it is addressed, it is 'guilty', and it drinks. F's 'Seat' is potentially absurd in relation to the following line.
13–16 **Now . . . Richard** Referring to 1.3.207–30. She did not curse Bucking-

ham, but Rivers might wish she had done so.
18 **for** in place of
21 **limit** prescribed time
3.4 For More's account, see Appendix E. This is one of the 'divided' councils, held

**HASTINGS**

My lords, at once: the cause why we are met
Is to determine of the coronation.
In God's name say when is this royal day.

**BUCKINGHAM**

Are all things fitting for that royal time?

**STANLEY EARL OF DERBY**

It is, and wants but nomination.                                    5

**BISHOP**

Tomorrow, then, I guess a happy time.

**BUCKINGHAM**

Who knows the Lord Protector's mind herein?
Who is most inward with the noble Duke?

**BISHOP** Why, you, my lord.
Methinks that you should soonest know his mind.          10

Q:

5 STANLEY EARL OF] *not in* Q1, F. *Similarly at ll.* 47, 59, 63.     6 BISHOP] Q3 (*Bish.*), F (*Ely.*);
*Ryu.* Q1     10 that] This edition; *not in* Q1. F *has variant wording.*

F:

1 My lords, at once] Now Noble Peeres     3 say] speake     this] the     4 Are . . . fitting for that]
Is . . . ready for the     6 BISHOP] *Ely. Similarly throughout the scene.*     guess a happy time] iudge
a happie day     9–10 Why . . . mind] Your Grace, we thinke, should soonest know his minde

in the Council Chamber at the Tower.
What happens at Crosby Place is left obscure. To make sense of the play one need
imagine no more than a brief off-stage
private conference between Richard and
Catesby (see note to l. 80.1).

0.1–2 *Hastings . . . Ely* There may be other
lords who have no speaking role. Q1 does
not specify who the lords are. F names the
first four, adding Norfolk, Ratcliffe and
Lovel. Norfolk is not individuated in 3.4
even in F, but later becomes a significant
supporter of Richard at Bosworth. At the
end of the scene (see note to l. 80.1) Q1's
Catesby is equivalent to Ratcliffe, who in
F breaks the 'law of re-entry' by exiting in
Yorkshire at the end of 3.3 to re-enter
immediately in London. Lovel does not
appear in Q1. The Lovel mentioned at
4.4.436 is—confusingly in F—another
historical figure.

0.2 *Bishop of Ely* The historical figure,
Bishop Morton, was More's source of
information about the meeting.

1 **HASTINGS** He presides as Lord Chamberlain.
**at once** without preamble

2 **In . . . of** about

3 **In . . . day.** Q1's 'say' permits this to be
an injunction, though the compositor set
a question mark. F's 'speake' avoids the
'say . . . day' chime but disallows an
injunction.

4 **fitting** prepared. For '-ing' as equivalent
to modern past participle, see Abbott
372.
**royal** Taylor avoids repetition by emending to 'solemn'.

5 **wants but nomination** only needs the
time to be fixed

6 **BISHOP** See Appendix D, Note 10.
**happy** propitious, favourable

8 **inward with** confided in by

10 **that** Omitted in Q1 perhaps to save space:
ll. 9–10 are set as a single line with a
turn-over.
**his mind** Can refer to Richard's specific intention over the date of the coronation, his
intentions as a whole, or his disposition.

BUCKINGHAM

    Who, I, my lord? We know each other's faces;

    But for our hearts, he knows no more of mine

    Than I of yours,

    Nor I no more of his than you of mine.

    Lord Hastings, you and he are near in love.       15

HASTINGS

    I thank his grace I know he loves me well;

    But for his purpose in the coronation

    I have not sounded him, nor he delivered

    His grace's pleasure any way therein.

    But you, my noble lord, may name the time,       20

    And in the Duke's behalf I'll give my voice,

    Which I presume he'll take in gentle part.

        *Enter Richard Duke of Gloucester*

BISHOP

    Now in good time here comes the Duke himself.

RICHARD DUKE OF GLOUCESTER

    My noble lord, and cousins all, good morrow.

    I have been long a sleeper, but I hope       25

    My absence doth neglect no great designs

    Which by my presence might have been concluded.

Q:

19 therein] Q2, F; the rein Q1   22 he'll] F; he will Q1   22.1 *Enter . . . Gloucester*] *position as in* F; *bracketed as turn-over right of l.* 24 Q1; *after l.* 22 Q3   *Richard Duke of* ] *not in* Q1, F

F:

11 Who, I, my lord?] *not in* F   12 But for] for   14 Nor I no more of his] Or I of his, my Lord   19 grace's] gracious   20 noble lord] Q1 (noble Lo:); Honorable Lords F (*altering* Q3 'L.')   23 Now in good time] In happie time   25 hope] trust   26 designs] designe

11–14 **We . . . mine** Proverbially, 'The face is (or is not) the index of the heart (or mind)' (Dent F1, not citing this passage).

19 **His grace's** According to Davison an aural error for F's 'His gracious', but Q1 can be taken as a displacement of the address 'your grace's'.

20, 24 **lord . . . lord** Q1 contracts to 'Lo:' and 'L.', either of which might be expanded to the plural, as F reads. It is at least as plausible that Hastings defers to Buckingham, and that Richard addresses the previous speaker first (anticipating l. 34, where he singles him out).

21 **in . . . voice** The Lord Chamberlain would often speak for the monarch in Council, but, even if this procedure is invoked here, Hastings is taking a risk in giving Richard's voice (or vote) when he does not know his mind.

24 **cousins** Not simply a friendly suggestion of kinship; a sovereign would use the word to address his nobles.

25 **I . . . sleeper** This pretence at unconcern with the matters in hand comes from More. The phrasing is closest in *True Tragedy*, 'I have been a long sleeper today'.

26 **neglect** cause neglect of

BUCKINGHAM

Had not you come upon your cue, my lord,

William Lord Hastings had now pronounced your part—

I mean, your voice for crowning of the King.                            30

RICHARD DUKE OF GLOUCESTER

Than my lord Hastings no man might be bolder.

His lordship knows me well, and loves me well.

HASTINGS  I thank your grace.

RICHARD DUKE OF GLOUCESTER  My lord of Ely.

BISHOP  My lord?                                                        35

RICHARD DUKE OF GLOUCESTER  When I was last in Holborn

I saw good strawberries in your garden there.

I do beseech you send for some of them.

BISHOP  I go, my lord.                                        *Exit*

RICHARD DUKE OF GLOUCESTER

Cousin of Buckingham, a word with you.                                  40

(*Aside to him*) Catesby hath sounded Hastings in our

    business,

✓ And finds the t͟e͟s͟t͟y gentleman so hot

As he will lose his head ere give consent

Q:

39 *Exit*] F (*Exit Bishop.*); *not in* Q1    40 of] F; *not in* Q1    43 ere] eare

F:

28 not you] you not    29 had now] had    33–6 HASTINGS . . . When] My Lord of Ely, when
39 I go, my lord] Mary and will, my Lord, with all my heart    43 As] That

29 **pronounced your part** spoken your role
(as in a play; compare 'cue', l. 28)

36–8 **When . . . them** The incident, from
More, develops Richard's seeming genial
indifference to matters of state. An emblem headed '*Latet anguis in herba*', showing a snake twined round the stem of a
strawberry plant, appears in (a) Geoffrey
Whitney's influential *A Choice of Emblems*
(1586), p. 24, with verses concluding,
'No foe so fell, nor yet so hard to scape, |
As is the foe that fawns with friendly
shape', (b) Claudius Paradin, *Heroical Devices*, trans. P.S. (1591), with the commentary, 'In gathering of flowers
and strawberries that grow low upon the
ground, we must be very careful for the
adder and snake that lieth lurking in
the grass, for look whomsoever she

stingeth, they hardly recover after. So in
reading of authors and books which carry
a fair show to the eye and yielding small
delight to the ear, we must be careful that we
run not into absurd and wrong judge-
ments and opinions, and by that means
make shipwreck of our souls' (pp. 83–4).
Some productions have brought the fruit
on stage, with sinister implication. Holloway 'proceeded to sort out the most lus-
cious of Ely's strawberries with unction'
after commanding 'Off with his head' at
l. 81 (*Times*, 27 January 1927, quoted in
Hankey, p. 177); Troughton 'pummels
the bishop's bag of strawberries' to a pulp
(*Observer*, 10 September 1995).

✓42 **testy** headstrong. Sardonically alludes to
t͟h͟e͟ w͟o͟r͟d͟'͟s͟ d͟e͟r͟i͟v͟a͟t͟i͟o͟n͟ from old French
*teste*, 'head'.

His master's son, as worshipful he terms it,
Shall lose the royalty of England's throne. 45
BUCKINGHAM (*aside to him*)
Withdraw you hence, my lord; I'll follow you.
    *Exit Gloucester [followed by Buckingham]*
STANLEY EARL OF DERBY
We have not yet set down this day of triumph.
Tomorrow, in mine opinion, is too sudden,
For I myself am not so well provided
As else I would be were the day prolonged. 50
 *Enter Bishop of Ely*

BISHOP
Where is my Lord Protector? I have sent
For these strawberries.

HASTINGS
His grace looks cheerfully and smooth today.
There's some conceit or other likes him well
When he doth bid good morrow with such a spirit. 55
I think there's never a man in Christendom
Can lesser hide his love or hate than he;
For by his face straight shall you know his heart.
STANLEY EARL OF DERBY
What of his heart perceive you in his face
By any likelihood he showed today? 60

Q:
46.1 *Exit . . . Buckingham*] F (*Exeunt.*), POPE (*Exe. Glo. and Buck.*); *Ex Gl.* Q1   50.1 *Enter Bishop of Ely*] position as in Q3, F; *right of ll. 49–50 in* Q1   56 there's] F; there is Q1   57 Can] F; That can Q1

F:
44 son, as worshipful] Child, as worshipfully   46 you . . . follow] your selfe a while, Ile goe with   46.1 *Exit . . . Buckingham*] *Exeunt.*   48 mine opinion] my iudgement   50.1 *Bishop*] *the Bishop*   51 Protector] the Duke of Gloster   53 today] this morning   55 he doth bid . . . such a] that he bids . . . such   60 likelihood] liuelyhood

44 **worshipful** Glances at 'worshipful master' as a form of address more appropriate to a magistrate or alderman than a king.
47 **set down** appointed the time for
 **triumph** public festivity
49 **provided** prepared, equipped
50 **prolonged** put off
53 **smooth** pleasant, friendly. Often implies insincerity in the person described. Hast-ings seems to have no such thought, though in Olivier's film Hastings is al-ready fearfully awaiting the trap to spring. Compare note to ll. 68–71.
54 **conceit** thought, fancy. It is actually 'the little surprise he has for Hastings' (Wilson).
 **likes** pleases
60 **likelihood** indication, sign

HASTINGS

Marry, that with no man here he is offended;

For if he were, he would have shown it in his looks.

STANLEY EARL OF DERBY

I pray God he be not, I say.

*Enter Richard Duke of Gloucester [and Buckingham]*

RICHARD DUKE OF GLOUCESTER

I pray you all, what do they deserve

That do conspire my death with devilish plots                    65

Of damnèd witchcraft, and that have prevailed

Upon my body with their hellish charms?

HASTINGS

The tender love I bear your grace, my lord,

Makes me most forward in this noble presence

To doom th'offenders, whatsoe'er they be.                    70

I say, my lord, they have deservèd death.

RICHARD DUKE OF GLOUCESTER

Then be your eyes the witness of this ill.

See how I am bewitched. Behold, mine arm

Is like a blasted sapling withered up.

This is that Edward's wife, that monstrous witch,                    75

Q:

63.1 *Richard Duke of Gloucester*] Glocester     *and Buckingham*] F;   *not in* Q1     70 th'offenders ] F;
the offenders Q1     whatsoe'er] whatsoeuer. *Compare F.*

F:

62 if . . . have] were he, he had     63 STANLEY . . . say.] *not in* F     63.1 *Richard . . . Buckingham*]]
*Richard, and Buckingham*     64 what do] tell me what     69 noble] Princely     70 whatsoe'er]
whatsoeuer Q1;   whosoe're F     72 this ill] their euill     73 See] Looke     75 This is that] And this is

63.1 *Enter . . . Gloucester* More's description of Richard here as 'changed, with a
wonderful sour angry countenance, knitting the brows, frowning and fretting,
and gnawing on his lips' (Holinshed,
p. 380) might have informed the original
staging.
65–6 **devilish . . . witchcraft** The accusation
is from More, but would have had topical
relevance to the trial and execution of
Scottish witches for allegedly attempting
to bewitch and drown King James VI in
1591. The title-page of the London pamphlet on the subject, *News from Scotland*
(*c*.1592), describes the sorcerer Doctor
Fian as 'damnable', 'register to the devil',
and in consort with 'notorious witches'.
68–71 **The . . . death** Hastings, knowing
privily of the executions at Pomfret,

might think he is in on the political game,
expecting the Queen with her faction but
not her sexual rival to be blamed.
70, 73 **whatsoe'er . . . See** Honigmann
points out that these Q1 readings corres-
pond with the chronicles against F's variants, 'whosoe're' and 'Looke'.
73–4 **Behold . . . up** More notes that the lords
knew that Richard had always had a
withered arm, and so that his display was
a pretence and a trap (see Appendix E,
Passage 2).
74 **blasted** shrivelled, blighted (with a suggestion of supernatural agency).
75–6 **that . . . Shore** An unlikely alliance, as
More noted.
75 **that Edward's wife** Contemptuously re-
fuses to mention her in her own right.
**monstrous** Suggests something both un-

Consorted with that harlot strumpet Shore,
That by their witchcraft thus have markèd me.

HASTINGS

If they have done this thing, my gracious lord—

RICHARD DUKE OF GLOUCESTER

'If', thou protector of this damnèd strumpet,
Tell'st thou me of 'if's? Thou art a traitor.                    80

     [*He claps his fist on the table.*
     *Enter Catesby and soldiers*]

Off with his head! Now by Saint Paul,
I will not dine today, I swear,
Until I see the same. Some see it done.
The rest that love me, come and follow me.

     *Exeunt; Catesby [and soldiers] remain with Hastings*

Q:
80.1–2 *He . . . soldiers*] This edition; *not in* Q1, F; Ratcliffe *and Soldiers rush in from different entrances* MACREADY    84.1 *Exeunt . . . Hastings*] *Exeunt manet* | *Cat with Ha.*

F:
78 thing . . . gracious] deed . . . Noble    80 Tell'st thou me] Talk'st thou to me    81–2 Paul . . . dine today, I swear] *Paul* I sweare . . . dine    83 Some see it] *Louell* and *Ratcliffe*, looke that it be    84 come] rise    84.1 *Exeunt . . . Hastings*] *Exeunt. (after l. 83)*, *Manet Louell and Ratcliffe, with the* | *Lord Hastings. (after l. 84)*

natural and wicked. Richard transfers the term from himself ('deformed in birth') to the Queen ('atrocious', 'transgressive of womanhood').

76 **harlot strumpet** Resort to synonyms suggests flustered indignation.
  **Shore** 'She is dragged in so as to catch Hastings, who falls into the trap' (Wilson).
80.1 *He . . . soldiers* 'And therewith, as in a great anger, he clapped his fist upon the board [table] a great rap, at which token one cried "treason" without the chamber. Therewith a door clapped, and in come there rushing men in harness, as many as the chamber might hold' (More, in Holinshed, p. 381). This moment is dramatized in *Ricardus Tertius* (p. 164). It is likely to have been realized in early stagings of *Richard III*, and was acted on by Macready, Phelps, and others after the scene was restored. Most editions follow F's alternative staging: Ratcliffe enters at the beginning of the scene and speaks instead of Catesby at ll. 99–100. Q1 provides no entry for Catesby. Davison has him on stage from the opening entry, but

Catesby has no role in the early part of the scene. If he is absent, Richard has an offstage accomplice with whom he might imaginarily confer about Hastings before entering late. This, then, is the meeting arranged at 3.1.185–6 (postponed to morning because Catesby does not question Hastings until early morning), and is the actuality of the other 'divided' council meeting at Crosby Place. The exit after l. 46 can be to give Catesby the go-ahead. In every respect Q1 seems designed to follow More.
81 **Off with his head** See end of note to ll. 36–8.
81–3 **by . . . same** Proverbial, and common in Tudor drama (Dent B627.2). Compare, for example, *Jack Straw*, ll. 933–4: 'By Him that died for me, I will not dine | Till I have seen thee hanged or made away'. But here directly from More (see Appendix E, Passage 2).
81 **by Saint Paul** See note to 1.2.34.
84.1 *Exeunt* A moment of deep culpability. Some productions highlight Stanley. More gives a different emphasis, saying that he was wounded by a soldier.

HASTINGS

Woe, woe for England!—not a whit for me,                    85
For I, too fond, might have prevented this.
Stanley did dream the boar did raze his helm,
But I disdained it, and did scorn to fly.
Three times today my footcloth horse did stumble,
And startled when he looked upon the Tower,                    90
As loath to bear me to the slaughterhouse.
O, now I want the priest that spake to me.
I now repent I told the pursuivant,
As 'twere triumphing at mine enemies,
How they at Pomfret bloodily were butchered,                    95
And I myself secure in grace and favour.
O Margaret, Margaret, now thy heavy curse
Is lighted on poor Hastings' wretched head.

CATESBY

Dispatch, my lord, the Duke would be at dinner. ⎱
Make a short shrift; he longs to see your head.   ⎰                    100

HASTINGS

O momentary state of worldly men,

Q:
93 pursuivant] Pursiuant

F:
87 raze his helm] rowse our Helmes    88 But . . . scorn] And I did scorne it, and disdaine
90 startled] started    92 want] need    94–5 'twere triumphing at . . . How they] too triumphing, how . . . To day    99 CATESBY] Q1 (*Cat.*); *Ra.* F    Dispatch, my lord] Come, come, dispatch    101 state of worldly] grace of mortall

86 **fond** naive
89 **Three . . . stumble** 'his horse twice or
  thrice stumbled with him, almost to the
  falling' (More, in Holinshed, p. 381)
  **footcloth horse** horse wearing a richly-
  ornamented cloth hanging over its
  flanks. Suggests a special occasion; compare Nashe, *Have With You*, p. 79: 'on
  his foot-cloth majestically he would pace
  it'.
90 **startled** shied
91 **As** as if
93–6 **I now . . . favour** More comments on
  Hastings's execution, 'O good God, the
  blindness of our mortal nature! When he
  most feared he was in good surety; when
  he reckoned himself surest he lost his life,
  and that within two hours after' (Holinshed, p. 382).

96 **secure** Alludes to the Calvinist usage:
  'distinguished from (proper) assurance of
  salvation as meaning self-generated over-
  confidence' (Stachniewski, p. 246).
98 **Is lighted** has fallen (as of a weapon-blow)
99–100 **Dispatch . . . head** Echoes Thomas
  Lodge, *Wounds of Civil War, 1594*, ed. J.
  Dover Wilson (1910), ll. 2050–5, where
  the tyrant Silla says, 'Dispatch . . . For
  sore I long to see the traitor's head', and
  More, where Richard tells Hastings to
  'speed and shrive him apace' (Holinshed,
  p. 381).
101–6 **O . . . deep** The immediate point of
  reference is More: 'O good God, the blindness of our mortal nature!' (Holinshed,
  p. 382).'Our mortal nature' corresponds
  with Q1's 'momentary state of worldly
  men'; the point concerns worldly men

Which we more hunt for than the grace of heaven!
Who builds his hopes in air of your fair looks
Lives like a drunken sailor on a mast,
Ready with every nod to tumble down                     105
Into the fatal bowels of the deep.—
Come, lead me to the block, bear him my head.
They smile at me that shortly shall be dead.    *Exeunt*

[3.5]    *Enter Richard Duke of Gloucester and Buckingham
in rotten armour, marvellous ill-favoured*

RICHARD DUKE OF GLOUCESTER
Come, cousin, canst thou quake and change thy colour?

Q:
3.5.0.1 *Richard Duke of Gloucester*] Duke of Glocester    0.2 *rotten*] F;  *not in* Q1      *marvellous
ill-favoured*] F;  *not in* Q1

F:
102 heaven] God    103 hopes . . . fair] hope . . . good    106 deep.—] F *adds 4 lines. See Appendix A, Passage F*.    108 that] who
3.5.0.1 *Richard Duke of Gloucester*] Richard

amongst whom Hastings is counted. In F, the 'grace' is conferred by princes, 'your good Lookes' is their favourable regard, and the thought is closer to that of Psalms, 146: 3: 'O put not your trust in princes, nor in any child of man, for there is no help in them' (Psalter). In Q1 *state* is 'prosperity, high rank', and 'lookes' dismisses it as a mere appearance.

102 **heaven** The variant Q1 'heauen' F 'God' runs against the tendency of F to remove Q1 profanity, but is consistent with Q1 'state' F 'grace'. *God* underscores F's parallel between the grace of (other) men and the grace of God, whereas in Q1 *of heaven* contrasts with *worldly*.

103–6 **Who . . . deep** The Homily against Gluttony and Drunkenness, echoing Proverbs 23: 34, says of the drunk 'He doubtless is in great danger that sleepeth in the midst of the sea . . . He is like to fall suddenly that sleepeth in the top of the mast.' There is perhaps also a suggestion of a bird building its nest in a high tree; compare 1.3.263–4. Hastings's image of tumbling into the sea recalls Clarence's dream (1.4.19) and anticipates the tumbling of his own head from his body. F's extra passage of four lines after 'deep' breaks the connection between the imagery and Hastings's final couplet on his

execution, though Taylor suggests they might have been censored.

103 **in air of** Thus all pre-1623 quartos and F. Q7 emends to 'in the air of', but to 'build in air' is acceptable, and *of* might mean 'out of, upon', qualifying *builds* rather than *air*.

108 **They . . . dead** There is continuity of theme but a switch of tone when Richard and Buckingham enter to talk about hamming the tragic actor.

3.5 The location is within the walls of the Tower, an important royal stronghold.

0.2 *rotten, marvellous ill-favoured* The details, from F, are closely based on More (see Appendix E). They suggest a comically grotesque appearance, and might also be morally emblematic. More's *brigander* was body armour for a foot-soldier, of a kind that would be antiquated to the play's early audiences. *Rotten* probably refers to the leather on to which the armour was sewn, and *marvellous ill-favoured* suggests 'amazingly scruffy'.

1 **change thy colour** i.e. make yourself look pale. Compare Richard's boast that he 'can add colours to the chameleon, | Change shapes with Proteus for advantages, | And set the murderous Machiavel to school' in *Richard Duke of York* 3.2.191–3. For another instance of Buckingham echoing this speech, see note to l. 93.

Murder thy breath in middle of a word,
And then begin again, and stop again,
As if thou wert distraught and mad with terror?
BUCKINGHAM  Tut, fear not me.                                              5
I can counterfeit the deep tragedian:
Speak, and look back, and pry on every side,
Tremble and start at wagging of a straw,
Intending deep suspicion. Ghastly looks
Are at my service, like enforcèd smiles;                                   10
And both are ready in their offices
To grace my stratagems.
          *Enter Mayor*
RICHARD DUKE OF GLOUCESTER  Here comes the Mayor.
BUCKINGHAM
Let me alone to entertain him.—Lord Mayor—
RICHARD DUKE OF GLOUCESTER [*calling*]
Look to the drawbridge there!
BUCKINGHAM
The reason we have sent for you—                                           15
RICHARD DUKE OF GLOUCESTER [*calling*]
Catesby, o'erlook the walls!
BUCKINGHAM                          Hark, I hear a drum!

Q:
8 Tremble . . . straw,] F; *not in* Q1     14, 16 *calling*] OXFORD; *not in* Q1, F     16 o'erlook] F;
ouerlooke Q1

F:
3 begin again] againe begin     4 wert] were     5 fear not me.] *not in* F     12 To grace my strata-
gems.] At any time to grace my Stratagemes. | But what, is *Catesby* gone?   *Enter Mayor*] *Enter
the Maior, and Catesby. (after l.* 13)     Here comes the Mayor] He is, and see he brings the Maior
along     15, 16 The reason we have sent for you . . . Hark, I hear a drum] Hearke, a Drumme
. . . Lord Maior, the reason we haue sent

2 **Murder thy breath** 'kill off' your speech
and breathing. With a slight quibble:
*Murder* suggests *breath* as 'life'.
6 **deep tragedian** grave tragic actor. On the
longer view, Buckingham and Richard
are acting out their own tragedies.
8 **Tremble . . . straw** Proverbial (Dent W5).
The line was inadvertently omitted in Q1.
Taylor accepted Capell's suggestion that
the line was misplaced in F and should
follow 'tragedian', l. 6, because looking
back and prying are consistent with *suspicion*, but so is edgy nervousness.
**wagging** twitching, shaking

9 **Intending** expressing, pretending
10 **like** as well as, equally
11 **offices** appointed duties; proper action of
a part of the body
12 *Enter Mayor* In F the Mayor enters with
Catesby, so that an on-stage Catesby is addressed at l. 16, and it is Lovel and Ratcliffe
(see note to 3.4.0.1–2) who bring in Hastings's head. Q1 simplifies by eliminating
Lovel and transferring Ratcliffe's function
to Catesby, as in 3.4. The Mayor is often
played as foolish, flustered or intimidated.
13 **entertain him** engage his attention
16 **o'erlook** look over, guard from

**RICHARD DUKE OF GLOUCESTER** [*to the Mayor*]
  Look back, defend thee! Here are enemies.

**BUCKINGHAM**
  God and our innocence defend and guard us!
    *Enter Catesby, with Hastings's head*

**RICHARD DUKE OF GLOUCESTER**
  O, O, be quiet. It is Catesby.

**CATESBY**
  Here is the head of that ignoble traitor,                    20
  The dangerous and unsuspected Hastings.

**RICHARD DUKE OF GLOUCESTER**
  So dear I loved the man that I must weep.
  I took him for the plainest-harmless man
  That breathed upon this earth a Christian—
  Look ye, my lord Mayor—                                       25
  Made him my book, wherein my soul recorded
  The history of all her secret thoughts.
  So smooth he daubed his vice with show of virtue
  That, his apparent open guilt omitted—
  I mean his conversation with Shore's wife—                    30
  He laid from all attainture of suspect.

Q:
18 and guard] F; *not in* Q1    31 attainture] attainder

F:
18 innocence] Innocencie (*from* Q2)    18.1 *Catesby*] *Louell and Ratcliffe*    19 O, O . . . Catesby]
Be patient, they are friends: *Ratcliffe*, and *Louell*    20 CATESBY] *Louell.*    23 man] Creature
24 this] the    25 Look . . . Mayor—] *not in* F    31 laid] liu'd    suspect] suspects

18.1 *Enter . . . head* It is possible that the *drum* (l. 16) attends Catesby. A march, perhaps with the *traitor*'s head on a pole, would reassert the appearance of order. The staging is often managed less formally, with Hastings's head in a bloodstained bag. In Hands's and other productions the head was tossed around the stage in grisly fooling (Hankey, p. 179).
19 **be quiet** calm down
23 **plainest-harmless** most plain and harmless man F's 'Creature' might be preferred.
25 **Look . . . Mayor** Richard thus involves the Mayor in the goings-on. He might even make him 'read' Hastings's features, though Richard 'Made him my book' in the different sense of recording his own thoughts. The part-line is not in F.

27 **history** Perhaps here best glossed 'annals'. The word has particular frisson because Richard is actively constructing a narrative that he intends to become the basis of historical record, and because the actual historical record on which the play is based decidedly rejects Richard's version.
28 **daubed** This line is quoted in *OED* under sense 7, 'To cover with a specious exterior; to whitewash, cloak, gloss'. Also suggests 'to cover with plaster' (see *OED* 1) and 'apply cosmetic make-up'. There is probably an allusion to the biblical 'whited sepulchre' (Matthew 23: 27).
29 **apparent** self-evident
30 **conversation** sexual relationship
31 **laid** would have lain. This, Q1's reading, anticipates l. 32 ('covert'st-sheltered'). F's 'liu'd' is picked up in l. 33.

BUCKINGHAM

Well, well, he was the covert'st-sheltered traitor

That ever lived.

Would you have imagined, or almost believed,

Were't not that by great preservation                    35

We live to tell it you, the subtle traitor

Had this day plotted in the Council House

To murder me and my good lord of Gloucester?

MAYOR  What, had he so?

RICHARD DUKE OF GLOUCESTER

What, think you we are Turks or infidels,                40

Or that we would against the form of law

Proceed thus rashly to the villain's death,

But that the extreme peril of the case,

The peace of England, and our persons' safety

Enforced us to this execution?                           45

MAYOR

Now fair befall you! He deserved his death,

And you, my good lords both, have well proceeded

To warn false traitors from the like attempts.

I never looked for better at his hands

After he once fell in with Mistress Shore.               50

Q:

34 believed] F; beleeue Q1    35 not that] F; not Q1    36–8 you, the . . . Gloucester] ~? The . . . ~.

F:

34 have imagined] imagine    36 it ∧ you,] ~, that ∧    37 Had this day] This day had    39 What, had he so] Had he done so    42 to] in    47 you, my good lords] your good Graces    49 I] *Buck.* I

31 **from** free from
**attainture** taint, imputation. Q1's and F's 'attainder' has a separate headword in *OED* but is etymologically related and can be regarded as a spelling variant. **suspect** suspicion

32 **covert'st-sheltered** most secretly hidden

34 **almost** even actually ('Used to intensify a rhetorical interrogative'—*OED* 4). Compare *K. John* 4.3.42–4, 'could you think, | Or do you almost think, although you see, | That you do see'.

40 **Turks** Named as heathens and with reference to Ottoman despotism. *Common Prayer*'s third collect for Good Friday petitions for 'Jews, Turks, infidels, and heretics' (p. 144).

41 **form** order, formality

42 **rashly** with undue haste

43 **extreme** (stressed on the first syllable)

46 **fair befall you** may you have good fortune

49–60 **I . . . death** F has the single speech-prefix '*Buck.*' at l. 49 for these speeches. Q1's continuation of the Mayor's speech in ll. 49–50 gives him a comic uptake from Richard's sly mention of Shore's wife at l. 30. Q1's erroneous prefix '*Dut.*' at l. 51 might arise from a carelessly marked alteration in the manuscript. The speech it initiates could be given to Richard or Buckingham. As is argued in *Textual Companion*, Richard seems the more plausible speaker, and probably uses the 'royal' *we*.

49 **looked . . . hands** expected better of him

RICHARD DUKE OF GLOUCESTER

Yet had not we determined he should die
Until your lordship came to see his death—
Which now the longing haste of these our friends,
Somewhat against our meaning, have prevented—
Because, my lord, we would have had you heard                    55
The traitor speak and timorously confess
The manner and the purpose of his treason,
That you might well have signified the same
Unto the citizens, who haply may
Misconster us in him, and wail his death.                    60

MAYOR

But, my good lord, your grace's word shall serve
As well as I had seen or heard him speak,
And doubt you not, right noble princes both,
But I'll acquaint our duteous citizens
With all your just proceedings in this cause.                    65

RICHARD DUKE OF GLOUCESTER

And to that end we wished your lordship here,
T'avoid the carping censures of the world.

Q:
51 RICHARD DUKE OF GLOUCESTER] Q4, Q6 (*Glo.*); *Dut.* Q1; *Clo.* Q3, Q5; *not in* F (*which instead has speech-prefix 'Buck.' at l.* 49)    59 haply] F; happily Q1    64 our] F; your Q1    67 T'avoid] F; To auoyde Q1

F:
51 RICHARD DUKE OF GLOUCESTER] *Dut.* Q1; *not in* F (*altering* Q4 *and* Q6 '*Glo.*')    not we] we not    52 death] end    53 longing] louing    54 Somewhat against our meaning] Something against our meanings    55 we] I    57 treason] Treasons    61 word] words    62 or] and    63 doubt you not] doe not doubt    65 cause] case (*altering* Q6 'ease')    67 carping . . . world] Censures of the carping World

51 **had . . . die** Either 'we had determined he should not die' or 'we would not have determined he should die'.

53 **longing** eager, prompted by strong desire. F's reading, 'louing', is more predictable. Compare 'longing haste' with 'longing tarriance' in *Passionate Pilgrim* 6.4 (in a sonnet usually accepted as by Shakespeare).

55 **heard** Wilson, following a conjecture by Keightley, emended to 'hear'. As the syntax of the whole sentence is obfuscatory, it seems preferable to retain the ambiguity between 'we would have had you hear' and 'we would that you had heard'. It corresponds with the ambiguity between deliberate decision and later rationalization noted in l. 51.

58 **well** effectively

59 **haply** perchance. Q1's form *happily* is interchangeable with F's *haply*, and is now misleading as to both sense and metre.

60 **Misconster** Metrical variant of *misconstrue*.
**in him** i.e. in 'reading' him when they see what we have done to him

62 **as** as if

64 **But** but that

65 **cause** affair, business

BUCKINGHAM

But since you come too late of our intents,
Yet witness what we did intend. And so,
My lord, adieu.                              *Exit Mayor*

RICHARD DUKE OF GLOUCESTER

            After, after, cousin Buckingham!                    70
The Mayor towards Guildhall hies him in all post.
There, at your meet'st advantage of the time,
Infer the bastardy of Edward's children.
Tell them how Edward put to death a citizen
Only for saying he would make his son                          75
'Heir to the Crown', meaning, indeed, his house,
Which by the sign thereof was termèd so.
Moreover, urge his hateful luxury,
And bestial appetite in change of lust
Which stretchèd to their servants, daughters, wives—           80
Even where his raging eye or savage heart
Without control lusted to make his prey.
Nay, for a need, thus far come near my person:
Tell them, when that my mother went with child
Of that unsatiate Edward, noble York                           85
My princely father then had wars in France,

Q:
70 *Exit Mayor*] *position as in* F; *after* 'Buckingham' *in* Q1          81 raging] F; lustfull Q1
82 lusted] F; listed Q1

F:
68 But . . . intents] Which . . . intent    69 what] what you heare    70 lord, adieu] good Lord
Maior, we bid farwell    After] Goe after    72 meet'st advantage] meetest vantage (*altering* Q6
'meetest aduantage')    80 stretched to] stretcht vnto    82 his] a    85 unsatiate] insatiate

68 **come too late of** This seems to combine
   idioms such as 'fall short of' (compare
   Abbott 166) with 'come too late in
   respect of'.
70 **My lord, adieu** An abrupt dismissal.
71 **post** haste
72 **your . . . time** the best opportunity the
   occasion affords you
73 **Infer . . . children** In More, two friars,
   John Shaw and Friar Penker, 'both of
   more learning than virtue', plotted to
   preach sermons supporting Richard,
   agreeing 'they should allege bastardy,
   either in King Edward himself, or in his
   children, or both' (Holinshed, p. 386).
   **Infer** allege
74–7 **Tell . . . so** More (in Hall but not Holinshed) describes how Buckingham ex-

ploited this incident in which Edward
'made to be misconstrued' the citizen's
innocuous words.
76 **house** i.e. both home and shop (hence
   the sign)
78 **luxury** lust
79 **change** changefulness
81 **Even where** wherever
   **raging** Q1's 'lusting' is perhaps a miscor-
   rection, aimed to change 'listed' (immediately below in l. 82) to 'lusted'. F's *raging* develops the animal image whilst
   drawing on the sense 'taking its sexual
   pleasure' (obsolete; *OED, rage, v.* 3).
83 **for a need** if need be
84–8 **Tell . . . begot** This 'proof' of Edward's
   bastardy goes beyond the charges Richard's
   supporters make in Shakespeare's sources.

And by just computation of the time
Found that the issue was not his begot,
Which well appearèd in his lineaments,
Being nothing like the noble Duke my father.          90
But touch this sparingly, as 'twere far off,
Because you know, my lord, my mother lives.

BUCKINGHAM
Fear not, my lord, I'll play the orator
As if the golden fee for which I plead
Were for myself.          95

RICHARD DUKE OF GLOUCESTER
If you thrive well, bring them to Baynard's Castle,
Where you shall find me well accompanied          *like Bill Clinton*
With reverend fathers and well-learnèd bishops.

BUCKINGHAM
About three or four o'clock look to hear what news
Guildhall affordeth. And so, my lord, farewell.          100
                              *Exit Buckingham*

RICHARD DUKE OF GLOUCESTER
Now will I in to take some privy order
To draw the brats of Clarence out of sight,
And to give notice that no manner of person
At any time have recourse unto the princes.          *Exeunt*

Q:
91 'twere] F; it were Q1    100.1 *Exit Buckingham] position as in* F; *after l.* 101 *in* Q1    104 *Exeunt*] F; *Exit* Q1

F:
87 just] true    91 But] Yet    92 you know, my lord] my Lord, you know    93 Fear] Doubt    95 myself] my selfe: and so, my Lord, adue    99–100 About . . . farewell.] F *has a variant version of these lines followed by 3 extra lines. See Appendix A, Passage G.*    101 in] goe    103 notice . . . manner of] order . . . manner    104 At any time have] Haue any time

87 **just** exact
88 **his begot** fathered by him
90 **Being . . . father** Richard's own claim to resemble his father is obviously vulnerable, suggesting another possible reason for reticence.
93 **play the orator** Probably proverbial (Dent O74.1). The phrase occurs three times in *Richard Duke of York*, most notably in Richard's soliloquy where it is amongst his qualities as Proteus and Machiavel (3.2.188).
94–5 **As . . . myself** The *golden fee* is the crown 'for' which the orator or advocate pleads on Richard's behalf (drawing on

*fee* as 'inherited estate'), but also, in l. 95, the reward in gold coin 'for' which he does his office. The slippage might disconcert Richard.
96 **Baynard's Castle** A residence, between Paul's Wharf and Blackfriars, owned by the Duchess of York and increasingly Richard's London base as he gained power.
99–100 **About . . . farewell** F's variant lines add instructions from Richard to Lovel and Ratcliffe.
101 **take some privy order** make some secret arrangements
104 **recourse** (stressed on the first syllable)

**[3.6]**    *Enter a Scrivener, with a paper in his hand*
SCRIVENER                                                    *post facto!*

This is the indictment of the good Lord Hastings,
Which in a set hand fairly is engrossed,
That it may be this day read o'er in Paul's.
And mark how well the sequel hangs together.
Eleven hours I spent to write it over,                                    5
For yesternight by Catesby was it brought me;
The precedent was full as long a-doing;
And yet within these five hours lived Lord Hastings,
Untainted, unexamined, free, at liberty.
Here's a good world the while! Why, who's so gross          10
That cannot see this palpable device?
Yet who's so bold but says he sees it not?
Bad is the world, and all will come to naught,
When such bad dealing must be seen in thought.    *Exit*

Q:

   **3.6.**1 SCRIVENER] F (*Scr.*); *speech-prefix not in* Q1    3 o'er] F; ouer Q1    11 cannot see] F;
sees not Q1    12 bold] F; blinde Q1

F:

   **3.6.**0.1 with . . . hand] *not in* F    1 This] Here    3 this day] to day    5 spent] haue spent
6 brought] sent    8 lived Lord Hastings] *Hastings* liu'd    10 Why, who's] Who is    12 who's]
who (*from* Q3)    14 bad] ill

---

**3.6** This little scene (often omitted in performance) explores the writing and falsification of history. 'The language of a legal
document . . . may impress or even intimidate us because we do not see how the
language got there': Eagleton, *Literary
Theory* (1983), p. 170. The Scrivener tells
us. He explores specifically the relation
between historical and documentary se-
quences (which relates to the scene's
own position at the end of the Hastings
episode but *after* Richard's plans have
moved on to other things). He also affirms
that some at least felt smothered indignation towards Richard's charades. For
More, see Appendix E.
 0.1 *Scrivener* professional scribe, especially
of legal documents
 1 **indictment** The document accusing
Hastings to explain why he has been
executed. It is here not, as the term might
suggest, the basis for a trial.
 2 **set hand** formal handwriting
   **engrossed** written out in a large script
suitable for legal documents. Glances off
the sense 'made morally gross': in fact a

gross act has been written *fairly*, though
the Scrivener thinks the falsification is
itself *palpable* (l. 11).
 3 **Paul's** St Paul's Cathedral. Proclam-
ations were often delivered there.
 4 **sequel** Apparently refers to the *sequence* of
events. The sense is unusual, and the
word draws attention to the lack of proper
sequence.
 5–8 **Eleven . . . Hastings** The scene must be
set mid-morning, perhaps about 10 a.m.
 7 **precedent** document from which the copy
was made (the manuscript that Catesby
brought)
 9 **Untainted** not formally accused. *OED*'s
first illustration of the word in this sense;
the unfamiliar usage perhaps again draws
attention to the abruption of due process.
   **free** Both synonymous with *at liberty* and
'innocent'.
 10 **the while** these days
   **gross** stupid (with play on the sense 'palpable' in l. 11; compare also *engrossed*, l. 2)
 11 **device** contrivance
 13 **naught** (a) bad, wickedness, (b) *nought*,
nothing. *Naught* and *nought* were not

**[3.7]**    *Enter Richard Duke of Gloucester at one door,*
            *Buckingham at another*

RICHARD DUKE OF GLOUCESTER

How now, my lord, what say the citizens?

BUCKINGHAM

Now by the holy mother of our Lord,

The citizens are mum, and speak not a word.

RICHARD DUKE OF GLOUCESTER

Touched you the bastardy of Edward's children?

BUCKINGHAM    I did, with                                                5

Th'insatiate greediness of his desires,

His tyranny for trifles, his own bastardy,

As being got your father then in France.

Withal I did infer your lineaments,

Being the right idea of your father                                    10

Both in your form and nobleness of mind;

Laid open all your victories in Scotland,

Q:
    3.7.0.1 *Richard Duke of Gloucester*] *Glocester*    6 Th'insatiate] the insatiate Q1; Th'vnsa-
tiate F

F:
    3.7.0.1–2 *Richard . . . another*] *Richard and Buckingham at seuerall Doores*    1 my lord] how
now    3 and speak] say    5–8 I . . . France.] F*'s version extends to 7 lines. See Appendix A,
Passage H.*

distinguished as separate words; both senses are strongly present.

14 **seen in thought** i.e. not openly acknowledged as seen (also 'seen in mental anguish')

3.7 The location is Baynard's Castle (see 3.5.96 and note). The main stage represents the courtyard, and the rear stage wall, the wall of the building. More records at length Buckingham's speech to the citizens; Shakespeare closely summarizes the upshot in ll. 20–36. For the Mayor and Citizens' visit to Baynard's Castle, see Appendix E.

2 **by . . . Lord** A distinctly Catholic oath by Shakespeare's time, but unremarkable in the pre-Reformation period of the play's setting.

3 **The . . . word** Proverbially, 'No word but mum' (Dent W767).
**mum** The word could not in the period mean 'mother', fortunately.
**and speak** F reads 'say'. Q1 disrupts

the metre of Buckingham's doggerelish rhyming couplet.

5–8 **I . . . France** Q1 sets ll. 5–6 as one type line, and altogether is four lines shorter than F's version. See Appendix D, Note 11.

7 **tyranny for trifles** despotic cruelty in response to trivialities

8 **got** begot, conceived

9–11 **Withal . . . mind** Echoes More's account of Dr Shaw's sermon, where Richard is called his father's 'very right heir, of his body lawfully begotten' and claiming he 'as well in all princely behaviour as in the lineaments and favour of his visage represented the very face of the noble Duke his father' (Holinshed, p. 389). Buckingham strains credulity in referring to Richard's *form*. In the BBC film he looked embarrassed. Taylor emends to 'face'.

10 **right idea** true image

12 **Laid open** Suggests the metaphor of a book.

Your discipline in war, wisdom in peace,
Your bounty, virtue, fair humility;
Indeed left nothing fitting for the purpose                    15
Untouched or slightly handled in discourse.
And when mine oratory grew to an end,
I bid them that did love their country's good
Cry, 'God save Richard, England's royal king!'
RICHARD DUKE OF GLOUCESTER
Ah, and did they so?
BUCKINGHAM                    No, so God help me,                    20
But like dumb statuës or breathing stones
Gazed each on other and looked deadly pale;
Which when I saw, I reprehended them,
And asked the Mayor what meant this wilful silence.
His answer was, the people were not wont                    25
To be spoke to but by the Recorder.
Then he was urged to tell my tale again:
'Thus saith the Duke', 'thus hath the Duke inferred';
But nothing spake in warrant from himself.
When he had done, some followers of mine own,                    30
At the lower end of the Hall, hurled up their caps,
And some ten voices cried 'God save King Richard!'
'Thanks, loving citizens and friends,' quoth I,

Q:
17 end,] ~.    20 Ah,] A_    21 statuës] statues

F:
15 the] your    17 mine] my (*from* Q3)        grew to an] drew toward (*altering* Q3 'grew to')
20 Ah, and] Q1 (A and); And F    me] me, they spake not a word        22 Gazed] Star'd
25 wont] vsed        29 spake] spoke (*altering* Q6 'speake')        31 At the] At        32 Richard!']
*Richard:* | And thus I tooke the vantage of those few.

20 **No, so God help me** In the theatre, the
anticlimax usually gets a laugh.
21 **statuës** Similarly pronounced as three
syllables in, for example, *Contention*
3.2.80.
**stones** Proverbially mute (Dent S878.1),
but the immediate source is the citizens'
response to Shaw's sermon in More, 'as
they had been turned into stones' (Holinshed, p. 390).
26 **spoke** Taylor conjectures 'so spoke',
which would regularize the metre.
**Recorder** officer appointed by the Mayor
and Aldermen of London to regulate their
proceedings and preserve the City's cus-

toms and institutions; according to More,
'the mouth of the city'. Stressed on the
first syllable.
28 **inferred** alleged
29 **in . . . himself** on his own authority
31 **At the . . . of the** Both pronounced as
monosyllables.
**the Hall** i.e. the Guildhall
32 **Richard!'** See F's extra line. Q1 could
omit by eyeskip from one 'And' at the beginning of the line to the other, but Taylor notes that the disparity between the
subdued acclaim of the 'ten voices' and
Richard's inclusive response is funnier
without the line.

'This general applause and loving shout
Argues your wisdoms and your love to Richard'—     35
And so brake off and came away.

RICHARD DUKE OF GLOUCESTER
What, tongueless blocks were they? Would they not
    speak?

BUCKINGHAM No, by my troth, my lord.

RICHARD DUKE OF GLOUCESTER
Will not the Mayor, then, and his brethren come?

BUCKINGHAM
The Mayor is here at hand. Intend some fear.     40
Be not you spoke with but by mighty suit;
And look you get a prayer book in your hand,
And stand betwixt two churchmen, good my lord,
For on that ground I'll build a holy descant.
Be not easily won to our request.     45
Play the maid's part: say 'no', but take it.

RICHARD DUKE OF GLOUCESTER
Fear not me. If thou canst plead as well for them
As I can say 'nay' to thee for myself,
No doubt we'll bring it to a happy issue.

Q:
40 BUCKINGHAM] Q3, F; *Glo.* Q1   hand. Intend] F; ~, and intend Q1   41 you spoke with but
by] F; spoken withall, but with Q1   48 myself,] ~?

F:
33, 34 loving . . . loving] gentle . . . chearefull   35 wisdoms] wisdome (*from* Q3)   36 so] euen
here   38–9 BUCKINGHAM . . . GLOUCESTER] *not in* F   43 betwixt] betweene   44 build] make
45 Be . . . request] And be . . . requests   46 say 'no', but] still answer nay, and   47 Fear not
me. If thou canst] I goe: and if you   49 we'll] we

33–5 **loving . . . loving . . . love** F's version is
more varied. Q1's repetition makes Buckingham self-parodic.
37 **What, . . . they?** Peter Alexander's pointing.
Q1 has 'What tonglesse blockes were they,'.
40 **The . . . hand** The change of heart *might*
suggest threats or bribes (in which case the
Baynard's Castle audience *might* need little
persuading). In Bill Alexander's production Buckingham paused then gave a conspiratorial laugh before saying the line.
**Intend** pretend
**fear** (a) intimidating manner; or (b) religious reverence; or (c) apprehension of
danger
41 **you spoke with but by** Q1's reading is
clumsily repetitive and anticipates l. 52.
44 **on . . . descant** An improvised musical

*descant* would be 'built' on a *ground* as a
simple repeated bass melody. There is
also a suggestion of erecting a building
(such as a church) on foundations in the
earth. Unmetaphorically, *ground* is the
basis for an argument. For 'build', F
more weakly has 'make'.
46 **Play . . . it** Proverbial advice encouraging
seduction, or even rape (Dent M34), but
it is Richard who will play the seducer,
standing in phallic domination over the
crowd traditionally being figured with 'female' attributes such as
fickle changeability).
48 **for myself** Equivocates between 'on my
own behalf' and 'for my own advantage'.
49 **issue** Complicated by the sense 'offspring',
which develops the sexual metaphor.

BUCKINGHAM

You shall see what I can do. Get you up to the leads.          50

*Exit Richard*

*Enter the Mayor and Citizens*

Now, my Lord Mayor. I dance attendance here;

I think the Duke will not be spoke withal.

*Enter Catesby*

Here comes his servant. How now, Catesby, what says
    he?

CATESBY

My lord, he doth entreat your grace

To visit him tomorrow or next day.          55

He is within with two right reverend fathers,

Divinely bent to meditation,

And in no worldly suit would he be moved

To draw him from his holy exercise.

BUCKINGHAM

Return, good Catesby, to thy lord again.          60

Tell him myself, the Mayor, and citizens

In deep designs and matters of great moment

No less importing than our general good

Are come to have some conference with his grace.

CATESBY

I'll tell him what you say, my lord.          *Exit*     65

BUCKINGHAM

Aha, my lord, this prince is not an Edward.

He is not lolling on a lewd day-bed,

Q:

50.1 *Richard*] *not in* Q1          50.2 *Enter the Mayor and Citizens* F;  *not in* Q1          51 here] heare
67 lolling] lulling

F:

50 You . . . leads] Go, go vp to the Leads, the Lord Maior knocks F     Get you] Go, go     50.1 *Exit
Richard*] *not in* F      51 Now, my Lord Mayor] Welcome, my Lord     53 Here . . . he?] Now
*Catesby*, what sayes your Lord to my request?     54 My . . . grace] He doth entreat your Grace,
my Noble Lord,     58 suit] suites     60 thy lord again] the gracious Duke     61 citizens]
Aldermen     62 and matters] in matter     65 tell . . . lord] signifie so much vnto him straight
67 day-bed] Loue-Bed

50 **leads** flat leaded roofing
51 **I dance attendance** I am waiting eagerly
    to attend. Proverbial (Dent A392).
52.1 ***Enter Catesby*** Catesby might be above,
    to indicate that he is stepping out onto the
    'leads' directly from the room where
    Richard is supposedly at prayer.

53–4 **Here . . . grace** The metre would be
    evened up if 'says he' were regarded as
    the first foot of the following line, but
    'what' would make a weak line-end.
59 **exercise** religious devotion
62 **deep** weighty
67 **day-bed** Later used by Shakespeare in

But on his knees at meditation;
Not dallying with a brace of courtesans,
But meditating with two deep divines;                    70
Not sleeping to engross his idle body,
But praying to enrich his watchful soul.
Happy were England would this gracious prince
Take on himself the sovereignty thereof.
But sure I fear we shall never win him to it.            75

MAYOR

Marry, God forbid his grace should say us nay.

BUCKINGHAM   I fear he will.

*Enter Catesby*

How now, Catesby, what says your lord?

CATESBY                                      My lord,

He wonders to what end you have assembled
Such troops of citizens to speak with him,               80
His grace not being warned thereof before.
My lord, he fears you mean no good to him.

BUCKINGHAM

Sorry I am my noble cousin should
Suspect me that I mean no good to him.
By heaven, I come in perfect love to him.                85
And so once more return and tell his grace.

*Exit Catesby*

When holy and devout religious men

Q:
74 thereof] F; thereon Q1   77.1 *Enter Catesby*] *position as in* Q3 (*similarly* F, *after added part-line*); *right of* 'Catesby', *l.* 78, *in* Q1   87 holy] hollie

F:
73 gracious] vertuous   74 himself] his Grace   75 never] not   76 forbid] defend   77 will] will: here *Catesby* comes againe   78 How now . . . your lord] Now . . . his Grace   My lord,] *not in* F   80 speak with] come to   82 My lord, he fears] He feares, my Lord   85 I . . . him] we come to him in perfit loue   86.1 *Exit Catesby*] *Exit.*

*Twelfth Night* 2.5.46–7, with a similar sexual implication: 'having come from a day-bed where I have left Olivia sleeping'. F's 'Loue-Bed' is found nowhere else in Shakespeare. *OED* records no use of either expression earlier than *Richard III*; both are probably Shakespearian and perhaps his coinages. Q1's version anticipates ll. 71–2: 'not in bed in the daytime, but praying as though wakefully at night'.

70 **deep** profoundly learned
71 **engross** make gross, fatten
72 **watchful** Both 'attentive' and 'sleepless' (see note to l. 67). Christ in the Garden of Gethsemane commanded Peter, as one of the *sleeping* disciples, to '*watch* and *pray*' (Matthew 26: 41).
75 **never** Pronounced as one syllable: 'ne'er'.
78 **How . . . My lord** The line is variant in F and unmetrical in both texts.

Are at their beads, 'tis hard to draw them thence,
So sweet is zealous contemplation.

>  [*Enter Catesby below.*] *Enter Richard Duke of Glouces-
>  ter, between two bishops, aloft*

MAYOR

See where he stands between two clergymen.                    90

BUCKINGHAM

Two props of virtue for a Christian prince,
To stay him from the fall of vanity;
And see, a book of prayer in his hand,
True ornaments to know a holy man.—
Famous Plantagenet, most gracious prince,                     95
Lend favourable ears to our request,
And pardon us the interruption
Of thy devotion and right Christian zeal.

RICHARD DUKE OF GLOUCESTER

My lord, there needs no such apology.
I rather do beseech you pardon me,                           100

Q:

89.1 *Enter Catesby below*] THEOBALD (*subs.*); *not in* Q1, F    89.1–2 *Duke of Gloucester*] *not in* Q1,
F    89.2 *between*] F; *with* Q1; *and* Q3    *aloft*] Q2, F; *a loste* Q1    93–4 And . . . man.—] F; *not
in* Q1

F:

88 hard] much    89.2 *between two bishops, aloft*] *aloft, betweene two Bishops* (*altering* Q3 '*and*' *to*
'*betweene*')    90 he . . . between] his Grace . . . tweene    96 ears . . . request] eare . . . requests
100 rather do beseech you] doe beseech your Grace to

88 **at their beads** i.e. at prayer. Perhaps
Richard carries rosary beads.
89 **zealous** pious
89.1 *Enter Catesby below* Q1 and F provide
no re-entry, but Catesby later (from
l. 185) seems to be playing the role of
*agent provocateur* in the crowd.
89.2 *between two bishops* From More (in
Hall but not Holinshed): 'with a bishop
on every hand of him'. The false piety
that Shakespeare elaborates from More
would have seemed textbook Machiavelli. It would have been politically safer
and theatrically more impressive to dress
the pair in red as cardinals. In the modern
theatre the effect is sometimes clowned
up by showing that they are stooges
dressed as clerics.
*aloft* i.e. on the gallery, or upper acting
space, on the wall between the stage and
the tiring-house. More says Richard
appeared 'in a gallery over them'

(Holinshed, p. 395). This is the only place
in the play where the upper acting space
is certainly used. The staging can be read
as indicating emblematically the high
point in Richard's fortunes.
91 **props of virtue** 'virtuous supporters', 'effective supporters', and 'sustainers of
virtue'
92 **stay him** hold him back, support him
**the fall of** i.e. falling into sin as a result of
93–4 **And . . . man** Kemble made famous use
of the property by flinging it away when
the citizens depart at the end of the scene
(Colley, p. 48). Though the prayer book
is unlikely to have been forgotten by actors
or to have become unmentioned through
choice, the lines are not in Q1. Compositorial omission of two lines is possible.
The prayer book and the lines referring to
it may, however, have never reached the
Shakespearian stage. The Office of the
Revels might have seen an anachronistic

Who, earnest in the service of my God,
Neglect the visitation of my friends.
But, leaving this, what is your grace's pleasure?

BUCKINGHAM
Even that, I hope, which pleaseth God above,
And all good men of this ungoverned isle.                    105

RICHARD DUKE OF GLOUCESTER
I do suspect I have done some offence
That seems disgracious in the City's eyes,
And that you come to reprehend my ignorance.

BUCKINGHAM
You have, my lord, would it might please your grace
At our entreaties to amend that fault.                       110

RICHARD DUKE OF GLOUCESTER
Else wherefore breathe I in a Christian land?

BUCKINGHAM
Then know it is your fault that you resign
The supreme seat, the throne majestical,
The sceptred office of your ancestors,
The lineal glory of your royal house,                        115
To the corruption of a blemished stock,
Whilst in the mildness of your sleepy thoughts,

Q:
109 it might] F; it Q1    116 blemished] Q2, F; blemishst Q1

F:
102 Neglect] Deferr'd    107 eyes] eye    110 At . . . that] On . . . your    112 Then know]
Know then    114 ancestors] Ancestors, | Your State of Fortune, and your Deaw of Birth
117 Whilst] Whiles (*altering* Q2 'Whilest')

reference to *Common Prayer* that affronted
the established church. The property appears nowhere else in a Shakespeare play
apart from Folio 3 *Henry VI* (*Richard Duke of
York*) 3.1.12.2, though there are less specific books. Henry VI appears reading a
book aloft ('*on the walls*') in the scene
where Richard murders him (*Richard
Duke of York* 5.6).

102 **visitation** visiting
107 **disgracious** *OED*'s earliest example of
the word, glossed 'Out of favour; in disfavour; disliked' (sense 2). This applies
well at 4.4.169, but here the sense might
instead be 'shameful, discreditable'.
108 **my ignorance** i.e. my unknown misde-
meanour
109 **You . . . please** Q1's punctuation, 'You

haue my Lord, . . .' permits either the po-
litely conditional reading suggested by
the comma after 'lord' (i.e. I would only
allege a fault if you were happy to recognize and amend it) or, more bluntly, 'You
have, my lord. Would it might please . . .'
111 **Else wherefore breathe I** to what other
end do I live (or 'what otherwise would be
the point of my living')
114 **ancestors,** F has a line not in Q1. There
is no particular mechanical explanation
for Q1 omitting by accident, but the line's
disruption of the rhetorical patterning,
together with a wish to tighten up some
of the longer speeches in the scene (compare 'Your right of birth', l. 129), could
account for a deliberate cut. For other
omissions in this speech, see notes to
ll. 120 and 125.

Which here we waken to our country's good,
This noble isle doth want her proper limbs,
Her face defaced with scars of infamy,                                    120
And almost shouldered in the swallowing gulf
Of blind forgetfulness and dark oblivion.
Which to recure, we heartily solicit
Your gracious self
To take on you the sovereignty thereof,                                   125
Not as Protector, steward, substitute,
Or lowly factor for another's gain,
But as successively from blood to blood
Your right of birth, your empery, your own.
For this, consorted with the citizens,                                    130
Your very worshipful and loving friends,
And by their vehement instigation,
In this just suit come I to move your grace.
RICHARD DUKE OF GLOUCESTER
I know not whether to depart in silence
Or bitterly to speak in your reproof                                      135

F:

119 This] The   her] his (*from* Q3)   120 Her] His   infamy] Infamie, | His Royall Stock grafft
with ignoble Plants   122 blind . . . dark] darke . . . deepe   125 sovereignty thereof] charge |
And Kingly Gouernment of this your Land   133 suit] Cause   134 know not whether] cannot
tell, if (*altering* Q5 'know not whither')

119 **want** lack
  **proper** own, due by right (also 'hand-some, well-proportioned')
120 **infamy** See F's extra line. It repeats and rephrases l. 116 (compare also *royal*, l. 115), and disallows the continuity of imagery as in Q1 between *face* and *shouldered* (l. 121).
121 **shouldered in** roughly shoved with the shoulders into (perhaps as one might be jostled into the sewerage ditch that ran down the middle of Elizabethan streets, especially as those of higher rank would usually pass securely on the side nearest the wall). Probably applies to the *isle* as a body, not just the *face* or head, but see following note.
  **swallowing gulf** Recalls Clarence's dream of drowning and Hastings's anticipation of execution at the end of 3.4.
123 **recure** cure, redress
125 **sovereignty thereof** F's reading is longer and different. The Q1 version saves 'kingly' for l. 221, where F has

'Royall' ('Royall' is also in the Folio line deleted after l. 120). Q1 needs relining to adjust for the cut; like F it divides ll. 123–5 after 'solicit'.
127 **factor** merchant's agent
128 **successively** by right of succession
129 **empery** absolute dominion
131 **worshipful** distinguished, honourable (glancing at the word's use as an honorific title for City dignitaries)
134–56, 186–9 **I . . . him, Alas . . . you** Shakespeare may have noted similar dissimulation in the future tyrant Tiberius in *Mirror for Magistrates* (1587 edn., in *Parts Added*), where Tiberius is made to speak of his 'Dissembling that which afterward was known. | For when the fathers' mind to me was shown | Of their electing mine imperial place, | I seemed to stay, refusing it a space' ('Claudius Tiberius Nero', ll. 67–70).
134–6 **I . . . condition** Unless 'or' in l. 136 is an error for 'and', Richard is using ambiguous syntax. It may be rationalized

Best fitteth my degree or your condition.
Your love deserves my thanks, but my desert,
Unmeritable, shuns your high request.
First, if all obstacles were cut away,
And that my path were even to the crown                    140
As my ripe revenue and due by birth,
Yet so much is my poverty of spirit,
So mighty and so many my defects,
As I had rather hide me from my greatness,
Being a barque to brook no mighty sea,                     145
Than in my greatness covet to be hid
And in the vapour of my glory smothered.
But, God be thankèd, there's no need of me;
And much I need to help you if need were.
The royal tree hath left us royal fruit,                   150
Which, mellowed by the stealing hours of time,
Will well become the seat of majesty,
And make, no doubt, us happy by his reign.
On him I lay what you would lay on me:

F:
136 condition.] F *adds* 10 *lines. See Appendix A, Passage I.*    141 my . . . by] the . . . of    144 As
I had] That I would    148 thankèd, there's] thank'd, there is    149 if need were] were there
need    154 what] that

(a) by taking 'or' in l. 136 to mean 'or for
that matter', (b) by paraphrasing the
whole, 'I know not whether to depart in
silence, as best fitteth my degree, or bitterly to speak in your reproof, as best fitteth your condition'.

136  **degree** Presumably refers to spiritual condition rather than social rank. There is the
same ambiguity in the meaning of
Richard's physical situation: between two
bishops and elevated above the citizens.
**condition.** F has ten extra lines in which
Richard expands on his dilemma.
137-8 **desert,  |  Unmeritable** Quibbles on
*desert* as suggesting positive value ('high
merit') and as lacking prior judgement
('what I deserve, meritable or not').
139-40 **if . . . crown** *Cut away* slips in a reminder of Richard's violence. Compare
his resolution, when seeing himself as
'like one lost in a thorny wood', to 'hew
my way out with a bloody axe' in order to
'catch the English crown' (*Richard Duke
of York* 3.2.174, 181, 179).

140  **even** straight and smooth
141  **my . . . birth** A slightly odd way of saying
'what is owing to me by birth and will
now come back to me in my maturity'.
*Revenue* in the usual sense 'income' cannot quite apply to the crown itself as an estate, but T. Thomas in 1587 defined Latin
*piscus* as 'a king's treasure or revenue'.
*OED* shows the word used in 1532 to indicate a king's return to his realm. This is
especially applicable in view of the
metaphor of a *path* in the previous line.
*Ripe* glances contrastively at the immatur-
ity of Prince Edward (compare ll. 150–1).
145  **brook** withstand
149  **much I need** I am greatly inadequate
**need were** help were needed
151  **stealing** moving stealthily on. There
may also be a suggestion that time would
have robbed Richard if Prince Edward
matured to become King.
153  **no doubt** 'The effect of the awkwardly
placed intrusion of this phrase into the
sentence is to make the hearers think
there is doubt' (Hammond).

The right and fortune of his happy stars,                    155
Which God defend that I should wring from him.
BUCKINGHAM

My lord, this argues conscience in your grace,
But the respects thereof are nice and trivial,
All circumstances well considerèd.
You say that Edward is your brother's son.            160
So say we too, but not by Edward's wife;
For first he was contract to Lady Lucy—
Your mother lives a witness to that vow—
And afterward by substitute betrothed
To Bona, sister to the King of France.                165
These both put by, a poor petitioner,
A care-crazed mother of a-many children,
A beauty-waning and distressèd widow,
Even in the afternoon of her best days,
Made prize and purchase of his lustful eye,          170
Seduced the pitch and height of all his thoughts
To base declension and loathed bigamy.
By her in his unlawful bed he got
This Edward whom our manners term the prince.
More bitterly could I expostulate,                   175
Save that for reverence to some alive
I give a sparing limit to my tongue.

Q:
173 got‸] ~.

F:
162 he was] was he   163 that] his   166 by] off   167 of a-many children] to a many Sonnes
(*altering* Q2 'of many children')   170 lustful] wanton   171 all his thoughts] his degree
174 term] call

155 **happy stars** i.e. astrologically auspi-
   cious birth. Richard shifts the issue away
   from that of entitlement to the crown.
156 **defend** forbid
158 **respects** considerations
   **nice** slight, fastidious
162 **first . . . Lucy** In More's account, Shaw
   declared that Edward 'was before God
   husband unto dame Elizabeth Lucy, and
   so his children [by the Queen] bastards'
   (Holinshed, p. 389).
   **contract** betrothed. Stressed on the second syllable.
164–5 **And . . . France** The episode is staged

   in *Richard Duke of York* 3.3.
164 **by substitute** The Earl of Warwick conducted the negotiations on Edward's
   behalf.
165 **sister** sister-in-law
166 **put by** thrust aside, discarded
166–9 **a poor . . . days** i.e. Elizabeth Grey.
   See *Richard Duke of York* 3.2.
170 **Made prize and purchase of** captured,
   made booty of
171 **pitch** the highest point to which a falcon
   flies before stooping
172 **base declension** descent to baseness
176 **some alive** Specifically, Richard's mother.

Then, good my lord, take to your royal self
This proffered benefit of dignity,
If not to bless us and the land withal,                              180
Yet to draw out your royal stock
From the corruption of abusing time
Unto a lineal, true-derivèd course.
MAYOR (*to Gloucester*)
Do, good my lord, your citizens entreat you.
CATESBY (*to Gloucester*)
O make them joyful, grant their lawful suit.                         185
RICHARD DUKE OF GLOUCESTER
Alas, why would you heap these cares on me?
I am unfit for state and dignity.
I do beseech you take it not amiss
I cannot nor I will not yield to you.
BUCKINGHAM
If you refuse it, as in love and zeal                                190
Loath to depose the child your brother's son—
As well we know your tenderness of heart
And gentle, kind, effeminate remorse,
Which we have noted in you to your kin
And equally, indeed, to all estates—                                 195
Yet, whether you accept our suit or no,
Your brother's son shall never reign our king,
But we will plant some other in the throne,
To the disgrace and downfall of your house.
And in this resolution here we leave you.                            200
Come, citizens. Zounds, I'll entreat no more.

Q:
195 equally] egallie

F:
181 out your royal stock] forth your Noble Ancestrie    182 time] times    184 you.] you. |
*Buck.* Refuse not, mightie Lord, this proffer'd loue.    186 these cares] this Care (*altering* Q2
'those cares')    187 dignity] Maiestie    194 kin] Kindred    196 whether] know, where
201 Zounds, I'll] we will

179 **benefit** bestowal
  **dignity** sovereignty
182 **abusing time** i.e. the impostures and
  ill-treatment of the present day
184 **entreat you.** In F Buckingham's subsequent line repeats from the end of his previous speech (especially 'proffered' as in
  l. 179).

193 **effeminate** The only instance in Shakespeare of the favourable sense 'tender,
  gentle'. Compare l. 46 and note.
  **remorse** pity
195 **all estates** people of all ranks
201 **Zounds** See note to 1.4.114. F deletes
  the profanity, and so omits Richard's
  response.

RICHARD DUKE OF GLOUCESTER

O do not swear, my lord of Buckingham.

*Exeunt Buckingham [and some Citizens]*

CATESBY

Call them again, my lord, and accept their suit.

ANOTHER

Do, good my lord, lest all the land do rue it.

RICHARD DUKE OF GLOUCESTER

Would you enforce me to a world of care?                          205

Well, call them again.                    *[Exit Catesby]*

I am not made of stones,

But penetrable to your kind entreats,

Albeit against my conscience and my soul.

*Enter Buckingham and the rest*

Cousin of Buckingham, and you sage, grave men,

Since you will buckle fortune on my back                          210

To bear her burden whe'er I will or no,

I must have patience to endure the load.

But if black scandal or foul-faced reproach

Attend the sequel of your imposition,

Your mere enforcement shall acquittance me                        215

From all the impure blots and stains thereof;

Q:

202.1 *Exeunt . . . Citizens*] F ('*Exeunt.*', *after l.* 201), CAPELL (*subs.*); *not in* Q1    206 *Exit Catesby*] THEOBALD; *not in* Q1, F    208.1 *Enter . . . rest*] F; *not in* Q1    211 whe'er] F (where); whether Q1    213 foul-faced] F; soule-fac't Q1; so foule fac't Q3

F:

202 RICHARD . . . Buckingham.] *not in* F    203 them again, my lord, and] him againe, sweet Prince,    204 ANOTHER Do, my good lord, lest . . . do] Q1 (*Ano . . . .*); If you denie them . . . will F (*no new speaker*)    205 Would . . . care] Will . . . Cares    206 Well, call] Call    207 entreats] entreaties    209 you sage] sage

204  **ANOTHER** Where F continues the speech to Catesby, Q1 makes Richard's apparent change of heart hinge on a minimal rejoinder from one citizen.
     **rue it** Presumably elided 'rue't', to rhyme with *suit*.
206  **stones** The proverb 'As hard as a stone' (Dent S878) was applied particularly to a hard heart. Pope's emendation 'stone' is often followed, though Q1 and F agree on 'stones'.
207  **entreats** entreaties. Similarly in *Titus* 1.1.446 and 480 (at the end of a line). As the scene in *Titus* may have been written

by Peele, F's 'entreaties' may be right; but a stylistic Peelism mistakenly modernized in F to the more familiar form seems at least as likely. Compare *gratulate*, 4.1.5.
210  **on my back** With a reference to Richard's hunch-back. The words make a joke at the speaker's expense.
215  **Your mere enforcement** (a) the fact that you and you alone have enforced it (a legal sense of *mere*: OED adj. 2; compare *acquittance*), (b) your absolute enforcement
     **acquittance** acquit

For God He knows, and you may partly see,
How far I am from the desire thereof.

MAYOR

God bless your grace! We see it, and will say it.

RICHARD DUKE OF GLOUCESTER

In saying so you shall but say the truth.                    220

BUCKINGHAM

Then I salute you with this kingly title:
Long live Richard, England's royal king!

MAYOR  Amen.

BUCKINGHAM

Tomorrow will it please you to be crowned?

RICHARD DUKE OF GLOUCESTER

Even when you will, since you will have it so.              225

BUCKINGHAM

Tomorrow, then, we will attend your grace.

RICHARD DUKE OF GLOUCESTER (*to the bishops*)

Come, let us to our holy task again.—
Farewell, good cousin. Farewell, gentle friends.  *Exeunt*


[4.1]  *Enter Queen, Duchess of York, Marquis Dorset, at
one door, Anne Duchess of Gloucester at another door*

DUCHESS OF YORK

Who meets us here? My niece Plantagenet?

Q:

4.1.0.1 *Queen*] F; *Quee. mother* Q1   0.2 *Anne*] F; *not in* Q1. *Compare F.*   1 DUCHESS OF
YORK] *Duch.* Q1; *Duch. Yorke.* F

F:

217 He knows] doth know   218 thereof] of this   221 kingly] Royall   222 Richard] King
*Richard (from* Q3)   royal] worthie   223 MAYOR] *All.*   224 will] may   225 will, since]
please, for   226 grace] Grace, | And so most ioyfully we take our leaue   227 task] Worke
228 good cousin] my Cousins

4.1.0.1–4.1.2 *Enter . . . fast?*] F *expands. See Appendix A, Passage J.*   0.1–2 *Enter . . .
another door*] *Enter the Queene, Anne Duchesse of Gloucester, the | Duchesse of Yorke, and Marquesse
Dorset.*   1 DUCHESS OF YORK] *Duch.* Q1; *Duch. Yorke.* F

221 **kingly** See note to l. 125. The tautolo-
gies of 'kingly . . . royal king' (compare F:
'Royall . . . worthie King') make Buckingham's flourish patronizing to his audience and almost self-parodic. Compare
note to ll. 33–5.
223 **MAYOR** F instead calls for a general response from '*All*'.
4.1 The location, as suggested by l. 3, is not
far from the Tower. The events are without basis in the chronicles, and the scene

has sometimes been cut entirely.
0.2 *Anne Duchess of Gloucester* Her first appearance since 1.2. In Q1 she is now
'*Duchesse of Glocest.*' without personal
name, as distinct from '*Lady Anne*' in
1.2. The disjunction is both suggestive
and confusing.
1 **My niece Plantagenet** This refers to
Anne, with *niece* in the general sense of
'female relative' (*OED* 2). She formerly
might have derived the title *Plantagenet*

279

QUEEN

Sister, well met. Whither away so fast?

ANNE DUCHESS OF GLOUCESTER

No farther than the Tower, and as I guess

Upon the like devotion as yourselves:

To gratulate the tender princes there.                              5

QUEEN

Kind sister, thanks. We'll enter all together.

　　　*Enter [Brakenbury,] Lieutenant of the Tower*

And in good time here the Lieutenant comes.

Master Lieutenant, pray you by your leave,

How fares the Prince?

LIEUTENANT

Well, madam, and in health. But, by your leave,               10

I may not suffer you to visit him.

The King hath straitly charged the contrary.

QUEEN　The King? Why, who's that?

LIEUTENANT

I cry you mercy, I mean the Lord Protector.

QUEEN

The Lord protect him from that kingly title.                     15

Hath he set bounds betwixt their love and me?

I am their mother; who should keep me from them?

Q:

2 Whither] whether　　3 ANNE DUCHESS OF GLOUCESTER] *Duch.* Q1; *Dut. Glo.* Q3; *Anne.* F
6.1 *Brakenbury*] CAPELL (*subs.*); *not in* Q1, F　　*of the Tower*] Q3; *not in* Q1, F

F:

3 ANNE . . . GLOUCESTER] *Dutch.* Q1; *Dut. Glo.* Q3; *Anne.* F　　5 tender] gentle　　6.1 *Lieutenant*]
*the Lieutenant* (*from* Q3)　　9 fares the Prince] doth the Prince, and my young Sonne of *Yorke*
10 Well . . . leave] Right well, deare Madame: by your patience　　11 him] them　　12 straitly]
strictly　　13 Why, who's] who's　　14 I cry you mercy,] *not in* F　　16 betwixt] betweene
17 should keep] shall barre

from her former husband Edward (of the
Lancastrian line), but now she presumably owes it to her present husband
Richard (see note to 1.2.140). See Appendix D, Note 12 for comment on F's
version of this passage.

　4　**devotion** devoted purpose (*OED*'s earliest
　　example of sense 7)
　5　**gratulate** greet. A word favoured by Peele
　　and found elsewhere in early Shake-
　　speare only in *Titus* in 1.1.221, in a scene
　　attributed to Peele (see note to 3.7.207).
　　**tender** young

6.1　**Brakenbury** Capell's identification is
　　overwhelmingly plausible even in the
　　Quarto text, in which Brakenbury is con-
　　flated with the Keeper in 1.4 and so is
　　potentially of lower rank than the
　　Lieutenant. Brakenbury's ahistorical
　　presence in the earlier scenes (as similarly
　　with the return of Anne in the present
　　scene) establishes a link between the
　　early and present events (see headnote to
　　1.4). Continuity of identity on stage
　　would be essential for this.
12　**straitly** strictly
14　**cry you mercy** beg your pardon

**DUCHESS OF YORK**

I am their father's mother; I will see them.

**ANNE DUCHESS OF GLOUCESTER**

Their aunt I am in law, in love their mother.

Then fear not thou; I'll bear thy blame,    20

And take thy office from thee on my peril.

**LIEUTENANT**

I do beseech your graces all to pardon me.

I am bound by oath, I may not do it.    *Exit*

*Enter Lord Stanley Earl of Derby*

**STANLEY EARL OF DERBY**

Let me but meet you ladies an hour hence,

And I'll salute your grace of York as mother    25

And reverend looker-on of two fair queens.

(*To Anne*) Come, madam, you must go with me to
Westminster,

There to be crownèd Richard's royal queen.

**QUEEN**

O cut my lace in sunder, that my pent heart

May have some scope to beat, or else I swoon    30

With this dead-killing news.

**ANNE DUCHESS OF GLOUCESTER**

Despiteful tidings! O, unpleasing news!

**DORSET**

Madam, have comfort.—How fares your grace?

**QUEEN**

O Dorset, speak not to me. Get thee hence.

Death and destruction dog thee at the heels.    35

Q:

18 father's ] F; Fathers, Q1; father, Q2    19 ANNE DUCHESS OF GLOUCESTER] *Duch. glo. Similarly
at ll. 61, 84, and 86.*    23 Exit] F (*Exit Lieutenant.*); *not in* Q1    23.1 *Earl of Derby*] *not in* Q1
24 EARL OF DERBY] *not in* Q1, F. *Similarly at ll. 43 and 52.*    30 swoon] sound    32 ANNE . . .
news!] F (*omitting title in speech-prefix*); *not in* Q1

F:

19 ANNE . . . GLOUCESTER] Q1 (*Duch. glo.*), F (*Anne.*). *Similarly ll. 61, 84, and 86.*    20 fear not
thou] bring me to their sights    22 I . . . me] No, Madame, no; I may not leaue it so    23 I may
not do it] and therefore pardon me    23.1 *Lord Stanley Earl of Derby*] *Stanley*    24 an] one
27 go with me] straight    29 O . . . in sunder] Ah . . . asunder    33 Madam . . . How] Be of good
cheare: Mother, how    34 hence] gone    35 dog] dogges    the] thy

19 **in law** i.e. by marriage
21 **take . . . thee** take on your official
    responsibility
25 **mother** i.e. mother-in-law

26 **looker-on** Hints at the spectacle of
    coronation.
29 **lace** cords tying up the bodice

Thy mother's name is ominous to children.
If thou wilt outstrip death, go cross the seas
And live with Richmond, from the reach of hell.
Go hie thee, hie thee from this slaughterhouse,
Lest thou increase the number of the dead　　　　40
And make me die the thrall of Margaret's curse:
Nor mother, wife, nor England's counted queen.

STANLEY EARL OF DERBY
Full of wise care is this your counsel, madam.—
(*To Dorset*) Take all the swift advantage of the time.
You shall have letters from me to my son,　　　　45
To meet you on the way and welcome you.
Be not ta'en tardy by unwise delay.

DUCHESS OF YORK
O ill-dispersing wind of misery!
O my accursèd womb, the bed of death,
A cockatrice hast thou hatched to the world,　　　　50
Whose unavoided eye is murderous.

STANLEY EARL OF DERBY (*to Anne*)
Come, madam; I in all haste was sent.

ANNE DUCHESS OF GLOUCESTER
And I in all unwillingness will go.
I would to God that the inclusive verge
Of golden metal that must round my brow　　　　55

Q:
50 hatched] Q2, F; hatch Q1　53 ANNE DUCHESS OF GLOUCESTER] *Duch.* Q1; *Anne.* F　54 that] thar

F:
44 time] howres　46 To . . . welcome you] In your behalfe, to meet you on the way　52 madam] Madame, come　53 ANNE . . . GLOUCESTER] Q1 (*Duch.*), F (*Anne.*)　in] with　54 I] O

37 **outstrip** Continues the image from *dog*, l. 35.
　**cross** Either the verb or 'across'.
38 **with Richmond** i.e. in Brittany, where Richmond was sent after the Battle of Tewkesbury (see *Richard Duke of York* 4.7.92–102).
　**from** away from
41 **And . . . curse** Q1 indents the line. Perhaps l. 42 should have been thus marked off, as a quotation.
42 **Nor . . . queen** Compare 1.3.206.
　**counted** acknowledged
45 **son** stepson

46 **To meet you** If Dorset is to bear the letters, Stanley must mean that they will enable Dorset to meet his son. The compressed expression may suggest Stanley's haste.
47 **ta'en tardy** caught by surprise
48 **ill-dispersing** scattering evils
49 **bed** i.e. birthplace
50 **cockatrice** basilisk (see note to 1.2.148). 'To hatch the cockatrice egg' was proverbial for bringing evil into the world (Dent C496.1).
51 **unavoided** unavoidable
54 **inclusive** enclosing (*OED*'s earliest example of the sense)

Were red-hot steel to sear me to the brain.
Anointed let me be with deadly poison,
And die ere men can say 'God save the Queen'.

QUEEN

Alas, poor soul, I envy not thy glory.
To feed my humour, wish thyself no harm.                    60

ANNE DUCHESS OF GLOUCESTER

No? When he that is my husband now
Came to me as I followed Henry's corpse,
When scarce the blood was well washed from his hands
Which issued from my other angel-husband
And that dead saint which then I, weeping, followed,         65
O when, I say, I looked on Richard's face,
This was my wish: 'Be thou,' quoth I, 'accursed
For making me, so young, so old a widow;
And when thou wedd'st let sorrow haunt thy bed,
And be thy wife—if any be so mad—                           70
As miserable by the life of thee
As thou hast made me by my dear lord's death.'
Lo, ere I can repeat this curse again,
Even in so short a space, my woman's heart
Grossly grew captive to his honey words,                    75
And proved the subject of my own soul's curse,

Q:
60 thyself] rhy selfe    62 corpse] course    66 Richárd's] Richatds    71 life] F; death QI
73 ere] eare

F:
56 brain] Braines    57 poison] Venome    59 Alas] Goe, goe    61 No] No: why    65 dead]
deare    71–2 As . . . As] More . . . Then    74 Even in so short a space] Within so small a time
76 my] mine

57 **Anointed** Playing between ceremonial oil and medicinal (but here poisonous) ointment.
60 **humour** disposition. 'To feed a humour' was proverbial (Dent H806.1).
62 **corpse** QI's spelling 'course' admits play on the sense 'way of life'.
64 **my other angel-husband** Implies her present husband Richard is a devil. The construction is poised between (a) my other husband, an angel, (b) my entirely different angel-husband (*OED*, *other*, *adj.* 7), (c) my other-angel (good angel, as opposed to bad angel) husband.
68 **so old a widow** i.e. so experienced in widowhood
70–2 **be . . . death** Compare her words at 1.2.24–6.
70 **so mad** See Appendix D, Note 13.
71 **life** The equivalent at 1.2.25 is 'death', as in QI here. Anne's lack of accurate foreknowledge makes 'death' acceptable in the earlier speech, but here it is conspicuously irrelevant.
75 **Grossly** (a) stupidly, (b) excessively, (c) lecherously

Which ever since hath kept my eyes from sleep;
For never yet one hour in his bed
Have I enjoyed the golden dew of sleep,
But have been wakèd by his timorous dreams.                    80
Besides, he hates me for my father Warwick,
And will, no doubt, shortly be rid of me.

QUEEN

Alas, poor soul, I pity thy complaints.

ANNE DUCHESS OF GLOUCESTER

No more than from my soul I mourn for yours.

DORSET

Farewell, thou woeful welcomer of glory.                      85

ANNE DUCHESS OF GLOUCESTER

Adieu, poor soul, thou tak'st thy leave of it.

DUCHESS OF YORK (*to Dorset*)

Go thou to Richmond, and good fortune guide thee;
⌐*Exit Dorset*⌐

(*To Anne*) Go thou to Richard, and good angels guard
thee;                      ⌐*Exeunt Anne and Stanley*⌐

(*To the Queen*) Go thou to sanctuary, good thoughts
possess thee;                      ⌐*Exit Queen*⌐

I to my grave, where peace and rest lie with me.              90

Q:

85 DORSET] Q1 (*Dor.*), F (*Dors.*); Qu. Q2    87–92.1 *Exit . . . Exit*] staggered exits OXFORD;  *not in*
Q1;  '*Exeunt.*' *after l.* 92 *and* 6 *extra lines* F

F:

77 ever since hath kept my . . . sleep] hitherto hath held mine . . . rest    79 Have I enjoyed]
Did I enioy    80 have . . . dreams] with his timorous Dreames was still awak'd    83 Alas, poor
soul . . . complaints] Poore heart adieu . . . complaining    84 from] with    86 thou] that
88 guard] tend    89 good] and good

79 **golden dew of sleep** Alluding to 'honey-
dew', a sweet and sticky substance on
leaves thought to form at night in the
same way as dew itself; also to the
proverb 'Morning sleep is golden' (Dent
S525.1). Compare 'the honey-heavy dew
of slumber', *Caesar* 2.1.229.

80 **his timorous dreams** More refers to
Richard's 'fearful dreams' after the murder of the Princes (Holinshed, p. 403).

81 **Warwick** whose desertion to the Lancastrian cause (see *Richard Duke of York*
3.3.167–233) led to Clarence following
suit (*Richard Duke of York* 4.1.116–21
and 4.2)

83 **complaints** laments

85 **DORSET** Q2's attribution to the Queen is
an improvement, as this and the following line make an effective exchange
between the erstwhile queen and the
queen-to-be. The reading could conceivably be authoritative, as Q2 authorita-
tively corrects Q1 at 1.1.102. Moreover,
the apparent manuscript linkage from
the manuscript behind F to the copy for
Q1 (see Introduction, 'Quarto and Folio
Compared') creates the theoretical possibility of Q1 and F sharing an error where
the printed copy for F has a correct reading. As error, the prefix for Dorset could
originate in confusion between, for instance, 'Qu' and 'Do', perhaps on the

Eighty odd years of sorrow have I seen,
And each hour's joy racked with a week of teen.

*Exit*

[**4.2**]    [*A throne is set forth.*] *The trumpets sound. Enter*
           *Richard, crowned, Buckingham, Catesby, with other*
           *nobles, and a Boy*

KING RICHARD

Stand all apart. ⌐Cousin of Buckingham,
Give me thy hand.

*Trumpets sound. Here he ascendeth the throne*
                    Thus high by thy advice
And thy assistance is King Richard seated;

Q:

92 racked] wrackt

**4.2.0.1** *A throne is set forth*] CIBBER (*subs.*); *not in* Q1, F    0.3 *and a Boy*] CAPELL (*Page*); *not in*
Q1, F    1 KING RICHARD] *King* Q1; *Rich.* F. *Similarly in his speech-prefixes throughout the rest of* Q1,
*and in* F *except at* 5.4.51 *and from* 5.4.187 *to* 5.5.76, *where* F *reads* '*King.*'    2 *Trumpets sound*]
F (*Sound.*); *not in* Q1

F:

92 teen.] F *adds a speech of* 7 *lines by the Queen. See Appendix A, Passage K.*

**4.2.0.1–3** *The . . . nobles*] *Sound a Sennet. Enter Richard in pompe, Buc-|kingham, Catesby,*
*Ratcliffe, Louel.*    1 KING RICHARD] *See* Q *collation*    Buckingham,] Buckingham. | *Buck. My*
*gracious Soueraigne.* | *Rich.*    2 *Here . . . throne*] *not in* F

part of someone regularizing the prefixes.
But attribution of the speech to Dorset
makes valid sense and, despite reserva-
tions, the Q1–F agreement has here been
respected.

92 **racked** tortured (and stretched out) as on
the rack. Q1's 'wrackt' is alternatively
modernized 'wrecked'.
    **of teen** of grief. Editors sometimes record
Q1 as reading 'ofteene'. But there is a
thin space between 'f' and 't', such as
was not usually set between the letters.
    **teen.** F gives the Queen a further speech
of seven lines in which she implores the
Tower to pity her 'babes'.

**4.2** Shakespeare reshapes events to seed
Richard's downfall in the moment his
reign begins. The interview with Buckingham is invented by Shakespeare; More's
Richard is directed to Tyrrell by his page at
a later date; Dorset's desertion to Richmond is also later. As sacraments, cor-
onations were not allowed to be shown on
stage, and the scene evidently begins immediately after the ceremony. The location at Court would be signalled when the

throne was put on stage (conventionally
positioned in the Elizabethan theatre in
front of the middle of the wall at the rear of
the stage). Though in More's account
Anne accompanies Richard in the coronation ceremonies, she is here conspicuously absent. Various productions have
brought her on stage, 'a wan and
sleepless spectre' in Olivier's: Audrey
Williamson, *Old Vic Drama* (1948), p. 175.

0.3 *a Boy* He is, as F and Holinshed specify,
a page. He might enter first to set out the
throne and/or bear Richard's train.
Probably the actor would also play one of
the two young princes, as three boy
actors playing the women's roles have
just left the stage. Such a doubling might
lend dramatic irony to ll. 30–40, in
which the Boy is instrumental in setting
up the murder of the Princes.

  1 **KING RICHARD** The usual speech-prefix in
Q1 becomes '*King.*'; F continues '*Rich.*'
(though sometimes '*King.*' in Act 5 to
avoid confusion with Richmond).
    **apart** i.e. away from Richard

1–3 **Cousin . . . seated** This seems to be a
public acknowledgement of Buckingham,

\ [*Aside to him*] But shall we wear these honours for a day?
Or shall they last, and we rejoice in them?                    5
BUCKINGHAM [*aside to him*]
Still live they, and for ever may they last.
       [*They continue to talk aside*]
KING RICHARD
O Buckingham, now do I play the touch,
To try if thou be current gold indeed.
Young Edward lives. Think now what I would say.
BUCKINGHAM  Say on, my gracious sovereign.                     10
KING RICHARD
Why, Buckingham, I say I would be king.
BUCKINGHAM
Why, so you are, my thrice-renownèd liege.
KING RICHARD
Ha, am I king? 'Tis so, but Edward lives.
BUCKINGHAM
True, noble prince.                    *That's what R. Thinks B is saying?*
KING RICHARD            O bitter consequence:
That Edward still should live 'true noble prince'.             15
Cousin, thou wert not wont to be so dull.
Shall I be plain? I wish the bastards dead,
And I would have it suddenly performed.
What sayst thou? Speak suddenly, be brief.

Q:
6.1 *They . . . aside*] This edition;  *not in* Q1, F

F:
4 honours] Glories   6 may they] let them    7 O] Ah    9 say] speake    10 gracious sovereign]
louing Lord    12 liege] Lord    16 wert] wast    19 thou] thou now

> though (a) 'Thus . . . seated' might
> be spoken aside to him, (b) in some
> productions Richard needs physical sup-
> port to ascend the throne, or he stumbles
> on his way to it.
>
> 4 **But** Doubles as conjunction and displaced
>   adverb ('. . . but for a day').
> 5 **rejoice in** Though *OED* lends no support,
>   the prefix 're-' might here suggest some-
>   thing repeated: 'continue to enjoy'.
> 6 **Still live they** Refers to Richard's *honours*,
>   but anticipates the threat picked up in
>   l. 9, 'Young Edward lives'.
> 7 **play the touch** act the touchstone.
>   Capell's emendation 'ply' (suggested by

> Warburton) might be considered were it
> not characteristic of Richard to *play* roles,
> especially the testing role of tempter.
> 14 **consequence** sequel
> 15 **'true noble prince'** Richard turns 'true
>   noble prince' into a *consequence* to 'but
>   Edward lives', making it clear there is one
>   true noble prince too many. The line
>   might alternatively be punctuated '. . .
>   live. "True, noble prince"!', quoting
>   Buckingham without alteration of the
>   phrasing, and with the *consequence* refer-
>   ring to 'but Edward lives'.
> 16 **dull** obtuse
> 19 **suddenly** Taylor follows Wilson's conjec-
>   ture 'immediately', which assumes (a) a

BUCKINGHAM  Your grace may do your pleasure. *He wants R. to implicate himself*  20

KING RICHARD

Tut, tut, thou art all ice, thy kindness freezeth.

Say, have I thy consent that they shall die?

BUCKINGHAM

Give me some breath, some little pause, my lord,

Before I positively speak herein.

I will resolve your grace immediately.            *Exit*   25

CATESBY

The King is angry. See, he bites the lip.

KING RICHARD

I will converse with iron-witted fools

And unrespective boys. None are for me

That look into me with considerate eyes.—

Boy!—                                             30

High-reaching Buckingham grows circumspect.

BOY  My lord.

KING RICHARD

Know'st thou not any whom corrupting gold

Would tempt unto a close exploit of death?

BOY

My lord, I know a discontented gentleman             35

Whose humble means match not his haughty mind.

---

F:
21 freezeth] freezes   23 breath . . . my] litle breath, some pawse, deare   24 herein] in this
25 your grace immediately] you herein presently   *Exit] Exit Buck. (restoring direction omitted
from* Q2)   26 bites the] gnawes his   30–1 Boy!— | High-reaching . . . circumspect.] Q1 (Boy,
high reaching . . . circumspect.); High-reaching . . . circumspect. | Boy. F   32, 35, 39 BOY]
*Page.*   34 Would] Will   35 My lord, I] I   36 mind] spirit

double memorial error in Q1 (also 'immedi-atelie' for F 'presently' at l. 25, on the basis that the word lost at l. 19 reappears at l. 25), and (b) uncorrected error in F. But the repetition of *suddenly* and 'be brief' correlates words and deeds as in the proverb 'Few words and many deeds' (Dent W797). Compare Shakespeare's correlation of words and deeds elsewhere ('Ill deeds is doubled with an evil word', *Errors* 3.2.20; 'his few bad words are matched with as few good deeds', *Henry V* 3.2.39–40).

23 **breath** breathing-space
26 **he bites the lip** 'When he stood musing, he would bite and chew busily his nether

lip' (Holinshed, p. 447). In Cooke's Richard it was a nervous mannerism in several scenes (Colley, p. 58). Othello behaves similarly shortly before killing Desdemona ('why gnaw you so your nether lip?', *Othello* 5.2.46).
27 **iron-witted** dull-witted
28 **unrespective** inattentive, disrespectful
29 **considerate** thoughtful, deliberative
30 **Boy** F instead places this call after l. 31. Q1 links 'Boy' more closely with the comment on 'unrespective boys'; Richard interrupts his meditation then resumes it.
33–40 For More's account, see Appendix E.
34 **close** secret
   **exploit** (stressed on the second syllable)

287

Gold were as good as twenty orators,
And will no doubt tempt him to anything.

KING RICHARD

What is his name?

BOY                        His name, my lord, is Tyrrell.

KING RICHARD

Go call him hither presently.                    *Exit Boy*        40
(*Aside*) The deep-revolving witty Buckingham
No more shall be the neighbour to my counsel.
Hath he so long held out with me untired,
And stops he now for breath?

    *Enter Lord Stanley Earl of Derby*

                How now, what news with you?

STANLEY EARL OF DERBY

My lord, I hear the Marquis Dorset is fled              45
To Richmond, in those parts beyond the seas
Where he abides.

KING RICHARD  Catesby.

CATESBY  My lord.

KING RICHARD (*aside to him*)  Rumour it abroad            50
That Anne my wife is sick and like to die;

---

Q:

40 *Exit Boy*] F (*Exit.*); *not in* Q1    44 *Lord Stanley Earl of Derby*] *Darby*    45 STANLEY EARL OF
DERBY] *Darby*.

F:

40 Go . . . hither presently.] I partly know the man: goe . . . hither, | Boy.    42 counsel] coun-
sailes    44 breath?] breath? Well, be it so.    *Lord Stanley Earl of Derby*] *Stanley*    what news
with you] Lord *Stanley*, what's the newes    45 STANLEY EARL OF DERBY] *Stanley*.    My lord, I
hear . . . is] Know my louing Lord, . . . As I heare, is    46 those parts beyond the seas] the parts
48–50 Catesby . . . Rumour] Come hither *Catesby*, rumor    51 sick and like to die] very
grieuous sicke

37 **Gold . . . orators** Perhaps proverbial (Dent
G285a, queried).
41 **deep-revolving** deeply meditating
**witty** cunning, crafty
43 **held out** kept up
45–7 **the . . . abides** This is the first mention
of Richmond in Richard's presence. He
appears not to respond, but he has heard
(see l. 86), and 'his self-protective plans
(ll. 50–65) betray the first traces of panic'
(Honigmann).
50–1 **Rumour . . . die** 'He procured a common rumour (but he would not have the
author known) to be published and

spread abroad among the common
people that the Queen [Anne] was dead
. . . either by inward thought and pen-
siveness of heart, or by infection of poison
(which is affirmed to be most likely)
within few days after, the Queen departed
out of this transitory life' (Holinshed,
pp. 430–1). To Shakespeare's contemporaries, Anne's suspicious death at the
time Richard was planning to marry Lady
Elizabeth might have resembled the
mysterious death of Leicester's wife
when he was courting Queen Elizabeth.
Leicester, like Richard, was often re-

288

I will take order for her keeping close.
Enquire me out some mean-born gentleman,
Whom I will marry straight to Clarence' daughter.
The boy is foolish, and I fear not him.                    55
Look how thou dream'st! I say again, give out
That Anne my wife is sick and like to die.
About it, for it stands me much upon
To stop all hopes whose growth may damage me.

> *Exit Catesby*

(*Aside*) I must be married to my brother's daughter,    60
Or else my kingdom stands on brittle glass.
Murder her brothers, and then marry her.
Uncertain way of gain, but I am in
So far in blood that sin will pluck on sin.
Tear-falling pity dwells not in this eye.                  65

> *Enter Tyrrell*

Is thy name Tyrrell?

**TYRRELL**

James Tyrrell, and your most obedient subject.

**KING RICHARD**

Art thou indeed?

**TYRRELL**                    Prove me, my gracious sovereign.

> [*They talk aside*]

Q:
59.1 *Exit Catesby*] CAPELL; *not in* Q1, F    68.1 *They talk aside*] This edition; *not in* Q1, F

F:
53 mean-born] meane poore    57 wife] Queene    68 sovereign] Lord

garded as a Machiavellian, especially
from a Catholic perspective; see Peter
Milward, *Shakespeare's Religious Back-
ground* (1973), p. 187, quoting *Leicester's
Commonwealth*, attrib. Thomas Morgan
(Paris, 1584).

52 **take order** make arrangements
**her keeping close** keeping her shut away
55 **The boy** i.e. Clarence's son
**foolish** an idiot
56 **Look how thou dream'st** Even Catesby
seems shocked.
58 **it stands me much upon** it is very important for me; I must ensure (see Abbott 204)
59 **hopes** i.e. both the people who elicit hope
and the hope they elicit
61 **brittle glass** Proverbial: 'As brittle as

glass' (Dent G134) and 'Who climbeth,
standeth on glass' (Lyly, *Sappho and Phao*,
1.1.4, quoted in Dent under G136.1).
63–4 I . . . on sin A well-recognized Senecan
proverb: 'Every sin brings in another'
(Dent S467.1; compare Seneca, *Agamem-
non*, l. 115, 'Per scelera semper sceleribus
tutum est iter', misquoted by Kyd,
*Spanish Tragedy*, 3.13.6, who goes on to
translate 'evils unto ills conductors be').
Richard's version anticipates *Macbeth*
3.4.135–7, 'I am in blood | Stepped in so
far that, should I wade no more, | Re-
turning were as tedious as go o'er'. In
Richard's line, however, the wading
metaphor is less intrinsic; *in* (l. 63) can
be simply 'engaged, involved'. *In blood*
glances at kinship as well as bloodshed.

KING RICHARD

 Dar'st thou resolve to kill a friend of mine?

TYRRELL

 Ay, my lord, but I had rather kill two enemies.    70

KING RICHARD

 Why, there thou hast it: two deep enemies, ·

 Foes to my rest and my sweet sleep's disturbers,

 Are they that I would have thee deal upon.

 Tyrrell, I mean those bastards in the Tower.

TYRRELL

 Let me have open means to come to them,   75

 And soon I'll rid you from the fear of them.

KING RICHARD

 Thou sing'st sweet music. Come hither, Tyrrell.

  *[Tyrrell comes closer and kneels]*

 Go by that token. Rise, and lend thine ear.

  *He whispers in his ear*

 'Tis no more but so. Say it is done,

 And I will love thee, and prefer thee too.   80

TYRRELL  'Tis done, my gracious lord.

KING RICHARD

 Shall we hear from thee, Tyrrell, ere we sleep?

  *Enter Buckingham*

TYRRELL  Ye shall, my lord.      *Exit*

BUCKINGHAM

 My lord, I have considered in my mind

 The late demand that you did sound me in.   85

KING RICHARD

 Well, let that pass. Dorset is fled to Richmond.

Q:
72 disturbers] F; disturbs QI 77.1 *Tyrrell . . . kneels*] *Kneeling* COLLIER *conj. in* Cambridge *(at l.* 75); *not in* QI, F 79 it is] Q3, F; is it QI 83 *Exit*] F; *not in* QI

F:
70 Ay, my lord] Please you 71 there] then 77 Come] Hearke, come 78 that] this 78.1 *He . . . ear*] *Whispers.* 79 'Tis] There is 80 too] for it 81 'Tis . . . lord] I will dispatch it straight 82–3 KING . . . lord.] *not in* F 82.1 *Enter Buckingham*] F *prints after Tyrrell's exit, l.* 83. 85 demand] request 86 pass] rest

69–71 **friend . . . enemies** *Friend* equivocates between the usual modern sense and 'relative'.
73 **deal upon** set to work upon
78 **token** Perhaps a ring, or a written warrant.

79 **'Tis no more but so** that's all there is to it. A semi-proverbial phrase (Dent M1158.1).
80 **prefer** advance
82–3 KING . . . lord. Echoes 3.1.185–6. See Appendix D, Note 8.

BUCKINGHAM  I hear that news, my lord.

KING RICHARD

Stanley, he is your wife's son. Well, look to it.

BUCKINGHAM

My lord, I claim your gift, my due by promise,

For which your honour and your faith is pawned,          90

Th'earldom of Hereford and the movables

The which you promisèd I should possess.

KING RICHARD

Stanley, look to your wife. If she convey

Letters to Richmond, you shall answer it.

BUCKINGHAM

What says your highness to my just demand?               95

KING RICHARD

As I remember, Henry the Sixth

Did prophesy that Richmond should be king

When Richmond was a little peevish boy.

A king—perhaps, perhaps.

BUCKINGHAM                    My lord.

KING RICHARD

How chance the prophet could not at that time            100

Have told me, I being by, that I should kill him?

BUCKINGHAM

My lord, your promise for the earldom.

---

Q:
88 son] Q4, F (*setting from* Q3); sonnes Q1      91 Th'earldom] F; The Earledome Q1

F:
87 that] the      88 to] vnto      89 your] the      91 Hereford] Q1 (Herford); Hertford F
92 The . . . should] Which you haue promised I shall      95 demand] request      96 As I remember] I doe remember me      99 perhaps, perhaps] perhaps      99–118 BUCKINGHAM . . . today.]
*not in* F

---

94  **answer** be answerable for

96–8  **Henry . . . boy** See *Richard Duke of York*
4.7.67–76.

98  **peevish** silly

99–118  **BUCKINGHAM . . . today** Not in F. Most
probably Shakespeare's later addition to
the play. W. J. Griffin, 'An Omission in
the Folio Text of *Richard III*', *RES* 13
(1937), 329–32, suggests that it was omitted from F because by 1622–3 a later

Buckingham was extorting favours from
James I, but Q6 (1622) was not similarly
affected, and there are no obvious comparable cuts for political reasons made
during the printing of F as a whole.

101  **him** i.e. Henry VI, whom Richard killed
saying 'Die, prophet' in *Richard Duke of
York* 5.6.57. But Richard may be eliding
this incident with his unprophetic hope
that he will kill Richmond.

**KING RICHARD**

Richmond! When last I was at Exeter,
The Mayor in courtesy showed me the castle,
And called it 'Rougemount', at which name I started,         105
Because a bard of Ireland told me once
I should not live long after I saw Richmond.

**BUCKINGHAM**  My lord.

**KING RICHARD**  Ay? What's o'clock?

**BUCKINGHAM**

I am thus bold to put your grace in mind         110
Of what you promised me.

**KING RICHARD**  Well, but what's o'clock?

**BUCKINGHAM**  Upon the stroke of ten.

**KING RICHARD**  Well, let it strike.

**BUCKINGHAM**  Why 'let it strike'?         115

**KING RICHARD**

Because that like a jack thou keep'st the stroke
Betwixt thy begging and my meditation.
I am not in the giving vein today.

**BUCKINGHAM**

Why then, resolve me whether you will or no.

**KING RICHARD**

Tut, tut, thou troublest me. I am not in the vein.         120
                   *Exit [followed by all but Buckingham]*

**BUCKINGHAM**

Is it even so? Rewards he my true service
With such deep contempt? Made I him king for this?

Q:
120.1 *followed . . . Buckingham*] CAPELL; *not in* Q1, F    121 Rewards] Q2; rewardst Q1; repayes F

F:
119 Why . . . no] May it please you to resolue me in my suit    120 Tut, tut, thou] Thou
121 Is it even so] And is it thus    Rewards] repayes    121–2 true service . . . deep contempt]
deepe seruice . . . contempt

103–7 **When . . . Richmond** Shakespeare
would have depended on the revised second edition of Holinshed for this incident.
107 **Richmond** The pronunciation, though
surely distinguishable from 'Rougemont',
may have been closer than one would
now expect.
116–17 **Because . . . meditation** Perhaps
meaning that once the hour has been

struck Richard can return to his meditation.
116 **jack** mechanical human figure that
struck the hour on the clock-bell
**keep'st the stroke** i.e. repeatedly marks
the time by striking (Buckingham's behaviour being over-prompt and irritating)
122 **With . . . this** Makes a hexameter with
the metrically redundant last syllable of
the previous line.

292

O let me think on Hastings, and be gone
To Brecon while my fearful head is on.

*Exit [at another door]*

**[4.3]**    *Enter Sir James Tyrrell*

TYRRELL

The tyrannous and bloody deed is done,
The most arch-act of piteous massacre
That ever yet this land was guilty of.
Dighton and Forrest, whom I did suborn
To do this ruthless piece of butchery—     5
Although they were fleshed villains, bloody dogs—
Melting with tenderness and kind compassion,
Wept like two children in their deaths' sad stories.
'Lo, thus,' quoth Dighton, 'lay those tender babes.'
'Thus, thus,' quoth Forrest, 'girdling one another     10

Q:

124 Brecon] Brecnock    124.1 *at another door*] OXFORD; *not in* Q1, F
    4.3.0.1 *James*] OXFORD; *Francis* Q1; *not in* F    10 one] on

F:

    4.3.0.1 *Sir James*] *not in* F    1–2 deed . . . arch-act] Act . . . arch deed     4 whom] who
5 ruthless piece of] Q1; ruthfull peece of Q2; p eece of ruthfull F    6 Although] Albeit    7 Melting . . . kind] Melted . . . milde    8 two] to     stories] Story    9 Lo . . . those tender] O . . . the
gentle

124 **Brecon** Buckingham's stronghold in
    south Wales.
4.3.0.1–35 *Enter . . . soon.* For More's ac-
    count, in which the murderers show no
    remorse, see Appendix E. The scene's
    location is presumably still the Court,
    though Marshall, reflecting Irving's
    Gothic staging, instead sets the scene on
    '*The Ramparts of the Tower*', which hints
    that Tyrrell might have risen from below
    the stage. The staging suggested in the
    present edition implies continuity of place
    by conjecturally retaining the throne on
    stage (see note to 4.4.455.2). If in the
    Elizabethan theatre there were a door on
    each side of the throne, Buckingham
    would probably have left by one door and
    Tyrrell have entered at the other, in which
    case Tyrrell would probably enter at the
    door by which Richard has just left. If the
    throne is on stage, Tyrrell might sit on it.
0.1 *James* Q1's error '*Francis*' is just possible
    as a misreading.
2–3 **The . . . of** Tyrrell recognizes the deed
    as the prime example within national

history, not far removed from the standard types of Western culture such as
Herod's Slaughter of the Innocents
(Matthew 2: 16), as staged in the medieval pageant plays.
2 **arch** pre-eminent
5 **piece** Probably not 'bit' but 'master-
piece', anticipating other suggestions of
artifice in the account.
6 **fleshed** inured to bloodshed (as of a hound
that has been conditioned to hunting by
reward of a piece of flesh)
8 **in . . . stories** in relating the sad stories of
their deaths (merging the non-specific
'children' with the young princes)
9 **tender babes** Not how they appear when
on stage in 3.1. Shakespeare amplifies
the pathos in More (Holinshed, p. 400,
'those babes') and added to More in Hall
(*Richard III*, 4ᵛ), in a passage Holinshed
omits ('innocent babes' and the Queen's
lament for 'her sweet babes'). The word
allows correlation with the children aged
two and under killed by Herod. See also
note to 1.3.180.

Within their innocent, alabaster arms.
Their lips were four red roses on a stalk
Which in their summer beauty kissed each other.
A book of prayers on their pillow lay,
Which once,' quoth Forrest, 'almost changed my mind.        15
But O, the devil—' There the villain stopped,
Whilst Dighton thus told on: 'We smothered
The most replenishèd sweet work of nature
That from the prime creation e'er she framed.'
Thus both are gone with conscience and remorse.              20
They could not speak; and so I left them both,
To bring this tidings to the bloody King.
    *Enter King Richard*
And here he comes. All hail, my sovereign liege!

KING RICHARD
Kind Tyrrell, am I happy in thy news?

TYRRELL
If to have done the thing you give in charge                 25
Beget your happiness, be happy then;
For it is done, my lord.

KING RICHARD                    But didst thou see them dead?

TYRRELL
I did, my lord.

KING RICHARD        And buried, gentle Tyrrell?

TYRRELL
The chaplain of the Tower hath buried them,
But how or in what place I do not know.                       30

Q:
11 alabaster] alablaster     16 devil—' There] ~ ‸ their     19 e'er she] F; euer he Q1

F:
11 innocent, alabaster] Alablaster innocent     13 Which] And     15 once] one     17 Whilst]
When     20 Thus] Hence (*line not in* Q3)     22 bring] beare     22.1 *King Richard*] *Richard*
23 hail . . . liege] health . . . Lord     25 give] gaue (*from* Q3)     27 my lord] *not in* F     30 how
or in what place] where (to say the truth)

---

11 **alabaster** white gypsum used particularly for human figures in funerary
  monuments
12 **Their . . . stalk** Perhaps a reminiscence of
  twining stems with flowers in ornamen-
  tal carving, painting, or tapestry.
17, 18 **smotherèd, replenishèd** The syllabic
  '-ed's might add to the artifice of the
  passage.

18 **replenishèd** perfect, complete
  **work of nature** The crucial difference between this and a 'work of art' lies in its
  capacity to be 'smotherèd'.
19 **prime** first
20 **gone** overcome; virtually dead
22 **this tidings** Either *tidings* is treated as
  singular (compare *news*), or 'this' is a
  spelling of *these*.

KING RICHARD

Come to me, Tyrrell, soon at after-supper,
And thou shalt tell the process of their death.
Meantime but think how I may do thee good,
And be inheritor of thy desire.
Farewell till soon.                    *Exit Tyrrell*    35
The son of Clarence have I pent up close.
His daughter meanly have I matched in marriage.    *Another reprise.*
The sons of Edward sleep in Abraham's bosom,
And Anne my wife hath bid the world goodnight.
Now, for I know the Breton Richmond aims    *she is the prize* 40
At young Elizabeth my brother's daughter,    *she is the*
And by that knot looks proudly o'er the crown,

Q:
31 KING RICHARD] Q3 (*King.*), F (*Rich.*); *Tir.* Q1    Tyrrell] *Tirre!*    35 *Exit Tyrrell*] *after* l. 34
39 goodnight] godnight    40 Breton] Brittaine

F:
31 at] and    32 And] When    35 soon.] then.  | *Tir.* I humbly take my leaue.  | *Rich.*    *Exit*
*Tyrrell*] *not in* F    39 the] this    42 o'er] on

31 **soon at** towards
   **after-supper** Can refer to either the dessert
   of the main evening meal (as in *Dream*
   5.1.34, where there are 'three hours' between it and bedtime) or a snack before
   going to bed. As the former would be a
   more public occasion, Richard may plan
   to indulge himself with bedtime stories.
32 **process** account, story
35 **till soon** for a while. A standard farewell,
   but echoing l. 31.
36–50 **The . . . army** There is an early example here of a double time-scheme such
   as has often been noted in *Othello*. By the
   'short' time-scheme Richard (in Q1) appoints Tyrrell on his coronation day to kill
   the princes 'ere we sleep', and it must now
   be the evening of the same day. On the
   'long' scheme some weeks at least must be
   supposed to have elapsed for the events
   mentioned here to have happened. Indeed
   Shakespeare is reaching past the end of
   More's account, squeezing in events from
   Hall's continuation recorded under 'The
   Third Year' of Richard's reign.
36 **The . . . close** Richard was less anxious
   about him at 4.2.55.
37 **meanly** i.e. to a man of low birth

38 **sleep in Abraham's bosom** Probably
   proverbial (Dent A8); from Luke 16: 22,
   where the dead Lazarus in Abraham's
   bosom contrasts with the dead rich man
   in the torments of hell.
39 **hath . . . goodnight** An ominous
   euphemism. See note to 4.2.50–1.
40 **for** because
   **Breton** Modernized from 'Britaine',
   which, as usual in Shakespeare (except in
   *Cymbeline*), signifies an inhabitant of
   Brittany, where Richmond is exiled. But
   there is also perhaps a suggestion of
   *Briton* (i.e. a Celtic inhabitant of Britain),
   alluding to Richmond as a Welshman;
   compare 4.4.394 and note. Richmond is
   repeatedly associated with Celtic Brittany
   and Wales.
42 **knot** marriage-tie
   **looks . . . crown** Richmond's vantage
   would become higher than the crown
   itself; he would have a stronger claim
   than its present possessor. For 'o'er', F
   has 'on', suggesting that the marriage
   would, more modestly, bring Richmond
   closer to the crown, but Q1's reading is
   consistent with *proudly* and Richard's
   intermittent sense of vulnerability.

To her I go, a jolly thriving wooer—
    *Enter Catesby [in haste]*
CATESBY  My lord.
KING RICHARD
Good news or bad that thou com'st in so bluntly?                    45
CATESBY
Bad news, my lord. Ely is fled to Richmond,
And Buckingham, backed with the hardy Welshmen,
Is in the field, and still his power increaseth.
KING RICHARD
Ely with Richmond troubles me more near
Than Buckingham and his rash-levied army.                           50
Come, I have heard that fearful commenting
Is leaden servitor to dull delay.
Delay leads impotent and snail-paced beggary.
Then fiery expedition be my wing,
Jove's Mercury an herald for a king.                                55
Come, muster men. My counsel is my shield.
We must be brief when traitors brave the field.
                                    *Exeunt*

Q:
43.1 *in haste*] OXFORD (*subs.*);  *not in* Q1, F    55 an] OXFORD (*conj.* Theobald); and Q1, F

F:
43 I go] go I    43.1 *Catesby*] *Ratcliffe*    44, 46 CATESBY] Q1 (*Cat.*, *Cates.*); *Rat.* F    45 news
or bad] or bad newes    46 Ely] *Mourton*    50 army] Strength    51 heard] learn'd    56 Come]
Go

43 **jolly** fresh, spirited, gallant
43.1 **Enter Catesby** From here on Holinshed
    no longer reproduces More, whose ac-
    count ends with the murder of the
    Princes.
46–8 **Ely . . . increaseth** The details are from
    Holinshed p. 413 and pp. 416–17.
46 **Ely** Here and at 4.4.385 F reads the
    Bishop's name '*Mourton*'. Q1 makes it
    clear that this is the strawberry-growing
    cleric of 3.4.
49 **near** deeply
51–4 **I . . . wing** The proverbial backdrop is
    'Not words but deeds' (Dent W820).
51 **fearful commenting** timorous discussion.
    *Commenting, delay, beggary,* and *expedition*

are half-personified emblematizations.
52 **dull** inert, drowsy
53 **snail-paced** Proverbial (Dent S579).
54 **fiery** Appropriate to a high-mettled horse.
    Compare 'fiery Pegasus' in *1 Henry IV*
    4.1.110, alluding to the winged horse of
    classical myth. That passage describes
    another prince's preparation for battle,
    and also makes reference to Mercury.
56 **My counsel is my shield** keeping my
    thoughts to myself is my best defence (in
    contrast with ll. 50–2); my best advice is
    to use my shield (to fight); I will have
    weapons instead of counsellors. Earlier,
    Buckingham was Richard's *counsel*
    (2.2.120).

**[4.4]**    *Enter old Queen Margaret, alone*

MARGARET

So now prosperity begins to mellow
And drop into the rotten mouth of death.
Here in these confines slyly have I lurked
To watch the waning of mine adversaries.
A dire induction am I witness to,                              5
And will to France, hoping the consequence
Will prove as bitter, black and tragical.
Withdraw thee, wretched Margaret; who comes here?
        *Enter the Queen and the Duchess of York*

QUEEN

Ah, my young princes! Ah, my tender babes!
My unblown flowers, new-appearing sweets!                     10

Q:
    4.4.0.1 *old*] F; *not in* QI    *alone*] sola    1 MARGARET] F (*Mar.*); *Q.Mar.* QI. *Similarly
throughout scene.*

F:
    4.4.0.1 *alone*] *not in* F    4 adversaries] enemies    9 young] poore    10 unblown] vnblowed

4.4 Editors usually accept Capell's location 'Before the Palace', but on a stage without fixed locations the throne can remain in place (see note to l. 455.2). Most of the scene is without basis in the sources, but Holinshed more briefly has Richard persuade the Queen to encourage Lady Elizabeth to marry him instead of Richmond (p. 429). For other details see notes to ll. 348–9, 351–451, and 412–14. A possible influence on the opening speech is Thomas Sackville's Induction in *Mirror for Magistrates*, placed between the tragedies of Hastings and Buckingham, and set in the 'cruel season' of approaching winter. In it, the poet meets the female figure of Sorrow.

0.1 *alone* See note to 1.1.0.1. There is point to the reminder that, unlike most queens, Margaret has no retinue.

2 **rotten mouth** The hollow in which fallen fruit rots is like the mouth of death as a rotting cadaver (drawing on associations of both death as devourer and earth as burial place). The autumnal imagery contrasts with the summer of Richard's opening soliloquy in 1.1.

3 **these confines** i.e. this country (England, as distinct from France). As *confines* can indicate a bounded place more generally, it can also apply to the Court, a walled

garden, or, anticipating ll. 5–7, the theatre. Less directly applicable is the idea of a place either of imprisonment for people (such as the Tower) or confinement for spirits. Margaret is an intruder; others are imprisoned within a physical place or caught within an inevitable process.

4 **waning** Might recall the Queen's description of herself as 'governed by the wat'ry moon' (2.2.68).
**adversaries** Seems to draw on the literal etymological sense of those turned towards or against her, as is consistent with the theatrical imagery. Perhaps also suggests the image of a malign astrological influence (compare *1 Henry VI* 1.1.53–4, where the ghost of Henry V is invoked to 'Prosper this realm; keep it from civil broils; | Combat with adverse planets in the heavens').

5 **induction** See Introduction, p. 25 and pp. 60–1.

7 **black** 'The emblematic colour of tragedy on the Elizabethan stage' (Hammond).

8.1 *Enter . . . York* They are perhaps both in mourning black. Richard's failure to recognize his mother (l. 130) might suggest that she is at that point wearing a veil.

10 **unblown** unblossomed. Alice Walker (in Wilson) plausibly attributes F 'vnblowed' here and 'blow'd' in *Othello* 3.3.186 (QI

297

If yet your gentle souls fly in the air
And be not fixed in doom perpetual,
Hover about me with your airy wings
And hear your mother's lamentation.

MARGARET (*aside*)

Hover about her, say that right for right                    15
Hath dimmed your infant morn to agèd night.

QUEEN

Wilt thou, O God, fly from such gentle lambs,
And throw them in the entrails of the wolf?
When didst thou sleep when such a deed was done?

MARGARET (*aside*)

When holy Harry died, and my sweet son.                      20

DUCHESS OF YORK

Blind sight, dead life, poor mortal living ghost,
Woe's scene, world's shame, grave's due by life usurped,
Rest thy unrest on England's lawful earth

blowne) to the Folio compositor, as Shakespeare elsewhere used the form only in a context that suggests unidiomatic English (MacMorris in *Henry V* 3.3.35).

10 **sweets** (a) darlings, (b) fragrant flowers

12 **doom perpetual** the place appointed by God's judgement (heaven or hell)

15 **right for right** 'justice answering to the claims of justice' (Johnson, complaining that 'This is one of these conceits which our author may be suspected of loving better than propriety')

16 **morn** Echoes as *mourn*?
**agèd night** (approximately 'living death')
**night.** F prints (a) the Duchess's speech that in Q1 appears at ll. 29–31, (b) a rhyming response to it from Margaret.

17–18 **Wilt . . . wolf** God is postulated as like (or worse than) the 'hireling' that 'seeth the wolf coming, and he leaveth the sheep and fleeth' (John 10: 12).

19 **When didst thou sleep** Compare 1.3.288 and note.

21–4 **Blind . . . blood** For the rhetorical patterning, see following note. It is not clear whether the Duchess speaks these lines to herself or the Queen. The latter (perhaps

suggested by the pitying epithet 'poor' and the description of the figure as a spectacle in a 'scene') would be more consistent with the women sitting down together, as in this edition and as defended by Taylor. An aside would lead on more readily to the Duchess sitting alone after her speech, to be joined by the Queen after l. 28, as indicated in other editions since Capell.

22 **usurped,** See F's extra line. The line's absence in Q1 may be accidental, but l. 23 follows more strongly without interruption after 'grave's due by life usurped'. Moreover, Q1's omission probably relates to a transposition in l. 21, which opens in F with 'Dead life, blind sight'. In Q1, *scene* occupies the same position in the line as *sight*, which allows *sight* to be picked up, in the sense 'spectacle', in *Woe's scene* (which might acquire a suggestion of *Woes seen*).

23 **Rest thy unrest** Echoes Kyd, *Spanish Tragedy* 1.3.5–10, in a passage that anticipates this one in other ways too: 'Then rest we here awhile in our unrest, | And feed our sorrows with some inward sighs, | For deepest cares break never

Unlawfully made drunk with innocents' blood.
[*The Queen and the Duchess sit*] on the ground, like the witches in Macbeth

QUEEN

O that thou wouldst as well afford a grave                   25
As thou canst yield a melancholy seat;
Then would I hide my bones, not rest them here.
O who hath any cause to mourn but I?

DUCHESS OF YORK

So many miseries have crazed my voice
That my woe-wearied tongue is mute and dumb.         30
Edward Plantagenet, why art thou dead?

MARGARET (*coming forward*)

If ancient sorrow be most reverend,
Give mine the benefit of seniory,
And let my woes frown on the upper hand.
If sorrow can admit society,                                 35

Q:
24.1 *The . . . sit*] OXFORD; *not in* Q1, F. CAPELL *has the Duchess sit here and the Queen at l.* 28.
32 *coming forward*] WILSON (*subs.*); *not in* Q1, F     33 seniory] signorie

F:
24 innocents'] innocent     25 O . . . as well] Ah . . . assoone     28 O . . . I] Ah . . . wee     29–31
DUCHESS . . . dead?] F *prints after l.* 16.     30 mute and dumb] still and mute     34 woes] greefes

into tears. | But wherefore sit I in a regal throne? | This better fits a wretch's endless moan. | *Falls to the ground*. | Yet this is higher than my fortunes reach . . .'; also 3.13.27–9.

23 **England's lawful earth** Both 'the earth that is lawfully England's' and *lawful* as 'law-abiding, righteous'.

23–4 **earth | Unlawfully made drunk** Compare the earth/mouth image in ll. 1–2.

24.1–27 *The . . .* **here** To sit on the earth is to be emblematically abased (see note to 'Rest thy unrest', l. 23), to assume a stance appropriate to *melancholy*, and to place oneself close to the earth as grave.

25 **thou** 'either the Duchess or "England's lawful earth"' (Honigmann).

29 **crazed** broken, rendered infirm

32–109 **If . . . France** In the theatre the rhetorical formality has often deterred. The passage has been frequently cut entirely or shortened, though Wolfit re-

garded the scene as 'the core of the play' (Colley, p. 169). It is a crucial episode for those who find a ritualistic quality in the play approaching that of Greek or Senecan tragedy. W. Clemen, *Commentary on Shakespeare's 'Richard III'* (1957), p. 186, notes that the three lamenting women recall the lament of the three Marys in medieval mystery plays. They also counterbalance the three sons of York (see note to 1.1.2) who have caused so much of the misery.

32–4 **If . . . hand** Her sorrow is more or less personified as an elderly figure. That figure corresponds with Margaret herself, especially if she is physically *on the upper hand* as the only woman standing.

33 **seniory** seniority (*OED*'s only example of the word in this sense)

34 **on the upper hand** Varies the proverb 'To get the upper hand' (Dent H95).

35 **admit society** be sociable. The melancholic would typically seek solitude.

Tell over your woes again by viewing mine.
I had an Edward, till a Richard killed him.
I had a Harry, till a Richard killed him.
(*To the Queen*) Thou hadst an Edward, till a Richard killed
    him.
Thou hadst a Richard, till a Richard killed him.                    40
DUCHESS OF YORK [*rising*]
I had a Richard too, and thou didst kill him.
I had a Rutland too, thou holp'st to kill him.
MARGARET
Thou hadst a Clarence too, and Richard killed him.
From forth the kennel of thy womb hath crept
A hell-hound that doth hunt us all to death.                        45
That dog that had his teeth before his eyes,
To worry lambs and lap their gentle bloods,
That foul defacer of God's handiwork
Thy womb let loose, to chase us to our graves.
O upright, just, and true-disposing God,                            50
How do I thank thee that this charnel-cur

Q:
38 Harry] CAMBRIDGE, *varying* 'Henry' RANN (*conj.* Capell); Richard Q1; Husband F      Richard]
Ricard      40.1 *rising*] OXFORD; *not in* Q1, F      42 holp'st] Q3; hopst Q1, F      51 charnel-
cur] carnal curre

F:
36 Tell . . . mine.] *not in* F (*with unpunctuated* 'hand', *l.* 34, *and full stop after* 'Society', *l.* 35)
38 had a Harry] had a Richard Q1; had a Husband F      47 bloods] blood      48 handiwork]
handy worke: | That reignes in gauled eyes of weeping soules: | That excellent grand Tyrant of
the earth,

36 **Tell . . . mine** F omits, presumably by
accident, though the passage could be
repunctuated to make sense without it.
**Tell over** Both 'count up' and 'narrate'.
37–42 **I . . . him** The victims, in order, with
their relationship to the grieving woman,
are: Prince Edward killed at Tewkesbury
(son), Henry VI (husband), the young
princes Edward and Richard (sons), Richard
Duke of York (husband), Rutland (son).
38 **Harry** Q1's 'Richard' is an error (compare l. 40). The personal name is more
plausible than F's 'husband'.
41 *rising* If the Duchess rises here she challenges Margaret's claim to pre-eminence
in sorrow.
46 **had . . . eyes** i.e. could bite before he
could see properly, was born with teeth
(as Richard himself relates in *Richard*

*Duke of York* 5.6.74–7, using the same
analogy with a dog)
48 **defacer** defiler, destroyer. With reference
to the literal sense of marring the face
(perhaps recalling Protestant iconoclasm
against images of saints). Also suggests
the sense 'defamer', in that Richard is a
discredit to humanity.
**God's handiwork** Recalls Isaiah 64: 8,
'We are all the work of thine hands', and
similar biblical phrases.
**handiwork** Editors since Capell have transposed F's extra two lines, and Hammond
also relocates them to before l. 48. The
image of the hell-hound is disrupted no
matter how the lines are arranged. 'Gallèd
eyes' occurs also in *Hamlet* at 1.2.155.
51 **charnel-cur** Suggests that Richard both
fills the charnel-houses and feeds on their

Preys on the issue of his mother's body,
And makes her pew-fellow with others' moan.

DUCHESS OF YORK

O Harry's wife, triumph not in my woes.
God witness with me, I have wept for thine.                    55

MARGARET

Bear with me, I am hungry for revenge,
And now I cloy me with beholding it.
Thy Edward, he is dead, that stabbed my Edward;
Thy other Edward dead, to quite my Edward.
Young York, he is but boot, because both they          60
Match not the high perfection of my loss.
Thy Clarence he is dead, that killed my Edward;
And the beholders of this tragic play,
Th'adulterate Hastings, Rivers, Vaughan, Grey,
Untimely smothered in their dusky graves.              65
Richard yet lives, hell's black intelligencer,

Q:
52 Preys] Praies    54 wife] Q2, F; wifes QI    59 quite] quitte    64 Th'adulterate] F; The
adulterate QI

F:
58 stabbed] kill'd    59 Thy] The    61 Match] Matcht    62 killed] stab'd    63 tragic] franticke

carrion. Taylor notes, in discussing his
modernization of QI's 'carnal' to 'charnel', that 'A unique, strained, and figurative sense "carnivorous" thus seems
less likely than a confusion of the doublets
*carnal* and *charnel*'. 'Carnal cur' has, perhaps, the advantage of alliteration.

52 Preys QI's 'Praies' is no more than a
spelling variant, but there is nonetheless
a half-realized pun: the cur *preys* on his
mother's children, while his lamenting
mother *prays* for them in the church-pew.
53 pew-fellow i.e. fellow mourner
   moan lamentation
58–61 Thy Edward . . . loss Edward IV and
Edward V, the Duchess's son and grandson, together make up a requital for the
murder of Margaret's son Edward. The
other grandson, young York, is thrown
in to make up the shortfall: even two
Edwards fail to match Margaret's Edward.
The repetition of 'Edward' makes it hard
for the audience to keep the figures distinct, though Margaret doubtless does so.

Young York, not an Edward, is seen as
little better than a cheap offcut of meat.
Richard had a hand in all the deaths, and
the tally of Edwards anticipates by postponement the need for requital against
him. This matter is held over until
ll. 66–7, where Margaret describes
Richard's life as 'reserved'.
58 stabbed my Edward i.e. caused him to be
   stabbed
59 quite requite
60 boot something thrown into the bargain
61 high perfection supreme excellence, flaw-
   lessness (of the lost one); large amount
   needed to *perfect*, or make up, the tally
   (of the loss)
63 this tragic play For Margaret's metatheatrical sense of tragedy, compare 'dire
   induction', l. 5. For 'tragic', F has
   'franticke', which lacks theatrical connotation but is otherwise plausible. Just
   possibly, F should read 'antic'.
66 intelligencer Literally 'information-
   gatherer, spy', but here 'secret agent'
   more actively: almost 'assassin'.

Only reserved their factor to buy souls
And send them thither; but at hand, at hand,
Ensues his piteous and unpitied end.
Earth gapes, hell burns, fiends roar, saints pray,          70
To have him suddenly conveyed away.
Cancel his bond of life, dear God, I plead,
That I may live to say, 'The dog is dead'.

QUEEN

O, thou didst prophesy the time would come
That I should wish for thee to help me curse
That bottled spider, that foul bunch-backed toad.

MARGARET

I called thee then vain flourish of my fortune;
I called thee then poor shadow, painted queen,
The presentation of but what I was,
The flattering index of a direful pageant,          80

*[handwritten marginalia: The Yorkist Q comports w/ the Lancastrian margaret]*

Q:

68 hand, at hand] Q2, F;  hand at handes Q1       72 plead] OXFORD (*conj.* Daniel);  pray Q1, F

F:

71 away] from hence       73 to] and

67 **Only reserved** (a) kept alive for the sole purpose of being, (b) uniquely set apart to be

**factor** commercial agent

70–1 **Earth . . . away** This couplet, rhyming eight paired monosyllables with a regular pentameter (see following note), is unapologetically melodramatic. Hammond recognizes the lines as 'Faustian'. 'Hell burns, fiends roar' echoes passages such as 'Hell calls for right, and with a roaring voice | Says "Faustus come! Thine hour is come"' (Marlowe, *Faustus*, A, 5.1.49–50). Where Faustus' Good Angel tries to preserve him from hell, Margaret sees saints co-operating with fiends. The alignment of earth with hell, and saints with fiends, retraces Faustus' final loss of alternatives to damnation.

70–3 **pray . . . dead** F's line-ends are 'pray', 'from hence', 'pray', and 'dead', hence there are no rhyming couplets but the repeated 'pray' in ll. 70 and 72 rhymes with itself. Q1 also reads 'pray' at l. 72, giving a triplet followed by an unrhymed

line. Contextually 'pray' is an easy error for 'plead'. Daniel's emendation, accepted, for example, by Wilson and Taylor, comes more fully into its own with Q1's 'away' at l. 71. The half-rhyme 'hand'/'end' leads naturally into a pair of rhyming couplets.

72 **Cancel his bond of life** Suggests that Richard's crimes offend the terms on which life is contractually leased. Echoed in *Macbeth* 3.2.50–1, where Macbeth calls on night to 'Cancel and tear to pieces that great bond | Which keeps me pale'.

74–6 **O . . . toad** See 1.3.242 and 246–7.

77–86 **I . . . scene** Elaborates on a single re-called line (1.3.241).

78 **shadow** (a) portrait, likeness, (b) actor (introducing a cluster of theatrical images), (c) ghost (compare l. 21 if it applies to the Queen)

79 **presentation** semblance, representation **but what I** what I alone

80 **flattering** pleasing but deceptive **index of** prologue to. Compare *induction*, l. 5.

One heaved a-high to be hurled down below,
A mother only mocked with two sweet babes—
A dream of which thou wert a breath, a bubble—
A sign of dignity, a garish flag
To be the aim of every dangerous shot,                    85
A queen in jest, only to fill the scene.
Where is thy husband now? Where be thy brothers?
Where are thy children? Wherein dost thou joy?
Who sues to thee, and cries 'God save the Queen'?
Where be the bending peers that flattered thee?
Where be the throning troops that followed thee?          90
Decline all this, and see what now thou art:
For happy wife, a most distressèd widow,
For joyful mother, one that wails the name,
For queen, a very caitiff crowned with care,              95
For one being sued to, one that humbly sues,
For one commanding all, obeyed of none,
For one that scorned at me, now scorned of me.
Thus hath the course of justice wheeled about,

*[handwritten marginal note:]* These are more than curses; they are maledictions w/ incantations, w/ sacramental overtones; conjurations + conjuring up the devils like Dr. Faustus.

Q:
82 only,] ~,

F:
82 sweet] faire    83–5 A dream . . . shot] A dreame of what thou wast, a garish Flagge | To be
the ayme of euery dangerous Shot; | A signe of Dignity, a Breath, a Bubble;    88 are] be (*from*
Q3)    children] two Sonnes    89 to thee, and cries] and kneeles, and sayes    95–6 For queen
. . . sues,] F *prints these lines in the opposite order*.    97–8 For one commanding . . . scorned of
me.] F *prints these lines in the opposite order, adding between them* 'For she being feared of all, now
fearing one:'.    one . . . one] she . . . she    99 wheeled] Q1 (whe'eld); whirl'd F

82 **mocked with** taunted with; having a false
illusion of
83–5 **A dream . . . shot** See Folio collation.
F puzzlingly puts 'a garish flag' in apposition to 'A dream', and 'A sign of dignity'
in apposition to 'a breath, a bubble'.
83 **A dream . . . bubble** Presumably a paren-
thetic comment on the spectacle of
mother and children (not a comment on
the Queen herself in parallel with *A mother*
and *A sign*).
  **a breath** Proverbially, 'Life is but breath'
(Dent B641.1).
84 **sign** (a) mere semblance, (b) ensign,
banner
86 **in jest** for amusement; in masquerade
90 **bending** bowing, obsequious
91 **troops** retinue
92 **Decline** The literal sense is 'go through the

inflections of a word', perhaps in response
to set questions ('Where be . . .?'), and
hence 'go through formally from beginning to end'. Compare 'I'll decline the
whole question' in *Troilus* 2.3.51. The
exercise traces out the Queen's formalized *decline* in fortunes.
95–8 **For queen . . . of me** For F, see Appendix D, Note 14.
95 **caitiff** poor wretch
99 **course of justice** Margaret sees the *course*
or turn of the wheel more usually associated with Fortune as a *course* or process of
divine justice. But to *wheel about* might
suggest also a wheeling change of direction, and *course* in conjunction with
*prey* hints at an image of hunting or
'coursing'. For 'wheeled', F more giddily
has 'whirl'd'.

And left thee but a very prey to time,                                    100
Having no more but thought of what thou wert
To torture thee the more, being what thou art.
Thou didst usurp my place, and dost thou not
Usurp the just proportion of my sorrow?
Now thy proud neck bears half my burdened yoke,         105
From which, even here, I slip my weary neck,
And leave the burden of it all on thee.
Farewell, York's wife, and queen of sad mischance.
These English woes will make me smile in France.

QUEEN [*rising*]

O thou well-skilled in curses, stay a while,                    110
And teach me how to curse mine enemies.

MARGARET

Forbear to sleep the nights; and fast the days.
Compare dead happiness with living woe.
Think that thy babes were fairer than they were,
And he that slew them fouler than he is.                       115
Bett'ring thy loss makes the bad causer worse.
Revolving this will teach thee how to curse.

QUEEN

My words are dull. O quicken them with thine.

MARGARET

Thy woes will make them sharp and pierce like mine.

                                                              *Exit*

Q:
110 *rising*] OXFORD; *not in* Q1, F    119.1 *Exit*] *position as in* F (*Exit Margaret*); *after l.*120 Q1
(*Exit Mar.*)

F:
101 wert] wast (*altering* Q3 'art')    106 weary] wearied (*from* Q6)    neck] head    109 will]
shall    112 nights . . . days] night . . . day (*from* Q3)    114 fairer] sweeter

101–2 **Having . . . art** A commonplace of
    medieval thought. Compare Chaucer,
    *Troilus and Criseyde*, 3.1625: 'For of for-
    tunes sharpe adversitee | The worste
    kynde of infortune is this, | A man to
    han ben in prosperitee', | And it remem-
    bren, whan it passed is'.
104 **just proportion** rightful portion; exactly
    corresponding amount
105–7 **Now . . . thee** Combines the yoke as a
    biblical figure for any abstract burden
    with the proverb 'To slip one's neck, or
    head, out of the collar' (Dent N69). For

'weary neck', F has 'wearied head', but
    Q1's repetition of *neck* is consistent with
    its repetition of *usurp* and *burden(ed)*, and
    with the symmetry of the yoke image.
110 **rising** The Queen might alternatively
    rise, for example, for her speech at l. 74,
    but in Margaret's speech beginning l. 77
    she has remained a spectacle of
    abasement.
116 **Bett'ring** exaggerating
117 **Revolving** deliberating upon (with a
    suggestion of turning over in one's mind
    the turns in the wheel of fortune)

**DUCHESS OF YORK**

  Why should calamity be full of words?       120

**QUEEN**

  Windy attorneys to your client woes,

  Airy succeeders of intestate joys,

  Poor breathing orators of miseries—

  Let them have scope. Though what they do impart

  Help not at all, yet do they ease the heart.       125

**DUCHESS OF YORK**

  If so, then be not tongue-tied, go with me,

  And in the breath of bitter words let's smother

  My damnèd son which thy two sweet sons smothered.

    *Drum within*

  I hear his drum; be copious in exclaims.

    *Enter King Richard [in arms] and his train, [amongst*

    *them Catesby,] marching, with drums and trumpets*

**KING RICHARD**

  Who intercepts my expedition?       130

**DUCHESS OF YORK**

  A she that might have intercepted thee

*[handwritten marginal note: R. is conjured up live … metstroples … something … wicked this way comes]*

Q:
122 Airy] Q2, F; A erie Q1    128.1 *Drum within*] CAPELL; *not in* Q1, F    129.1 *in arms*] This edition; *not in* Q1, F    *and his train*] F; *not in* Q1    129.1–2 *amongst them Catesby*] HAMMOND (*subs.*); *not in* Q1, F

F:
121 your client] Q1, Q5; your clients Q4; their Clients F (Q6 *copy*)    122 intestate] intestine    124 do] will    125 not at all] nothing els    128 which] that    129 I hear his drum] The Trumpet sounds    129.1–2 *Enter . . . trumpets*] *Enter King Richard, and his Traine.*    130 my] me in my    131 A] O

121 **your client woes** 'Your' relates to 'woes'; 'client' is adjectival.

122 **succeeders** Taylor (following Wilson's conjecture) emends to 'recorders', as *succeeders* creates a difficult reading and fails to provide an equivalent to *attorneys* and *orators*. The general sense is clear enough: the *joys* have died intestate, and the only inheritance derived from them is insubstantial words that recall them. The lack of equivalence with *attorneys* and *orators* may be to the point: woes and miseries are actively promoted, joys merely remembered.
  **intestate** F reads 'intestine'. Wilson thinks the compositor was thinking about flatulence, but the word can mean 'inward'.

125 **yet . . . heart** Compare proverbial 'Grief is lessened when imparted to others' (Dent G447).

127–8 **smother . . . smothered** The person speaking and her reference to sons might suggest that these words themselves 'smother' the word *mother*.

129 **exclaims** outcries

129.1 **in arms** The Duchess's comment at l. 179 suggests full body armour. The others are probably more lightly armed.

130 **Who . . . expedition** See note to l. 8.1.
  **expedition** (a) haste, speed, (b) military enterprise

131 **A she** a woman (Abbott 224). Alternatively, 'Ah, she'; compare F's 'O she'.
  **might have** should have

By strangling thee in her accursèd womb
From all the slaughters, wretch, that thou hast done.
QUEEN (*to King Richard*)
Hid'st thou that forehead with a golden crown,
Where should be graven, if that right were right,                    135
The slaughter of the Prince that owed that crown
And the dire death of my two sons and brothers?
Tell me, thou villain slave, where are my children?
DUCHESS OF YORK (*to King Richard*)
Thou toad, thou toad, where is thy brother Clarence?
And little Ned Plantagenet, his son?                                 140
QUEEN (*to King Richard*)
Where is kind Hastings, Rivers, Vaughan, Grey?
KING RICHARD                            *The Q's brothers*
A flourish, trumpets! Strike alarum, drums!
Let not the heavens hear these tell-tale women
Rail on the Lord's anointed. Strike, I say!
      *The trumpets and drums sound*
Either be patient and entreat me fair                                145

Q:
144.1 *The trumpets and drums*] *The trumpets* Q1. *Compare F.*    *sound*] Q2; *not in* Q1

F:
135 *Where should be graven*] *Where't should be branded*    137 *two*] *poore*    141 *kind Hastings, Rivers, Vaughan, Grey?*] *the gentle* Riuers, Vaughan, Gray? | *Dut.* Where is kinde *Hastings?*    144.1 *The trumpets and drums sound*] *Flourish. Alarums.* (*altering* Q3 '*The trumpets sounds*')

133 **From** i.e. so as to prevent
134–7 **Hid'st . . . brothers** Compare the proverb 'Your faults are not written in your forehead' (Tilley F120, first recorded 1609, but compare *True Tragedy* ll. 1175–6, 'If thy faults were so written in thy forehead as mine is'). There is probably a glance at the Whore of Babylon: 'And in her forehead was a name written, "A mystery, that great Babylon, that mother of whoredoms and abominations of the earth"' (Revelation 17: 5), especially as she is described in the following verse as 'drunken with the blood of the saints'. That Richard's mother might be comparing *him* with the mother of whoredoms connects with the episode's insistence on gender positions.
135 **graven** There is a hint of a pun on *grave*. F reads 'branded'.

135 **if that right were right** i.e. if what is morally right were properly observed
136 **owed** owned
141 **kind Hastings** F instead makes it the Duchess of York who asks 'Where is kinde *Hastings*?' The Queen has no reason to speak well of Hastings. Q1 makes her baldly follow Margaret's advice that 'Bett'ring thy loss makes the bad causer worse' (l. 116).
142 **alarum** the call to arms
143–4 **Let . . . anointed** The suggestion that the heavens would be offended at treasonous gossip justifies drowning out the truth. 'The Lord's anointed' is a biblical phrase for a king (1 Samuel 16: 3, etc.), applied to English monarchs through the sacramental coronation ceremony of applying oil.
145 **entreat me fair** treat me nicely

Or with the clamorous report of war
Thus will I drown your exclamations.
DUCHESS OF YORK  Art thou my son?
KING RICHARD
Ay, I thank God, my father, and yourself.
DUCHESS OF YORK
Then patiently hear my impatience.                                    150
KING RICHARD
Madam, I have a touch of your condition,
Which cannot brook the accent of reproof.
DUCHESS OF YORK
I will be mild and gentle in my speech.
KING RICHARD
And brief, good mother, for I am in haste.
DUCHESS OF YORK
Art thou so hasty? I have stayed for thee,                           155
God knows, in anguish, pain and agony—
KING RICHARD
And came I not at last to comfort you?
DUCHESS OF YORK
No, by the holy rood, thou know'st it well,
Thou cam'st on earth to make the earth my hell.
A grievous burden was thy birth to me;                               160
Tetchy and wayward was thy infancy;
Thy schooldays frightful, desp'rate, wild, and furious;
Thy prime of manhood daring, bold and venturous;

Q:
150 hear] here    155 hasty?] ~ ∧    162 desp'rate] F; desperate Q1

F:
152 Which] That    reproof] reproofe. | *Dut*. O let me speake. | *Rich*. Do then, but Ile not
heare.    153 speech] words    156 anguish, pain, and] torment, and in

146 **report of war** The phrase suggests the sound of gunfire and explosions, but Richard is drawing on *report* as 'musical sound' (*OED sb*. 6a) and 'testimony'.
152 **brook** endure
  **accent** speech, idiom
  **reproof**. F's following exchange in itself is effective, but Q1 seems to have been edited down to avoid repetition; compare the variants at ll. 171–2.
155–9 **I . . . hell** Richard perhaps opens up the suggestion of childbirth latent in

'anguish, pain, and agony'. The Duchess certainly develops the idea.
155 **stayed** waited
158 **by the holy rood** An ironically appropriate oath: Christ's death on the *rood* brought salvation; Richard's birth makes earth a hell.
160 **grievous burden** (a) painful birth, (b) oppressive weight of sorrow
162 **frightful** causing terror
  **desp'rate** reckless

Thy age confirmed proud, subtle, bloody, treacherous.
What comfortable hour canst thou name                          165
That ever graced me in thy company?

KING RICHARD

Faith, none but Humphrey Hour, that called your grace
To breakfast once forth of my company.
If I be so disgracious in your sight,
Let me march on, and not offend your grace.                    170

DUCHESS OF YORK

O hear me speak, for I shall never see thee more.

KING RICHARD  Come, come, you are too bitter.

DUCHESS OF YORK

Either thou wilt die by God's just ordinance
Ere from this war thou turn a conqueror,
Or I with grief and extreme age shall perish,                  175
And never look upon thy face again.
Therefore take with thee my most heavy curse,
Which in the day of battle tire thee more

Q:
172 are] Q2; art Q1; speake F (*confirming formal* 'you')      174 Ere] Eeare

F:
164 bloody, treacherous.] slye, and bloody, | More milde, but yet more harmfull; Kinde in
hatred:      166 in] with      169 sight] eye      170 your grace.] you Madam. | Strike vp the
Drumme.      171 O . . . more.] I prythee heare me speake.      172 Come . . . bitter.] You speake
too bitterly. | *Dut.* Heare me a word: | For I shall neuer speake to thee againe. | *Rich.* So.
176 never look upon] neuer more behold      177 heavy] greeuous

164  **age confirmed** maturity
     **bloody, treacherous** F reads 'slye, and
     bloody', adding a perhaps confusing line,
     'More milde, but yet more harmfull;
     Kinde in hatred'.
165  **comfortable** cheering, cheerful
167  **Humphrey Hour** Q1's 'Humphrey
     houre' and F's '*Humphrey Hower*' have
     puzzled commentators. Some accept
     Steevens's suggestion of a reference to
     the expression 'to dine with Duke
     Humphrey' (first recorded 1592; Dent
     D637), meaning to go hungry, but the
     line recalls the phrase only vaguely and
     makes little sense with reference to it. F's
     spelling is unusual for Compositor B (only
     two other instances), and departs from
     printed copy. This may be a deliberate at-
     tempt to differentiate the reading from
     'hour(e)'. Taylor emends to 'Humphrey
     Hewer', suggesting a strong-limbed serv-

ingman, or perhaps a spelling variant of
'ewer', indicating a servant who brought
in the ewer of water for washing the
hands before meals: see G. Taylor,
'*Humphrey Hower*', *SQ* 33 (1982), 95–7.
167, 169  **your grace, disgracious** Sarcastic
     responses to the Duchess's *graced*.
169  **disgracious** See note to 3.7.107.
171–2  **O . . . bitter** See Folio collation for F's
     more expansive text. The reviser might
     have considered ll. 141–72 as in F too
     repetitious. The drums may nevertheless
     be struck up after l. 170.
173  **die . . . ordinance** Alludes to the biblical
     death penalty for murder: 'Whoso shed-
     deth man's blood, by man shall his blood
     be shed' (Genesis 9:6).
     **Either** Pronounced as one syllable.
175  **extreme** Stressed on the first syllable.
178  **tire thee** Subjunctive: 'may [it] tire
     thee'. *Tire* is 'exhaust', but possibly plays

Than all the complete armour that thou wear'st.
My prayers on the adverse party fight,                    180
And there the little souls of Edward's children
Whisper the spirits of thine enemies,
And promise them success and victory.
Bloody thou art, bloody will be thy end.
Shame serves thy life, and doth thy death attend.    *Exit*    185

QUEEN
Though far more cause, yet much less spirit to curse
Abides in me; I say 'Amen' to all.

KING RICHARD
Stay, madam, I must speak a word with you.

QUEEN
I have no more sons of the royal blood
For thee to murder. For my daughters, Richard,            190
They shall be praying nuns, not weeping queens,
And therefore level not to hit their lives.

KING RICHARD
You have a daughter called Elizabeth,
Virtuous and fair, royal and gracious.

QUEEN
And must she die for this? O let her live,                195
And I'll corrupt her manners, stain her beauty,
Slander myself as false to Edward's bed,
Throw over her the veil of infamy.

Q:
183 victory] victoric    189 more] moe    190 murder. For] ~ ‸ for

F:
187 all] her    188 speak] talke    190 murder] slaughter

on the sense 'attire' (compare *wear'st*, l. 179). Wilson's suggestion of a quibble on the sense 'prey' seems impossible without a preposition such as *upon*.

179 **complete** Stressed on the first syllable.
182 **Whisper** whispers to
185 **doth . . . attend** The present tense suggests shame is *waiting for* Richard's death rather than *serving* it, but as his death is seen as imminent both senses may be present.
186 **spirit** Pronounced as one syllable.

188–350 **KING . . . woman.** In Holinshed, the Queen promises Lady Elizabeth (her daughter by Edward IV) to Richmond before Richard persuades her to change her mind; in the play she seems to change her mind in the opposite direction (see 4.5).
191 **nuns** As, according to More, was Bridget, another of the Queen's daughters.
192 **level** aim (as with a gun)
196 **manners** Might mean 'politeness of behaviour', as in modern usage, or 'morals'.
198 **veil** Usually associated with modesty or mourning.

So she may live unscarred from bleeding slaughter,
I will confess she was not Edward's daughter.     200
KING RICHARD
Wrong not her birth; she is of royal blood.
QUEEN
To save her life I'll say she is not so.
KING RICHARD
Her life is only safest in her birth.
QUEEN
And only in that safety died her brothers.
KING RICHARD
Lo, at their births good stars were opposite.     205
QUEEN
No, to their lives bad friends were contrary.
KING RICHARD
All unavoided is the doom of destiny—
QUEEN
True, when avoided grace makes destiny.
My babes were destined to a fairer death,
If grace had blessed thee with a fairer life.
KING RICHARD Madam, so thrive I in     210
My dangerous attempt of hostile arms
As I intend more good to you and yours
Than ever you or yours were by me wronged.

*[Margin handwriting:]* Every time makes a prop'n his sins are recounted – & he confesses & & obsolves himself

F:
199 from] of     201 of royal blood] a Royall Princesse     203 only safest] safest onely
205 births] Birth     206 bad] ill     210 life.] F *adds a passage of* 14 *lines. See Appendix A, Passage
L.*     212 dangerous attempt of hostile arms] enterprize | And dangerous successe of
bloody warres. *See Appendix C.*     214 or] and (*from* Q6)     were by me wronged] by me were
harm'd

199 **So** if thereby
203 **only** Qualifies 'in her birth'.
205 **Lo** Suggests a gestural appeal to
the heavens. Pope emended to 'No',
which Alice Walker (in Wilson) thought
'improves the sense and verbal
patterning'.
    **opposite** astrologically adverse
206 **contrary** actively opposed, hostile
207 **All . . . destiny** Proverbial (Dent F83).
    **unavoided** unavoidable, inevitable

208 **avoided** Probably in the active sense
'ejected, expelled'.
209 **were** would have been
210 **life.** F has 14 extra lines, in which the
Queen accuses Richard of responsibility
for killing her sons.
211–14 **Madam . . . wronged** Compare
ll. 317–19, and see Appendix D, Note 15.
211 **thrive I** may I thrive
212 **attempt of** military enterprise against
213 **As** to the extent that

QUEEN

What good is covered with the face of heaven                215
To be discovered that can do me good?

KING RICHARD

Th'advancement of your children, mighty lady.

QUEEN

Up to some scaffold, there to lose their heads.

KING RICHARD

No, to the dignity and height of honour,
The high imperial tipe of this earth's glory.                220

QUEEN

Flatter my sorrows with report of it.
Tell me what state, what dignity, what honour
Canst thou demise to any child of mine?

KING RICHARD

Even all I have, yea, and myself and all,
Will I withal endow a child of thine,                       225
So in the Lethe of thy angry soul
Thou drown the sad remembrance of those wrongs
Which thou supposest I have done to thee.

Q:
215 the] rhe    217 Th'advancement] F;  The aduancement Q1    220 tipe] Q1 (tipe), F (Type)

F:
217 mighty] gentle    219 No, to . . . honour] Vnto . . . Fortune    221 sorrows] sorrow
224 yea] I

215 **What . . . heaven** Based on the proverb
'The face is (or is not) the index of the
mind' (Dent F1; compare 3.4.11–14).
Events have made heaven look malignant.
  **with** by
216 **discovered** uncovered
220 **tipe** utmost point. Q1's 'tipe' could be
modernized *tip* (literally 'point'), *tipe*
(literally 'cupola'), or *type* (as in F and
most editions; 'emblem, symbol'). *OED*
indicates that *tip* and *tipe* both meant
'apex' figuratively, with particular reference to power or dignity. The underlying
images of a point and a cupola might both
be present. This edition, by printing
'tipe', favours the latter, on the grounds
that (a) it allows a strong emblematic
contrast between a 'high imperial' edifice

and another high structure, the scaffold
of l. 218; (b) despite the synonymity of *tip*
and *tipe* in the figurative sense, *OED* does
not record 'tipe' as a spelling of *tip*;
(c) 'tipe' recognizes aurally that *type* also
has relevance.
221 **Flatter my sorrows** Might imply either
'encourage me into further sorrows'
or, with irony, 'cheer me up from my
sorrows'.
222 **state** dignity, rank, majesty
223 **demise** transmit. 'The legal term ironically suggests that his claims are illegal'
(Wilson).
225 **endow** The original sense 'give a dowry
to' seems relevant.
226 **So** provided that
  **Lethe** The river of forgetfulness in the
underworld of classical myth.

QUEEN

Be brief, lest that the process of thy kindness

Last longer telling than thy kindness' date.                    230

KING RICHARD

Then know that from my soul I love thy daughter.    *singular &
                                                     not named,*

QUEEN

My daughter's mother thinks it with her soul.

KING RICHARD  What do you think?

QUEEN

That thou dost love my daughter 'from' thy soul,

So from thy soul's love didst thou love her brothers;                    235

And from my heart's love I do thank thee for it.

KING RICHARD

Be not so hasty to confound my meaning.

I mean that with my soul I love thy daughter,

And do intend to make her queen of England.

QUEEN

Say then, who dost thou mean shall be her king?                    240

KING RICHARD

Even he that makes her queen; who should be else?

QUEEN  What, thou?

KING RICHARD

Ay, even I. What think you of it, madam?

QUEEN

How canst thou woo her?

KING RICHARD                    That would I learn of you,

As one that are best acquainted with her humour.                    245

QUEEN

And wilt thou learn of me?

KING RICHARD                    Madam, with all my heart.

Q:

230 date] F; doe Q1    239 do intend] F; meane Q1    243 Ay] I

F:

240 Say] Well    241 should be else] else should bee (*altering* Q2 'should else')    243 Ay . . .
madam] Euen so: How thinke you of it    244 would I] I would (*from* Q3)    245 that are] being
(*altering* Q3 'that were')

229 **process** story
230 **date** end, expiry
232 **with her soul** with all her heart
234 **thou . . . soul** i.e. it is far away 'from'
   your soul to love my daughter
239 **do intend** Q1's unmetrical 'meane'

seems to have been caught from the previous line.
240 **Say . . . king?** Could be taken to show
   that the Queen is one step ahead, having
   her own intentions.
245 **humour** temperament

QUEEN

Send to her, by the man that slew her brothers,
A pair of bleeding hearts; thereon engrave ⌐
'Edward' and 'York'. Then haply she will weep.
Therefore present to her, as sometimes Margaret          250
Did to thy father, steepèd in Rutland's blood,
A handkerchief, which, say to her, did drain          ✓ Lord Grey
The purple sap from her sweet brother's body,
And bid her dry her weeping eyes therewith.
If this inducement force her not to love,          255
Send her a story of thy noble acts.
Tell her thou mad'st away her uncle Clarence,
Her uncle Rivers, yea, and for her sake
Mad'st quick conveyance with her good aunt Anne.

KING RICHARD

Come, come, you mock me; this is not the way          260
To win your daughter.

QUEEN          There is no other way,

Q:
248 hearts;] ~ₐ     249 haply] happelie     251–3 steepèd . . . body] F; a handkercher steept
in Rutlands blóud Q1     252 handkerchief] handkercher

F:
249 she will] will she     250 sometimes] sometime (*from* Q3)     254 dry . . . therewith] wipe
. . . withall     255 force] moue     256 story . . . acts] Letter . . . deeds     258 yea] I     260 Come,
come, you] You (*altering* Q3 'Come, come, ye')     me; this is] me Madam, this

248 **engrave** Suggests that the hearts are
emblematic jewels (in Catholic iconography the bleeding heart was a symbol of
Christ's suffering to redeem humankind). Also puns grimly on the idea of
putting Edward and York 'in' their
'graves', as the Q1 spelling 'ingraue' emphasizes.
249 **haply** Perhaps with an ironic pun on
*happily*.
250–4 **Therefore . . . therewith** Recalls
*Richard Duke of York* 1.4.80–4; see
1.3.171–5 and note.
250 **sometimes** once
251–3 **steepèd . . . body** From F. Q1 carelessly has 'a handkercher steept in Rutlands bloud'. Historically, Rutland died
before Elizabeth was born; dramatically,
they have no connection.
253 **her sweet brother's body** As Capell com-
mented, 'Smother'd bodies, as were the
princes', emit no "purple sap"; therefore

body is meant of another "brother," Lord
Grey, who had a death to wet many
"handkerchiefs"' (*Notes*, ii. 188). But a
passing inconsistency is just as likely.
256 **story** historical narrative (apparently
both written in a book proposedly sent to
her, and told by Richard)
**noble acts** Implies a putative book-title:
'The Noble Acts of Richard . . .'
259 **conveyance** riddance by underhand
means. *OED* quotes the line under sense 3,
'Carrying away, removal, riddance', but
sense 4, 'Furtive or light-fingered carrying
off; stealing', and sense 11b, 'Cunning
management or contrivance; underhand
dealing, jugglery, sleight of hand' are also
relevant. There is a sexual undertow that
harks back to Richard's seduction of
Anne, *conveyance* suggesting 'seduction'
or 'arrangements for a sexual liaison', and
also a glance at the legal conveyance of
property; compare *demise*, l. 223.

313

Unless thou couldst put on some other shape
And not be Richard that hath done all this.

KING RICHARD

Infer fair England's peace by this alliance.

QUEEN

Which she shall purchase with still-lasting war.          265

KING RICHARD

Say that the King, which may command, entreats.

QUEEN

That at her hands which the King's King forbids.

KING RICHARD

Say she shall be a high and mighty queen.

QUEEN

To wail the title, as her mother doth.

KING RICHARD

Say I will love her everlastingly.          270

QUEEN

But how long shall that title 'ever' last?

KING RICHARD

Sweetly enforce unto her fair life's end.

QUEEN

But how long fairly shall her sweet life last?

KING RICHARD

So long as heaven and nature lengthens it.

QUEEN

So long as hell and Richard likes of it.          275

Q:
272 enforce] inforce     life's] lyues

F:
263 this.] F *adds a passage of 55 lines. See Appendix A, Passage M.*     266 Say that . . . which] Tell her . . . that     269 wail] vaile     272 enforce] Q1 (inforce); in force F     274–5 So . . . So] As . . . As

262 **shape** Glances both at Richard's physical deformity and the sense 'theatrical role' or 'costume'.

263 **this.** F prints 55 extra lines in which Richard presses the advantages to the Queen of her daughter marrying him and providing children as 'a comfort to your age'.

264 **Infer** adduce, allege (though *OED* glosses this instance 'bring about, cause')

267 **That . . . forbids** Referring to the prohib-

itions on incestuous marriage in the Table of Kindred and Affinity in *Common Prayer*.

269 **wail** Alternatively F's 'vaile', meaning 'lower'.

271 **title** appellation, claim

272 **enforce** urge forcibly. Q1's 'inforce' is altered in F to 'in force', which editors usually follow.

273 **last** Wilson, noting the repetition from l. 271, conjectures 'stretch'.

KING RICHARD

Say I her sovereign am her subject love.

QUEEN

But she your subject loathes such sovereignty.

KING RICHARD

Be eloquent in my behalf to her.

QUEEN

An honest tale speeds best being plainly told.

KING RICHARD

Then in plain terms tell her my loving tale.                    280

QUEEN

Plain and not honest is too harsh a style.

KING RICHARD

Madam, your reasons are too shallow and too quick.

QUEEN

O no, my reasons are too deep and dead:

Too deep and dead, poor infants, in their grave.

KING RICHARD

Harp not on that string, madam; that is past.                    285

QUEEN

Harp on it still shall I till heartstrings break.

KING RICHARD

Now by my George, my Garter, and my crown—

Q:
285 on] one

F:
276 love] low    280 in plain terms tell her] plainly to her, tell    282 Madam, your] Your
284 grave] graues    285–6 KING . . . break.] F *transposes these lines, to continue the Queen's
speech from l.* 283 *with* 'Harpe on . . .', *printing speech-prefix* 'Rich.' *before* 'Harpe not . . .' (*altering* Q2's *omission of l.* 285).

276 **subject love** subjected lover. 'Love . . . loathes' combines aural similarity with antithesis; F's 'low . . . lothes' depends entirely on aural interplay.
279 **An . . . told** Proverbial ('Truth's tale is simple', Dent T593).
282–3 **your . . . dead** Based on the proverb 'Shallow brooks murmur most, | Deep silent slide away' (Dent W123 and W130; here quoted from Sidney, *Arcadia* (1590), 1st Eclogues, 7, l. 11, Sidney supplying the only recorded examples of W130 before Shakespeare; compare also *Lucrece* 1329, 'Deep sounds make lesser noise than shallow fords'). The present ex-

change adds the quibble on *quick* (fast-flowing; alive) and *dead* (profoundly quiet and still; concerning dead people).
286 **heartstrings** tendons or nerves supposed to brace the heart (*OED* 1), hence the most intense feelings (*OED* 2). Wordplay on the strings of a *harp*.
287–316 **KING . . . o'erpast** Wilson compares the thwarted swearing in *Leir*, ll. 1625–33: '*Mes⟨senger⟩*. That to be true in sight of heaven I swear. | *Leir*. Swear not by heaven, for fear of punishment. | The heavens are guiltless of such heinous acts. | *Mes*. I swear by earth, the mother of us all. | *Leir*. Swear not by earth, for

315

QUEEN

Profaned, dishonoured, and the third usurped.

KING RICHARD

I swear—

QUEEN         By nothing, for this is no oath.

The George, profaned, hath lost his holy honour;                    290

The Garter, blemished, pawned his knightly virtue;

The crown, usurped, disgraced his kingly dignity.

If something thou wilt swear to be believed,

Swear then by something that thou hast not wronged.

KING RICHARD

Now by the world—

QUEEN              'Tis full of thy foul wrongs.                    295

KING RICHARD

My father's death—

QUEEN                    Thy life hath that dishonoured.

KING RICHARD

Then by myself—

QUEEN                    Thyself thyself misusest.

KING RICHARD

Why then, by God—

QUEEN                    God's wrong is most of all.

If thou hadst feared to break an oath by him,

Q:
289 swear] F; sweare by nothing Q1

F:
290–2 The . . . The . . . The] Thy . . . Thy . . . Thy    290 holy] Lordly    292 dignity] Glory
293 wilt] would'st    296 that] it    297 KING . . . misusest.] F *prints before l.* 295.    thyself mis-
usest] is selfe-mis-vs'd    298 God . . . God's] Heauen . . . Heanens    299 hadst feared . . . by]
didd'st feare . . . with

she abhors to bear | Such bastards as are
murderers of her sons. | *Mes.* Why then,
by hell and all the devils I swear. | *Leir.*
Swear not by hell, for that stands gaping
wide | To swallow thee an if thou do this
deed.'

287 **George** A jewelled ornament representing St George; part of the insignia of
the Order of the Garter, the highest order
of English knighthood.
**Garter** A decorative leg-band that was
badge of the Order of the Garter.

288 **Profaned** Appropriate to the George as
an image of a saint.

289 **I swear** Q1's addition 'by nothing'
is probably an error anticipating the
Queen's reply.

290, 291, 292 **his** its

291 **knightly** Taylor objects that *knightly* is
too humble for a king, and emends to
'lordly', F's reading instead of 'holy' in
the previous line. But *knightly* here
means 'chivalric', and applies exactly to
the kind of honour associated with the
Garter. There is, moreover, wordplay
between *pawned* and *knightly* alluding to
chess-pieces.

297 **Thyself thyself misusest** Compare
l. 319.

The unity the king thy brother made 300
Had not been broken, nor my brother slain.
If thou hadst feared to break an oath by him,
The imperial metal circling now thy brow
Had graced the tender temples of my child,
And both the princes had been breathing here, 305
Which now, two tender bedfellows for dust,
Thy broken faith hath made a prey for worms.

KING RICHARD

˙ By the time to come—

QUEEN                    That thou hast wronged in time o'erpast,
For I myself have many tears to wash
Hereafter-time for time past wronged by thee. 310
The children live whose parents thou hast slaughtered,
Ungoverned youth, to wail it in their age.
The parents live whose children thou hast butchered,
Old withered plants, to wail it with their age.
Swear not by time to come, for that thou hast 315
Misused, ere used, by time misused o'erpast.

Q:

300 thy brother] Q6b; my brother Q1; my husband F   306 bedfellows] F; plaie-fellowes Q1
310 past wronged by thee] F; by the past wrongd Q1   thee] the   316 ere] eare

F:

300 thy brother] Q6b; my brother Q1, Q6a; my husband F (*altering* Q6a or b);   301 Had not
been . . . brother slain] Thou had'st not . . . Brothers died   303 brow] head   307 a] the
307–8 worms. | KING RICHARD By the] Wormes. | What can'st thou sweare by now. |
*Rich.* The   308 wronged in] wronged [= -èd] in the   311 parents] Fathers   312 in their]
with their Q5, F; with her Q6 (Q6 *copy*)   314 withered] barren   316 time misused o'erpast]
times ill-vs'd repast

300  **thy brother** This edition follows the Q6
press correction rather than F. It supposes slighter error in Q1, and 'thy
brother . . . my brother' is echoed in 'thy
brow . . . my child' in ll. 303–4.
306–7  **two . . . worms** Echoes Job 21: 26:
'They shall sleep both in the dust, and the
worms shall cover them'.
306  **bedfellows for** Thus F. Q1's substitution
'plaie fellowes for' was probably influenced by 'praie for' in the next line.
307–8  **worms . . . o'erpast,** F has an
extra part-line.

308  **the time to come** An unwitting reminder
that Lady Elizabeth and the future will be
taken up by Richmond, not Richard.
310  **time past wronged by thee** Q1's 'time by
the past wrongd' might just be glossed
'time that you wronged in the past', but
the expression 'time past' seems required
in opposition to 'Hereafter-time'. Confusion between 'the' as a spelling of *thee*
and as article ('the past') may have contributed to the error.
314  **withered** (so past their time of flowering
and seeding)

KING RICHARD

As I intend to prosper and repent,

So thrive I in my dangerous attempt

Of hostile arms. Myself myself confound,

Heaven and fortune bar me happy hours,                    320

Day, yield me not thy light, nor, night, thy rest,

Be opposite all planets of good luck

To my proceedings, if with pure heart's love,

Immaculate devotion, holy thoughts,

I tender not thy beauteous princely daughter.            325

In her consists my happiness and thine.

Without her follows to this land and me,

To thee, herself, and many a Christian soul,

Sad desolation, ruin, and decay.

It cannot be avoided but by this,                        330

It will not be avoided but by this.

Therefore good mother—I must call you so—

Be the attorney of my love to her.

Plead what I will be, not what I have been;

Not by deserts, but what I will deserve.                 335

Urge the necessity and state of times,

And be not peevish-fond in great designs.

Q:
320 Heaven . . . hours,] F; *not in* Q1    331 by] Q2, F; *not in* Q1

F:
318 attempt] Affayres    323 proceedings . . . pure] proceeding . . . deere    327–8 this land and me, | To thee, herself] my selfe, and thee; | Her selfe, the Land    329 Sad] Death,    332 good] deare    335 by] my    337 peevish-fond] peeuish found

317–19 **As . . . arms** See ll. 211–14 and Appendix D, Note 15. The word *repent* is new (but Richard used it hypocritically at 1.3.307). *Prosper* and *repent* lack equivalence, as Richard intends the one but not the other.

319 **Myself myself confound** The distinction between subject and object is itself confounded by the use of *myself* as (a) emphatic for 'I', (b) reflexive. *Confound* is subjunctive, as probably also are *bar* (l. 320) and *Be* (l. 322), but the direct addresses in l. 321 indicate imperative *yield*.

320 **Heaven . . . hours,** From F; not in Q1. The omission seems accidental. Hammond emends 'Heauen' to 'God', urging expurgation of F as at l. 298, but the resulting line is less metrical.

324 **Immaculate** unblemished. The religious imagery may hint that the word can transfer to the object of devotion, picturing her as the Virgin Mary.

325 **tender** have tender feelings for

326 **consists** inheres, resides. In view of the religious language, there is probably a blasphemous echo of Colossians 1:17, 'in Him all things consist'.

329 **decay** destruction

332 **good mother** Or *good-mother*, 'mother-in-law'; but *mother* in itself can have the same meaning.

336 **times** the present day

337 **peevish-fond** stubbornly sentimental; wilful and silly
**great designs** i.e. affairs of state

QUEEN

Shall I be tempted of the devil thus?

KING RICHARD

Ay, if the devil tempt thee to do good.

QUEEN

Shall I forget myself to be myself? 340

KING RICHARD

Ay, if your self's remembrance wrong yourself.

QUEEN

But thou didst kill my children.

KING RICHARD

But in your daughter's womb I bury them,
Where in that nest of spicery they shall breed
Selves of themselves, to your recomforture. 345

QUEEN

Shall I go win my daughter to thy will?

KING RICHARD

And be a happy mother by the deed.

QUEEN

I go. Write to me very shortly.

Q:

343 I bury] Q3, F (*setting from* Q6); I buried Q1; Ile burie Q4     345 recomforture] F; recomfiture Q1

F:

339 thee] you     342 But] Yet     344 shall] will     348 shortly.] shortly, | And you shal vnderstand from me her mind.

338 **tempted of the devil** The phrase used to describe Christ's temptation in Matthew 4: 1 and Luke 4: 2. *Of* is 'by'.

340 **Shall . . . myself** Meaning, presumably, 'Shall I forget my soul and myself as wronged mother, to be myself as stateswoman?' Richard's seemingly most effective flattery is to offer the Queen a new role as Queen Mother.

341 **your self's remembrance** Presumably a compacted way of saying 'yourself's self-remembrance'. Or Q1's 'selfes' might be an error for 'selfe', but if so it is uncorrected in F.

343–5 **But . . . recomforture** A grotesque extension of the common womb/tomb conceit, complicated by an allusion to the burning and rebirth of the phoenix (as in *Metamorphoses*, 15.438–42). See Introduction, p. 65.

344 **spicery** A common collective for 'spices'.

345 **to your recomforture** to renew your emotional well-being. *OED* glosses *recomforture* as 'consolation, comfort', citing this line as the only example of the word, but there seems to be a stronger sense of returning her to what she was. In Holinshed's account of the Battle of Bosworth, Sir William Stanley 'recomforted' (strengthened, put new spirit in) the hard-pressed Richmond (p. 444). Q1's 'recomfiture' suggests a further train of thought leading from spices to comfiture; *recomfiture* as 'preservation', however, seems strained.

348–9 **I go . . . *Kissing her*** Modern productions have sometimes highlighted the erotic possibilities of the surrogate wooing. In Hall's production the Queen 'kisses Richard passionately. Richard breaks away' (prompt book); in the 1969 Warsaw production he was 'practically

KING RICHARD

Bear her my true love's kiss. [*Kissing her*] Farewell—

*Exit Queen*

Relenting fool, and shallow, changing woman.                    350

*Enter Ratcliffe*

RATCLIFFE

My gracious sovereign, on the western coast
Rideth a puissant navy. To the shore
Throng many doubtful, hollow-hearted friends,
Unarmed, and unresolved to beat them back.
'Tis thought that Richmond is their admiral.                     355
And there they hull, expecting but the aid
Of Buckingham to welcome them ashore.

KING RICHARD

Some light-foot friend, post to the Duke of Norfolk.
Ratcliffe, thyself—or Catesby, where is he?

Q:
349 *Kissing her*] JOHNSON (*subs.*);  *not in* Q1, F    349.1 *Queen*] F (*Q.*);  *not in* Q1

F:
349 Farewell] and so farewell    349.1 *Exit Queen*] *after* 'mind' (*see note to* l. 348)    350.1 *Enter Ratcliffe*] How now, what newes? | *Enter Ratcliffe*.    351 My gracious] Most mightie    352 the shore] our Shores

seducing her—all to her visible loathing'
(B. F. Dukore, quoted in Hassel, *Songs*,
p. 24). Holinshed says that the promise of
'promotions innumerable and benefits'
to her and Dorset caused her 'somewhat
to relent . . . insomuch that she faithfully
promised to submit and yield herself fully
and frankly to the King's will and pleasure. And so she, putting in oblivion the
murder of her innocent children' and
other harms, and, forgetting her oath to
the Countess of Richmond that Elizabeth should marry Richmond, 'blinded
by avaricious affection and seduced by
flattering words, delivered into King
Richard's hands her five daughters'
(p. 429). Shakespeare's play, though it
makes the Queen a strong disputant,
leaves her finally inscrutable. In Cibber's
version she explicitly bides her time:
'What shall I say? Still to affront his love
| I fear will but incense him to revenge, |
And to consent I should abhor myself.
| Yet I may seemingly comply . . .'.

348 **shortly**. See F's extra line. Q1 may be
deliberately even more enigmatic.

350 **shallow, changing woman** For *shallow*,

compare ll. 282–3. By the proverbial
male view, 'Women are as changeable as
the wind' (Tilley W698), from Virgil,
*Aeneid*, 4.569–70: 'Varium et mutabile
semper Femina'. Holinshed noted of the
Queen, 'Surely the inconstancy of this
woman were much to be marvelled at'
(p. 430), and marginal note, 'The inconstancy of Queen Elizabeth' (p. 429). But
the comment is more applicable in his account (see note to ll. 348–9), and the
Queen can be played in this scene (as by
Duchêne) as a desperate and emotionally
open figure who makes Richard's sneer
seem cheap and even untrue. As for
Richard's constancy, see l. 373.

351–451 **My . . . told** Shakespeare runs together two separate expeditions by Richmond: (a) the failed invasion that led to
Richmond's appearance off the county of
Dorset after his fleet had been dispersed
(in 1483), and (b) the later successful
landing in Wales (in 1485).

352 **puissant** powerful
353 **doubtful** unreliable; apprehensive
356 **hull** float with sails furled, drift
358–73 **Some . . . changed.** The early 17th-
century annotator of the Kodama copy of

CATESBY  Here, my lord.                                          360
KING RICHARD
    Fly to the Duke. (*To Ratcliffe*) Post thou to Salisbury.
    When thou com'st there—(*To Catesby*) Dull, unmindful
        villain,
    Why stand'st thou still, and goest not to the Duke?
CATESBY
    First, mighty sovereign, let me know your mind,
    What from your grace I shall deliver him.                    365
KING RICHARD
    O, true, good Catesby. Bid him levy straight
    The greatest strength and power he can make,
    And meet me presently at Salisbury.          *Exit Catesby*
RATCLIFFE
    What is it your highness' pleasure I shall do
    At Salisbury?                                                370
KING RICHARD
    Why, what wouldst thou do there before I go?   *He's rattled !*
RATCLIFFE
    Your highness told me I should post before.
KING RICHARD
    My mind is changed, sir, my mind is changed.            *l₁*
        *Enter Lord Stanley Earl of Derby*
    How now, what news with you?

Q:
365 him] Q3; them Q1; to him F   368 Exit Catesby] F ('Exit.', after Catesby's 'I goe.'); *not in*
Q1   373.1 Enter . . . Derby] *position as in* F; *after l.* 374 *in* Q1   Lord Stanley Earl of Derby]
*Darbie*

F:
360 my] my good   361 Fly] *Catesby*, flye   Duke.] Duke. | *Cat*. I will, my Lord, with all con-
uenient haste. | *Rich. Catesby* come hither,   Post thou] poste   362 there] thither
363 stand'st thou still] stay'st thou here   364 sovereign, let me know your mind] Liege, tell
me your Highnesse pleasure   365 him] Q3; them Q1; to him F   367 power] power that
368 presently] suddenly   Salisbury.] Salisbury. | *Cat*. I goe.   369 is . . . shall] may it
please you, shall I. *For* 'is it' Q5 *reads* 'is is', Q6 'is'.   373 sir, my mind is changed] *not in* F
373.1 Lord Stanley Earl of Derby] Lord Stanley   374 How now] Stanley

F noted 'Richard's confused mind upon the news of Richmond's landing with forces' (Yamada, p. 159).

361 **Duke.** In F, Richard's address to '*Catesby*' is an error for '*Ratcliffe*', as Rowe emended.
373 **My . . . changed.** F reads 'My minde is chang'd' without repetition, giving a regular pentameter with the following part-line. For the metre in Q1, compare l. 348, which is the same in F. The Quarto line would become metrically regular if emended 'changèd, sir', but the repetition is more effective with mono-syllabic 'changed' each time, and the irregularity is fitting in view of Richard's perplexity.

321

STANLEY EARL OF DERBY

   None good, my lord, to please you with the hearing,        375
   Nor none so bad but it may well be told.

KING RICHARD

   Hoyday, a riddle: neither good nor bad!
   Why dost thou run so many mile about
   When thou mayst tell thy tale a nearer way?
   Once more, what news?

STANLEY EARL OF DERBY        Richmond is on the seas.        380

KING RICHARD

   There let him sink, and be the seas on him,
   White-livered runagate! What doth he there?

STANLEY EARL OF DERBY

   I know not, mighty sovereign, but by guess.

KING RICHARD   Well, sir, as you guess, as you guess?

STANLEY EARL OF DERBY

   Stirred up by Dorset, Buckingham, and Ely,        385
   He makes for England, there to claim the crown.

KING RICHARD

   Is the chair empty? Is the sword unswayed?
   Is the king dead? The empire unpossessed?
   What heir of York is there alive but we?
   And who is England's king, but great York's heir?        390
   Then tell me, what doth he upon the sea?

STANLEY EARL OF DERBY

   Unless for that, my liege, I cannot guess.

Q:

375 STANLEY EARL OF DERBY] *Dar. Similarly in the rest of* 4.4.

F:

375 STANLEY EARL OF DERBY] *Sta. Similarly in the rest of* 4.4.    lord] Liege    it may well be told]
well may be reported    378 Why dost . . . mile] What need'st . . . miles    379 a nearer] the
neerest    384 Well, sir, as you guess, as you guess] Well, as you guesse    385 Ely] *Morton*
386 there] here    391 doth . . . sea] makes . . . Seas

377   **Hoyday** An exclamation of impatience.
382   **White-livered** Proverbial (Dent F180).
    **runagate** A form of *renegade*. It here alludes
    to the sense 'runaway' (arising by associa-
    tion with *run* and *agate*, 'on the way'), im-
    plying 'coward'. The phrase is levelled at
    Richmond, whose mobility as an invader
    ironically suggests it. But it might also
    glance vocatively at Stanley, who has sup-
    posedly 'run . . . about' verbally (l. 378). A
    parallel for *White-livered* offers confirmation:
    Macbeth calls a messenger bringing bad

news a 'lily-livered boy' (*Macbeth* 5.3.16).
The line thus also anticipates Richard's suspicions of Stanley as they emerge at l. 393.
387   **chair** throne
388   **The empire** command over the state
389   **What . . . we?** Other claimants include
    Lady Elizabeth and Clarence's children.
    Richard is probing Stanley's loyalty. The
    following line is another apparently
    rhetorical question that actually chal-
    lenges Stanley, for it ignores the claim of
    the house of Lancaster.

KING RICHARD

   Unless for that he comes to be your liege.

   You cannot guess wherefore the Welshman comes?

   Thou wilt revolt and fly to him, I fear.               395

STANLEY EARL OF DERBY

   No, mighty liege; therefore mistrust me not.

KING RICHARD

   Where is thy power, then, to beat him back?

   Where are thy tenants and thy followers?

   Are they not now upon the western shore,

   Safe-conducting the rebels from their ships?         400

STANLEY EARL OF DERBY

   No, my good lord, my friends are in the north.

KING RICHARD

   Cold friends to Richard. What do they in the north,

   When they should serve their sovereign in the west?

STANLEY EARL OF DERBY

   They have not been commanded, mighty sovereign.

   Please it your majesty to give me leave,           405

   I'll muster up my friends and meet your grace

   Where and what time your majesty shall please.

KING RICHARD

   Ay, ay, thou wouldst be gone, to join with Richmond.

   I will not trust you, sir.

STANLEY EARL OF DERBY      Most mighty sovereign,

   You have no cause to hold my friendship doubtful.    410

   I never was nor never will be false.

Q:
408 wouldst] Q2, F; wouldest Q1

F:
396 mighty liege] my good lord    398 are] be   402 Richard] me   404 sovereign] King
405 Please it] Pleaseth   408 Ay, ay] I   409 I will not trust you, sir] But Ile not trust thee

393 **for that** because. Richard characteristically plays back the idiom with altered meaning.

394 **the Welshman** Richard is contemptuous towards Richmond's stock, but the play's audience would have been aware that the Tudor monarchs made much of their Welsh ancestry.

396 **therefore** in respect of that

397 **power** army

398 **tenants** (under feudal obligation to give military service to their overlords)

401 **friends** military allies
**in the north** The Stanleys were the chief family in Lancashire and Cheshire.

402 **Cold** Because (a) physically distant, (b) unenthusiastic, (c) living in a chilly climate.

KING RICHARD

Well, go muster men. But hear you, leave behind
Your son George Stanley. Look your heart be firm,
Or else his head's assurance is but frail.

STANLEY EARL OF DERBY

So deal with him as I prove true to you.                    *Exit*      415

    *Enter a Messenger*

FIRST MESSENGER

My gracious sovereign, now in Devonshire,
As I by friends am well advisèd,
Sir Edward Courtenay and the haughty prelate
Bishop of Exeter, his brother there,
With many more confederates, are in arms.                             420

    *Enter another Messenger*

SECOND MESSENGER

My liege, in Kent the Guildfords are in arms,
And every hour more competitors
Flock to their aid, and still their power increaseth.

    *Enter another Messenger*

THIRD MESSENGER

My lord, the army of the Duke of Buckingham—

Q:
413 heart] F; faith Q1    415 *Exit*] Q3 (*Exit. Dar.*); *not in* Q1    416 FIRST] CAPELL; *not in* Q1, F.
*Similarly with the numbering of other Messengers in the rest of* 4.4.    418 Edward] F; William Q1
420 more] mo

F:
412 Well, go . . . But hear you] Goe then, and . . . but    415 *Exit*] *Exit Stanley. (altering* Q3 '*Exit.
Dar.*')    419 brother there] elder Brother    421 My liege, in Kent] In Kent, my Liege
423 their aid . . . increaseth] the Rebels, and their power growes strong    424 the Duke of]
great

412–14 **But . . . frail** 'Amongst the noblemen whom he most mistrusted, these
   were the principal: Thomas Lord Stanley,
   Sir William Stanley his brother, Gilbert
   Talbot, and six hundred other . . . For
   when the said Lord Stanley would have
   departed into his country to visit his family and to recreate and refresh his spirits,
   as he openly said—but the truth was to
   the intent to be in a perfect readiness to
   receive the Earl of Richmond at his first
   arrival in England—the King in no wise
   would suffer him to depart before he had
   left as an hostage in the court George
   Stanley Lord Strange, his first-begotten

   son and heir' (Holinshed, p. 431).
413 **heart** F is preferred to Q1's 'faith', a
   weak substitution.
414 **assurance** security
417 **advisèd** informed (stressed on the
   second and fourth syllables)
418 **Edward** Q1 has 'William'. F's reading is
   upheld by Hall and Holinshed, where the
   brothers (historically cousins) are named
   as supporters of Buckingham's uprising.
   It is just conceivable that Q1 was deliberately altered to preserve the overused
   'Edward' for the kings and princes.
422 **competitors** allies

KING RICHARD

Out on you, owls! Nothing but songs of death.　　　425

　　*He striketh him*

Take that, until thou bring me better news.

THIRD MESSENGER

Your grace mistakes; the news I bring is good.

My news is that by sudden flood and fall of water

The Duke of Buckingham's army is dispersed and

　　scattered,

And he himself fled, no man knows whither.　　　430

KING RICHARD

O, I cry you mercy, I did mistake.

Ratcliffe, reward him for the blow I gave him.

Hath any well-advisèd friend given out

Rewards for him that brings in Buckingham?

THIRD MESSENGER

Such proclamation hath been made, my liege.　　　435

　　*Enter another Messenger*

FOURTH MESSENGER

Sir Thomas Lovel and Lord Marquis Dorset,

'Tis said, my liege, are up in arms.

Yet this good comfort bring I to your grace:

The Breton navy is dispersed. Richmond in Dor'shire

Sent out a boat to ask them on the shore　　　440

If they were his assistants, yea or no,

Who answered him, they came from Buckingham

Q:
425.1 *He striketh him*] *position as in* F; *after l.* 424 *in* Q1　　430 whither] whether　　439 Breton] Brittaine

F:
425 you] ye (*also* Q6, *but copy probably* Q3)　　426 Take that, until thou bring me] There, take thou that, till thou bring　　427–8 Your . . . that] The newes I haue to tell your Maiestie, | Is, that　　428 flood . . . water] Floods . . . Waters　　429 The Duke of] *not in* F　　430 fled] wandred away alone　　431 O . . . mistake] I cry thee mercie　　432 Ratcliffe . . . gave him] There is my Purse, to cure that Blow of thine　　433–4 given out | Rewardes for] proclaym'd | Reward to 434 in Buckingham] the Traytor in　　435 liege] Lord　　437 are up] in Yorkeshire are 438 Yet . . . grace] But . . . Highnesse　　439 dispersed] dispers'd by Tempest　　Dor'shire] Dorsetshire　　440 to ask them on the shore] Vnto the shore, to aske those on the Banks

425 **owls . . . death** The belief that the owl's cry 'betokeneth some heavy news and is most execrable and accursed' and utters 'a heavy groan of doleful mourning' goes back to Pliny (and see Dent R33). Compare *Lucrece* 165, 'No noise but owls' and wolves' death-boding cries'.

427–31 **Your . . . mistake** See Appendix D, Note 16.

433 **given out** proclaimed

439 **Dor'shire** the county of Dorset

Upon his party. He, mistrusting them,
Hoised sail, and made away for Brittany.

KING RICHARD

March on, march on, since we are up in arms,                   445
If not to fight with foreign enemies,
Yet to beat down these rebels here at home.
    *Enter Catesby*

CATESBY

My liege, the Duke of Buckingham is taken.
That's the best news. That the Earl of Richmond
Is with a mighty power landed at Milford          450
Is colder tidings, yet they must be told.

KING RICHARD

Away towards Salisbury! While we reason here,
A royal battle might be won and lost.
Someone take order Buckingham be brought
To Salisbury. The rest march on with me.            455
       *[Trumpets and drums sound.] Exeunt.*
          *[The throne is removed]*

Q:
444 Hoised] Hoist   Brittany] Brittaine   455.1 *Trumpets and drums sound.] not in* Q1. *Compare
F.*   455.2 *The throne is removed*] This edition; *not in* Q1, F

F:
444 away] his course againe   449 That's] That is   451 tidings,] Newes, but (*altering* Q6
'newes')   455.1 *Trumpets and drums sound*] *Florish.*

443 **his** i.e. Richmond's
444 **Hoised** hoisted. *Hoise* is the earlier form
   of *hoist*.
   **Brittany** Compare the modernization of
   'Brittaine' at 5.5.53. At 4.4.444 three
   syllables are required.
448–52 **My . . . Salisbury** Richard can
   scarcely keep track of the confused and
   contradictory reports (for Shakespeare's
   compression of events, see note to
   ll. 351–451). In Holinshed events are differently ordered and already confusing in
   themselves. Richard heads for Salisbury
   to intercept Buckingham; Buckingham's
   forces are dispersed by the River Severn
   flooding; Buckingham is captured in
   Shropshire and taken to Shrewsbury,
   'where Richard then kept his household', then executed at Salisbury
   (p. 418). Salisbury would be en route to
   the county of Dorset, but seems a point-
   less destination by the end of the scene.

448 **My . . . taken** In Cibber's adaptation
   this line prompts Richard's famous reply
   'Off with his head. So much for Buckingham'. Peter Holland (SHAKSPER inter-
   net conference, SHK 9.0897, 25 Sept.
   1998) points out that in Cibber the line is
   printed in italic, the font usually reserved
   for passages 'entirely Shakespeare'. Cibber's choice of font leaves open the possibility that the line was part of earlier stage
   tradition.
450 **Milford** Milford Haven, a fiord-like inlet
   on the coast of south-west Wales.
452 **reason** debate
453 **A . . . lost** Proverbially, 'In war, some
   win and some lose' (Dent W43.1).
455.2 *The throne is removed* This seems a
   more convenient and theatrically appropriate point to remove the throne than
   the end of 4.2 or 4.3. In Morahan's production Margaret emerged from lurking
   behind it at the beginning of 4.4. In Bog-

<br>

**[4.5]**    *Enter Stanley Earl of Derby, Sir Christopher*

STANLEY EARL OF DERBY

Sir Christopher, tell Richmond this from me:
That in the sty of this most bloody boar
My son George Stanley is franked up in hold.
If I revolt, off goes young George's head.
The fear of that withholds my present aid.                                    5
But tell me, where is princely Richmond now?

SIR CHRISTOPHER

At Pembroke or at Ha'rfordwest, in Wales.

STANLEY EARL OF DERBY

What men of name resort to him?

SIR CHRISTOPHER

Sir Walter Herbert, a renownèd soldier,
Sir Gilbert Talbot, Sir William Stanley,                                        10
Oxford, redoubted Pembroke, Sir James Blunt,

Q:
  4.5.0.1 *Enter*] Q2, F; *Entee* Q1    *Stanley Earl of*] *not in* Q1, F    1 STANLEY EARL OF DERBY] *Dar.*
Q1, F. *Similarly to the end of the play.*    7, 9 SIR CHRISTOPHER] *Chri.*

F:
  4.5.0.1 *Sir*] *and Sir*    2 this most bloody] the most deadly    5 withholds] holds off    aid.]
ayde. | So get thee gone: commend me to thy Lord. | Withall say, that the Queene hath heartily
consented | He should espouse *Elizabeth* hir daughter. (*Compare ll.* 16–18.)    7 Ha'rfordwest]
Q1 (Harford-west); Hertford West F (*from* Q3 *and* Q6)

danov's modern-dress *Wars of the Roses* an anachronistic throne appeared specifically for the scene. In this and other productions Margaret sat in it while delivering her first speech, and Richard filled it when at 4.4.387 he pointedly asked 'Is the chair empty?' Much of 4.4 concerns its future occupancy.

**4.5** Holinshed supplies the priest's name (conspicuous because printed in a marginal note, p. 414) and the names of Richmond's allies (pp. 434–5).

**0.1 *Enter Stanley Earl of Derby*** Stanley has travelled to his family seat in the northwest of England. This is therefore the only scene before the battle sequence set outside London but not in a prison.
  ***Sir Christopher*** Identifiable from Holinshed as Christopher Urswick, a chaplain to the Countess of Richmond's household employed by him as a messenger, and later chaplain to Richmond as Henry VII. 'Sir' is thus a form of address to an ordained priest.

**3 franked** penned
  **hold** custody

**7 At Pembroke or at Ha'rfordwest** On southerly (Pembroke) and northerly (Haverfordwest) branches of Milford Haven.

**8 name** Both 'good family, title' and 'honourable reputation'.

**9 Herbert** Early audiences would have recognized the family name of the Earls of Pembroke.

**10 Talbot** The Stanleys of Shakespeare's day were descended from the Talbots.
  **William Stanley** There is no apparent recognition that he is Stanley's brother. Historically, he led the Stanley forces at Bosworth Field. 'By [otherwise] omitting William Stanley, Shakespeare manages to suggest that the direct ancestor of his patron, Lord Strange, decisively aided Queen Elizabeth's grandfather when he became king': Honigmann, *Lost Years*, p. 64.

**11 Pembroke** Jasper Tudor, Richmond's uncle. See Introduction, 'Date, Theatre Companies, and Patrons'.

Rhys ap-Thomas with a valiant crew,
With many more of noble fame and worth;
And towards London they do bend their course,
If by the way they be not fought withal.                    15

STANLEY EARL OF DERBY

Return unto thy lord; commend me to him.
Tell him the Queen hath heartily consented
He shall espouse Elizabeth her daughter.
These letters will resolve him of my mind.
Farewell.                              *Exeunt [severally]*    20

[**5.1**]    *Enter Buckingham, with Ratcliffe and guard, to*
            *execution*

BUCKINGHAM

Will not King Richard let me speak with him?

RATCLIFFE

No, my lord, therefore be patient.

BUCKINGHAM

Hastings, and Edward's children, Rivers, Grey,
Holy King Henry, and thy fair son Edward,
Vaughan, and all that have miscarrièd                        5
By underhand, corrupted, foul injustice,
If that your moody, discontented souls

Q:
12 Rhys ap-Thomas] Rice vp Thomas    13 more] moe    20 *severally*] OXFORD;  *not in* Q1, F
   **5.1**.0.1 *with Ratcliffe and guard*] DAVISON (*subs.*);  *not in* Q1;  *and Guard* MALONE. *Compare F.*

F:
12 Rhys] And *Rice*    13 With many more of noble fame] And many other of great name
14 they do bend their course] do they bend their power    16 Return . . . him] Well hye thee to
thy Lord: I kisse his hand    17–18 Tell . . . daughter] F *instead prints after l.* 5, *with variants.*
19 These letters] My Letter
   **5.1**.0.1 *Ratcliffe and guard*] Halberds,led    2, 11 RATCLIFFE] Q1 (*Rat.*); *Sher⟨iff⟩*. F    2 lord]
good Lord    3 Rivers, Grey] *Gray & Riuers*

11 **Blunt** Ancestor of a Stratford landowner
   (Hammond).

12 **Rhys ap-Thomas** Leader of a force of
   Welshmen. According to Holinshed, Sir
   Walter Herbert and he 'then ruled Wales
   with equal power and like authority'
   (p. 436).
   **crew** band, company

17–18 **Tell . . . daughter** F places these lines
   after 4.5.5. As Taylor notes, Q1's transposition to the end of the scene gives them

more emphasis. They are our first inkling
that the Queen is outmanoeuvring
Richard. But she does not appear on stage
again.

**5.1** Holinshed reports that Buckingham
confessed hoping for an interview with
Richard, either 'to sue for pardon and
grace' or to have 'sticked him with a dagger', but was summarily executed in
Salisbury market place (p. 418).

5 **miscarrièd** perished

7 **moody** angry

Do through the clouds behold this present hour,
Even for revenge mock my destruction.
This is All-Souls' Day, fellows, is it not?    *Nov. 2*    10
RATCLIFFE It is, my lord.
BUCKINGHAM
Why then, All Souls' Day is my body's doomsday.
This is the day that in King Edward's time
I wished might fall on me when I was found
False to his children or his wife's allies.    15
This is the day wherein I wished to fall
By the false faith of him I trusted most.
This, this All Souls' Day to my fearful soul
Is the determined respite of my wrongs.
That high all-seer that I dallied with    20
Hath turned my feignèd prayer on my head,
And given in earnest what I begged in jest.
Thus doth he force the swords of wicked men
To turn their own points on their master's bosom.
Now Margaret's curse is fallen upon my head.    25

Q:
15 wife's] wiues

F:
10 fellows] Fellow    11 is, my lord] is    13 that] which    15 or] and    17 I trusted most] whom most I trusted    20 that I] which I    24 on] in    bosom] bosomes    25 Now . . . is fallen upon my head] Thus . . . falles heauy on my necke

9 **Even for revenge mock** As Vaughan pointed out (conjecturing 'mark' for 'mock') some of the dead figures have no cause for revenge against Buckingham and some are not of a revengeful disposition. But Buckingham sees himself chorically and almost impersonally as an agent of Richard, his former 'other self', and the function of the speech is to foreshadow Richard's doom.
10 **All Souls' Day** The day in the Church calendar (2 November) when God was petitioned on behalf of the souls of the faithful dead. Shakespeare compresses events over two years apart to make the occasion of Buckingham's death anticipate the appearance of the ghosts of Richard's victims at Bosworth. 'Throughout the Middle Ages it was a popular belief that the souls in purgatory could appear on this day . . . to persons who had wronged them during their life': *New Catholic Encyclopedia*

(1967), cited in Jones, pp. 228–9.
12 **All . . . doomsday** The day of Buckingham's execution, when judgement and death are inflicted on his body, stands in analogy with the Last Judgement, when the souls of the dead will be judged. Commemoration of earlier deaths and Buckingham's own impending death are also connected, in that the 'Dies Irae' (a hymn imagining the Last Judgement) was obligatory in the Catholic church on All Souls' Day and was also used in the requiem mass to mark a death or burial.
13–17 **This . . . most** See 2.1.32–40.
19 **determined respite of** preordained end to the postponement in punishing
20 **dallied** trifled, prevaricated
22 **in earnest** (a) in all seriousness, (b) to secure the bargain
23–4 **Thus . . . bosom** Compare Psalms 37: 15, 'Their sword shall go through their own heart'.

'When he,' quoth she, 'shall split thy heart with sorrow,
Remember Margaret was a prophetess.'
Come, sirs, convey me to the block of shame.
Wrong hath but wrong, and blame the due of blame.

*Exeunt*

[5.2]    *Enter Richmond [with a letter] and lords, with drums*
        *and trumpets*

RICHMOND

Fellows in arms, and my most loving friends,
Bruised underneath the yoke of tyranny,
Thus far into the bowels of the land
Have we marched on without impediment,
And here receive we from our father Stanley                    5
Lines of fair comfort and encouragement.
The wretched, bloody, and usurping boar,
That spoils your summer fields and fruitful vines,
Swills your warm blood like wash, and makes his
        trough
In your inbowelled bosoms, this foul swine                    10

Q:
26 quoth] quorh    sorrow,] ~.    29 Exeunt] *not in* Q1. *Compare F.*
**5.2.0.1 with a letter**] OXFORD; *not in* Q1, F    **and lords**] DAVISON (*subs.*); *not in* Q1. *Compare F.*
8 spoils] CAPELL; spoild Q1, F

F:
28 sirs, convey] leade me Officers    29.1 Exeunt] *Exeunt Buckingham with Officers.*
**5.2.0.1–2 with drums and trumpets**] *Oxford, Blunt, Herbert, and | others, with drum and*
*colours*    10 inbowelled] embowel'd

26–7 **When . . . prophetess** See 1.3.300–1.
**5.2** Line 13 implies that Tamworth in the
east Midlands is the location. Short,
geographically dispersed scenes lead towards the battlefield.
0.1 **Richmond** According to Holinshed, 'he
was a man of no great stature, but so
formed and decorated with all gifts and
lineaments of nature that he seemed
more an angelical creature than a terres-
trial personage. His countenance and aspect was cheerful and courageous, his
hair yellow like the burnished gold, his
eyes grey [i.e. blue], shining, and quick'
(p. 441). In production he might variously be: well proportioned; idealized;
impersonal; Welsh-accented.
*lords* F names them as Oxford, Blunt, and

Herbert. Their anonymity in Q1's stage
directions and speech-prefixes is consistent with their anonymity on stage, but
Blunt, who speaks and is named by Richmond in 5.4, is likely to be one of them.
2 **yoke** A common biblical image for oppression; compare, for example, Gal-
atians 5: 1, 'entangled again with the
yoke of bondage', in contrast with 'the
liberty wherewith Christ hath made us
free'.
3 **the bowels** i.e. the 'heart'. Compare
ll. 9–11.
5 **father** stepfather
7 **wretched** hateful, loathsome
8 **spoils** despoils
9 **wash** pig-swill
10 **inbowelled** Suggests *embowelled* (as in F's

Lies now even in the centre of this isle,
Near to the town of Leicester, as we learn.
From Tamworth thither is but one day's march.
In God's name, cheerly on, courageous friends,
To reap the harvest of perpetual peace                    15
By this one bloody trial of sharp war.

FIRST LORD
Every man's conscience is a thousand swords
To fight against that guilty homicide.

SECOND LORD
I doubt not but his friends will fly to us.

THIRD LORD
He hath no friends but who are friends for fear,          20
Which in his greatest need will shrink from him.

RICHMOND
All for our vantage. Then, in God's name, march!
True hope is swift, and flies with swallows' wings.
Kings it makes gods, and meaner creatures kings.

                                          *Exeunt*

Q:
18 guilty] F;  bloudie Q1     24 makes] Q6, F (*setting from* Q3);  make Q1     24.1 *Exeunt*] *Exit*. Q1.
*Compare* F.

F:
11 Lies . . . centre] Is . . . Centry     12 Near] Ne're     17 FIRST LORD] Q1 (1 *Lo*.);  *Oxf*⟨*ord*⟩. F
swords] men     18 that] this     19 SECOND LORD] Q1 (2 *Lo*.);  *Her*⟨*bert*⟩. F     fly] turne     20 THIRD
LORD] Q1 (3 *Lo*.);  *Blunt*. F     who] what     21 greatest] deerest     shrink] flye     24.1 *Exeunt*]
*Exeunt Omnes*. (*altering omission of stage direction in* Q2)

'embowel'd'), meaning 'disembowelled',
and perhaps also *inbowed*, meaning 'bent
inwards', like a *trough* (compare 'inbowed
bosom' in Sidney, *Arcadia*, 1593 edn.,
H6). Richard's disembowelling of England
with the boar's tusks compares and
contrasts with Richmond's unimpeded
thrust 'into the bowels of the land' (l. 3).

11 **in the centre of this isle** Leicester lies at
the 'centre' of England and Wales (as
governed by Richard and the Tudors),
though not the 'isle' as a whole including
Scotland. The geography can be read
symbolically.
**centre** Taylor argues, speculatively, that
F's 'Centry' is a portmanteau of *centre*
and *sentry* (watchtower; sanctuary).

15 **reap the harvest** Compare l. 8.

17 **conscience . . . swords** Proverbially,

'Conscience is a thousand witnesses'
(Dent C601).

18 **guilty** F's 'guilty' importantly takes into
account Richard's spiritual state as well
as his enemies' sense of mission. Q1's
'bloudie' might be caught from l. 16.

19 **friends** allies. The reply in l. 20 opens the
gap between the political–military and
personal senses.

21 **shrink from** slink away from, desert

23 **True . . . wings** Varies the proverbs 'As
swift as a swallow' (Dent S1023)
and 'swift as thought' (T240), hope
being a kind of thought. Shakespeare describes thought as winged in *Lucrece*
1216, *As You Like It* 4.1.134, and *Hamlet*
1.5.29.

24 **Kings . . . kings** Perhaps a hubristic
claim, and disconsonant with hope as a
Christian virtue.

331

[**5.3**]    *Enter King Richard, Norfolk, Ratcliffe, Catesby, with*
*others, in arms*

KING RICHARD

Here pitch our tents, even here in Bosworth field.
    [*Soldiers begin to pitch two open tents*]
Why, how now, Catesby, why look'st thou so sad?
CATESBY

My heart is ten times lighter than my looks.
KING RICHARD   Norfolk, come hither.

Norfolk, we must have knocks, ha, must we not?                5
NORFOLK

We must both give and take, my gracious lord.
KING RICHARD (*to soldiers*)

Up with my tent there! Here will I lie tonight.—
But where tomorrow? Well, all's one for that.—
Who hath descried the number of the foe?
NORFOLK

Six or seven thousand is their utmost number.                10
KING RICHARD

Why, our battalion trebles that account.

Q:

**5.3.0.2** *in arms*] F (*after 'Richard'*); *not in* Q1    1.1 *Soldiers . . . tents*] This edition; *Tent set*
*up.* (*after l.* 11), *Soldiers of Richmond's Army . . . set up his tent* (*at opening of* 5.4) CAPELL; *not in*
Q1, F    2 sad] Q2, F; bad Q1    8 all's] F; all is Q1    10 utmost] Q1 (*British Library, Bodleian,*
*Folger*), F; greatest Q1 (*Huntington*), Q2

F:

**5.3.0.1–2** *Norfolk . . . others*] with Norfolke, Ratcliffe, | *and the Earle of Surrey*    1 tents] Tent
2 *Why . . . thou*] My Lord of Surrey, why looke you (*altering* Q2 '. . . lookest . . .'')    3 CATESBY]
Q1 (*Cat,*); *Sur*⟨*rey*⟩. F    4 Norfolk, come hither.] My Lord of Norfolke. | *Nor.* Heere most gra-
cious Liege.    6 gracious] louing    7 tent there] Tent    9 foe] Traitors    10 number] power
11 battalion] Battalia

5.3.1.1 **Soldiers . . . tents** 'It is no doubt
contrary to probability that their tents
only should be separated by so small a
space; but Shakespeare could reckon on
poetical spectators who were ready to
take the breadth of the stage for the distance between two hostile camps, if for
such indulgence they were to be recom-
pensed by beauties of so sublime a nature
as this series of spectres and Richard's
awakening soliloquy' (A. W. von
Schlegel, 1808, in Bate, ed., *Romantics*,
p. 507). For the staging, see R. J. Fusillo,
'More about "Tents" on Bosworth Field',
*SQ* 7 (1956), 458–9, arguing for imaginary tents, Albert Weiner, 'Two

Tents in *Richard III*?', *SQ* 13 (1962),
258–60, arguing for a single one, and
Hammond, pp. 65–6, arguing for two.
Hammond has Richmond's tent pitched
after he enters, but no command is given.
Richard's commands are repeated, and
in Q1 at least he stipulates, in l. 1, more
than one tent.
  1 **Bosworth field** Near Leicester. Named
'field' as if already known as a battlefield.
  6 **give and take** Proverbial (Dent G121).
10, 11 **Six or seven thousand . . . trebles** In-
flates Holinshed: 'exceeded not five thousand men . . . double so much and more'
(p. 439). But Holinshed counts Stanley's
force of three thousand separately.

Besides, the King's name is a tower of strength,
Which they upon the adverse party want.—
Up with my tent there!—Valiant gentlemen,
Let us survey the vantage of the field.                              15
Call for some men of sound direction.
Let's want no discipline, make no delay,
For, lords, tomorrow is a busy day.                    *Exeunt*

[5.4]    *Enter Richmond with the Lords and others, amongst*
         *them Blunt*

RICHMOND

The weary sun hath made a golden set,
And by the bright track of his fiery car
Gives signal of a goodly day tomorrow.
Where is Sir William Brandon? He shall bear my standard.
The Earl of Pembroke keeps his regiment;                            5
Good Captain Blunt, bear my goodnight to him,
And by the second hour in the morning
Desire the Earl to see me in my tent.
Yet one thing more, good Blunt, before thou goest:
Where is Lord Stanley quartered, dost thou know?                    10

Q:
    **5.4.**0.1 *and others*] *&c.* Q1; *not in* Q3    0.1–2 *amongst them Blunt*] CAPELL (*subs.*); *not in* Q1.
*Compare F.*    1 sun] sonne    5 keeps] F; keepe Q1

F:
    13 party] Faction    14 my tent there!—Valiant] the Tent: Come Noble    15 field] ground
17 want] lacke
    **5.4.**0.1–2 *with . . . Blunt*] *Sir William Brandon, Ox–|ford, and Dorset (altering* Q3's '*with the*
*Lordes*')    2 track] Tract    3 signal] token    4 Where . . . He] *Sir William Brandon*, you
standard.] F *goes on to print ll.* 20–3, *reading* 'Power' *instead of* 'strength', *and then printing:* 'My
Lord of Oxford, you Sir *William Brandon*, | And your Sir *Walter Herbert* stay with me:'. F2 *cor-*
*rects* 'your' *to* 'you'.    9 good Blunt, before thou goest] (good Captaine) do for me    10 dost
thou] do you

12 **the . . . strength** A blasphemous para-
    phrase of Proverbs 18: 10, 'the name of
    the Lord is a strong tower'.
16 **direction** qualities of leadership and tac-
    tical planning
**5.4–5.7** Holinshed gives a full account of
    the battle.
**5.4.**0.1 **the Lords** They might include
    Dorset, as F specifies, but if Dorset and
    Grey are a single role in 1.3. and 2.1,
    Dorset may have been excluded from an
    active role to avoid confusion when the
    ghost of Grey appears.

1–3 **The . . . tomorrow** Proverbially, the sky
    red in the evening foreshadows a fair
    morning (Dent S515; from Matthew
    16: 2). Contrast 5.5.7–16, where gloomy
    weather reflects Richard's outlook.
2 **car** carriage
4 **Where . . . Brandon** Q1, unlike F, keeps
    the on-stage lords anonymous, apart
    from Blunt. In lines printed in F only,
    Richmond goes on to address Oxford,
    Brandon, and Herbert.
5 **keeps** stays with

BLUNT

    Unless I have mista'en his colours much,

    Which well I am assured I have not done,

    His regiment lies half a mile, at least,

    South from the mighty power of the King.

RICHMOND

    If without peril it be possible,                  15

    Sweet Blunt, make some good means to speak with him,

    And give him from me this most needful scroll.

BLUNT

    Upon my life, my lord, I'll undertake it.

RICHMOND  Farewell, good Blunt.         *Exit Blunt*

    Give me some ink and paper in my tent.         20

       [*Soldiers bring a table, chairs, ink, and paper into*

        *his tent*]

    I'll draw the form and model of our battle,

    Limit each leader to his several charge,

    And part in just proportion our small strength.

    Come, let us consult upon tomorrow's business.

    Into our tent; the air is raw and cold.         25

                    *They withdraw into his tent*

       *Enter King Richard, Norfolk, Ratcliffe, Catesby, and*

       *others*

Q:

16 Sweet . . . him] F; Good captaine Blunt beare my good night to him Q1    19 *Exit Blunt*] CAPELL; *not in* Q1, F    20.1–2 *Soldiers . . . tent*] This edition; *not in* Q1, F    25.1 *They . . . tent*] F ( *. . . the Tent*); *not in* Q1    25.2–3 *and others*] *&c.*

F:

17 scroll] Note    18 it.] it, | And so God giue you quiet rest to night.    19 Farewell, good] Good night good Captaine    20–3 Give . . . strength.] *Not printed here in* F. *See note to* 'standard.', l. 4.    24 Come, let] Come Gentlemen, | Let    25 our . . . air] my . . . Dew    25.2 *King Richard*] Richard (*altering* Q3 '*R. Richard*')    25.2–3 *Norfolk . . . others*] Ratcliffe, Norfolke, & Catesby (*following* Q3 *for omission of* Q1 '*&c.*')

16 **Sweet . . . him** Q1 repeats l. 6; perhaps memorial substitution for the line in F.

21 **the form and model** i.e. a plan of the formal layout

    **battle** army

22 **Limit** appoint

    **several** separate, distinct

25.1 *They . . . tent* The distinction between

this direction (from F) and '*Exeunt*' at the end of 5.2 is consistent with the distinction between '*Enter king Richard . . .*' (l. 25.2) and '*Enter Darby to Richmond in his tent*' (Q1 and F, l. 57.2). Whereas Richard leaves the stage, Richmond remains in view in his tent. The editorial scene divisions have been established on this basis.

KING RICHARD
  What is o'clock?
CATESBY     It is six of clock, full supper time.
KING RICHARD
  I will not sup tonight. Give me some ink and paper.
      [*Soldiers bring a table, a chair, ink, paper, and a light*
        *into his tent*]
  What, is my beaver easier than it was,
  And all my armour laid into my tent?
CATESBY
  It is, my liege, and all things are in readiness.                30
KING RICHARD
  Good Norfolk, hie thee to thy charge.
  Use careful watch, choose trusty sentinel.
NORFOLK  I go, my lord.
KING RICHARD
  Stir with the lark tomorrow, gentle Norfolk.
NORFOLK  I warrant you, my lord.          *Exit*      35
KING RICHARD  Catesby.
CATESBY  My lord.
KING RICHARD
  Send out a pursuivant-at-arms
  To Stanley's regiment. Bid him bring his power
  Before sun-rising, lest his son George fall               40
  Into the blind cave of eternal night.     [*Exit Catesby*]
  Fill me a bowl of wine. Give me a watch.     [*Exit soldier*]

Q:
27. 1–2 *Soldiers . . . tent*] This edition;  *not in* Q1, F   34 KING RICHARD Stir] Q1 (*text: King.* Stur);
Sturr Q1 (*catchword*)   35 *Exit*] F;  *not in* Q1   37 CATESBY] POPE;  *Rat.* Q1 (*and* F, *but in* F *Ratcliffe
is addressed*)   38 pursuivant] Pursiuant   41 *Exit Catesby*] CAMBRIDGE;  *not in* Q1   42, 44
*Exit soldier*] This edition;  *not in* Q1

F:
26 is] is't  It is . . . time] It's Supper time my Lord, it's nine a clocke (*altering* Q3 '. . . sixe of the
. . .')   32 sentinel] Centinels   36–7 Catesby. | CATESBY] Catesby. | *Rat.* Q1;  *Ratcliffe.* | *Rat.* F

26 **What is** The absence of 'it' is usual
  enough in Q1.
  **It is** F's 'It's' was not in Shakespearian
  or general use in the 1590s ('*tis* was the
  standard contraction).
27. 1 **a light** See l. 159. For a possible alternative cue for bringing it on stage, see
  note to l. 42.
28 **beaver** face-guard of a helmet
  **easier** The hinging or leather must have

  been too stiff.
32 **Use careful watch** make sure to guard
  carefully
34 **Stir with the lark** Proverbial (Dent B186).
41 **Into . . . night** Compare 1.4.44 and note.
42–4 **Fill . . . heavy** The call for wine, naming of a white horse, and avoidance of
  heaviness all resolutely combat melancholy. The last call for wine was from
  Clarence before his murder (1.4.140).

Saddle White Syrie for the field tomorrow.
Look that my staves be sound and not too heavy.

*[Exit soldier]*

    Ratcliffe.                                            45

RATCLIFFE  My lord.

KING RICHARD

Saw'st thou the melancholy Lord Northumberland?

RATCLIFFE

Thomas the Earl of Surrey and himself,

Much about cockshut time, from troop to troop

Went through the army cheering up the soldiers.      50

KING RICHARD

So, I am satisfied.

*[Enter soldier with wine]*

        Give me a bowl of wine.

---

Q:

43 White Syrie] white Surrey    44 heavy.] F; ~ ‸ Q1 (*without line-break*)    51 *Enter soldier with wine*] ECCLES *and* RIVERSIDE (*subs., after l.* 53); *not in* Q1

F:

47 Saw'st thou] Saw'st

42  **watch** Might mean either a guard (compare l. 55) or a slow-burning candle (but *OED* does not support the latter, and even *watch-light* is not recorded before 1628). Perhaps more likely to be a small portable clock with a chiming mechanism, the '*clock*' that strikes at 5.5.5.1. The (anachronistic) property would be a reminder that Richard's last hours are passing (as, more dramatically, with Marlowe's Faustus).

43  **White Syrie** In Q1 'white Surrey' seems oddly to anticipate mention of the Earl of Surrey five lines later, but 'Surrey' is a spelling of *Syrie* (Syria), as in Chaucer's 'Man of Law's Tale', l. 1, etc. ('Surrye'); here it probably indicates a fast and graceful horse from Syria (compare the staves, 'not too heavy'). Holinshed reports that Richard entered Leicester on a 'great white courser' (p. 437), suggesting a powerful battle-horse that could bear the weight of medieval armour. A White Syrie evidently appears amongst Richard's horses recorded in BL MS Harleian 433 (f. 4), a register of Richard's

secretariat and a major historical source for the period (P. M. Kendall, *Richard the Third* (1955), p. 492 n. 1; I am grateful to Christine Buckley for this reference). How Shakespeare might have come to know of this detail and apply it to the horse Richard chose at Bosworth is uncertain. Coincidence is possible: Syria was a major source for horses, so the name is not in itself remarkable, and Shakespeare later invented a name for another royal horse based on its colour and origin, 'Roan Barbary' (*Richard II* 5.5.78).

44  **staves** lance-shafts

47  **melancholy** It is Richard whom Holinshed describes as melancholy soon after sending messages to Northumberland, Surrey, and others (p. 436). The epithet hints that Richard mistrusts Northumberland. But it perhaps attached to him through association with the 'deep-searching' Elizabethan earl.

49  **cockshut time** twilight (the time when poultry were shut up for the night)

51  **a bowl of** Taylor emends to 'some' to regularize metre and avoid repetition from l. 42.

I have not that alacrity of spirit
Nor cheer of mind that I was wont to have.
Set it down. Is ink and paper ready?

RATCLIFFE

It is, my lord.

KING RICHARD    Bid my guard watch. Leave me.    55
About the mid of night come to my tent,
Ratcliffe, and help to arm me. Leave me, I say.

*Exit Ratcliffe [and others]*

*[Richard withdraws into his tent. He writes, and*
*later sleeps.]*
*Enter Stanley Earl of Derby to Richmond and*
*Lords in his tent*

STANLEY EARL OF DERBY

Fortune and victory sit on thy helm!

RICHMOND

All comfort that the dark night can afford
Be to thy person, noble father-in-law.    60
Tell me, how fares our loving mother?

STANLEY EARL OF DERBY

I, by attorney, bless thee from thy mother,
Who prays continually for Richmond's good.
So much for that. The silent hours steal on,
And flaky darkness breaks within the east.    65
In brief—for so the season bids us be—

Q:
56–7 About . . . Ratcliffe, and] OXFORD; Ratliffe about . . . And Q1    57.1 *and others*] OXFORD
(*subs.*); *not in* Q1    57.2 *Richard . . . tent*] HAMMOND (*subs.*); *not in* Q1    57.2–3 *He . . . later*]
OXFORD (*subs.*); *not in* Q1    57.3 *sleeps*] F; *not in* Q1    57.4 *Stanley Earl of*] *not in* Q1. *Similarly*
*l. 86.1.*    57.4–5 *and Lords*] CAPELL (*subs.*); *not in* Q1    58 sit] set    64 that. The] ~ ˌ the

F:
61 loving] Noble (*from* Q3)

52–3 **I . . . to have** Follows Holinshed's description of Richard after his dream: '. . . not
using the alacrity and mirth of mind and
countenance as he was accustomed to do
before he came toward the battle' (p. 438).

57.2–3 **and later sleeps** 'Given the formality
of the sequence, Richard may not fall
asleep until Richmond does' (Taylor).

57.4 **Enter Stanley** In Holinshed, Richmond
secretly left the camp to meet Stanley in
the town of Atherstone (p. 435).

58 **Fortune . . . helm** Suggests a heraldic
emblem.

60 **father-in-law** stepfather

62 **attorney** proxy

64 **So much for that** Commonplace tag (Dent
M1289.1).

65 **flaky darkness** the darkness with flakes of
light thought to be the first sign of dawn.
Compare 'fleckeld darknesse' (or in the
variant passage 'darknesse fleckted'),
*Romeo and Juliet* 2.2.3.

Prepare thy battle early in the morning,
And put thy fortune to th'arbitrament
Of bloody strokes and mortal-shearing war.
I, as I may—that which I would, I cannot—                    70
With best advantage will deceive the time
And aid thee in this doubtful shock of arms.
But on thy side I may not be too forward,
Lest, being seen thy brother, tender George
Be executed in his father's sight.                           75
Farewell. The leisure and the fearful time
Cuts off the ceremonious vows of love
And ample interchange of sweet discourse
Which so long-sundered friends should dwell upon.
God give us leisure for these rites of love!                 80
Once more adieu. Be valiant, and speed well.

RICHMOND

Good lords, conduct him to his regiment.
I'll strive with troubled thoughts to take a nap,
Lest leaden slumber peise me down tomorrow
When I should mount with wings of victory.                   85
Once more, good night, kind lords and gentlemen.

                        *Exeunt Stanley Earl of Derby and Lords*
        [*Richmond kneels*]

Q:

68 th']F; the Q1    69 mortal-shearing] This edition (*varying Oxford's* 'mortal sharing'); mortal staring Q1    72 doubtful] doubful    79 sundered] Q3 (sundired); sundried Q1    80 rites] rights    82 lords, conduct] lords conduct Q1 (*British Library, Bodleian, Folger*); lords conduct Q1 (*Huntington*)    86.1 *Exeunt . . . Lords*] HAMMOND (*subs.*); *Exunt.* Q1. *Compare F.*    86.2 *Richmond kneels*] CAPELL (*subs.*); *not in* Q1

F:

83 thoughts] noise    86.1 *Exeunt . . . Lords*] *Exeunt. Manet Richmond.*

69  **mortal-shearing** Q1's 'mortal staring' requires war to be an indiscriminate basilisk. The reading is possible but strained, and could result from simple typographical error of ligature 'ſt' for ligature 'ſh'. Taylor prints 'mortal-sharing', taking the primary sense of *sharing* to be 'apportioning in shares', but the form is better in context as a recognized spelling of *shearing*. The allusion is to Atropos, the mythological Fate whose shears cut the thread of life. War determines destiny.

70  **as I may** in so far as I am able. Proverbially, 'Men must do as they may, not as they would' (Dent M554).

71  **With best advantage** taking the best opportunity
    **the time** the contingencies of the moment
72  **doubtful** of uncertain outcome (perhaps also 'giving cause for apprehension')
    **shock** The military sense 'clash of armed opponents' was the only one current.
74  **being seen** Refers to 'I' (Abbott 378).
76, 217  **leisure** time available before it is too late
81  **speed well** be successful
83  **with** against
84  **peise** weigh. 'To weigh like any lead' was a proverbial simile (Dent L136.1).

O thou whose captain I account myself,
Look on my forces with a gracious eye.
Put in their hands thy bruising irons of wrath,
That they may crush down with a heavy fall                    90
Th'usurping helmets of our adversaries.
Make us thy ministers of chastisement,
That we may praise thee in the victory.
To thee I do commend my watchful soul
Ere I let fall the windows of mine eyes.                       95
Sleeping and waking, O defend me still!            *He sleeps*

*Enter the Ghost of young Prince Edward, son to Harry
the Sixth, to Richard*

Q:
91 Th'usurping] F; The vsurping Q1    95 Ere] Eare    96 *He sleeps*] F (*Sleeps.*); *not in* Q1
96.1 *son to*] Q2; *sonne* Q1    96.2 *Richard*] Ri.

F:
93 the] thy (*from* Q3)    96.1 *young*] *not in* F (*following* Q3)    *Harry*] Henry (*from* Q2)    96.2 *to
Richard*] *not in* F (*following* Q3)

87 **thou . . . myself** Jones, pp. 229–31, suggests that the episode might reflect the
dream of Constantine, who established
Christianity in the Roman Empire. On the
eve of battle for control of the Empire an
angel appeared to Constantine who
showed him the sign of the cross, saying,
'In this sign thou shalt overcome the
battle'. The dream and the battle were
depicted on the walls of the Guild Chapel
in Stratford-upon-Avon.

89–90 **Put . . . fall** Echoes Psalms 2: 9,
where God says to 'his anointed', 'Thou
shalt bruise them [the heathen kings of
the earth] with a rod of iron, and break
them in pieces like a potter's vessel'
(Psalter); 'Thou shalt crush them with a
sceptre of iron . . .' (Geneva).

92 **Make . . . chastisement** Richmond already sees himself in the role of the civil
ruler whom St Paul described as 'the
minister of God to take vengeance on him
that doth evil' (Romans 13: 4), 'A well-
known Tudor doctrine that was often rehearsed in the homilies' (Shaheen).

93 **That . . . victory** Victory will be taken to
testify to God's blessing and so refute
Richard's charge that he is a rebel
(4.4.400, 447).

96.1 **Enter the Ghost** In Holinshed, Richard
had 'a dreadful and terrible dream' of 'diverse images like terrible devils, which
pulled and haled him', described as 'no
dream, but a punction and prick of his
sinful conscience' (p. 438). In *True
Tragedy* Richard narrates his dream, in
which, as in Shakespeare, he is visited by
the ghosts of his victims. Shakespeare
pairs this with the motif of Constantine's
dream of an angel (see note to l. 87). The
ghosts enter in the order of their
deaths, except that Hastings is brought
on between the Princes and Anne, probably because one of the boy actors played
both a young prince and Anne. Q3's
normalization of the sequence was transmitted to F and is accepted by most editors.
Capell had the ghosts 'rising between the
Tents' on a trap, and the same staging is
suggested in Rowe's illustration of 1709;
both may have been influenced by the
Cibber version, in which there are fewer
ghosts and the arrangement would have
been more practical (S. Wells, 'Staging
Shakespeare's Ghosts', in *The Arts of
Performance*, ed. M. Biggs *et al.* (1991),
pp. 50–60). In contrast, Taylor puts
them '*above*'; but they are more likely to

339

GHOST (*to Richard*)

Let me sit heavy on thy soul tomorrow.

Think how thou stabb'st me in my prime of youth

At Tewkesbury. Despair therefor, and die.

(*To Richmond*) Be cheerful, Richmond, for the wrongèd
        souls                                                                100

Of butchered princes fight in thy behalf.

King Henry's issue, Richmond, comforts thee.      [*Exit*]

    *Enter the Ghost of Henry the Sixth*

GHOST (*to Richard*)

When I was mortal, my anointed body

By thee was punchèd full of deadly holes.

Think on the Tower and me. Despair and die.                   105

Harry the Sixth bids thee despair and die.

(*To Richmond*) Virtuous and holy, be thou conqueror.

Harry that prophesied thou shouldst be king

Doth comfort thee in thy sleep. Live and flourish.   [*Exit*]

    *Enter the Ghost of Clarence*

GHOST (*to Richard*)

Let me sit heavy in thy soul tomorrow:                        110

Q:
97 (*to Richard*)] *to Ri. Similarly at ll.* 103 *and* 125.     100 (*To Richmond*)] *To Rich. Similarly at*
*ll.* 107, 115, 129, 136, 143, *and* 152.     102 *Exit*] WILSON; *not in* Q1. *Similarly at ll.* 109, 117.1,
137, 145 (*following* CIBBER, '*sinks*'), *and* 155.

F:
100 *To Richmond*] *Ghost to Richm.*            103 *to Richard*] *not in* F (*altering* Q3 '*to K. Ri.*')
104 deadly holes] holes (*from* Q2)            107 *To Richmond*] *To Richm. Similarly at ll.* 115, 123.
109 thy sleep] sleepe

enter through Richard's tent or by a door
to the side of it. There seems to have been
no standard ghost costume in the Elizabethan theatre (Hamlet's father is evidently in armour in the early scenes and,
according to Q1, in his nightgown in
3.4). Ghosts would probably have been
whited with flour. The figures could have
been individually recognizable by face
and costume (especially as the Elizabethan theatre had no lights to dim),
though in modern productions they are
often shrouded or underlit. Bogdanov
gave them individuating gestures or
properties: Clarence drinks wine, Anne
spits, and so on.

97–185 **Let . . . Richard** Elizabethan Calvin-
ists understood the despair experienced

by those whom God rejected to be a fore-
taste of hell (Stachniewski, pp. 23–4).
See note to 1.4.40–60.
97 **tomorrow.** Taylor adds as a verse-line the
words from the stage direction, 'Prince
Edward, son to Henry the Sixth', on the
basis that he is inadequately identified.
But Edward has been strongly associated
with Tewkesbury, and does reveal himself to Richmond as 'King Henry's issue'.
98 **prime** See 1.2.132 and note.
99 **Despair . . . die** Death on the battlefield is
here associated with suicide through spiritual despair.
**therefor** on that account
103 **anointed** See notes to 4.4.143–4 and
5.4.89–90.
104 **punchèd** stabbed, pierced
109 **thy** Metrically emphasized.

I that was washed to death with fulsome wine,
Poor Clarence, by thy guile betrayed to death.
Tomorrow in the battle think on me,
And fall thy edgeless sword. Despair and die.
(*To Richmond*) Thou offspring of the house of Lancaster,    115
The wrongèd heirs of York do pray for thee.
Good angels guard thy battle. Live and flourish.

                                                     *⌐Exit⌐*

       *Enter the Ghosts of Rivers, Grey, Vaughan*
GHOST OF RIVERS (*to Richard*)
Let me sit heavy in thy soul tomorrow,
Rivers that died at Pomfret. Despair and die.
GHOST OF GREY (*to Richard*)
Think upon Grey, and let thy soul despair.    120
GHOST OF VAUGHAN (*to Richard*)
Think upon Vaughan, and with guilty fear
Let fall thy lance. Despair and die.
ALL (*to Richmond*)
Awake, and think our wrongs in Richard's bosom
Will conquer him. Awake and win the day.

                                          *⌐Exeunt Ghosts⌐*

       *Enter the Ghosts of the two young Princes*
GHOSTS (*to Richard*)
Dream on thy cousins smothered in the Tower.    125
Let us be lead within thy bosom, Richard,
And weigh thee down to ruin, shame, and death.
Thy nephews' souls bid thee despair and die.

Q:
118, 120 GHOST OF] CAMBRIDGE; *not in* Q1    118 RIVERS] Q3 (*Riu.*);    *King* Q1    sit] set    123 *to Richmond*] Q1 (*to Ri.*), Q3 (*to Rich.*)    124 Will] Q2; Wel Q1    124.1 *Exeunt Ghosts*] WILSON; *not in* Q1    125 GHOSTS] F; *Ghost.* Q1; *Gho.* Q3

F:
117.1 *Vaughan*] *and Vaughan*    124.2–132 *Enter . . . flourish.*] *Printed instead after l.* 137 (*as in* Q3)    125 *to Richard*] *not in* F (*altering* Q3 '*to K. R.*')    126 lead] laid (*from* Q2)    128 souls bid] soule bids

111  **washed** Ironic in relation to *fulsome*, and glancing at the expression *to wash one's brain*, to get drunk.
    **fulsome** foul, disgusting; excessive
114  **fall . . . sword** Probably imperative 'drop your edgeless sword' (compare l. 122).
    **edgeless** blunt, ineffectual (first recorded in *OED* 1617)
117  **guard** May be subjunctive, imperative, or indicative.

122  **Let . . . die** Metre and the parallel with l. 114 suggest a word may be missing. Capell emended to 'hurtless lance'. Wilson conjecturally emended to 'think, despair'.
123  *Richmond* Q1's direction is the one case where the contractions '*Ri*' and '*Rich*' fail to discriminate between Richard and Richmond respectively.

    *(To Richmond)* Sleep, Richmond, sleep in peace, and
        wake in joy.
    Good angels guard thee from the boar's annoy.        130
    Live, and beget a happy race of kings.
    Edward's unhappy sons do bid thee flourish.
                                   *[Exeunt Ghosts]*
          *Enter the Ghost of Hastings*
GHOST *(to Richard)*
    Bloody and guilty, guiltily awake,
    And in a bloody battle end thy days.
    Think on Lord Hastings. Despair and die.        135
    *(To Richmond)* Quiet, untroubled soul, awake, awake.
    Arm, fight, and conquer for fair England's sake.
                                *[Exit]*
          *Enter the Ghost of Lady Anne, his wife*
GHOST *(to Richard)*
    Richard, thy wife, that wretched Anne thy wife,
    That never slept a quiet hour with thee,
    Now fills thy sleep with perturbations.        140
    Tomorrow in the battle think on me,
    And fall thy edgeless sword. Despair and die.
    *(To Richmond)* Thou quiet soul, sleep thou a quiet sleep.
    Dream of success and happy victory.
    Thy adversary's wife doth pray for thee.    *[Exit]*   145
          *Enter the Ghost of Buckingham*
GHOST *(to Richard)*
    The first was I that helped thee to the crown.
    The last was I that felt thy tyranny.
    O in the battle think on Buckingham,
    And die in terror of thy guiltiness.
    Dream on, dream on, of bloody deeds and death.    150
    Fainting, despair. Despairing, yield thy breath.

**Q:**

132.1 *Exeunt Ghosts*] WILSON (*following* CIBBER, '*Vanish*'); *not in* Q1    137 England's] Engiands
138 GHOST (*to Richard*)] F; *not in* Q1    140 perturbations] Q2; preturbations Q1    146 GHOST]
*speech-prefix not in* Q1    *to Richard*] F (*to Rich.*); *not in* Q1

**F:**

129 *To Richmond*] Ghosts to Richm.    132.2 Hastings] Lord Hastings (*from* Q3)    136 *To Rich-*
*mond*] Hast. to Richm.    137.2 *Lady Anne*] Anne (*altering* Q3 '*Queene Anne*')    143 *To Richmond*]
Ghost to Richm. *Similarly at l.* 152.

        129 **sleep in peace** The same words occur in Psalms 4: 8.

(*To Richmond*) I died for hope ere I could lend thee aid,
But cheer thy heart, and be thou not dismayed.
God and good angels fight on Richmond's side,
And Richard falls in height of all his pride.          [*Exit*]    155
        *Richard starteth up out of a dream*
KING RICHARD
Give me another horse! Bind up my wounds!
Have mercy, Jesu!—Soft, I did but dream.
O coward conscience, how dost thou afflict me!
The lights burn blue. It is now dead midnight.
Cold fearful drops stand on my trembling flesh.          160
What do I fear? Myself? There's none else by.
Richard loves Richard; that is, I and I.
Is there a murderer here? No.—Yes, I am.
Then fly.—What, from myself?—Great reason why:
Lest I revenge.—What, myself upon myself?               165
Alack, I love myself.—Wherefore?—For any good
That I myself have done unto myself.—

Q:
154 Richmond's] Richmons

F:
155 falls] fall       155.1 *Richard starteth up*] *Richard starts* (*altering* Q3 'K. *Richard starteth*')
a] his      156 KING RICHARD] *King Ri.* Q1; *Rich.* F       159 now] not (*from* Q2)       161 What‸ . . .
fear?] ~? . . . ~‸ (*altering* Q2, ~‸ . . . ~‸)       162 and] am (*from* Q2)

152 **for . . . aid** i.e. for aspiring to lend you
aid before I could do so. Wright instead
took *for hope* as 'as regards hope', virtually 'for want of hope'.
155 **And . . . pride** Proverbially, 'Pride will
have a fall' (Dent P581).
156–85 **Give . . . Richard** The early 17th-
century annotator of the Kodama copy of F
noted, 'Despair of conscience and memory
of abominable cruelties and perjuries make
Richard mad' (Yamada, p. 160).
157 **Soft** stay, be quiet
158 **coward conscience** Richard differs from
the sinner of repentance literature whose
temporary despair causes him to follow
the promptings of conscience. His is 'the
wounded *conscience*' by which 'a man ap-
prehends himself to be wholly destitute of
true *grace*, and deserted and forsaken of
God' (John Sym, 1637, quoted by Stachniewski, p. 47). Compare 5.5.38–9 and
note. Proverbially, 'A guilty conscience

is a self-accuser' (Dent C606). *Conscience*
may also suggest 'consciousness'.
159 **The lights burn blue** Thought to be a
sign that a spirit was present.
**It . . . midnight** A surprising statement
after l. 65, but in this episode the time,
like the weather, is more symbolic than
realistic.
162 **and** Editors often follow Q2's and hence
F's 'am', which is either a deliberate but
guessed emendation or eyeskip to 'I am'
in the next line. In contrast with 'I am
myself alone' (*Richard Duke of York*
5.6.84), the emphasis is now on division,
not autonomy. The conscious, fearful,
and morally aware self perceives the murderous other self.
165, 166 **What, Wherefore** Some editors
delete to regularize the metre (following
Capell, l. 165, and Maxwell, l. 166), but
the verse-flow is in any case broken up in
this passage.

O no, alas, I rather hate myself
For hateful deeds committed by myself.
I am a villain.—Yet I lie; I am not.                                170
Fool, of thyself speak well.—Fool, do not flatter.
My conscience hath a thousand several tongues,
And every tongue brings in a several tale,
And every tale condemns me for a villain.—
Perjury, perjury, in the high'st degree!—                           175
Murder, stern murder, in the dir'st degree.
All several sins, all used in each degree,
Throng to the bar, crying all, 'Guilty, guilty!'
I shall despair. There is no creature loves me,
And if I die, no soul will pity me.                                  180
And wherefore should they, since that I myself
Find in myself no pity to myself.
Methought the souls of all that I had murdered
Came to my tent, and every one did threat
Tomorrow's vengeance on the head of Richard.                        185
    *Enter Ratcliffe*
RATCLIFFE My lord.

Q:
175–6 high'st . . . dir'st] F;  highest . . . dyrest Q1

F:
175 Perjury, perjury] Periurie (*from* Q3)    178 Throng] Throng all (*from* Q3)    to the bar]
to'th'Barre    180 will] shall (*from* Q3)    181 And] Nay

170–1 **Yet . . . well** Richard attempts to sustain the illusion that he can decide for himself what he is.

172–85 **My . . . Richard** Samuel Johnson found this passage 'truly tragical' (*Johnson on Shakespeare*, ed. Arthur Sherbo (1968), ii. 631).

172 **My . . . tongues** Proverbially, 'Conscience is a thousand witnesses' (Dent C601). There could be a suggestion that Richard's conscience resides with the play's audience.

172, 173, 177 **several** separate

173 **brings in** introduces, adduces as evidence. Compare *History of Lear*, 13.31, 'I'll see their trial first. Bring in the evidence' (cited in *OED* as earliest example of the sense).

175 **Perjury . . . degree** The defiant Richard's defence, answered by his conscience in the next line.

176 **degree** The specific legal sense, as in 'first degree murder', is not recorded before 1676 (Wilson).

177 **used** practised

178 **bar** court, tribunal (specifically, the wooden rail bounding the precinct of the judge's seat). Used figuratively by writers such as John Wyclif and William Perkins to refer to the Last Judgement.

179 **creature** created being. Both as a self-constituting being ('Richard loves Richard') and more mundanely as a dire murderer, he is without affinity. 'Likeness generates love' (Ficino, quoted by Neill, p. 106).

181–2 **since . . . to myself** Echoes the excessive and fragmenting self-reference of Petrarch's famous 'di me medesmo meco mi vergogno' (*Canzoniere*, 1.11); reductively translated as 'I am ashamed of myself', but note the recurrence of 'me' and 'mi'.

KING RICHARD  Zounds, who is there?

RATCLIFFE

  Ratcliffe, my lord; 'tis I. The early village cock

  Hath twice done salutation to the morn.

  Your friends are up, and buckle on their armour.                190

KING RICHARD

  O Ratcliffe, I have dreamed a fearful dream.

  What think'st thou, will our friends prove all true?

RATCLIFFE

  No doubt, my lord.

KING RICHARD                    O Ratcliffe, I fear, I fear.

RATCLIFFE

  Nay, good my lord, be not afraid of shadows.

KING RICHARD

  By the Apostle Paul, shadows tonight                              195

  Have struck more terror to the soul of Richard

  Than can the substance of ten thousand soldiers

  Armèd in proof and led by shallow Richmond.

  'Tis not yet near day. Come, go with me.

  Under our tents I'll play the eavesdropper,                       200

  To see if any mean to shrink from me.

                *Exeunt Richard and Ratcliffe*   ·

     *Enter the Lords to Richmond, sitting in his tent*

LORDS  Good morrow, Richmond.

---

Q:
200 eavesdropper] ease dropper     201.1 *Richard and Ratcliffe*] F;  *not in* Q1     201.2 *sitting in his tent*] F;  *not in* Q1     202 LORDS] Q1 (*Lo.*), Q3 (*Lords.*)

F:
187 Zounds, who is] Who's     191–3 KING . . . lord.] *not in* F     201 see] heare (*from* Q3)
202 LORDS] Q1 (*Lo.*); *Richm*. F

187 **Zounds, who is there?** Presumably he fears more ghosts. The position of ll. 183–5 has puzzled some editors, but they prepare for this response.

191–3 **KING . . . lord.** F's omission is an error of eyeskip caused by copy repetition of '*King*. O Ratcliffe'.

192 **think'st** 'thinkest' (Capell) regularizes the metre. Wilson also transposed: '. . . will our friends prove true?'

194 **shadows** phantasms

198 **Armèd in proof** in tested armour

200 **Under . . . eavesdropper** The tents are probably imagined as having a pitched roof overhanging vertical walls. The eavesdrop, in the literal sense, is the ground that the rainwater drips on from the eaves. In the theatre it could refer to the shallow gutter surrounding the stage below the edge of the stage roof, and it is not impossible that Richard and Ratcliffe would have gone down to this area instead of exiting.

201 **see** Editors who accept Q3's 'heare' take 'see' over-literally.

RICHMOND

Cry mercy, lords and watchful gentlemen,

That you have ta'en a tardy sluggard here.

LORD  How have you slept, my lord?                                                    205

RICHMOND

The sweetest sleep and fairest-boding dreams

That ever entered in a drowsy head

Have I since your departure had, my lords.

Methought their souls whose bodies Richard murdered

Came to my tent and cried on victory.                                                 210

I promise you, my soul is very jocund

In the remembrance of so fair a dream.

How far into the morning is it, lords?

LORD  Upon the stroke of four.

RICHMOND [*coming forward*]

Why then, 'tis time to arm and give direction.                                        215

    *His oration to his soldiers*

More than I have said, loving countrymen,

The leisure and enforcement of the time

Forbids to dwell upon. Yet remember this:

God and our good cause fight upon our side;

The prayers of holy saints and wrongèd souls,                                         220

Q:
205, 214 LORD] Q1 (*Lo.*)      208 departure] depature      215 *coming forward*] HAMMOND (*subs.*);
*not in* Q1

F:
205 LORD] Q1 (*Lo.*); *Lords.* Q3, F      211 soul] Heart

203  **Cry mercy** I beg your pardon
204  **you . . . here** Compare Richard's pre-
    tence at 3.4.25.
    **ta'en** caught
    **tardy** dilatory (but compare *ta'en tardy*,
    4.1.47)
210  **cried on** invoked
215  **direction** leadership
215.1  *His . . . soldiers* Richmond's and
    Richard's orations should perhaps be de-
    livered to the play's audience as im-
    aginary soldiers. Both follow the
    chronicles, probably Holinshed. Hassel
    (*Songs*, pp. 36–45) suggests Shake-
    speare's exclusions tend to diminish
    Richard and exalt Richmond. In Holin-
    shed, Richard's oration is given before
    Richmond's, and Richard is first to be
    embattled. Holinshed gives headings that

anticipate Q1's directions, 'The oration
of King Richard the III to the chieftains of
his army' (p. 439) and 'The oration of
King Henry the VII to his army' (p. 441).
The King's set-speech exhortation before
battle was a standard rhetorical feature of
Tudor historiography. See Appendix D,
Note 17.
216  **More . . . said** Taylor emends to 'Much
    that I could say', but Richmond probably
    means '. . . said previously'.
    **loving countrymen** A Tudor elision of dif-
    ference: as claimant to the English crown
    Richmond, though elsewhere regarded
    as Welsh, speaks as if he were English.
217  **leisure** See note to l. 76.
220–1  **The . . . forces** Echoes Revelation
    6: 9–10, 'I saw . . . the souls of them that
    were killed for the word of God . . . and they

Like high-reared bulwarks, stand before our forces.
Richard except, those whom we fight against
Had rather have us win than him they follow.
For what is he they follow? Truly, gentlemen,
A bloody tyrant and a homicide;                                    225
One raised in blood, and one in blood established;
One that made means to come by what he hath,
And slaughtered those that were the means to help him;
A base, foul stone, made precious by the foil
Of England's chair where he is falsely set;                        230
One that hath ever been God's enemy.
Then if you fight against God's enemy,
God will, in justice, ward you as his soldiers.
If you do sweat to put a tyrant down,
You sleep in peace, the tyrant being slain.                        235
If you do fight against your country's foes,
Your country's fat shall pay your pains the hire.
If you do fight in safeguard of your wives,
Your wives shall welcome home the conquerors.
If you do free your children from the sword,                       240
Your children's children quites it in your age.
Then, in the name of God and all these rights,
Advance your standards, draw your willing swords.
For me, the ransom of my bold attempt
Shall be this cold corpse on the earth's cold face.                245

---

Q:
221 forces] OXFORD;  faces Q1    222 Richard except,] ~, ~,    233 in] ln    241 quites] quits

F:
229 foil] soyle (*from* Q3)    234 sweat] sweare (*from* Q3)

---

cried with a loud voice, saying "How long,
Lord which art holy and true? Dost not
thou judge and avenge our blood?"' and
Revelation 5: 8, 'the prayers of the saints'.

221 **bulwarks** defensive earthworks and/or
ramparts
229 **foil** setting for a jewel
230 **chair** throne
   **set** Applies to both a jewel and a king on a
   throne.
233 **ward** defend
237 **fat** wealth, surplus; as in Genesis
45: 18, 'the fat of the land'

237 **hire** recompense
241 **quites** requites. None of the early editions found need to correct the lack of
concord with *children*.
244 **ransom** i.e. the unransomed penalty for
failure. It was a sore point amongst foot-
soldiers that their leaders were often captured and ransomed, rather than killed as
they were.
245 **this cold corpse** i.e. this living body
anticipated as cold in death. 'Living
body' was a current sense of *corpse*. Taylor transposes 'my' (l. 244) and 'this' to
avoid Richmond's apparent reference to

347

But if I thrive, the gain of my attempt
The least of you shall share his part thereof.
Sound drums and trumpets bold and cheerfully!
God and Saint George! Richmond and victory!
                              [*Drums and trumpets. Exeunt*]

**[5.5]**    *Enter King Richard, Ratcliffe, and others*
KING RICHARD

What said Northumberland as touching Richmond?
RATCLIFFE

That he was never trainèd up in arms.
KING RICHARD

He said the truth. And what said Surrey then?
RATCLIFFE

He smiled and said, 'The better for our purpose.'
KING RICHARD

He was in the right, and so indeed it is.                    5
        *The clock striketh*

Tell the clock there. Give me a calendar.

Who saw the sun today?
RATCLIFFE                       Not I, my lord.
KING RICHARD [*looking in an almanac*]

Then he disdains to shine, for by the book

Q:
248 bold] STAUNTON; boldlie QI    249.1 *Drums and trumpets*] OXFORD; *Shouts, &c.* CAPELL;
*not in* QI    *Exeunt*] CAPELL; *not in* QI
    **5.5**.0.1 *and others*] *&c.*    5 so indeed] so in deede QI (*Huntington, Folger*); soin deede QI
(*British Library*)    5.1 *The clock striketh*] *right of* 'there', *l.* 6, *in* QI    8 *looking in an almanac*] *A
Calendar brought* COLLIER 1853 (*after* 'today', *l.* 7); *not in* QI

F:
    **5.5**.0.1 *others*] Catesby    5.1 *The clock striketh*] *Clocke strikes.* (*position as in* QI)

himself as already dead. An alternative
emendation would be 'this corpse cold on
the earth's cold face'. But the licence
with logical sense in QI does not obscure
the meaning.

249.1 *Exeunt* Not in QI or F. Richmond
is on his way to the battlefield ahead of
Richard.
**5.5** Richard's recovery of confidence was a
strong point in many Victorian productions, and even George Bernard Shaw ap-
proved 'the magnetic moment when all
the dreadful joy of the fighting man

surges up in him': *Shaw on Shakespeare*,
ed. Edwin Wilson (1961), p. 167. But
Richard may instead be shown as desperate or uncertain, as by Sher.
    0.1 *Enter . . . others* The action remains cen-
tred on the tent, as the properties of the
clock and the book indicate. The *others*
(soldiers) need be very few if Richard's
oration is addressed to the audience.
With a small retinue the opening dialogue plausibly refers to the eavesdrop-
ping (see 5.4.199–201).
    6 **Tell** count
    **a calendar** i.e. a pocket almanac

He should have braved the east an hour ago.
A black day will it be to somebody. Ratcliffe.                    10
RATCLIFFE
  My lord.
KING RICHARD  The sun will not be seen today.
  The sky doth frown and lour upon our army.
  I would these dewy tears were from the ground.
  Not shine today: why, what is that to me
  More than to Richmond? For the selfsame heaven            15
  That frowns on me looks sadly upon him.
     *Enter Norfolk*
NORFOLK
  Arm, arm, my lord! The foe vaunts in the field.
KING RICHARD
  Come, bustle, bustle! Caparison my horse.
     ⌈*Richard arms*⌉
  Call up Lord Stanley, bid him bring his power.
                     ⌈*Exit a soldier*⌉
  I will lead forth my soldiers to the plain,                      20
  And thus my battle shall be orderèd:
  My foreward shall be drawn out all in length,
  Consisting equally of horse and foot;
  Our archers shall be placèd in the midst;
  John Duke of Norfolk, Thomas Earl of Surrey,                    25
  Shall have the leading of this foot and horse.
  They thus directed, we will follow

Q:
10 somebody. Ratcliffe.] some bodie Rat.    11 not] Q2; nor Q1    16.1 *Norfolk*] *Norffolke*. Q1
(*Huntington, Folger*); ~ Q1 (*British Library*)    18.1 *Richard arms*] HAMMOND; *not in* Q1
19 Stanley] Q2 (Stanlie); Standlie Q1    19.1 *Exit a soldier*] OXFORD (*subs.*); Exit *Catesby* CIBBER
(*Catesby here equivalent to Ratcliffe*); *not in* Q1

F:
22 drawn out all] drawne (*from* Q2)    26 this] the (*from* Q3)

  9  **braved** made splendid
  10  **A . . . somebody** Similar predictive interpret-
    ations of nature were found in almanacs.
  11–14  **The sun . . . today** In Holinshed the
    day is sunny, but in *True Tragedy* 'you
    wat'ry heavens roll on my gloomy day,
    and darksome clouds close up my cheerful
    soul [misprinted 'sownde']. Down is thy
    sun, Richard, never to shine again' (his
    final speech, without self-consolation;

    ll. 1989–91).
  18  **Caparison** put trappings on, harness
  20–9  **I . . . horse** Closely based on Holinshed,
    p. 438.
  22  **My . . . length** The purpose, as Holinshed
    explains, was to dishearten the enemy by
    giving the impression of a huge army.
    **foreward** first line of troops
  27  **we** Probably 'royal' plural for 'I'. Pope
    remedied the metre by adding 'ourself'.

In the main battle, whose puissance on each side
Shall be well wingèd with our chiefest horse.
This, and Saint George to boot! What think'st thou,
    Norfolk?                                       30

NORFOLK

A good direction, warlike sovereign.
    *He showeth him a paper*
This found I on my tent this morning:
    'Jocky of Norfolk, be not so bold,
  ✓ For Dickin thy master is bought and sold.'

KING RICHARD

A thing devisèd by the enemy.                      35
Go, gentlemen, each man unto his charge.
Let not our babbling dreams affright our souls.
Conscience is but a word that cowards use,
Devised at first to keep the strong in awe.
Our strong arms be our conscience, swords our law.    40

---

Q:
28 main] matne    each side] This edition; either side Q1; both sides OXFORD    30 boot] Q3;
bootes Q1    31 NORFOLK A good] Q1 (*text: Nor.* A good); A good Q1 (*catchword*)    34 Dickin]
*Dickon*    36 each] POPE; euery Q1    40 conscience, swords$_\wedge$] $\sim_\wedge \sim$,

F:
31.1 *He showeth him a paper*] *not in* F    36 unto] to    38 Conscience] For Conscience    but a] a
(*from* Q3)

28 **battle** body of troops
29 **horse** cavalry
30 **to boot** as well, into the bargain (i.e. also
    on our side)
32 **This** Pope plausibly added 'paper' to re-
    store the metre.
33–4 **Jocky . . . sold** Editors often follow
    Capell in reassigning the reading of the
    paper to Richard, but (a) '*showeth*'
    (l. 31.1) does not mean 'gives', (b) it
    seems unsafe to emend, as does Wilson,
    on the ground that the lines would be too
    insulting to be read to a king, for the
    King's authority is itself in question.
33 **Jocky** Contraction of diminutive 'John-
    kin', John being the Duke of Norfolk's
    Christian name. Subversively overfamil-
    iar, mildly cryptic, and perhaps distinct-
    ively Scottish (compare 'Jock').
    **so** Capell, noting the reading in the
    chronicles, emends to 'too'. Many edi-
    tors agree, but E. A. J. Honigmann cites
    the passage as an example of Shake-
    speare's fondness for tinkering: *Stability*

*of Shakespeare's Text* (1965), pp. 42–3.
✓34 **Dickin** Diminutive of 'Dick', for Richard.
    **bought and sold** i.e. betrayed for a bribe.
    Historically, Stanley was rewarded with
    the title of Earl of Derby after the victory
    at Bosworth. The unofficial view that
    Richmond owed his victory to a bribe sur-
    faces momentarily in doggerel, both in
    the play and in Holinshed (p. 444).
35 **A . . . enemy** The alternative reading
    would be that it is an example of popular
    prophecy, much feared by monarchs.
37, 40 **our** Refers to Richard and the 'gentle-
    men' collectively, but particularly appro-
    priate (as 'royal' plural) to Richard
    himself.
38–9 **Conscience . . . awe** *Conscience* can be
    tantamount to religion, as in Christian
    teaching a sense of good and evil depends
    on knowledge of God's laws. The use of
    religion to political ends was advocated
    by Machiavelli in *Discorsi* 1.11–15. There
    are various Elizabethan parallels, in par-
    ticular Marlowe's views as reported in

March on, join bravely! Let us to it, pell-mell:
If not to heaven, then hand in hand to hell.
   *His oration to his army*
What shall I say more than I have inferred?
Remember whom you are to cope withal:
A sort of vagabonds, rascals and runaways,            45
A scum of Bretons, and base lackey peasants
Whom their o'ercloyèd country vomits forth
To desperate ventures and assured destruction.
You sleeping safe, they bring to you unrest.
You having lands and blessed with beauteous wives,    50
They would restrain the one, distain the other.
And who doth lead them but a paltry fellow,
Long kept in Bretagne at our mother's cost,
A milksop, one that never in his life
Felt so much cold as over shoes in snow?        55

the Baines Note, 'the first beginning of religion was only to keep men in awe': in *Complete Plays and Poems*, ed. E. D. Pendry and J. C. Maxwell (1976), p. 513.

40 **Our . . . law** Compare Marlowe, *Jew of Malta*, Pro. 19–21, 'What right had Caesar to the empire? | Might first made kings, and laws were then most sure | When like the Draco's they were writ in blood'. The play was unpublished when Shakespeare wrote, but he clearly knew it on the stage.

42.1 **His . . . army** See notes to 5.4.215.1 and 5.5.0.1. As Wilson notes, the oration seems to follow awkwardly after the summons to march on and join battle. There may have been a flourish of trumpets and drums while Richard and his followers marched forward to address the (imagined?) army at large.

43 **inferred** alleged
44 **cope withal** encounter
45 **sort** crew, band
   **runaways** See note to 4.4.382.
51 **restrain** withhold (referring to the whole phrase 'you [from] having lands'). War-

burton's emendation *distrain*, meaning 'seized', is often accepted, perhaps rightly.
**distain** defile

53 **mother's** Capell and some subsequent editors, including Hammond and Taylor, emend to 'brother's', as the historically correct referent is Richard's brother-in-law the Duke of Burgundy. The factual error originates in the second edition of Holinshed, where the first edition's 'brother' is misprinted 'moother'. Richard's insult 'milksop' was no doubt the source for an error of association by the compositor. Accepting his source, Shakespeare made the association significant in its own right. Richmond is equivalent to a renegade brother: presumably a bastard one (compare l. 62). The reading 'mother's' might even become 'the final sign of Richard's own matriarchal perversion' (Hodgdon, p. 115).

54 **milksop** Holinshed (p. 440) supports the emendation.
55 **over shoes** 'To be over shoes' (i.e. to get wet feet) was proverbial (Dent S380): an inconsequential sort of going too far.

Let's whip these stragglers o'er the seas again,
Lash hence these overweening rags of France,
These famished beggars, weary of their lives,
Who, but for dreaming on this fond exploit,
For want of means, poor rats, had hanged themselves.      60
If we be conquered, let men conquer us,
And not these bastard Bretons, whom our fathers
Have in their own land beaten, bobbed, and thumped,
And in record left them the heirs of shame.
Shall these enjoy our lands, lie with our wives,      65
Ravish our daughters?
     *Drum afar off*
                     Hark, I hear their drum.
Fight, gentlemen of England; fight, bold yeomen.
Draw, archers, draw your arrows to the head!
Spur your proud horses hard, and ride in blood!
Amaze the welkin with your broken staves!      70
     *Enter a Messenger*
What says Lord Stanley? Will he bring his power?
MESSENGER
My lord, he doth deny to come—
KING RICHARD    Off with his son George's head!
NORFOLK
My lord, the enemy is past the marsh.
After the battle let George Stanley die.      75
KING RICHARD
A thousand hearts are great within my bosom.

---

Q:
66 *Drum afar off* ] F; *not in* Q1      70.1 *Enter a Messenger*] F; *not in* Q1

F:
64 in] on (*from* Q3)      67 Fight] Right (*from* Q3)      bold] boldly (*from* Q2)

57 **Lash . . . France** Vagabonds were whipped and returned to their home parish.
59 **fond** foolish
62 **our fathers** Alludes primarily to Henry V's campaigns in France.
63 **bobbed** beaten with fists
64 **record** (stressed on the second syllable)
69 **in blood** (a) in hot pursuit of the prey (as a hunting term), (b) through spilt blood

70 **Amaze** stupefy, craze (as with a blow, and perhaps referring to the visual effect of the rebounding staves slashing the sky chaotically); astonish
**welkin** sky
**broken** i.e. shattered on striking their targets
71–5 **What . . . die** Closely based on Holinshed.
76 **great** swollen

Advance our standards! Set upon our foes!
Our ancient word of courage, fair Saint George,
Inspire us with the spleen of fiery dragons.
Upon them! Victory sits on our helms.                *Exeunt*      80

[**5.6**]    *Alarum, excursions. Enter Catesby*
CATESBY [*calling*]
Rescue! My lord of Norfolk, rescue, rescue!—
The King enacts more wonders than a man,
Daring an opposite to every danger.
His horse is slain, and all on foot he fights,
Seeking for Richmond in the throat of death.—                    5
Rescue, fair lord, or else the day is lost!
       [*Alarums.*] *Enter Richard*
KING RICHARD
A horse, a horse! My kingdom for a horse!

Q:
80 them! Victory] ~ ˄ victorie
    **5.6.**1 *calling*] *not in* Q1     6.1 *Alarums.*] F; *not in* Q1

F:
80 helms] helpes (*from* Q3)     *Exeunt*] *not in* F (*following* Q3)
    **5.6.**7, 9 KING RICHARD] *King* Q1; *Rich.* F

78 **Saint George** There might be dramatic
   irony in view of Richard's intention to
   kill the George discussed in the previous
   exchange.
79 **spleen** fiery impetuosity
   **dragons** Richard's rhetoric surely betrays
   him into putting himself on the wrong side.
   For Richmond and Richard as St George
   and the Dragon, see Illustration 1.
80 **Victory . . . helms** Compare 5.4.58 and
   note.
**5.6.**0.1 *Alarum, excursions* summons to
   battle by drums and trumpets, and skirmishes between groups of soldiers
   **Catesby** Editors often follow Capell in
   adding Norfolk, but Catesby may be
   searching and calling for him, and so
   speak ll. 2–5 as a soliloquy—or perhaps
   to an anonymous soldier.
2 **a man** i.e. what is humanly possible
3 **an opposite** an opponent. Q8's 'and opposite' is attractive.
7 **A . . . for a horse** A famous and often
   parodied line. Holinshed relates that
   Richard's supporters brought him 'a

swift and a light horse to convey him
away', which he rejected to 'make an
end of all battles or else there finish his
life' (p. 445). *True Tragedy* offers a closer
parallel: Richard calls for 'A horse, a
horse, a fresh horse', without staking his
kingdom for it; his Page responds 'Ah,
fly, my lord, and save your life', to which
Richard replies 'Fly, villain? Look I as
though I would fly?' (ll. 1985–7). In
Peele's *Alcazar*, which probably ante-
dates both Richard plays, the Moor says,
'A horse, a horse, villain, a horse', intending to 'fly', ll. 1413–14). Though
Richard's cry has sometimes been interpreted to mean that the loss of his horse
has lost him the kingdom, it is more likely
that he is calling for a fresh horse to continue fighting at any cost, as in *True
Tragedy*. Expressions such as 'I'd give my
life for/ the world for . . .' are not meant
literally. For Richard to stake his kingdom has obvious irony, and it substitutes
fittingly for his almost finished life, or his
unpromising soul.

CATESBY

Withdraw, my lord. I'll help you to a horse.

KING RICHARD

Slave, I have set my life upon a cast,

And I will stand the hazard of the die. 10

I think there be six Richmonds in the field.

Five have I slain today instead of him.

A horse, a horse! My kingdom for a horse! [*Exeunt*]

[**5.7**] *Alarum. Enter Richard and Richmond, [meeting].*
*They fight. Richard is slain. [Exit Richmond.] Then,*
*retreat and flourish being sounded, enter Richmond,*
*Stanley Earl of Derby, bearing the crown, with other*
*lords and soldiers*

RICHMOND

God and your arms be praised, victorious friends,

The day is ours; the bloody dog is dead.

Q:

13 *Exeunt*] CIBBER; *not in* Q1

**5.7**.0.1 *meeting*] CIBBER; *not in* Q1   0.2 *Exit Richmond*] HAMMOND; *not in* Q1   0.3 *and flourish*] F; *not in* Q1   0.4 *Stanley Earl of*] *not in* Q1, F   0.5 *and soldiers*] HAMMOND; *&c.* Q1

F:

**5.7**.0.1 *Alarum*] Alatum   0.2–3 *Then . . . sounded,*] Retreat, and Flourish.   0.4–5 *other lords, and soldiers*] diuers other Lords (*altering* Q3 *'s omission of* Q1 *'s '&c.'*)

9 **cast** throw of the *die*

10 **the die** i.e. the singular of *dice*, though with play on the idea of death

11–12 **I . . . him** Richmond, like Henry IV (*1 Henry IV* 5.3.25 and 5.4.24–7) has other soldiers dressed as him to confuse the enemy and protect himself. Shakespeare invents this.

**5.7**.0.1 **Alarum** This direction for the trumpet call to battle may be accompanied with skirmishes between soldiers, so as to avoid an immediate re-entry for Richard.

0.2 **They fight** The single combat, found also in *True Tragedy*, is a fiction. In Holinshed, Stanley's brother Sir William arrived suddenly with 3,000 men, now supporting Richmond; Richard's soldiers were driven back and fled, and 'he himself, manfully fighting in the middle of his enemies, was slain' (p. 444). The combat has often been impressive and sustained in the theatre. See Introduction, pp. 69–70, 92.

**Richard is slain.** Capell altered the Q1 and F direction and had Richard and

Richmond exeunt fighting, and this arrangement has sometimes been followed on stage.

[*Exit Richmond.*] If Richard's body is for a moment alone on stage, the wheel has come full circle from the play's opening.

0.3 **retreat and flourish** Implying a trumpet call for retreat and a flourish for victory, probably sounded off-stage from opposite sides of the stage. The tents, or the framework of them, might still be in place, and even if they have been removed the audience would still be able to identify one side of the stage with Richard, the other with Richmond.

0.4, 7.1 **bearing the crown, He . . . head** According to Holinshed, Stanley 'took the crown of King Richard, which was found amongst the spoil in the field, and set it on the Earl's head, as though he had been elected king by the voice of the people' (p. 446). Stanley says at ll. 4–6 that he took the crown directly from Richard's head. It is not clear whether Richard's body remains on stage.

STANLEY EARL OF DERBY

Courageous Richmond, well hast thou acquit thee.

Lo here, this long usurpèd royalty

From the dead temples of this bloody wretch                    5

Have I plucked off, to grace thy brows withal.

Wear it, enjoy it, and make much of it.

⌈*He sets the crown on Richmond's head*⌉

RICHMOND

Great God of heaven say 'Amen' to all.

But tell me, is young George Stanley living?

STANLEY EARL OF DERBY

He is, my lord, and safe in Leicester town,                   10

Whither, if it please you, we may now withdraw us.

RICHMOND

What men of name are slain on either side?

STANLEY EARL OF DERBY ⌈*reading a paper*⌉

John Duke of Norfolk, Walter Lord Ferrers,

Sir Robert Brakenbury, and Sir William Brandon.

RICHMOND

Inter their bodies as become their births.                    15

Proclaim a pardon to the soldiers fled

That in submission will return to us,

And then, as we have ta'en the sacrament,

We will unite the white rose and the red.

Smile, heaven, upon this fair conjunction,                    20

Q:

4 royalty‸] ~.      7.1 *He . . . head*] CAPELL (*subs.*); *not in* Q1      8 RICHMOND Great] Q1 (*text*: *Richm.* Great); But Q1 (*catchword, anticipating the next line*)      11 Whither] Whether      13 STANLEY EARL OF DERBY] F (*Der.*); *speech-prefix not in* Q1      *reading a paper*] OXFORD (*subs.*); *not in* Q1, *but suggested by* Q1's *centred layout of ll.* 13–14      13 Ferrers] *Ferris*

F:

4 this] these      royalty] Royalties (*from* Q2)      7 enjoy it, and] and (*from* Q3)      11 if . . . now] (if you please) we may

3  **acquit** acquitted
4  **royalty** emblem of sovereignty
9  **But . . . living** Metrically deficient and variously emended: 'young' to 'your son' (Capell) or 'the young' (Marshall); 'is . . . living' to '. . . young George Stanley, is he living' (Taylor), etc.
13  **STANLEY EARL OF DERBY** F has '*Der.*'; in Q1 there is no speech-prefix, but '*Rich.*' is printed before l. 12 and l. 15. Richmond

might himself read the names (which are from Holinshed).
15  **as become their births** in accordance with their social standing by birth
18–41  **And . . . 'Amen'** Loosely based on Holinshed's account of Richmond's marriage in 'Henry VII': 'By reason of which marriage peace was thought to descend out of heaven into England, considering that the lines of Lancaster and York were

That long have frowned upon their enmity.
What traitor hears me and says not 'Amen'?
England hath long been mad, and scarred herself:
The brother blindly shed the brother's blood,
The father rashly slaughtered his own son,                    25
The son, compelled, been butcher to the sire.
All this divided York and Lancaster,
Deformèd in their dire division.
O now let Richmond and Elizabeth,
The true succeeders of each royal house,                      30

Q:
28 Deformèd] This edition; Deuided Q1;  United OXFORD

now brought into one knot and connexed
together, of whose two bodies one heir
might succeed to rule and enjoy the
whole monarchy and realm of England,
which before was rent and divided into
factions and partakings, whereby many a
man's life was lost, great spoils made of
people's goods, waste of wealth,
worship, and honour, all which ended in
this blessed and gracious connection, authorized by God' (p. 482). Davison suggests the influence of plays such as *Nice
Wanton* (1560), which has a final address
to the audience with a summary of the
action and its moral, and a prayer for the
Queen: *Popular Appeal in English Drama to
1850* (1982), pp. 81–2. *Ricardus Tertius*
also offers a model: the Epilogue cele-
brates 'the happy unity of both houses,
of whom the Queen's majesty came'
(p. 200). See Introduction, pp. 70–1.

18 **as . . . sacrament** i.e. in accordance with
an oath confirmed by holding a special
mass (held, according to Holinshed, at
Rheims Cathedral)

19 **the white rose and the red** i.e. the houses
of York and Lancaster, identified by their
emblems. Cibber highlights Richmond's
meaning by having Blunt inform him
that the Queen and Princess Elizabeth are
'On their way to gratulate your victory'.

20 **fair conjunction** Suggests a favourable
astrological conjunction, as well as
marriage.

23–34 **England . . . days** These lines are
more persuasive as a close to the First
Tetralogy than to *Richard III*, in which the
aggressor has been a single figure and

both he and most of his victims belong to a
single *house*.

25–6 **The . . . sire** As dramatized in *Richard
Duke of York* 2.5.

27–8 **All . . . division** Johnson, following
Rann's conjecture, reads 'All that divided . . .' and alters the punctuation after
'division' to a comma, which produces
an attractive reading (with 'All' the
object of 'conjoin', l. 31); but the difficulty addressed in the following note remains, as it does even after Wilson
additionally emends 'their' to 'this'.

28 **Deformèd** Q1's 'Deuided in their dire
deuision' is a dire tautology, especially
after 'deuided' in l. 27. It seems likely
that the context has produced a substitution, involving either association of ideas
or similarity in the form of the words.
Taylor's 'United' gives a neat paradox,
but undermines *conjoin* in l. 31. Other
possibilities include 'Debasèd', 'Declinèd',
'Defilèd', and 'Despisèd'. The reading
adopted here, *Deformèd*, links the Wars of
the Roses with their final physical mani-
festation in Richard; it harks back to
Richard's opening soliloquy, and makes
Richmond's address more relevant in relation to the play's action. The first and last
speeches share in their contrast between
war and peace, and the description of
peace as 'smooth-faced' at l. 33 indicates
the appropriateness of calling civil war
the cause of deformity.

29–41 **O now . . . Amen** Compare Richard's
ironic celebration of peace after war in 1.1.

30 **The true succeeders** Both were descended
from Edward III, Richmond on his
mother's side via the Lancastrian John of

By God's fair ordinance conjoin together,
And let their heirs, God, if thy will be so,
Enrich the time to come with smooth-faced peace,
With smiling plenty, and fair, prosperous days.
Abate the edge of traitors, gracious Lord,                       35
That would reduce these bloody days again
And make poor England weep in streams of blood.
Let them not live to taste this land's increase
That would with treason wound this fair land's peace.
Now civil wounds are stopped, peace lives again.                 40
That she may long live here, God say 'Amen'.

                                              *Exeunt*

   *FINIS*

Q:
41 here] heare     41.1*Exeunt*] F;  *not in* Q1

F:
32 their] thy (*from* Q3)

Gaunt by his third wife, and Elizabeth via
Richard Duke of York. Historically Richmond had a weaker claim to the
Lancastrian line than Clarence's children. Within the play his lineage is not
properly established.

31 **God's fair ordinance** Compare 4.4.173.
32 **their heirs** *Ricardus Tertius* and *True
   Tragedy* specifically name Elizabeth I
   (Richmond and Elizabeth's granddaughter) in their closing speeches.
35–9 **Abate . . . peace** Elizabethans might
   have related these lines to the Catholic
   threat.
35 **Abate the edge** blunt the sword
36 **reduce** restore
37 **in** with

38–9 **Let . . . peace** Interpretable as a threat
   to execute enemies.
38 **increase** harvest plenty, growth in prosperity. Land as nation is idealized as nurturing farmland. Stressed on the second
   syllable.
40 **are stopped** (a) have had their bleeding
   checked, (b) have ceased to be inflicted
41–41.1 **'Amen'.** *Exeunt* Productions often
   introduce an affirmation absent in the
   texts such as a general 'Amen' (as specified in Barton and Hall's *The Wars of the
   Roses*) and/or a flourish of trumpets. Jane
   Howell's BBC version ironized the ending
   by adding a tableau in which the camera
   moved across a pile of corpses to discover
   Queen Margaret presiding over it, cack-
   ling, with dead Richard in her arms.

APPENDIX A

# PASSAGES FIRST PRINTED IN THE 1623 FOLIO

THESE passages were probably deleted for stage performance.

A. After 1.2.152:

These eyes, which never shed remorseful tear,
No, when my father York and Edward wept
To hear the piteous moan that Rutland made
When black-faced Clifford shook his sword at him;
Nor when thy warlike father, like a child,                    5
Told the sad story of my father's death,
And twenty times made pause to sob and weep,
That all the standers-by had wet their cheeks
Like trees bedashed with rain. In that sad time
My manly eyes did scorn an humble tear;                    10
And what these sorrows could not thence exhale,
Thy beauty hath, and made them blind with weeping.

B. After 1.4.65:

O God, if my deep prayers cannot appease thee,
But thou wilt be avenged on my misdeeds,
Yet execute thy wrath in me alone.
O spare my guiltless wife and my poor children.

C. After 1.4.236:

Which of you, if you were a prince's son,
Being pent from liberty, as I am now,
If two such murderers as yourselves came to you,
Would not entreat for life? As you would beg
Were you in my distress—                    5

---

A.2–9 **when . . . rain** Staged in *Richard Duke of York* 1.4 and 2.1.

A.3 **hear** i.e. hear about

A.8 **That** so that

A.11 **exhale** draw out

C.4 **As** The interrupted sentence makes little sense if the passage is placed as in F, or if

relocated to 1.4.238 as in Hammond's edition (see commentary note to 1.4.236), but can be retained if the passage is relocated to after 1.4.242. Editors wishing to stabilize the sentence emend to 'Ah' (Theobald) or 'Ay' (Hammond).

# Appendix A

**D.** After 2.2.87:

DORSET

> Comfort, dear mother. God is much displeased
> That you take with unthankfulness his doing.
> In common worldly things 'tis called ungrateful
> With dull unwillingness to repay a debt
> Which with a bounteous hand was kindly lent;          5
> Much more to be thus opposite with heaven
> For it requires the royal debt it lent you.

RIVERS

> Madam, bethink you like a careful mother
> Of the young prince your son. Send straight for him,
> Let him be crowned; in him your comfort lives.          10
> Drown desperate sorrow in dead Edward's grave,
> And plant your joys in living Edward's throne.

**E.** After 2.2.109:

RIVERS

> Why with some little train, my lord of Buckingham?

BUCKINGHAM

> Marry, my lord, lest by a multitude
> The new-healed wound of malice should break out,
> Which would be so much the more dangerous
> By how much the estate is green and yet ungoverned.          5
> Where every horse bears his commanding rein
> And may direct his course as please himself,
> As well the fear of harm as harm apparent,
> In my opinion, ought to be prevented.

RICHARD DUKE OF GLOUCESTER

> I hope the King made peace with all of us;          10
> And the compact is firm and true in me.

RIVERS

> And so in me, and so, I think, in all.
> Yet since it is but green, it should be put
> To no apparent likelihood of breach,

E.1 Why . . . Buckingham] *2 lines*: train/

D.7 **For** because
D.8 **careful** caring
D.11 **Drown** i.e. bury (the sorrow envisaged as tears). The verb could conceivably be subjunctive, allowing an image of

suicide: 'let desperate Sorrow drown herself'.
E.5 **estate** political administration; state of things
**green** new, inexperienced

Which haply by much company might be urged.                    15
Therefore I say with noble Buckingham
That it is meet so few should fetch the Prince.
HASTINGS  And so say I.


**F.** After 3.4.106:

LOVEL
Come, come, dispatch. 'Tis bootless to exclaim.
HASTINGS
O bloody Richard! Miserable England,
I prophesy the fearful'st time to thee
That ever wretchèd age hath looked upon.


**G.** Lovel and Ratcliffe, instead of Catesby, bring on Hastings's
head at 3.5.18.1. At 3.5.99–100 Buckingham's parting speech
is variant, and is followed by lines in which Richard addresses
Lovel and Ratcliffe:

BUCKINGHAM
I go, and towards three or four o'clock
Look for the news that the Guildhall affords.               *Exit*
RICHARD DUKE OF GLOUCESTER
Go, Lovel, with all speed to Doctor Shaw—
Go thou to Friar Penker—bid them both
Meet me within this hour at Baynard's Castle.                  5
                              *Exeunt Lovel and Ratcliffe*


**H.** Expanding 3.7.5–8:

I did, with his contract with Lady Lucy,
And his contract by deputy in France,
Th'unsatiate greediness of his desire,
And his enforcement of the City wives,
His tyranny for trifles, his own bastardy,                      5
As being got your father then in France,
And his resemblance, being not like the Duke.

G.2 *Exit*] *Exit Buckingham*.    G.4 Penker] CAPELL; *Peuker* F    G.5.1 *Exeunt Lovel and Ratcliffe*]
*Exit*.

F.1 **bootless** futile                           notes to 3.5.73 and 3.7.9–11.
G.3 **Lovel** A minor character systematically    H.1–2 These charges are repeated more fully
    removed from Q1.                                  at 3.7.161–5.
G.3–4 **Doctor Shaw . . . Friar Penker** See

**I.** After 3.7.136:

> If not to answer, you might haply think
> Tongue-tied ambition, not replying, yielded
> To bear the golden yoke of sovereignty,
> Which fondly you would here impose on me.
> If to reprove you for this suit of yours,                    5
> So seasoned with your faithful love to me,
> Then, on the other side, I checked my friends.
> Therefore to speak, and to avoid the first,
> And then in speaking not to incur the last,
> Definitively thus I answer you.                              10

**J.** Expanding 4.1.0.1–4.1.2:

> *Enter the Queen, the Duchess of York, and Marquis Dorset,*
> *at one door, Anne Duchess of Gloucester with Clarence's*
> *daughter at another door*

DUCHESS OF YORK

> Who meets us here? My niece Plantagenet,
> Led in the hand of her kind aunt of Gloucester?
> Now, for my life, she's wand'ring to the Tower,
> On pure heart's love to greet the tender Prince.—
> Daughter, well met.

ANNE                          God give your graces both        5

> A happy and a joyful time of day.

QUEEN

> As much to you, good sister. Whither away?

**K.** After 4.1.92:

QUEEN

> Stay, yet look back with me unto the Tower.—
> Pity, you ancient stones, those tender babes
> Whom envy hath immured within your walls.
> Rough cradle for such little pretty ones,
> Rude, ragged nurse, old sullen playfellow                    5

J.0.1–3 *Enter . . . another door*] *Enter the Queene, Anne Duchesse of Gloucester, the | Duchesse of Yorke, and Marquesse Dorset.*     J.1 *Who . . . Plantagenet*] *2 lines:* here/     J.5–6 God . . . day] happy/

I.4 **fondly** foolishly
I.7 **checked** rebuked

K.2 **tender babes** Compare 4.3.9 and commentary note.

For tender princes, use my babies well.
So foolish sorrows bids your stones farewell.


## L. After 4.4.210:

KING RICHARD
  You speak as if that I had slain my cousins.
QUEEN
  Cousins indeed, and by their uncle cozened—
  Of comfort, kingdom, kindred, freedom, life.
  Whose hand soever lanced their tender hearts,
  Thy head, all indirectly, gave direction.      5
  No doubt the murd'rous knife was dull and blunt
  Till it was whetted on thy stone-hard heart
  To revel in the entrails of my lambs.
  But that still use of grief makes wild grief tame,
  My tongue should to thy ears not name my boys    10
  Till that my nails were anchored in thine eyes,
  And I, in such a desp'rate bay of death,
  Like a poor barque of sails and tackling reft,
  Rush all to pieces on thy rocky bosom.


## M. After 4.4.263:

KING RICHARD
  Say that I did all this for love of her.
QUEEN
  Nay then indeed she cannot choose but hate thee,
  Having bought love with such a bloody spoil.
KING RICHARD
  Look what is done cannot be now amended.
  Men shall deal unadvisedly sometimes,     5
  Which after-hours gives leisure to repent.
  If I did take the kingdom from your sons,
  To make amends I'll give it to your daughter.
  If I have killed the issue of your womb,

L.4 lanced] lanch'd

K.7 **sorrows** Rowe and others emend to 'sorrow', which admits a personification suggestive of the Queen herself.
L.5 **all** entirely. Or perhaps for 'albeit' or 'although'.

L.9 **But that** were it not that
  **still** constant
  **use** i.e. rehearsal in words
L.14 **Rush** Perhaps an error for 'Rushed'.
M.4 **Look what** whatever

To quicken your increase I will beget 10
Mine issue of your blood, upon your daughter.
A grandam's name is little less in love
Than is the doting title of a mother.
They are as children, but one step below;
Even of your mettle, of your very blood; 15
Of all one pain, save for a night of groans
Endured of her for whom you bid like sorrow.
Your children were vexation to your youth,
But mine shall be a comfort to your age.
The loss you have is but a son being king, 20
And by that loss your daughter is made queen.
I cannot make you what amends I would,
Therefore accept such kindness as I can.
Dorset your son, that with a fearful soul
Leads discontented steps in foreign soil, 25
This fair alliance quickly shall call home
To high promotions and great dignity.
The king that calls your beauteous daughter wife
Familiarly shall call thy Dorset brother.
Again shall you be mother to a king, 30
And all the ruins of distressful times
Repaired with double riches of content.
What? We have many goodly days to see.
The liquid drops of tears that you have shed
Shall come again, transformed to orient pearl, 35
Advantaging their love with interest
Of ten-times double gain of happiness.
Go then, my mother, to thy daughter go.
Make bold her bashful years with your experience.
Prepare her ears to hear a wooer's tale. 40
Put in her tender heart th'aspiring flame
Of golden sovereignty. Acquaint the Princess
With the sweet silent hours of marriage-joys.
And when this arm of mine hath chastisèd
The petty rebel, dull-brained Buckingham, 45

M.10 **quicken your increase** (a) propagate your living offspring, (b) bring your offspring back to life
M.14 **They** i.e. grandchildren
M.16 **all one** just as much
**pain** trouble, effort (shifting to the pain of childbirth in 'night of groans')
M.17 **of** by
**like** similar, the same

M.29 **Familiarly** as a member of the family
M.36 **love** Many editors follow Theobald in emending to 'loan', positing confusion between 'lone' and 'loue'.
M.37 **Of ten-times** Thus F, though the space between 'f' and 't' is narrow (leading some editors to record 'Of ten-times' as an emendation).
M.44 **chastisèd** punished

Bound with triumphant garlands will I come,
And lead thy daughter to a conqueror's bed;
To whom I will retail my conquest won,
And she shall be sole victoress, Caesar's Caesar.

QUEEN

What were I best to say?—Her father's brother          50
Would be her lord? Or shall I say her uncle?
Or he that slew her brothers and her uncles?
Under what title shall I woo for thee,
That God, the law, my honour, and her love
Can make seem pleasing to her tender years?          55

M.48  **retail** tell over (and/or, perhaps, 'be-          M.51  **lord** husband
stow'). See note to 3.1.77.

APPENDIX B

# QUARTO COPY FOR F

THE Folio collation (printed in the second sequence below the text of the play) includes notes recording Folio readings that were first introduced in the quarto editions standing between Q1 and F. It is here complemented by a list of readings that were altered in one of the intervening quartos but restored to the Q1 reading in F. The information is important because it provides a relatively controlled view of the process of annotation that made F a substantively distinct text from the quartos. It also affords independent confirmation from F where Q1 has an authoritative reading, for at least where the correction is not self-evident it will very probably reflect the independent testimony of the manuscript that the annotator was following.

This appendix arranges this listing under headings that identify the likely copy for different sections of F, as determined by Taylor in *Textual Companion*, pp. 229–30. It is not designed to contribute to a full record of derivative quarto readings, and so does *not* record (a) derivative quarto readings that are altered back to the Q1 reading in subsequent pre-1623 quarto reprints and that are rejected by editors; (b) readings from quartos that appeared after the quarto that is presumed to be the Folio copy at the point in question. For information on these matters, see Kristian Smidt's 1969 parallel text edition.

### Title

Q2 adds '*By William Shakespeare*'; Q3 adds 'Newly augmented.' between the title and '*By William Shakespeare*'.

### 1.1.0.1–1.2.151: Q3 Copy

1.1.1 our] *not in* Q3    1.1.9 wrinkled] wringled Q3    1.1.21 scarce] *not in* Q3    1.1.51 what's] what is Q3    1.1.133 buzzards] buzars Q3    1.1.143 you.] yon. Q3    1.2.14 these] the Q3    1.2.29 weary] awearie Q3    1.2.92 bloody] bloodly Q3    1.2.94 brothers] brother Q3    1.2.108 you] ye Q3    1.2.113 keen] kinde Q2    1.2.140 that] what Q3

### 1.2.152–210: Q6 Copy

1.2.153 friend] friends Q6    1.2.163 the] thy Q6    1.2.173 thy] the Q3    1.2.177 shalt thou] thou shalt Q2    1.2.185 shall I] I shall Q2

366

1.2.190 my] me Q5    1.2.192 devoted] *not in* Q2    1.2.207 Berkeley]
Bartley Q3

### 1.2.210.1–1.3.6: Q3 Copy

1.2.216 his] her Q3    1.2.217 hate] heate Q2    1.2.242 adorn] adore
Q3    1.2.244 some] a Q3

### 1.3.7–126: Q6 Copy

1.3.14 Is it] It is Q6    1.3.24 arrogance] arrogancie Q3    1.3.25 do]
*not in* Q3    1.3.26 false] *not in* Q3    1.3.30 of] *not in* Q6    1.3.39 to]
ot Q6    1.3.44 and] *not in* Q6    1.3.52 his] in Q5    1.3.54 all] *not in* Q6
1.3.69 ground] grounds Q6    1.3.71 make] may Q3    1.3.75 envy my]
enuy mine Q2    1.3.77 grants] grant Q3    1.3.113 of] Q1, Q3; or Q2;
*not in* Q6    1.3.117 my] when Q6

### 1.3.127–256: Q3 Copy

1.3.159 sharing] sharing out Q2    1.3.170 are] is Q3    1.3.175 faultless]
*not in* Q3    1.3.177 all] *not in* Q3    1.3.187 all . . . now] now . . . all Q2
1.3.195 ours] our Q3    1.3.203 rights] glorie Q2    1.3.208 wast] was Q3
1.3.236 That] *not in* Q2    1.3.245 that] when Q2    1.3.246 poisonous]
poisoned Q2

### 1.3.257–74: Q6 Copy

### 1.3.275–312: Copy uncertain

1.3.278 still] shall Q6    1.3.280 MARGARET] Q1 (*Q.M.*), Q3 (*Q. Mar.*); *Q.
Mary* Q5    1.3.286 those] them Q6    1.3.298 soothe] soothd Q6

### 1.3.313–1.4.10: Q3 Copy

1.3.321 grace] noble Grace Q3    1.3.325 mischiefs] mischiefe Q3
1.3.334 I] *not in* Q3    1.3.339 come] comes Q2    1.3.341 you] ye Q3

### 1.4.11–75: Q6 Copy

1.4.12 toward] towards Q6    1.4.30 wooed] wade Q5    1.4.41 to] of Q6
1.4.51 Dabbled] Dadled Q6    1.4.71 titles] tiles Q6    1.4.75 their] your
Q3

### 1.4.76–207: Q3 Copy

1.4.85 hereby] thereby Q3     1.4.89 charge] place Q3     1.4.125 swear] steale Q3     1.4.129 purse] piece Q3     1.4.142 thy] my Q3 1.4.144 sop] scoope Q3     1.4.153 speak] spake Q3     1.4.164 that] *not in* Q3     1.4.177 the] his Q3     1.4.198 lawless] lawfull Q2     1.4.201 springing] spring Q2

### 1.4.208–35: Q6 Copy

1.4.208 meed] neede Q2     1.4.233 by] for Q3     1.4.233 murd'ring] murdering Q2

### 1.4.236–49: Q3 Copy

1.4.238 devilish] and diuelish Q2

### 1.4.250–2.1.132: Q6 Copy

2.1.0.1 Dorset] *not in* Q3     2.1.6 friends] friend Q6     2.1.10 heart's] hears Q6     2.1.11 truly] *not in* Q3     2.1.26 This] Thus Q2     2.1.30 embracements] embracement Q6     2.1.52 my] *not in* Q3     2.1.61 true] *not in* Q3     2.1.62 will] *not in* Q6     2.1.65 Lord Rivers] my Lord Riuers Q5 2.1.74 your] you Q6     2.1.97 is it thou demand'st] it is thou demaundest Q6     2.1.115 garments] armes Q6     2.1.131 yours] your Q6

### 2.1.133–2.2.32.1: Q3 Copy

2.1.133 rashness] rawnes Q3

### 2.2.33–2.3.42: Q6 Copy

2.2.35 soul] selfe Q5     2.2.60 thy cries] the cries Q5     2.2.75 stays] stay Q6     2.2.77–8 never . . . never] euer . . . euer Q2     2.2.84 so do not] and so do Q2     2.2.93 your] you Q6     2.2.96 And] *not in* Q6     2.2.97 a] my Q2     2.2.102 of] for Q2     2.2.103 son] soone Q6     2.2.106 gently] greatly Q2     2.2.116 stay] be Q2     2.2.118 late] lately Q2     2.3.10 good] *not in* Q2     2.3.26 Will] Which Q2     2.3.29 not to] not Q6     2.3.35 men] may Q6

### 2.3.43–3.1.139: Q3 Copy

2.4.12 Gloucester] Clo. Q3     2.4.27 say] say that Q2     2.4.28 old] hold

Q3    2.4.30 biting] pretie Q2    2.4.33 His nurse?] *not in* Q2    2.4.43
thy] the Q2    3.1.29 have come] come Q3    3.1.33–8 to send . . . winne
the] thesend . . . winne to Q3    3.1.123 as] as as Q3    3.1.133 gives]
giue Q3


## 3.1.140–66: Q6 Copy


## 3.1.167–3.4.108: Q3 Copy (3.2.7–44, 3.2.84–118, and 3.4.91–108 queried)

3.1.170 thou] *not in* Q3    3.1.182 Mistress] gentle Mistresse Q3
3.1.195 all] *not in* Q2    3.2.5 these] the Q2    3.2.17 Go] Good Q3
3.2.23 instance] instancie Q2    3.2.32.1 *Catesby*] *Catesby to L. Hastings*
Q3    3.2.39 How] Who Q3    3.2.84 they] *not in* Q3    3.2.92 hats] hat
Q2    3.2.93.1 *Enter . . . Hastings*] *before l. 95 in* Q3    3.2.96 your] your
good Q3    3.3.8 ominous] dominious Q2    3.4.5 wants] let Q3    3.4.25
but] but now Q2    3.4.48 sudden] soone Q2    3.4.62 looks] face Q2
3.4.77 witchcraft] witchcrafts Q2    3.4.102 the] for the Q3


## 3.5.0.1–3.6.11: Q6 Copy (3.5.0.1–58 queried)

3.5.18.1 *Enter . . . head*] *after l. 19 in* Q3    3.5.26 Made] I made Q5
3.5.35 Were't] were Q6    3.5.40 you] ye Q3    3.5.41 form] course Q3
3.5.60 Misconster] Misconstrue Q6    3.5.61 But, my] My Q3    3.5.66
wished] wish Q6    3.5.68 come] came Q3    3.5.86 wars] wares Q6
3.5.92 my mother] my brother Q5; me brother Q6


## 3.6.12–3.7.16: Q3 Copy (queried)

3.7.9 lineaments] lienaments Q2    3.7.11 your] one Q3


## 3.7.17–55: Q6 Copy

3.7.17 an end] end Q3    3.7.18 I bid] I bad Q5 *catchwords and text*
3.7.18 did love] loues Q3    3.7.21 breathing] breathlesse Q3    3.7.24
meant] meanes Q6    3.7.35 love] loues Q3    3.7.40 at hand] *not in* Q3
3.7.40 some] somes Q6    3.7.45 easily] easie Q2    3.7.52 spoke]
spoken Q3


## 3.7.56–108: Q3 Copy

3.7.56 right] *not in* Q3    3.7.96 our] my Q2

### 3.7.109–4.1.0.2: Q6 copy

3.7.118 our] your Q5    3.7.121 the] this Q3    3.7.123 recure] recouer Q6    3.7.126 steward] Stweward Q3; Swteard Q6    3.7.127 Or] Nor Q3    3.7.131 very worshipful . . . loving] worshipfull . . . very louing Q3    3.7.141 ripe] right Q2    3.7.148 of] for Q3    3.7.162 contract] contracted Q6    3.7.164 afterward] afterwards Q6    3.7.167 a-many] many Q2    3.7.171 Seduced] Seduce Q6    3.7.173 his] this Q6    3.7.175 could I] could Q6    3.7.196 accept] except Q6    3.7.211 her] the Q3

### 4.1.1–4.4.50: Q3 Copy

4.1.18 DUCHESS OF YORK] *not in* Q2    4.1.18 I will] and will Q2    4.1.23.1 *Stanley*] *Standly* Q3    4.1.47 ta'en] taken Q2    4.1.52 sent] sent for Q3    4.1.57 be] *not in* Q3    4.1.70 mad] badde Q3    4.1.73 ere] euen Q2    4.1.75 Grossly] Crosselie Q2    4.1.76 subject] subiectes Q2; subsects Q3    4.1.82 no doubt,] *not in* Q2    4.1.85 DORSET] *Qu.* Q2    4.2.7 do I] I do Q3    4.2.32 My lord] Lord Q3    4.2.64 will] *not in* Q2    4.2.70 enemies] deepe enemies Q2    4.3.12 were] *not in* Q2; like Q3    4.3.20 Thus . . . remorse.] *line not in* Q3    4.3.45 com'st] comest Q2    4.3.54 wing] wings Q3    4.3.55 Jove's] Ioue Q3    4.4.20 Harry] *Mary* Q3    4.4.42 thou] and thou Q3    4.4.43 and] till Q2

### 4.4.51–199: Q6 Copy

4.4.55 thine] thee Q2    4.4.70 hell] hels Q6    4.4.76 bunch-backed] hunch-backt Q2    4.4.128 sweet] *not in* Q3    4.4.143 women,] ~. Q2    4.4.163 Thy . . . venturous;] *line not in* Q3    4.4.169 I] it Q2, Q5; *not in* Q4    4.4.169 disgracious] gratious Q3    4.4.184 art, ] art, and Q6

### 4.4.200–10: Q3 Copy

### 4.4.211–63: Q6 Copy

4.4.213 I intend] Intend Q6    4.4.220 high] height Q2    4.4.235 soul's love] soule Q6    4.4.235 thou love] thou Q2    4.4.244 woo] woe Q6    4.4.259 Mad'st] Madest Q2

### 4.4.264–94: Q3 Copy

4.4.267 forbids] forbid Q2    4.4.273 her sweet life] that title Q3    4.4.285 KING . . . past.] *line not in* Q2    4.4.286 QUEEN] *King.* Q2; *not in* Q3

#### 4.4.295–390: Q6 Copy

4.4.296 life] selfe Q3     4.4.300 thy] my Q6 (*some copies*)     4.4.307 worms] worme Q6     4.4.314 plants] plaints Q6     4.4.324 Immaculate] Immaculatd Q2; Immaculated Q3     4.4.325 tender] render Q3     4.4.344 they] there Q3     4.4.362 com'st] comest Q2     4.4.362 villain] villanie Q6

#### 4.4.391–442: Q3 Copy

#### 4.4.443–5.1.23: Q6 Copy (4.4.443–9 queried)

4.4.455.1 *Exeunt*] *not in* Q2     4.5.16 thy] my Q2     5.1.23 swords] sword Q3

#### 5.1.24–5.3.16: Q3 Copy

5.1.24 own] *not in* Q3     5.2.8 fields] field Q3     5.2.14 cheerly] cheere Q2

#### 5.3.17–5.4.19: Q6 Copy

5.4.1 set] seate Q2     5.4.13 lies] liet Q3, Q5;  lieth Q4, Q6

#### 5.4.20–5.7.41: Q3 Copy

5.4.67–8 early . . . arbitrament] eatly . . . arbrittement Q3     5.4.79 sundered] sundired Q3     5.4.107 *Richmond*] *K. Ri.* Q3     5.4.108 shouldst] shouldest Q2     5.4.117.2 *Ghosts*] *Ghoast* Q3     5.4.155.1 *Richard*] *K. Richard* Q3     5.4.183 I had] I Q2     5.4.184 Came] Came all Q3     5.5.30 think'st] thinkest Q2

# ALTERATIONS TO LINEATION

THIS Appendix records departures from the lineation of Q1. Editorial differentiation between verse and prose in the situation where Q1 prints a speech consisting of a single unjustified line is unrecorded. In the text, the verse lineation is clarified by dropping the first line of a speech below the speech-prefix when it is a verse line, as in other modern editions. The first line of a speech is indented when it completes a verse line that begins at the end of the previous speech (as, for example, at 1.1.43), a practice that stems from Capell. However, where part-lines could potentially be paired up in more than one pattern (as at 1.2.178–88), indentation has not been imposed.

Relineations involving Buckingham's speeches (see Introduction, p. 126) have been identified with 'B' in parentheses.

| | |
|---|---|
| 1.1.41 | Dive . . . comes] F; soul/ Q1 |
| 43–5 | His . . . Tower] POPE; *2 lines*: appointed/ Q1; *2 lines*: safety/ F |
| 94–5 | A cherry . . . tongue] STEEVENS; *1 line* Q1, F |
| 103–4 | I . . . Duke] CAPELL; forbear/ Q1; *3 lines*: grace/ forbear/ F |
| 1.2.142 | Here . . . me] *2 lines* Q1: Here/. Q's arrangement is not immediately affected by the stage direction as it is printed right of 'Where is he', but in the manuscript the direction was probably supposed to follow 'Here', as in the edited text. F interposes the stage direction. POPE prints as one line with the stage direction after it. |
| 1.4.78–9 | I would . . . legs] F; *verse-line?* Q1. In 1.4, Q1 repeatedly sets prose as verse. This might reflect marks in the manuscript copy to calculate the prose as type-lines. |
| 92–3 | No . . . wakes] F; cowardly/ Q1 |
| 94–5 | When . . . day] F; wakes/ Q1 |
| 98–9 | The . . . me] F; bred/ Q1 |
| 101–3 | Not . . . us] POPE; damned/ Q1; warrant/ (*omitting* 'for it') which/ F |
| 106–8 | I pray . . . twenty] POPE; will/ Q1; *verse with variant wording and line-breaks* F |
| 110–11 | Faith . . . me] F; *verse-line* Q1 |
| 118–19 | So . . . out] F; reward/ Q1 |
| 123–32 | I'll . . . without it] F; thing/ steal/ checks him/ detects/ mutinies/ obstacles/ found/ all/ every/ trust to/ Q1 |
| 133–4 | Zounds . . . Duke] F; me/ Q1 |

| | |
|---|---|
| 135–6 | Take . . . sigh] POPE; not/ Q1, F |
| 137–8 | Tut . . . thee] CAMBRIDGE; me/ Q1; F *variant* |
| 139–40 | Spoke . . . gear] POPE; reputation/ (*but end of sentence and justified type-line*) Q1; *similarly but unjustified* F |
| 141–3 | Take . . . room] F; *verse* Q1: sword/ |
| 3.1.156–7 | Well . . . intend] POPE (*omitting* 'hither'), STEEVENS; Catesby/ Q1, F |
| 3.4.9–10 | Why . . . mind] This edition; 1 *line* Q1; F *variant* |
| 13–14 | Than . . . mine] CAMBRIDGE; 1 *line* Q1; F *variant* (B) |
| 51–2 | Where . . . strawberries] CAPELL; 1 *line* Q1; F *variant* |
| 3.5.33–5 | That . . . preservation] F (*with variant wording*); 2 lines: imagined/ Q1 (B) |
| 69–70 | Yet . . . adieu] This edition; 1 *line* Q1; intend/ F (*with variant wording*) (B) |
| 99–100 | About . . . farewell] This edition; hear/ Q1; o'clock/ F (*with variant wording*) (B) |
| 3.7.5–6 | I . . . desires] This edition; 1 *line* Q1; F *variant* (B) |
| 77–8 | I . . . your lord] CAMBRIDGE; Catesby/ Q1; F *variant* (B) |
| 78–9 | My . . . assembled] This edition; 1 *line* Q1; F *variant* |
| 124–5 | Your . . . thereof] This edition; 1 *line* Q1; F *variant* (B) |
| 4.2.2–3 | Give . . . seated] ROWE; 3 lines: hand/ advice/ Q1; 3 lines: hand/ assistance/ F |
| 30–1 | Boy . . . circumspect] DAVISON; 1 *line* Q1; High . . . circumspect/ Boy F |
| 45–7 | My . . . abides] Q7; 2 lines: Dorset/ Q1; F *variant* |
| 4.4.211–12 | Madam . . . arms] This edition; 1 *line* Q1; F *variant* |
| 252–3 | A . . . body] F; 1 *line* (*variant text*) Q1 |
| 369–70 | What . . . Salisbury] CAMBRIDGE; 1 *line* Q1; F *variant* |
| 5.4.44–5 | Look . . . Ratcliffe] ROWE 1709; 1 *line* Q1, F |
| 5.5.6–7 | Tell . . . today] POPE; there/ (*with stage direction to the right*) Q1, F |
| 5.7.13–14 | John . . . Brandon] F; *centred, dividing* 'sir | Robert' Q1 |

Q1 sets parts of two speeches as a single type-line as follows:

*Printed by Simmes*: 1.2.99 Didst . . . yea    1.2.109 LADY . . . bedchamber    1.2.140 LADY . . . Plantagenet    1.3.232–3 MARGARET . . . Ha    1.4.155 CLARENCE . . . Ay    2.3.8–9 FIRST . . . world    3.1.124–5 RICHARD . . . Little    3.2.8 HASTINGS . . . word    3.2.58–9 I . . . lord    3.4.34–5 RICHARD . . . My lord

*Printed by Short*: 4.2.48–9 KING . . . lord    4.2.99 A . . . lord

# LONGER TEXTUAL NOTES

## 1. Act and Scene Divisions

The divisions are based on F's Latin divisions ('*Actus Primus. Scoena Prima.*', '*Scena Secunda.*', etc.) with the following exceptions:

(a) in Act 3, F is undivided after 3.4;
(b) in Act 4, F continues 4.2 where this edition begins 4.3; 4.4 and 4.3 are therefore in F '*Scena Tertia.*' and '*Scena Quarta.*';
(c) in Act 5, F is undivided after 5.2.

The regularization of F was effected by Pope, following a classical system that admitted more frequent scene divisions but ran on the scene at 3.6 and 5.4; Theobald, who initiated a scene-break at 5.4; and Capell, most of whose divisions have been accepted by subsequent editors. I follow the Oxford *Complete Works* in beginning a new scene in Act 5 whenever the stage is evidently cleared of actors except at 5.4.25, where Richmond and others remain on stage in their tent; the *Complete Works* begins a new scene here. The correspondence of modern editions is as follows:

| This edition | 5.1 | 5.2 | 5.3 | 5.4 | 5.4 | 5.5 | 5.6 | 5.7 |
|---|---|---|---|---|---|---|---|---|
| Oxford *Complete Works* | 5.1 | 5.2 | 5.3 | 5.4 | 5.5 | 5.6 | 5.7 | 5.8 |
| Most others (following Capell) | 5.1 | 5.2 | 5.3 | 5.3 | 5.3 | 5.3 | 5.4 | 5.5 |

The Folio act divisions have some relation to the play's structure in terms of its use of source material. However, one would not expect them to have been marked for performance before Shakespeare's company began to play at the indoor Blackfriars playhouse in 1608 or thereafter. Moreover, it is by no means clear that the manuscript consulted had been used in the theatre in connection with Jacobean revival.

Act 1 is largely fictional, with 1.4 drawing on a shortish passage in Holinshed. The following three acts are based on the events of 1483, with Act 2 using sporadic passages from More, Act 3 treating the source material much more closely, and Act 4 collating various details from More and Holinshed. Act 5 concentrates on the events of 1485, though they are conflated and rearranged at the beginning of Act 5, as they are too towards the end of Act 4. All this is enough to intimate that the play might have been written with the five-part structure loosely in mind, though the play's organization as dramatic action generates other structural formations.

## 2. Derby/Stanley

In stage directions and speech-prefixes, Lord Stanley is sometimes referred to as Stanley and sometimes as Derby. In both Q1 and F there is consistency within individual scenes but variation between scenes. The pattern of variation is similar in the two texts. The correspondence, though not exact throughout the play, is striking, and it cannot be dismissed as coincidence. It is independent of variations in the naming of the same character in the dialogue. This area of unexpected agreement between Q1 and F anomalously resists the persistent variation between them that prevails through the text generally.

The situation in the dialogue is easily summarized. In 1.3 the figure is five times called Derby. In the rest of the play, from 3.1 onwards, he is consistently 'Stanley'. There is therefore a single shift, consistent with a change of authorial practice during the course of composition, and it is common to Q1 and F. The theatrical identifiers show a more complicated pattern, and there is variation in that pattern between Q1 and F. In both texts there are five sections, occurring in the pattern ABCBC. The difference between Q1 and F lies in the altered boundary between the second 'B' and the second 'C'. Here, in brief, is the pattern in F:

A. In 1.3, 2.1, and 2.2, these scenes containing the character's only appearances in the first two acts, he is Derby, as in the dialogue for 1.3.
B. In the section from 3.1 to 4.4 he is consistently Stanley, as in dialogue, except in 3.4.
C. In 3.4, and again from 4.5 to the end, he is Derby, in conflict with the dialogue.

Q1 follows the same pattern, with the important exception that the second and longer section following pattern C begins at 4.2 instead of 4.5. For the theatrical identifiers Q1 and F agree in 1.3 (Derby), 2.1 (Derby), 3.2 (Stanley), 3.4 (Derby), 4.1 (Stanley), 4.5 (Derby), and all of Act 5 (Derby). As I argue more fully elsewhere, the agreement seems to represent a transcriptional link between MSF and MSQ; in other words it weighs against memorial transmission ('"Derby", "Stanley", and Memorial Reconstruction in Quarto *Richard III*', *Notes and Queries*, 245 (2000), 75–9).

## 3. Dorset/Grey

There are several anomalies in the treatment of the Queen's family and supporters in Q1 and F that are largely interrelated and need considering together:

(a) In 1.3, the first scene involving the Queen's allies, her son Dorset is given an entry in neither F nor Q1, though F gives an expanded and therefore independent version of the stage direction; Dorset has speeches at ll. 183, 254, and 262.

(b) At 1.3.7 and 1.3.54, lines given to Grey in F are spoken by Rivers in Q1, and at 1.3.30 a line is similarly transferred from the Queen to Rivers.

(c) At 1.3.207 the play in Q1 and F departs from its sources in naming Rivers and Dorset rather than Grey and Dorset as standers-by at the murder of Prince Edward.

(d) At 1.3.333, after the Queen's faction has left the stage, Richard refers to Rivers, Dorset, and Grey in F, but Rivers, Vaughan, and Grey in Q1.

(e) In 2.1, the next scene involving these characters, the King's injunction to Dorset and Rivers to make peace with each other (l. 7) is changed in Q1 to Rivers and Hastings.

(f) Later in the scene, at l. 65, Richard addresses Rivers and Dorset, then Woodville and Scales, in F, but simply Rivers and Grey in Q1.

(g) At 2.1.80 a line is transferred from the King in F to Rivers in Q1.

(h) In 2.4, the Messenger who in F announces the arrest of Rivers, Grey, and Vaughan becomes Dorset in Q1; Q1 introduces dialogue changes to make it clear that the arriver is the Queen's son.

A couple of the F/Q1 variants can be and usually are regarded as initial mistakes by Shakespeare that were later rectified. Dorset and Rivers need no reconciliation, whereas Rivers has been instrumental in Hastings's recent imprisonment; hence Q1's alteration at 2.1.7 is a necessary correction. At 2.1.65 Shakespeare seems to have been confused by Hall's misleading punctuation 'Lord Antony Wooduile erle Ryuers and lorde Scales, brother to the quene' (*Edward V* 5.12; Holinshed does not here refer to Scales); he evidently concluded that Woodville and Scales were independent characters, whereas they are further titular names of the figure more regularly called Rivers (the Folio entry opening 2.1 names Rivers and Woodville separately but not Scales). In writing the expository scenes for the Queen's allies, Shakespeare therefore had some difficulties in establishing the dramatic roles.

The variant in 1.3 involving a switch from Dorset to Vaughan is not quite so readily explained, as either text might stand. Vaughan plays no part in 1.3, and in F at l. 333 Richard simply names the figures of the Queen's party who have been on stage. But Richard will not direct his revenge against Dorset as he here anticipates; it is, as Q1 has it, Rivers, Vaughan, and Grey who will become his next victims after Clarence. Later these three are repeatedly mentioned as a single group; they appear together on their way to execution at Pomfret, and return together to haunt Richard as ghosts in Act 5. Q1's introduction of Vaughan in 1.3 prepares for the news of his arrest in 2.4, which otherwise refers to a figure who has been neither shown on stage nor mentioned in dialogue. Several of the other changes can similarly be seen as part of a process of textual adjustment to consolidate dramatic roles. Four speeches are transferred to Rivers, who will take the leading role amongst the arrested lords at Pomfret in 3.3. Rivers also benefits from the alteration at 2.1.7. Grey is brought more explicitly into association with Rivers at 2.1.65. By the time of their execution, Rivers, Vaughan and Grey are in Q1 more firmly established both as individuals and as a group.

In F, Dorset's role early in the play is stable but not particularly clear. At 1.3.255 he is addressed as 'master Marquis', but he is not identified as the Queen's son in that scene. He is 'your son Dorset' at 2.1.19, and is named a few times; his dramatic function is becoming clearer, at least after the error in l. 7. However, his role is diminished in Q1 in that two addresses to him are redirected to other characters. His replacement of the messenger in 2.4 is therefore purposeful. It reaffirms that he is the Queen's son, and it actively separates him from the victims at Pomfret by bringing him to the Queen as the bearer of the ill tidings of their fate.

The alterations from F to Q1 at 2.1.65 involve, as well as cancellation of the redundant titles for Rivers, a switch from Dorset to Grey. Whereas the removal of Dorset at 2.1.7 seems necessary, there is no reason why he should not be included here. Because Grey is addressed, he needs to be on stage throughout the scene, as would be allowed—though not required— by Q1's permissive '*&c.*' at the end of the scene's opening entry. As Taylor notes, Grey may have been introduced to compensate for the diminishment of the Queen's retinue once it was realized that Woodville and Scales needed deleting. Another explanation would be a memorial confusion, but, even assuming memorial transmission, this seems less likely, partly because it is unparsimonious. It would be highly uncharacteristic of Q1, which is an efficient text in terms of the number of actors' parts, to introduce a new but superfluous character unless by design.

Q1's change in 2.1 causes the scene to mirror 1.3. In 1.3 there is no entry for Dorset and no indication that he is on stage in F or Q1 until l. 183. Long before he becomes involved in the action, Grey has fallen silent and may as well not be there. In 2.1 there is no explicit entry for Grey in either text. By the time he is mentioned in Q1, Dorset has long been silent. Shakespeare can scarcely have drafted 1.3 with a view to playing two characters who are on stage at the same time by one actor, but it is plausible that he began the scene with no plan to introduce Dorset, or even that he initially thought of Grey and *Rivers* as the Queen's sons. And this would be consistent with the fact that F makes no reference to Vaughan, and hence to the grouping Rivers, Vaughan, Grey, until 2.4. It is only at this point that the play as presented in F starts to distinguish between a son who will become a member of a group of Richard's victims and a son, Dorset, who will survive.

I suggest, therefore, that F reflects Shakespeare's initial confusion between Dorset and Grey, which was part of a larger uncertainty as to the number of the Queen's allies and their plot functions. In 1.3 and 2.1 he consistently referred to only one of them at a time; the one named in the initial entry has the first speaking part and his other self takes over later in each scene. Thus when Rivers instead of Grey is paired with Dorset as a stander-by at 1.3.207, there would be a very practical reason for making this change if Dorset and Grey could not be identified in one breath as separate figures. By the time the play reached the stage various other difficulties had been resolved, but it looks as though considerations of doubling actors' roles led to the play retaining Shakespeare's temporary conflation of Grey and Dorset into a single figure in 1.3 and 2.1. In 2.1, Richard's change of address from Dorset in F to Grey in Q1 can now be seen as purposeful in a different way from that suggested by Taylor. It keeps alive the doubleness of referent for the single figure on stage, and it anticipates the execution scene in naming Grey alongside Rivers.

The renaming of the Folio's Messenger in 2.4 as Dorset means that Dorset, unequivocally identified as the Queen's son, can speak of his brother's fate, and this would have been particularly needful if the two brothers had not been distinguished previously. Yet the theatrical economy need not have stopped here. If Dorset and Grey effectively were a single figure in 1.3 and 2.1, they can still be played by the same actor in 2.4 (the message scene: Dorset), 3.3 (the execution scene: Grey), and 3.7 (Dorset's last appearance before fleeing from the play's action).

For further details, see John Jowett, 'Pre-Editorial Criticism and the Space for Editing: Examples from *Richard III* and *Your Five Gallants*', in *Problems of Editing*, ed. Christa Jansohn, *Beihefte zu Editio*, 14 (1999), pp. 127–49.

### 4. 'inductious' (1.1.32)

This is clearly Q1's reading, though it sometimes passes unrecorded. Editors, including Davison in his edition of Q1, follow the Folio reading 'Inductions' without comment, though it actually derives from a correction in Q3. It should be kept in mind that Q3 might occasionally introduce corrections with reference to an authoritative source (see Introduction, 'Quarto Reprints'), though it might be ill-advised to accept an emendation of a valid Q1 reading on this basis. F shows no sign of copy annotation between l. 26 and l. 40.1; moreover, an annotator could easily fail to notice a discrepancy between printed copy 'inductions' and manuscript 'inductious'. Hence it is impossible to have any confidence that F confirms the reading by reference to the manuscript.

For an editor whose text is based primarily on Q1, the variant needs careful consideration not least because the Q3–F reading is universally accepted and commands assent through its familiarity. Q1's *Inductious* would probably be a Shakespeare coinage, readily made on the analogy of 'danger-ous'. It may be compared with *Timon* 4.3.188, where *conceptious* occurs evidently as a nonce word (as pointed out by P. Maas, in 'Two Passages in *Richard III*', in *Review of English Studies*, 18 (1942), 315–17, p. 317). *Inductious* is similar in meaning as well as form to *conceptious*. The word is cited in *OED* on account of its later use by John Ford (1620), but failed to enter the language more widely from the Shakespearian precedent if only because it was unavailable in editions of *Richard III* from 1602 onwards. As early as 1606 Marston's *The Fawn* (1604–6) at 2.1.196 parodically quotes the Q3 reading.

The theatrical sense of Q3's *inductions* is at first sight a point in its favour. Adjectival *inductious*, however, is very precisely applicable to Richard and his plots, and it is appropriate too that the plot-maker should be a word-maker. Though technically less metatheatrical, *inductious* may in practice be more so, as it describes more precisely and urgently this inductive moment in which the plots initiating the play's action are brought into view. It would, then, be a mistake to take the fact that *induction* occurs at 4.4.5 as a point in Q3's favour, for where Margaret in 4.4 describes a fated and unalterable structure of events, Richard's emphasis is on an evolving process that he himself is very actively shaping.

### 5. 'yea' (1.3.98 etc.)

The first of eight variants where Q1 'yea' becomes 'I', for 'ay', in F is at 1.3.98. E. A. J. Honigmann ('On the Indifferent and One-Way Variants in Shakespeare', *The Library*, V, 22 (1967), 189–204) pointed to a Folio editor's distaste for 'yea', but Taylor explains the variant as Simmes's Compositor A's distaste for 'ay'. The latter theory is insufficient in itself, as for two of the variants Short rather than Simmes was the Quarto printer. Authorial or scribal tinkering is also possible. As the only certainty is that not all the variants were introduced in Simmes's shop, and as it is impossible to arbitrate as to the origin of each variant in Simmes's section, Q1 has not been emended.

### 6. 'broken rancour . . . splinted' (2.2.104–6)

An understanding of the overdetermined imagery rests on the following considerations of individual words:

(a) *Broken*: *OED*, sense 2, 'Rent, ruptured, torn, burst'; sense 6, '. . . subdued, humbled'; sense 8, 'Reduced to obedience . . .'; sense 11, 'Routed, dispersed'.

(b) *Rancour*: i.e. 'rankness', in various senses of *rank*: sense 1, 'Proud, high-minded, haughty; froward, rebellious' (last recorded *c*.1560, but surely relevant); sense 5, 'Vigorous or luxuriant in growth . . . large and coarse'; sense 6, '. . . swollen . . .'; sense 14b, 'Corrupt, foul; festering'.
(c) *Splinted*: The critical word in determining that the mixed metaphor of ll. 104–6 is primarily of bone-setting. The word could be accommodated to the figure of a lanced swelling if it could itself mean 'lanced', but *OED* does not support such a gloss. *OED* does record Richard Carew in 1594 using *splint* to mean specifically 'Of the heart: to burst or split'. This, however, is of little help in that the sense, if current, would not accord with the process of healing suggested by 'knit and joined together'. Carew's usage does at least suggest how the word might, in a confused way, find company with *broken* and *hearts*, but still leaves *splinted* without a place in the metaphor of a swollen wound.

## 7. The Cardinal (2.4.0.1)

In Holinshed there is only one prelate involved in these events—though he is Archbishop of York rather than Cardinal Archbishop of Canterbury. Hall indicates that Rotherham, Archbishop of York, was the cleric who encouraged the Queen to take sanctuary. This might have influenced F, which has the 'Archbishop' in 2.4 and the 'Cardinal' in 3.1.

However, as F (like Q1) identifies neither episcopal sees nor personal names, its designations could merely be different ways of referring to the Cardinal Archbishop. Moreover, as Taylor points out, it is entirely possible that the manuscript behind F read 'Archbishop' throughout: for most of 3.1 there is evidently no recourse to the manuscript, so it is inevitable that F prints 'Cardinal' in this scene; in doing so it is merely following the Quarto copy. The only scrap of evidence that might suggest the text was altered to establish a single dramatic figure *after* the Folio manuscript version had been written is the Cardinal's exit and re-entry in Q1 at 2.4–3.1, but re-entry in procession might have been acceptable.

## 8. 'Shall we hear from you, Catesby, ere we sleep?' (3.1.185)

Compare 4.2.82–3, where virtually the same words and reply are spoken in dialogue between Richard and Tyrrell, but in Q1 only. This adds further urgency to the time sequence in 4.2, and the lines' addition may be connected with its addition of the 'clock' passage several lines below. The exchange is less appropriate in 3.1, the scene where it is printed in both Q1 and F, in that Catesby will in the event visit Hastings in the early morning, not 'ere we sleep'. Where F elsewhere gets the time-scheme confused, Q1 usually straightens it, but here does not. A shared error would be hard to explain, especially as F alters copy speech-prefix '*Glo.*' to '*Rich.*', a change that could not derive from the manuscript if the lines were not in it.

The exchange probably always stood in 3.1. It seems to me that Q1's repetition is purposefully echoic, drawing attention to the compulsively repetitive nature of Richard's crimes. And this would explain why the inconsistency in the time sequence in 3.1–3.2 had to stand.

### 9. 'razed his helm' (3.2.9)

The sense of *razed* in More and Q1, slashed (*OED*, *raze*, 1; *rase*, 1), is the same as the altered form *rash* in *History of Lear* 14. 56, 'In his anointed flesh rash boarish fangs'. Q1 in this passage is closer to the source, as F has 'rased off', which seems to disallow More's sense (see Commentary). The meaning in F, and perhaps additionally in Q1, is 'pulled off', as in *OED*'s one instance (*c*.1400) of the altered form *rache*, 'His head was bare, his helme was rached'. Hammond understands *raze* as 'scrape off, erase' and *helm* as the figure of a helmet on a coat of arms, but *OED*'s first instance of *helm* in this sense is 1864 (and even *helmet* in this sense is not before 1610), and Hammond's reading seems a poor alternative to the bloody image in More.

### 10. BISHOP (3.4.6)

Q1's '*Riu.*' is the same as the speech-prefix the compositor had set for Rivers eight lines previously. As he had not found the Bishop of Ely named in the stage direction, he could easily have misread 'Bi.' as 'Ri.' The next speech-prefix for the Bishop (l. 9), on the second line of a new page (G1ᵛ), reads 'B*i.*', which lends some support to this conjecture of the reading in the copy. Further, the irregular Roman 'B' at l. 9 may have arisen because a '*Ri.*' prefix on the new page was corrected. Hammond's suggestion that the parts were doubled seems less likely, and would involve the actor immediately re-entering in the new role.

### 11. Edward's Faults ('I did . . . France', 3.7.5–8)

Thus Q1. For F's more expansive version, see Appendix A, Passage H. It is tempting to argue that Q1 was cut in the printing house to allow the text to be accommodated to the page, because the passage occurs near the foot of the last page of inner sheet G, which was the final sheet printed by Simmes. However, a compositor would be more likely to cut whole typelines than make the adjustment seen in ll. 5–6 (which Q1 prints as one line). An alternative explanation is that 'The allegations made against Edward were very similar to those made with more truth against Henry VIII'

(Marshall) and so might have been censored, though it is not clear on what basis Q1's lines (here and in 3.5) might have been permitted but those excluded from Q1 disallowed. The cuts more probably result from theatrical adaptation. They reduce the amount of repetition between this passage and (a) Richard's instructions to Buckingham at the end of 3.5, (b) Buckingham's speech beginning 3.7.157. And, typical of Q1 as a whole, they avoid reference to incompletely explained historical events of which the audience might have had little knowledge, or for which their understanding might have depended on their remembering details from *Richard Duke of York*.

### 12. 'My niece Plantagenet' (4.1.1)

In F *niece* must be taken specifically in the recorded sense 'granddaughter', because it refers to an unspecified girl who is 'Led in the hand of her kind Aunt of Gloster'. Theobald identified her as Clarence's daughter. Barton and Hall, in *Wars of the Roses* (1970), interestingly named her as the Queen's daughter Princess Elizabeth, though there is no reason why Anne should lead her. Either girl would be *Plantagenet* as a granddaughter of Richard Duke of York. The potentially touching but unintegrated detail of Anne caring for Clarence's daughter may have been eliminated because it caused confusion, and it often disappears in modern performance too. The identity of the *niece* cannot be inferred directly from the text, and there is plenty of information for the audience to assimilate without this added complication.

F has some characteristics of a duplication, as can be seen by breaking it into two sections (TLN 2473–7, as in Appendix A, Passage J.1–4; and TLN 2478–84, as in J.5–7, then 4.1.3–6):

A:      *Duch. Yorke.*  Who **meetes** [1] vs heere?
        My **Neece** [2] *Plantagenet*,
        Led in the hand of her kind Aunt of Gloster?
        Now, **for my Life** [3], shee's **wandring to the Tower** [4],
        **On pure hearts loue** [5], **to greet the tender Prince** [6].

B:      [*Duch. Yorke.*] **Daughter** [2], **well met** [1].
        *Anne.*  God giue your Graces both, a happie
        And a ioyfull time of day.
            *Qu.*  As much to you, good Sister: whither away?
            *Anne.*  **No farther then the Tower** [4], and **as I guesse** [3],
        **Vpon the like deuotion** [5] as your selues,
        **To gratulate the gentle Princes** [6] there.

One explanation of F would be that Shakespeare redrafted the passage to eliminate the business with Clarence's daughter, in which case he did so

immediately as he wrote, because 'Kind sister, thanks' in l. 6 responds to
Anne's speech in version B. To judge by Q1, the final outcome was to re-
vert to the first verse-line of A before switching to a necessarily reworked
fourth line of B and thence following B more closely.

### 13. 'so mad—' (4.1.70)

The early texts read 'so madde,' (Q1), 'so badde,' (Q3), 'so mad,' (F).
Wilson, following a conjecture by Ferrers, emends 'so, made'. Compare
1.2.24, where, in the words recapitulated here, the equivalent word is
'made'. Q1's 'so madde' is unexpected as a literal recollection of the earlier words, yet there is no reason why it should not be a retrospective and
self-recriminating 'aside'. As Taylor points out, F's correction of Q3 copy
'badde' to 'mad' confirms 'mad' as the required reading. Taylor emends
by introducing 'made' after 'miserable' in l. 71; this seems unnecessary.

### 14. Declining the Queen ('For queen . . . of me', 4.4.95–8)

In F, ll. 95 and 96 are transposed, as are ll. 97 and 98, and F prints between the second pair a line not in Q1, 'For she being feared of all, now
fearing one:'. D. L. Patrick, *Textual History of 'Richard III'* (1936), defend-
ing F, noted that its sequence 'wife . . . mother . . . sued to . . . queen' corresponds with the questions in ll. 87–9, 'husband . . . children . . . sues
. . . the Queen'. But (a) neither text responds to 'Where be thy brothers?';
(b) F's line following this sequence '. . . scorned at me' disrupts the
parallel, whereas Q1's equivalent 'commanding all' corresponds with
'the bending peers that flattered thee'; (c) Q1 establishes its own logic: the
'wife . . . mother . . . queen' sequence of ll. 93–5 and the 'sued to . . .
commanding' sequence in ll. 96–7, neither of which cohere in F. F closes
the passage with a firm rhyming couplet 'one . . . none', whereas Q1 leads
into the 'thou'/'me' comparisons of ll. 103–7.

### 15. So thrive I ('Madam . . . wronged', 4.4.211–14)

Compare ll. 317–19 and Commentary. Both passages, especially the present one, are variant in F, where l. 211 is preceded by a passage not in Q1
(see Appendix A, Passage L). Q1's alteration of 'successe' to 'attempt'
avoids the strained logic of 'So thrive I in my . . . success'. F's 'enterprize
| And' before 'dangerous' disappears (at the cost of leaving an unassim-
ilated part-line of verse or, as Q1 prints it, a single sixteen-syllable line
'Madam . . . arms') probably because the noun is synonymous with
'attempt' (though it is not impossible that 'enterprise' was accidentally
deleted along with the previous speech). Later, at l. 318, the word

'attempt' again replaces a Folio reading, 'Affayres'. The two 'attempt' variants and the emendation of 'bloody warres' to 'hostile arms' at l. 212 alike reinforce the parallels between the passages. As the parallels are intrinsic even to F and are clearly deliberate, it seems best to regard the reinforcement of them as deliberate too.

## 16. The Dispersal of Buckingham's Army ('Your . . . mistake', 4.4.427–31)

F's version is:

> *Mess.* The newes I haue to tell your Maiestie,
> Is, that by sudden Floods, and fall of Waters,
> *Buckinghams* Armie is dispers'd and scatter'd,
> And he himselfe wandred away alone,
> No man knowes whither.
>     *Rich.* I cry thee mercie:

Q1's version of the Messenger's speech is more dramatically effective in its opening, and the Messenger's risky 'Your grace mistakes' is neatly picked up in Richard's 'I did mistake' at l. 431. The singular 'flood' in Q1 at l. 428 is consistent with 'fall', and singular 'water' is consistent with Hall's and Holinshed's accounts. But Q1's two successive hexameters with feminine endings strain metrical credibility. Its 'fled' is also metrically irregular, and less poetic, perhaps, than F's 'wandred away alone'; but is more to the point, and closer to Hall's and Holinshed's report that he 'was of necessity compelled to fly'. The shortening here connects with Q1's expansion of l. 431: F's unmetrical 'No man knowes whither. | I cry thee mercie' becomes a more regular line with the last syllable of 'whither' lending the initial unstressed syllable (a development that is particularly hard to reconcile with memorial transmission by actors). The temptation to conflate Q1 and F in this passage is strong, but has been resisted. Q1 is fully adequate, in some respects better than F, and deficient mainly by way of metre.

## 17. The Orations (5.4.215.1–249, 5.5.42.1–70)

Davison suggests that Shakespeare belatedly revised a corrupted text by reconstructing both Richmond's and Richard's orations from Holinshed, citing (a) the unusual form of the stage directions ('They are not announcements to be spoken, they do not indicate action, and what they describe is self-evident'), (b) the unusually close verbal correspondences with the source, and (c) a cluster of specific details favouring Holinshed over Hall (Holinshed's phrases indentifying the addressees, the plural *pains* where Hall has the singular at 5.4.237, and the factual error shared with the second edition of Holinshed noted at 5.5.53).

Yet 5.4.216–47 and 5.5.43–70 are more likely to be late additions than replacements of originals. In this they might be like the 'clock' passage at 4.2.99–118, which also contains a detail found only in Holinshed (see Commentary to 4.2.103–7). The orations are out of historical sequence in that Hall and Holinshed have them spoken on the battlefield, not in the camp, and the play reverses their order. They both make a rather awkward transition from a small group of on-stage leaders to an 'army'. Moreover, as Wilson noted, Richard's oration follows oddly after his resolute couplet at 5.5.41–2. The orations are completely separable, in that the immediate dialogue and action proceed unimpaired without them, and there is no moment elsewhere in the play that anticipates, recalls, or presupposes them. They retrieve the sense of historical actuality, but they do so at the expense of imposing major set-piece speeches between Richard's 'conscience' soliloquy and his death, thus diminishing the impact of the soliloquy on the play's ending.

As for the stage directions, which are unique in Shakespeare, an obvious though speculative interpretation of them would be that, as they are literary in quality, the speeches they head might have been supplied specifically for the printed text, the only context in which the words could function in a way comparable with Hall's and Holinshed's marginal notes. It may be significant that there are similar stage directions in *Ricardus Tertius* (pp. 216–17), where they are part of the classicized presentation of the text.

In short, the oration speeches seem belated and in some respects extraneous to the play on stage. In defence of them, they are dramatic in the particular sense that they can and probably should be taken to address the theatre audience, which is thereby implicated in the action. They sustain the sense of balance and formality that runs throughout the battle sequence, most obviously in the dream episode, again developing the contrast between Richard and Richmond through similarities of situation. In these respects they are well integrated.

# PASSAGES FROM SIR THOMAS MORE'S
## *HISTORY OF RICHARD III*

THE following passages from More as printed in Raphael Holinshed's *Chronicle* (1587 edition) are modernized in spelling and punctuation. Headings here printed in round brackets are set out as marginal notes in Holinshed. Notes in square brackets are editorial.

### Passage 1 (p. 362)

(*The description of Richard III*:) Richard, the third son, of whom we now entreat, was in wit and courage equal with either of them [Edward and Clarence], in body and prowess far under them both, little of stature, ill-featured of limbs, crook-backed, his left shoulder much higher than his right, hard-favoured of visage, and such as is in states [i.e. among people of rank] called a warly [i.e. a warlike (visage)], and in other men otherwise. He was malicious, wrathful, envious, and from afore his birth ever froward. It is for truth reported that the Duchess his mother had so much ado in her travail that she could not be delivered of him uncut, and that he came into the world with the feet forward, as men be born outward, and, as the fame runneth also, not untoothed, whether men of hatred report above the truth or else that nature changed her course in his beginning, which in the course of his life many things unnaturally committed. So that the full confluence of these qualities, with the defects of favour and amiable proportion, gave proof to this rule of physiognomy: 'Distortum vultum sequitur distortio morum' [distortion of character follows a distorted countenance].

None evil captain was he in the war, as to which his disposition was more meetly than for peace. Sundry victories had he, and sometimes overthrows, but never on default as for his own person, either of hardiness or politic order. Free was he called of dispense, and somewhat above his power liberal. With large gifts he gat him unsteadfast friendship, for which he was fain to pill and spoil in other places, and got him steadfast hatred. He was close and secret, a deep dissembler, lowly of countenance, arrogant of heart, outwardly companionable where he inwardly hated, not letting to kiss whom he thought to kill, dispiteous and cruel, not for evil will alway, but ofter for ambition, and either for the surety or increase of his estate.

Friend and foe was muchwhat indifferent. Where his advantage grew, he spared no man's death whose life withstood his purpose. (*The death of*

*King Henry VI:*) He slew with his own hands King Henry VI, being prisoner in the Tower, as men constantly said, and that without commandment or knowledge of the King, which would undoubtedly, if he had intended that thing, have appointed that butcherly office to some other than his own born brother. Some wise men also ween that his drift covertly conveyed lacked not in helping forth his brother of Clarence to his death, which he resisted openly, howbeit somewhat, as men deemed, more faintly than he that were heartily minded to his wealth [well-being].

### Passage 2 (pp. 379–83)

Thus many things coming together, partly by chance, partly of purpose, caused at length not common people only, that wound with the wind, but wise men also, and some lords eke, to mark the matter and muse thereon, so far forth that the Lord Stanley, that was after Earl of Derby, wisely mistrusted it, and said unto the Lord Hastings that he much misliked these two several councils. 'For while we', quoth he, 'talk of one matter in the t'one place, little wot we whereof they talk in the t'other place.'

'My lord,' quoth the Lord Hastings, 'on my life, never doubt you. For while one man is there which is never thence, never can there be thing once moved that should sound amiss toward me but it should be in mine ears ere it were well out of their mouths.' This meant he by Catesby, which was of his near secret counsel and whom he very familiarly used [. . .]

But surely great pity was it that he [Catesby] had not had either more truth or less wit. For his dissimulation only kept all that mischief up; in whom, if the Lord Hastings had not put so special trust, the Lord Stanley and he had departed with diverse other lords and broken all the dance for many ill signs that he saw, which he now construes all to the best, so surely thought he that there could be none harm toward him in that council intended where Catesby was. And of truth the Protector and the Duke of Buckingham made very good semblance unto the Lord Hastings, and kept him much in company. And undoubtedly the Protector loved him well and loath was to have lost him, saving for fear lest his life should have quailed their purpose.

For which purpose he moved Catesby to prove with some words cast out afar off whether he could think it possible to win the Lord Hastings unto their part. But Catesby, whether he assayed him or assayed him not, reported unto them that he found him so fast, and heard him speak so terrible words, that he durst no further break. And of truth, the Lord Chamberlain, of very trust, showed unto Catesby the distrust that others began to have in the matter. And therefore he, fearing lest their motion might with the Lord Hastings minish his credence, whereunto only all the matter leaned, procured the Protector hastily to rid him. And much the rather for that he trusted by his death to obtain much of the rule that the Lord Hastings bare in his country, the only desire whereof was the allective [enticement] that induced him to be partner and one special contriver of all this horrible treason.

(*An Assembly of Lords in the Tower*:) Whereupon soon after, that is to wit on the Friday, being the 13th of June, many lords assembled in the Tower, and there sat in council, devising the honourable solemnity of the King's coronation, of which the time appointed then so near approached that the pageants and subtleties were in making day and night at Westminster, and much victuals killed therefore that afterward was cast away. These lords so sitting together communing of this matter, the Protector came in amongst them, first about nine of the clock, saluting them courteously, and excusing himself that he had been from them so long, saying merrily that he had been a sleeper that day.

After a little talking with them, he said unto the Bishop of Ely, 'My lord, you have very good strawberries at your garden in Holborn. I require you let us have a mess of them.' 'Gladly, my lord,' quoth he, 'Would God I had some better thing as ready to your pleasure as that!' And therewithal in all the haste he sent his servant for a mess of strawberries. The Protector set the lords fast in communing, and thereupon praying them to spare him for a little while, departed thence. (*The behaviour of the Lord Protector in the assembly of the lords*:) And soon after one hour, between ten and eleven, he returned into the chamber amongst them all, changed, with a wonderful sour angry countenance, knitting the brows, frowning and fretting, and gnawing on his lips, and so sat him down in his place.

All the lords were much dismayed, and sore marvelled at this manner of sudden change, and what thing should him ail. Then, when he had sitten still a while, thus he began: 'What were they worthy to have that compass and imagine the destruction of me, being so near of blood unto the King, and Protector of his royal person and his realm?' At this question, all the lords sat sore astonied, musing much by whom this question should be meant, of which every man wist himself clear. Then the Lord Chamberlain, as he that for the love between them thought he might be boldest with him, answered and said that they were worthy to be punished as heinous traitors, whatsoever they were. And all the other affirmed the same. 'That is', quoth he, 'yonder sorceress my brother's wife, and other with her,' meaning the Queen.

At these words many of the other lords were greatly abashed that favoured her. But the Lord Hastings was in his mind better content that it was moved by her than by any other whom he loved better, albeit his heart somewhat grudged that he was not afore made of counsel in this matter, as he was of the taking of her kindred and of their putting to death, which were by his assent before devised to be beheaded at Pomfret this selfsame day in which he was not ware that it was by other devised that he himself should be beheaded the same day at London. Then said the Protector, 'Ye shall all see in what wise that sorceress and that other witch of her counsel Shore's wife, with their affinity, have by their sorcery and witchcraft wasted my body.' And therewith he plucked up his doublet sleeve to his elbow upon his left arm, where he showed a wearish [shrivelled] withered arm, and small, as it was never other.

Hereupon every man's mind sore misgave them, well perceiving that this matter was but a quarrel. For they well wist that the Queen was too wise to go about any such folly. And also, if she would, yet would she of all folk least make Shore's wife of her counsel, whom of all women she most hated as that concubine whom the King her husband had most loved. And also, no man was there present but well knew that his arm was ever such since his birth. Natheless, the Lord Chamberlain, which from the death of King Edward kept Shore's wife, on whom he somewhat doted in the King's life, saving, as it is said, he that while forbear her of reverence toward the King, [catchword 'or'] else of a certain kind of fidelity to his friend, answered and said, 'Certainly, my lord, if they have so heinously done, they be worthy heinous punishment.'

'What,' quoth the Protector, 'thou servest me, I ween, with ifs and with ans. I tell thee, they have so done, and that I will make good on thy body, traitor.' And therewith, as in a great anger, he clapped his fist upon the board a great rap, at which token one cried 'treason' without the chamber. Therewith a door clapped, and in come there rushing men in harness, as many as the chamber might hold. And anon the Protector said to the Lord Hastings, 'I arrest thee, traitor.' 'What, me, my lord?' quoth he. 'Yea, thee, traitor,' quoth the Protector. (*The Lord Stanley wounded*:) And another let fly at the Lord Stanley, which shrunk at the stroke and fell under the table, or else his head had been cleft to the teeth, for, as shortly as he shrank, yet ran the blood about his ears.

Then were they all quickly bestowed in diverse chambers, except the Lord Chamberlain, whom the Protector bade speed and shrive him apace, 'For by St Paul,' quoth he, 'I will not to dinner till I see thy head off.' It booted him not to ask why, but heavily took a priest at adventure and made a short shrift, for a longer would not be suffered, the Protector made so much haste to dinner, which he might not go to until this were done, for saving of his oath. (*Lord Hastings Lord Chamberlain beheaded*:) So was he brought forth to the green beside the chapel within the Tower and his head laid down upon a long log of timber, and there stricken off, and afterward his body with the head interred at Windsor beside the body of King Edward, both whose souls our Lord pardon. Thus began he to establish his kingdom in blood, growing thereby in hatred of the nobles, and also abridging both the line of his life and the time of his regiment; for God will not have bloodthirsty tyrants' days prolonged, but will cut them off in their ruff, according to David's words: 'Impio, fallaci, avidoque caedis | Fila mors rumpet viridi in iuventa' [For the man who is wicked, false, and eager for slaughter, death breaks the thread of life in vigorous youth] (*Buchanan, in Psalm* 55).

A marvellous case is it to hear either the warnings of that he should have voided or the tokens of that he could not void. For the self night next before his death, the Lord Stanley sent a trusty messenger unto him at midnight in all the haste, requiring him to rise and ride away with him, for he was disposed utterly no longer to bide, he had so fearful a dream; (*The Lord Stanley's dream*:) in which him thought that a boar with his tusks so razed them both by the heads that the blood ran about both their shoulders. And forsomuch as the Protector gave the boar for his cognizance, this dream made so fearful an impression in his heart that he was throughly determined no longer to tarry, but had his horse ready, if the Lord Hastings would go with him, to ride yet so far the same night that they should be out of danger ere day.

'Ha, good lord,' quoth the Lord Hastings to this messenger, 'leaneth my lord thy master so much to such trifles, and hath such faith in dreams, which either his own fear fantasieth or do rise in the night's rest by reason of his day's thought? Tell him it is plain witchcraft to believe in such dreams, which if they were tokens of things to come, why thinketh he not that we might be as likely to make them true by our going if we were caught and brought back, as friends fail fliers?—for then had the boar a cause likely to raze us with his tusks, as folk that fled for some falsehood. Wherefore, either is there peril or none there is indeed; or if any be, it is rather in going than biding. And in case we should needs fall in peril one way or other, yet had I rather that men should see that it were by other men's falsehood than think it were either by our own fault or faint heart. And therefore go to thy master, man, and commend me to him, and pray him be merry and have no fear. For I ensure him I am as sure of the man that he woteth of as I am of mine own hand.' 'God send grace, sir,' quoth the messenger, and went his way.

(*Foretokens of imminent misfortune to the Lord Hastings*:) Certain is it also that in riding towards the Tower, the same morning in which he was beheaded, his horse twice or thrice stumbled with him, almost to the falling. Which thing, albeit each man wot well daily happeneth to them to whom no such mischance is toward, yet hath it been of an old rite and custom observed as a token oftentimes notably foregoing some great misfortune. Now this that followeth was no warning, but an envious scorn. The same morning, ere he was up, came a knight unto him, as it were of courtesy to accompany him to the council, but of truth sent by the Protector to haste him thitherwards, with whom he was of secret confederacy in that purpose; a mean man at that time, and now of great authority.

This knight, I say, when it happened the Lord Chamberlain by the way to stay his horse and commune a while with a priest whom he met in the Tower Street, brake his tale, and said merrily to him, 'What, my lord! I pray you come on. Whereto talk you so long with that priest? You have no need of a priest yet,' and therewith he laughed upon him, as though he would say, 'Ye shall have soon'. But so little wist the t'other what he meant, and so little mistrusted, that he was never merrier nor never so full of good hope in his life, which self thing is oft seen a sign of change. But I shall rather let anything pass me than the vain surety of man's mind so near his death, flattering himself with deceitful conceits of inward motions of life to be prolonged, even in present cases of deadly danger and heavy misfortunes offering great mistrust; as he did that is noted for speaking like a fool: 'Non est, crede mihi, sapientis dicere "Vivam"; | Nascentes morimur, finisque ab origine pendet' [It is not, believe me, for the wise to say 'I shall live'. Being born we die, and the end hangs upon the beginning.] (*Manilius, 'Astronomica', lib. 4*).

Upon the very Tower Wharf, so near the place where his head was off soon after, there met he with one Hastings, a pursuivant, of his own name. And at their meeting in that place he was put in remembrance of another time, in which it had happened them before to meet in like manner together in the same place. At which other time the Lord Chamberlain had been accused unto King Edward by the Lord Rivers the Queen's brother, in such wise as he was for the while, but it lasted not long, far fallen into the King's indignation, and stood in great fear of himself. And forsomuch as he now met this pursuivant in the same place, that jeopardy so well passed, it gave him great pleasure to talk with him thereof, with whom he had before talked thereof in the same place while he was therein.

And therefore he said, 'Ha, Hastings, art thou remembered when I met thee here once with an heavy heart?' 'Yea, my lord,' quoth he, 'that remember I well, and thanked be God they gat no good nor you no harm thereby.' 'Thou wouldst say so,' quoth he, 'if thou knewest as much as I know, which few know else as yet, and more shall shortly.' That meant he by the lords of the Queen's kindred that were taken before and should that day be beheaded at Pomfret, which he well wist, but nothing ware that the axe hung over his own head. 'In faith, man,' quoth he, 'I was never so sorry nor never stood in so great dread of my life as I did when thou and I met here. And lo how the world is turned: now stand mine enemies in the danger, as thou mayest hap to hear more hereafter, and I never in my life so merry, nor never in so great surety.'

O good God, the blindness of our mortal nature! When he most feared, he was in good surety; when he reckoned himself surest, he lost his life, and that within two hours after. (*The description of the Lord Hastings*:) Thus ended this honourable man, a good knight and a gentle, of great authority with his prince, of living somewhat dissolute, plain and open to his enemy, and secret to his friend; easy to beguile as he that of good heart and courage forestudied no perils; a loving man, and passing well beloved; very faithful, and trusty enough, trusting too much. Now flew the fame of this lord's death swiftly through the city, and so forth further about like a wind in every man's ear. But the Protector, immediately after dinner, intending to set some colour upon the matter, sent in all the haste for many substantial men out of the city into the Tower.

Now at their coming, himself with the Duke of Buckingham stood harnessed in old ill-faring briganders, such as no man should ween that they would vouchsafe to have put upon their backs except that some sudden necessity had constrained them. And then the Protector showed them that the Lord Chamberlain and other of his conspiracy had contrived to have suddenly destroyed him and the Duke there the same day in the council. And what they intended further was as yet not well known. Of which their treason he never had knowledge before ten of the clock the same forenoon, which sudden fear drave them to put on for their defence such harness as came next to hand. And so had God holpen them that the mischief turned upon them that would have done it. And this he required them to report. [. . .]

Now was this proclamation made within two hours after that he was beheaded, and it was so curiously indited and so fair written in parchment, in so well a set hand, and therewith of itself so long a process, that every child might well perceive that it was prepared before. For all the time between his death and the proclaiming could scant have sufficed unto the bare writing alone, all had it been but in paper and scribbled forth in haste at adventure. So that upon the proclaiming thereof, one that was schoolmaster of Paul's of chance standing by, and comparing the shortness of the time with the length of the matter, said unto them that stood about him, 'Here is a gay goodly cast foul cast away for haste.' And a merchant answered him that it was written by prophecy.

## Passage 3 ( pp. 393–6)

(*The election of King Richard hardly to be preferred*:) But were it for wonder or fear, or that each looked that other should speak first, not one word was there answered of all the people that stood before, but all was as still as the midnight, not so much as rounding [whispering] amongst them by which they might seem to commune what was best to do. When the Mayor saw this, he with other partners of that council drew about the Duke, and said that the people had not been accustomed there to be spoken unto but by the Recorder, which is the mouth of the city, and happily to him they will answer. (*Fitzwilliam Recorder*:) With that, the Recorder, called Fitzwilliam, a sad man and an honest, which was so new come into that office that he never had spoken to the people before, and loath was with that matter to begin, notwithstanding thereunto commanded by the Mayor, made rehearsal to the commons of that the Duke had twice rehearsed to them himself.

But the Recorder so tempered his tale that he showed everything as the Duke's words, and no part his own. But all this noting no change made in the people, which alway after one stood as they had been men amazed. Whereupon the Duke rounded unto the Mayor and said, 'This is a marvellous obstinate silence,' and therewith he turned unto the people again [. . .]

At these words the people began to whisper among themselves secretly, that the voice was neither loud nor distinct, but as it were the sound of a swarm of bees, till at the last in the nether end of the hall an ambushment of the Duke's servants and Nashfield's, and other belonging to the Protector, (*King Richard's election preferred by voices of confederacy*:) with some prentices and lads that thrust into the hall amongst the press, began suddenly at men's backs to cry out as loud as their throats would give, 'King Richard, King Richard!', and threw up their caps in token of joy. And they that stood before cast back their heads, marvelling thereof, but nothing they said. Now when the Duke and the Mayor saw this manner, they wisely turned it to their purpose, and said it was a goodly cry and a joyful, to hear every man with one voice, no man saying nay. [. . .]

(*The Mayor's coming to Baynard's Castle unto the Lord Protector*:) Then on the morrow after, the Mayor with all the aldermen and chief commoners of the city, in their best manner apparelled, assembling themselves together, resorted unto Baynard's Castle, where the Protector lay. To which place repaired also, according to their appointment, the Duke of Buckingham and diverse noblemen with him, beside many knights and other gentlemen. And thereupon the Duke sent word unto the Lord Protector of the being there of a great and honourable company to move a great matter unto his grace. Whereupon the Protector made difficulty to come out unto them but if he first knew some part of their errand, as though he doubted and partly mistrusted the coming of such a number unto him so suddenly, without any warning or knowledge whether they came for good or harm.

Then the Duke, when he had showed this to the Mayor and other, that they might thereby see how little the Protector looked for this matter, they sent unto him by the messenger such loving message again, and therewith so humbly besought him to vouchsafe that they might resort to his presence to propose their intent, of which they would unto none other person any part disclose, that at the last he came forth of his chamber, and yet not down unto them, but stood above in a gallery over them, where they might see him and speak to him, as though he would not yet come too near them till he wist what they meant. And thereupon the Duke of Buckingham first made humble petition unto him on the behalf of them all that his grace would pardon them and license them to propose unto his grace the intent of their coming, without his displeasure, without which pardon obtained they durst not be bold to move him of that matter.

In which albeit they meant as much honour to his grace as wealth to all the realm beside, yet were they not sure how his grace would take it, whom they would in no wise offend. Then the Protector, as he was very gentle of himself, and also longed sore to wit what they meant, gave him leave to propose what him liked, verily trusting, for the good mind that he bare them all, none of them anything would intend unto himward wherewith he ought to be grieved. When the Duke had this leave and pardon to speak, then waxed he bold to show him their intent and purpose, with all the causes moving them thereunto, as ye before have heard, and finally to beseech his grace that it would like him, of his accustomed goodness and zeal unto the realm, now with his eye of pity to behold the long continued distress and decay of the same, and to set his gracious hands to redress and amendment thereof.

All which he might well do by taking upon him the crown and governance of this realm, according to his right and title lawfully descended unto him, and to the laud of God, profit of the land, and unto his noble grace so much the more honour and less pain, in that that never prince reigned upon any people that were so glad to live under his obeisance as the people of this realm under his. When the Protector had heard the proposition he looked very strangely thereat, and answered that all were it that he partly knew the things by them alleged to be true, yet such entire love he bare unto King Edward and his children (*O singular dissimulation of King Richard!*) that so much more regarded his honour in other realms about than the crown, of any one of which he was never desirous, that he could not find in his heart in this point to incline to their desire. [. . .]

[. . .] Notwithstanding, he not only pardoned them the motion that they made him, but also thanked them for the love and hearty favour they bare him, (*King Richard spake otherwise than he meant*:) praying them for his sake to give and bear the same to the prince under whom he was and would be content to live. [. . .]

[. . .] And after that, upon like pardon desired and obtained, he [the Duke of Buckingham] showed aloud unto the Protector that for a final conclusion, that the realm was appointed King Edward's line should not any longer reign upon them, both for that they had so far gone that it was now no surety to retreat, as for that they thought it for the weal universal to take that way, although they had not yet begun it. Wherefore, if it would like his grace to take the crown upon him, they would humbly beseech him thereunto. If he would give them a resolute answer to the contrary, which they would be loath to hear, then must they needs seek and should not fail to find some other nobleman that would. These words much moved the Protector, which else, as every man may weet, would never of likelihood have inclined thereunto.

But when he saw there was none other way, but that either he must take it or else he and his both go from it, he said unto the lords and commons, 'Sith we perceive well that all the realm is so set, whereof we be very sorry, that they will not suffer in any wise King Edward's line to govern them, whom no man earthly can govern against their wills, and we well also perceive that no man is there to whom the crown can by just title appertain as to ourselves, as very right heir lawfully begotten of the body of our most dear father Richard late Duke of York, to which title is now joined your election, the nobles and commons of this realm, which we of all titles possible take for the most effectual, we be content and agree favourably to incline to your petition and request, and, according to the same, here we take upon us the royal estate, pre-eminence, and kingdom of the two noble realms, England and France, (*The Protector taketh upon him to be king:*) the one from this day forward by us and our heirs to rule, govern, and defend, the other by God's grace and your good help to get again and subdue and establish forever in due obedience unto this realm of England, the advancement whereof we never ask of God longer to live than we intend to procure.'

With this there was a great shout, crying 'King Richard, King Richard!' And then the lords went up to the king, for so was he from that time called, and the people departed, talking diversely of the matter, every man as his fantasy gave him. But much they talked and marvelled of the manner of this dealing, that the matter was on both parts made so strange, (*A made match to cozen the people:*) as though neither had ever communed with other thereof before, when that themselves wist there was no man so dull that heard them but he perceived well enough that all the matter was made [artificially contrived] between them. Howbeit, some excused that again, and said all must be done in good order though, and men must sometime for the manners' sake not be aknown what they know—though it be hard to outreach the circumspect, wise, and vigilant-minded man, as the poet saith: '. . . non facile est tibi | Decipere Ulyssem' [it is not easy for you to deceive Ulysses] (*Juvenal, Satire 2*).

For at the consecration of a bishop, every man woteth well by the paying for his bulls [papal mandate] that he purposeth to be one, and though he pay for nothing else. And yet must he be twice asked whether he will be bishop or no, and he must twice say nay, and the third time take it, as compelled thereunto by his own will. And in a stage play, all the people know right well that one playing the sultan is percase a souter [cobbler], yet if one should can [know] so little good to show out of season what acquaintance he hath with him, and cast him by his own name while he standeth in his majesty, one of his tormentors might hap to break his head—and worthy—for marring of the play. And so they said that these matters be kings' games, as it were stage plays, and for the more part played upon scaffolds, in which poor men be but the lookers on. And they that wise be will meddle no further. For they that sometime step up and play with them, when they cannot play their parts they disorder the play, and do themselves no good.

# A PROLOGUE FOR THE THEATRE

In the English Shakespeare Company production of *The Wars of the Roses*, 1988–9, *Richard III* began with a Prologue in which the Narrator identified guests at a cocktail party as the play's main figures. It is reprinted here both for the benefit of the reader who needs a quick if slanted guide to the characters, and as a model of how the historical ice can be broken in the theatre. From Michael Bogdanov and Michael Pennington, *The English Stage Company* (1990).

**Narrator:**

THE LATE KING HENRY VI.
Deposed by Edward IV, imprisoned in the Tower, then murdered by Edward's brothers Richard and Clarence. Only a few months earlier, Henry's only son had been stabbed to death by Edward, Clarence and Richard at the Battle of Tewkesbury.

EDWARD IV, KING OF ENGLAND, THE SUN IN SPLENDOUR, AND ELIZABETH HIS QUEEN.
By overthrowing and murdering Henry VI, Edward has settled an uneasy peace on the houses of York and Lancaster.

GEORGE DUKE OF CLARENCE, BROTHER TO THE KING AND RICHARD.
Joint murderer with Richard of Henry and Henry's only son.

RICHARD DUKE OF GLOUCESTER, THE BOAR.
Brother to the King and the Duke of Clarence; his father and younger brother were murdered by Henry and Henry's queen, Margaret.

EARL RIVERS.
Brother to Queen Elizabeth. Later he will be executed.

LORD GREY.
Son of Queen Elizabeth (by her first husband). Later he will be executed.

THE MARQUIS OF DORSET—HIS BROTHER.
He will escape execution and fly to France.

THE DUKE OF BUCKINGHAM.
Richard's confidant and right-hand man. Peer of the realm and a politician at the heart of the struggle for power. Later he will be executed.

LORD HASTINGS, THE LORD CHAMBERLAIN.
Supporter of King Edward IV, arrested, released, arrested again and finally executed.

LORD STANLEY.

Supporter of those in power. Supporter of Henry VI, Edward IV, Richard of Gloucester and the Earl of Richmond. He will live to a ripe old age.

And now the ladies.

MARGARET, HENRY VI's WIDOW AND FORMER QUEEN.

Her husband was murdered in the Tower. Her only son was stabbed to death at the Battle of Tewkesbury.

THE DUCHESS OF YORK.

Mother to Edward, Clarence and Richard. Her husband, three of her sons and her two grandsons are murdered.

LADY ANNE.

Her father, father-in-law and her husband were all killed by Richard of Gloucester. Later, she herself will be killed by him.

The sons and heirs to the throne—THE PRINCE OF WALES AND THE DUKE OF YORK.

THE WOODVILLES, related to the Crown through marriage, not blood.

THE LADIES IN MOURNING:

MARGARET, mourning her son and her late husband, King Henry VI.

LADY ANNE, mourning her late husband and her father-in-law, the late king.

THE DUCHESS OF YORK, mourning everybody.

And there you have it.

THE POLITICIANS, THE LADIES, THE WOODVILLES, THE PLANTA-GENETS.

Simple.

# INDEX OF ACTORS, DIRECTORS, AND OTHERS

[Actors played Richard unless otherwise stated.]

# INDEX

This selective index is primarily a guide to the Commentary. It excludes names entered in Appendix G, modern critics, and proverbial and biblical allusions. Dramatic roles are recorded mainly in relation to historical sources. Abbreviations include 'hn.' (headnote) and 'App.' (Appendix). An asterisk indicates that a note supplements information in *OED*.

doubtful 4.4.353; 5.4.72
dragons 5.5.79
draw me in 1.3.89
dubbed 1.1.82
dugs 2.2.29
dull 1.3.193; 4.2.16; 4.3.51
Du Maurier, George p. 30
duty 1.3.251

eagle(s) 1.1.132; 1.3.71
earnest 5.1.22
eavesdropper 5.4.200
*edgeless 5.4.114
Edward of Lancaster 1.1.153; 1.4.50
Edward, Prince of Wales pp. 12, 18;
  2.2.108, 119
*Edward III* 1.3.229; 2.2.104
Edward IV 1.1.1–31, 153; 1.3.194;
  2.1 hn.
effeminate 3.7.193
Eleanor of Aquitaine 3.1.92
Elizabeth, Lady p. 71; 4.2.50–1;
  4.4 hn., 188–350; 5.7.18–41
Elizabeth, Queen to Edward IV
  1.1.62–5, 82; 4.4.348–9, 350
Elizabeth I pp. 70–1; 5.7.32
else wherefore 3.7.111
elvish-marked 1.3.225
Ely, Bishop of 3.4.0.2; 4.3.46
embassage 2.1.1–6
empery 3.7.129
empire 4.4.388
emulation 2.3.25
endow 4.4.225
ends 1.3.337
enforce 4.4.272
enfranchise 1.1.110
*England's Parnassus* p. 81
engrave 4.4.248
engross(ed) p. 59; 3.6.2; 3.7.71
entail 3.1.75
entertain 1.2.241; 1.4.121; 3.5.13
entreat(s) (*sb*) 3.7.207; (*vb*) 4.4.145
envious 1.3.26; 1.4.34
Erasmus, Desiderius p. 56; 2.2.120
erroneous vassal 1.4.176
estate(s) 3.7.195; App. A (E.5)
even where 3.5.81
evidence 1.4.164
evil 1.1.139
exclaims 1.2.50; 4.4.129
excursions 5.6.0.1
*executioner 1.2.117, 171

exercise 3.2.107; 3.7.59
exhales 1.2.56
expedient duty 1.2.202
expedition 4.4.130
eyrie 1.3.264

factor 3.7.127
fair(ly) p. 59; 3.1.106; 4.4.145
fair befall 1.3.282; 3.5.46
falchion 1.2.92
familiarly App. A (M.29)
fascism pp. 98–9, 107
fat 5.4.237
father 1.1.155; 1.3.135; 5.2.5
father-in-law 5.4.60
faultless 1.3.175
fear 3.7.40
fearful 1.1.11; 4.3.51
feature 1.1.19
field 1.4.53; 5.3.1
fiery 4.3.54
figure 1.2.5
figured in 1.2.179
fitting 3.4.4
flakey darkness 5.4.65
flatter my sorrows 4.4.221
flattering 4.4.80
fleeting 1.4.52
fleshed 4.3.6
flint 1.3.140
flood 1.4.34, 42
flourish of my fortune 1.3.241
foil 5.4.229
fond 3.4.86; 5.5.59
Fontane, Theodor p. 91
fool 1.4.94
foolish 4.2.55
footcloth horse 3.4.89
for a need 3.5.83
for that 4.4.393
Ford, John (*Perkin Warbeck*) p. 82
foreward 5.5.22
forfeit 2.1.98
form 3.5.41; 3.7.9–11; 5.4.21
formal 3.1.82
forswearing 1.4.183
forward 3.1.94
France 3.1.92
franked 1.3.314; 4.5.3
fraud 1.4.137
free 3.6.9
French 1.3.49
Freud, Sigmund pp. 55 n., 95

friend(s) 1.3.75; 4.2.69–71;
4.4.401; 5.2.19
frightful 4.4.162
front 1.1.9
Furies 1.4.54

gallant-springing 1.4.201
Garter, Order of the 4.4.287
Gascoigne, George (*Posies*) 1.1.94
gear 1.4.140
gentle villain 1.3.163
George 4.4.287, 288
given out 4.4.433
God's dreadful law 1.4.190–1
God's handiwork 4.4.48
golden dew of sleep 4.1.79
golden fee 3.5.94–5
gone 4.3.20
good days 1.1.42
goodman 1.1.66
good-mother 4.4.332
gossips 1.1.83
got 3.7.8
government 2.3.12
grace 1.3.55, 321; 2.1.75; 2.4.13
Grafton, Richard pp. 13–14
gramercy 3.2.105
grannam 2.2.1
gratulate 4.1.5
graven 4.4.135
Great Seal 2.4.74–5
great 5.5.76
*Greene's Groatsworth* pp. 3, 8
Grey, Lady, *see* Elizabeth, Queen
Grey, Lord p. 76; 1.3.183; 2.1.0.2;
2.4.44; 4.4.253; App. D (3)
grief 3.1.114
grievous burden 4.4.160
gross(ly) p. 59; 2.4.13; 3.6.10;
4.1.75
ground 3.7.44
Guildhall 3.7.31
gulls 1.3.328

halberdier 1.2.0.1–3
Hall, Edward, *Union* pp. 13–14, 22,
121–2; 2.2.119; 3.1.163, 176;
4.3.36–50; 4.4.418; App. D (16, 17)
Hall, the 3.7.31
halt 1.1.23
*Hamlet* pp. 73, 120; 1.4.51; 4.4.48
hap 1.3.84
haply, happily 3.5.59; 4.4.249

happiness 1.3.41
happy 2.1.47; 3.4.6
hardly 2.1.56
Hardyng, John p. 14
harlot strumpet 3.4.76
hastes 3.1.22
Hastings, Lord 1.1.153; 2.1 hn.;
3.1.23.1; 3.2.9, 93–106; 3.4.93–6
hatches 1.4.12
hats 3.2.92
haught 2.3.28
have 1.2.215
Haverfordwest 4.5.7
Hazlitt, William pp. 70, 87–8
heap 2.1.53
hearse 1.2.0.2
heartstrings 4.4.286
heaven 1.3.216
heavenly 1.2.168
heavy, heavily 1.3.228; 1.4.1, 67
hedgehog 1.2.100
held out 4.2.43
hell 1.2.107–9
helpless balm 1.2.13
Henslowe, Philip pp. 7 n., 8
Henrietta Maria, Queen pp. 81–2
1 *Henry IV* pp. 115, 117; 4.3.54;
5.6.11–12
*Henry V* p. 117; 4.2.19
Henry VI 1.1.1–31, 153; 1.2.0.1–3,
4; 2.3.11
1 *Henry VI* p. 7 n.; 2.3.11, 20; 4.4.4
2 *Henry VI, see Contention*
3 *Henry VI, see Richard Duke of York*
Henry VIII pp. 14–17, 56
herb of grace 2.4.13
Herbert, Henry pp. 81–2
Herod pp. 16, 18; 4.3.2–3, 9
Heywood, Thomas (2 *Edward IV*)
1.4.87
hilts 1.4.141
hire 5.4.237
history 3.5.27; 3.6 hn.
Hogarth, William pp. 86–7
hoised 4.4.444
hold (*sb*) 4.5.3; (*vb*) 3.2.104
holp 1.2.105
Homilies pp. 17, 51–2; 2.3.11;
3.4.103–6
horse 5.5.29; 5.6.7
house 3.5.76
hoyday 4.4.377
hull 4.4.356